# OREGON

## JUDY JEWELL & W. C. McRAE

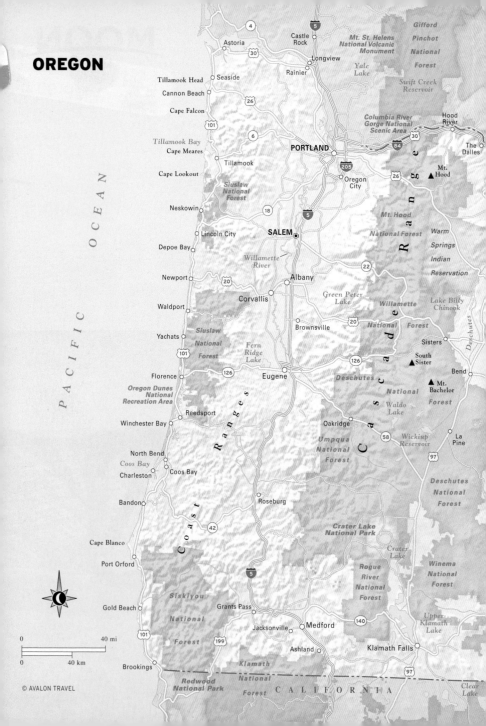

# Contents

# DISCOVER
# Oregon

Truly epic in its breadth, Oregon's landscape is diverse and dramatic. A broad deep-green swath, lush with farmland and studded with old-growth Douglas firs, runs between the rugged Pacific coast and the volcanic peaks of the Cascades. Farther east, you'll find high desert, mountains, and deep river canyons—spectacular country that's largely unexplored by visitors.

But Oregon is much more than a scenic abstraction. In few places has human civilization meshed so agreeably with the natural environment. What helps make Oregon unique is the attitude of its citizens, who are fiercely proud of their state, its culture, and its open spaces. Equal to the great outdoors, the arts are cherished and draw crowds by multitudes. The state also celebrates its historical heritage, ethnic makeup, and straightforward high spirits with a thousand festivals. And the food? Much of Oregon is a huge garden where vegetables, fruit, wine grapes, and farm and ranch products reach perfection. Mighty rivers and 360 miles of Pacific coast provide shellfish, salmon, tuna, and halibut.

Whether it's "three days and four plays" at the Oregon Shakespeare Festival in Ashland, shopping for wild morel mushrooms at the Sisters farmers market,

**Clockwise from top left:** Shore Acres State Park; Crux Fermentation Project in Bend; a vineyard in southern Oregon; Chinese dragon boats docked in downtown Portland; fly-fishing on the Deschutes River; bridge at Latourell Falls.

dueling pinot noir tastings in Carlton, or kiteboarding near Hood River, you'll find that Oregonians engage with everyday life with a verve that's at once intensely local yet tied to a larger, more universal perspective. In Portland, where "organic" and "local" are assumptions, not exceptions, life is rich with the culture and cuisine options of a cosmopolitan center, yet as comfortable and cozy as in a small town.

Oregonians tell a fable about a crossroads on the old Oregon Trail. Pointing south toward the California goldfields was a sign with a drawing of a bag of gold. Pointing north was another sign with the words "To Oregon." The punch line? Only those pioneers who could read continued to Oregon.

Of course, the Oregon Trail is history now, but that doesn't mean that the movement to Oregon is over. The same vaguely agrarian and utopian ideals that drew the pioneers still work magic on a new crop of immigrants eagerly moving to the Beaver State to seek the good life.

**Clockwise from top left:** Corvallis farmers market; kiteboarding on the Columbia River; John Day Fossil Beds and the Painted Hills; yurt at a coastal Oregon campground.

# 10 TOP EXPERIENCES

**1 Portland:** The quirky, welcoming spirit of this flannel-clad, rain-scrubbed city makes it feel like a small town (page 33).

**2 Columbia River Gorge:** Waterfalls tumble from the mountain's edge and deep-green forests cling to cliff walls in this living Pacific Northwest postcard (page 102).

>>>

**3 Crater Lake:** High in the Cascades, the deepest lake in the country is Oregon's crown jewel (page 418).

>>>

**4** **Mount Hood:** The state's highest peak is an all-season recreation playground (page 133).

**5** **Coastal Road Trip:** With highlights like Astoria, Cannon Beach, Cape Perpetua, and Yaquina Head, a drive along scenic U.S. 101 can be the trip of a lifetime (pages 207, 273, and 327).

**6** **Shakespeare in Ashland:** The soul of the Bard lives on during the "three days and four plays" at this charming town's annual theater festival (page 385).

<<<

**7** **Hiking and Biking:** The best way to experience Oregon is with a set of wheels (page 22) or a pair of hiking boots (page 29).

>>>

**8** **Pacific Northwest Cuisine:** Fresh from the farm and the sea, Oregon's bounty achieves perfection on a plate.

<<<

**9** **Craft Brews:** Portland is the epicenter of the craft brewing revival, but the aftershocks continue throughout the state (pages 26 and 78).

>>>

**10** **Wine-Tasting:** Oregon's long, sunny summer days, followed by the slow-cooling days of fall, produce wines with a unique complexity of flavor. Taste them for yourself (pages 24 and 148).

# Planning Your Trip

## Where to Go

### Portland

Graced by the presence of the Columbia and Willamette Rivers and nearby Mount Hood, Portland is the state's green urban core. Just north of downtown, find the vibrant **Pearl District.** To the west, **Washington Park** is home to rose gardens; trails here connect to **Forest Park,** the nation's largest urban forested park. Cross the Willamette River to the east side to explore thriving neighborhoods.

### Columbia River Gorge and Mount Hood

This is the Pacific Northwest's primal landscape: towering waterfalls, moss-draped rainforests, snowcapped volcanoes—all in a chasm 5 miles wide, 80 miles long, and 3,000 feet deep. The **Historic Columbia River Highway** ushers

travelers to hiking trails. Hood River has a lovely setting at the foot of **Mount Hood;** drive up the mountain to the landmark **Timberline Lodge** to more hiking trails and nearly year-round skiing.

### The Willamette Valley

The historic end of the Oregon Trail, this valley is still agriculturally rich, with the emphasis now on **wine grapes.** Nearly the entire west side of the valley is a wine lover's pilgrimage route, accessible by car or bicycle. Hike past some of the state's prettiest waterfalls at **Silver Falls State Park.**

### North Coast

Sandy beaches along the northern coastline are separated by headlands, most traced by a hiking trail. Beach towns range from quirky spots lost in

rose garden in Washington Park

# If You Have...

- **A LONG WEEKEND:** Visit Portland with day trips to the Willamette Valley wine country and the Columbia River Gorge.

- **ONE WEEK:** Add a trip down the coast from Astoria to Newport, then head east to Bend and

central Oregon's alpine lakes and volcanoes. Return to Portland via Mount Hood.

- **TWO WEEKS:** Add eastern Oregon (catch the Wallowa Mountains in late summer), Crater Lake, and Ashland's Shakespeare Festival.

time to sophisticated resorts, so everyone can find a place to adopt as their own. Vibrant **Astoria** has a rich history; **Cannon Beach** is Portlanders' favorite getaway; and the **Three Capes Scenic Loop** provides access to spectacular beaches, including the one at **Cape Kiwanda.**

## Central Coast

The central coast is anchored at its northern end by sprawling **Lincoln City** and exemplified by **Newport,** with charming neighborhoods, an active fishing port, and the **Oregon Coast**

**Aquarium.** At the southern end, **Florence** and **Reedsport** are great bases for visits to the otherworldly sandscape of the **Oregon Dunes.**

## South Coast

The south coast feels far from everything, a landscape of mountains, dense forest, wild rivers, and beaches punctuated with dramatic rock formations. West of **Coos Bay** are wild and beautiful natural areas. **Bandon** is cozy and full of visitors, many there for the world-class golf courses at **Bandon Dunes.** The southernmost part of

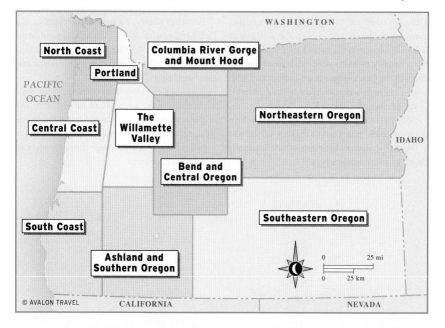

Oregon's coastline may be its most scenic, especially the stretch between **Gold Beach** and **Brookings.**

## Ashland and Southern Oregon

This land of opposites ranges from the arts town of **Ashland,** known for its **Shakespeare Festival,** to secluded backcountry. The valleys of the **North Umpqua and Rogue Rivers** are attractive to hikers, anglers, and white-water rafters, and **Crater Lake** is a gem.

## Bend and Central Oregon

This high desert is cut through by the **Deschutes and Crooked Rivers** and dotted with volcanic peaks. In **Bend,** visitors can find good food, comfortable lodging, and easy access to **hiking, mountain biking,** and **skiing.** Raft trips vary from tame floats to the rip-roaring rapids outside **Maupin.** Visit the **Warm Springs Indian Reservation** to get a sense of Native American history and culture.

## Northeastern Oregon

Here you'll hear echoes of the Old West, whether you're touring Chief Joseph's homeland, tracing the Oregon Trail, or cheering rodeo athletes at the **Pendleton Round-Up.** Go farther into the past at the **John Day Fossil Beds,** or explore the geology of **Hells Canyon** with a boat ride down the **Snake River.**

## Southeastern Oregon

This high-desert region boasts deep-blue skies, geologic marvels, and plenty of elbow room. Soak in natural **hot springs,** view migrating birds at the vast **Malheur National Wildlife Refuge,** and get to know your fellow travelers at the **Frenchglen Hotel.** Reconnect with nature and enjoy time and space for reflection.

# When to Go

Although **summer** weather is usually beautiful, June can be cloudy and cool in the Willamette Valley. When the Willamette Valley heats up, the coast usually remains cool, with morning fog. Trails in the Cascades are often snowy until mid-July—find early summer hikes in the Columbia Gorge or along the Rogue River Trail.

**Spring** is ideal for touring southeastern Oregon, unless you want to make it all the way to the top of Steens Mountain, which is usually closed by snow until early July.

**Autumn's** first rains appear in September, but October's weather often starts off clear and beautiful. Even after the rains start, remember that cloudy days with scattered rain are the norm, and that "sun breaks" are common.

Although the mountainous parts of the state accumulate huge amounts of snow during the **winter,** snowfall is rare on the coast and in the western valleys. Wintertime temperatures are usually above freezing, though the dampness can make it seem colder.

# The Best of Oregon

It's almost impossible to cover all of Oregon in a week, so we've crafted a 10-day tour that hits most of the highlights. Don't hesitate to stay longer at one site or discover your own favorites along this route. Wild and remote eastern Oregon gets an itinerary of its own (see page 31).

## Day 1
### PORTLAND

Fly into **Portland International Airport** and either pick up a rental car or take the MAX Light Rail train into town and arrange to get a rental car in downtown Portland. Spend the afternoon strolling around downtown, visiting **Powell's City of Books** and the **Pearl District.** Spend the night at the Heathman Hotel and dine nearby at old fave Higgins or, a slightly longer walk away, at Tasty n Alder.

## Day 2
### NORTH COAST

Head northwest from Portland on U.S. 30 to **Astoria.** Explore this historic town at the mouth

of the Columbia River, including a visit to the replica of Fort Clatsop, which served as Lewis and Clark's winter home in 1805-1806. Then continue south and spend the night in **Cannon Beach** at the Stephanie Inn.

## Day 3
### NORTH COAST TO CENTRAL COAST

Head south out of town on U.S. 101 and stop for a walk at **Oswald West State Park,** where you can follow a short trail through an old-growth forest to Short Sands Beach to watch the surfers. Then drive down the coast as far as **Yachats** and spend the night at Overleaf Lodge. Stop at Yachats Brewing for a beer and a plate of pickled veggies, then eat dinner and catch some live music at the Drift Inn Pub.

## Day 4
### CENTRAL COAST TO THE WILLAMETTE VALLEY

Spend the morning exploring the tide pools and old-growth forest around **Cape Perpetua.** Take

Cannon Beach

# Best Bike Rides

## PORTLAND AREA
### Waterfront Park and the Eastbank Esplanade
3-5 miles, easy

In downtown Portland, **Waterfront Park and the Eastbank Esplanade** run along either bank of the Willamette River. Cross the Steel Bridge's pedestrian and bike bridge at the northern end of the loop, and ride the Hawthorne Bridge's sidewalk at the loop's south end. It's a car-free three-mile loop, good for the whole family. If you want to ride a couple of miles farther, continue south on the east side to the car-free **Tilikum Crossing bridge.** Bike lanes on the west side of the bridge usher you back north to Waterfront Park.

More ambitious cyclists should stay on the east side and continue south; the trail will jog a couple of blocks east and become the **Springwater Corridor,** which runs 21 miles to the town of Boring.

### Banks-Vernonia Trail
42 miles round-trip, moderate

The **Banks-Vernonia State Trail** runs along the route of an old logging train and includes 80-foot-high railroad trestles, one of which is safety-improved for cyclists. Catch the trail west of Portland; Banks is on Highway 47 just south of U.S. 26. The trail passes through sprawling L. L.Stub Stewart State Park, which has a campground and great mountain biking. If you want to cut a few miles off your ride, turn around at Stub Stewart.

## COLUMBIA GORGE
### Mosier Twin Tunnels
7 miles round-trip, easy

Another family-friendly ride is along the five-mile **Mosier Twin Tunnels** stretch of the Historic Columbia River Highway between Hood River and Mosier. This is a restored portion of the old road, now open only to bike and foot traffic. Park at the Mark O. Hatfield Trailhead at the east end of Hood River, near I-84's exit 64 (parking $3) or ride up from town (it's a steep approach).

## WILLAMETTE VALLEY
### Aufderheide National Scenic Byway
60 miles one-way, challenging

Oakridge is known for its network of mountain bike trails, but a wonderful road ride starts here too and goes north along the **Aufderheide National Scenic Byway** to Rainbow, a site on the McKenzie River Highway (Hwy. 126). Near the northern end of the ride, you'll pass Terwilliger Hot Springs. You'll be too tired to turn around and ride back the way you came, so a car drop is recommended.

## SOUTHERN OREGON
### Crater Lake Loop
33 miles, challenging

Don't plan to ride the loop around **Crater Lake's rim** too early in the summer, or you'll run into snow. And don't count on riding it too fast, either—most of the ride is above 7,000 feet, and you'll be stopping not only to suck air but also to admire the great views of the lake. There's a window, usually in late June, when most of the snow has melted but the road is not yet entirely open to cars. A car-free weekend is also held during the third weekend of September.

## OREGON COAST
### Oregon Coast Bike Highway
342 miles one-way, challenging

The **Oregon Coast Bike Highway,** a hilly 342-mile ride along the shoulder of busy U.S. 101, is popular for its spectacular ocean views and ample opportunities for eating and sleeping. Do this ride from north to south for the best views and to take advantage of the prevailing winds.

## STATEWIDE
### Cycle Oregon
Usually about 400 miles, challenging

**Cycle Oregon** has mapped out some great routes over the years for its weeklong mid-September tours. One of the best makes a 365-mile loop through northeastern Oregon, starting in Baker City, heading east to Halfway, north to Joseph, northwest through Enterprise and Lostine to Elgin, then south through Cove and Union back to the starting point. Train well for this ride: It's wild, rugged, and beautiful country, and the stretch from Halfway to Joseph climbs over 7,000 feet in 61 miles.

## RIDE OREGON
Find a ride anywhere in the state at **www.rideoregonride.com.** Here you can find notices of upcoming bicycling events as well as rides along scenic bikeways, mountain trails, and roads. Each ride includes detailed directions and cue sheets, elevation profiles, and maps. Try the 38-mile Covered Bridges Scenic Bikeway out of Cottage Grove, a challenging 79-mile mountain bike ride along the North Umpqua Trail, or a 135-mile figure-eight tour of northeastern Oregon's back roads, starting and ending in La Grande.

Mount Hood

a tour of **Sea Lion Caves** (or just peer down from the road with your binoculars). From the seaside town of Florence, cut east on Highway 126 to **Eugene,** with a detour to the King Estate Winery tasting room. Spend the night near Eugene's riverside trails at the elegant Inn at the 5th.

## Days 5-6
### ASHLAND AND SOUTHERN OREGON
Drive south along I-5 to **Ashland** to attend a world-class play. Dine at New Sammy's Cowboy Bistro (reserve well in advance) or Amuse, and spend the night at the Ashland Springs Hotel. From Medford, just north of Ashland, drive up the Rogue River on Highway 62 through the tiny towns of Prospect and Union Creek to **Crater Lake National Park,** and spend the night at the Crater Lake Lodge.

## Day 7
### BEND AND CENTRAL OREGON
Head north on U.S. 97 to **Bend,** visiting the **Lava Lands Visitors Center** and **High Desert Museum** on the way. Stay downtown at the Oxford Hotel or a few miles out of town

along the Deschutes River at the Mount Bachelor Village Resort.

## Day 8
### CENTRAL OREGON TO MOUNT HOOD
Continue north to **Maupin** to meet your raft guide for a daylong float down the Deschutes. At the end of the day, drive up **Mount Hood** and spend the night at Timberline Lodge.

## Day 9
### COLUMBIA RIVER GORGE
### AND MOUNT HOOD
Hike along the **Timberline Trail** (or spend the morning skiing—even in August) and then drive to Hood River. Take a hike to **Upper Horsetail Falls** and then continue west to **Troutdale,** where you'll spend your final night at McMenamins' **Edgefield.**

## Day 10
### RETURN TO PORTLAND
It doesn't take long—about 20 minutes—to get from Edgefield to the Portland airport. If you have a late flight, spend the day in **Portland,** visiting Washington and Forest Parks.

Portland residents love how easy it is to get out of town. The following places are within a couple of hours of downtown Portland:

- **Columbia River Gorge:** It only takes 45 minutes to drive to the gorge. If all you want to do is see Multnomah Falls, go early in the day (the parking lot fills up on nice days) and you'll be back in town by lunchtime. Extend your trip by hiking to the top of the falls, catching the Larch Mountain trail to the Wahkeena Falls Trail (Trail 420), and hiking down via Wahkeena Falls. The final 0.5 miles of this 5-mile loop is on the road.

- **Oregon Coast:** Head west on U.S. 26, and within an hour and a half you'll be gazing at tide pools at the base of Haystack Rock. Grab lunch in Cannon Beach, then head south to Oswald West State Park for hiking or surfing (rent surf gear in Cannon Beach). Finish with a visit to Manzanita for a burrito or some pizza; hang around long enough to miss the evening rush hour into Portland.

- **Mount Hood:** In the winter, a ski trip is a no-brainer. Mount Hood Meadows is our favorite place for downhill, but a day on the slopes at Timberline Ski Area is enhanced by an après-ski hot cocoa or beer in the lodge. Cross-country and snowshoe trails abound; stop at Otto's in the town of Sandy for rental gear and maps.

- **Pacific Crest Trail:** In summer, hike the Pacific Crest Trail in the area around Mount Hood's Timberline Lodge.

- **Willamette Valley Wine Country:** A loop that includes Dundee, McMinnville, and Carlton makes a good day trip in the wine country. Don't be tempted to stop at every tasting room you see on the way, and remember that all three of these towns have excellent places to eat. Consider taking back roads on your return to Portland (you'll need a map!).

- **Silverton:** East of Salem, the area around Silverton has a number of lovely places to visit. Hike the trails at Silver Falls State Park—they're especially attractive in the winter—or visit the Oregon Garden, with cultivated gardens and a house designed by Frank Lloyd Wright. Before heading home, stop at the Mount Angel Abbey for a visit to the library there (designed by Finnish architect Alvar Aalto). The views and the peaceful atmosphere will chill you out for the drive back to Portland.

# The Wine Route

**TOP EXPERIENCE**

There are over 700 wineries in the state, with an emphasis on small family operations: 70 percent of Oregon wineries produce fewer than 5,000 cases a year. Wine grape production takes place across the state, even in the dry rangelands of eastern Oregon. Planning a trip through Oregon's many wine regions is a good way to explore the state and track down little-known vintages that don't make it across state lines.

## Ashland and Southern Oregon

### DAY 1

Start your wine odyssey in Ashland, where Shakespeare and fine restaurants make good companions for wine exploration. Just south of town, **Weisinger Family Winery** produces fine viognier and cabernet sauvignon. The area's best wines, and the greatest concentration of wineries, are over the ridge in the Applegate Valley. High summer heat here enables the production of red wines such as cabernet and syrah as well as some California-style chardonnays; check out the wines at **Valley View Winery** or **Troon Vineyard.**

Spend the night at the **Ashland Creek Inn,** a luxury inn right on the water, and dine at **Peerless Restaurant,** known for its wine cellar and lovely garden setting.

a vineyard in Willamette Valley

## DAY 2

Travel north toward Roseburg, central for the wines of the Umpqua Valley. **Abacela** is noted for the many varieties of wine grapes it grows, offering unusual-for-Oregon varietals such as tempranillo, dolcetto, and sangiovese. **Henry Estate Winery** is one of the state's oldest, and has lovely gardens that make an excellent picnic destination. The wines range from full-bodied pinot noir and merlot to refreshing riesling. **Girardet** produces a range of wines, such as chardonnay, cabernet sauvignon, and pinot noir, and also makes wine from more unusual grapes such as baco noir.

The historic, riverside **Steamboat Inn,** 38 miles up the North Umpqua River, is the region's best dining and lodging choice.

## The Willamette Valley

The Willamette Valley is Oregon's primary wine-growing region. Here the weather is cooler than in the Umpqua and Applegate Valleys, favoring the production of pinot noir and chardonnay, the grapes of France's Burgundy valley, and pinot gris from northern Italy and the French Alsace region.

## DAY 1

Near Eugene, stop at **King Estate Winery,** with a hilltop tasting and winemaking facility that is literally palatial. **Territorial Vineyards & Wine Company** has vineyards near the Coast Range, but a winemaking facility and tasting room in downtown Eugene. From its estate-grown pinot noir grapes, Territorial makes a series of regular pinot noir bottlings and a fantastic rosé. Make dinner reservations at **Marché** restaurant and spend the night a few steps away at the **Inn at the 5th.**

## DAY 2

Between Rickreall and Carlton is the greatest concentration of wineries in the state and the pinot noir vineyards that have put Oregon on the world wine map. With over 200 wineries in a relatively compact area, there's no single route to recommend, so pick up a copy of the widely available Willamette Valley Winery Association's winery map, and follow your instincts.

That said, here are a few tips: Not to be missed is **Sokol Blosser Winery,** with a stunning tasting room perched on a hill just above Dundee. **Domaine Drouhin,** also near Dundee, is the

# Best Craft Breweries

If you're serious about craft brews, plan your trip around the **Oregon Brewers Festival,** held in Portland during the last full weekend of July.

## PORTLAND

- **Cascade Brewing Barrel House:** Try the gose—a lemony, herbal beer that may have a slightly salty finish. It's a good summer beer, and it's also relatively low in alcohol.

- **Hair of the Dog:** HOTD, known for bold, rich flavors and alcohol contents of about 10 percent, also brews some lower-alcohol beers that leave you able to bike home. It's right near the Eastbank Esplanade, making it a good biking destination.

- **Hopworks Urban Brewery:** HUB is just about as Portland as it gets, with a commitment to bikes and environmental issues—as well as very good beer.

## COLUMBIA RIVER GORGE

Hood River has two great brewpubs, and the **Hood River Hotel** is an easy walk from both of these spots.

- **Double Mountain Brewery:** Stop here for pizza and a Double Mountain Hop Lava.

- **Full Sail Brewery:** Brewery tours, good beer, and a spectacular river view from the deck make this a great place to spend the afternoon.

## WILLAMETTE VALLEY

- **Ninkasi Brewing Company:** Ninkasi was the ancient Sumerian goddess of fermentation, and she's easy to worship with a glass of Believer Double Red Ale in your hand.

- **Rogue Farms Hopyard:** If you've never seen hops growing, head to this Willamette River-side farm in Independence, where, if you visit around the fall harvest time, you'll be able to drink fresh-hopped brew.

- **Brewers Union Local 180** in Oakridge is a favorite with the mountain bikers who come to ride the local trails.

## NORTH COAST

- **Fort George Brewery and Public House** in downtown Astoria brews some of the state's best beers. Even if you can't make it to the pub, pick up a can of Belgian-style Quick Wit at a grocery store.

- **Pelican Pub and Brewery** in Pacific City has a spectacular oceanside setting at the foot of Cape Kiwanda and a popular cream ale in addition to the requisite IPAs.

## SOUTH COAST

- **Arch Rock Brewing Company:** Fill your growler or simply stop in for a taste at this tiny Gold Beach brewery that turns out the best local beers.

## SOUTHERN OREGON

- **Caldera Tap House:** Tucked away near Ashland Creek, Caldera is just a couple of blocks from the Oregon Shakespeare Festival's theaters.

- **Portal Brewing Company:** This Medford brewpub is housed in a historic fire station.

## CENTRAL OREGON

- **Deschutes Brewery and Public House:** The Mirror Pond pale ale is an Oregonian staple.

- **10 Barrel:** You'll want the award-winning S1NIST0R black ale.

- **Boneyard Brewing** is only a tasting room, but look for Boneyard on tap around town.

- **GoodLife Brewing:** Bring your dog, sit outside, and get to know the locals over a pint of Descender IPA.

## NORTHEASTERN OREGON

Some would say northeastern Oregon is itself off the beaten path, but plenty of brewpubs await to quench your thirst.

- **Prodigal Son Brewery and Pub:** Cowboy up at this lively and pleasant pub on the edge of downtown Pendleton.

- **Terminal Gravity Brewing:** Enjoy a mighty IPA in a creek-side setting in Enterprise.

- **Barley Brown's Brew Pub:** Make a pilgrimage to Baker City for a pint of Barley Brown ales—if you see a BB brew on tap elsewhere around the state, order it!

Oregon outpost of France's famed Drouhin family and makes excellent pinot noirs in the Burgundy style. **Anne Amie Vineyards** makes fine pinot noirs and has a beautiful facility with one of the most panoramic views in the valley. The **Rex Hill Vineyards**, just east of Newberg, it is one of the closest to Portland, with premium pinot noir and a lovely garden setting.

### DAY 3

If it seems like there are just too many wineries to choose from, consider a stop at **Carlton Winemakers Studio**, a cooperative where small winemakers share a winemaking facility and tasting room. Stay at the **Allison Inn** near Newberg and plan to dine at **Thistle**, in nearby McMinnville.

## Columbia River Gorge

Microclimates in the Columbia River Gorge create niches where cool-climate grapes like pinot noir thrive, while just up the road vineyards of syrah and merlot, which require intense summer heat to ripen, may be planted.

### DAY 1

There are wineries on both the Oregon and Washington sides of the gorge, so don't hesitate to cross bridges to taste wine. Across the Columbia are such notable producers as **Syncline Wine Cellars** and **Domaine Pouillon.**

Stay at the grand and historic **Columbia Gorge Hotel** in Hood River, and dine at **Celilo Restaurant and Bar** for sophisticated fine dining and a wine list rich in local vintages.

## Northeastern Oregon

### DAY 1

Highway 11 runs north from Pendleton toward Walla Walla, Washington. About a third of the official Walla Walla wine-growing area is in Oregon, and several tasting rooms in Walla Walla call for serious attention from lovers of cabernet and merlot. On the Oregon side, stop in Pendleton at **Great Pacific Wine and Coffee Co.,** where wines from Walla Walla and the Columbia Valley are featured. Book a room at **Pendleton House Bed and Breakfast** for the night.

# High Adventure in Bend

Central Oregon's high-desert landscape is a magnificent setting for outdoor recreation. A friendly town with more than its fair share of good restaurants and hotels, not to mention great coffee and fine microbrews, Bend makes a great home base. High-adrenaline recreation and stunning geologic sites are within an hour's drive.

## Day 1

If you're starting from Portland, drive east on U.S. 26 over the hump of Mount Hood and spend your first afternoon at **Smith Rock State Park.** Hike the trails and watch climbers scale the rocks, then drive down to Bend and settle into your hotel at **McMenamins Old St. Francis School.**

## Day 2

Begin the day with an ocean roll (and a sandwich to go) at **Sparrow Bakery** and a stroll or bike ride along the Deschutes River Trail in town. Then head about seven miles up the Cascade Lakes Highway and turn off onto Forest Road 41 to hike a more outlying section of the Deschutes trail to Lava Island Falls, Dillon Falls, and Benham Falls. Return to Bend and spend another night at the McMenamins Old St. Francis School.

## Days 3-4

Now get serious about heading up the Cascade Lakes Highway to hike, fish, or just hang out on a lakeshore. Camp at a hike-in site at **Todd Lake,** or find a more convenient car-camping site at one of the other lakes along the road. (If you're not camping, reserve a cabin at Elk Lake Resort.) Consider spending more than one night here; once you've found the perfect lakeside

Todd Lake

cabin or camping spot, it seems a shame to leave it, and there are plenty of trails to hike, including the tough but rewarding hike from Devils Lake to the top of **South Sister.**

## Day 5

Drive down to Sunriver on Highway 42 (catch it just past Crane Prairie Reservoir), then south a few miles on U.S. 97 to the turnoff for **Newberry Volcano.** Head up to the caldera, where you can hike the trail through the **Big Obsidian Flow,** and then find your new campground at either **Paulina** or **East Lake** (or a cabin at one of the rustic lakeside resorts).

## Day 6

After you break camp, head back down the volcano and north on U.S. 97. Stop to explore the **Lava River Cave.** Continue north and spend the afternoon at the **High Desert Museum** (don't worry, they have a café), then splurge with a night at Bend's **Oxford Hotel.**

## Day 7

Finish your week with a river trip. Get up early and drive north of Madras to Maupin, where you'll meet your river guide for a day trip on the **Deschutes River.** Wear sunscreen and quick-dry shorts, and take a swim down the **Elevator Rapids.**

# Best Camping and Hiking

## COLUMBIA RIVER GORGE

- **Eagle Creek Campground:** The tent campground here is the U.S. Forest Service's oldest. The classic gorge trail starts down the hill from the campground and follows Eagle Creek past waterfalls and springtime wildflowers. Your face will be misted with spray, and in places you'll need to grab hold of cables bolted into the basalt cliffs as the trail narrows. This trail was the epicenter of a wildfire in 2017, so check its status before hiking.

## WILLAMETTE VALLEY

- **Silver Falls State Park:** Ten waterfalls cascade off canyon walls in a forest of Douglas firs, ferns, and bigleaf and vine maple. Come during fall foliage season when there are few visitors. The campground here offers easy access to hiking and biking trails.

- **Paradise Campground:** This campground provides access to the 26.5-mile McKenzie River National Recreation Trail and the nearby Belknap Lodge and Hot Springs.

## NORTH COAST

- **Fort Stevens State Park:** The campground here is large and family-oriented, with lots of yurts. The trails are best for biking around the sprawling park. Hiking is mostly along the beach.

## CENTRAL COAST

- **Carl G. Washburne State Park:** Pile your gear into a wheelbarrow (provided) and trundle it to one of the great walk-in campsites. After pitching your tent, take a hike down the Hobbit Trail.

## SOUTH COAST

- **Humbug Mountain State Park:** The campground here is pretty close to the road, but traffic quiets down at night. Stay here, and in the morning you'll beat the crowds on the hike up Humbug Mountain, an excellent trail along which to acquaint yourself with native plants.

## CENTRAL OREGON

- **Devils Lake:** These prime lakeside campsites, along the Cascade Lakes Highway, are set away from the parking area, so you'll have to schlep your gear. Across the highway is the climbers' trail for South Sister.

- **Metolius River Campgrounds:** The many campgrounds here, especially those downstream from Camp Sherman, offer a chance to linger by central Oregon's most magical river. Take a short walk to the headwaters of the Metolius or a longer hike along the river.

- **Smith Rock State Park:** The campground here is a rough-and-ready climber's bivouac, but anyone who's willing to leave their car in the parking area—and return to the parking area to cook dinner, as no fires are allowed in the tent area—is welcome. Majestic spires tower above the Crooked River at this state park. Seven miles of well-marked trails follow the Crooked River and wend up the canyon walls.

## NORTHEASTERN OREGON

- **Strawberry Campground:** This campground offers a quick 1.25-mile hike to Strawberry Lake. Make sure your car has a bit of clearance and good tires before heading up the bumpy dirt access road.

- **Grande Ronde Lake Campground:** Small Grande Ronde Lake lies in a meadow of tiny streams that is the headwaters of the Grande Ronde River. Hiking trails into the Elkhorn Mountains start nearby.

## SOUTHEASTERN OREGON

- **Hart Mountain National Antelope Refuge:** This hot springs campground is four miles south of the refuge headquarters. Soak in the hot springs, then explore the area on foot or by mountain bike.

- **Page Springs:** This campground is just a few miles from Frenchglen, at the base of Steens Mountain. Get up early to check out the birds on a hike along the Donner und Blitzen River.

# River Running

There are great river trips in every corner of the state:

- **Portland:** Paddle the Willamette with a sea kayak or stand-up paddleboard from **Portland Kayak Company** (6600 SW Macadam Ave., 503/459-4050, www.portlandkayak.com) on the west side of the Willamette River. An easy afternoon tour circumnavigates Ross Island and offers a chance to see bald eagles nesting just a couple of miles from downtown.

- **The Willamette Valley:** In mid-August join the Willamette Riverkeepers' **Paddle Oregon** (www.paddleoregon.org) event to run 107 miles of the Willamette in a canoe or sea kayak. It's also easy to do this trip, or a shorter one, on your own.

- **Columbia Gorge and Mount Hood:** Catch some wind on the mighty Columbia. **Big Winds** (207 Front St., Hood River, 541/386-6086, www.bigwinds.com) offers board and full rig rentals, lessons, and all the necessary windsurfing equipment. Or give kiteboarding a try.

- **North Coast:** Rent a surfboard and wetsuit at **Cleanline Surf** (171 Sunset Blvd., Cannon Beach, 503/436-9726), drive a few miles south, and hike down to Short Sands Beach at Oswald West State Park.

- **Central Coast:** Set out to sea on a fishing or crabbing charter. Several charter services, including **Living Waters** (541/584-2295, www.fishinglivingwaters.com) and **Winchester Bay Charters** (541/361-0180, www.winchesterbaycharters.com) operate from Winchester Bay.

- **South Coast:** Board a jet boat and travel upstream from the mouth of the Rogue River through a designated Wild and Scenic stretch that's loaded with wildlife and lush vegetation. **Jerry's Rogue Jets** (29985 Harbor Way, Gold Beach, 541/247-4571 or 800/451-3645, www.roguejets.com) has been running these trips for many years, and the boat pilots are known for their excellent commentary.

- **Southern Oregon:** Take a multiday raft trip on the Rogue River starting seven miles west of Grants Pass. This stretch not only has some of the best white water in the United States, but also backcountry riverside lodges. The Rogue is also ideal for half- and full-day rafting trips, with most outfitters putting in near the town of Merlin and continuing downstream as far as Foster Bar. **Morrison's Rogue River Lodge** (8500 Galice Rd., Merlin, 541/476-3825 or 800/826-1963, www.rogueriverraft.com) leads a variety of trips.

- **Central Oregon:** Spend a day rafting the Deschutes River surrounded by sage-covered grasslands and wild rocky canyons, where you might see bald eagles, pronghorn, and other wildlife. The town of Maupin is home base for many outfitters, including **All Star Rafting and Kayaking** (405 Deschutes Ave., 541/395-2201 or 800/909-7238, www.asrk.com).

- **Northeastern Oregon:** The undammed John Day River winds through unpopulated rangeland and scenic rock formations; plan to spend a few days away from everything. It's easy enough for almost everybody to paddle on their own; **Kellie Frech's Service Creek** (38686 Hwy. 19, Fossil, 541/468-3331, www.servicecreek.com) rents rafts and can set you up with a car shuttle. Farther east, an early-summer raft trip on the **Wallowa and Grande Ronde Rivers** starts in Minam and heads into a rugged remote canyon. Find rentals, shuttles, and a guide at **Minam Raft Rentals** (541/437-1111, www.minamraftrentals.com).

- **Southeastern Oregon:** The Owyhee River is a prime springtime destination for whitewater enthusiasts. The 53 miles from Rome to the Owyhee Reservoir have two sections of exceptionally heavy rapids, but the many pools of short, intense white water alternating with easy drifts make for a well-paced trip. **Ouzel Outfitters** (541/385-5947 or 800/788-7238, www.oregonrafting.com) is one of several companies with guided Owyhee trips.

Wallowa Lake

# The Oregon Outback

Get set for expansive views, lots of wildlife, and a dose of Western adventure in this area sometimes referred to as "Oregon's outback." If you're flying in for this trip, consider using the airport in Boise, Idaho; it's much closer to Baker City, where this itinerary begins and ends, than the Portland airport.

## Day 1

Start your tour of eastern Oregon in **Baker City,** but don't linger in town for too long; head west to the near-ghost town of **Sumpter** (30 miles) and then up a ways into the Elkhorns for more gold-era history and mining ghost towns. North of Sumpter, follow the **Elkhorn Drive National Scenic Byway** to the near-ghost town of **Granite.** If you're enjoying the drive, continue north and east to Anthony Lakes; from there, continue east back to I-84 and Baker City.

## Day 2

Visit the **National Historic Oregon Trail Interpretive Center** near Baker City, then head about 70 miles east on Highway 86 to **Hells Canyon** at Oxbow, where you can take a look at the Snake River's gorge by car, jet boat, or on foot. Backtrack and stay the night in **Halfway,** just beneath the southern edge of the **Wallowa Mountains.**

## Day 3

From Halfway, head about 15 miles east on Highway 86, then turn north on Forest Road 39. This 54-mile summer-only road will take you up the eastern edge of the Wallowas—and past the area's most accessible viewpoint onto **Hells Canyon**—to lodgings in the artsy town of **Joseph** or at nearby **Wallowa Lake.**

Malheur National Wildlife Refuge

## Day 4

Take the **Wallowa Lake Tramway** from Wallowa Lake. The tram lets you off at the top of Mount Howard, where there is a network of hiking trails. Then head west to I-84 at La Grande and follow the interstate to Pendleton. Tour the **Pendleton Underground** and spend the night in town.

## Day 5

Hop back on I-84 and take it west to Arlington. From Arlington, drive south on Highway 19 to the **John Day Fossil Beds.** Just south of the Thomas Condon Paleontology Center, turn west onto U.S. 26 and take it to your night's lodging in John Day.

## Day 6

It's a pretty drive south from John Day on U.S. 395 through Burns to the **Malheur National Wildlife Refuge.** Visit the refuge headquarters a few miles east of Highway 205, then continue south on Highway 205 to lodgings in **Frenchglen.**

## Day 7

If the snows have melted, drive the **Steens Mountain Byway.** Spend another night in Frenchglen, or head north to Burns before driving back to Boise to fly home.

埠華崙砵

# Portland

# Highlights

★ **Portland Art Museum:** Portland's green and shady South Park Blocks are home to this excellent collection of art and artifacts (page 44).

★ **Tom McCall Waterfront Park:** This riverside park is home to lots of summer festivals, great people-watching, a fountain, and over a mile of seawall to stroll (page 45).

★ **International Rose Test Garden:** The most spectacular sights in Washington Park are these famed gardens containing 10,000 rose plants (page 46).

★ **Portland Japanese Garden:** Five gardens in one, this is one of the most authentic Japanese gardens in the United States (page 47).

★ **Lan Su Chinese Garden:** A magical enclave in historic Chinatown, this replica of a Ming Dynasty garden was built by craftspeople from Suzhou, China (page 49).

★ **Pearl District:** This upscale shopping and dining district is Oregon's most densely populated neighborhood, home to many of the city's top galleries and restaurants (page 50).

★ **Hawthorne District:** This neighborhood, with its kick-back hippie vibe, is a good place to sip coffee and people-watch (page 54).

★ **Forest Park:** In the nation's largest forested urban park, you can mountain bike or walk on Leif Erikson Drive or explore part of the 30-mile-long Wildwood Trail (page 55).

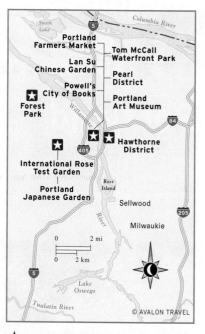

© AVALON TRAVEL

★ **Portland Farmers Market:** On Saturday, the South Park Blocks explode with the fresh bounty of the Willamette Valley (page 72).

★ **Powell's City of Books:** As the Pearl District has flourished, so has this huge bookstore, known for its mix of new and used titles (page 74).

# This friendly, flannel-clad, rain-scrubbed city has vaulted to a new place in the popular culture firmament, becoming a major trendsetter in cuisine, wine, arts, design, and up-to-the-second lifestyles.

Oregon's largest city, metro Portland has a population of 2.34 million, although its easygoing and quirky spirit makes it feel like a much smaller town. It's extremely easy to feel at home here—many are the tales of visitors coming to stay for a few days and finding a few pleasant years later that they forgot to leave. Newcomers are drawn here to live out their dream of launching a startup, opening a coffee shop, founding a clothing design firm, or establishing a micro-distillery. Portland's combination of youthful idealism and entrepreneurial zeal makes it a top destination for young creatives.

And then there's the politics. Portland is famously liberal and irreverent. In fact, even as the city grows, its reputation as a center of unconventional lifestyles and alternative and populist politics increases. But there's more to Portland than tribal tattoos and indolent coffee shops. Amid lush greenery, top-notch cultural institutions such as a first-rate

symphony and an opera company lend an air of worldly sophistication. A latticework of bridges spanning the Willamette River adds a distinctive profile, while parks, plazas, and other public spaces give Portland a heart and a soul.

Local Native Americans, referred to in general as the Chinook people, have lived near the confluence of the Columbia and Willamette Rivers for millennia. Sauvie Island, northwest of the city, was the site of Wal-lamt, the village whose name inspired explorer William Clark to name the Willamette in 1805. Portland's early growth was fueled by shipping and trade, which boomed after the California gold rush of 1849. At the same time, Oregon Trail settlers brought agriculture to the Willamette Valley, and mining and ranching developed throughout the West.

Today's Portland is a small city with lots of personality; an urban area equally suffused with green space and creative energy. A recent

**Previous:** Chinatown Gate; Crystal Springs Rhododendron Garden. **Above:** koi pond at the Portland Japanese Garden.

# Greater Portland Area

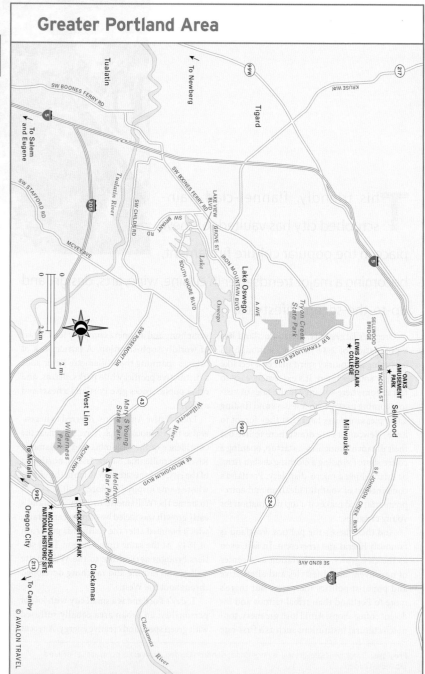

© AVALON TRAVEL

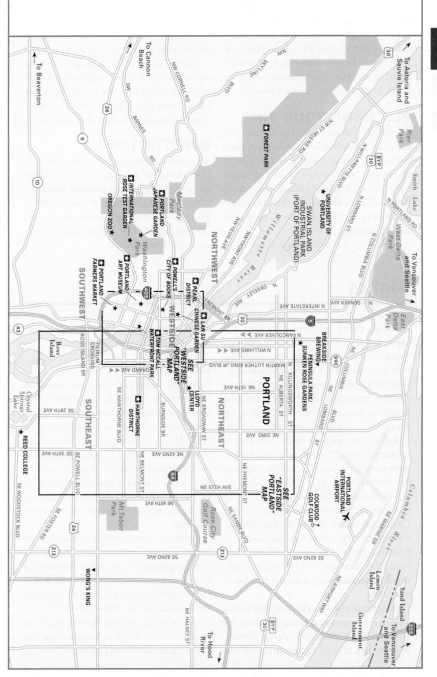

To Astoria and Sauvie Island

30

To Cannon Beach

NW CORNELL RD

SW 26

BARNES RD

8

To Beaverton

10

43

Pier Park

BYP 30

Smith Lake

N WILLAMETTE BLVD

N LOMBARD ST

N PORTLAND RD

West Delta Park

To Vancouver and Seattle

N COLUMBIA BLVD

N DENVER AVE

East Delta Park

SKYLINE BLVD

NW ST HELENS RD

FOREST PARK

Macleay Park

Washington Park

INTERNATIONAL ROSE TEST GARDEN
OREGON ZOO
PORTLAND JAPANESE GARDEN

SOUTHWEST

PORTLAND ART MUSEUM

PORTLAND FARMERS MARKET

NORTHWEST

SWAN ISLAND INDUSTRIAL PARK (PORT OF PORTLAND)

UNIVERSITY OF PORTLAND

PENINSULA PARK/ SUNKEN ROSE GARDENS

Willamette River

NW YEON AVE

NW FRONT AVE

N GREELEY AVE

FREMONT BR

N INTERSTATE AVE

30

I5

N VANCOUVER AVE
N WILLIAMS AVE

99E

NE COLUMBIA BLVD

NE LOMBARD ST

BREAKSIDE BREWING

MARTIN LUTHER KING JR BLVD

NE KILLINGSWORTH ST

NE ALBERTA ST

NE 15TH AVE

PORTLAND

POWELL'S CITY OF BOOKS
PEARL DISTRICT
LAN SU CHINESE GARDEN
WESTSIDE PORTLAND
TOM McCALL WATERFRONT PARK

SEE "WESTSIDE PORTLAND" MAP

Ross Island

ROSS ISLAND BR

TILIKUM CROSSING

Crystal Springs Lake

RED COLLEGE

SOUTHEAST

SE POWELL BLVD

SE WOODSTOCK BLVD

SE FOSTER RD

SE 28TH AVE

SE 39TH AVE

SE HAWTHORNE BLVD

HAWTHORNE DISTRICT

GRAND AVE

LLOYD CENTER

BURNSIDE ST

BURNSIDE BR

NE BROADWAY ST

NE 33RD AVE

NE 42ND AVE

NE BELMONT ST

NE 57TH AVE

NE 60TH AVE

NE FREMONT ST

NORTHEAST

Mt Tabor Park

26

SE 82ND AVE

213

SE 82ND AVE

Rose City Golf Course

NE SANDY BLVD

213

NE 82ND AVE

NE HALSEY ST

WONG'S KING

SEE "EASTSIDE PORTLAND" MAP

84

COLWOOD GOLF CLUB

PORTLAND INTERNATIONAL AIRPORT

NE MARINE DR

NE AIRPORT WAY

BYP 30

205

Columbia River

Lemon Island

Sand Island

Government Island

To Vancouver and Seattle

To Hood River

*New York Times* article declared Portland to be the most European city in the United States, but most Portlanders were too busy biking, drinking handcrafted ale, and buying local cheese at the farmers market to have noticed. Portland isn't like other places in the United States, and of that its citizens are proud.

## PLANNING YOUR TIME

Portland is different from London and San Francisco, cities filled with loads of top-notch destinations that serve as pilgrimage sights for every visitor. Aside from a handful of unique institutions and sights, Portland is more a city that you explore for its way of life. To capture Portland's potent allure, you need to do some serious hanging out.

Make a checklist of sights and activities, but leave time for spontaneous in-the-moment detours. Check out downtown institutions such as Powell's Books and the Portland Art Museum, but also visit the city's parks and let yourself relax in verdant beauty. Likewise, explore the city's varied neighborhoods, but take time to chat with new friends in a brewpub or coffee shop. The Portland experience is more a lifestyle than a set of destinations.

## ORIENTATION

Avenues run north-south and streets run east-west. The line of demarcation between north and south in addresses is Burnside Street; between east and west it's the Willamette River. These give reference points for the address prefixes southwest, southeast, north, northwest, and northeast.

# Sights

Portland offers a wealth of attractions and experiences, from cultural and historic to hands-on and avant-garde. Alongside the built environment are Portland's myriad beloved parks, which range from meticulously tended to sprawling and untamed. Portland has all the amenities you expect from a city, but with a healthy dose of the great outdoors.

Before you arrive, check out **Travel Portland** (503/275-8355 or 877/678-5263, www.travelportland.com) for free maps and its informative magazine-like publication *Travel Portland*. When you get to town, stop by its **visitor information center** (Pioneer Courthouse Square, 701 SW 6th Ave., 8:30am-5:30pm Mon.-Fri., 10am-4pm Sat. Nov.-Apr., 8:30am-5:30pm Mon.-Fri., 10am-4pm Sat., 10am-2pm Sun. May-Oct.) to pick up additional information and a map of the downtown area.

For a fun overview of Portland's top sights, join Big Pink Sightseeing's **Hop-On Hop-Off Trolley Tour** (503/241-7373, www.graylineofportland.net, $37). A daylong ticket lets you jump off and on an open-air covered bus anywhere along its 12-stop route.

## DOWNTOWN

Portland's modern downtown is located on a broad ledge of land between the north-flowing Willamette River and a steep volcanic ridge just to the west called the West Hills. More accurately called the Tualatin Mountains, they form a backdrop that towers 1,000 feet above downtown. The forested West Hills are home to one of Portland's oldest and most beautiful residential neighborhoods and to Washington Park, the city's grandest.

Portland's city center is a pleasant area dotted with green spaces. Cafés and bars spill onto the pavement, and a handsome blend of modern office towers, turn-of-the-20th-century storefronts, and office buildings lends architectural interest. What Portland doesn't have is a lot of massive skyscrapers. City blocks are only 200 feet long, making the city more accessible and pedestrian-friendly.

## Pioneer Courthouse Square

The nominal center of Portland is **Pioneer Courthouse Square** (SW 6th Ave. at Morrison St.), a block-square redbrick plaza that serves as an urban park and entertainment venue Always busy, in good weather the square is filled with brown-bag lunchers, chess players, political activists, and dozens of free spirits that defy characterization. The square is ringed by fanciful columns supporting nothing in particular, and a portion of the plaza is a hillside of steps that serve as seating or stairways, depending on your needs. Food carts line the south edge of the square, and many more are within a few blocks, making this a good destination for an open-air lunch. In summer, free midday concerts add to the zest.

A waterfall fountain (not always working) flanks the doors of the **TriMet office** (701 SW 6th Ave., 503/238-7433, www.trimet. org, 8:30am-5:30pm Mon.-Fri.), and **Travel Portland's Visitor Information Center** (701 SW 6th Ave., 503/275-8355 or 877/678-5263, www.travelportland.com, 8:30am-5:30pm Mon.-Fri., 10am-4pm Sat. Nov.-Apr., 8:30am-5:30pm Mon.-Fri., 10am-4pm Sat., 10am-2pm Sun. May-Oct.). Through the same doors you'll find access to public restrooms. Just east, across 6th Avenue, the **Pioneer Courthouse** (555 SW Yamhill St.) is the oldest public building in the state, constructed between 1869 and 1873.

Pioneer Courthouse Square is also at ground zero for downtown shopping. Immediately west, across Broadway, is Nordstrom, and one block east along Morrison or Yamhill Streets is Pioneer Place, a two-section upscale shopping development that is linked by a skywalk to fashion bargains at H&M. The lower level of Pioneer Place features a food court with a wide array of fast-food concessions.

## The South Park Blocks

Southwest of the square, one block west of Broadway, is **Director Park,** another open plaza that's a hub of lunchtime activity. A block south marks the start of the **South Park Blocks Cultural District,** a delightful thread of tree- and statuary-filled greenways established in the 1850s. The stands of American elms found here (and in the Pearl District's North Park Blocks) are among the largest remaining in North America, most of the rest having succumbed to Dutch elm disease.

Strolling the lanes of the South Park Blocks, which are flanked by many of Portland's most important museums and early landmark churches, evokes European parks. Portland's founders established this park in 1852, when wilderness stretched in every direction for thousands of miles.

Twice weekly, the **Portland Farmers Market** (Sat. and Wed. spring-fall) fills the South Park Blocks with the agricultural bounty of the Willamette Valley. Many vendors purvey freshly prepared food in addition to fruits, vegetables, cheeses, and meats. Also opening onto the park is the Portland Art Museum and the Oregon Historical Society Museum. The southern edges of the parks dissolve into Portland State University, an urban campus with the state's largest higher-education enrollment.

### PORTLAND'5 CENTERS FOR THE ARTS

Backing up to the South Park Blocks are two units of **Portland's Centers for the Arts** (503/248-4335, www.portland5.com), including the ornate **Arlene Schnitzer Concert Hall** (1037 SW Broadway), home to the Oregon Symphony. This jewel-box concert venue was once a 1920s vaudeville hall, but you'd never know it after a 1980s makeover turned the neglected theater into the city's premier concert space. Directly across Main Street is the **Antoinette Hatfield Hall** (SW Broadway at Main St.), which houses theaters and a soaring lobby topped by a confetti-like glass dome. You'll need a concert ticket to see its glittering interior of the Schnitzer Concert Hall, but the Antoinette Hatfield Hall is open all day and during the evening when

# Portland

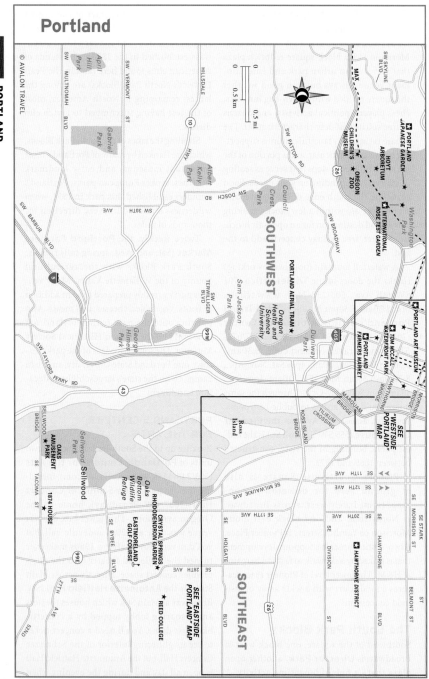

© AVALON TRAVEL

SW SKYLINE BLVD

MAX

SW SKYLINE BLVD

HILLSDALE

SW VERMONT ST

SW MULTNOMAH BLVD

April Hill Park

Gabriel Park

10

SW PATTON RD

SW DOSCH RD

Albert Kelly Park

Council Crest Park

SW 30TH AVE

SOUTHWEST

PORTLAND JAPANESE GARDEN

HOYT ARBORETUM

OREGON ZOO

CHILDREN'S MUSEUM

26

INTERNATIONAL ROSE TEST GARDEN

Washington Park

SW BROADWAY

PORTLAND AERIAL TRAM

SW TERWILLIGER BLVD

Sam Jackson Park

Oregon Health and Science University

PORTLAND ART MUSEUM

TOM McCALL WATERFRONT PARK

PORTLAND FARMERS MARKET

PORTLAND

SW BARBUR BLVD

5

George Himes Park

99W

405

Dunniway Park

"WESTSIDE PORTLAND" MAP

MORRISON BRIDGE

HAWTHORNE BRIDGE

SEE "WESTSIDE PORTLAND" MAP

SW TAYLORS FERRY RD

43

MARQUAM BRIDGE

TILIKUM CROSSING

Ross Island

ROSS ISLAND BRIDGE

SELLWOOD BRIDGE

Sellwood Park

OAKS AMUSEMENT PARK

SE TACOMA ST

Sellwood

Oaks Bottom Wildlife Refuge

1874 HOUSE

SE MILWAUKIE AVE

SE 11TH AVE

SE 12TH AVE

SE 17TH AVE

SE 20TH AVE

SE MORRISON ST

SE STARK

SE STARK ST

MORRISON ST

HAWTHORNE

BELMONT ST

HAWTHORNE DISTRICT

HAWTHORNE BLVD

99E

SE BYBEE BLVD

CRYSTAL SPRINGS RHODODENDRON GARDEN

EASTMORELAND GOLF COURSE

SE 28TH AVE

SE HOLGATE

DIVISION

DIVISION ST

BELMONT ST

SE 27TH AVE

SE 22ND AVE

REED COLLEGE

SEE "EASTSIDE PORTLAND" MAP

SOUTHEAST

26

BLVD

0    0.5 mi

0    0.5 km

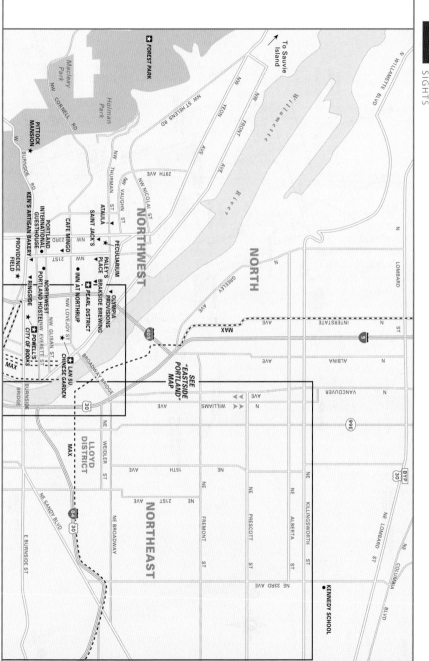

FOREST PARK

To Sauvie
Island

Macleay
Park

Holman
Park

NW CORNELL RD

PITTOCK
MANSION ★

NW BURNSIDE RD

W

NW ST HELENS RD

NW YEON AVE

NW FRONT AVE

NW NICOLAI ST

NW THURMAN ST

NW VAUGHN ST

29TH AVE

W i l l a m e t t e   R i v e r

NORTH

N

N WILLAMETTE BLVD

N LOMBARD ST

N INTERSTATE AVE

N GREELEY AVE

MAX

(5)

N ALBINA AVE

N VANCOUVER AVE

(99E)

NORTHWEST

ATAULA ▼
SAINT JACK'S ▼

CAFE MINGO ▼

NW 23RD

PECULIARIUM ★

PALEY'S
PLACE ▼

NW 21ST

BRAKSIDE BREWING ★

KEN'S ARTISAN BAKERY ▼

PORTLAND
INTERNATIONAL
GUESTHOUSE ●

PROVIDENCE
FIELD ★

INN AT NORTHRUP ●

NW LOVEJOY ST

NW NORTHRUP ST

PEARL DISTRICT ★

OLYMPIA
PROVISIONS ▼

405

NW EVERETT ST

NW GLISAN ST

RINGSIDE ▼

NORTHWEST
PORTLAND HOSTEL ●

POWELL'S
CITY OF BOOKS ★

MAX

BURNSIDE
BRIDGE

LAN SU
CHINESE
GARDEN ★

BROADWAY BRIDGE

(30)

SEE
"EASTSIDE
PORTLAND"
MAP

N WILLIAMS AVE

◄◄
► ►

MAX

NE WEIDLER ST

LLOYD
DISTRICT

NE 15TH AVE

NE 21ST AVE

NE SANDY BLVD

84 (30)

NE BROADWAY

NORTHEAST

E BURNSIDE ST

NE FREMONT ST

NE PRESCOTT ST

NE ALBERTA ST

NE KILLINGSWORTH ST

NE 33RD AVE

● KENNEDY SCHOOL

NE LOMBARD ST

NE COLUMBIA BLVD

BYP (30)

# Westside Portland

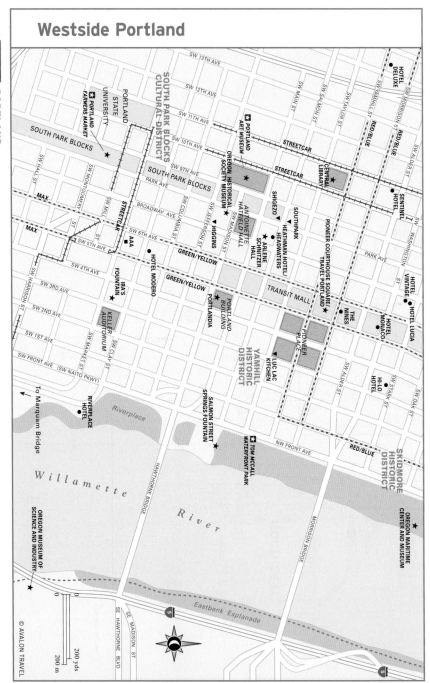

SW 13TH AVE
SW 12TH AVE
SW 11TH AVE
SW 10TH AVE
SW 9TH AVE

SW MAIN ST
SW SALMON ST
SW TAYLOR ST
SW YAMHILL ST
SW MORRISON ST

HOTEL DELUXE

PORTLAND STATE UNIVERSITY

PORTLAND FARMERS MARKET

SOUTH PARK BLOCKS CULTURAL DISTRICT

SOUTH PARK BLOCKS

PORTLAND ART MUSEUM

OREGON HISTORICAL SOCIETY MUSEUM

STREETCAR

STREETCAR

CENTRAL LIBRARY

RED/BLUE
RED/BLUE

SW WASHINGTON ST
SW ALDER ST

SENTINEL HOTEL

PARK AVE

MAX
MAX

SW HALL ST
SW MONTGOMERY ST
SW MILL ST
SW 5TH AVE

PARK AVE
BROADWAY AVE
SW COLUMBIA ST
SW JEFFERSON ST
SW MADISON ST

SHIGEZO

SOUTHPARK

ANTOINETTE HATFIELD HALL

HIGGINS

HEATHMAN HOTEL

HEADWATERS

ARLENE SCHNITZER HALL

PIONEER COURTHOUSE SQUARE / TRAVEL PORTLAND

HOTEL VINTAGE

HOTEL LUCIA

SW 6TH AVE
STREETCAR
AAA
GREEN/YELLOW
GREEN/YELLOW
TRANSIT MALL

HOTEL MODERO

IRA'S FOUNTAIN

HOTEL MONACO

THE NINES

SW 4TH AVE
SW 3RD AVE
SW 2ND AVE
SW 1ST AVE

SW HARRISON ST

KELLER AUDITORIUM

PORTLANDIA

PORTLAND BUILDING

PIONEER PLACE

YAMHILL HISTORIC DISTRICT

LUC LAC KITCHEN

HI-LO HOTEL

SW STARK ST
SW OAK ST

SW ALDER ST

SW FRONT AVE (SW NAITO PKWY)
SW MARKET ST
SW CLAY ST

To Marquam Bridge

RIVERPLACE HOTEL

Riverplace

SALMON STREET SPRINGS FOUNTAIN

TOM McCALL WATERFRONT PARK

NW FRONT AVE

RED/BLUE

SKIDMORE HISTORIC DISTRICT

HAWTHORNE BRIDGE

Willamette

River

MORRISON BRIDGE

OREGON MUSEUM OF SCIENCE AND INDUSTRY

OREGON MARITIME CENTER AND MUSEUM

Eastbank Esplanade

SE HAWTHORNE BLVD
SE MADISON ST

0       200 yds
0       200 m

© AVALON TRAVEL

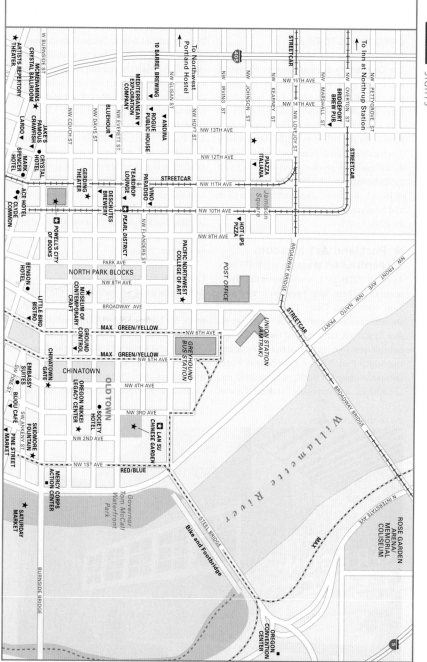

performances are scheduled; the lobby bar makes a nice spot for a drink.

## OREGON HISTORICAL SOCIETY MUSEUM

The **Oregon Historical Society Museum** (1230 SW Park Ave., 503/222-1741, www.ohs.org, 10am-5pm Mon.-Sat., noon-5pm Sun., $11 adults, $9 seniors and students, $5 ages 6-18, free for Multnomah County residents) tells the rich story of the state's Native American and settler heritage; special exhibits are mounted regularly and often focus on topics beyond local history, such as the legacy of John F. Kennedy. The combined gift shop and bookstore is a good place to pick up quality gifts.

## ★ Portland Art Museum

The **Portland Art Museum** (1219 SW Park Ave., 503/226-2811, www.portlandartmuseum.org, 10am-5pm Tues.-Wed. and Sat.-Sun., 10am-8pm Thurs.-Fri., $20 adults, $17 students and over age 54, free under age 18, free 5pm-8pm 1st Thurs. of the month) encompasses two grand structures along the South Park Blocks, the original Pietro Belluschi-designed building from 1932 and the adjacent and imposing Portland Masonic Temple, which together offer 112,000 square feet of galleries housing 42,000 objects. Dating from 1892, it's the oldest art museum on the West Coast and houses Oregon's most significant art collection, including a small selection of Old Masters and Impressionists and a noteworthy Asian art collection. In 2001, the museum acquired the private collection of renowned New York art critic Clement Greenberg, which is on permanent display. The Pacific Northwest Native Art collection is excellent, and at least one major traveling exhibition is presented most of the time, usually with separate admission. A major expansion of the museum, housing paintings by native son Mark Rothko, begins construction in 2018. The Rothko Pavilion will tie together the existing museum buildings and create a new central entrance.

## Central Library

Portland is a city of readers, with the busiest library system in the United States. A landmark for bibliophiles, Multnomah County Library system's **Central Library** (801 SW 10th Ave., 503/988-5123, www.multcolib.org, 10am-8pm Mon., noon-8 Tues.-Wed., 10am-6pm Thurs.-Sat., 10am-5pm Sun.) is an architecturally stunning renovation of a 1913

the Portland Art Museum

# Portland Architecture

Portland has many notable buildings, both old and new. From its beginnings in the 1840s to the 1870s, Portland was built mostly of wood. However, after a series of fires in the 1870s, which together burned much of the original downtown, Portland was rebuilt in brick and stone. By this time the merchant kings of Portland felt like displaying their affluence, and a brand-new and glamorous city went up between 1880 and 1915.

From Pioneer Courthouse Square you can see a number of notable buildings, including the **American Bank Building** (SW Morrison St. between 6th Ave. and Broadway), built in 1913 from a design by famed architect A. E. Doyle. Doyle is also responsible for the building just east, the block-square **Meier & Frank Building,** now housing the Nines Hotel, built in 1909. Both buildings, and the 1912 **Jackson Tower/Oregon Journal Building** (Broadway and SW Yamhill St.) across the square, are faced in white-glazed terra-cotta tile.

Immediately east of the Square is the **Pioneer Courthouse** itself. Begun in 1869, it's the oldest public building in Oregon and the second-oldest west of the Mississippi. Kitty-corner to the square to the southwest is one of Portland's most pleasing modern buildings, the 27-story **Fox Tower,** built in 2000 with a curving facade that looks like a cruise ship.

North on Broadway are two other handsome historic structures. The **Hotel Vintage** (SW Washington St. and Broadway), a marvelous example of late Victorian (1894) Romanesque, is built of local basalt and red brick. The 1917 **U.S. National Bank Building** (SW Broadway and Stark St.; main entrance on SW 6th Ave.) is a grand neoclassical structure faced with 54-foot Corinthian columns. Just around the corner, **U.S. Bancorp Tower** (SW 6th Ave. and Burnside St.) is the city's second-tallest building, at 43 stories. Commonly called "Big Pink" for its pink granite and rose glass facade, it's one of Portland's most distinctive buildings.

The **Dekum Building** (SW 3rd Ave. and Washington St.), with its massive basalt columns, arches, and gargoyles, is a prime example of Richardson Romanesque from 1891. The striking 1893 **Haseltine Building** (133 SW 2nd Ave.) was once a hansom cab stable, its arches open for the carriages.

building designed by Albert Doyle, architect of the Benson Hotel and the U.S. National Bank Building downtown. Climb the sweeping staircases to the top floor to get a sense of the scale of this building—three stories have never seemed so monumental.

## Portland Building

Raymond Kaskey's *Portlandia,* a statue that is said to symbolize the city, ranks right behind the Statue of Liberty as the world's largest hammered copper sculpture. Located outside Michael Graves's postmodern **Portland Building** (SW 5th Ave. between Main St. and Madison St.), the crouching female figure holding a trident recreates the Lady of Commerce on the city seal. Although the birthday-cake design of the building caused much acclaim and scorn when it was built in the 1980s, it hasn't held up well; it's

undergoing a major remodel through 2020 to address structural problems.

## ★ Tom McCall Waterfront Park

**Tom McCall Waterfront Park** is named for the governor credited with helping to reclaim Oregon's rivers. In the early 1970s the park's grassy shore replaced Harbor Drive, a freeway that impeded access to the Willamette River. Today, the park is frequently the scene of summer festivals, while the wide, paved riverside esplanade is a favorite for joggers, cyclists, and strolling families.

Begin your introduction to mile-long Tom McCall Waterfront Park at **RiverPlace,** an attractive string of restaurants, specialty shops, and boating facilities overlooking the Willamette River in the shadow of the Marquam Bridge. Follow the paved riverside walkway north to the **Salmon Street Springs Fountain** at the base of Salmon Street. The fountain water's ebb and flow are meant to evoke the rhythms of the city and provide a refreshing shower on a hot day.

North along the seawall is the sternwheeler USS *Portland,* which houses the **Oregon Maritime Center and Museum** (foot of SW Pine St., 503/224-7724, www.oregonmaritimemuseum.org, 11am-4pm Wed. and Fri.-Sat., $7 adults, $5 seniors, $4 ages 13-18, $3 ages 6-12). The museum offers a window into the fascinating maritime heritage of Portland and the Columbia and Willamette River systems, and it features ship models, historic diving equipment, and other artifacts.

Farther north in the shadow of the Burnside Bridge is the home of the **Portland Saturday Market** and the **Battleship *Oregon* Memorial,** which commemorates the famed 1893 fighting ship; its block juts out of the grass. Also north of the Burnside Bridge, the **Japanese American Historical Plaza** is dedicated to the memory of those who were deported to internment camps during World War II. This is also the site of a gorgeous swath of cherry trees.

### Old Town and the Skidmore Fountain Historic District

From the 1870s through the 1920s, **Old Town** was the heart of Victorian-era Portland. After a disastrous fire in 1873 burned Portland's original wood-built commercial district, the city was rebuilt with multistory brick buildings, many with cast-iron facades. Iron could be cast in myriad forms, and the most popular in this period were Italianate columns with elaborate plinths and capitals. Portland has the second-largest inventory of cast-iron-fronted buildings in the country.

Portland's original harbor area fell on hard times after commercial shipping traffic moved to docks farther downriver and passenger trains replaced boats. Today, even though there's still a scruffy edge to Old Town, many of the city's hottest nightclubs

and bars are here. At the heart of Old Town is **Skidmore Fountain** (SW 1st Ave. and SW Ankeny St.). Built at great expense with a bequest from an early Portland dentist, it was intended as a source of water for "horses, men, and dogs."

Just north of the Skidmore Fountain is the **Mercy Corps Action Center** (28 SW 1st Ave., 503/896-5002, www.actioncenter.org, 11am-5pm Mon.-Fri.), where you can learn about many of the projects sponsored by Mercy Corps, a Portland-based aid organization.

## WASHINGTON PARK

The crown jewel of Portland's magnificent park system is **Washington Park,** which encompasses 130 acres of forest, formal gardens, and such civic institutions as the Oregon Zoo, the International Rose Test Garden, the Portland Japanese Garden, and the Portland Children's Museum. Adjacent to the park is the Hoyt Arboretum.

The park had its beginnings in 1871, and in its early years was modeled on European parks, with winding drives, shady walkways, fountains, noble statuary, formal plantings, lawns, and ornamental flower displays. To reach the park from downtown, take TriMet bus 63, with weekday service, or the MAX Light Rail Blue or Red Lines. Parking is limited, so it's really best to avoid driving. A free summertime shuttle runs between the MAX station at the zoo and other Washington Park destinations. If you do drive, bike, or walk, take Park Place west from SW Vista Avenue and wind up the hill. The road passes a number of fountains and statues as it loops upward. From NW 23rd Avenue and Burnside, it's about a one-mile walk to the Rose Garden and Japanese Garden.

### ★ International Rose Test Garden

Encompassing 4.5 acres of roses, manicured lawns, other formal gardens, and an outdoor concert venue, the **International Rose Test Garden** (400 SW Kingston Ave.) is wedged

the International Rose Test Garden

rose gardens must pay zoo admission in addition to train fare.

Just beyond the rose gardens is the **Rose Garden Children's Park,** a large and elaborate play area with quite fantastic play structures.

## ★ Portland Japanese Garden

Just up the slope from the rose gardens, the **Portland Japanese Garden** (611 SW Kingston Ave., 503/223-1321, www.japanesegarden.com, noon-7pm Mon., 10am-7pm Tues.-Sun. mid-Mar.-Sept., noon-4pm Mon., 10am-4pm Tues.-Sun. Oct.-mid Mar., $15 adults, $13 seniors, $12 students, $10.45 ages 6-17) is a magical five-acre Eden with tumbling water, bonsai, and elaborately manicured shrubs and trees. Winding paths link six separate gardens. Architect Kengo Kuma designed the striking on-site Cultural Village in modern Japanese style, with a courtyard and dry-stacked rock wall, a gallery, a library, and a café.

From the rose gardens, you can walk up the short but relatively steep trail to the Japanese Garden, or hop on the free open-air shuttle that runs every 15 minutes or so.

## Oregon Zoo

The **Oregon Zoo** (4001 SW Canyon Rd., 503/226-1561, www.oregonzoo.org, 9:30am-6pm daily Memorial Day-Labor Day, 9:30am-4pm daily Sept.-May, $15 ages 12-64, $13 seniors, $10 ages 3-11, $5 discount Oct.-Feb.) has exhibits representing various geographic areas of the world. A series of major expansions through 2019 will see new rhino, primate, and polar bear habitats; nearly half the zoo grounds will get an upgrade. The zoo collection contains nearly 2,000 individual animals representing 232 species. The zoo is especially noted for its elephant program, which has one of the most successful breeding programs in the world. The zoo features two year-round eating establishments, a series of educational events for children, and summertime concerts. The zoo is easily reached from

onto the steep slopes of the West Hills in Washington Park. In addition to intoxicating scents and incredible floral displays, the garden also offers the classic view of Portland—Mount Hood rising above the downtown office towers. Bring a camera. Today, the rose garden features over 10,000 rose bushes of 650 varieties, both old and new. A charming annex to the rose garden is the **Shakespeare Garden,** which includes only herbs, trees, and flowers mentioned in Shakespeare's plays.

Free tours of the rose garden (1pm daily June-Labor Day, donation) are led by trained volunteers. Meet at the sign outside the Rose Garden Store.

Just above the rose gardens are a set of tennis courts, beautifully situated beneath towering firs, and up a flight of steps is the terminus for the 30-inch narrow-gauge Washington Park and Zoo Railway, which links these two popular family destinations with a trip through Washington Park's dense forests. Riders who take the train from the

the MAX Light Rail Blue and Red Lines or, on weekdays, via bus number 63 from downtown.

If you plan to visit both the zoo and the rose garden, consider linking these two family-favorite sites along the 30-inch narrow-gauge **Washington Park and Zoo Railway** (503/226-1561, 10:30am-5:30pm daily Memorial Day-Labor Day, weather permitting, $4, free under age 3), a two-mile trip through Washington Park's dense forests. Since the train's upper station is within the zoo precincts, riders who board the train at the rose gardens must also purchase admission to the zoo.

The train also runs during the holiday ZooLights season (5pm-8pm Sun.-Thurs., 5pm-8:30pm Fri.-Sat.) from the Friday after Thanksgiving through the Sunday after New Year's Day, when you can visit the zoo with the added enhancement of a holiday display with over one million LED lights. You can also visit the zoo via public transportation or private car during the same hours.

### Portland Children's Museum

Adjacent to the zoo is the **Portland Children's Museum** (4015 SW Canyon Rd., 503/223-6500, www.portlandcm.org, 9am-5pm Fri.-Wed., 9am-8pm Thurs. Mar. 1-Labor Day, 9am-5pm Tues.-Sun. Labor Day-Feb., $10.75 adults and children, $9.75 military and over age 54), featuring events and activities for kids ages six months to 10 years.

### Hoyt Arboretum

Along the crest of the West Hills above Washington Park is **Hoyt Arboretum** (4000 SW Fairview Blvd., 503/865-8733, www.hoytarboretum.org, 6am-10pm daily, free), with 12 miles of trails winding through an expansive 187-acre tree garden boasting the world's largest collection of conifers. The arboretum's collection is made up of over 6,000 individual trees and plants that represent over 2,000 species from all corners of the globe. Most of the collection is linked by trails and labeled with botanical names. The trees throughout are presented in taxonomically organized groups:

oaks are with oaks; maples are with other maples. Stop by the visitors center and pick up a trail map before setting out. A one-mile trail is paved and suitable for wheelchairs.

## NORTHWEST

Northwest Portland is an entire quadrant of the city, but when most Portlanders talk about the Northwest, they are talking about a rather compact set of neighborhoods just north of downtown.

### Old Town and Chinatown

From the 1870s through the 1910s, the entire Willamette River waterfront was the city's harbor, an extended area now called **Old Town.** By the 1870s, the more northerly neighborhoods of Old Town, roughly bounded by NW 2nd and 4th Avenues and Burnside and Everett Streets, became known as **Chinatown,** an enclave of historic redbrick buildings that was home to Chinese and Japanese immigrants.

At its peak, around 1890, Portland's Chinatown had a population of around 5,000, second in size only to San Francisco's. As the Chinese moved on, they were replaced by Japanese people, and Chinatown became **Japantown;** by 1940, Portland's Japantown had over 100 Japanese-owned businesses and a population of some 3,500.

Portland's thriving Japanese community came to a sudden end in 1942, when President Franklin D. Roosevelt issued Executive Order 9066, leading to the evacuation and internment of thousands of Japanese American citizens. Almost overnight, Japantown became a ghost town. Chinese businesses moved back in, and the area once again became known as Chinatown; but in many ways, this neighborhood has never recovered. Today's Asian community in Portland is along SE 82nd Avenue.

Wandering the streets of Old Town and Chinatown late at night is probably not a good idea, but traveling safely to and from the restaurants and clubs is simple. Taxis are easy to find in this entertainment hotbed; MAX Light Rail trains run along 1st, 5th, and 6th

Avenues; and buses pass along 5th and 6th Avenues and on Everett Street.

## OREGON NIKKEI LEGACY CENTER

For insights into Portland's Japanese community and the wartime internment, visit the **Oregon Nikkei Legacy Center** (121 NW 2nd Ave., 503/224-1458, www.oregonnikkei. org, 11am-3pm Tues.-Sat., noon-3pm Sun., $5 adults, $3 students and seniors), in the heart of old Japantown; it is one of the most fascinating small museums in Portland.

## CHINATOWN GATE

Presented as a gesture of goodwill from the Chinese community to the city of Portland, the colorful **Chinatown Gate** (W. Burnside St. and SW 4th Ave.) is the largest of its kind in the United States and marks the entrance to historic Chinatown. Dedicated in 1986, the Chinatown Gate comprises five roofs, 64 dragons, and two huge lions.

## ★ LAN SU CHINESE GARDEN

Colorful in a different way, the **Lan Su Chinese Garden** (239 NW Everett St., 503/228-8131, www.lansugarden.org, 10am-7pm daily Apr.-Oct., 10am-5pm daily Nov.-Mar., $10 adults, $9 seniors, $7 ages 6-18 and college students) is a formal Chinese garden built in the style of the Ming Dynasty. The block-square green space is the result of a joint effort between two famed gardening centers, Portland and its Chinese sister city, Suzhou. Over 60 landscape designers and craftspeople from Suzhou lived and worked in Portland for a year to complete the gardens, which are the largest traditional Chinese gardens in the United States. Nearly all the materials and tools used were also brought from China, including roof and floor tiles, all of the hand-carved woodwork, the latticed windows, and over 500 tons of Swiss cheese-like Taihu granite boulders. A tea shop keeps the same hours as the gardens and is a delightful spot for a light lunch.

## UNION STATION

To the north, Old Town and Chinatown ends at **Union Station** (800 NW 6th Ave.), the glorious Italianate rail station that still serves as Portland's Amtrak depot. The station has been in continuous use since it was built in 1896 and is the second-oldest still-operating train station in the country. With its terracotta tile roof and 150-foot campanile with a four-sided Seth Thomas clock, this is one of Portland's most beloved landmarks.

The Lan Su Chinese Garden is a quiet spot in the middle of busy Old Town.

## ★ Pearl District

A former warehouse district, the **Pearl District** is lined with upscale condos, home decor boutiques, fine restaurants, and art galleries. A good place to begin your exploration is along NW 10th and 11th Avenues. **Powell's Books** (W. Burnside St. and 10th Ave.) is one of the nation's largest bookstores and a classic place for Portlanders to spend rainy weekend afternoons. Continuing north on 11th Avenue, you pass the castellated **Gerding Theater** (128 NW 11th Ave.), a former armory and home to Portland Center Stage. If you're looking to decorate your home, the myriad furniture and decor stores along NW Glisan Street between 10th and 14th Avenues ought to provide inspiration.

Farther north is **Jamison Square** (bounded by NW 10th Ave., 11th Ave., Johnson St., and Kearney St.), a public park with a fountain that's a favorite destination for the neighborhood's children to get wet and cool down. Three blocks north is quieter **Tanner Springs Park**, which recalls the wetland that once covered the Pearl District.

From downtown, the Pearl District is easily reached on the Portland Streetcar, which travels along NW 10th and 11th Avenues.

## NW 21st and 23rd Avenues

Sometimes referred to as Nob Hill, the lovely Victorian neighborhoods around NW 21st and 23rd Avenues represent an island of upscale dining and shopping. Victorian homes have been remodeled into boutiques to join stylish clothing shops, restaurants, bars, and theaters. Generally speaking, NW 21st Avenue has the greater number of restaurants, while NW 23rd Avenue has more shops—a mix of upper-end locally owned boutiques and national chains.

Coffee shops and unique little stores are abundant, and on a nice day, the streets are absolutely thronged with intriguing-looking people. Street parking can be difficult to find in Northwest Portland; if you're coming from downtown or the Pearl District, consider taking the Portland Streetcar, which crosses both NW 21st and 23rd Avenues along Marshall and Lovejoy Streets.

## Peculiarium

From the bloody Frankenstein dummy dozing in a wheelchair outside the entrance to the creepy fake-alien dolls, Bigfoot exhibit, and gross-out ice cream sundaes ("Crime Scene Massacre," anybody?), the **Peculiarium** (2234 NW Thurman St., 503/227-3164, www.peculiarium.com, 11am-6pm Tues.-Thurs., 11am-8pm Fri.-Sat., 11am-7pm Sun., $5, free with "decent costumes") does its bit to keep Portland weird. Even weirder, it's right around the corner from tony 23rd Avenue.

## Pittock Mansion

Occupying a 1,000-foot promontory on 46 acres in the West Hills is **Pittock Mansion** (3229 NW Pittock Dr., 503/823-3623, http://pittockmansion.org, 11am-4pm daily Feb.-May and Sept.-Dec., 10am-5pm daily June-Labor Day, $10 adults, $9 seniors, $7 ages 6-18), a grand 1914 home built by the then editor of the *Oregonian* newspaper. The 22-room mansion was designed to contemporary tastes and is a showcase of early-20th-century style and design. Guided tours of the mansion are available, but it's also worth the trip up to this pinnacle vantage point simply to enjoy the lush gardens, the fabulous views of Portland and the Cascades, and the easy access to Forest Park's Wildwood Trail (bring a picnic).

## NORTHEAST

North and Northeast Portland cover an enormous area, all the way from East Burnside Street north to the Columbia River, and from the Willamette River east to beyond Portland's airport. However, for visitors, the quadrant's main draws are the inner Northeast neighborhoods directly across from downtown as well as a handful of districts that represent the outposts of Portland's DIY nation.

## Lloyd District

Just east of Old Town, across the Willamette

# Portland Bridges

Of all the metro areas in the United States, Portland is arguably *the* City of Bridges, with 13 on the Willamette and two on the Columbia. The three oldest—the Broadway, Steel, and Hawthorne—were built before World War I. Bridge fans can also revel in the broad array of types on view; all were designed by the preeminent engineers of their day. Many of the Willamette River crossings are illuminated at night by strategically placed floodlights, adding yet another pleasing visual dimension. The two spans of the **Steel Bridge** (1912) can be raised and lowered independently. The lovely **St. John's Bridge** (1931) is the only steel suspension bridge in Portland and one of only three suspension bridges in Oregon.

From the newest, the **Tilikum Crossing** (2015), to the oldest, the **Hawthorne Bridge** (1910), downtown bridges are 0.3 miles from each other and are, for the most part, safe and accessible for bicyclists and pedestrians; only the I-5 Marquam and I-405 Fremont Bridges are off-limits to nonmotorized vehicles and pedestrians.

the Tilikum Crossing

River, is the **Lloyd District.** Named for Lloyd Center—Oregon's first shopping mall, which lies in the district's middle—it is basically an extension of downtown, with towering office buildings, major public buildings, sports stadiums, convention facilities, and a number of midrange hotels. The monumental **Oregon Convention Center** (777 NE M. L. King Jr. Blvd., 503/235-7575, www.oregoncc.org) is easy to spot, with its twin glass steeples. Encompassing nearly 20 square blocks, this massive structure is the largest convention facility in the Pacific Northwest.

All of these destinations are easily reached by the MAX Light Rail Red and Blue Lines and the eastside Portland Streetcar. On the north edge of Lloyd District is NE Broadway, a major arterial linking the northeast residential neighborhoods with downtown Portland via the Broadway Bridge (take bus 17 from downtown).

## NE Alberta Street

Once a thriving commercial strip, by the late 1980s Alberta Street had become a symbol of neglect, redlining, drug dealing, and gang activity. A decade later, the surrounding neighborhood was among the most rapidly gentrifying in the country, with all the change that entails. Nowadays Alberta Street, between NE Martin Luther King Jr. Boulevard and NE 33rd Avenue, is known to a new generation as a trendy arts district and a center for drinking and fine dining, perhaps the closest thing you'll find in Portland to a Latin Quarter of bohemian artists, cafés, bars, and bonhomie.

Part of the charm of Alberta Street is that it hasn't been razed and remade; there are still barbershops and body shops, storefront churches and comfortably seedy bars amid all the new construction and renovation. Alberta Street is also home to several art galleries, which play host along with studios and street vendors to thousands of revelers the last Thursday evening of every month for the Art Walk, otherwise known as Last Thursday.

The best way to get to Alberta Street by public transport is by bus 6, which crosses Alberta Street on NE Martin Luther King Jr. Boulevard, or bus 8, which crosses Alberta Street on NE 15th Avenue. Once on Alberta

# Eastside Portland

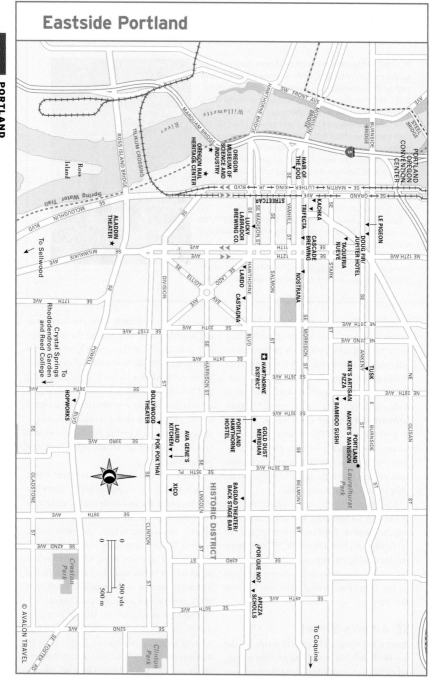

SW FRONT AVE

Willamette River

Ross Island

MARQUAM BRIDGE

HAWTHORNE BRIDGE

MORRISON BRIDGE

BURNSIDE BRIDGE

STEEL BRIDGE

PORTLAND OREGON CONVENTION CENTER

TILIKUM CROSSING

ROSS ISLAND BRIDGE

MCLOUGHLIN BLVD

Spring Water Trail

To Sellwood

MILWAUKIE AVE

ALADDIN THEATER ★

OREGON RAIL HERITAGE CENTER ★

OREGON MUSEUM OF SCIENCE AND INDUSTRY ★

SE MARTIN LUTHER KING JR. BLVD

SE GRAND AVE

NE 12TH AVE

HAIR OF THE DOG

STREETCAR

SE LUCKY LABRADOR BREWING CO.

SE MADISON ST

YAMHILL

KACHKA

TRIFECTA

CASCADE BREWING

DOUG FIR/ JUPITER HOTEL

TAQUERIA NUEVE

LE PIGEON

SE 6TH AVE

11TH

12TH

HAWTHORNE

SALMON

STARK

NOSTRANA

SE 20TH AVE

NE 20TH AVE

NE 22ND AVE

SE LADD AVE

SE ELLIOT AVE

DIVISION

LARDO

CASTAGNA

ANKENY

KEN'S ARTISAN PIZZA

TUSK

PORTLAND MAYOR'S MANSION

BAMBOO SUSHI

NE 28TH AVE

E BURNSIDE ST

GLISAN ST

Laurelhurst Park

SE 17TH AVE

SE 21ST AVE

POWELL

To Crystal Springs Rhododendron Garden and Reed College

MORRISON ST

BLVD

✚ HAWTHORNE DISTRICT

SE 24TH AVE

HARRISON ST

SE 26TH AVE

SE 30TH AVE

SE 35TH AVE

BELMONT ST

HOPWORKS

SE 28TH AVE

BLVD

BOLLYWOOD THEATER

POK POK THAI

LAURO KITCHEN

AVA GENE'S

XICO

GOLD DUST MERIDIAN

PORTLAND HAWTHORNE HOSTEL

BAGDAD THEATER/ BACK STAGE BAR

HISTORIC DISTRICT

LINCOLN

CLINTON

SE 33RD AVE

SE 39TH

GLADSTONE

Creston Park

SE 42ND AVE

ST

43RD

¿POR QUE NO?

APIZZA SCHOLLS

SE 49TH AVE

SE 50TH AVE

To Coquine

0    500 yds
0    500 m

© AVALON TRAVEL

SE 52ND AVE

SE FOSTER RD

Clinton Park

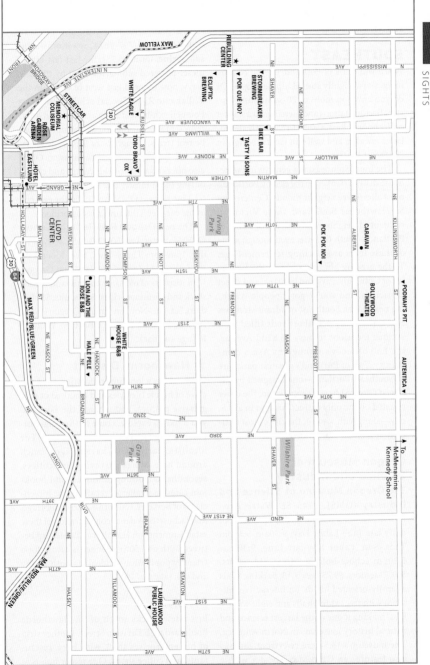

MAX YELLOW

REBUILDING CENTER ★

ECLIPTIC BREWING ▼

POR QUÉ NO? ▼

STORMBREAKER BREWING ▼

SHAVER ST

NE SKIDMORE ST

MISSISSIPPI AVE

N

NE

N INTERSTATE AVE

NW

BROADWAY BRIDGE

FRONT AVE

STREETCAR

WHITE EAGLE ▼

N RUSSELL ST

30

N WILLIAMS AVE

N VANCOUVER AVE

NE RODNEY AVE

BIKE BAR ▼

TASTY N SONS ▼

MALLORY AVE

NE

NE

TORO BRAVO ▼

OX ▼

BLVD

MARTIN LUTHER KING JR

NE

MEMORIAL COLISEUM ★

ROSE GARDEN ARENA

HOTEL EASTLUND

NE GRAND AVE

HOLLADAY ST

7TH AVE

Irving Park

NE 10TH AVE

NE 17TH AVE

POK POK NOI ▼

KILLINGSWORTH ST

CARAVAN ●

NE ALBERTA ST

▼ PODNAH'S PIT

LLOYD CENTER

MULTNOMAH ST

WEIDLER ST

NE 12TH AVE

KNOTT ST

SISKIYOU ST

THOMPSON ST

TILLAMOOK ST

NE 15TH AVE

FREMONT ST

NE 21ST AVE

NE MASON ST

PRESCOTT ST

BOLLYWOOD THEATER ■

NE 30TH AVE

AUTENTICA ▼

30

84

MAX RED/BLUE/GREEN

LION AND THE ROSE B&B ●

NE WASCO ST

HANCOCK ST

WHITE HOUSE B&B ●

HALE PELE ▼

NE 28TH AVE

BROADWAY

NE 32ND AVE

NE 33RD AVE

SHAVER ST

Wilshire Park

NE 42ND AVE

To McMenamins Kennedy School

NE SANDY BLVD

NE 39TH AVE

Grant Park

NE 36TH AVE

BRAZEE ST

NE 41ST AVE

NE 39TH AVE

MAX RED/BLUE/GREEN

NE 47TH AVE

HALSEY ST

TILLAMOOK ST

STANTON ST

NE 51ST AVE

LAURELWOOD PUBLIC HOUSE ▼

NE 57TH AVE

Street, take bus 72, which travels on Alberta between NE Martin Luther King Jr. Boulevard and NE 30th Avenue.

# SOUTHEAST

When you think of Portland, do you conjure images of a slightly stoned hippie utopia? Or do you envision mobs of 20-something hipsters flashing tattoos and piercings in a slacker coffeehouse? Rest assured that both stereotypes are alive and well—in fact thriving—in Southeast Portland.

The inner Southeast is a gentrifying warehouse district flanked to the east by Portland's most alternative neighborhoods. Centered on SE Hawthorne Boulevard, these Victorian residential neighborhoods are still home to Portland's Youth Culture, even though some of these folks are reaching retirement age. To the graying hippies, add in a thick overlay of Goth kids, gays and lesbians, and street musicians, and you've got a people-watching nexus. The Southeast quadrant stretches east across leafy neighborhoods filled with antique mansions to busy SE 82nd Avenue, the hub of today's immigrant Asian community. Two of Portland's greatest parks are in Southeast Portland—one designed by the famed Olmsted firm a century ago, the other situated on the only extinct volcano in a U.S. city—along with some of the city's most critically acclaimed independent restaurants.

## Oregon Museum of Science and Industry

The **Oregon Museum of Science and Industry** (OMSI, 1945 SE Water Ave., 503/797-4000, www.omsi.edu, 9:30am-7pm daily late June-Labor Day, 9:30am-5:30pm Tues.-Sun. Labor Day-late June, 9:30am-5:30pm school-holiday Mon., $14 adults, $10.75 seniors, $9.75 ages 3-13, parking $5) is a family-oriented hands-on interactive museum with five exhibit halls and eight science labs, making it one of the largest science and natural history museums in North America. The museum's 18.5-acre riverfront campus also features an OmniMax Theater with a

five-story-high domed screen ($7 adults, $6 seniors and youth), the Pacific Northwest's largest planetarium ($5.75), and the **USS Blueback** (503/797-4624, www.omsi.edu/submarine, tours $6.75), the last fast-attack diesel-powered submarine built by the U.S. Navy, now moored just west of OMSI in the Willamette River. Special exhibits, such as a Pompeii exhibit featuring artifacts and a 4-D representation of the volcanic eruption, can be real treats, though extra fees, which vary, can nearly double the cost of admission. OMSI also offers a variety of kids camps and classes during the summer. The Portland Streetcar's CL Line stops at OMSI, and it's at the east end of the car-free Tilikum Crossing bridge.

The new **Oregon Rail Heritage Center** (2250 SE Water Ave., 503/233-1156, www.orhf.org, 1pm-5pm Thurs.-Sun., free) focuses on the railroad history of Portland and Oregon, with displays of old-time engines and rolling stock and 45-minute rides ($10 adults, $5 children, Sat. Jan.-Nov.) on vintage Oregon Pacific Railroad trains to Oaks Bottom Wildlife Refuge and back.

## ★ Hawthorne District

Portland has a longtime reputation as an enclave of hippie lifestyles and a hotbed of progressive politics, and if that's the Portland you'd like to explore, come to the neighborhoods along SE Hawthorne Boulevard. The idealistic early 1970s haven't aged much around here. Stores purveying fine coffees, secondhand clothing, antiques, and books join cafés and galleries recalling the hip enclaves of Berkeley, California, and Cambridge, Massachusetts. A dense concentration of these establishments on Hawthorne Boulevard between 30th and 50th Avenues is catnip for a friendly population of idealists both young and old; take bus 14.

## Division

Just a few blocks south of SE Hawthorne Boulevard is SE Division Street, another strip of hip enterprises thick with bars, restaurants, and coffee shops. One major hub is at

**D Street Village** at SE 30th Avenue, where you'll find some of the city's best casual dining and a few shops; take bus 4.

## Laurelhurst Park

Until 1909, the land that would become **Laurelhurst Park** (SE 39th Ave. and Stark St.)—one of the most beautiful and beloved of Portland's many parks—was part of the then mayor's stock farms, and blue-ribbon cows drank from the property's small spring-fed lake. The city bought 30 acres of the farmland to create Laurelhurst Park based on plans drawn up by the Olmstead Brothers for the development of Portland's parks. The original watering hole was enlarged and deepened into a small lake, and the rest of the park was divided into a series of distinct sections. In 2001 the park was put on the National Register of Historic Places, the first city park ever listed. The south side has tennis, volleyball, and basketball courts; nearby is a large playground.

## Mount Tabor Park

**Mount Tabor Park** (SE 60th Ave. and Salmon St.) rises above Southeast Portland, and its distinctive cone shape reveals its primary attribute: The park contains the country's only extinct volcano within the city limits of a major population center. Roping in nearly 200 acres, Mount Tabor Park is large enough to offer several miles of hiking trails and a large off-leash dog park. During July, you can catch free Wednesday-evening concerts at a natural amphitheater. A looping road leads to the summit.

## Crystal Springs Rhododendron Garden

Ten-acre **Crystal Springs Rhododendron Garden** (SE 28th Ave. and Woodstock Blvd., daily 6am-10pm daily) is a colorful place mid-April-June, when some 600 varieties of rhododendrons and azaleas, represented by about 2,500 individual specimens, are in bloom. The floral display peaks in mid-May; strolling the woodland trails on Mother's Day is a Portland tradition. An **admission fee** ($5) is charged during **peak blooming season** (10am-6pm Wed.-Sun. March-Labor Day).

# Sports and Recreation

## PARKS

Portland is famous for more park acreage per capita than any other major U.S. city—more than 37,000 acres are preserved as parkland, with 8 percent of the city's area devoted to public recreational venues. **Portland Parks and Recreation** (503/823-7529, www.portlandparks.org) operates the city's 250 parks.

## Waterfront Park and the Eastbank Esplanade

A 2.8-mile loop trail rings the Willamette River in the heart of Portland, linking two bridges and Waterfront Park with a floating walkway on the river's eastern bank. The trail can be accessed at many points; to follow the loop clockwise from downtown, walk the riverfront embankment trail north through Waterfront Park to the Steel Bridge. Cross the lower span of the bridge, a pedestrian- and cyclists-only crossing called the Steel Bridge RiverWalk.

On the east side of the Willamette, the trail heads south, dropping onto the Eastbank Esplanade, about half of which is a floating walkway (at 1,200 feet, the longest in the country) and the rest a paved path along the riverbank. At the Hawthorne Bridge, climb up the stairs and cross the bridge to downtown, completing the loop. Or add a couple more miles to your walk or ride by continuing south and crossing on the car-free Tilikum Crossing bridge.

## ★ Forest Park

The largest urban wilderness in the United

**56**

States, with over 5,100 acres and 70 miles of trails, **Forest Park** stretches along the crest of Portland's West Hills. It is 8.5 miles long and 1.5 miles wide. As much a statement of Portland's priorities and values as a leafy refuge for hikers, joggers, and cyclists, Forest Park is home to an abundance of wildlife (more than 112 bird and 62 mammal species, including bears, elk, deer, and cougars), all found just minutes from the urban center.

For hikers, the park's centerpiece is 30-mile **Wildwood Trail,** which links various parklands in the West Hills with Forest Park. The southern end of the trail starts just past the Vietnam Veterans of Oregon Memorial near the Oregon Zoo. From here it runs through Washington Park and Hoyt Arboretum and past Pittock Mansion. At Cornell Road, the trail crosses the edge of the **Audubon Sanctuary** (5151 NW Cornell Rd., 503/292-6855, www.audubonportland.org, dawn-dusk daily, free), where the Audubon Society of Portland administers a 148-acre nature preserve that is a showcase for native flora and fauna, with four miles of forested hiking trails in the verdant West Hills.

From the Audubon Sanctuary, the Wildwood Trail enters Forest Park and runs north for another 22 miles. The trail can be accessed at the points described above or at several more northerly trailheads, including the western end of NW Upshur Street at Macleay Park, and the end of NW Thurman Street (the Thurman Street bus, number 15, from downtown stops about 0.25 miles downhill from this entrance to the park).

### Tryon Creek State Park

The only Oregon state park within the metro area, 645-acre **Tryon Creek State Park** (11321 SW Terwilliger Blvd., 503/636-9886, http://oregonstateparks.org) offers a nature center and eight miles of trails in a vernal woodland setting. Cyclists bike along the paved trail on the park's eastern edge. The park's many events include summer day camps for kids, guided nature walks, and special activities; for a list of events, go to www.

The Wildwood Trail runs for 30 miles through Forest Park.

tryonfriends.org. Streamside wildlife includes beavers and songbirds. In late March there are wondrous displays of trilliums, a wild marsh lily. To reach the park, take I-5's exit 297 south of Portland, follow SW Terwilliger Boulevard for 2.5 miles past Lewis and Clark College, and watch for signs for the park.

### BICYCLING

Portland has twice been selected by *Bicycling* magazine as the most bike-friendly city in the nation, and indeed the city has a comprehensive infrastructure devoted to cycling. Unless you're from Amsterdam, you'll be amazed at the number of people who get around Portland on bikes.

The website of the **City of Portland's Office of Transportation** (www.portland-oregon.gov) lists up-to-date information for cyclists. Keep up on local cycling issues at **Bike Portland** (http://bikeportland.org), an excellent bike blog; find fun rides and details on **Pedalpalooza** (http://shift-2bikes.org) events, held throughout June.

An indispensable map called *Bike There!*, published by the government agency Metro, is sold at bike shops and bookstores across town and is available online (www.oregon-metro.gov).

Not all bridges are recommended for cyclists. A river-level foot-and-bike bridge forms the lower deck of the Steel Bridge and connects Waterfront Park and downtown to the Eastbank Esplanade; otherwise, the Hawthorne, Broadway, and Burnside Bridges are best, although bikes must share sidewalks with pedestrians. The new Tilikum Crossing bridge is dedicated to cyclists, pedestrians, and public transportation. TriMet buses have bike racks mounted on the front of every bus, and bikes are allowed on the MAX trains and the Portland Streetcar.

For a recreational ride that's almost entirely on bike paths, check out the 16.8-mile **Springwater Corridor,** a bike thoroughfare built on a reclaimed rail line from the east base of the Tilikum Crossing bridge through Gresham to Boring. Views of Mount Hood abound along much of the route, which has easy access to Leach Botanical Gardens, Powell Butte, and other worthy detours.

An easy choice for mountain bikers is **Leif Erikson Road** in Forest Park. From the park gate at the end of NW Thurman Street, the dirt road is closed to motor vehicles; it's a steady but gentle six-mile climb through mature forest to the junction at Salzman Road, and another six miles to the trail's end at Germantown Road. Bikes are not allowed on the park's hiking trails, but they can go on selected steep fire lanes, as marked by signs.

North of Portland at the confluence of the Columbia and Willamette Rivers is **Sauvie Island** (http://sauvieisland.org), a perfectly flat island where farms and truck gardens share space with wildlife refuges. The island's 12-mile loop road is a scenic delight reminiscent of rural France. Sauvie Island is 10 miles north of Portland, off U.S. 30.

## Bike Rentals

Although bike sharing took a while to come to Portland, it's now easy to pick up an orange (sometimes white) **Biketown** bike (www.biketownpdx.com, $2.50 per 30-minute trip, $12 per day). Sign up online, via the mobile app, or at a Biketown station kiosk, located every few blocks around the central city area. Take care to test ride the bike in a quiet area before heading out into traffic; they're a little clunky to ride and may handle quite differently than your normal ride.

biking the Eastbank Esplanade

# Escape to Sauvie Island

Ten miles northwest of Portland, at the confluence of the Willamette and Columbia Rivers, is the rural enclave of **Sauvie Island** (http://sauvieisland.org), a scant 20 minutes from downtown. On clear days, views of the snowcapped Cascades backdrop oceangoing freighters and cruise ships. Visitors enjoy horseback riding, swimming, and U-pick farms. A favorite spot for bird-watching, the island sees eagles, great blue herons, geese, and sandhill cranes among the 250 species that pass through on the Pacific Flyway. Wildlife aficionados may glimpse red foxes and black-tailed deer on the island's northern half. In addition, anglers come to Sauvie's lakes and sloughs for panfish and bass, and to the Columbia side for sturgeon, salmon, and steelhead. Bikers are drawn to the flat 12-mile biking loop. Nearby is **Collins Beach** (4am-10pm daily), which is clothing-optional.

Be aware that if you park at one of Sauvie Island's public beaches or wildlife viewing areas, you'll need a parking certificate, available for $7 per vehicle at the Cracker Barrel Convenience Store on Sauvie Island Road; turn left after exiting the bridge. Also remember to gas up and hit the ATM before heading to the island as neither is here. To reach Sauvie Island, take U.S. 30 northwest.

When you're done riding, lock it up at any station.

It's no problem to rent a bike from a shop, either, and with this option you'll also get a helmet (you have to supply your own with Biketown bikes); average rates run $35-60 for a 24-hour rental, depending on the model. Convenient to Waterfront Park and with a large rental fleet is **Waterfront Bikes** (10 SW Ash St., 503/227-1719, www.waterfrontbikes. com, 10am-6pm Mon.-Fri., 9am-6pm Sat.-Sun.). On the way to Forest Park trails is **Fat Tire Farm** (2714 NW Thurman St., 503/222-3276, www.fattirefarm.com, 11am-7pm Mon.-Fri., 10am-6pm Sat., noon-5pm Sun.). Just east of the Hawthorne Bridge, **Clever Cycles** (900 SE Hawthorne Blvd., 503/334-1560, http://clevercycles.com, 11am-6pm Mon.-Fri., 11am-5pm Sat.-Sun.) rents Brompton folding bikes, cargo bikes, and electric-assist bikes. At **Pedal Bike Tours** (133 SW 2nd Ave., 503/243-2453, www.pedalbiketours.com, 9am-6pm daily), you can rent a bike or join a tour around town (possibly focusing on food carts or brewpubs) or out to the Columbia Gorge.

## BIRD-WATCHING

To the far south of the Southeast district, the Sellwood neighborhood offers access to wetlands along the Willamette River. **Oaks** Bottom Wildlife Refuge (SE 7th Ave. and Sellwood Blvd., www.portlandonline.com, 5am-midnight daily) is a 163-acre area of woods, open fields, and wetlands. This is a popular spot for birders, since it attracts some 125 species of birds, including blue herons, red-tailed hawks, and eight species of warblers. To explore the bottoms, hike down the bluff from the parking lot at the north end of Sellwood Park.

Just a little farther afield is **Sauvie Island,** home to over 250 bird species, including lots of bald eagles, migrating ducks and other waterfowl, nesting great blue herons and ospreys, and a variety of raptors. One nice hike that has varied marsh, river, lake, and forested habitats is the **Wapato Access State Greenway.** To reach this trail turn left off the bridge and follow Sauvie Island Road about three miles to the parking area.

## CLIMBING

The top inner-city destination for climbers is **Portland Rock Gym** (21 NE 12th Ave., 503/232-8310, http://portlandrockgym.com, 7am-11pm Mon.-Fri., 9am-9pm Sat., 9am-6pm Sun.), with a 12,000-square-foot climbing area, 40-foot top-rope and lead walls, and a large bouldering area. A day pass ($17 adults, $9 seniors, $12 under age 14) includes unlimited access to the climbing gym and workout room.

## PADDLING

If you're tempted to get out onto the Willamette River, take a tour or rent a sea kayak, paddleboard, or canoe from **Portland Kayak Company** (6600 SW Macadam Ave., 503/459-4050, www.portlandkayak.com, 10am-6pm Mon.-Fri., 9am-6pm Sat., 9am-5pm Sun., $14-22 per hour, 2-hour minimum) on the west side of the Willamette River near Willamette Park. Three-hour beginner-friendly tours around Ross Island leave from **RiverPlace Marina** (1816 SW River Dr., 10am and 2pm daily, $49); on these tours, paddlers have a chance to see great blue herons and, oftentimes, ospreys and eagles.

About 30 minutes northwest of town, past Sauvie Island, the **Next Adventure Scappoose Bay Paddle Center** (57420 Old Portland Rd., Warren, 503/397-2161, www.nextadventure.net, 8am-6pm daily) rents kayaks, canoes, and paddleboards from a marina on a quiet backwater of the Columbia River ($16-27 per hour). On an easygoing three-hour kayak tour ($50) of the area's wetlands, you're pretty much guaranteed to see wildlife.

## SWIMMING

Public beaches and swimming along the Willamette and Columbia Rivers are popular in summer. **Poet's Beach,** a short walk south of the **RiverPlace Marina** (1816 SW River Dr.), is easy to get to from downtown. **Sellwood Riverfront Park,** at the east end of the Sellwood Bridge, is a good place for a picnic and a wade in the Willamette River; there's also an outdoor pool in **Sellwood Park** (7951 SE 7th Ave., 503/823-3679). Strong swimmers can join the **River Huggers** (www.humanaccessproject.com) for regular summertime swims in the Willamette, right in the heart of the city.

Ten miles north of Portland, the beaches along the east side of **Sauvie Island** are popular; they are reached from U.S. 30. Once on the island, nude sunbathing becomes more the norm the farther north you go along its beaches. If you're headed up the Columbia River Gorge, **Rooster Rock State Park** (I-84, exit 25) has three miles of sandy beaches on the Columbia River, with the easternmost beaches being clothing-optional.

## GOLF

Portland Parks and Recreation runs a couple of exceptionally good golf courses, with peak rates topping out at $40-45. **Heron Lakes** (3500 N. Victory Blvd., 503/289-1818, http://heronlakesgolf.com) is the premier public golf facility, with 36 holes (the Greenback and Great Blue courses), a grass driving range, and good short-game practice areas. The two courses offer varying challenges for different greens fees. The easier and shorter Greenback is good for beginners and moderate players, though it doesn't drain as well. The more challenging and costlier Great Blue, designed by Robert Trent Jones Jr., is better manicured and drains better in wet weather.

**Eastmoreland Golf Course** (2425 SE Bybee Blvd., 503/775-2900, www.eastmorelandgolfcourse.com) is Oregon's second-oldest course and one of the most beautiful. Located near Reed College in Southeast Portland, the 100-year-old and lengthy (6,529 yards) 18-hole course is lined with statuesque trees and gardens. Eastmoreland features a two-tier driving range, a pro shop, and a full bar and restaurant. The course was designed by former U.S. amateur champion H. Chandler Egan, who later helped redesign Pebble Beach Golf Links in the early 1900s.

## SPECTATOR SPORTS

Portland is more a town for athletes than for devotees of spectator sports. Nonetheless, a couple of professional sports teams have ardent fans. Directly across the Willamette River from downtown in Northeast Portland, the Rose Quarter area is home to two of Portland's sports stadia. The larger and newer is the **Rose Garden Arena** (east end of the Steel Bridge, 503/235-8771, www.rosequarter.com), which is home to pro basketball's

Portland Trailblazers. While most seats are reserved for season ticket holders, some are available at Ticketmaster outlets or through the box office (503/797-9619). Of course, there are always the offerings on Craigslist (www.craigslist.org) and the scalpers who may be found beyond a four-block radius of the Rose Garden. You can also buy tickets directly from the Blazers website (www.nba.com/blazers). Regular season play is October-April.

Adjacent to the Rose Garden Arena is the 12,000-seat **Memorial Coliseum** (1401 N. Wheeler Ave., 503/235-8771), which hosts concerts and sporting events, including those of the **Winter Hawks** (503/238-6366, www.winterhawks.com), a minor-league ice-hockey team. Both venues are easily reached on the Red, Green, Yellow, and Blue MAX trains (get off at the Rose Quarter Transit Center).

Across the river, **Providence Park** (1844 SW Morrison St., 503/553-5400, www.timbers.com) is home to pro soccer's **Portland Timbers.** The stadium's 20,000 seats are usually filled, with a substantial number occupied by the Timbers Army, an enthusiastic legion of green-scarfed fans. The **Portland Thorns** (www.timbers.com/thornsfc), owned by the same franchise, is Portland's National Women's Soccer League team and also plays at Providence Park stadium. Tickets for all of these teams' games are available through **Ticketmaster** (800/277-1700, www.ticketmaster.com).

# Entertainment and Events

As Portland has grown in recent years, its arts scene has become more diverse and sophisticated. The traditional institutions of symphony, opera, and classical ballet are strong, and contemporary dance and theater are represented by eclectic and adventurous companies. In addition to these listings, there's an active summer festival itinerary that includes the superb Chamber Music Northwest series, Portland Opera's summer performances, and blues and jazz festivals.

In Portland, bars are allowed to stay open until 2:30am, though few do so on weekdays, while brewpubs often close earlier. During the week, most places close at midnight or 1am, though may stay open later if there's entertainment. If there's live music, cover charges usually kick in at 9pm.

## NIGHTLIFE

Portland has a full-bodied live music and club scene: On any given night, some 300 clubs offer live music, and with typical Portland character, what you'll find in these venues is often a bit different than you might expect. In addition to live music and dancing, you'll also find lots of theme nights, often accompanied by a combination of cabaret, performance art, magic, and burlesque—think *Cabaret*'s Kit Kat Klub. These unscripted evenings provide diverting entertainment.

Much of the nightlife is concentrated in a few easily reached neighborhoods, most with safe and dependable public transportation. Pick up a copy or check the websites of *Willamette Week* or the *Portland Mercury,* two free weeklies that follow the music and nightlife scene closely. Most music events in bars are restricted to ages 21 and older. Cover charges, $5-10 in most nightclubs, are frequently levied, though there's often no cover charge for live music early in the week or even early in the evening. Also note that smoking is not permitted in Oregon bars, though nudity is: Because of Oregon's liberal laws regarding nudity, Portland is home to many strip clubs.

## Brewpubs

Portland, also known as Beervana, is the epicenter of the craft brewing revival in North America, boasting more breweries than any

# The McMenamins Brewpub Empire

Whether or not you're a beer drinker, you're likely to run into a McMenamins brewpub during a trip to Portland. This highly successful local enterprise now has over 50 pubs in Washington and Oregon, and whenever a historic venue goes on sale, there's at least a large minority of Pacific Northwesterners who hope that it will become a McMenamins brewpub. The McMenamins are in fact brothers Brian and Mike, who are equally devoted to brewing beer, designing fun spaces to drink it in, and preserving distinctive buildings.

The **Crystal Ballroom** (1332 W. Burnside St., 503/225-0047), a former dance hall, is a singular place to catch a concert or have a beer. Constructed in 1914, the top-story ballroom has a mechanical "floating on air" dance floor (there's a layer of ball bearings and springy rubber beneath the hardwood flooring). One block away is another extension of this massive entertainment citadel: the **Crystal Hotel** (303 SW 12th Ave., 503/972-2670), set in a former gay bathhouse, with an appropriately labyrinthine set of basement bars culminating in the just-right **Ringler's Annex,** a tiny subterranean bar in a flatiron-like structure for the in-the-know.

The **Kennedy School** (5736 NE 33rd Ave., 503/249-3983 or 888/249-3983) is an unusual enterprise—a block-square 1915 grade school that's been converted into a brewpub, restaurant, and hotel, plus a movie theater (think couches in the auditorium). In the suburbs of Portland is one of the grandest extensions of the McMenamins' dream. On the way to the Columbia Gorge, **Edgefield** (2126 SW Halsey St., Troutdale, 503/669-8610 or 800/669-8610) began its existence as the Multnomah County Poor Farm and now contains multiple restaurants and drinking establishments, plus a delightful period hotel, movie theater, winery, and "pub golf" course.

Lest we forget, the McMenamins pioneered the notion of cinema brewpubs, where you can buy a microbrew, chow down on a burger, and watch a recent movie. The **Bagdad Theater & Pub** (3702 SE Hawthorne Blvd., 503/236-9234) is in the thick of the Hawthorne neighborhood. For more info on locations and music and movie offerings within the McMenamins empire, visit www.mcmenamins.com or call 503/249-3983.

other city in the world—105 were in operation at last count.

All brewpubs are required to serve food, and many double as restaurants. This means that in almost all cases, families are welcome in brewpubs within dining hours and sometimes in designated nonbar areas. Portland brewpubs come in all shapes and sizes, from garden tents to converted warehouses to funeral chapels. Locally brewed beer is one of the pillars of Portland life—cheers!

## NORTHWEST

Portland's first microbrewery, **BridgePort Brewing** (1313 NW Marshall St., 503/241-3612, www.bridgeportbrew.com, 11:30am-10pm Sun.-Wed., 11:30am-11 Thurs.-Sat., 11:30am-10pm Sun.), started out in an old rope factory in the then-derelict Pearl District. It's no longer on the cutting edge, but it's still worth stopping in for pint of the Ebenezer or a fresh-hopped IPA.

Oregonians shrieked when **10 Barrel** (1411 NW Flanders St., 503/224-1700, www.10barrel.com, 11am-11pm Sun.-Thurs., 11am-midnight Fri.-Sat.) was sold to Anheuser-Busch, but almost immediately thereafter a Pearl District branch of this Bend brewery opened, and there's rarely been an open seat on the rooftop deck since. Come by for an Apocalypse IPA. A poblano-laced farro salad ($12) goes with beer just as well as the pizza and burgers offered.

Right across the street is **Rogue Distillery & Public House** (1339 NW Flanders St., 503/222-5910, www.rogue.com, 11am-12:30am Mon.-Thurs., 11am-1:30am Fri.-Sat., 11am-10:30pm Sun.), a Portland outlet of Rogue Brewing in Newport. Most of the elixirs here are wonderful, but check out the Maibock-style Dead Guy Ale and St. Rogue Red.

Although its headquarters is in Bend, **Deschutes Brewery's Portland Public House** (210 NW 11th Ave., 503/296-4906, www.deschutesbrewery.com, 11am-11pm Sun.-Thurs., 11am-midnight Fri.-Sat.), in the midst of the Pearl District, is large and well located. While much of the space is dedicated to restaurant service, there's also a large bar area for these local brewing gods, creators of the classic Mirror Pond Pale Ale and Black Butte Porter. This is a great place to come before or after a play at neighboring Portland Center Stage.

## NORTH AND NORTHEAST

If your local pub has a children's play area, you know you must be in Portland. **Laurelwood Public House & Brewery** (5115 NE Sandy Blvd., 503/282-0622, www. laurelwoodbrewpub.com, 11am-10pm Mon.-Tues., 11am-11pm Wed.-Thurs., 11am-11pm Fri., 10am-11pm Sat., 10am-10pm Sun.) is a family-friendly brewpub with restaurant-quality food and Workhorse IPA, a favorite of many Portlanders, in Northeast Portland's Hollywood district.

For our 2017 eclipse camping trip, there was only one beer to bring, and it came from **Ecliptic Brewing** (825 N. Cook St., 503/265-8002, www.eclipticbrewing.com, 11am-10pm Sun.-Thurs., 11am-11pm Fri.-Sat.), where the brewer is as passionate about astronomy as he is about beer (and he's worked for Oregon's best breweries and developed some of their finest beers). Although the outside tables at this spot just off busy North Mississippi Avenue are warm-weather destinations, step inside to check out the lighting fixture describing the earth's path.

At **Breakside Brewery** (820 NE Dekum St., 503/719-6475, www.breakside.com, 11:30am-10pm Sun.-Thurs., 11:30am-11pm Fri.-Sat.), Portlanders prove they can drink something besides IPA; the pilsner here is excellent. Food is also good, but if you want something more, there's a good Italian restaurant in the old fire station across the street. Breakside also has a large brewpub in Northwest Portland (1570 NW 22nd Ave., 503/444-7597, 11am-11pm Sun.-Thurs., 11am-midnight Fri.-Sat.).

## SOUTHEAST

**Hopworks Urban Brewery** (2944 SE Powell Blvd., 503/232-4647, http://hopworksbeer. com, 11am-11pm Sun.-Thurs., 11am-midnight

Ecliptic Brewing is right off North Mississippi Avenue.

Fri.-Sat.), or HUB, is about as Portland as you can get; it's an "ecopub" combining a bicycle theme with good beer and pizza. Along one of the city's busiest bike corridors, find Hopworks' **Bike Bar** (3947 N. Williams Ave., 503/287-6258), where bike frames from local custom builders are displayed over the bar. The atmosphere is great, but the beer is even better.

Most beers made in Portland are strongly hopped, but there's starting to be a trend toward sour beers, such as the summer gose you'll find at **Cascade Brewing Barrel House** (939 SE Belmont St., 503/265-8603, http://cascadebrewingbarrelhouse.com, noon-11pm Sun.-Thurs., noon-midnight Fri.-Sat.). **Hair of the Dog Brewing Company** (61 SE Yamhill St., 503/232-6585, www.hairofthedog.com, 11:30am-10pm Tues.-Sat., 11:30am-8pm Sun.), famous for its commitment to unusual and high-alcohol beers that are meant to be aged and drunk like fine wines, does serve up a wide range of beers with lower alcohol content, from Little Dog Fred (3.5% ABV) to Adam from the Wood (12% ABV).

A huge outdoor patio with a fire pit is one reason to visit **Wayfinder** (304 SE 2nd Ave., 503/708-2337, www.wayfinder.beer, 11am-11pm Sun.-Wed., 11am-midnight Thurs.-Sat.), tucked down into the old warehouse district just south of the Burnside Bridge. Another reason is the beer, brewed by an alum of Hood River's Double Mountain. And then there's the food—ranging from vegan sweet-potato hash to chicken schnitzel or grilled trout. It's one of Portland's best new pubs.

A longtime favorite of the Southeast Portland crowds is **Lucky Labrador Brewing Company** (915 SE Hawthorne Blvd., 503/236-3555, 11am-midnight Mon.-Sat., noon-10pm Sun.). This former sheet-metal warehouse is a comfortable and unpretentious place—slip on your flip-flops, bring your dog, and head down to the large shady patio for some brews.

## Bars

Portland is a nightlife kind of city, with bars everywhere. It's never difficult to find places to drink, but here's a primer on some of the city's best bars.

The most sought-after bar stools in Portland are at the **Multnomah Whisk{e}y Library** (1124 SW Alder, 503/954-1381, www.mwlpdx.com, 4pm-midnight Mon.-Thurs., 4pm-1am Fri.-Sat.), an ornate, membership-driven bar with an extensive collection of liquors: This library has some 1,500 bottles on its shelves, almost 1,000 of them whiskies. The bar room is attractive and clubby, and the service top-notch. Nonmembers can have a drink at the street-level bar or ask if there's room in the library up the stairs; at night, the lines can be long.

In the hip Ace Hotel, **Clyde Common** (1014 SW Stark St., 503/228-3333, www.clydecommon.com, 3pm-midnight daily) is where young downtown execs enjoy hand-crafted cocktails and nicely curated local ales in a bright, bustling bar. There's quite a different vibe in the Ace's other bar, **Pépé Le-Moko** (407 SW 10th, 503/546-8537, http://pepelemokopdx.com, 4pm-2:30am daily), a tiny subterranean speakeasy-type joint with classic cocktails, oysters on the half shell, and the sense of traveling back in time to the 1920s.

In the Pearl District, the **Teardrop Lounge** (1015 NW Everett St., 503/445-8019, www.teardroplounge.com, 4pm-close daily) is a small and stylish see-and-be-seen bar where creative drinks are crafted from handmade elixirs, hard-to-find liquors, and tinctures of a local variety. Everything is sourced locally.

One of Northeast Portland's top cocktail bars is **Expatriate** (5424 NE 30th Ave., 503/867-5309, 5pm-midnight daily), a moody candlelit lounge with a romantic travel theme. Drinks are excellent, and the Asian fusion snacks are from recipes of Naomi Pomeroy, the award-winning chef whose Beast restaurant is just across the street.

Along a humdrum stretch of NE Broadway is Portland's top tiki bar, **Hale Pele** (2733 NE Broadway, 503/662-8454, 4pm-midnight Sun.-Thurs., 4pm-1am Fri.-Sat.), a hole-in-the-wall decorated with shrunken heads, puffer-fish lights, and a smoking volcano. The tropical-themed drinks are delicious, and the collection of rums is formidable.

There's a cluster of bars in inner Southeast Portland (near the east end of the Morrison Bridge, just across the river from downtown) where you can stumble from bar to excellent bar and have a completely different experience in each. Here are some favorites. **Bit House Saloon** (727 SE Grand Ave., 503/954-3913, www.bithousesaloon.com, 3pm-2:30am daily) is a large and rollicking redbrick bar with a nice patio. The specialties here are barrel-stored spirits poured through a tap system and highfalutin cocktails both fresh-squeezed and draft-style. Across the street is **Kachka** (720 SE Grand Ave., 503/235-0059, http://kachkapdx.com, 4pm-midnight daily), with vodka flights and delicious Russian snacks. One block farther east is **Trifecta Tavern** (726 SE 6th Ave., 503/841-6675, http://trifectapdx.com, 5pm-9pm Mon., 5pm-10pm Tues.-Thurs., 4pm-11pm Fri.-Sat., 4pm-9pm Sun.), an excellent bakery and restaurant with a bar up front. The cocktails are updated classics, accompanied by fresh oysters, thin-sliced American hams, and wonderful breads.

Of the dozens of McMenamins locations in Portland, the **Back Stage Bar** (3702 SE Hawthorne Blvd., 503/236-9234, 4pm-1:30am Mon.-Thurs., 4pm-2:30am Fri., noon-2:30am Sat., noon-1:30am Sun.) is the most amazing. At the front of the building is the **Bagdad Theater,** a former vaudeville hall converted to a pub-movie theater. In the old days, when the painted scrims and backdrops that set the scene for its live song-and-dance routines weren't in use, they were hung in the Back Stage, a seven-story curtain storehouse directly behind the theater. Today's Back Stage Bar makes the most of this narrow towering space. On the ground floor is the handsome bar and pool tables, but catwalks and staircases lead to secluded spots tucked into the walls. And there's nothing like a bar with a seven-story-high ceiling to start a conversation.

The **Crow Bar** (3954 N. Mississippi Ave.,

503/280-7099, 3pm-2am daily) feels comfortable and slightly old-fashioned, a narrow space with exposed redbrick, high ceilings, and a long wooden bar. However, the crowds are anything but old-fashioned—this is a favorite watering hole for the many 20- and 30-somethings who have refashioned the adjoining North Portland neighborhoods in their image.

**Gold Dust Meridian** (3267 SE Hawthorne Blvd., 503/239-1143, http://golddustmeridian.com, 2pm-2:30am daily) started out as a 1960s-era accountant's office, which it remained until it was transformed into a swank temple of drink. This is a lively spot, with a pool table, good cocktails, and a high-energy vibe. The young, attractive crowd, chatting above blaring techno-pop, is easy on the eyes as well.

You don't have to drink to have fun at **Ground Kontrol** (115 NW 5th Ave., 503/796-9364, http://groundkontrol.com, noon-2am daily), a fantastically popular video game and pinball arcade. Kids are welcome until 4:30pm; IDs are checked starting at 5pm. In addition to the arcade games, there are regular "geeks who drink" quiz nights and stand-up comedy.

## Gay and Lesbian

Portland's gay bar scene used to be concentrated along SW Stark Street downtown, but the scene has dispersed, both into new neighborhoods (there are now as many gay bars on the East Side as downtown) and to regular bars. Lesbian bars, as such, are currently nonexistent in Portland. Gay people are welcome pretty much anywhere in town, and you don't need to seek out a gay bar just to have drinks with gay friends.

SW Stark Street is the traditional hub of Portland's gay bar scene, and **Scandals** (1038 SW Stark St., 503/227-5887, www.scandalspdx.com, noon-2:30am daily) has been a fixture here since the 1970s. The bar is bright and airy, and in summer the floor-to-ceiling windows slide open and the scene spills onto the sidewalk. While there are pool tables

# The *Real* Portland Spirit

Portland is famed as a center for brewing, with more breweries than any city in the world, and it's a short drive from world-class wineries in the northern Willamette Valley and the Columbia Gorge. What you may not know is that Portland is also a major center for artisanal **micro-distilleries.** There are over a dozen small distilleries in Portland, producing specialty vodka, gin, whiskey, rum, and eau-de-vie. Several offer tasting rooms where you can sample the Portland spirit.

In addition to the following distilleries, also check out the small-batch liquors at brewpubs **Edgefield** (2126 SW Halsey St., Troutdale, 503/669-8610 or 800/669-8610, www.mcmenamins. com) for Hogshead whiskey, Penney's gin, and various brandies; and **Rogue Distillery & Public House** (1339 NW Flanders St., 503/241-3780, www.rogue.com) for three kinds of rum, a Scotch-style whiskey, and gin made with spruce rather than juniper.

- **Clear Creek Distillery** (2389 NW Wilson St., 503/248-9470, www.clearcreekdistillery.com, noon-6pm Sun.-Fri., 10am-6pm Sat.): Famous for pear brandy and other fruit-based eaux-de-vie; check out the Oregon Single Malt Whiskey, if the year's tiny production isn't already sold out.

- **House Spirits Distillery** (2505 SE 11th Ave., 503/235-3174, www.housespirits.com, noon-6pm daily): Most noted for its Aviation Gin, but also try the Medoyeff vodka and aquavit.

- **Eastside Distilling** (1512 SE 7th Ave., 503/926-7060, www.eastsidedistilling.com, noon-8pm Sun.-Thurs., noon-10pm Fri.-Sat.): Check out the popular Burnside Bourbon and potato vodka, and investigate three types of rum.

- **New Deal Distillery** (900 SE Salmon St., 503/234-2513, http://newdealdistillery.com, noon-6pm Wed.-Sun.): This operation specializes in vodka and gin.

- **Stone Barn Brandy Works** (3315 SE 19th Ave., 503/775-6747, www.stonebarnbrandy-works.com, noon-6pm Fri.-Mon.): Unsurprisingly, there's brandy, but so much more, such as grappa, ouzo, rye whiskey, oat whiskey, and strawberry, apricot, cranberry, and coffee liqueur.

and DJs spinning tunes, this is an easygoing, cruisy bar where mostly men come to hang out and meet friends.

At the longtime favorite **CC Slaughters** (200 NW 3rd Ave., 503/248-9135, http://cc-slaughterspdx.com, 3pm-2am daily), the Rainbow Room, in the front of the building, is a frosty-cool cocktail lounge, a place to sip cocktails and play pool in high-style surroundings; food is available as well. The nightclub is entered along NW Davis Street and contains a large bar and dance floor where DJs keep the rhythms pounding. The crowd is mostly male and of all ages, but all are welcome.

**Crush** (1400 SE Morrison St., 503/235-8150, www.crushbar.com, noon-2am Mon.-Sat., noon-1am Sun.) is a bar that defies easy categorization. There are three separate bar areas, each with its own ambience, including the lounge with its old-fashioned curved bar and the Blue Room for dancing and live music; other evenings may feature theme nights, burlesque, or tarot card readers. Crush is a fun, high-energy place to hang.

**Darcelle XV Showplace** (208 NW 3rd Ave., 503/222-5338, www.darcellexv.com, shows at 8pm Wed.-Thurs., 8pm and 10:30pm Fri.-Sat.) is one of those Portland institutions, like biking and brewing, that may not make sense until you get here. Darcelle is a female impersonator extraordinaire who has, over the years, cozied up to all of the political leaders in Oregon and whose outsize personality has made her an entertainment legend for over 40 years. The stage show ($20), a combination of lip-synching and comedy by a bevy of lovely queens, is funny and rather raunchy, just as it should be. Reservations are recommended, especially on weekends. If it's midnight on Friday or Saturday, bring on the male strippers!

In a city as accepting and welcoming as Portland, it's easy to ask why gay bars still even exist. Well, places like **Embers** (110 NW Broadway, 503/222-3082, 11am-2:30pm daily) hang on because they are so much damn fun. Part drag showcase (up front), part disco inferno (the back room), Embers is a Portland institution from the days when dancing all night beneath a mirrored ball to "I Will Survive" seemed like an act of defiant liberation. This is still Portland's premier gay dance club, though the crowds here are inclusive of gays and straights and everyone in between.

In the heart of Old Town, **Hobo's** (120 NW 3rd Ave., 503/224-3285, www.hobospdx. com, 4am-close daily) combines the classic redbrick good looks of an authentic 1890s bar with the courtly rhythms of a contemporary piano lounge. Starting at 8pm Wednesday-Sunday, pianists tickle the ivories (jazz, show tunes, occasional classical numbers) while the well-dressed clientele—a friendly mix of gays, lesbians, and their straight friends—enjoy cocktails. Hobos is a classy spot for an after-dinner drink.

## Live Music

One of the pioneers along gentrifying North Mississippi Avenue is tiny, acoustically rich **Mississippi Studios** (3939 N. Mississippi Ave., 503/288-3895, www.mississippistudios. com, hours vary), where local and regional bands go to record music and perform in the studio's intimate space. Check the website to find out what concerts may be offered during your visit; this is a great spot to catch rising stars. The **Alberta Rose Theatre** (3000 NE Alberta St., 503/719-6055, www.albertarosetheatre.com, hours vary) hosts a selection of folk, world music, cabaret and circus music, comedy, and whatever else is slightly alternative and cool.

If you're looking for the punk edge of the Portland live music scene, one good place to start is **The Know** (3728 NE Sandy Blvd., 503/473-8729, 3pm-2am daily), sometimes

The back view of Kells gives an indication of the high spirits inside.

referred to as Portland's CBGB. Speaking of the cool kids, you'll find them on NE Russell Street, in the wood-paneled Victorian-era bar at the **Secret Society** (116 NE Russell St., 503/493-3600, thesecretsocietylounge. com, 5pm-midnight Sun.-Thurs., 5pm-1am Fri.-Sat.) or smoking outside the **Wonder Ballroom** (128 NE Russell St., 503/284-8686, wonderballroom.com, hours vary). The upstairs ballroom at the Secret Society hosts shows ranging from choro to bluegrass to jazz; the ground-level Wonder's shows tend to be rock or acoustic, including some pretty big names on the indie circuit.

At **Holocene** (1001 SE Morrison St., 503/239-7639, www.holocene.org, hours vary), the nightly entertainment can be live music, DJs, performance art, or regularly scheduled evening events. Many events hover at the intersection of music, performance, and technology, including storytelling with *The Moth,* and the crowds are fun and varied.

Before you hit town, check out the performers scheduled at the **Aladdin Theater** (3017

SE Milwaukie Ave., 503/233-1994, www.aladdin-theater.com, hours vary). This 1920s burlesque house has been gussied up to host an eclectic array of touring performers, including Steve Earle, the Buena Vista Social Club, and Rufus Wainwright. Many folk, world beat, and indie rock bands play here, and it's a wonderful small theater for taking in a concert.

**Kells Irish Restaurant and Pub** (112 SW 2nd Ave., 503/227-4057, www.kellsportland.com, 11am-2am Sun.-Thurs., 11am-2pm Fri.-Sat.) is a landmark not just because of its Victorian good looks but also thanks to live Celtic music. The musicians are usually local—Portland has a large Celtic music community—although touring bands are also featured.

## JAZZ AND BLUES

In the basement of the Rialto Lounge, find the **Jack London Revue** (529 SW 4th Ave., 866/777-8932, http://jacklondonrevue.com), one of Portland's newest jazz venues. There's live music several nights a week, with a focus on jazz and its outgrowths, as well as national touring jazz groups. The lounge at the back of the old-school steakhouse **Clyde's** (5474 NE Sandy Blvd., 503/281-9200) has live music almost every evening at 9pm; especially popular are the Sunday-evening jazz jam sessions (beginning at 8:30pm) led by local drummer extraordinaire Ron Steen. The atmosphere is friendly and inclusive.

Located in historic Union Station, **Wilf's** (800 NW 6th Ave., 503/223-0070, www.wilfsrestaurant.com) is another swanky but truly retro spot to take in live jazz. The large, high-ceilinged, redbrick space was created as the formal dining room for rail travelers during the golden age of the railroad. Jazz is normally offered starting at 7pm Wednesday-Saturday. Many of Portland's top local performers cycle through.

The music is often as good as the excellent food at **Andina** (1314 NW Glisan St., 503/228-9535, www.andinarestaurant.com), where there's Latin-inspired music, including Gypsy swing and Latin jazz, in the classy

and comfortable bar every night. With live jazz and blues seven nights a week, **Blue Diamond** (2016 NE Sandy Blvd., 503/230-9590, www.bluediamondpdx.net) is a laid-back insider's place to enjoy top local bands.

## ROCK

Just west of the Burnside Bridge is **Dante's** (SW 3rd Ave. and Burnside St., 503/226-6630, www.danteslive.com, 11am-2:30am daily), where, in addition to live alternative bands, you'll find often outrageous cabaret and burlesque shows. One stronghold of the concert scene is the **Crystal Ballroom** (1332 W. Burnside St., 503/225-0047, www.mcmenamins.com, hours vary), where a mix of rock, indie, and world beat artists play in a large ballroom. There, you can "dance on air" thanks to the floating dance floor—perhaps the only one in the United States.

Portland's East Side has a lively music scene. A major destination in any tour of Portland's music hotbeds would include **Doug Fir** (830 E. Burnside St., 503/231-9663, www.dougfirlounge.com, 7am-2:30pm daily), which attracts some of Portland's most interesting acts and is part of a hip development that includes a vintage motor court motel and late-night restaurant.

If you came to Portland to find the remnant of its hippie Grateful Dead roots, then the **Laurelthirst Public House** (2958 NE Glisan St., 503/232-1504, 4pm-midnight Mon., 10:30am-midnight Tues.-Wed., 10:30am-1am Thurs., 10:30am-2am Fri.-Sat., 10:30am-midnight Sun.) is where you need to be. This venerable and funky tavern has excellent local folk and country swing bands along with a feel-good vibe that takes you back to the Summer of Love.

## Comedy

For rollicking comedy improv, go to **ComedySportz** (1963 NW Kearney St., 503/236-8888, www.portlandcomedy.com, 8pm Fri.-Sat., $15), where two teams compete for laughs using suggestions from the audience. If you're into standup, check out

**Curious Comedy Theater** (5225 NE M. L. King Jr. Blvd., 503/477-9477, www.curious-comedy.org, $5-15), a nonprofit theater that offers a variety of shows, including "comedy showdowns," audience-participation "random acts of cruelty," and more.

Newest on the scene is the ultra-hip **Helium Comedy Club** (1510 SE 9th Ave., 888/643-8669, www.portland.heliumcomedy. com, $15-30) which caters to the edgier "alt comedy" side of humor. Each weekend, stars perform to a packed house of Portland's hip bespectacled locals.

## CANNABIS

Since it became legal to buy cannabis (marijuana) in 2015, retail outlets, known as dispensaries, have popped up in almost every neighborhood. Perhaps the highest concentration of green crosses, which signify a cannabis dispensary, is along NE Sandy Boulevard, which has earned the nickname of Portland's "Green Mile," though it stretches way farther than a mile. Shoppers who'd like to explore the medical benefits of cannabis might want to head out to **Panacea** (6714 NE Sandy Blvd., 503/477-5083, http://panaceapdx.com, 10am-9pm Mon.-Sat., 11am-6pm Sun.), where a nurse is sometimes available for consultation and all the profits are donated to social justice groups.

In Southeast Portland, just across the Hawthorne Bridge from downtown, find **Farma** (916 SE Hawthorne Blvd., 503/206-4357, http://farmapdx.com, 10am-10pm Mon.-Sat., 11am-7pm Sun.), with a good selection of flower, including high-CBD strains that may help with pain and anxiety but won't get you too high, as well as more THC-heavy bud, edibles, and concentrates. Farma's budtenders are some of the best in town; this is a great place to go if you're not sure what to try.

Just across from the convention center, **Oregon's Finest** (736 NE M. L. King Jr. Blvd., 503/239-1150, www.oregons-finest.com, 8am-10pm daily) has a particularly wide assortment of pre-rolls (a.k.a. joints), which are handy for visitors who didn't pack a pipe.

The Oregon Symphony performs at Arlene Schnitzer Concert Hall.

If you're shopping, dining, or listening to music on North Mississippi Avenue, you're not far from **Nectar** (4125 N. Mississippi Ave., 503/206-4818, www.nectarpdx.com, 7am-10pm daily), housed in a little bungalow with a wall full of flower-filled jars and just as many concentrates.

Downtown, **Serra** (220 SW 1st Ave., 971/279-5613, http://shopserra.com, 10am-10pm Mon.-Sat., 11am-7pm Sun.) is a stylish high-end dispensary that encourages customers to shop by the experiences they're seeking from cannabis: happy, focused, relaxed, creative, etc.

Be sure to read the rules and cautions about cannabis use in the Essentials chapter.

## THE ARTS
### Performing Arts

The **Oregon Symphony** (503/228-1353, www.orsymphony.org) is the oldest orchestra west of the Mississippi, and it performs in a historic jewel-box of an auditorium, the **Arlene Schnitzer Concert Hall** (1037

SW Broadway). **Portland Opera** (503/241-1802, www.portlandopera.org) has moved to a summer festival format, with four operas presented May through July. The opera also hosts traveling Broadway shows. Other classical music organizations include the **Portland Baroque Orchestra** (503/222-6000, www.pbo.org), led by Monica Huggett and presenting 18th-century music on period instruments; **Portland Piano International** (503/228-1388, www.portlandpiano.org), which presents world-renowned pianists in recital; and the **Third Angle New Music Ensemble** (503/331-0301, www.thirdangle.org), presenting contemporary classical music.

**Oregon Ballet Theatre** (503/222-5538, www.obt.org) is the city's classical dance troupe, usually performing at Keller Auditorium. **White Bird Dance** (503/245-1600, www.whitebird.org) brings an impressive number of world-class modern dance troupes to Portland. White Bird sponsors two different series each year, one at Arlene Schnitzer Concert Hall that features established troupes such as Paul Taylor or Mark Morris, the other featuring edgier and more intimate dance pieces held at various venues in Portland. Portland's homegrown modern dance troupe, **BodyVox** (1201 NW 17 Ave., 503/229-0627, http://bodyvox.com), is known for its energy and wit.

## Theater

More than a dozen theatrical troupes make up a significant presence on Portland's cultural scene. Cutting-edge **Imago Theatre** (17 SE 8th Ave., 503/231-9581, www.imagotheatre.com) is an internationally acclaimed troupe that employs multimedia visuals, masks, puppets, dance, and animation to achieve dramatic resonance. Imago performs in an intimate, old Masonic hall.

For more traditional theater, **Portland Center Stage** (PCS, 503/445-3700, www.pcs.org) operates out of the renovated **Portland Armory Building** (128 NW 11th Ave.) in the Pearl District. PCS productions encompass classical, contemporary, and premiere works in addition to an annual summer playwrights' festival. Portland's other major theater group, **Artists Repertory Theater** (1515 SW Morrison St., 503/241-1278, www.artistsrep.org), produces intimate, often edgier productions from its black-box theater just west of downtown.

## Art Galleries

Portland has a dynamic fine art scene. Many of the top galleries are in the Pearl District and other neighborhoods in Northwest Portland. To preview some of Portland's leading galleries, go to the **Portland Art Dealers Association** website (www.padaoregon.org), which has details of monthly shows at a dozen of the city's top galleries.

One of the best times to explore Portland's galleries is on the first Thursday of every month during the **First Thursday Gallery Walk.** More than 30 gallery owners coordinate show openings, and many offer complimentary refreshments. Visit the agglomeration of galleries in the Pearl District, where the biggest crowds gather. In this neighborhood, **Elizabeth Leach Gallery** (417 NW 9th Ave., 503/224-0521, www.elizabethleach.com) is one of Portland's most successful and long-established galleries, presenting challenging and inventive art pieces from top regional and national artists. Also check out the nearby **Augen Gallery** (716 NW Davis St.) and the cluster of galleries on that two-block stretch of NW Davis Street.

For something completely different, plan to attend **Last Thursday,** an event at month's end that highlights the dynamic district of galleries and independent designers on Northeast Alberta Street. A mix of street fair, performance art, and gallery tour, Last Thursday is much more raucous than First Thursday, with live bands, fire-eaters, and other high jinks adding a circuslike atmosphere to the Alberta Street art scene.

**Portland Institute for Contemporary Art** (PICA, 224 NW 13th Ave., 503/242-1419, www.pica.org) is Portland's leader in cutting-edge performance, experimental theater, new music, and dance. Throughout the year PICA offers lectures, performances, and exhibitions at many venues throughout the city, but the organization's top event, September's **Time-Based Art Festival** (TBA), is a contemporary art festival of regional, national, and international artists presenting theater, dance, music, film, visual exhibitions, and installations.

## CINEMA

Portland has a rich selection of alternative and repertory cinemas that feature independent, foreign, and vintage movies. **Cinema 21** (616 NW 21st Ave., 503/223-4515, www.cinema21. com) is the city's principal independent arthouse movie theater. **Hollywood Theatre** (NE 41st Ave. and Sandy Blvd., 503/281-4215, www.hollywoodtheatre.org) showcases off-beat, foreign, and cult movies in a vintage movie palace. The **Clinton Street Theater** (2522 SE Clinton St., 503/238-8899, www.cst-pdx.com) features films that generally would not have a market elsewhere, from vintage concert and Cold War propaganda films to *The Rocky Horror Picture Show* (showing every Saturday night since 1978).

The **McMenamins brewpubs** (www. mcmenamins.com) screen just-past-first-run flicks ($2-10) along with pub grub and beer at several restored vintage theaters. The most convenient to central Portland neighborhoods are the **Mission Theater** (1624 NW Glisan St., 503/223-4527) and the neo-Moorish **Bagdad Theater & Pub** (3710 SE Hawthorne Blvd., 503/236-9234). Other options in the drinks-with-movies trend are the budget-priced **Laurelhurst Theater** (NE 28th Ave. and Burnside St., 503/232-5511, www.laurel-hursttheater.com), offering beer and pizza, and **Living Room Theaters** (341 SW 10th Ave., 971/222-2010, www.livingroomtheaters.com), with a high-end cocktail bar.

Part of the Portland Art Museum, the **Northwest Film Center** (934 SW Salmon St., 503/221-1156, ext. 10, www.nwfilm. org) offers an ongoing series of foreign,

classic, experimental, and independent films. Included are thematic series (for example, contemporary films of Egypt), special retrospectives (Rainer Werner Fassbinder, David Lynch), and visiting artist programs. Most films are screened at the Whitsell Theater at the Portland Art Museum.

## FESTIVALS AND EVENTS

The February **Portland International Film Festival** (503/221-1156, www.nwfilm.org) is a two-week-plus showcase of foreign and art films that are screened in various theaters across the city.

The **Cinco de Mayo Fiesta** (www.cinco-demayo.org, $8 adults, $4 ages 6-12) celebrates Latino heritage at Tom McCall Waterfront Park the first weekend (Thurs.-Sun.) in May. This has become one of the largest celebrations of its kind in the country. Mariachis, folk dance exhibitions, a large selection of Mexican food, and fireworks displays are included in the festivities.

The **Waterfront Blues Festival** (503/282-0555, www.waterfrontbluesfest.com, $15) is the largest festival of its kind on the West Coast. It takes place the first weekend in July at Tom McCall Waterfront Park and features some of the biggest names in the blues. Profits go to the Oregon Food Bank.

From late June through July, **Chamber Music Northwest** (503/294-6400, www. cmnw.org, from $25) presents five weeks of classical music concerts in two locations: Reed College in Southeast Portland and the Catlin Gabel School in Northwest Portland.

Portland hosts many running and walking events, including the early-October **Portland Marathon** (503/226-1111, www.portlandma-rathon.org). To find out about these and other events, contact the **Oregon Road Runners Club** (www.orrc.net).

Portland is a bicycle town that loves a festival, but it questions authority. Put this all together and you get **Pedalpalooza** (www. shift2bikes.org/pedalpalooza), a decentralized, even anarchic celebration of Portland's

# Portland Rose Festival

the Rose Queen and her court

The **Portland Rose Festival** (503/227-2681, www.rosefestival.org) has been the city's major summer event for over a century. The Rose Queen and her court (chosen from among local high school entrants), navy sailors, and floats from several parades clog Portland's traffic arteries during this 18-day citywide celebration each June. Check out the website for a schedule of what is essentially a small-town festival done with big-town flair.

Two of the more colorful events of the June fete are the **Grand Floral Parade** and the **Festival of Flowers** at Pioneer Courthouse Square. In the latter, all manner of colorful blossoms fill the square to overflowing during the first week of the festival. The Grand Floral Parade usually begins the Saturday following the opening of the festival. You can reserve seats in the Memorial Coliseum ahead of time, but save your money and station yourself on an upper floor along the parade route or visit the floats at Oregon Square between Lloyd Center and the Convention Center during the week following the parade. Any lofty perch is sufficient for taking in all the hoopla, drill teams, the Rose Queen, and equestrian demonstrations. This procession is the second-largest all-floral parade in the United States.

bike culture. The festival is extremely free-form and is held in multiple locations, with only a few organized annual events, the most notable of which is the **World Naked Bike Ride** (http://pdxwnbr.org), drawing up to 10,000 riders.

Held on Father's Day weekend in June, the **Pride Festival** (503/295-9788, www.pridenw.org) celebrates Stonewall and affirms the city's LGBTQ community. The Waterfront Park main stage has entertainment all weekend, but Sunday is the big day, when some 50,000 people attend the Pride Parade.

Taking place the last full weekend in July in Portland's Tom McCall Waterfront Park, the **Oregon Brewers Festival** (www.oregon-brewfest.com) is North America's largest gathering of independent brewers. The four-day event showcases the wares of more than 100 breweries and attracts more than 90,000 beer lovers. Admission is free, but you'll need to spend $11 for a souvenir mug and four drink tokens (bring cash). Live musical entertainment accompanies the beer.

Kick off August with a weekend at **Pickathon** (www.pickathon.com), a low-key but ambitious independent music festival held in a woodsy setting on the outskirts of Portland. If you can't commit to a weekend of camping (weekend pass $310), catch a shuttle bus and come out for a day ($125) of acts ranging from rootsy bluegrass to dreamy electronica. Much of the fun is discovering new acts.

The citywide **Music Fest Northwest** (www.projectpabst.com, age 21 and over) is Portland's answer to Austin's SXSW festival. Over the course of a weekend in late August, about 20 bands play for large and enthusiastic audiences at Waterfront Park. Along with the up-and-coming bands, expect to hear big names ranging from Iggy Pop to Beck to Father John Misty. To attend the concerts, you'll need to buy a wristband ($65 per day, 2-day pass $99).

**Art in the Pearl** (503/722-9017, www.artinthepearl.com) is an outdoor arts and crafts fair held over Labor Day weekend in the North Park Blocks, bounded by NW Park and 8th Avenues and Burnside and Glisan Streets along the eastern edge of the Pearl District. This street fair showcases the creations of the local artistic community and also features food and music.

Portland's biggest food festival, the mid-September **Feast Portland** (http://feastportland.com, $35-185, age 21 and over), brings chefs from all over the country to prepare meals and teach classes alongside local chefs. A couple of the most popular of the 40-plus events are the Night Market and the Sandwich Invitational. Events sell out quickly, so check the website and buy tickets ahead of time.

# Shopping

Oregon has no sales tax, so you'll find Portland shopping especially satisfying.

## DOWNTOWN AND SOUTHWEST
### Shopping Centers and Malls

In the heart of the downtown shopping district, **Pioneer Place** (SW 5th Ave. and Morrison St., 503/228-5800, www.pioneerplace.com) is an upscale shopping development that features a number of national merchandisers, including Eddie Bauer, J. Crew, Coach, and more. The lower level features a vast food court amid pleasant fountains.

**Nike Portland** (638 SW 6th Ave., 503/221-6453, www.nike.com/NikePortland, 10am-8pm Mon.-Sat., 11am-6pm Sun.) is the flagship store of Oregon's largest sportswear manufacturer, and you'll find a large selection of elite shoes and sports gear in a temple-like retail environment. If you're looking for Nike goods at a lower price, head to the **Nike Factory Store** (2650 NE M. L. King Jr. Blvd., 503/281-5901) in inner Northeast Portland.

### Farmers Markets
★ **PORTLAND FARMERS MARKET**

One of the institutions that characterize Portland, the **Portland Farmers Market** (South Park Blocks, www.portlandfarmersmarket.org, 8:30am-2pm Sat. Mar.-Nov., 9am-2pm Sat. Nov.-Feb.) attracts throngs of people, and not just for food shopping. Every Saturday, upward of 15,000 people come for breads and baked goods, locally grown fruits and vegetables, artisanal cheeses, wild mushrooms, and freshly caught fish. There's always live music, and local chefs give cooking demonstrations. In addition, this is a great place to have breakfast or lunch, as a number of food carts offer freshly made food. People-watching is of the highest caliber.

On Wednesday (10am-2pm), there's a smaller version of this farmers market a few blocks to the north, at the end of the South Park Blocks near SW Salmon and Park. Pets are not allowed at either market. There are other farmers markets in Portland neighborhoods throughout the week. During summer and fall, Monday is the only day without a market somewhere. For a complete list, see www.oregonfarmersmarkets.org.

## Clothing and Accessories

You don't have to be in Oregon very long before plaid woolen shirts begin to look sensible and stylish. Pendleton Woolen Mills is an Oregon company, and at downtown's **Pendleton Store** (825 SW Yamhill St., 503/242-0037, 10am-8pm Mon.-Sat., 11am-7pm Sun.) you can pick up distinctive wool shirts, skirts, and blankets that will last for years.

Portland's most upscale menswear store is **Mario's** (833 SW Broadway, 503/227-3477, http://marios.com, 10am-6pm Mon.-Sat., noon-5pm Sun.), with the best of casual and formal wear from the world's top designers.

A Portland women's fashion leader for over 40 years, **The Mercantile** (729 SW Alder St., 503/223-6649, www.mercantileportland.com, 10am-6pm Mon.-Sat., noon-5pm Sun.) is a top choice for sophisticated clothing, both hip and professional. The Mercantile carries many New York and LA clothing lines, and has exclusive representation of several Portland-based designers.

Downtown's West End is home to a number of small, somewhat edgier clothing shops. **Radish Underground** (414 SW 10th Ave., 503/928-6435, http://radishunderground.com, 11am-7pm Mon.-Sat., noon-6pm Sun.) features dresses, cute cotton undies, and jewelry from local designers. **Wildfang** (404 SW 10th Ave., 503/967-6746, www.wildfang.com, 10am-6pm Mon.-Sat., noon-5pm Sun.) stocks streetwear and menswear-inspired styles for tomboys and wild feminists. **Frances May** (1003 SW Washington St., 503/227-3402, www.francesmay.com, 11am-7pm Mon.-Sat., noon-6pm Sun.) has a lovely selection from independent designers for women, men, and kids.

## Crafts

**Real Mother Goose** (901 SW Yamhill St., 503/223-9510 or 800/968-1070, www.therealmothergoose.com, 10am-5:30pm, Mon.-Thurs., 10am-6pm Fri.-Sat.) is a quality crafts gallery that presents jewelry, pottery, woodcrafts, and other goods from hundreds of Pacific Northwest artists and craftspeople. It's an excellent place to buy one-of-a-kind gifts. A smaller shop is at the Portland airport, outside of the TSA screening area.

Pick up a gift for your dog-sitter or a Portland-inspired souvenir at **Crafty Wonderland** (808 SW 10th Ave., 503/224-9097, 10am-6pm Mon.-Sat., 11am-6pm Sun.), a fun shop with handmade cards, zines, jewelry, and T-shirts from over 200 local artists.

In operation since 1974, **Portland Saturday Market** (just south of the Burnside Bridge in Waterfront Park, www.portlandsaturdaymarket.com, 10am-5pm Sat., 11am-4:30pm Sun. Mar.-Dec. 24) is the largest outdoor arts and crafts fair in the United States, attracting an estimated 750,000 visitors each year. The handicrafts range from exquisite woodwork at reasonable prices, pottery, and jewelry to more uniquely Portland items like tie-dyed baby clothes and handmade juggling equipment. The high quality is astonishing.

## Outdoor Clothing and Gear

Based in the Portland metro area, **Columbia Sportswear** (911 SW Broadway, 503/226-6800, 9:30am-7pm Mon.-Sat., 11am-6pm Sun.) has its flagship store downtown on SW Broadway. This is the place to go for fashionable, hardworking outerwear for recreation and heavy weather. For discounts on the same quality clothing and gear, go to the **Columbia Sportswear Outlet** (1323 SE Tacoma St., 503/238-0118, 9am-7pm Mon.-Sat., 11am-6pm Sun.) in Sellwood.

Synonymous with earth-friendly and socially responsible manufacturing and high-quality outdoor clothing, **Patagonia** (1106 W. Burnside St., 503/525-2552, 10am-7pm Mon.-Sat., 10am-6pm Sun.) is across from Powell's City of Books.

# NORTHWEST
## Clothing and Accessories

If all Portland hipsters had money, they'd be shopping at **Lizard Lounge** (1323 NW Irving St., 503/416-7176, www.lizardloungepdx.com,

11am-7pm Sun.-Fri., 10am-7pm Sat.), which celebrates the relaxed panache that requires just the right plaid shirt. A Portland-based company with functional, eco-friendly, stylish duds, **Nau** (304 NW 11th Ave., 503/224-9697, www.nau.com, 10am-6pm Mon.-Sat., 11am-6pm Sun.) is the place to find the perfect bike-to-work outfit.

**Popina Swimwear Boutique** (318 NW 11th Ave., 503/243-7946, www.popinaswimwear.com, 11am-6pm Mon.-Wed., 11am-7pm Thurs.-Sat., noon-5pm Sun.) is a fabulous shop for women's bathing suits, with 25 international brands and Popina's own line of updated retro-chic swimwear.

Founded in Portland in 1983, **Hanna Andersson** (327 NW 10th Ave., 503/321-5275, www.hannaandersson.com, 10am-6pm Mon.-Fri., 10am-5pm Sat., 11am-5pm Sun.) sells clothing for kids in bright, simple Swedish-inspired designs and soft, durable cotton. It's decidedly upscale but high quality and long lasting, destined to be handed down.

Head north to Thurman Street to find unique independent stores. **Betsy & Iya** (2403 NW Thurman St., 503/227-5281, http://betsyandiya.com, 10am-6pm daily) sells not-too-expensive jewelry (some inspired by Portland's bridges) made in the upstairs studio as well as a small selection of clothing and gifts. For a larger selection of stylish but wearable women's clothing (including a great front-porch sale rack), head around the corner to **Oxalis** (1824 NW 24th Ave., 503/206-8568, 10am-6pm daily). Hike a few blocks up Thurman to **Neapolitan** (2773 NW Thurman St., 415/671-9754, www.neapolitanshop.com, noon-6pm Wed.-Fri., noon-4pm Sat.-Sun.), where you can commission a pair of shoes (or take a sandal-making class) and visit the artists' studios farther back in the building.

## Books
### ★ POWELL'S CITY OF BOOKS
For many visitors, **Powell's City of Books** (1005 W. Burnside St., 503/228-0540 or 800/878-7323, www.powells.com, 9am-11pm daily) is one of Portland's primary attractions. A block square and three stories tall, Powell's combines new, used, and out-of-print books and is usually absolutely thronged with bibliophiles. In addition to miles of bookshelves, Powell's offers a coffee shop as well as free author events and book signings.

## Outdoor Clothing and Gear
The Northwest Portland outpost of **REI** (1405 NW Johnson St., 503/221-1938, 10am-9pm

Prepare to spend some time browsing at Powell's City of Books.

Mon.-Sat., 10am-7pm Sun.) is where to head if you forgot your bike helmet or crampons, or if you are shopping for functional, all-weather clothing for active lifestyles.

## NORTHEAST

Built in 1960, **Lloyd Center** (NE 15th Ave. and Weidler St., 503/282-2511, www.lloydcenter.com) was Oregon's first shopping center and is still one of Portland's major shopping destinations. Centered around an Olympic-size indoor ice-skating rink (Tonya Harding once trained here), Lloyd Center boasts more than 200 retail outlets (including Ross and Macy's), a food court, and two multiplex cinemas.

One of Northeast Portland's top destinations for strolling and window shopping is North Mississippi Avenue between Fremont and Skidmore Streets, with dozens of locally own boutiques, bars, restaurants, and food carts, and excellent people-watching. Favorite shops include **Gypsy Chic** (3966 N. Mississippi Ave., 503/234-9779, http://shop.gypsy-chic.com, 11am-7pm Mon.-Wed., 11am-8pm Thurs.-Fri., 10am-8pm Sat., 10am-7pm Sun.) for casual but elegant women's clothing and **PedX North** (3806 N. Mississippi Ave., 503/546-0910, www.pedx-shoes.com, 11am-6pm Mon.-Sat., 11am-5pm Sun.) for men and women's shoes. You'll need to stop in at **Meadow** (3731 N. Mississippi Ave., 503/288-4633, www.atthemeadow.com, 10am-7pm daily). What's not to like in a shop that sells dozens of different wines, flowers,

artisanal chocolate, and the largest selection of bitters imaginable?

A few blocks east on Williams Avenue is another hotbed of hip shops, pubs, and restaurants. If you wonder where Portland's "put a bird on it" aesthetic hails from, look no further than **Queen Bee Creations** (3961 N. Williams Ave., 503/232-1755, www.queenbee-creations.com, 10am-6pm Mon.-Fri., 10am-7pm Sat., 11am-5pm Sun.) where you'll find handmade bags, wallets, bike packs, and other fun leather cases, many in fact with whimsical birds on them.

## SOUTHEAST
### Music

A quintessential Portland business, **Music Millennium** (3158 E. Burnside St., 503/248-0163, www.musicmillennium.com, 10am-10pm Mon.-Sat., 11am-9pm Sun.) is a vast and funky music store of the sort that typified the 1970s. You'll find almost every kind of music, and next door is Classical Millennium, which offers the same expansive selection for opera and classical music fans.

## SELLWOOD

Sellwood, about five miles south of downtown Portland on the east banks of the Willamette River, is synonymous with antiques stores. Walk along Southeast 13th Avenue between Marion and Malden Streets and check out its many shops, starting at **1874 House** (8070 SE 13th Ave., 503/233-1874). Take bus 70 from the Rose Quarter.

# Food

Portland restaurants focus on locally sourced ingredients, and visitors increasingly structure their trips around eating. Even if you're not a foodie, restaurants have strong associations with their locale, and each neighborhood has a strong dining character of its own. A good online source for Portland restaurant news, openings, and best-of listings is **Eater Portland**'s site (http://pdx.eater.com).

## Food Carts

If you're on a budget or looking for inexpensive alfresco dining, join the bus commuters, cyclists, and pedestrians on the go who eat at street food carts, scattered all over the city and purveying all sorts of food. The selection is staggering; an estimated 800 food carts operate around Portland. Downtown, find a hub, or "pod," of 60 carts at SW Alder Street at 9th and 10th Avenues; on the bus mall around SW 5th Avenue and Stark Street; along SW 3rd Avenue between Stark and Washington Streets; and at SW 4th and Hall Streets near Portland State University (PSU). Other major pods include **Cartopia** (SE 12th Ave. and Hawthorne Blvd.), where half a dozen carts remain open until late at night, and the **Mississippi Marketplace** (N. Mississippi Ave. and N. Skidmore St.). If you're serious about exploring Portland cart culture, visit www.foodcartsportland.com for maps, reviews, and apps for your smartphone.

## DOWNTOWN AND SOUTHWEST
### Pacific Northwest Cuisine

A pioneer of Portland's seasonal, regional, locavore food movement, **Higgins** (1239 SW Broadway, 503/222-9070, http://higgins-portland.com, 11:30am-9:30pm Sun.-Thurs., 5pm-10:30 Fri.-Sat., $20-39) is the best exemplar of Pacific Northwest cuisine in downtown Portland. Although Higgins specializes in charcuterie, this is also a good spot for vegetarians, as there's usually a broad selection of meat-free dishes. Budget tip: The classy wood-paneled bar is a great spot for a light meal from the bistro menu ($8-26) and a beer from the one of the carefully curated taps.

## Seafood

The large, comfortably informal dining room at **SouthPark Seafood** (901 SW Salmon St., 503/326-1300, http://southparkseafood.com, 11:30am-3pm and 5pm-10pm daily, $20-32) is, as its name suggests, just a block from the South Park Blocks—and the busy cultural venues at Portland's Centers for the Arts. The focus is on the Pacific Northwest's bounty of fresh seafood, with a 13-seat raw bar and Portland's largest selection of oysters. The adjacent cocktail bar is a favorite for a pre- and post-symphony quaff.

The acclaimed **Headwaters at the Heathman** (1001 SW Broadway, 503/790-7752, www.headwaterspdx.com, 6:30am-10pm daily, $13-33) is helmed by celebrity chef Vitaly Paley—both an Iron Chef and James Beard Best Chef winner. It's a temple of casually elegant dining focused on Northwest fish and seafood, ranging from octopus carpaccio to plank-roasted salmon with squid carbonara and pea tendrils.

**Roe** (515 SW Broadway, 503/232-1566, www.roepdx.rest) is Portland's most exclusive fish restaurant, known for big Asian flavors, refined French technique, and lavish presentation. Choose a three-course pre-theater menu or the more leisurely seven-course tasting menu.

**Jake's Famous Crawfish** (401 SW 12th St., www.mccormickandschmicks.com, 503/226-1419, 11:30am-10pm Mon.-Thurs., 11:30am-11pm Fri.-Sat., 10am-10-pm Sun., $17-41) has been one of Portland's most popular restaurants since 1892. This old-fashioned fish and steak house is emblematic of traditional Pacific Northwest cooking at its best—dozens of fresh fish choices, hefty cuts of beef, and oysters on the half shell served up by a knowledgeable white-jacketed staff. The dining room is full of character, and the adjacent bar is simply full of characters.

## French

Portland chef Gabriel Rucker has gained national attention for his cooking at Le Pigeon on East Burnside and his downtown outpost, ★ **Little Bird** (219 SW 6th Ave., 503/688-5952, http://littlebirdbistro.com, 11:30am-midnight Mon.-Fri., 5pm-midnight Sat.-Sun., $14-29), where French bistro favorites such as steak tartare and duck confit are served up in a dining room that looks like a Parisian bistro staffed by hip, friendly Pacific Northwesterners. Don't skip the not-quite-French Le Pigeon burger.

## Japanese

Portland has gone *izakaya* crazy, and these casual Japanese-style pubs are everywhere. At **Shigezo** (910 SW Salmon St., 503/688-5202, www.shigezo-pdx.com, 11:30am-2:30pm and 4pm-10pm Mon.-Thurs., 11:30am-11pm Fri.-Sat., 11:30am-10pm Sun., $8-15), craft cocktails and local beers mix with excellent sushi rolls, *nigiri,* sashimi, grilled skewers, and ramen with house-made noodles and stocks. Shigezo was the first U.S. restaurant opened by the popular Japanese chain Kichinto, which now operates four other *izakaya* in the city.

## Vietnamese

Portland is undergoing an explosion of excellent Asian cooking, but few of these outstanding restaurants are downtown. **Luc Lac Kitchen** (835 SW 2nd Ave., 503/222-0047, http://luclackitchen.com, 11am-2:30pm and 4pm-midnight Sun.-Thurs., 11am-2:30pm and 4pm-4am Fri.-Sat., $9-16) is a happy exception. The food (excellent pho, banh mi, peanut curry stir-fry) is fresh and big on flavor, as are the cocktails. The only downside is the line at the door (no reservations).

## Breakfast and Lunch

A longtime favorite for a hearty morning meal, the **Bijou Café** (132 SW 3rd Ave., 503/222-3187, http://bijouxcafepdx.com, 7am-2pm Mon.-Thurs., 7am-2pm and 6pm-10pm Fri.-Sun., 8am-2pm Sat.-Sun., breakfast $8-16) is a friendly, light-filled little diner that has staked its reputation on perfecting breakfast classics. While fried cinnamon bread, red snapper, or roast beef hash are morning mainstays in this cheery café, ordinary breakfast foods are done

Jake's is the gold standard if you're looking for an old-fashioned fish-and-steak-house experience.

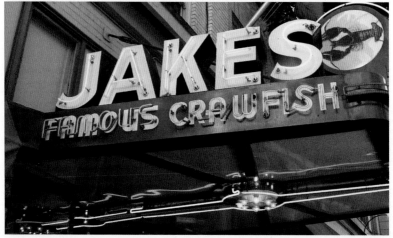

# Tasty, Family-Friendly Brewpubs

According to Oregon law, brewpubs are licensed as restaurants, so all Oregon brewpubs also offer food service for diners of all ages. While some pubs serve pretty ordinary food, it's more common for Portland brewpubs to feature upscale fare to match their ales. Brewpubs are also good for late-night dining. While no one would accuse the local **McMenamins** (www.mcmenamins.com) chain of offering high-end food, most of their 20-some Portland pubs serve a full menu until 1am daily.

Brewpubs with notable food include **Breakside Brewing** (1570 NW 22nd Ave., 503/444-7597, www.breakside.com, 11am-11pm Sun.-Thurs., 11am-midnight Fri.-Sat., $10-20), with excellent British-style ales and great sandwiches (fried green tomato and pork belly) and main courses such as grilled albacore tuna with wild mushroom and bean ragout. There's a second location of Breakside (820 NE Dekum St., 503/719-6475, 11:30am-10pm Sun.-Thurs., 11:30am-11pm Fri.-Sat., $10-20).

**10 Barrel Brewing** (1411 NW Flanders St., 503/224-1700, http://10barrel.com, 11am-11pm Sun.-Thurs., 11-midnight Fri.-Sun., $10-19) is an import from Bend that has found a lovely home on the edge of the Pearl District. Their rooftop deck is a great place to sample delicious brews and eat elevated pub food, such as steak and gorgonzola nachos and great thin-crust pizza.

**Ecliptic Brewing** (825 N. Cook St., 503/265-8002, http://eclipticbrewing.com, 11am-10pm Sun.-Thurs., 11am-11pm Fri.-Sat., $8-16) makes serious beer (IPAs and porters in addition to fruit-based sour beers) and serves serious food. There's nothing ordinary about sweet and spicy confit chicken drumsticks, beet and goat-cheddar-melt sandwiches, or smoked beef-tongue BLT.

Though it's not a brewpub, **Altabira City Tavern** (1021 NE Grand Ave., 503/963-3600, www.altabira.com, 11:30am-9pm Mon.-Thurs., 11:30am-10pm Fri., 5pm-10pm Sat., 5pm-9pm Sun., $19-29), at the top of the Hotel Eastlund, offers over a dozen taps from the region's top brewers and cider makers. Both the dining room (dinner $19-29) and tavern ($9-18) menus are designed to match the beer selection, with dishes like spinach salad with smoky blue cheese, and herb-roasted chicken with tarragon gnocchi and fava beans. Best of all, Altabira has one of the best views of Portland from its Eastside ninth-story rooftop perch.

Because they are licensed as restaurants, all brewpubs have an area where families with children can eat, and some pubs really roll out the welcome mat for kids. **Laurelwood Public House** (5115 NE Sandy Blvd., 503/282-0622, www.laurelwoodbrewpub.com, 11am-10pm Mon.-Thurs., 11am-11pm Fri., 10am-11pm Sat., 10am-10pm Sun., $10-16) has a children's play area with toys and books, plus a children's food menu. Their hearty Northwest-style ales are a good match for burgers.

**Hopworks Urban Brewery** (2944 SE Powell Blvd., 503/232-4677, http://hopworksbeer.com, 11am-11pm Sun.-Thurs., 11am-midnight Fri.-Sat., $12-15) is a bike-themed brewpub with excellent German and Belgian-style beers plus good pizza and sandwiches. Hopworks welcomes kids with toys, puzzles, crayons, and a dozen-item kids menu. A second location, the **BikeBar** (3947 N. Williams Ave., 11am-11pm Sun.-Thurs., 11am-midnight Fri.-Sat.) is equally kid-friendly.

perfectly with the freshest local ingredients. The Bijou is open for dinner only on Friday evenings, when a seasonal menu is accompanied by live jazz.

Meaty sandwiches, including the tasty pork meatball banh mi, are specialties at **Lardo** (1205 SW Washington St., 503/241-2490; 1212 SE Hawthorne Blvd., 503/234-7786, http://lardosandwiches.com, 11am-10pm daily, $8-12),

a casual sandwich shop with a good beer list. Vegetarians should come in for the broccoli rabe sandwich and the absolutely delicious kale Caesar salad.

The famous **Voodoo Doughnut** (22 SW 3rd Ave., 503/241-4704, www.voodoodoughnut.com, 24 hours daily) is in the thick of the Old Town bar zone and offers all-night doughnuts to club kids and anyone else who stumbles by. But by now, Portlanders tend to roll their eyes when they see folks at the airport flying home with Voodoo's pink to-go boxes; locals line up at **Blue Star Donuts** (1237 SW Washington St., 503/265-8410, www.bluestardonuts.com, 8am-7pm daily), where the treats are made with brioche dough. Try the *matcha* doughnut for a nice blend of bitter and sweet.

## Food Courts

If you like the idea of food carts but not eating on the street, head to **Pine Street Market** (126 SW 2nd Ave., 503/299-2000, www.pinestreetpdx.com, market 8am-11pm daily, vendor hours vary). Nine of Portland's top chefs and restaurants operate food stalls in this bustling food court, with plenty of room at communal tables. You'll find excellent ramen, burgers, pizza, rotisserie chicken, and a Korean smokehouse, plus local beers and craft cocktails.

## NORTHWEST

Northwest Portland begins just north of downtown across Burnside Street. Three of the city's most vibrant dining districts are here, within minutes of downtown hotels. **Old Town** also encapsulates historic Chinatown and is a hotbed of music clubs and late-night bars. The Portland Streetcar travels through the **Pearl District,** with its wealth of restaurants, linking it with downtown. Another restaurant destination along the streetcar line is **NW 21st and 23rd Avenues,** two pedestrian-friendly streets that are at the heart of an attractive 19th-century neighborhood.

## Pacific Northwest Cuisine

**Bluehour** (250 NW 13th Ave., 503/226-3394, www.bluehouronline.com, 4pm-9pm Sun.-Wed., 4pm-10pm Thurs.-Fri., 10am-10pm Sat., 10am-9pm Sun., $21-44) is one of Portland's few really swanky restaurants. The cooking is nominally Italian, though the kitchen is fluent in many cuisines, resulting in sophisticated dishes that are flavor-focused, revelatory, and fun all at the same time. If you

don't feel like getting dressed up for the dining room, the bar has its own menu and a more relaxed vibe.

There's no better place to taste the terroir of Oregon than ★ **Paley's Place** (1204 NW 21st Ave., 503/243-2403, www.paleysplace.net, 5:30pm-10pm Mon.-Thurs., 5pm-11pm Fri.-Sat., 5pm-10pm Sun., $26-42), an intimate bastion of fine dining. Chef Paley has a firm grasp of traditional French techniques and uses the best local ingredients in dishes such as hazelnut-shell-roasted salmon with herbed butter and creamed corn. The wine list features many hard-to-find Oregon pinot noirs. This is one of Portland's best special-occasion restaurants; for an affordable treat, eat in the less romantic bar or order the half-portions offered on the dining room menu.

Tucked beneath the Fremont Bridge, you'll find one of two locations of **Olympia Provisions** (1632 NW Thurman St., 503/894-8136; 107 SE Washington St., 503/954-3663, www.olympiaprovisions.com, 11am-10pm Mon.-Fri., 9am-10pm Sat.-Sun., $20-27), known for excellent sausages and charcuterie but also serving up some wickedly good fish dishes, such as pan-roasted halibut with forest mushrooms and cabbage. The southeast location (107 SE Washington St., 503/954-3663) has a different but similar menu; the Thurman Street location is also a butcher shop, with most of the building taken up by production of chorizo and the like.

## Steak House

Portland has a full contingent of upscale expense-account steak houses, but if you're hungry for beef, go to one of the city's originals, the **Ringside** (2165 W. Burnside St., 503/223-1513, www.ringsidesteakhouse.com, 5pm-11:30pm Mon.-Wed., 5pm-midnight Thurs.-Sat., 4pm-11:30pm Sun., reservations recommended, $33-75). Family owned for over 75 years, the Ringside retains its 1960s look of red Naugahyde and dark lighting even after a remodel. The steaks, prime rib, and seafood are excellent, and James Beard once proclaimed the onion rings "the best I ever had." Come before 6pm for a special three-course dinner menu ($40).

## French

Reserve a table at ★ **Saint Jack's** (1610 NW 23rd Ave., 503/360-1281, http://stjack-pdx.com, 9am-9:30pm Sun.-Thurs., 9am-10:30pm Fri.-Sat., $25-40) for dinner or, as is our preference, drop by for a light meal ($11-27) or late-evening drink and snack at the bar. Either way, you'll feel like you've landed in a Paris bistro, with food inspired by the meaty cuisine of Lyons, such as pan-roasted sweet-breads with figs, arugula, and onion. No surprise that this is also a good place for a glass of wine.

## Italian

**Café Mingo** (807 NW 21st Ave., 503/226-4646, http://caffemingonw.com, 11am-2pm and 5pm-10pm Tues.-Fri., 5pm-10pm Sat.-Sun., $17-29) is an always-bustling trattoria (with an equally popular bar alongside) on a busy section of NW 21st Avenue. The dining room is intimate yet casual, with the kitchen opening out to diners. The menu is a bit idio-syncratic; don't expect to dine in traditional *antipasti, primi,* and *secondi* courses. The dishes are well-prepared, however, and the service is gracious.

Italian cooking "like Mama used to make" conjures up associations of red-checkered tablecloths and a rosy-cheeked maternal presence in the kitchen. **Piazza Italiana** (1129 NW Johnson St., 503/478-0619, www.piazzaportland.com, 11:30am-3pm and 5pm-9:30pm Sun.-Tues., 11:30am-3pm and 5pm-10pm Wed.-Thurs., 11:30am-3pm and 5pm-11pm Fri.-Sat., $11-17) isn't like that. This is a hearty trattoria with European league soccer on the TV, effusive Italian conversation bouncing off the walls, and a persistent bustle that verges on rowdiness. Everyone comes for the pasta, particularly bucatini *all'Amatriciana* (bucatini pasta with pancetta, onion, and pecorino in a red wine and tomato reduction sauce).

Mediterranean Exploration Company

## Middle Eastern

★ **Mediterranean Exploration Company** (133 NW 13th Ave., 503/222-0906, www.med-iterraneanexplorationcompany.com, 4pm-10pm Sun.-Thurs., 4pm-11pm Fri.-Sat., small plates $8-19) is a hotspot for modern Eastern Mediterranean cooking. The warm *freekeh* salad with pistachio oil, the grilled octopus salad, and the *chreime,* or Tripolitany Jewish fish stew, go far beyond Middle Eastern standards such as hummus or falafel (though that's here too, with tasty twists that make them special).

## Latin American

At **Andina** (1314 NW Glisan St., 503/228-9535, www.andinarestaurant.com, 11:30am-2:30pm and 5pm-9:30pm Sun.-Thurs., 11:30am-2:30pm and 5pm-10:30pm Fri.-Sat., bar open later, $17-35), the take on South American cooking is unexpectedly delicious. The many small plates are rich in vegetar-ian choices, like quinoa-stuffed piquillo pep-pers, and can make a meal. Alternately, go

# Local Chains

If you're out exploring and need a decent bite to eat without too much fuss or expense, chances are you'll find one of these local chains around. You can feed yourself for $5-10 at any of these informal restaurants.

A simple pleasure of summer is sitting on the deck outside the Pearl District's Ecotrust Building with a slice of **Hotlips Pizza** (NW 10th Ave. and Irving St., 503/595-2342, 11am-9pm Sun.-Thurs., 11am-10pm Fri.-Sat.) and a beer or a bottle of Hotlips's homemade fruit soda. Other convenient Hotlips outlets are near PSU (1909 SW 6th Ave., 503/224-0311), at Southeast Hawthorne Street and 22nd Avenue (503/234-9999), and across from Providence Field (SW 18th Ave. and Morrison St., 503/517-9354).

Eugene-based **Café Yumm** (301 SW Morrison St., 503/222-9866, 10:30am-7pm Mon.-Fri., 11am-7pm Sat.-Sun.) offers tasty Yumm bowls, packed with veggies, rice, beans, and the secret Yumm sauce that will have you coming back for more. Though chicken and turkey are available, this is a great spot for vegetarians, vegans, and the gluten-free crowd. Soup, salad, wraps, sandwiches, and bento boxes also available. Other locations are near PSU (1806 SW 6th Ave., 503/226-9866); near Lloyd Center (1010 NE 7th Ave., 503/236-9866) and on Concourse C at the airport.

If you're near the convention center, don't fear the fast food at **Burgerville** (1135 NE M. L. King Jr. Blvd., 503/235-6858, 6:30am-11pm daily), where you can dine on the seasonal (celebrate spring with batter-fried asparagus and a strawberry shake) and the local (beef from an eastern Oregon ranchers' cooperative and smoked salmon from Astoria). In Portland, other locations to stop by for Walla Walla onion rings (in season) are at 1122 SE Hawthorne Boulevard (503/230-0479), 3432 SE 25th Avenue at Powell Boulevard (503/239-5942), and in Concourse D at the airport.

A simple, relatively quick, and inexpensive place to eat downtown is **Pastini Pastaria** (911 SW Taylor St., 503/863-5188, 11am-9pm Mon.-Thurs., 11am-10pm Fri.-Sat., 3pm-9pm Sun.). The tasty pasta dishes are served with Pearl Bakery ciabatta bread. Pastini also has restaurants at 2027 SE Division Street (503/595-6400) and 1426 NE Broadway (503/288-4300).

Although it's not a restaurant, **New Seasons Market** (2170 NW Raleigh St., 503/224-7522, 8am-10pm daily) is a great place to grab deli food to go. Of the nearly 20 stores in greater Portland, many are in central neighborhoods where visitors may find themselves looking for a bakery, a salad and burrito bar, and organic groceries: Sellwood (1214 SE Tacoma St., 503/230-4949), Seven Corners (1954 SE Division St., 503/445-2888), Hawthorne (4034 SE Hawthorne Blvd., 503/236-4800), inner Northeast (3445 N. Williams Ave.), Hollywood (3210 NE Broadway, 503/282-2080), and inner Northwest (2170 NW Raleigh St., 503/224-7522).

for traditional Peruvian such as lamb shanks braised in black beer, or a hybrid like quinoa-crusted diver scallops with wilted spinach and potato-parsnip puree.

## Spanish

Find the city's best Spanish food on a side street at the far north end of Northwest Portland, where ★ **Ataula** (1818 NW 23rd Place, 503/894-8904, http://ataulapdx.com, 4:30pm-10pm Tues.-Sat.) serves beautifully presented and exquisitely flavored tapas ($4-17) and cocktails (special sangria!) in a relaxed gastropub atmosphere. If you can resist ordering more and more tapas, it's good to

know that the paella (serves two, $34-39) is also excellent.

## Bakeries and Cafés

With Portland's profusion of excellent bakeries, it's easy to get into a squabble by asking people to identify their favorite. One thing's for certain: **Ken's Artisan Bakery** (338 NW 21st Ave., 503/248-2202, www.kensartisan.com, 7am-9:30pm Mon., 7am-6pm Tues.-Sat., 8am-5pm Sun.) is always among the top choices for wonderful French-style breads and pastries; the croissants—light, flaky, and crunchy—are masterful. At this busy fixture, you can also pick up a lunchtime sandwich

(11am-3pm daily, $7-10). Monday evenings only, Ken's stays open late and serves delectable pizza ($11-15).

# NORTH AND NORTHEAST

Linked to downtown by MAX Light Rail trains and near the Lloyd Center hotels, the area along **NE Broadway** (between NE 8th Ave. and NE 28th Ave.) is the hub of close-in Northeast Portland. Other Northeast Portland destinations for diners looking for casual yet cutting-edge food are **North Mississippi Avenue** and **NE Alberta Street.** Out past the Hollywood neighborhood along **Sandy Boulevard** is the heart of today's Vietnamese community, where you'll find inexpensive and delicious pho and other Southeast Asian specialties.

## Classic American

Join Portland's late-rising hipsters for breakfast at **Tasty n Sons** (3808 N. Williams Ave., 503/621-1400, http://tastynsons.com, 9am-10pm Sun.-Thurs., 9am-11pm Fri.-Sat., $7-19) and you'll almost certainly plan to return for dinner. This popular spot is a great place for robustly flavored brunch, happy-hour snacks, or dinner. Dishes are divided into small plates (like foie gras torchon with apricot jam) and bigger plates, such as Alabama barbecue chicken with white barbecue sauce—all designed to be shared. Downtown you'll find another location, **Tasty n Alder** (580 SW 12th Ave., 503/621-9251, www.tastynalder.com, 9am-10pm Sun.-Thurs., 9am-11pm Fri.-Sat., $7-19).

## Barbecue

**Podnah's Pit** (1625 NE Killingsworth St., 503/281-3700, http://podnahspit.com, 11am-9pm Mon.-Thurs., 9am-10pm Sat., 11am-9pm Sun., $11-20) serves up Texas-style barbecue, slow-cooked over oak in a pit. With one exception, Podnah's takes "Don't mess with Texas" to heart—tasty North Carolina-style pulled pork. Although smoked trout and sides of pinto beans and "Texas caviar" (black-eyed

pea salad) are available, non-meat-eaters will feel a little lonely here.

## Mexican

Like an unassuming beach taqueria in Baja, ★ **¿Por Qué No?** (3524 N. Mississippi Ave., 503/467-4149; 4635 SE Hawthorne Blvd., 503/954-3138, www.porquenotacos.com, 11am-10pm Mon.-Sat., 11am-9:30pm Sun., $3-13) has a relaxed hole-in-the-wall vibe to go with its excellent house-made corn tortilla tacos and other south-of-the-border street foods. You can't go wrong with any of the tacos; the guacamole is outstanding, as is the ceviche. Fresh-squeezed margaritas are utterly addictive. This place is tiny—line up to order your food, then find a seat. Most people end up sitting at outdoor tables, rain or shine.

The Mexican food at **Autentica** (5507 NE 30th Ave., 503/287-7555, www.autenticaportland.com, 5pm-10pm Tues.-Fri., 10am-2pm and 5pm-10pm Sat.-Sun., $18-23) is complex and sophisticated, but the restaurant doesn't take itself so seriously as to suck the fun out of the experience. The whole place is warm and colorful, and the patio out back is one of the best places to celebrate a warm evening in Portland. Although you can order enchiladas here, Autentica is a good place to stretch your idea of Mexican food, perhaps to include grilled cactus leaf with seasonal vegetables and wild mushrooms.

## Spanish

**Toro Bravo** (120 NE Russell St., 503/281-4464, www.torobravopdx.com, 5pm-10pm Sun.-Thurs., 5pm-11pm Fri.-Sat., $4-25) serves the kind of food that would be native to Portland had it been colonized by the Spanish: rich, seasonal, and full of vigorous flavor. The menu is extensive, covering many regions of Spain and offering everything from a bowl of olives to heaping platters of paella.

## Argentinian

Fire is the raison d'être of **Ox** (2225 NE M. L. King Jr. Blvd., 503/284-3366, http://oxpdx.com, 5pm-10pm Sun.-Thurs., 5pm-11pm

Fri.-Sat., $10-59), where meats, seafood, and vegetables get licked by flames and are served in a style that recalls the hearty, smoky flavors of Argentina. Try the crispy beef, olive and raisin empanadas, or the clam chowder enriched with a beef bone marrow. Seared steaks are the stand-out main courses, but if you're not into beef, you can enjoy the house-made chorizo sausages or pan-roasted sea scallops with Dungeness crab risotto.

## SOUTHEAST

Southeast Portland is filled with restaurant enclaves, where it's a good idea to just park the car and wander the streets before making a dining choice. Some neighborhoods, such as the six-block stretch of **28th Avenue** near East Burnside Street or **SE Division Street,** especially from SE 27 to SE 38 Avenues, seem almost totally devoted to dining.

### Pacific Northwest Cuisine

No need to dust off your high school French when calling for reservations at ★ **Le Pigeon** (738 E. Burnside St., 503/546-8796, www.lepigeon.com, 5pm-10pm daily, $17-39, 5-course tasting menu $85)—rhymes with smidgen—a highly touted hot spot of meaty gastronomy. This lack of pretension is characteristic of chef-owner Gabriel Rucker's full-flavored cooking style and his slightly manic, pocket-size dining room. His cooking embraces a breadth of rarely encountered ingredients: lambs' tongues, beef cheeks, and (yes) pigeon, all from local sources and prepared with a passion for robust flavors and inventive contrasts.

At **Castagna** (1752 SE Hawthorne Blvd., 503/231-7373, www.castagnarestaurant.com, 5:30pm-10pm Wed.-Sat., 7-course prix fixe dinner menu $100, 13-course tasting menu $165) each dish is an epiphany of taste and texture. Expect a succession of small, exquisite tastes, such as hot-smoked halibut belly with roe and nasturtium cream and aged duck with black garlic and toasted alliums. This is some of Portland's most cutting-edge dining. The dining room presents a minimalist decor that some find austere, others soothing. Immediately next door is **Café Castagna** (1758 SE Hawthorne Blvd., 503/231-9959, 5pm-10pm Tues.-Sat., 10am-2pm and 5pm-1pm Sun., $13-30), offering a less formal, more affordable dining experience.

Ken Forkish is as close as Portland has to a celebrity baker, noted for his French-style breads and pizza. **Trifecta Tavern** (726 SE 6th Ave., 503/841-6675, www.trifectapdx.com, 5pm-9pm Mon., 5pm-10pm Tues.-Thurs., 4pm-10:30 Fri.-Sat., 4pm-9pm Sun., $10-26) is his first full-on restaurant. The large, eclectic menu focuses on the seasonal bounty: grilled ear corn with chili-lime butter, fava bean fritters, and duck confit with brandied cherries. This is a lively spot to share family-style dishes with friends.

### Chinese

Portland's contemporary Chinese community is centered in the SE 82nd Avenue and Division Street neighborhood, where Portland's best Chinese food can be found at **Wong's King** (8733 SE Division St., 503/788-8883, http://wongsking.com, 10am-10pm Mon.-Thurs., 10am-11pm Fri., 9:30am-11pm Sat., 9:30am-10pm Sun., $8-21). The chef has won prestigious cooking awards in China, and the huge dining room is always thronged with Chinese families, but the staff is solicitous to non-Chinese diners who may be confounded by the extensive menu. The dim sum (10am-3pm Mon.-Fri., 9:30am-3pm Sat.-Sun.) is terrific.

### Japanese

**Bamboo Sushi** (310 SE 28th Ave., 503/232-5255, http://bamboosushi.com, 4:30pm-10pm daily, rolls $8-17), with a stylish dining room and a vast selection of fish that has been harvested according to "green" and sustainable practices, has become Portland's top sushi restaurant. Indeed, with non-sushi dishes such as sesame-crusted tuna with caramelized eggplant, it's one of the city's best seafood restaurants. Find other outposts at 836 NW 23rd Avenue (971/229-1925), 1409 NW

Alberta Street (503/889-0336), and downtown at 404 SW 12th Avenue (503/444-7455).

## Thai

One of the most exciting Thai restaurants in Portland is not the fanciest. In fact, ★ **Pok Pok Thai** (3226 SE Division St., 503/232-1387, www.pokpokpdx.com, 11:30am-10pm daily, $13-20) started out with just outdoor seating and a kitchen that was more a shed than a restaurant. Nonetheless, the Thai food produced here—specializing in the cuisine of the Chiang Mai region—is incredible. The roast game hen with dipping sauces is delicious, as is the *muu sateh* (charcoal-grilled pork loin skewers marinated in coconut milk and turmeric and served with cucumber relish). In Northeast Portland? Head to sister restaurant **Pok Pok Noi** (1469 NE Prescott St., 503/287-4149, www. pokpoknoi.com, 5pm-midnight daily, $9-23), which offers many of the same dishes.

A restaurant hidden within another restaurant is a treasure, particularly if it's **Langbaan** (6 SE 28th St., 971/344-2564, http://langbaanpdx.com, seatings 6pm and 8:45pm Thurs.-Sat., 5:30pm and 8:15pm Sun., prix fixe $75), Make your way through PaaDee (itself a fine Thai restaurant) and turn right at the bookcase to find the exclusive 25-seat dining room. The monthly changing menu features a dozen or so courses, a pageant of extremely refined dishes. Reservations are highly coveted, so call as soon as you know your travel dates.

## Indian

At ★ **Bollywood Theater** (3010 SE Division St., 503/477-6699; 2039 NE Alberta St., 971/200-4711, www.bollywoodtheaterpdx. com, 11am-10pm daily, $6-17) the focus is on Indian street food—the Dahi Papri Chaat (house-made crackers topped with chickpeas, potatoes, yogurt, cilantro, and tamarind chutney) is outrageously delicious, and other top dishes include pork vindaloo and egg masala. Order at the counter and take a free table, inside or out, to eat your meal. Expect long lines on weekends and food that's worth the wait.

## Middle Eastern

The stylish and acclaimed ★ **Tusk** (2448 E. Burnside St., 503/894-8082, www.tuskpdx. com, 5pm-10pm Mon.-Wed., 5pm-midnight Thurs.-Fri., 10am-2pm and 5pm-midnight Sat., 10am-2pm and 5pm-10pm Sun., $11-29) refines hearty Middle Eastern flavors with superlative Oregon ingredients. Most dishes come in two sizes so you can sample your way across the menu. Unusual salads and vegetable dishes are particularly good (try a salad of broccoli, peaches, fennel, and mint), but don't ignore Tusk's version of hummus (made with hominy) or meat dishes such as roasted pork shoulder.

## French

Much lauded **Coquine** (6839 SE Belmont St., 503/384-2483, www.coquinepdx.com, 8am-2:30pm Mon.-Tues., 8am-2:30pm and 5pm-10pm Wed.-Sun., $20-32), takes French comfort food to new heights. In a charming old storefront on the flanks of Mount Tabor, chef Katy Millard cooks casual but refined food that tunes French techniques on the freshest of local ingredients.

## Russian

Don't let preconceptions about Russian food keep you from visiting **Kachka** (720 SE Grand Ave., 503/235-0059, http://kachkapdx.com, 4pm-10pm daily, $13-20); if nothing else, go for a flight of vodkas, perhaps infused with dill flower or marigold. While at the bar, studying the Soviet-era posters on the walls, you may find yourself ordering a plate of pickled veggies. That might lead to a *zakuski* (appetizer) spread, including *taranka* (aptly described as "something like fish jerky"), and on to pork-stuffed cabbage rolls. The food is shockingly good, and the atmosphere pure Portland.

## Italian

**Nostrana** (1401 SE Morrison St., 503/234-2427, http://nostrana.com, 11:30am-2pm and 5pm-10pm Mon.-Thurs., 11:30am-2pm and 5pm-11pm Fri., 5pm-11pm Sat., 5pm-10pm

Sun., $16-28, pizza $9-18) is part wood-fired pizza joint and part rustic Italian home-cooking restaurant. Order one of the excellent pizzas—perhaps prosciutto and arugula—and augment it with a selection of wonderful salads, soups, house-cured meats, and wood-oven-cooked meats. The menu changes nightly to ensure that everything is fresh and seasonal.

**Ava Gene's** (3377 SE Division St., 971/229-0571, http://avagenes.com, 5pm-11pm daily, $19-38) focuses on Rome and its traditional cooking traditions, translated for the Pacific Northwest. Start with vegetable small plates, such as peach, padrone pepper, preserved lemon, and feta salad, move on to a hearty plate of tagliolini with white wine chicken ragù; and if you're still hungry, perhaps a *secondi* of roast lamb, eggplant, and pine nuts. The handsome tiled dining room lends a perfect touch of formality.

## Pizza

The staff at **Apizza Scholls** (4741 SE Hawthorne Blvd., 503/233-1286, http://apizzascholls.com, 5pm-9:30pm Mon.-Fri., 11:30am-2:30pm and 5pm-9:30pm Sat.-Sun., pizzas $19-26) have earned the reputation as pizza snobs for their formidable resistance to allowing patrons to add more than three toppings. But they're right: The handmade crusts won't char properly if they're loaded up. The Diablo Blanco, with ricotta, tomato pesto, and pumpkin seeds, is a great house specialty. Reserve online or expect a wait.

## Mexican

Forget American-style Mexican food; **Xico** (3715 SE Division St., 503/548-6343, www.xicopdx.com, 5pm-9:30pm Sun.-Thurs., 5pm-11pm Fri.-Sat., $18-29) serves sophisticated Mexican cuisine, with tortillas handmade from corn ground in-house; the same masa is used to make tamales. A specialty is the rotisserie chicken dinner for two with optional side dishes, but don't overlook Oregon lamb roasted in peanut-chocolate adobo, with tomato-chili broth.

Start with a wild boar taco or some chips and excellent guacamole at **Taqueria Nueve** (737 SE Washington St., 203/954-1987, www.taquerianueve.com, 5pm-10pm Tues.-Sat., 5pm-9pm Sun., $4-15). From there, keep going with tacos or order a plate of enchiladas or a grilled hanger steak with smoky chili sauce. Along with good food, enjoy a fun, high-energy atmosphere.

Kachka

# Accommodations

Portland has a broad range of lodging choices. Many of the best are downtown, close to the arts, restaurants, and nightlife, though prices can be steep. Northeast Portland, near Lloyd Center and the Convention Center, offers a wide selection of chain motels at somewhat lower prices with convenient links to downtown by MAX Light Rail. The rates quoted are for double-occupancy summer high-season rooms. Winter off-season rates are usually about 25 percent lower. Shopping for rooms on Internet discount lodging sites can yield unexpected deals, even in high season.

## DOWNTOWN

Unless otherwise noted, you'll pay to park at downtown hotels. Fees range $20-45 per night—and you'll be charged lodging tax, currently 13.5 percent on lodgings with more than 50 rooms. Remember that MAX Light Rail trains will deliver you to Lloyd Center, the Convention Center, and downtown, so think twice before automatically renting a car at the airport.

### $100-150

★ **McMenamins Crystal Hotel** (303 SW 12th Ave., 503/972-2670 or 855/205-3930, www.mcmenamins.com/CrystalHotel, $125-205, parking $25), has stories to tell. The McMenamins crew has rehabilitated this once notorious building with the company's trademark whimsy and Oregonian informality (guests in the less expensive rooms will find baths down the hall). The ground floor is dominated by the Zeus Café. In the basement, you'll find Al's Den, with live music nightly and a huge soaking pool, in memory of when this building housed downtown's liveliest gay baths.

**Mark Spencer Hotel** (409 SW 11th Ave., 503/224-3293 or 800/548-3934, www.markspencer.com, $129-339, parking $25), is a former residential hotel that's now a comfortable lodging just a few blocks from shopping and dining in the Pearl District. The rooms once rented as apartments, so even the standard guest rooms are spacious and have complete kitchens. Rates include continental breakfast.

McMenamins Crystal Hotel

## $150-200

The renovation of the 1912 ★ **Ace Hotel Portland** (1022 SW Stark St., 503/228-2277, www.acehotel.com/portland, $195-365, parking $34) has turned a historic but down-at-heel property in an unbeatable downtown location into a distinctive, quintessentially Portland hotel. Spare but stylish guest rooms reflect the city's recycling ethic with a mix of salvaged fir, vintage fixtures, and army surplus, while custom-made Pendleton blankets and eclectic murals by local artists enhance the unique sense of place. The less expensive rooms share a bath, while the top-floor deluxe rooms offer understated luxury.

The **Benson Hotel** (309 SW Broadway, 503/228-2000 or 800/663-1144, www.bensonhotel.com, $195-367, valet parking $40) was built in 1913 as the city's most luxurious hotel, and thankfully this grande dame retains nearly all of its spectacular early-20th-century fittings, particularly the grand lobby with its walnut paneling, chandeliers, and massive oriental carpets. If you're feeling VIP, go for the Presidential Suite: Every U.S. president since Taft (but one) has stayed here. Facilities include a restaurant and a cozy lobby bar.

## $200-250

At the vintage but beautifully updated ★ **Hotel deLuxe** (729 SW 15th Ave., 503/219-2094 or 866/895-2094, www.hoteldeluxeportland.com, $200-309, self-parking $29, valet $35) a Hollywood theme prevails throughout, with hundreds of movie stills and other photos celebrating the golden age of film in guest rooms, hallways, and on a screen that dominates the lobby. The least expensive rooms are rather small, but well appointed, and service is strong on details. The hotel is just west of downtown.

Chic and conveniently located, **Hotel Lucia** (400 SW Broadway, 503/225-1717 or 866/986-8086, www.hotellucia.com, $220-381, valet parking $43) is a top choice for travelers looking for high-design comfort and a frisson of cool urban style. Edgy art fills the lobby along with modern furniture that bespeaks cool elegance. Standard guest rooms aren't large but are comfortable and beautifully furnished; consider stepping up to a Superior or Deluxe room if you need space.

Sleek and stylish, **Hotel Modera** (515 SW Clay St., 503/484-1084 or 877/484-1084, www.hotelmodera.com, $235-385, valet parking $38) showcases an updated mid-century aesthetic. The large art-draped lobby, lined with marble and dark woods, opens onto a spacious courtyard with lots of outdoor seating, three fire pits, and a "living wall" of greenery. Guest rooms carry on the Euro-chic look, with a streamlined aesthetic that's both bold and whimsical. Hotel Modera is at the center of downtown and right on the MAX rail line. Guests can use the nearby 24-Hour Fitness.

A historic hotel with a stunning Romanesque facade, ★ **Hotel Vintage** (422 SW Broadway, 503/228-1212 or 800/263-2305, www.hotelvintage-portland.com, $212-347, valet parking $43) is a temple of discreet luxury, perfect for a romantic weekend or a highly civilized business stay. Standard rooms are sumptuous, but if you're here for a special occasion, the many unique suites make this a top choice—check out the two-story townhouse suites and the Garden Spa rooms, with a flower-decked rooftop patio and outdoor hot tub. Amenities include the Pazzo Ristorante and bar, a manager's wine reception, an honor bar, fitness and business centers, and free Wi-Fi. Pets are welcome.

Don't let the corporate moniker mislead you. ★ **Embassy Suites Portland** (319 SW Pine St., 503/279-9000, www.embassyportland.com, $219-313, valet parking $45, self-parking $35) is in fact the palatial Multnomah Hotel, built in 1912 as the largest and grandest hotel in the Pacific Northwest. When Embassy Suites remodeled this aging beauty, the company reduced the number of guest rooms from 700 to just 276 suites. These are the largest standard rooms in downtown Portland. Amenities include a free breakfast, and an indoor pool and fitness center that resembles a Roman bath.

In true Portland tradition, the **Hi-Lo Hotel** (320 SW Stark St., 971/222-2100, www.hi-lo-hotel.com, $246-379, parking $43) was "crafted" from a vintage 1910 office building. The conversion saw the removal of everything but the ground floor and the building's historic facade; all the upper-floor guest rooms are new. "Raw and refined" forms the hotel's aesthetic, with high-end amenities playing off against reclaimed barn wood. Facilities include a restaurant, a bar, and a fitness center.

## Over $250

A true Portland landmark, ★ **The Sentinel** (614 SW 11th Ave., 503/224-3400 or 800/554-3456, www.sentinelhotel.com, $254-374, parking $43) has two wings: the original 1909 hotel with an imposing white tile facade (look for the Transformer-like figures along the roofline) and the adjoining Portland Elks Lodge, an ornate structure built in 1932 to resemble the Farnese Palace in Rome. This is one of Portland's most regal hotels. The standard deluxe-level guest rooms are large and nicely furnished, but the suites are really outstanding. Amenities include Jake's Grill restaurant, a Starbucks, and a large and airy fitness center.

The interior of the historic and luxurious ★ **Heathman Hotel** (1009 SW Broadway, 800/551-0011, www.heathmanhotel.com, $300-389, parking $44), built in 1927, offers a tantalizing balance between old and new, between its old-fashioned opulence and the refreshing brio of the hotel's vast collection of modern art. The entry-level Deluxe rooms aren't huge but offer refined furnishings and every luxury. For more room, book an Executive King or a Symphony Suite. Facilities include the **Headwaters Restaurant,** one of Portland's finest seafood spots; and a wonderful two-story wood-paneled tea-room with daily high tea and live jazz music Wednesday-Saturday.

The conveniently located **Hotel Monaco** (506 SW Washington St., 503/222-0001 or 888/207-2201, www.monaco-portland.com, $335-395, valet parking $42) is a showcase of vivid color, oversize art, and unconventional furnishings. The zippy decor continues into the large, stylish guest rooms, which are designed with a sense of humor, using color and fabric to create a mood of relaxed whimsy. Amenities include a day spa, fitness and business centers, and the **Red Star Tavern** restaurant.

**The Nines** (525 SW Morrison St., 877/229-9995, www.thenines.com, $607-729, valet parking $43) occupies the top nine floors of the former Meier and Frank department store, a magnificent glazed terra-cotta landmark from 1908. A dramatic nine-story interior atrium is flanked by large stylish guest rooms. Guest rooms feature original art from students at the Pacific Northwest College of Art. Facilities include fitness and business centers, the organic steak house Urban Farmer, and the rooftop Departures, which has cocktails and lighter Asian-influenced fare.

One of the few hotels right on the Willamette River, the lodge-like **RiverPlace Hotel** (1510 SW Harbor Way, 503/228-3233 or 800/227-1333, www.riverplacehotel.com, $239-475, valet parking $37) sits above a marina at the edge of Waterfront Park, yet it's just moments from downtown shopping and activities. A warm and pleasing arts and crafts aesthetic pervades the lobby and bar, and guest rooms are large and comfortable. RiverPlace also offers one- and two-bedroom condos. With the notable position right on the river, the bar and restaurant, both with large outdoor decks, are very popular.

## NORTHWEST
### Under $50

**Northwest Portland Hostel** (425 NW 18th Ave., 503/241-2783 or 888/777-0067, http://nwportlandhostel.com, bunks $29 for Hostelling International members, $39 non-members, private rooms $71-104, parking permit $2 per day) has a great location at the heart of Northwest Portland's most exciting neighborhoods. The hostel consists of three adjacent buildings with a mix of four- to six-bed dorms, private rooms, a fully equipped kitchen, a café open for three meals daily, plus common rooms and courtyards.

## $50-100

Another simple place to stay in Northwest Portland is the **Portland International Guesthouse, Northwest** (2185 NW Flanders St., 503/224-0500 or 877/228-0500, www.pdxguesthouse.com, $80-100), a historic home with six rooms sharing three baths, a sitting room, and a kitchen.

In the heart of the Old Town-Chinatown district, the **Society Hotel** (203 NW 3rd Ave., 503/445-0444, bunks $50, private rooms with shared bath $115, suites with private baths $169-189, self-parking $15, valet $20) is a revitalization of an 1881 sailors' boardinghouse that has seen a lot of history, including stints as a Chinese tong lodge and a hospital. This simple but comfortable hotel has been rebuilt with hipster chic, with a 24-bed dorm, plus a mix of hotel rooms with shared and private baths. The large living room-like lobby has a café-bar (7am-11pm daily), and in good weather you can take your drinks up to the rooftop deck.

## Over $250

One of Portland's most engaging lodging choices, the ★ **Inn at Northrup Station** (2025 NW Northrup St., 503/224-0543 or 800/224-1180, www.northrupstation.com, $255-370, free parking) is an older motel in Northwest Portland that has been totally renovated into a retro-hip showcase with a wild color palette. Each room has a kitchen and boldly designed furniture, and there's a rooftop garden. The inn is right on the Portland Streetcar line, so you can get to the Pearl District or downtown in minutes without having to worry about parking.

## NORTH AND NORTHEAST

Between downtown Portland and the Lloyd Center are the Portland Oregon Convention Center and the Rose Garden sports arena, along with a number of good-value chain hotels. There are often deep discounts on these hotels at Internet reservation sites. Most of the hotels are no more than five minutes' walk from the MAX line. The downside is that many of these close-in hotels are in a busy neighborhood with lots of traffic, but that's the price you pay for convenience.

The historic Irvington neighborhood north of Broadway, studded with lovely vintage homes, offers a couple of fine bed-and-breakfast options.

## $50-100

A historic saloon and hotel near the foot of the Fremont Bridge in a gentrifying industrial neighborhood, **McMenamins White Eagle** (836 N. Russell St., 503/335-8900 or 866/271-3377, www.mcmenamins.com, $94-99, free street parking) is one of the best lodging deals in town. The 11 sparsely furnished but comfortable rooms share two restrooms and two showers, European style. The saloon features live music nightly, so it's loud until at least midnight. Earplugs are available for free.

## $150-200

The historic Irvington neighborhood north of the Lloyd Center has several fine B&Bs. The landmark **Lion and the Rose Victorian Bed and Breakfast Inn** (1810 NE 15th Ave., 503/287-9245 or 800/955-1647, www.lionrose.com, $185-235) is a 1906 Queen Anne mansion listed on the National Register of Historic Places. The seven guest rooms and apartment, all with private baths, are each unique, charming in an authentically Victorian way, and up-to-date with air-conditioning and cable TV. The B&B is within walking distance of good restaurants and shopping on Northeast Broadway.

The opulent ★ **White House Bed and Breakfast** (1914 NE 22nd Ave., 503/287-7131 or 800/272-7131, www.portlandswhitehouse.com, $175-345) gives you the presidential treatment. Located just off Broadway near an avenue of shops and restaurants and only 5 to 10 minutes from the Lloyd Center and downtown, this lovingly restored 1912 lumber baron's mansion is one of the city's top B&Bs. It really does look like its namesake in DC.

Portland is epicenter for the tiny house movement, so **Caravan** (5015 NE 11th Ave., 503/228-5225, http://tinyhousehotel.com, $165-175), a tiny house hotel, makes perfect sense. Rent one of six custom-made houses on wheels gathered around a central fire pit and common area. Each of the tiny houses (which range 120-170 square feet) has a flush toilet and shower, kitchen, and electric heat. Best of all, you'll wake up in the midst of the Alberta arts neighborhood, with great dining and galleries within steps.

## $200-250

Just across the street from the Oregon Convention Center and immediately on the MAX line, **Hotel Eastlund** (1021 NE Grand Ave., 503/235-2100 or 800/343-1822, http://hoteleastlund.com, $229-279, parking $25) offers recently updated rooms in a convenient location. The rooftop Altabira City Tavern offers fantastic views over Portland.

★ **Kennedy School** (5736 NE 33rd Ave., 503/249-3983 or 888/249-3983, www.kennedyschool.com, $225-245, free parking) is a quirky McMenamins hotel in the Concordia neighborhood, about six miles northeast of downtown. The hotel is set in an old elementary school that has been transformed into a brewpub, movie theater, restaurant, several school-themed bars (including the Detention Lounge), and a concert venue. You have a choice of rooms: whimsically decorated former classrooms that have become guest rooms, complete with chalkboards and private baths, and king bedrooms in the "English Wing," a newly built addition in a lush courtyard behind the school.

## SOUTHEAST
### Under $50

No other lodgings capture the eco-friendly vibe of Portland—and especially the woolly Hawthorne neighborhood—quite like

**Portland Hawthorne Hostel** (3031 SE Hawthorne Blvd., 503/236-3380 or 866/447-3031, www.portlandhostel.org, bunks $34-37 for Hostelling International members, $37-40 nonmembers). Among its most prominent features is an eco-roof over the front porch, a runoff filtering system to capture rainwater for landscaping and flushing toilets. The 1909 house offers men's, women's, and coed dorm rooms, plus two private rooms ($74 members, $77 nonmembers). Amenities include a fully equipped kitchen (make your own pancakes for $1), lockers, and bike rentals.

### $150-200

On the east side of the Burnside Bridge, as Burnside Street mounts the hill, are a number of older motor-court motels, some of dubious quality. However, one of these older properties has an interesting story. The **Jupiter Hotel** (800 E. Burnside St., 503/230-9200 or 877/800-0004, www.jupiterhotel.com, $161-309, parking $15) is what you might call a boutique motel, an older motor court that has been totally updated with a chic modern look and such stylish accoutrements as fine linens, eye-grabbing art, and high-end toiletries. Best of all, the Jupiter Hotel is also home to the Doug Fir Restaurant and Lounge, one of Portland's top music clubs, with a popular dining room open till 4am daily. Weekends can get pretty noisy, so bring earplugs, or just dance till dawn.

On the edge of beautiful Laurelhurst Park, the opulent **Portland Mayor's Mansion** (3360 SE Ankeny St., 503/232-3588, http://pdxmayorsmansion.com, $175-280) is indeed the home of a former Portland mayor. Built in 1912 of redbrick in colonial revival style, the mansion is filled with intriguing period detail and offers four lodging options, all with private baths, including a three-room executive suite. This mansion is at the heart of one of early Portland's most exclusive neighborhoods, and a walk in any direction will reveal dozens of beautiful architectural specimens.

# CAMPING

Portland isn't particularly convenient for campers. South of Portland, with easy access off I-5, is **Champoeg State Heritage Area** (503/678-1251, www.oregonstateparks.org, reservations 800/452-5687, http://oregonstateparks.reserveamerica.com, $19-29), a lovely park along the Willamette River. Campsites are in shaded groves alongside the river, and bike and hiking paths and museums make this park a worthy recreational destination. In addition to year-round tent ($19) and RV ($28-31) sites, there are also yurts ($43-53) and rustic cabins ($41-51). Champoeg is about 30 miles south of downtown Portland, off I-5 at exit 278.

For those who enjoy rural serenity within commuting distance of downtown, there's camping in **Milo McIver State Park** (503/630-7150 or 800/551-6949, www.oregonstateparks.org, reservations 800/452-5687, http://oregonstateparks.reserveamerica.com,

mid-Mar.-Oct., $18 tents, $26 RVs). This retreat, set on the banks of the Collowash River five miles northwest of Estacada, is 25 miles (but about 45 minutes) from downtown Portland. To get to the park, take I-84 east to I-205 south and follow it to the exit for Highway 224 and Estacada. The road forks right at the town of Carver to go 10 miles (look for Springwater Road) to the campground.

East of Portland, a few miles north of I-84 on the Sandy River, is **Oxbow Park** (503/797-1850, reservations 800/452-5687, www.reserveamerica.com, $22, vehicle entrance fee $5), operated by Metro, the Portland regional government agency. Oxbow Park is right on a bend in the river in a quiet woodsy setting and offers flush toilets but no showers. There's a strict no-dog policy. To reach Oxbow Park, take I-84's exit 17, follow 257th Avenue to Division Street, turn east (right), and follow signs to the park.

# Information and Services

## VISITOR INFORMATION

Portland's visitor information resources are far-reaching and extensive. Begin at Travel Portland's **Visitor Information Center** (701 SW 6th Ave., 503/275-8355 or 877/678-5263, www.travelportland.com, 8:30am-5:30pm Mon.-Fri., 10am-4pm Sat. Nov.-Apr., 8:30am-5:30pm Mon.-Fri., 10am-4pm Sat., 10am-2pm Sun. May-Oct.), located in Pioneer Courthouse Square. Sharing the space with the visitor information center is the **TriMet Ticket Office** (www.trimet.org, 8:30am-5:30pm Mon.-Fri.), where you can buy bus tickets and pick up schedules.

## NEWSPAPERS

The *Oregonian* (www.oregonlive.com), Portland's longtime newspaper, is joined by a host of alternative or community papers that circulate around the city. Of all the free weeklies, most useful to travelers are the

*Willamette Week* (http://wweek.com) and the *Portland Mercury* (www.portlandmercury.com). Both publications have live music and entertainment listings; their websites have archives of restaurant reviews.

*Portland Monthly* (www.portlandmonthlymag.com) is a glossy magazine dedicated to the good life in Portland. The magazine keeps an eye trained on the city's burgeoning dining scene and offers fairly comprehensive restaurant listings.

## RADIO STATIONS

Portland is very much a public and community radio kind of city. **OPB** (91.5 FM) is the local NPR station. Of the top 50 public radio news stations in the nation, OPB has the largest share of listeners in its broadcast area. That doesn't mean that Portland is the most public radio-listening city in the United States (some cities have more than one NPR station), but almost.

For a taste of Portland's more alternative side, tune into **KBOO** (90.7 FM) for community radio, Oregon style. KBOO's mission statement just about says it all: "Volunteer-powered, noncommercial, listener-sponsored, full-strength community radio for Portland, Oregon, Cascadia, and the world!"

Other noncommercial radio stations include **KMHD** (89.1 FM) for jazz and **KBPS** (89.9 FM) for classical music and the Metropolitan Opera radio broadcasts.

# Transportation

## GETTING THERE
### Air

**Portland International Airport** (PDX, 877/739-4636, www.flypdx.com), known by its airport code, PDX, has been selected twice in recent years as the top airport in the country by readers of *Condé Nast Traveler* magazine, for its easy MAX connections to downtown, free Wi-Fi, and great shopping and dining, with a focus on airport outposts of local businesses.

PDX is 15 miles from downtown Portland, but if you're driving, allow at least half an hour to make the trip, more if you are traveling during rush hour. From downtown, take I-84 east toward The Dalles, then take I-205 north toward Seattle. Take Airport Way West, exit 24 from I-205.

**Airport MAX** (www.trimet.org) makes it easy to avoid traffic with frequent light-rail train service to and from PDX and downtown and other stops on the MAX system. The airport service is called the Red Line, and it runs every 15 minutes from Beaverton Transit Center through downtown Portland to PDX. Depending on the day, the earliest trains begin operation from the airport around 5am; the final trains of the day leave PDX by midnight. Travel downtown to or from the airport is $2.50. The trip to or from the airport and the city center takes approximately 40 minutes.

To find the MAX station at PDX, proceed to the lower level (follow signs for baggage claim), then turn right (south) at the base of the escalators. Proceed to the end of the terminal; at the final set of doors, you'll find automated ticketing machines for MAX, and right outside the doors is the train itself.

Several cab companies and shuttle services serve the airport, as do Uber and Lyft; look for them at the center section of the airport terminal's lower roadway—go out the doors from the baggage-claim level. Taxi fare to downtown is roughly $40 from the airport.

To drive to Portland from PDX, exit the airport and follow signs to Portland. This takes you first to I-205 south; then, at exit 21B, follow signs to Portland, via I-84 west. In six miles, at the junction of I-5, take the exit for I-5 south, but remain in the on-ramp lane, which exits onto the Morrison Bridge and downtown.

### Train

Portland is served by three **Amtrak** (800/872-7245, www.amtrak.com) routes. The Coast Starlight travels between Los Angeles and Seattle, with a daily stop each way in Portland. The Cascades route operates multiple trains daily between Eugene, Portland, Seattle, and Vancouver, British Columbia. The Empire Builder links Portland and Chicago with once-daily service in each direction. Handsome **Union Station** (800 NW 6th Ave.) is a glorious 1890s vestige of the glory days of rail travel that's still in service as Portland's Amtrak station.

### Bus

**Greyhound** (550 NW 6th Ave., 503/243-2361 or 800/231-2222, www.greyhound.com) provides intercity bus service from the Greyhound depot, one block south of Amtrak's Union Station.

A great addition to Pacific Northwest intercity bus transport is **Bolt Bus** (877/265-8287, www.boltbus.com), with direct service between Portland, Seattle, Bellingham, and Vancouver, British Columbia. Tickets between Portland and Seattle range $17-27 one-way.

## Car

Portland is near several interstate highways. I-5 runs from Seattle to San Diego, and I-84 goes east to Salt Lake City. I-405 circles downtown Portland to the west. I-205 bypasses the city to the east. U.S. 26 heads west to Cannon Beach on the coast and east to the Cascades.

# GETTING AROUND

The city's layout is fairly straightforward, with most streets conforming to an easily understood grid. Most streets are named and run east-west; most avenues are numbered and run north-south. Generally speaking, the city is divided into quadrants by the Willamette River and Burnside Street. Therefore, streets and avenues with an SE (Southeast) prefix are south of Burnside and east of the river; streets and avenues prefixed by NW (Northwest) are north of Burnside Street and west of the Willamette, and so on. There is also a section of Portland with the single prefix, N., for north; it's best thought of as the part of Northeast Portland that is west of Williams Avenue. Also worth noting: Northwest Portland streets proceed in alphabetical order from Ankeny, moving north with streets keyed to the names of early settlers (hence Burnside, Couch, Davis, Everett, all the way to Yeon).

Bridges are a major part of getting around in a river city. The east and west sides of Portland are linked by a dozen bridges, 11 of them in the core of the city, including the public transit, pedestrian, and bike bridge linking OMSI and the South Waterfront. Some of these are drawbridges and regularly lift to allow boats to pass. This is particularly a feature of everyday life during the Rose Festival,

when the naval fleet arrives at and departs from downtown moorages.

## Public Transportation

Portland has an excellent public transportation system called **TriMet** (503/238-7433, www.trimet.org), which includes buses, light rail (MAX), and commuter rail. There is also the Portland Streetcar and an aerial tram operated by the city. Nearly all of Portland's primary destinations are easily reached by this system, so unless you actually need a rental car for your visit, consider using public transportation. In fact, riding MAX, the Portland Streetcar, and the tram can be part of the fun of visiting Portland.

The most widespread of TriMet's transport services are **buses,** with over 90 bus lines, most of which connect to MAX. For most lines, bus service begins 5am-5:30am; selected lines continue service until about 1:30am. Throughout downtown, 5th and 6th Avenues are referred to as the Portland Mall or simply the **Bus Mall.** Most buses run along these two one-way streets as they pass through downtown.

**Streetcar service** currently links the Nob Hill district of NW 23rd Avenue, the Pearl District, and downtown (along 10th Ave. and 11th Ave.); Lloyd Center, the inner east side, and OMSI; and Portland State University, the South Waterfront development, and the Portland Aerial Tram. **MAX** is the light-rail system, with four different lines, the longest being the 33-mile Blue Line that connects Gresham on the east through downtown and west to Beaverton and Hillsboro. The Red Line travels some of the same route from Beaverton in the west through downtown to the Gateway Transit Center, but then it turns north and travels to the airport. The Yellow Line runs between downtown and the Portland Expo Center via the Rose Quarter Transit Center and North Portland along Interstate Avenue. The MAX Green Line runs between Gateway Transit Center and Clackamas Town Center, and on 5th and 6th Avenues in downtown Portland between Union Station and Portland

State University. The Orange Line links downtown Portland to the southern suburb of Milwaukie.

Each part of the transit system uses the same **tickets** or fare structure, and bus transfers and streetcar or MAX tickets can be used throughout the system. Tickets are valid for a maximum of 2.5 hours of travel. Keep your ticket (or transfer, as it's also called) with you, as it is your proof of payment, and you can ride the system until the expiration time shown. Basic ticket prices are $2.50 adults; $1 for seniors, disabled, and people on Medicaid; $1.65 ages 7-17 and students; and $2.45 for lift or paratransit. Bus operators do not give change, but the ticketing machines accept both coins and bill. At the MAX stations, including transit centers, machines accept cash and credit or debit cards and will give change. In addition, an all-day ticket is available and is valid for unlimited rides on buses, MAX, and the Portland Streetcar until the end of the service day when the ticket was purchased; these cost $5 adults, $2 senior citizens, and $3.30 children, and are a great deal if you're going to use public transportation more than once a day.

Regular per-ride tickets can be purchased at TriMet's primary ticket and information center in Pioneer Courthouse Square (SW Yamhill St. and SW 6th Ave.), and as you board any bus or streetcar. In addition, there are ticket vending machines at all MAX stops. All-day tickets can be purchased from MAX ticket machines, from the TriMet office, and from bus operators; all-day passes are not available from streetcars. You'll need to insert and validate your all-day ticket in the validator machine if you're traveling on MAX or the streetcar.

The **Portland Aerial Tram** (5:30am-9:30pm Mon.-Fri., 9am-5pm Sat. Oct.-May, 5:30am-9:30pm Mon.-Fri., 9am-5pm Sat., 1pm-5pm Sun. June-Sept.) is a gondola that travels 3,300 linear feet between the South Waterfront District and the upper campus of the Oregon Health and Science University (OHSU). Round-trip tickets are $4.70; the tram is not part of the TriMet system, so bus transfers and MAX or streetcar tickets are not valid on the tram. Tickets are available from ticket machines at the lower terminal and are checked only on boarding at the lower terminal. The tram is easily reached via public transport, as the lower tram station is adjacent to the Westside streetcar line SW Moody Avenue and Gibbs Street stop.

one of Portland's streetcars

## Car

Apart from ever-increasing gridlock on the freeways and major arterials, driving in Portland is mostly straightforward. Avoid taking the interstates at rush hour (which can start as early as 3pm), if at all possible. Because Portland is a city of bridges, traffic tends to back up when approaching the rivers, particularly on the I-5 and I-205 bridges across the Columbia River.

You must pay to **park** downtown and in close-in Northwest, Northeast, and Southeast neighborhoods. Pay at a parking meter kiosk with change, a credit or debit card, or using the Parking Kitty smartphone app and receive a ticket to place on the street-side window as proof of payment (no ticket needed with the phone app). Valid tickets (those with time left on them) can be used at more than one parking place. In addition, the city is filled with parking garages; the seven city-owned SmartPark parking garages are usually the cheapest options and also accept merchant validation stamps (on the garage receipt) for a limited period of free parking. Street parking is free 7pm-8am daily.

## Taxi

In addition to **24-hour taxi service** (Broadway Cab, 503/333-3333; Radio Cab, 503/227-1212), Portland has Uber and Lyft.

## Bike

Portland's bike share program, **Biketown** bike (www.biketownpdx.com, $2.50 for 30 minutes, $12 per day) has racks of bikes throughout downtown and the inner neighborhoods. Sign up online, via the mobile app, or at a Biketown station kiosk. Note that these bikes don't come with helmets; be careful, especially when riding in traffic! When you're done riding, lock up at any station.

## Tours

If you want to get the Portland Big Picture before setting out to explore on your own, consider Big Pink Sightseeing's **Hop-On Hop-Off Trolley Tour** (503/241-7373, www.

graylineofportland.net, $37). A daylong ticket lets you jump off and on an open-air, covered bus anywhere along its 12-stop route, which includes many of Portland's top sights. This is an excellent introduction to Portland for first-time visitors.

**Portland Walking Tours** (503/774-4522, www.portlandwalkingtours.com) offers a variety of tours related to art, architecture, history, and food of the downtown area. Most depart from the visitors center at Pioneer Courthouse Square. The 2.5-hour Best of Portland tour ($23 adults) visits public art, downtown parks, and the waterfront; the Underground Portland tour ($23 adults) captures the spirit of the city's historic Old Town and Chinatown, culminating in a visit to an underground business district and a Shanghai tunnel.

Join up with the folks at **Pedal Bike Tours** (133 SW 2nd Ave., 503/243-2453, www.pedalbiketours.com, from $59, includes bike) and you'll not only get some exercise, but you'll get a feel for Portland life. The downtown tour provides a good orientation to the city's layout and sights; other tours visit local breweries and food carts.

Get out on the Willamette aboard the **Portland Spirit** (503/224-3900, www.portlandspirit.com), which offers a variety of sightseeing and dining cruises aboard a 150-foot yacht with three public decks. The usual tour route is between downtown and Lake Oswego, south (upstream) from Portland. Choose from a two-hour lunch cruise (11:30am Mon.-Sat., $44 adults), 2.5-hour dinner cruise (6:30pm daily, $74 adults), and two-hour brunch cruise (11:30am Sun., $52). Sightseeing passengers may also accompany any dining cruise (lunch and brunch sailings $30 adults, dinner sailings $40), with drinks and snacks available on board. Most cruises depart from the dock at Salmon Street Springs Fountain (at the base of SW Salmon St. at Waterfront Park). Call or check the website for departure times and to learn about other cruise options.

**Willamette Jetboat Excursions** (503/231-1532 or 888/538-2628, www.

willamettejet.com) offers jet-boat tours of the Willamette River. A two-hour cruise (daily May-Sept., $44 adults, $30 ages 4-11) travels up to Willamette Falls at Oregon City, while a one-hour Bridges and Harbor Tour (daily mid-June-early Sept., $31 adults, $21 ages 4-11) explores the waterfront and all 11 of downtown Portland's bridges. Tours depart from the OMSI dock (1945 SE Water Ave.).

**Ecotours of Oregon** (3127 SE 23rd Ave., Portland 97202, 503/475-0226, www.ecotours-of-oregon.com) runs tours blending ecological understanding with good times. Door-to-door van transport from anywhere in the Portland area, lunch, and commentary are included in itineraries such as Portland microbrewery tours ($70) and whale-watching ($109). Packages focusing on winery tours, Mount St. Helens, and the Columbia Gorge typify the focus of this small company. Trips are usually confined to vans for six people,

accompanied by a professional naturalist-historian guide.

If you're just interested in Portland beers, you have several brewpub tour options, including the minivan tours offered by **Brewvana** (503/729-6804, www.experiencebrewvana.com, $69-89, beer included). A more participatory option is **Brewcycle Portland** (1425 NW Flanders St., 971/400-5950, www.brewgrouppdx.com, $25-30, not including beer) where you'll join up to 14 other beer lovers on a specially designed "brewcycle" that you'll help peddle from pub to pub. These same folks also offer the BrewBarge, which gets you out on the Willamette on 1.5 hour cruises ($35), but you need to bring your own beer.

Sign on with **High Five Tours** (503/303-2275, www.high5tours.com, $65-95) to learn about the cannabis business in Portland or to simply fuel up on coffee, weed, and snacks and head to Multnomah Falls.

# Columbia River Gorge and Mount Hood

Look for ★ to find recommended sights, activities, dining, and lodging.

# Highlights

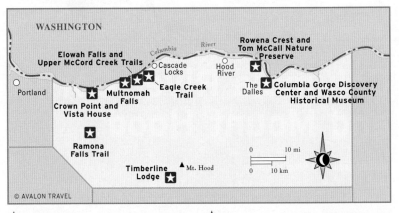

★ **Crown Point and Vista House:** This viewpoint provides the classic vista of the Columbia River and its mountain canyon (page 104).

★ **Multnomah Falls:** Plunging 620 feet, the highest drop in the state, this is one waterfall you can't miss (page 106).

★ **Elowah Falls and Upper McCord Creek Trails:** Leading to two fantastic overviews of the same beautiful waterfall, these trails are one of the Columbia Gorge's lesser-known hiking routes (page 108).

★ **Eagle Creek Trail:** The one trail you must hike in the Columbia Gorge leads to numerous waterfalls along a steep-sided valley (page 113).

★ **Rowena Crest and Tom McCall Nature Preserve:** One of the few drive-to vistas in the Columbia Gorge, this promontory is famed for its spring wildflower displays (page 128).

★ **Columbia Gorge Discovery Center and Wasco County Historical Museum:** The best museum in the Columbia Gorge relates the complex and fascinating history of the region (page 131).

★ **Timberline Lodge:** A fantastic log lodge built by hand in the 1930s, Timberline Lodge is an icon for the Pacific Northwest (page 134).

★ **Ramona Falls Trail:** An easy hike leads to a dramatic weeping-wall waterfall, one of the most beautiful near Mount Hood (page 135).

To Native Americans, the Columbia River Gorge was the great gathering place. To Lewis and Clark, it was the gateway to the Pacific. To visitors today, the Columbia River's enormous canyon carved through the Cascade Mountains is

one of the Pacific Northwest's most dramatic and scenic destinations. The river, over a mile wide, winds through a 3,000-foot-deep gorge flanked by volcanic peaks and austere bands of basalt. Waterfalls tumble from the mountain's edge and fall hundreds of feet to the river. Clinging to the cliff walls are deep-green forests filled with ferns and moss. It's the living rendition of a Pacific Northwest postcard.

While most visitors confine themselves to the cliffs and dense woodlands at the western end of the gorge, a surprise awaits the newcomer venturing farther east. Halfway through this cleft in the Cascades, the greenery parts to reveal tawny grasslands and sage-covered deserts under an endless sky. This 80-mile-long, 5-mile-wide chasm has as much variety in climate, topography, and vegetation as terra firma can muster.

Visitors can revel in a cornucopia of attractions: the world's largest concentration of high waterfalls, one of the planet's most diverse botanical communities, and a wide spectrum of recreational opportunities that includes skiing, fishing, hiking, rock climbing, windsurfing, and more—much of which can be enjoyed all in the same day.

Immediately south of the Columbia River Gorge rises 11,240-foot Mount Hood, Oregon's highest peak. Mount Hood is an all-season outdoor playground. Besides boasting five popular ski areas, the mountain attracts hikers, mountain climbers, and those who come to marvel at the extravagant Works Progress Administration-era Timberline Lodge.

If there's one word to describe the forces that created the Columbia River Gorge, it's *cataclysmic*. During the last ice age, a 2,000-foot ice dam formed Lake Missoula, a vast inland sea in what is now northern Idaho and western Montana. Its collapse some 15,000 years ago released a wall of water that steamrolled westward at 60 mph. These torrents

**Previous:** hiking trail leading to Mount Hood; bridge at Latourell Falls in spring. **Above:** Wahclella Falls.

# Columbia River Gorge and Mount Hood

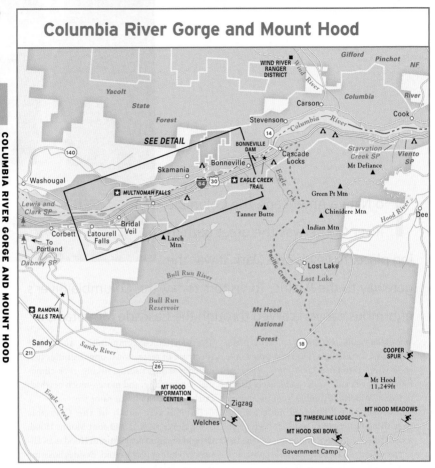

entered the eastern gorge at depths exceeding 1,000 feet. The floodwaters submerged what is now Portland and then surged 120 miles south, depositing rich alluvial sediments in the Willamette Valley. Scientists estimate there were at least 40 such inundations between 12,000 and 19,000 years ago.

## THE COLUMBIA RIVER

The 1,243-mile Columbia River has its primary headwaters at Lake Columbia in British Columbia, and from there it flows north and west from Canada's Kootenay Range. Glacial runoff, snowmelt, and such impressive tributaries as the Kootenay and Snake Rivers guarantee a fairly consistent flow year-round. At peak flows, the river pumps 250,000 cubic feet of water per second into the Pacific Ocean after draining 259,000 square miles, an area larger than France.

Flow peaks in spring and early summer, coinciding with the region's irrigation needs. Another leading use of the river is hydropower. The Columbia River Basin is the most hydroelectrically developed river system in the world, with more than 400 dams in place throughout the main stem and tributaries. As a result, the current incarnation

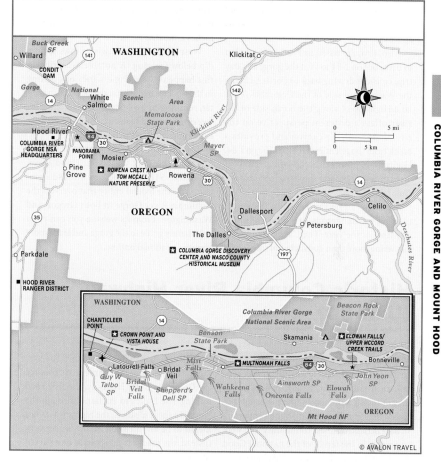

© AVALON TRAVEL

of the Columbia is a stark contrast to the white water that filled its channel before the dams. Back in that era, spawning salmon had to jump over several sets of roiling cascades, and shipping was a hazardous enterprise. Floods were commonplace; the flood of 1894, for example, inundated Hood River and The Dalles. Although the Columbia no longer exerts so pervasive an influence on the topography, it is still more powerful than any river in North America except the Mississippi.

## PLANNING YOUR TIME

The heart of the Columbia Gorge is just an hour from Portland, making this a major getaway for residents and travelers alike. Any trip to the gorge should include a drive along the Historic Columbia River Highway, with hikes to waterfalls and a drive up the "Fruit Loop" (Hwy. 35) from Hood River to Mount Hood. Even though the gorge is very popular, it's also vast, so it's easy to lose the crowds if you hike a lesser-known trail or get off the main routes.

While most people visit the gorge as a day trip from Portland, consider spending a night in Hood River or at Mount Hood to make this a more relaxing trip—and to get a feel for the youthful culture of windsurfers and cyclists that use this stunning landscape as their playground. In addition to excellent hotels and restaurants, you'll find wine-tasting rooms aplenty.

Also, if you're based in Portland and plan to drive out on I-84 to visit the gorge as a day trip, consider driving back to Portland along the Washington side of the Columbia. Two-lane Highway 14 along the north side of the river offers a different perspective on the river and its mighty canyon and provides a break from the relentless truck traffic on I-84. Highway 14 joins I-205 east of Portland for an easy detour back to the Oregon side of the Columbia.

Weather can be capricious in the gorge, making for dangerous driving conditions any time of the year. The Cascade summits can wring more than 200 inches of rain yearly from eastward-moving cloud masses, yet in The Dalles the annual rainfall is just six inches annually.

West of the Cascades, winter lows seldom dip below freezing. A notable exception to this happens when frigid winds originating in the Rockies blow through the gorge in winter, resulting in ice storms that can make for freezing rain and black ice, with the weather sometimes closing the interstate.

The **Columbia River Gorge National Scenic Area** (902 Wasco St., Hood River, OR 97031, 541/308-1700, www.fs.usda.gov/crgnsa) is the federal entity that oversees the Columbia River Gorge in both Oregon and Washington. From its website you can print out a handy guide to the gorge and learn more about recreational options.

# Historic Columbia River Highway (U.S. 30)

**TOP** EXPERIENCE

In 1911, Samuel Hill, a wealthy and eccentric railroad lawyer, began promoting a dream for an automobile route through the Columbia River Gorge. Hill found supporters in the Portland business community who were caught up in the fervor of the national Good Roads campaign of the time. This movement supported the construction of paved highways with scenic qualities to foster tourism.

As the first Model T rolled off Henry Ford's assembly line in 1913, Hill's dream began to take form. Timber magnate and hotelier Simon Benson coordinated the project's fiscal management and promotion, and mill owner John Yeon volunteered as road master of the work crews. Samuel Lancaster, a visionary Tennessee engineer recruited by Hill, added the artistic inspiration for what came to be known as "a poem in stone." Together Hill and Lancaster journeyed to Italy, Switzerland, and Germany to view European mountain roads.

Hill and Lancaster were able to convince the Oregon government to finance the Columbia River Highway, the first road linking The Dalles to Portland through the gorge. To these idealists, the highway was not meant to be an intrusion on the wilderness; instead, the road was designed to be a part of the landscape.

This would not only be the Pacific Northwest's first paved public road but one of the defining events in the growth of modern U.S. tourism. Following the 1915 completion of this highway's first section, from Troutdale to Hood River, scores of middle-class Portland families in their Model T's took to the cliffs above the Columbia on this architecturally aesthetic thoroughfare. After the stretch between Hood River and The Dalles was completed in 1922, it was dubbed "king of roads" by the *Illustrated London News*.

Service stations, roadside rest stops, motor courts (later called "motels"), and resort hotels that catered to the motorized carriage trade developed, contributing to the gorge's economic growth. Of the several dozen roadhouses that lined this highway from 1915 to 1960, only a few structures remain today. A new interstate was constructed in the 1950s and 1960s that made gorge travel faster, but the charm of the earlier era was lost. Some sections of the old highway became part of the interstate; two sections remained open to car travel as U.S. 30.

Fortunately, the "king of roads" experienced a renaissance in the 1980s. Political activists, volunteers, government agencies, and federal legislation provided the spadework for the creation of the Historic Columbia River Highway, the first federally designated scenic highway in the United States. Thanks to its inclusion on the National Register of Historic Places (the only road on the list) as well as listings as an All-American Road, National Scenic Byway, National Heritage Road, and National Historic Landmark, the restoration has become a reality.

Currently, the old highway's sections from Troutdale to Ainsworth State Park and Mosier to The Dalles attract millions of motorists annually. Other segments of the old road are being rebuilt with attention to architectural nuance and potential recreational and interpretive uses. The reconstructed Mosier Twin Tunnels east of Hood River as well as restored sections between Cascade Locks and Eagle Creek and in the Bonneville-Tanner Creek corridor exemplify how parts of the highway have been rededicated as hiking and biking trails.

### Access Points

There are several options for getting onto U.S. 30 from Portland. If you're in no hurry, head east on I-84 and take exit 17, turning right at the outlet mall, left at the blinking light up the hill from the outlets, and onto the Historic Columbia River Highway (follow the signs to Corbett). This route snakes up the Sandy River and through the pleasant small towns of Troutdale and Corbett before reaching the Columbia Gorge's big attractions. The next

20 miles traverse historic bridges and stonework, lush orchard country, rainforested slot canyons, six large waterfalls, and cliffside views of the Columbia River Gorge. The attractions between Corbett and Horsetail Falls explain why both the American Automobile Association and Rand McNally rate the Historic Highway as one of the top 10 scenic roads in the country.

For quicker access to waterfalls and hikes from the west, take I-84's exit 22 at Corbett, which joins U.S. 30 just before the first major viewpoints. To reach this section of U.S. 30 from the east, take exit 35 at Ainsworth State Park.

## SIGHTS
### Portland Women's Forum State Scenic Viewpoint
The view east from Chanticleer Point, as this vista point is also called, is the first cliffside panorama of the Columbia and its gorge that most travelers experience on U.S. 30. This classic tableau features Crown Point's domed Vista House jutting out on an escarpment about a mile to the east, giving human scale to the cleft in the Cascades 725 feet below.

### Larch Mountain Turnoff
If you veer right on the road marked "Larch Mountain" at the Y intersection with the highway, you'll go 14 miles to an overlook featuring views of the snowcapped Cascades as well as the Columbia all the way west to Portland. There are also picnic tables and trailheads for hikes to the gorge below, and gorgeous bear grass blossoms in June. Later, August's huckleberries and mushrooms await foragers after the first rains.

To enjoy one of Oregon's classic sunsets, head to the northeast corner of the Larch Mountain parking lot around dusk and follow a gently rolling 0.25-mile paved path through forests of old-growth noble fir. The trail's last 100 yards are a steep climb up to an outcropping. This is **Sherrard Point,** and it has preeminent alpine views on a clear day.

# Mount Hood Loop

By far the most popular day trip from Portland is the so-called Mount Hood Loop, which connects many of the sights in this area into a single day's driving adventure. Depending on side trips, the loop is about 160 miles—not too stressful if you get an early start and make frequent stops. Most travelers begin by heading out I-84 up the Columbia River Gorge and detouring onto U.S. 30, the Historic Columbia River Highway, which passes towering waterfalls and hiking trailheads—you should definitely make time for a short walk to an otherwise hidden waterfall to appreciate the gorge's striking natural history. After spending the morning in the mists of waterfalls, continue to Hood River for lunch. From here, head south on Highway 35 through orchards and farmland toward Mount Hood, which by this time will be filling the horizon. In summer and fall, this road is lined with farm stands selling fruit and vegetables. At Mount Hood, drive up to Timberline Lodge to go eye-to-eye with the mountain, Oregon's highest at 11,249 feet. Have a hot chocolate in the historic lodge and take a short hike around the base of the ski lifts (chances are you will be panting due to the elevation). Then drop down the west face of Mount Hood on U.S. 26, following signs in Gresham, Portland's easternmost suburb, back to I-84 and Portland.

## ★ Crown Point and Vista House

Driving I-84, you might notice the distinctive outline of an octagonal structure 733 feet above the Columbia on a high bluff in the western gorge. This is the **Vista House Visitors Center at Crown Point** (40700 E. Historic Columbia River Hwy., 503/695-2240, www.vistahouse.com, 9am-6pm daily Apr.-Oct.). Construction began in 1916 when the Columbia River Highway was formally dedicated. As President Woodrow Wilson pressed a button in the White House, Old Glory was electrically unfurled at the flat circular dirt area that was to become the visitors center.

Vista House was completed two years after the highway's official dedication. The outside observation deck up the steps from the main rotunda showcases 30 miles of the Columbia River Gorge. A plaque outside pays homage to Samuel Lancaster for the "poetry and drama" the highway embodies. Photos of the various stages of the road's construction are displayed in the main rotunda, as are wildflower cuttings of the region's native plants. In the gallery of Vista House, volunteers run an information desk, while educational exhibits relate the history of the building and the highway.

## Figure-Eight Loops

The highway between Crown Point and Latourell Falls drops 600 feet in elevation in several miles. As you wind downhill from Vista House, it becomes apparent that Lancaster softened the grade of the road by means of switchbacks. With a grade never exceeding 5 percent and curve radii of not less than 100 feet, this section presents few problems for modern vehicles, but it challenged period cars and trucks during the highway's first decades. During construction, Scottish stonecutters and Italian masons sometimes hung suspended on ropes, singing while they worked on the precipitous roadbed.

## Latourell Falls

**Latourell Falls** is the first of six roadside waterfalls seen by motorists. When the highway was built, special care was taken to ensure the bridge crossing Latourell Creek provided a good view of the waterfall. Nonetheless, you can take the paved 150-yard trail from the parking lot to the base of this 249-foot cataract for a closer look. The shade and cooling spray create a microclimate for fleabane, a delicate bluish member of the aster family, and other flowers normally common to alpine biomes. The misty tendrils of water against the columnar basalt formations on

# Indigenous People of the Gorge

Archaeological findings indicate that indigenous people have lived in the Columbia River Gorge for some 10,000 years. When Meriwether Lewis and William Clark first came through in 1805, they found a gathering of Native Americans near present-day Wishram, Washington, whose numbers and variety surpassed any other Native American trading center on the continent, hosting indigenous people from as far away as Alaska and the Great Lakes, who would come for barter fairs during salmon fishing season. Gambling, races, and potlatches (festivities in which individuals gave away possessions to gain status) supplemented trade and fishing.

Lewis and Clark encountered evidence of foreign contact on the Columbia from such disparate sources as a Chinook chieftain with red hair and local people with swords, coins, and other European and Asian goods. Certain artifacts suggested that Native American trade links stretched as far as present-day Missouri and the U.S. Southwest. Lewis and Clark observed trade currency consisting of shells from Vancouver Island and blankets crafted by the British Hudson's Bay Company rather than indigenous articles.

When Lewis and Clark passed through, an estimated 13,500 Native Americans lived in the Columbia River region. However, with the waves of European settlers and traders in the early 19th century came diseases to which local people had no resistance. Measles and smallpox epidemics killed up to three-quarters of the region's population, greatly reducing their ability to resist the influence of European and American colonists. While the arrival of settlers on the Oregon Trail brought isolated conflicts, far more damaging to the long-term survival of Native Americans culture here was the destruction of their dietary staples, including the camas root and salmon. Native Americans were removed to reservations outside the gorge as a result of treaties enacted in 1855.

the cliffs make Latourell a favorite with photographers. Foragers appreciate maidenhair ferns and thimbleberries, but not enough to denude the slope.

Another trailhead begins in the middle of the parking lot and climbs around and above the waterfall, although bushes may obscure the overhang from which the water descends when you're looking down from the top. You'll probably be more inclined to stop after 50 yards and take in the distant perspective of Latourell from across the chasm. Latourell Creek flows from the waterfall underneath the highway bridge toward Guy Talbot State Park, where there are picnic tables shaded by an ancient forest.

## Shepperd's Dell

A lush, forested canyon cut by a waterfall, **Shepperd's Dell** is one of the visual highlights of the gorge—despite the fact that little of this splendor is apparent from the road. It was named for a settler who retreated here for spiritual renewal because of the lack of good

roads to a nearby church. An 80-yard paved walkway descends from a small parking lot east of a bridge, the intricate architecture of which can be appreciated with a glance over your shoulder. Chances are, however, your gaze will be riveted by Shepperd's Dell Falls coursing down out of the forest to plummet sharply over a precipice.

## Bishop's Cap

**Bishop's Cap** embodies the highway engineering genius of Samuel Lancaster. The base of a basalt outcropping was undercut as little as possible to accommodate traffic. Locals call this altered formation "mushroom rock" due to its similarity to a stem connecting to a mushroom cap. The same motif is repeated around the bend. More highway architecture is visible in the form of dry masonry walls and stone guardrails.

## Bridal Veil Falls State Park

The 1926-era Bridal Veil Lodge across from **Bridal Veil Falls State Park** is another legacy from the past. This establishment is one of the few lodgings from the heyday of the Columbia River Highway still operating.

Across from Bridal Veil Lodge is the waterfall for which the state park is named, reached by a trailhead at the east end of the parking lot. A short 0.7-mile round-trip hike takes you to the observation platform at the base of this voluminous gushing bi-level cascade.

Bridal Veil Falls State Park is also the western trailhead for the 33.5-mile **Gorge Trail 400.** Between here and Wyeth, this largely level trail takes in the gorge's highest waterfalls as well as newly opened sections of the old Columbia River Highway that are closed to vehicular traffic.

In addition to tree-shaded picnic tables and restrooms open all year, the park features the largest camas patch in the Columbia River Gorge. Blue-flowering camas and wapato were once the leading food staples for local Native Americans. The camas bulb looks like an onion and tastes very sweet after it is slowly baked. Leave the camas alone, out of respect for a traditional food source as well as for your own safety— camas with white flowers are poisonous, a fact that is not always established when the bulb is being harvested.

If you're here in April, look for patches of camas along the short **Overlook Trail** to the Pillars of Hercules, a pair of giant basalt monoliths with I-84 and the Columbia River in the background. These formations are also called Spilyai's children, after the Native American coyote demigod. According to legend, Spilyai transformed his wife into Latourell Falls and his children into these volcanic formations to keep them from leaving him. Overlook Trail is about 20 yards west of the Bridal Veil Falls trailhead.

## Wahkeena Falls

The name means "most beautiful," and **Wahkeena Falls,** a 242-foot series of cascades that descends in staircase fashion to the parking lot, is certainly a contender. To the right of the small footbridge abutting

Multnomah Falls is the tallest waterfall in Oregon.

the road is a trailhead for the 0.6-mile hike to upper Wahkeena Falls. Follow this largely paved trail to a bench just beyond the waterfall and take in views of both the upper and lower falls. Higher up are panoramic vistas of the Columbia River and Gorge and the ridgeline pathway connecting Wahkeena to Multnomah. This trail is especially striking in October, when the cottonwoods and the bigleaf and vine maples sport colorful fall foliage. A picnic area is north of the Historic Highway, across from the waterfall.

## ★ Multnomah Falls

At 620 feet, **Multnomah Falls** is the tallest waterfall in the state. This huge cascade pours down from above with the authority worthy of the prominent Native American chief for whom it is named. The waterfall drops twice: once over 550 feet from a notch in an amphitheater of vertical rock, and then another 70 feet over a ledge of basalt. A short trail leads to an arch bridge directly over the second waterfall.

# Cruising the Columbia River

Thanks to a revival of interest in Lewis and Clark's journey, Columbia River cruises are more popular than ever. Most of these small cruise ships carry 80 to 180 people and offer weeklong trips, primarily from Portland or Vancouver, Washington. These are rather pricey packages, but offer a highly scenic and relaxing alternative to a lengthy road trip. The well-appointed ships boast gourmet meals and ideal sightlines on the shipping locks and dam facilities. Add expert commentary by professional interpreters and you have a trip to remember.

**Un-Cruise Adventures** (888/862-8881, www.uncruise.com) offers a seven-night, eight-day cruises on the Columbia, Snake, and Willamette Rivers from April through November. Departing from Portland, Un-Cruise offers itineraries such as wine-tasting or history and adventure. Rates start at $3,395 per person double occupancy and include all meals and lodging.

**Linblad Expeditions** (800/762-0003, www.expeditions.com) packages trips in conjunction with National Geographic on state-of-the-art craft with groups small enough to guarantee individualized attention from an attentive crew. In addition to luxury, these cruises offer an in-depth experience into the human and natural history of the region thanks to visiting authors, historians, and professors. There are frequent trips ashore, plus Zodiac explorations to remote side canyons. The ship is equipped with kayaks, which allow guests the freedom to explore on their own. The seven-day itinerary travels between Portland and ends at Clarkston, Washington, on the Snake River; cruises run in September and October, with prices starting at $4,890 per person double occupancy.

The **American Queen Steamboat Company** (888/749-5280, www.americanqueen-steamboatcompany.com) offers sternwheeler tours aboard the *American Empress,* the largest overnight riverboat west of the Mississippi, with over 100 staterooms and suites. Nine-day cruises travel up and down the Columbia between Astoria and Clarkston, Washington, from the ship's home port in Vancouver, Washington (across the river from Portland). The price for a nine-day trip is $3,499 per person double occupancy.

The 0.5-mile-long uphill trail to the bridge should be attempted by anyone capable of a small amount of exertion. You can bathe in the cool mists of the upper waterfall and appreciate the power of Multnomah's billowy flumes. The more intrepid can reach the top of the waterfall and beyond, but even the view from the base of the waterfall is astonishing. While some of the waterfalls in the surrounding area emanate from creeks fed by melting snows on Larch Mountain, Multnomah is primarily spring fed, enabling it to run year-round. Roughly two million visitors per year make Multnomah Falls the most-visited natural attraction in the state.

The waterfall area has a snack bar as well as **Multnomah Falls Lodge** (503/695-2376, www.multnomahfallslodge.com, 8am-9pm daily). A magnificent structure, the lodge was built in 1925 as one of the original hostelries along the Columbia River Highway, and today is operated by a private concessionaire. The day lodge has an on-site restaurant, snack bar, and gift shop but no overnight accommodations. There's also a U.S. Forest Service visitors center.

## Oneonta Gorge

Just east of Multnomah Falls, **Oneonta Gorge** is a narrow chasm cut into a thick basalt flow by Oneonta Creek. Walls more than 100 feet high tower over the stream, the cliff walls in some spots being just 20 feet apart. This peculiar ecosystem, preserved as **Oneonta Gorge Botanical Area,** is home to a number of rare cliff-dwelling plants that thrive in the moist, shadowy chasm. There's no room along the sheer walls of Oneonta Gorge for a trail, but for those unperturbed by the thought of wet sneakers, the shallow stream can be waded for about 0.5 miles to

Oneonta Falls, where Oneonta Creek drops 75 feet into the gorge.

## Horsetail Falls

Only a few hundred feet east of Oneonta Gorge is **Horsetail Falls,** which drops 176 feet out of a notch in the rock. While the waterfall is easily seen from the turnout along U.S. 30, hikers should consider the three-mile **Horsetail-Oneonta Loop Trail.** Starting at Horsetail Falls, the trail quickly climbs up the side of the gorge wall and along the edge of a lava flow. The trail continues *behind* Ponytail Falls (also called Upper Horsetail Falls), which pours out of a tiny crack into a mossy cirque. The trail then drops down to Oneonta Creek, with great views over the narrow gorge and waterfalls. The trail returns to U.S. 30 about 0.5 miles west of the Horsetail Falls trailhead.

## HIKING

There are many wonderful hikes along the Historic Highway. In addition to those described here, check out the U.S. Forest Service's "Short Hiking Loops" map, available free at the Multnomah Falls Lodge.

### Angel's Rest Trail

In 1991, massive fires engulfed portions of the Mount Hood National Forest off the Historic Highway. Today, Angel's Rest Trail 415 offers a good example of reforestation, as well as a great view of the gorge. To get here from I-84, take eastbound exit 28 and follow the exit road 0.25 miles to its junction with the Historic Highway. At this point, hang a sharp right as if you were going to head up the hill toward Crown Point, but pull over into the parking area on the north side of the highway instead. The trailhead is on the south side of the road.

The steep 2.3-mile path to the top of this rocky outcropping gains 1,600 feet and takes you from an unburned forest through wildflower meadows and patches of lush young fir trees beneath live evergreens with singed bark. Charred conifers dominate as you near the summit.

From the top you can enjoy a balcony-seat view overlooking the action. The stage in this case juts out over the Columbia River, with sweeping views toward Portland; to the northeast the snowcapped carapace of the Washington Cascades plays peekaboo behind a series of smaller ridges.

### Wahkeena-Multnomah Loop

This is a hike of about five miles with panoramic river views, perspectives of four waterfalls, and ancient forests. To get to Wahkeena Falls, drive I-84 to exit 28 for Bridal Veil Falls. Several miles later, you'll come to the waterfall parking area and trailhead. If you take the trail to the right of the bridge, in about one mile you'll come to Fairy Falls, so named for its ethereal quality. Just past Fairy Falls, leave Trail 420 for Vista Point Trail 419 to see panoramas from 1,600 feet above the river. Old-growth Douglas firs usher you through higher elevations on this trail.

Rejoin Trail 420 one mile east of where Trail 419 began. Once you get past the first 1.5 miles of this trail's initial steep ascent, the rest of the route is of moderate difficulty. As you begin your descent, the junction of Trail 420 and the Larch Mountain Trail is unsigned; hang a sharp left on Trail 441 to head west and down along Multnomah Creek. At the rear of this gorge is pretty Ecola Falls. There are several other cascades along the route.

When you hit the blacktopped section of Trail 441, hang a left to enjoy views from the top of Multnomah Falls; then descend, crossing the bridge and heading down into the parking area.

### ★ Elowah Falls and Upper McCord Creek Trails

To avoid the crowds while taking in spectacularly varied gorge landscapes, try the Elowah Falls and Upper McCord Creek Trails. From Portland, take I-84 past Multnomah Falls east to exit 35, Ainsworth State Park. As you come off the access road, you'll have a choice of left turns. Take Frontage Road, with signs for Dodson. This road may also be accessed from the Historic Highway after driving five miles east of Multnomah Falls. Drive about two miles to the small parking lot of John Yeon State Park, named for one of the major advocates of the Columbia River Highway. In the western corner of the lot is the trailhead. Follow it 0.5 miles up the hill. When you reach a junction of two trails, turn right for Upper McCord Creek and left for Elowah Falls.

The Upper McCord Creek Trail leads to a mossy glade framing a creek at the top of a waterfall just under a mile from the junction. En route, the trail narrows to a ledge carved out of a cliff. From behind a railing, gaze hundreds of feet down at the Columbia River in the foreground of 12,306-foot Mount Adams. Across the chasm, layered basalt strata indicate successive lava flows. This is a good place to look for ospreys riding the thermals before they dive down to the Columbia for a fish. The trail continues to a view of dual cascades descending the rock face.

Retrace your steps to where the trail forks and descend 0.5 miles from the junction to Elowah Falls. This 289-foot feathery cascade is set in a steep rock amphitheater amid hues of green that conjure the verdant lushness of Hawaii.

## SWIMMING

Swim in the Columbia River at historic and scenic **Rooster Rock State Park** ($5 per vehicle), at exit 25 off I-84 near Troutdale. West of the parking area is the monolith for which the park is named. According to some sources, Lewis and Clark labeled the cucumber-shaped promontory on November 2, 1805. Playing fields and a gazebo front a sandy beach on the banks of the Columbia. The water in the roped-off swimming area is shallow but refreshing. A mile or so east is one of only two nude beaches officially sanctioned by the state (the other is Collins Beach on Sauvie Island).

## FOOD AND ACCOMMODATIONS

Columbia River Gorge sights are no more than 30 miles from Portland or Hood River,

so most travelers will visit the waterfalls of the Columbia Gorge from the comfort of these cities. For a special escape, however, there are several wonderful accommodations in this area that deserve special consideration.

Imagine a 38-acre estate featuring a restaurant, a hotel, a brewery, a spa, a winery, a distillery, a tasting room, a movie theater, and a "pub golf" course amid lavish gardens and artwork at every turn. That's the McMenamins' ★ **Edgefield** (2126 SW Halsey St., Troutdale, 503/669-8610 or 800/669-8610, www.mcmenamins.com, $145-205). Oregon's preeminent brewpubmeisters have transformed what had been the Multnomah County Poor Farm and later a convalescent home into a base from which to explore the Columbia Gorge or Portland. This is truly the best of the country near the best of the city. Guests may choose from rooms with private baths or with common baths down the hall. None of the rooms have TVs or phones—remember, you're here to relax. There is also no air-conditioning, but window fans are available. The **Black Rabbit Restaurant and Bar** (7am-10pm daily, $14-24) in the hotel offers McMenamins' version of fine dining, with main courses such as grilled lamb porterhouse with garbanzos and chimichurri, or local chinook salmon with romesco and piquillo pepper relish. The **Power Station Pub** (11am-1am daily, $8-11) is in a separate building that once housed an electric power plant. Now it's where you go to enjoy a pint and dine on burgers, sandwiches, and pizza. In summer, a large open-air dining area sits just east of the pub.

Also unique is **Bridal Veil Lodge Bed & Breakfast** (46650 E. Historic Columbia River Hwy., Bridal Veil, 503/695-2333, http://bridalveillodge.com, $195). The lodge, across the road from Bridal Veil Falls State Park, is one of the last surviving accommodations from the 1920s "roadhouse" era on this part of the Historic Columbia River Highway. Knotty pine walls, antique quilts, and historic photos set the mood. While the historic lodge retains its rusticity, the comfortable, modern guest rooms are in duplex cabins amid towering evergreens. **Tad's Chicken 'n' Dumplins** (1325 E. Historic Columbia River Hwy., Troutdale, 503/666-5337, 5pm-10pm Mon.-Fri., 4pm-10pm Sat., 4pm-9pm Sun., $11-22) is an original. Right on the Sandy River, its classic weather-beaten roadhouse facade has graced this highway since the 1930s. If you decide to forgo the restaurant's namesake dish, try the fried oysters, fried chicken, steak, or salmon. It's good ol' American food that'll taste even better with drinks on the deck overlooking the Sandy.

Service in the dining room at historic **Multnomah Falls Lodge** (503/695-2376, www.multnomahfallslodge.com, 8am-9pm daily, $16-26) can be uneven, but the food is surprisingly good when the kitchen isn't overwhelmed. A cheery solarium adjacent to the wood-and-stone dining room makes a great setting to begin or end a day of hiking. On warm days the outside patio is delightful, and if you crane your neck, you can see the waterfall.

## INFORMATION

The **Multnomah Falls Information Center** (Multnomah Falls Lodge, 503/695-2372, 9am-5pm daily) has a ranger and volunteers on duty year-round to recommend campgrounds and hikes. Ask about nearby hikes to Horsetail Falls, Triple Falls, and Oneonta Gorge. Request the "Short Hiking Loops Near Multnomah Falls" map for a visual depiction of the network of trails.

# Cascade Locks

The sleepy appearance of modern-day Cascade Locks belies its historical significance. The town is perched on a small bluff between the river and I-84, and its services and creature comforts are mostly confined to the main drag, Wa-Na-Pa Street. Below the town were rapids—called the Cascades—that blocked steamboat traffic between Portland and The Dalles and caused hardship for raft-bound Oregon Trail pioneers. Before the shipping locks that inspired the burg's utilitarian name were constructed in 1896 to help steamboats navigate around hazardous rapids, most boats had to be portaged overland.

**The Bridge of the Gods,** a steel cantilever bridge spanning the Columbia River at Cascade Locks, was built in 1926, the modern realization of a legendary bridge that, according to Native American myth, spanned this same channel.

The construction of the Bonneville Dam in the late 1930s inaugurated boom times in the area. The dam created 48-mile Lake Bonneville, which submerged the shipping locks. Reasonably priced food and lodging, a historical museum, the Bonneville Dam, and sternwheeler tours along with superlative hiking trails nearby make Cascade Locks a nice stopover.

In 2017, the rugged valleys behind Cascade Locks, including Eagle Creek, were the site of devastating wildfires, damaging trails and facilities. Recovery is ongoing, but in the Pacific Northwest, fire danger is ever-present. Contact the local ranger station or tourism office before making plans for hiking in this area to determine if it's open for recreation.

## SIGHTS
### Bonneville Dam

The **Bonneville Dam** (541/374-8820, www.nwp.usace.army.mil/bonneville) can be reached via I-84's exit 40. The signs lead you under the interstate and through a tunnel to the site of the complex on Bradford Island. En route to the visitors center, you drive over a retractable bridge above the modern shipping locks. On the other side are the powerhouse and turbine room. Downriver on the Washington side, abutting the shoreline, is an 848-foot lava promontory (one of the tallest in the country) known as **Beacon Rock,** a moniker bestowed by Lewis and Clark.

Beyond the generating facilities is a bridge, underneath which is the fish-diversion canal. These fishways cause back eddies and guide the salmon, shad, steelhead, and other species past turbine blades. You'll want to stop for a brief look at the spillways of the 500-foot-wide Bonneville Dam, especially if they're open.

While it isn't anywhere near the largest or the most powerful dam on the river, Bonneville Dam was one of the largest and most ambitious of the Depression-era New Deal projects. Completed in 1937, it was the first major dam on the Columbia River. The building of the dam brought Oregon thousands of jobs on construction crews, and the cheap electricity that it produced promised future industrial employment. President Franklin D. Roosevelt officiated at the dam's opening in 1938, attended by a cheering throng of thousands. The two hydroelectric powerhouses together produce over one million kilowatts of power, and they back up the Columbia River for 15 miles.

**Tours of Powerhouse 1** (541/374-8820, 11am, 1pm, and 3pm daily June 15-Labor Day, call for info Sept.-June, free), but be aware that the dam may close to visitors without warning due to security alerts. The five-level **visitors center** (503/374-8820, 9am-5pm daily year-round) has exhibits on dam operations, pioneer and navigation history on the Columbia, and fish migration. A long elevator ride takes you down to the fish-viewing windows, where the sight of lamprey eels—which accompany the mid-May and mid-September salmon runs—is particularly fascinating. Outside the facility there's access to an overlook above the fish ladders. A walkway back to the parking lot is decorated with gorgeous roses spring through fall. Ask the Army Corps of Engineers personnel at the reception desk about public campgrounds, boat ramps, swimming, and picnic areas.

Retrace your route back to the mainland from Bradford Island and turn right, following the signs to the **fish hatchery** (7:30am-5pm daily, free). Visit during spawning season (May and Sept.) to see the salmon make their way upriver. During spawning season, head to the west end of the hatchery, where steps lead down to a series of canals and holding pens. So great is the zeal of these fish to spawn that they occasionally leap more

the fish ladder at Bonneville Dam

# Dams and Salmon

Beginning with Bonneville in 1938, the construction of the great dams on the Columbia changed the course of one of the world's mightiest rivers. Bonneville and Grand Coulee Dams supplied power for the World War II shipyards in Portland and Vancouver, Washington, and Boeing in Seattle. Besides billions of dollars' worth of pollution-free renewable energy at the lowest cost in the western United States, other Bonneville by-products include 370 miles of lucrative inland shipping, irrigation water for agriculture, and perfect windsurfing conditions.

Today, Pacific Northwest businesses and residents still benefit from hydropower, but at the possible cost of the greatest salmon runs ever known. Salmon are anadromous fish, meaning they live most of their lives in the ocean, but they breed in freshwater. They are hatched in rivers and then swim to the ocean where they mature. They then swim back up the same rivers they were born in, spawning in exactly the same spot where they were hatched, after which effort the fish die. The great salmon migrations up the Columbia were once so vast and strong that in the 1850s it was considered dangerous to row across the Columbia near Portland—the size and number of salmon were so great that they could inadvertently capsize small boats as they struggled upriver.

During the 1880s, 55 canneries operated on the Columbia, employing such then-new technologies as the salmon wheel, a Ferris wheel-like scooping device that extracted salmon from the river in such large numbers that the wheels were banned in the first decades of the 20th century. Starting with Bonneville Dam, the hydroelectric dams on the Columbia served as enormous barricades to the natural migrations of these fish, resulting in drastically smaller salmon populations.

than three feet out of the water. This shady spot is a lovely place for a picnic.

Inside the building, you can see the beginnings of a process that produces the largest number of salmon fry in the state. Fish culturists sort the fish and extract the bright-red salmon roe from the females. These eggs are taken to the windowed incubation building, where you can view trays holding millions of eggs that will eventually hatch. Once these fry grow into fingerlings, they are moved to outdoor pools where they live until being released into the Columbia River by way of the Tanner Creek canal. The whole process is annotated by placards above the windows inside the incubation building.

The salmon and trout ponds and the floral displays are worth a visit at certain times of the year, but the sturgeon pools to the rear of the visitors center are always interesting. Bonneville is the nation's only hatchery for white sturgeon, and the government has made this facility user-friendly. The white sturgeon species of the Columbia River, with bony plates instead of scales, has remained unchanged for 200 million years.

## Cascade Locks Marine Park

Down near the river is the **Cascade Locks Marine Park** (exit 44, I-84 east). Look for it on your left going east on Wa-Na-Pa Street; just follow the signs. Here the sternwheeler *Columbia Gorge* (reservations 503/224-3900 or 800/224-3901, www.portlandspirit.com, May-Oct.) makes it possible to ride up the river in the style of a century ago. This 145-foot, 330-ton replica carries 599 passengers on three decks. There are several packages of varying themes and duration. The two-hour sightseeing cruise ($30 adults and seniors, $20 children, plus $4 pp landing fee) departs at varying times; check the website for schedules. Lunch, dinner, and weekend brunch cruises are also available.

**Port of Cascade Locks** (541/374-8619, http://portofcascadelocks.org) houses the ticket office as well as an information center and gift shop, which sells an excellent map of local hiking trails.

About 0.25 miles west of the visitors center, **Cascade Locks Historical Museum** (503/374-8535, 10am-5pm daily May-Sept., free) is housed in an old lockkeeper's residence and exhibits Native American artifacts and pioneer memorabilia. Information about the fish wheel, a paddlewheel-like contraption that conveyor-belted salmon out of the river and into a pen, is especially fascinating. This diabolical device was perfected in Oregon in the early 20th century and was so successful at denuding the Columbia of fish that it was outlawed. Outside the museum is the diminutive *Oregon Pony,* the first steam locomotive on the Pacific coast. Its maiden voyage dates back to 1862, when it replaced the 4.5-mile portage with a rail route around the Cascades.

Take a walk over to the old locks. Construction began in 1878 to circumnavigate the steep gradient of the river; they were completed in 1896. By the time the Cascade shipping locks were completed, however, river traffic had decreased because cargo was being sent by train, so the impact of altering the river flow was negligible.

## HIKING

The following hikes require a $5-per-vehicle day pass or a $30 annual Northwest Forest Pass.

### Wahclella Falls and Old Columbia River Highway Hiker-Biker Trail

The best short hike in the Columbia Gorge that doesn't involve significant elevation gain is the walk along Tanner Creek to Wahclella Falls. After a mile of walking, you reach the terminus of the canyon framing the creek. En route, the gently hilly pathway shows off this pretty steep-walled arroyo to great advantage, but the destination is better than the journey.

In a scene evocative of a Japanese brushstroke painting, a waterfall pours down dramatically at the canyon's end, best seen from a bridge over the creek. While the trail on the other side of the stream is worthwhile, it doesn't loop all the way back to the parking lot, so you'll have to retrace your steps. From I-84 eastbound, reach the trailhead by taking exit 40 for Bonneville Dam and making a right at the bottom of the exit ramp into a

small parking lot (instead of a left under the highway to Bonneville Dam).

From this same parking lot you can access a resuscitated portion of the Columbia River Highway by heading east. However, with lanes barely wide enough to accommodate a golf cart, you'll have to leave the car behind. The state decided to repave this section of the old road for hikers and bikers, re-creating the arched guardrails, bridges, viaducts, and tunnels between here and Moffet Creek to join the surviving ones. In addition to the ornate stonework, the undulating roadbed—which was blasted out of the mountainside before 1920—offers unsurpassed views.

The highlight of the route is a reproduction of the Toothrock Viaduct, annotated by plaques and heritage markers. After exiting this section of the highway via a stairway into the parking lot of the Eagle Creek Fish Hatchery, head east a short distance to the second leg of this hiker-biker trail. The Eagle Creek-Cascade Locks section is highlighted by a pretty waterfall at the beginning and a well-rendered tunnel near the end. The distance between Bonneville and Moffet Creek is about seven miles.

### ★ Eagle Creek Trail

Hikes up a spectacular side canyon of the Columbia Gorge are the highlight of this popular recreational area. The Eagle Creek Trail 440, constructed in 1915, was an engineering feat. Volunteers blasted ledges for trails along vertical cliffs, spanned a deep chasm with a suspension bridge, and burrowed a 120-foot tunnel behind a waterfall. If you have time for only one day hike in the gorge, this should be it.

The classic Eagle Creek day hike leads up along the face of a cliff to a viewpoint over Metlano Falls. Part of the trail then drops back streamside near Punchbowl Falls, a good spot to break for lunch and splash in pools of cool water. Casual day hikers can return at this point, making for an easy 4.5-mile round-trip stroll.

More ambitious hikers can continue along to High Bridge, a suspension bridge spanning a deep crevice, and Tunnel Falls, so named because of the tunnel blasted into the rock behind the waterfall. Through the tunnel are great views up and down Eagle Creek's canyon. The round-trip hike from the trailhead to High Bridge is 6.5 miles; to Tunnel Falls and back it is a strenuous 12 miles.

The Eagle Creek Trail is very popular. Try to avoid summer weekends, when the trail is thronged with hikers. Some sections of the trail inch along vertical cliffs with cable handrails drilled into the cliff side for safety. Other steep sections lack handrails altogether. This isn't a good trail for unsupervised children or unleashed pets.

## FOOD AND ACCOMMODATIONS

Forget health food and haute cuisine until you get to Hood River. In Cascade Locks, you get reasonably priced down-home cooking. The **Cascade Locks Ale House** (500 Wa-Na-Pa St., Cascade Locks, 541/374-9310, 11am-9pm Wed.-Mon., $6-16) is a small, dark brewpub whose smoked salmon chowder, pizza, and sandwiches fill you up on the cheap. Along the old locks in the historic Marine Park, **Thunder Island Brewing** (515 NW Portage Rd., 971/231-4599, http://thunderislandbrewing.com, 11am-9pm Mon.-Wed., 11am-10pm Thurs.-Sun., $7-10) has an off-the-beaten-path location and excellent beers. The menu is simple (salads and excellent sandwiches) but the park-like location and the friendly welcome make this idyllic spot worth seeking out. Note that Thunder Island Brewing plans to move to a new location in downtown Cascade Locks by late 2018; call ahead. **East Wind Ice Cream** (395 Wa-Na-Pa St., Cascade Locks, 541/374-8380, 7am-7pm Mon.-Fri., 7:30am-7:30pm Sat.-Sun.) is a traditional stop for families on a Columbia River Gorge Sunday drive.

If the best view of the Columbia from a hotel room is important to you, then make reservations at Cascade Locks's **Best Western Columbia River Inn** (735 Wa-Na-Pa St., 541/374-8777 or 800/595-7108, www.bestwestern.com, $152-214). Some

along the Eagle Creek Trail

rooms have hot tubs, and all rooms have microwaves and fridges. Many rooms also have balconies. In addition to views, there's a fitness room with a whirlpool, a pool, and exercise facilities. With the Cascade Locks Marine Park down the street, this property is in an excellent location.

### Camping

There's no shortage of options for campers in this area. Keep in mind that the western gorge gets crowded, so avoid peak times when possible. The following have been chosen for their location near attractions or a prime trailhead, or for special amenities. **Ainsworth State Park** (503/695-2301 or 800/452-5687, www.oregonstateparks.org, mid-May-Oct., $17-26) has a great location and is very popular, so reserve in advance. The Nesbit Point Trail leaves directly from the campground, climbing the gorge walls to reach epic vistas near St. Peter's Dome, a towering basalt pinnacle.

**Eagle Creek Campground** (541/386-2333, mid-May-Oct., $15) can be noisy and crowded, but it's an ideal base camp for hiking, as it's close to several trailheads. Established in 1915, this is the first campground ever created by the U.S. Forest Service. Reservations (www.recreation.gov, $15) are essential on weekends. There are sites for tents and RVs up to 22 feet as well as picnic tables, grills, and flush toilets. Drinking water and flush toilets are available. Eagle Creek is located between Bonneville Dam and Cascade Locks off I-84. At the seven-mile point on the Eagle Creek Trail, there's a free primitive campground, but it fills up on summer weekends.

At I-84's exit 51 is the **Wyeth Campground** (no phone, reservations www.recreation.gov, $20), a beautiful and secluded U.S. Forest Service site that was used as a Civilian Conservation Corps (CCC) camp in the 1930s. Today it's popular as a windsurfing spot, and has piped water and flush toilets. **Cascade Locks Marine Park** (355 Wa-Na-Pa St., Cascade Locks, 509/637-6911, www.

portofcascadelocks.org, year-round, $15-35) has campsites close to the center of town. The museum and the sternwheeler are housed in the complex. Amenities not available on-site are within walking distance.

Two miles east of town near the banks of the Columbia is the **Cascade Locks KOA Kampground** (841 NW Forest Lane, Cascade Locks, 541/374-8668, reservations 800/562-8698, Feb.-Nov., $30 tents, $41-47 RVs, $3 per extra person). This private campground features the basics plus a hot tub and sauna, hot showers, and a heated swimming pool. Kamping Kabins with one room (a queen and a set of bunk beds, $70) or two rooms (a queen and two sets of bunks, $80) with shared baths, are available, as are two-bed cottages ($110-130) with private baths; bring your own linens and towels. Kabins fill up quickly, especially on weekends, so reserve well in advance. To get here, take U.S. 30 east from Cascade Locks and turn left onto Forest Lane. Proceed 1.2 miles; the KOA is on the left.

# Hood River

Hood River was once known as a scenic place to grow fruit. In the 1980s, well-heeled adherents of windsurfing began the town's transformation into an outdoor recreation mecca. In addition to its traditional industry of cherry, apple, peach, and pear production, Hood River now rakes in tens of millions of dollars annually from the presence of windsurfers, kiteboarders, paddlers, and mountain bikers.

Bounded by picturesque orchard country and the Columbia River, with snowcapped volcanoes serving as a distant backdrop, this town of 6,500 enjoys a magnificent setting. The main thoroughfare, Oak Street, which becomes Cascade Street as you head west, is on a plateau between the riverfront Marina Park to the north and streets running up the Cascade foothills to the south. Boutiques and hip restaurants dress up old

storefronts; this can be a busy place on summer weekends.

Pick up a map to the **Fruit Loop** (www. hoodriverfruitloop.com), a 45-mile stretch of meandering highways and back roads, through some of the richest farmland and most breathtaking scenery in the state, along the Hood River with Mount Hood as the backdrop. Vineyards, orchards, farm stands, and country stores dot the route that crisscrosses the river, inviting picnics and sampling of fresh produce.

## SIGHTS

Downtown Hood River is a lively place, with many shops and restaurants along Oak Street. A sense of fun and youthfulness pervades the town, the result of the many tanned, buff visitors who come here for the world-class windsurfing and kiteboarding. A good spot to catch

# Hood River

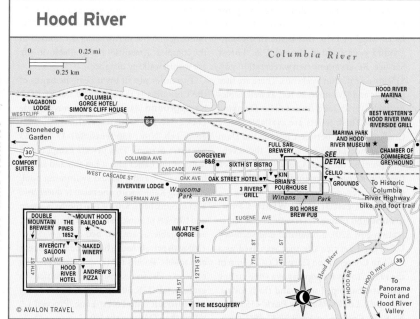

© AVALON TRAVEL

the spirit of the windsurfing scene is at Marina Park, just past the Hood River Museum, at the mouth of the Hood River. From here, lots of river athletes set sail and trade stories.

## Hood River Museum

At the **Hood River Museum** (300 E. Port Marina Dr., 541/386-6772, 11am-4pm Mon.-Sat. Apr-Aug., noon-4pm Mon.-Sat. Sept.-Oct., $5, free under age 11), exhibits trace life in the Hood River Valley, including prehistoric times and the first pioneer settlement in 1854. Native American stone artifacts, beadwork, and basketry as well as pioneer quilts and a Victorian parlor set are on display. The story of the area's development as a renowned fruit-growing center is told, and the contributions of the local Finnish and Japanese communities, along with World War I memorabilia, introduce the first half of the 20th century. Photos and implements related to fruit harvesting and packing methods round out the historical collections on the first floor.

## Western Antique Aeroplane and Automobile Museum

The **Western Antique Aeroplane and Automobile Museum** (1600 Air Museum Rd., 541/308-1600, www.waaamuseum.org, 9am-5pm daily, $16 adults, $14 seniors and veterans, $7 ages 5-18, free under age 5) presents a vast collection of historic conveyances, including cars, planes, gliders, motorcycles, and military vehicles. The dozens of restored antique aircraft on display in this 3.5-acre hangar still fly. On the second Saturday of the month, volunteers take the vintage airplanes and vehicles out for a spin. To reach the museum, follow 13th Avenue south (uphill) from central Hood River until it becomes Tucker Road (Hwy. 281). The museum, which is at the municipal airport, is five miles from Hood River.

## Panorama Point

If you don't have time to drive up the Hood River Valley to enjoy the fantastic vistas of Mount Hood above the orchards, here's a close-to-town alternative. Drive to the east end of town and turn south on Highway 35. Head south until you see the sign for **Panorama Point.** After a left turn, head south about a mile on East Side Road, then make a left on a road that takes you to the top of a knoll; the views south and west do justice to the name. Panoramic vistas here afford a distant perspective on the orchards below Mount Hood that have for decades served as a visual archetype of the Pacific Northwest.

## The Hood River Valley

South of the town of Hood River, the river of the same name drains a wide valley filled with orchards. During the spring, nearly the entire region brims with the scent and color of pink and white blossoms. Later on, fruit stands spring up along roadsides, selling apples, pears, cherries, berries, and vegetables. Watch for wineries, as grapes are the most recent crop in this famously fertile valley. Highway 35, which traverses the valley, leads up the south and east flanks of Mount Hood, only 25 miles south. On a clear day, this is one of the most scenic drives in Oregon, and it is one leg of the popular Mount Hood Loop.

Driving south on Highway 35 to Parkdale, visit the **Hutson Museum** (4967 Baseline Rd., Parkdale, 541-352-6808, 11am-4pm Wed.-Fri., 11am-6pm Sat.-Sun., $1 adults, $0.50 children, free under age 7). Native American artifacts, pioneer hand tools, and one of the better rock collections in the Pacific Northwest make it worthwhile.

## Mount Hood Railroad

Train buffs will be delighted to ride the **Mount Hood Railroad** (541/386-3556 or 800/872-4661, www.mthoodrr.com, June-Oct., $35-55 adults and seniors, $30-50 ages 2-12, depending on car), which runs from the old Hood River railroad depot (at I-84, exit 63) up the scenic Hood River Valley to its terminus in Parkdale—seemingly at the base of Mount Hood due to the volcano's immensity and proximity. Riders sit in restored enclosed Pullman coaches or in more exclusive domed coaches. Also featured are an antique concession car and, of course, the obligatory red caboose. The standard ride takes about four hours round-trip, including a stop in Parkdale. The railroad also features dinner and brunch trains and many special-event rides, such as the Western Train Robbery, with entertainment and a villainous holdup.

## Wine-Tasting

The moderate climate in the Hood River

the Mount Hood Railroad engine at its layover in Parkdale

# Hood River's Japanese Settlers

The first orchards were planted in the Hood River Valley in the 1850s, and the valley's rich volcanic soil, glacier-fed rivers and streams, and mild climate were perfect for apples, pears, stone fruit, berries, and vegetables. Strawberry farming was so successful at the turn of the 20th century that the Hood River Railroad was established in 1906 largely to hasten the delivery of the delicate berries to the main rail line at Hood River, where they were shipped to markets across the country.

Many of the workers who built the Hood River Railroad were immigrants from Japan, and many stayed on in the Hood River area to establish farms and businesses. By 1920, over 350 Japanese people lived in Hood River, and of these, 70 were land-owning farmers. The Japanese were successful and hardworking, and by 1940 there were 88 Japanese-owned farms in the valley.

In 1942, during World War II, Executive Order 9066, issued by President Roosevelt, declared that all people of Japanese ancestry were excluded from the entire Pacific coast. In a period of just two weeks, all the people in the Hood River of Japanese ancestry, including U.S. citizens, were forced onto trains and sent to internment camps in California.

After the war, about 40 percent of Hood River's Japanese attempted to return to the valley and their businesses, but most found their property stolen, vandalized, or untended. Many moved on, but some persevered; several large farms and orchards are still owned by Japanese American families.

Valley favors production of cool-weather grapes such as pinot noir and pinot gris, while just across the Columbia River near Bingen and Lyle in Washington, the microclimate makes possible heavier reds such as syrah and whites such as viognier. There are now some 30 wineries in the gorge, all open daily for tasting May-October (call to confirm opening times during winter), and all easily found with the **Columbia Gorge Wine map** (www.columbiagorgewine.com).

Here are some of our favorite stops. **Naked Winery** (102 2nd St., 800/666-9303, www.nakedwinery.com, 11am-7pm Sun.-Thurs., 11am-9pm Fri.-Sat.) has a tasting room in downtown Hood River. The wines are moderately priced and marketed with a slightly naughty edge: Penetration Cabernet, anyone? **Cathedral Ridge Winery** (4200 Post Canyon Rd., 541/386-2882, www.cathedralridgewinery.com, 11am-6pm daily) is just west of town near the golf course, and is noted for its award-winning pinot noir. Italian varietals are featured at **Marchesi Vineyards and Winery** (3955 Belmont Dr., 542/386-1800, www.marchesivineyards.com, 11am-6pm daily May-mid Nov., 11am-6pm Fri.-Sun. mid-Nov.-Apr.).

Probably the oldest vineyard in Oregon—a plot of century-old zinfandel planted by an Italian stonemason near The Dalles—forms the foundation for the best wines at **The Pines 1852** (202 Cascade Ave., 541/993-8301, www.thepinesvineyard.com, noon-6pm Mon., noon-5pm Tues.-Wed., noon-10pm Fri., noon-7pm Thurs. and Sat.-Sun.). Rhône-style wines and an ice wine are other sure bets. On Friday evenings, live bands accompany winetasting (6pm-9pm). Although the historic vineyards are near The Dalles, the tasting room is in Hood River.

## Lost Lake

The postcard photo of Mount Hood from **Lost Lake,** with the white mountain peak rising above a deep-blue reflecting pool amid a thick green forest, is probably the most famous image of Oregon's most famous volcano. The lake, about 25 miles southwest of Hood River, is a popular getaway when Hood River temperatures spike.

The 25-mile drive to Lost Lake from Hood River begins on 13th Street, which changes names (Hwy. 281, Tucker Rd., and Dee Hwy.) on its way up the flanks of Mount Hood. About 12 miles from downtown, take a right at the Dee Lumber Mill, where a green "Lost Lake" sign points the way. From here, bear left and follow the signs.

**Lost Lake Resort** (P.O. Box 90, Hood River, 541/386-6366, http://lostlakeresort.org, some sites reservable through www.reserveamerican.com, early May-late Oct., $8 day-use, lodge rooms $120-205, cabins with pit toilets $80-190, yurts $70, campsites $27-32) offers rowboat rentals (no power boats allowed on the lake) and a small store along with campsites and cabins. In addition, there are standard guest rooms in the second story of the lodge (bedding is provided, but bring your own towels). Come prepared; the closest gas station is 20 miles away, in Parkdale.

Late August huckleberry season is a highlight at Lost Lake, but September's weather and diminished crowds make it a preferable time to visit. The rangers have campfire programs on Saturday nights in July-August. The Lakeshore Trail features a 0.5-mile boardwalk through an old-growth cedar grove; the boardwalk is two miles into the trail, where you pass eight-foot-thick cedars. Pick up a map with natural history captions that correspond to numbered posts along the route.

## SPORTS AND RECREATION

The **Hood River Marina** offers an excellent family swim area and boat marina, and it also has personal watercraft rentals. **The Hook** recreation area with a protective cove offers gentle canoeing or kayaking when the winds and windsurfers are absent. **Koberg Beach State Park,** one mile east of town off I-84 but accessible from the westbound lanes only, offers a sandy swimming beach in a pretty setting. Be warned, however, that the drop-off is steep and not safe for young kids or weak swimmers.

### Windsurfing

Hood River is recognized around the world as a major center for windsurfing and related sports for its gusty sailing sites, related businesses, and the sport's unique subculture.

With a propitious mix of geography, climate, and river currents, the Columbia Gorge has strong, reliable summer westerlies (which blow west to east) countered by the strong westbound Columbia River current.

Three of the top-rated sites for advanced windsurfers are accessed from the Washington side of the river: Doug's Beach, the Hatchery, and Swell City are just across the Hood River Bridge. Three distinct windsurfing **beaches** (541/386-1645, $7 per vehicle day-use) are within Hood River city limits. The **Hood River Marina Sailpark** is the largest and most developed of the three, including baths with showers, food concessions, a picnic area, a grassy lawn for rigging, an exercise course, and a great family swimming beach area with sheltered shallow water for tykes. As the name implies, you'll find the largest marina and boat launches. Beware of shallow sandbars off the shore as well as the boats entering and exiting the marina. Due to its amenities, including ample close-by parking, this can be one of the most crowded sites around.

The **Event Site** (near I-84 exit 63, north end of 2nd St.), a newer and somewhat smaller site, is to the west of the Hood River's confluence with the Columbia. Major events, including well-known windsurfing competitions, happen here. It has a lawn for rigging and lots of lawn space for spectators. These amenities, plus a location convenient to downtown, make this an ideal spot for casual onlookers. It provides quicker access to deeper water than the marina, but it can also be quite crowded at times. Restrooms, water, and food carts are available on-site.

Several windsurfing schools in **The Hook** provide instruction in the gentle basin, an ideal location for beginners; once you're out in the main channel, winds can be strong. Conditions are variable, particularly as some places are in the wind shadow of nearby Wells Island, a sensitive wildlife area vulnerable to human impact. The views to the west (and hence the sunsets) are grand. Access to The Hook is at the west end of Portway

# The Other Side of the Gorge

Although this guide focuses on the sights of Oregon, it's clear that the Columbia River has two shores. Cross a bridge and you're on the Washington side, which offers a number of excellent destinations.

Across the Columbia from Hood River, the **White Salmon River** cuts a narrow canyon down through the gorge walls as it rushes to meet the Columbia. A number of white-water rafting guides offer half-day trips on the White Salmon, which bounces down through near-constant Class IV rapids. It's a short but exhilarating rafting trip and easily added to a gorge itinerary. Guided half-day trips ($60-65 pp) are available from **River Drifters** (800/972-0430, www.river-drifters.net) and **All Star Rafting and Kayaking** (800/909-7238, www.asrk.com).

The area around Lyle is transforming into a wine-producing mecca. The hot summer weather is perfect for growing syrah, grenache, viognier, and other wine grapes from France's Rhône Valley. Two notable wineries here are **Syncline Wine Cellars** (111 Balch Rd., Lyle, 509/493-4705, http://synclinewine.com, tasting 11am-6pm Thurs.-Sun. summer) and **Domaine Pouillon** (170 Lyle Snowden Rd., 509/365-2795, http://domainepouillon.com, noon-7pm Sat.-Sun. summer). For both, call to confirm winter hours.

Down the road, **Maryhill Winery** (9774 Hwy. 14, 877/627-9445, www.maryhillwinery.com, 10am-6pm daily) is an impressive clifftop tasting room 25 miles east of Lyle and directly across the Columbia from Biggs, Oregon, with a summer series of outdoor concerts in a natural amphitheater. The **Maryhill Museum** (509/773-3733, www.maryhillmuseum.org, 10am-5pm daily Mar. 15-Nov. 15, $9 adults, $8 seniors, $3 ages 6-16) is an idiosyncratic collection of art and artifacts in a grand country estate. The 20,000-square-foot manor house was built by early-20th-century mogul Sam Hill, whose family controlled the Great Northern Railway and who was instrumental in building the Columbia River Highway in the 1910s. Atop an 800-foot cliff above the Columbia, Maryhill was designed to resemble a French château as home to Hill and his wife, Mary, and as the center of a utopian Quaker community. Construction began in 1913 but it wasn't completed until 1926, as Hill lost interest in the project after it became clear that Mary was unwilling to live here and the immigrant Belgian Quakers found the arid cliffs unsuitable for agriculture. Maryhill opened as a museum in 1940 and has a good collection of Native American artifacts, an impressive set of 19th-century landscape and portrait paintings, sculpture and drawings by Auguste Rodin, and French fashion mannequins from the early 20th century. The museum also offers classes, lectures, and concerts, and has a museum café (10:30am-4:30pm).

Just east of Maryhill is another of Hill's eccentric constructions. Dedicated to the area's fallen World War I soldiers, a full-scale replica of **Stonehenge** looms above the gorge.

Avenue, the paved road that first takes you to the Event Site.

About eight miles west of town, **Viento State Park** (I-84, exit 56) offers good river access for sailing in a beautiful natural setting. The park has a campground, a picnic area, restrooms, and water. Spectators won't have a lot of room, but the wind and wave action can get spicy.

In the opposite direction, six miles east of Hood River, you'll find the **Rock Creek** launch site in Mosier. Amenities are sparse but include chemical toilets. The river here is wide, and the chop can get high. Take I-84's exit 69; at the top of the ramp, turn right, then take the first left, Rock Creek Road. The site is on the right, just past the dry creek bed.

**Big Winds** (207 Front St., 541/386-6086, www.bigwinds.com) offers board and full rig rentals (from $69 per day, $389 per week). Big Winds also has two levels of beginner lessons ($89), or choose the "First Timer" package ($149) that includes both lessons. Rates include use of a wetsuit, booties, and all the necessary windsurfing equipment. There are many other windsurfing lessons and rental operations in Hood River with similar price ranges and options. In addition to windsurfing, all the water sports outfitters also have rental gear for other sports, such as kiteboarding and stand-up paddling.

Adepts will tell you that windsurfing is best in the fall. It's less crowded, the water's warm, and the winds are lighter. It's easier to find parking and rigging space at launching areas, and there are enough clear days to add aesthetic appeal. Best of all, for beginners, is the availability of individualized instruction. While conditions are generally good at most locations along the river during the fall season, the best places are at the east end of the gorge, notably around Three Mile Canyon and other launch sites around Arlington, Oregon, and Roosevelt, Washington.

## Hiking

While the most famous gorge hikes tend to cluster around the west-end waterfall area, the environs of Hood River have their fair share of great trails. Three of these trails are right on the gorge, eight miles west of town on the south side of the highway, accessible via I-84's exit 56 for Viento Park.

The **Starvation Creek to Viento Trail** hike is the shortest and by far the easiest of the three. Actually a restored segment of the Historic Columbia River Highway, this mostly paved path runs a little over one mile each way. It offers some decent gorge views but will be of more interest to history buffs who want to retrace extant remnants of the old highway. This trail also provides access to the other two trails in the area.

Both the **Mount Defiance Trail** (Trail 413) and **Starvation Ridge Trail** (Trail 414) used to be accessible through the Starvation Creek rest stop exit off I-84, which is now closed. So walk the Starvation Creek to Viento Trail, then look for signs for either of the other trails once you get to the west side of the rest stop. Both trails eventually converge at the same place, high above the gorge just below the top of Mount Defiance. The highest point on the gorge proper at 4,960 feet, Mount Defiance presents a strenuous workout for anyone up for the challenge.

Either route rewards with spectacular views of the gorge as well as old-growth woods and pristine Warren Lake. The Starvation Ridge Trail is somewhat steeper than the Mount Defiance Trail. This long loop is about 12 miles round-trip. A short two-mile loop is also possible by following Trail 413 for one mile, then heading east (left) onto Trail 414. This eventually takes you back to the highway where you started. These trails are really best only for experienced hikers due to their steepness and narrowness.

The **Wygant Trail** is reached from the eastbound-only exit 58 on I-84 at Mitchell Point. Go right (west) at the top of the ramp, then follow the road heading west. This eventually becomes the trail, and it follows the old route of the Historic Highway for a stretch. The trail eventually winds its way for almost four miles to the top of 2,214-foot Wygant Peak. Along the way you'll pass through some native Oregon white oak groves, mixed conifer forests, and some openings with lovely views.

There are many beautiful trails south of Hood River off Highway 35 in Mount Hood National Forest. The **East Fork Trail** offers an easy but scenic amble along the swift glacial-fed East Fork of the Hood River. Accessed from either the Robin Hood or Sherwood Campgrounds (24 miles south of Hood River) along Highway 35, this trail is great on foot or mountain bike. It is about four miles between the two campgrounds, and the trail continues beyond the Sherwood Campground north into the Mount Hood Wilderness. **Tamanawas Falls Trail** leads off from the East Fork Trail about 0.5 miles north of the Sherwood Campground. A short but steeper hike, this trail is uphill all the way to the reward—beautiful 150-foot-high Tamanawas Falls.

Perhaps the best place to experience the transition from western alpine conifer forest to interior high desert is **Lookout Mountain** in the Badger Creek Wilderness. This aptly named 6,525-foot peak is the second-highest in the Mount Hood National Forest. To get here, drive 25 miles south of Hood River on Highway 35 to Forest Road 44 (the Dufur cut-off). Follow it east for five miles up a steep hill to Forest Road 4410, marked for "High Prairie." This route takes you six miles to a parking area opposite the trailhead to High Prairie Trail (Trail 493).

The 20-minute walk to the top of Lookout Mountain on Trail 493 takes you through wildflower meadows to the former site of a fire spotter's cabin. Directly west looms Mount Hood. Turn 180 degrees and you face the sagebrush and wheat fields of eastern Oregon. To the south are the Three Sisters and Broken Top. West and north of those peaks rises Mount Jefferson's tricorn hat. The body of water to the southwest is Badger Lake. To the north, views of Mounts Adams, St. Helens, and Rainier (on a clear day) will have you reeling with visual intoxication.

## Mountain Biking

Just west of the town of Hood River is a network of old gravel and dirt roads that local mountain bikers love. **Post Canyon Road** starts out as a typical paved rural road, with houses scattered along each side. Shortly past its start at Country Club Road, the pavement ends and the fat-tire fun begins. Several side roads branch off from Post Canyon Road into the Cascade foothills. You can ride for a long time without seeing any buildings, but you will undoubtedly encounter some clear-cuts and other logged areas, so don't expect pristine forests. Also, be warned: The road is used by groups of motorbikers at times, so stay alert. To get here, take I-84's exit 62, turn south at the top of the ramp, then make an immediate right onto Country Club Road. Follow this road about a mile as it bends to the south, then turn right into the well-signed Post Canyon.

**Surveyor's Ridge Trail** (Trail 688) traverses the ridgeline on the east side of the upper Hood River Valley for 17 miles. It offers some great Mount Hood and valley views and is especially fun for mountain bikers. The trailhead is off Forest Road 17, which intersects Highway 35 about 11 miles south of

Hood River just past the big lumber mill to the left of the highway.

Stop by **Discover Bicycles** (116 Oak St., 541/386-4820, www.discoverbicycles.com, 10am-6pm Mon.-Sat., 10am-5pm Sun.) for advice on mountain bike trails and bike rentals (from $30 per day).

## Fishing

The area offers two different types of fishing. You can go for trout in several beautiful small mountain lakes, most of which are west and south of the Hood River Valley. Notable among the latter are Wahtum, Rainy, and North Lakes, all about 45 minutes west of downtown Hood River on good gravel roads. Then there is Lost Lake, whose popularity might detract from the quality of the fishing in some seasons. Pick up licenses in any Hood River sports shop.

The other option is the Hood River, with good trout fishing, or the Columbia; both have good seasonal steelhead and salmon fishing. The Hood can be accessed from several county parks. Contact the **Gorge Fly Shop** (201 Oak St., 541/386-6977, www.gorgeflyshop.com, 9:30am-6pm Mon.-Sat., 10am-4pm Sun.) for information; this operation can also arrange fly-fishing lessons.

## Golf

Offering great views of Mount Hood is the popular 6,150-yard 18-hole **Indian Creek Golf Course** (3605 Brookside Dr., 541/386-3009, www.indiancreekgolf.com, $30-59). A little farther from town is **Hood River Golf Course** (1850 Country Club Rd., 541/386-3009, www.hoodrivergolf.net, $35). It has 18 holes that are a bit hillier than Indian Creek, as well as beautiful views of Mount Hood, Mount Adams, elk, and geese. Come in fall if only to see the spectacular foliage.

# ENTERTAINMENT AND EVENTS
## Brewpubs

Hood River and environs have spawned a mini microbrew scene, the most famous of which is the **Full Sail Brewery** (506 Columbia St., 541/386-2247, www.fullsailbrewing.com, 11am-9:30pm daily, $7-15), offering beautiful river views to accompany its renowned ales and soups, salads, and sandwiches. The **Big Horse Brew Pub** (115 State St., 541/386-4411, www.bighorsebrewpub.com, 11:30am-8:30pm Mon.-Thurs., 11:30am-9:30pm Fri.-Sat., 11:30am-8pm Sun., $9-16), in addition to selling its delicious ales (the IPA is recommended) also serves up a full menu of lunch and dinner items at pub prices; grab a seat by the window for good views.

★ **Double Mountain Brewery** (8 4th St., 541/387-0042, 11am-10pm daily, www.doublemountainbrewery.com, 16-inch pizza $16-22) offers excellent beers and a bustling hipster scene in a taproom with thrift store-chic decor. Food choices are simple—mostly grilled sausages and tasty wood-fired pizza. Lines can get long on weekends—have a plan B if you're in a hurry.

**Pfriem Family Brewers** (707 Portway Ave., 541/321-0490, www.pfriembeer.com, 11:30am-9pm daily, $10-18) has gained a big reputation for its Belgian-style brews and a small menu of soups, salads, and sandwiches in Hood River's industrial park. Up in tiny Parkdale is **Solera Brewery** (4945 Baseline Dr., 541/352-5500, www.solerabrewery.com, 4pm-10pm Mon.-Tues. and Thurs., noon-10pm Fri. and Sat.-Sun., $6-10), offering sandwiches, good beers, and a postcard view of Mount Hood from the back patio.

## Festivals and Events

The second weekend in April brings the **Hood River Hard-Pressed Cider Fest** (3315 Stadelman Drive, 541/386-2000, http://hoodriver.org/cider-fest, $20, includes 5 drink tokens, free under age 21), which gives seasoned and novice cider drinkers alike the chance to sample cider from Hood River County's very own cider makers, as well those from a variety of additional Northwest cideries. More than 25 cider makers usually participate, with more than 50 ciders on tap. The daylong event also features local food vendors,

produce and arts vendors, a kids' area, and a lineup of local music. April is also prime apple and pear blossom season, depending on the year, so a drive up through Hood River orchards should also be part of the celebration—before imbibing the cider.

For fans of the exciting Columbia Gorge beer and ale scene, the **Hood River Hops Fest** (541/386-2000 or 800/366-3530, http://hoodriver.org/hops-fest, $10 over age 20, $20 with 5 drink tickets) celebrates the hop harvest season with one of the largest fresh-hops beer selections in the nation. The festival, usually held noon-8pm the last Saturday in September, offers more than 75 fresh-hops beers from over 50 breweries. The event takes over about four blocks of downtown around the Columbia Parking Lot (between 5th St. and 7th St. at Cascade Ave.). The one-day festival also features arts and crafts vendors from the region, a selection of gorge wines, a children's play area, fun contests, and a daylong lineup of live music. Those under age 21 are welcome with free admission until 5pm.

## FOOD

Hood River's status as the premier windsurfing town in North America has brought sophisticated tastes to the gorge, with a resulting spike in restaurant quality. A cluster of casual deli, lunch, and coffee places are located along Oak Street in the downtown area; it's pleasant just to saunter the street and browse the menus. Few other small towns in the Pacific Northwest can boast such a roster of fine restaurants, not to mention options for vegetarians and gourmet coffee.

### Pacific Northwest Cuisine

Although the name makes it sound like a brewpub, ★ **Brian's Pourhouse** (606 Oak St., 541/387-4344, www.brianspourhouse.com, 5pm-10pm Mon.-Thurs., 11:30am-11pm Fri.-Sat., 11:30am-10pm Sun., $12-27) combines the virtues of a cocktail bar and a casual eatery. Brian's is a hangout for the under-30 outdoor sports-oriented crowd, and the chef offers inventive dishes that blend Northwest ingredients with traditional Asian, European, and nouvelle elements, always with a flair for freshness. Chile-crusted calamari is served with lemon aioli, and the halibut burger comes with roasted red peppers on a house-made brioche bun.

A stalwart of the Hood River fine-dining scene is ★ **Celilo Restaurant and Bar** (16 Oak St., 541/386-5710, www.celilorestaurant. com, 5pm-9pm Mon.-Thurs., 11:30am-3pm and 5pm-9pm Fri.-Sun., $14-24), with a daily changing menu and an updated lodge look that features hefty wood beams and splashes of soothing color. The food is well executed, with up-to-the-minute preparations such as skillet-roasted clams with garlic, chili, and fennel pollen, and roasted porcini mushrooms with shaved beets and fresh mint over couscous.

**Simon's Cliff House** (Columbia Gorge Hotel, 4000 Westcliff Dr., 541/386-5566 or 800/345-1921, www.columbiagorgehotel.com, 7am-2pm and 5pm-10pm Mon.-Sat., 9am-2pm and 5pm-10pm Sun., $18-36) looks east at the Columbia River rolling toward the hotel from out of the mountains, and west toward sunset alpenglow. The menu includes pasta, steaks, Columbia River steelhead and trout, and specialties such as chicken chardonnay and smoked duck breast with sour cherry glaze.

## Classic American

The **Sixth Street Bistro** (509 Cascade Ave., 541/386-5737, http://sixthstreetbistro.com, 11:30am-9:30pm daily, $8-20) has a good selection of microbrews on tap and an eclectic menu featuring fresh locally grown organic ingredients. Sample dishes ranging from red coconut curry to grilled rib eye with gorgonzola and port sauce. The deck is a shady refuge on a hot summer day.

For great views of the gorge, climb the steps up to **3 Rivers Grill** (601 Oak St., 541/386-8883, www.threeriversgrill.com, 11am-10pm daily, $10-37), with expansive decks overlooking downtown and the Columbia. The selection of Pacific Northwest seafood and steaks is large and well prepared.

A classic old bar in the center of town has been refurbished into the **River City Saloon** (207 Cascade Ave., 541/387-2583, www.waucomaclub.com, 11am-3pm and 6pm-2:30am Mon.-Thurs., noon-2:30am Fri.-Sun., $9-13). This handsome spot is perfect for lunch or early evening dinner, with lots of sandwich and steak options. This is also Hood River's primary sports bar and late-night hangout, so the crowds can get intense late in the evening, which isn't a problem if that's what you're looking for.

On "The Heights" (the plateau a few hundred feet above downtown), you'll find **The Mesquitery** (1219 12th St., 541/386-2002, www.thebestinhoodriver.com, 4:30pm-9pm daily, $8-19), where wood-smoke and barbecue flavors issue a wake-up call to your taste buds. You'll find the best ribs in town, not to mention steaks, fish, and even a barbecue pizza.

In Parkdale, 16 miles up the valley toward Mount Hood, is another outpost of barbecue. The **Apple Valley BBQ** (4956 Baseline Dr., 541/352-3554, www.applevalleybbq.com, 11am-8pm Wed.-Sun. summer, call to confirm winter hours, $8-24) is a hopping spot with St. Louis-Style ribs smoked over local cherry wood, plus local beers and wines.

## Italian

**Andrew's Pizza** (104 Oak St., 541/386-1448, 11am-9pm Sun.-Thurs., 11am-9:30pm Fri.-Sat., large pizzas from $14) easily wins our vote for best pizza in the gorge. Lots of extravagant toppings are available, as well as microbrews and great coffee. Andrew also now offers his excellent pizza and brews at the **Skylight Theater** (541/386-4888, www.skylighttheater.com), an expansion into two movie theaters immediately next door to the pizzeria.

**Romul's West** (315 Oak St., 541/436-4444, www.romuls.com, 4pm-9pm Sun.-Thurs., 4pm-10pm Fri.-Sat., $13-23) offers high-quality pasta and traditional Italian main courses (osso buco and veal piccata) in a stylized Roman dining room.

## Czech

An intimate sanctuary of continental European fine dining fortified with stellar local ingredients, **Kin** (110 5th St., 541/387-0111, 5pm-9pm Wed.-Sun., $16-21) offers a selection of shareable small plates plus seasonal main courses and Czech classics such as duck confit with purple potatoes and sauerkraut. The food and atmosphere here is refined, perfect for a romantic dinner.

## Breakfast and Coffee

Hood River has a number of excellent coffee shops with good pastries and other options for breakfast. Here are a few of our favorites. Just east of the major downtown intersection, **Ground** (12 Oak St., 541/386-4442, http://groundhoodriver.com, 6am-6pm daily) is the quirky kind of caffeinated outpost that you'd expect in Oregon. The coffee and ambience are great, and at lunch you'll find good panini sandwiches and fresh salads. Just to the west, **Dog River Coffee** (411 Oak St., 541/386-4502, 6am-6pm Mon.-Fri., 7am-6pm Sat.-Sun.) offers excellent Stumptown coffee and sustenance like breakfast burritos and muffins. For a hearty old-fashioned breakfast, a top choice is **Egg River Café** (1313 Oak St., 541/386-1127, 6am-2pm daily, $10-19), which serves scratch-cooked omelets, Benedicts, skillets, and such house specialties as a garlic, basil, and Brie cheese scramble.

## ACCOMMODATIONS

Finding a room in Hood River in the summer isn't easy, and the rates reflect the area's popularity. In fact, don't set out to Hood River in summer or on weekends without room reservations; there are a limited number of rooms and a large influx of visitors. Some lower-end motels can be pretty battered—the young ski and windsurfing crowd can be hard on rooms. All prices listed reflect summer rates; remember to add the 9 percent room tax in Hood River. Weekend rates can be substantially higher than those for weekdays.

### $50-100

In the heart of downtown is the ★ **Hood River Hotel** (102 Oak St., 541/386-1900 or 800/386-1859, www.hoodriverhotel.com, $91-209), an impeccably restored turn-of-the-20th-century hotel with a good restaurant (Cornerstone Cuisine, 7am-9pm daily, $12-20). Vacation packages are also featured. The oak-paneled, high-ceilinged lobby, with a cozy fireplace and an adjoining lounge and restaurant, is particularly inviting. Rooms that face the river also face the rail lines, so if you're a light sleeper, you may want to opt for a lower-priced town-view room; the least expensive rooms face an internal light shaft. "The Hotel" (as locals call it) is a nexus of activity and the most charming in-town digs to be found.

**Riverview Lodge** (1505 Oak St., 541/386-8719, www.rvlhoodriver.com, $95-140) has basic rooms, a pool, and some units with kitchens. It's within easy walking distance of Hood River's shopping center, Cascade Commons, with several grocery stores and eating options.

### $100-150

The ★ **Westcliff Lodge** (4070 Westcliff Dr., 541/386-2992, www.vagabondlodge.com, $132-203) is the new name of the well-loved Vagabond Lodge, which served the traveling public from its cliffside location west of downtown for over 60 years. The Westcliff has the same owners, but with updated rooms and the same lovely landscaped five-acre grounds with a playground for kids. Three guest rooms have full kitchens, and a number have large stone fireplaces. The best are the view rooms (extra charge), which take in a spectacular vista of the gorge. Queen bed "glamping tents" (actually canvas wall tents with river views) share modern restroom facilities and open-air showers.

A large 1909 house right on the edge of downtown is home to the **Oak Street Hotel** (610 Oak St., 541/386-3845 or 866/386-3845, www.oakstreethotel.com, $149-199), a small boutique hotel with just nine rooms, all stylishly furnished. The hotel also represents a number of rental vacation homes in the area, if you are traveling with a group or require the extra comforts of a private home.

Two B&Bs are located in the leafy old neighborhood near the historic center of Hood River. **The Inn at the Gorge** (1113 Eugene St., 541/386-4429, www.innatthegorge.com, $119-159) is a nicely refurbished 1908 Victorian that offers the informality of a windsurfer hangout in the form of a classy B&B. Three of the five guest rooms are suites, and have large rooms with full kitchens. All rooms have private baths.

Windsurfer-friendly, the **Gorgeview Bed and Breakfast** (1009 Columbia St., 541/386-5770, www.gorgeview.com, May-Oct.) is in a historic house with a great porch view and a hot tub. You'll have a choice of regular private rooms ($130-145) or hostel-style bunk rooms ($60 pp).

Up at Parkdale near Mount Hood, the **Old Parkdale Inn** (4932 Baseline Rd., Parkdale, 541/352-5551, www.hoodriverlodging.com, $145-160) has three rooms, two of which are spacious suites. All have private baths, TVs, DVD players, microwaves, coffeemakers, and fridges. The breakfast is gourmet quality, and the peaceful village will satisfy those looking for an escape from the rat race. The gardens, full kitchens, mountain views, and rural setting will get you in relaxation mode.

## $150-200

Immediately adjacent to the Columbia Gorge Hotel, **Columbia Cliff Villas** (3880 Westcliff Dr., 541/436-2660 or 866/912-8366, www.columbiacliffvillas.com, $195-339) shares its stellar views and offers hotel and condo lodgings with one- to three-bedroom units. The guest rooms can be put together into almost any layout, from basic hotel-style rooms to multi-bedroom suites with full kitchens.

**Best Western's Hood River Inn** (1108 E. Marina Way, 541/386-2200 or 800/828-7873, www.hoodriverinn.com, $170-250) is the only place in town to boast direct river frontage and even a small private beach. The rooms provide great opportunities to watch

windsurfers. There's a lounge and a decent restaurant (the Riverside Grill). Best of all are the heated outdoor pool and spa. The only downside is that the hotel is a bit of a trek to downtown. Room rates fluctuate wildly, so it's worth visiting the website before making reservations.

**Comfort Suites** (2625 W. Cascade Ave., 541/308-1000, $179-209) is at the west end of Hood River, about a mile from downtown. It offers immaculate guest rooms and amenities, such as a pool and spa, as well as some suites with kitchens.

## $200-250

Built in 1921 by lumber magnate Simon Benson, the ★ **Columbia Gorge Hotel** (4000 Westcliff Dr., 541/386-5566 or 800/345-1921, www.columbiagorgehotel.com, $219-329) has been called the "Waldorf of the West" for its neo-Moorish facade, glittering chandeliers, and 207-foot waterfall on the grounds. Large wing chairs around the fireplace and fresh-cut bouquets in the dining room bespeak the hotel's enduring refinement. In addition to a fine restaurant offering breakfast, lunch, and dinner, the hotel has lovely gardens. To get here, take I-84's exit 62, drive over the bridge to the north side of the highway, and follow Westcliff Drive west.

## Camping

Hood River County offers parks with campgrounds in the Hood River Valley. **Tucker Park** (2440 Dee Hwy., 541/386-4477, no reservations) is only four miles from town, in a lovely spot along the banks of the gurgling boulder-strewn Hood River. It's the more developed campground, with a store, a restaurant, laundry, and an ice machine. It has 14 RV sites with water and electricity ($30) and 80 tent sites ($20).

**Tollbridge Park** (Hwy. 35, 541/387-6888) is also along the Hood River in the upper valley. It's 17 miles south of Hood River and offers showers and two grocery stores a short distance away. Rates are $30 for full-hookup sites, and $20 for tent sites.

Reservations are available for some sites (www.co.hood-river.or.us).

**Oregon State Parks** (www.oregonstateparks.org, reservations 800/452-5687, http://oregonstateparks.reserveamerica.com) offers two full-service campgrounds right on the Columbia River. **Viento State Park** (800/551-6949 or 800/452-5687, mid-Apr.-late Oct.) is eight miles west of Hood River on the river side of I-84. There are 57 sites with water and electric ($22) and 18 for tents ($17). Viento offers direct recreational access to the mighty Columbia.

**Memaloose State Park** (800/452-5687, $19-24) is 11 miles east of Hood River on I-84, accessible from the highway's westbound lanes only. On the Columbia, but with limited river access, the park offers 43 full-hookup sites ($30) and 67 tent spaces ($19), showers, and an RV dump station. It's only fair to mention that both of these campgrounds are not far from a main rail line; in other words, expect to hear the freight trains go by, even at night.

There are several semiprimitive U.S. Forest Service campgrounds in the Mount Hood National Forest, which surrounds the valley on three sides. All are in pleasant settings. Call the **Hood River Ranger Station** (6780 Hwy. 35, 541/352-6002) for information. Some of the U.S. Forest Service campgrounds south of town are Sherwood and Robin Hood (both on Hwy. 35, $14), Laurence Lake (off Forest Rd. 2840, free), and Lost Lake ($25-30).

## INFORMATION

The **Hood River County Chamber of Commerce** (Hood River Expo Center, 405 Portway Ave., 541/386-2000 or 800/366-3530, www.hoodriver.org) has an extensive array of maps, pamphlets, and other information about the area. It also has a huge 3-D model of the gorge's terrain to get oriented to local geography. Take I-84's exit 63 and head north (toward the river), following the signs to the Expo Center. Another source of local visitor information, although limited to outdoor recreation, is the **U.S. Forest Service Scenic Area Office** (902 Wasco Ave., 541/386-2333). To get here, head down 7th Street until it winds around to the left, becoming Wasco Avenue, then follow the signs.

## GETTING THERE AND AROUND

**Greyhound** (www.greyhound.com) serves Hood River with three buses daily in each direction, stopping at the former rail station (110 Railroad Ave.). There are no services here, so plan on buying your ticket online or from the bus driver. **Hood River Taxi and Transportation** (1107 Wilson St., 541/386-2255) provides taxi service in and around the city.

## HISTORIC COLUMBIA RIVER HIGHWAY AND ROWENA CREST

East of Hood River, the highly scenic route up and over Rowena Crest is another segment of the Historic Columbia River Highway that remains open to motorists. Another section between Hood River and Mosier, the western gateway to Rowena Crest, was closed in the 1950s. However, in the 1990s public officials reopened a five-mile stretch of the route, which contains a number of tunnels, to hikers and bikers, making it possible to view the amazing engineering and craftsmanship of the original 1920s highway.

### Historic Columbia River Highway Trail

This five-mile-long segment of the Historic Columbia River Highway is worth exploring. It provides a great walking and biking experience (car traffic is prohibited) with the spectacular engineering feat of the reopened **Mosier Twin Tunnels** in the middle. Carved out of solid basalt and adorned with artful masonry work, the highway has become famous for its tunnels. They are about a mile from the trail's east end and 600 feet above the river. To start on the east end, take I-84's exit 69, then take the first left on Rock Creek Road. Go under the highway and continue for less than a mile. The parking area is on your left; the highway segment begins across the road.

Access the west-side parking area from downtown Hood River by going to the junction of State Street and Highway 35, then head up the hill on Old Columbia River Drive. This road is actually the Historic Columbia River Highway, officially U.S. 30. The west-side parking area has a small visitors center with restrooms.

Going west to east allows a hiker, in a mere five miles, to witness a rapid climate and vegetation transition rarely encountered in such a short distance. Starting on the Hood River side, the highway winds its way through lush towering Douglas fir groves. By the time you reach the east side of the tunnels by Mosier, you're in a dry oak savanna-grassland ecosystem.

About halfway down the trail, a short interpretive loop trail has been developed, rewarding hikers with stunning views of this varied and beautiful part of the gorge. Amateurs of geology will marvel at the dramatic precipice located across the river in Washington, visible from the east end. Locally called "Coyote Wall," it's technically part of a big syncline-anticline system in the area.

## ★ Rowena Crest and Tom McCall Nature Preserve

East of Mosier, a section of the Historic Columbia River Highway begins again for automobile traffic, climbing up over a spectacular volcanic promontory called **Rowena Crest.** For eastbound traffic, this route begins at Mosier, at I-84's exit 69, while westbound traffic can pick up the route at I-84's exit 76.

The **Tom McCall Nature Preserve,** a 2,300-acre sanctuary on part of Rowena Crest created by the Nature Conservancy, is the site of a mid-May pilgrimage by wildflower lovers. Because the preserve lies in the transition zone between the wet west and the dry east, several hundred species flourish here, including four that occur nowhere else. In the spring display you'll find yellow wild sunflowers, purple blooms of shooting stars, scarlet Indian paintbrush, and blue-flowered camas. Beware of ticks and poison oak, and enjoy the flowers, but leave them behind for the next person to view as well.

Tom McCall Nature Preserve

# The Dalles

It hits you shortly after leaving Hood River. Verdant forests give way to scrub oak, which transition to sage and the grasslands of central Oregon. You've come to The Dalles, a place Lewis and Clark called the "Trading Mart of the Northwest" in 1805. Instead of seeing a Native American potlatch on the Columbia River, however, the modern visitor will see 10,000 souls living in the industrial hub of the gorge. If you look carefully, you'll also glimpse Google's multimillion-dollar processor farms near the river.

These days, The Dalles (the name derives from the French word for flagstone) focuses on historical tourism as well as an emerging red-wine grape industry and already thriving cherry agriculture. The Google facilities provide about 250 jobs in the community.

For a traveler interested in Northwest history, gaining a complete perspective of Oregon's past is impossible without a day trip to The Dalles. Downtown is awash in bits of Oregon's heritage—the Oregon Trail Marker, the stunning 1897 Old St. Peters Landmark church, and the historic Baldwin Saloon. Explore the old Fort Dalles grounds and the Fort Dalles Museum, housed in the original surgeon's quarters from the days when the fort was active. Another early landmark, Pulpit Rock, still stands in the middle of 12th Street, just as it did in the 1800s when the Methodist ministers preached to the Native American population and settlers. Enjoy the work of local artists at The Dalles Art Center, located in the historic Carnegie Library.

The Dalles played a preeminent role in Oregon's early history. Five hundred years ago, nowhere in the Northwest boasted such a cosmopolitan mix of peoples. During the great fall and spring migrations of salmon, the banks of the Columbia River—and particularly those near Celilo Falls, just upstream and now smothered by The Dalles Dam—were lined with many Native American groups

trading, fishing, gambling, and socializing. Lewis and Clark first passed The Dalles in 1805, and in the 1840s the land route of the Oregon Trail terminated at The Dalles, as the gorge's high cliffs and rapids precluded further wagon travel along the Columbia.

The first colonial settlement at this transport hub was a Methodist mission, established in 1838. In 1854, the town of The Dalles was platted, and a town charter was granted in 1857. Then as now, the gorge was the principal corridor between eastern and western Oregon, and almost all freight bound in either direction passed through The Dalles. Steamboats docked at the riverfront; stagecoaches rattled off to far-flung desert communities. The streets were crowded with miners, ranchers, and traders.

The completion of the railroad and later barge lines through Columbia River reservoirs served to increase freight transport through The Dalles. The area is also the nation's largest producer of sweet cherries, and orchard workers from Latin America impart the community with cultural influences. Despite the recreational boom of the last 20 years, The Dalles remains largely hardworking and practical.

## SIGHTS

**Klindt's Booksellers** (315 E. 2nd St., 541/296-3355, www.klindtsbooks.com, 8am-6pm Mon.-Sat., 11am-4pm Sun.) represents a bit of history in The Dalles. Established in 1870, it is the oldest bookstore in Oregon, complete with original wood floors, a high ceiling, and oak and plate-glass display cases.

### Fort Dalles Museum

Established in 1850, **Fort Dalles** (15th St. and Garrison St., 541/296-4547, www.fortdallesmuseum.org, 10am-4pm daily Mar. 15-Oct., $8 adult, $5 senior, $1 ages 7-17) was meant to protect the incoming settlers

# The Dalles

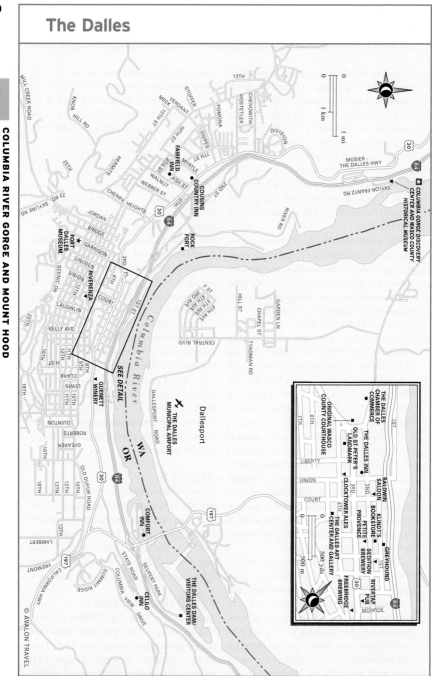

© AVALON TRAVEL

The Surgeon's Quarters at Fort Dalles Museum date from 1856.

along the Oregon Trail from the large Native American presence in the area. At the time it was built, Fort Dalles was the only U.S. Army garrison between the Pacific coast and Wyoming.

Of the original 10-square-mile encampment, only a grassy park with the Surgeon's Quarters, dating back to 1856, remains. The wooden structure serves as a museum for armaments, period furniture, and other pioneer items, as well as a collection of vintage vehicles from The Dalles's past. This is Oregon's oldest historic museum, dating back to 1905. On an adjacent block, three buildings (circa 1895) from a local homestead have been relocated and are available for touring.

Just down the hill, **Pulpit Rock** (near 12th St. and Court St.), a curious thumb of rock, combines geology and theology. From this natural pulpit, early Methodist missionaries preached to indigenous people. The rock still serves as a pulpit for local Easter services.

## ★ Columbia Gorge Discovery Center and Wasco County Historical Museum

The **Columbia Gorge Discovery Center and Wasco County Historical Museum** (5000 Discovery Dr. N., Crates Point, 541/296-8600, www.gorgediscovery.org, 9am-5pm daily, $9 adults, $7 seniors, $5 ages 6-16), three miles west of The Dalles on U.S. 30, brings together the rich historical, geological, biological, and cultural legacies of this region, articulating a 40-million-year timeline with scale models, videos, and simulated hands-on experiences that begins with the cataclysms that created the gorge on through its Native American occupation to the coming of the pioneers and subsequent domination by European Americans. Along the way, native plants and animals are given attention, along with such diverse activities as road building, orchards, and windsurfing. A cafeteria is located on-site.

### Wine-Tasting

The arid hills around The Dalles are home to a number of vineyards, and there's one standout winery right in town. **Quenett Winery** (901 E. 2nd St., 541/298-8900, noon-6pm daily) pours excellent wines in a tasting room that occupies a fantastic space: a renovated, century-old flour mill that has been brought back to life with all of its belts, pulleys, and chutes in place. It's worth a stop just to take in the magnificent infrastructure, but the wine is also a big draw, particularly the round and quenching viognier and velvety Grenache. On most Friday evenings, the winery remains open until 8pm with live music and light food service.

## FOOD

In the heart of downtown, **Petite Provence** (408 E. 2nd St., 541/506-0037, 7am-3pm daily, $5-12) is a French-style bakery and coffee shop that also offers sandwiches, soup, and light entrées at lunch.

★ **Baldwin Saloon** (1st St. and Court St., 541/296-5666, http://baldwinsaloon.

com 11am-10pm Mon.-Sat., $12-33) is in an 1876 building that has seen a bit of history—it was built as the dining hall for the local railroad crews. The redbrick interior houses a repository of early-20th-century oil paintings and an 18-foot mahogany bar. Fresh oysters are the house specialty, but the sandwiches, salads, steaks, and burgers are also good.

Just up the hill from downtown is one of The Dalles's most captivating breakfast and lunch options, **Riverenza** (401 E. 10th St., 541/980-5001, 7am-4pm Mon.-Sat., $5-8). In a century-old stone church, this small café offers excellent coffee, pastries, and lunch paninis and soups in a transformed religious space, with lovely shady patios off to the side. It's a great spot to recalibrate and realize you're in one of the West's oldest settlements.

Downtown, The Dalles has its share of handsome historic structures, and one of the most notable is the 1881 Wasco County Courthouse, topped with a bell tower. After serving as a Masonic hall and funeral parlor, this landmark is now home to **Clock Tower Ales** (311 Union St., 541/705-3590, http:// clocktowerales.com, 11am-9pm Tues. and Sun., 11am-10pm Wed.-Sat., $7-14), a taproom serving over 30 regional brews and light meals such as sandwiches and salads.

The **RiverTap Pub** (703 E 2nd St., 541/296-7870, www.rivertap.com, 11am-10pm Sun.-Thurs., 11am-midnight Fri.-Sat., $8-17) is a convivial tap house with about 20 local brews on draft and a bar, dining room, and large outdoor seating area right on Main Street. The menu includes a well-prepared selection of pub grub, with burgers, wraps, and salads.

**Sedition Brewery** (208 Laughlin St., 541/296-2337, noon-8pm Tues.-Thurs., noon-9pm Fri.-Sat., noon-6pm Sun.) is a new craft brewery right downtown in the historic Stadelman Ice House. Favorite brews include a dry-hopped pale ale and an IPA with both flaked and malted rye. Food choices include meat and cheese platters and sandwiches.

Another new arrival, **Freebridge Brewing** (710 E. 2nd St., 541/769-1234, 11:30am-9pm Sun.-Thurs., 11:30pm-10pm Fri.-Sat., $11-14) focuses on Northwest ales and German-style pilsners—check out the Weizenbock, a classic strong lager. The pizza here, made with dough moistened with house-brewed stout instead of water, is excellent, as are the sandwiches. The 1869 building was built to house an outpost of the U.S. Mint.

Though The Dalles is right on the Columbia, there are few opportunities to even get close to the river. **The Bent River Restaurant** (1535 Bargeway Rd., 541/370-2368, 11am-10pm Tues.-Thurs. and Sun., 11am-midnight Fri.-Sat., $11-26) solves that with a riverfront restaurant and patio and good casual dining. The menu tilts toward burgers and sandwiches, but you'll also find wild boar tortellini and grilled salmon with honey mint sauce.

## ACCOMMODATIONS

Conveniently located off I-84's exit 87, the **Comfort Inn** (351 Lone Pine Dr., 541/298-2800, $155-166) has a pool, a fitness facility, and continental breakfast included. Rooms come equipped with microwaves and coffeemakers. Also located near I-84, **Cousins Country Inn** (2114 W. 6th St., 541/298-5161 or 800/848-9378, www.cousinscountryinn. com, $89-139) is a quality motel with an indoor hot tub and an outdoor pool. Guest rooms have microwaves, fridges, and coffeemakers; some have fireplaces. The on-site restaurant and lounge is one of The Dalles's most popular.

The **Fairfield Inn and Suites** (2014 W. 7th St., 541/769-0753, $156-169) has spacious and stylish rooms on the west side of town. It also has an indoor pool, guest laundry, and free hot breakfast.

At the west end of the historic downtown is **The Dalles Inn** (112 2nd St., 541/296-9107 or 888/935-2378, www.thedallesinn.com, $99-149), a well-maintained motor court with a pool and guest rooms with microwaves, fridges, and coffeemakers. It's also within easy walking distance of downtown bars and restaurants. For clean, basic rooms at good rates, consider the **Budget Inn Motel** (118 West 4th St., 541/296-5464, http://budgetinnthedalles.com, $90-119), convenient to the historic downtown.

The area's top lodging choice, particularly if you're looking for gorge views and a cool, sophisticated decor, is the ★ **Celilo Inn** (3550 East 2nd St., 541/769-0001, www.celiloinn.com, $129-149 and up). This unlikely boutique motel sits atop cliffs just east of The Dalles, and makes the most of its modest mid-20th-century heritage through a stylish transformation. Rooms are nicely furnished with a hip retro-urban design—not something you expect in The Dalles. There's also a patio, an outdoor pool, and a fitness center. All rooms come with mini fridges and microwaves. The only problem is that the Celilo Inn is far from pubs and restaurants, but you can't beat the stylish atmosphere.

## INFORMATION AND SERVICES

Shortly after you enter town via exit 82 (the "City Center" exit), stop off at **The Dalles Area Chamber of Commerce** (404 W. 2nd St., at Portland St., 541/296-2231 or 800/255-3385, www.thedalleschamber.com) and pick up its pamphlets *The Dalles: Historic Gateway to the Columbia Gorge* and *Walking Tours to Historic Homes and Buildings*. Take a gander at the restored Wasco County Courthouse next door, which was moved from its original location. This court presided over much of the country west of the Rockies in the mid-1800s. At the time, Wasco County comprised 130,000 square miles and included parts of Idaho and Wyoming.

## GETTING THERE

**Greyhound** provides bus service from its terminal (201 Federal St., 541/296-2421) in The Dalles west to Portland and east to Spokane and Boise.

# Mount Hood

**TOP EXPERIENCE**

Oregon's highest peak, Mount Hood (or Wy'east, as the region's Native Americans knew it), rises 11,249 feet above sea level less than an hour's drive from Portland and dominates the city's eastern horizon. Like Japan's Mount Fuji, California's Shasta, and Washington's Rainier, Adams, and St. Helens, Hood is a composite volcano (or stratovolcano), a steep-sided conical mountain built up of layers of lava and ash over millennia.

Mount Hood was formed about 500,000 years ago and has since erupted repeatedly, most recently during two periods over the last 1,500 years. Centuries before the first Europeans entered the region, the indigenous people of the Pacific Northwest witnessed the mountain's eruptions, and the retelling of the events became lore handed down over generations. According to one legend, Wy'east and

Pahto were sons of the Great Spirit, Sahale, who both fell in love with a beautiful maiden named Loowit. She was unable to choose between the two, and the braves fought bitterly to win her affection, laying waste to forests and villages in the process. In his anger at the destruction, Sahale transformed the three into mighty mountains: Loowit became Mount St. Helens, Pahto became Mount Adams, and to the south, Wy'east became Mount Hood.

The first European to report seeing the mountain was British navy lieutenant William E. Broughton, who viewed it in 1792 from the Columbia River near the mouth of the Willamette River. Broughton named the peak after the British navy admiral Samuel Hood, who would never see the mountain himself.

Hood's most recent volcanic episode ended in the 1790s, just prior to the arrival of Lewis and Clark in 1805. But since record-keeping began in the 1820s, no significant volcanic activity has been noted, though in 1859, 1865, and 1903 observers mentioned the venting of steam accompanied by red glows or "flames." Although the mountain is quiet, volcanologists keep a careful watch on Mount Hood.

Today, the mountain is the breathtaking centerpiece of the Mount Hood National Forest, which embraces 1,067,043 acres of natural beauty and recreational opportunities right in Portland's backyard. Five downhill ski resorts and numerous cross-country and hiking trails, jewel-like alpine lakes, and more than 80 campgrounds are just the beginning.

## SIGHTS
### ★ Timberline Lodge

**Timberline Lodge** (6 miles north of Government Camp, 503/622-7979 or 800/547-1406, www.timberlinelodge.com) is one of the unquestioned masterpieces of rustic Craftsman design and an object of veneration for those who look back to the Depression-era building boom as a golden age of social and artistic idealism. Over two million people visit Timberline each year, making it one of the top tourism destinations in the state.

When it was built in 1936 and 1937, the four-story 43,700-square-foot log and stone lodge was the largest of the federal Works Progress Administration (WPA) projects in Oregon. It employed up to 500 workers and artists, for whom building Timberline was more than just a job; it was an expression of a cultural ideal. In a pamphlet from that time, one observer noted: "In Mount Hood's Timberline Lodge the mystic strength that lives in the hills has been captured in wood and stone, and in the hands of laborer and craftsman, has been presented as man's effort at approximating an ideal in which society, through concern for the individual, surpasses the standard it has unconsciously set for itself."

Nearly every part of the structure and its decor was handcrafted, from the selection of stones in the massive lobby fireplaces to the hand-loomed coverlets on the beds. Every effort was made to harmonize with the natural splendor of the location; stonecutters quarried local stone for the walls, and builders employed locally harvested timber for the floors, staircases, and monumental three-story lobby. The six-sided central tower was designed to echo the peak of Mount Hood; the steeply slanted rooflines are meant to resemble mountain ridges. Even the exterior paint

hikers setting out from Timberline Lodge

color was specially created to match the hue of mountain frost.

The results of this astonishing attention to detail and handcraftsmanship is vividly on display in the lobby and central foyer. The massive fireplace built of local basalt rises 92 feet through three floors of open lobby; all the furniture in the hotel was made by hand in WPA carpentry halls, fanciful hand-carved animals adorn newel posts and stairways, and murals and paintings of stocky stylized workers grace the walls. It's hard to imagine a more powerful relic of the 1930s glorification of the worker than this.

The lodge is open to nonguests, so stop by for a hot chocolate or a meal (there are three dining rooms and two bars). The **Rachael Griffin Historic Exhibition Center,** on the main floor, displays some of the history of the lodge in tools, drawings, weavings, and photographs. A free 30-minute video that illustrates the construction of the lodge is shown upon request.

## Cascade Streamwatch

Near the village of Welches, on the west side of Mount Hood, pull off U.S. 26 to visit the **Cascade Streamwatch** at the Wildwood Recreation site (between mileposts 39 and 40). This 0.75-mile, gently rolling and accessible wetlands trail goes through a beautiful second-growth mixed conifer forest along the Salmon River to several viewing windows built into the shoreline embankment, giving visitors a great opportunity to view fish in a natural river. The Streamwatch trail is one of several wetlands trails here; picnic tables and restrooms are available. While spring and fall spawning seasons are optimal times to see the coho, it's possible to spot fish at other times of the year. The trail is located 39 miles east of Portland on the south side of the highway in the Bureau of Land Management's **Wildwood Recreation corridor** (503/375-5646), near the town of Zigzag. A nearby pullout offers information about Barlow Road, the final leg of the Oregon Trail, which went through these woods.

# HIKING

Hikes in the **Zigzag Ranger District** (70220 U.S. 26 E., Zigzag, 541/666-0704 or 503/622-3191) are an excellent introduction to the wealth of recreation options in the Mount Hood National Forest off U.S. 26. Whether you're driving the whole **Mount Hood Loop** (U.S. 26, Hwy. 35, and I-84) or just looking for a nice day trip from the Portland area, the Zigzag District's relatively low elevation and spectacular views of the state's highest mountain can be enjoyed by neophyte hikers or trail-wise veterans.

Coming from the west on U.S. 26, stop at the **Zigzag Ranger District Visitor Information Center** (70220 E. U.S. 26, 503/622-3191, 7:45am-4:30pm daily) to get your bearings with a wealth of pamphlets and an information desk. Pick up the free U.S. Forest Service flyer *Mount Hood Hikes.*

## Salmon River Trail

The **Salmon River Trail** is pretty, easy, and at low elevation, meaning that there's no excuse not to hike it. The 33-mile Salmon River is one of the few waterways protected as a federal Wild and Scenic River for its entire length—from its headwaters on Mount Hood to its confluence with the Sandy River near Brightwood. This trail, which runs 14 miles in the Salmon-Huckleberry Wilderness Area but is most often hiked in much smaller sections, runs right alongside the river; hikers can expect to see wildflowers, old-growth Douglas firs, and a number of campgrounds. In fall, enjoy red and gold maples; year-round, giant cedars and firs dominate. Access is easy, especially to the lower portion of the trail. From Sandy, follow U.S. 26 east for 17.9 miles and turn right (south) onto the Salmon River Road. Follow this road five miles to the trailhead.

## ★ Ramona Falls Trail

The **Ramona Falls Trail,** a 4.5-mile loop to a stunning waterfall, is one of the most popular on Mount Hood. From the trailhead, it initially parallels the Sandy River. In a little more than a mile you'll come to a seasonal bridge over the river with a pretty view of Mount Hood. On the other side of the river, Trail 797 passes Ramona Falls in about two miles. The grade of the slope is gentle throughout, and while much of the trail isn't especially scenic (except for the bridge over the Sandy River, rhododendrons in June, and views of Mount Hood), Ramona Falls itself makes it worthwhile.

A multitude of cascades course over a 100-foot-high, 50-foot-wide series of basalt outcroppings. This weeping wall is set in a grove of gargantuan Douglas firs. The spray beneath this canopy of trees can reduce the temperature by 20°F, making the place a popular retreat on hot summer days. This trail connects with the Pacific Crest Trail, and backpackers often use it as part of a longer trip.

To reach Ramona Falls, drive 18 miles east of Sandy on U.S. 26 to Lolo Pass Road, close by the ranger station. Turn left (north) and go five miles up Lolo Pass Road; stay right onto Forest Road 1825. From here, you'll take the road about four miles to its end.

Ramona Falls cascades down a wall of columnar basalt.

### McNeil Point Shelter

Although the **McNeil Point Shelter** hike is gorgeous and culminates at a cool old stone shelter, it has some tricky trail nuances and requires a map and consultation, both available at the Zigzag Ranger District Visitor Information Center (70220 E. U.S. 26, 503/622-3191, 7:45am-4:30pm daily). The trailhead is not far from Ramona Falls, making this is a nice follow-up to that hike. (Between the two hikes, you can camp at the McNeil Campground.)

Start at the Top Spur Trailhead. A half-mile up the hiking trail, take a right on the Pacific Crest Trail and keep right, continuing up the trail to a four-way intersection. Views of Mount Hood—and in June, a spectacular wildflower display—will greet you.

The remaining three miles contain some twists and turns (essentially, you're skirting Bald Mountain) that need cartographic clarification from the U.S. Forest Service. Ask the information center, as the trail can change from year to year, depending on conditions. Your reward will be breathtaking above-timberline views of the Mount Hood National Forest. This excursion is four miles each way and tame enough for weekenders. Start early to give yourself sufficient daylight.

To reach the McNeil Point trailhead from U.S. 26, turn north onto Lolo Pass Road at Zigzag and follow it four miles. Veer right onto Forest Road 1828 and proceed 13 miles until you reach the Top Spur Trailhead 785.

### Mirror Lake Trail

It's easy to find the trailhead for the popular **Mirror Lake Trail**—it's right on U.S. 26, and it's usually marked by a fleet of parked cars. There's good reason for the crowd: The 1.5-mile trail gains 700 feet in elevation and passes wild rhododendrons and a passel of other wildflowers on the way up to the lake that, as its name suggests, forms a perfect reflecting mirror for Mount Hood. A trail

# Bigfoot

One of the secrets the Columbia Gorge might share if it could talk would be the whereabouts of Bigfoot, or Sasquatch.

Whether it exists outside the mind or not, the King Kong of the Pacific Northwest forests has attracted to the region everyone from hunters and academics to curiosity seekers and *National Enquirer* reporters. Although the notion of a half-man, half-ape eluding human capture seems implausible at first, a brief look at some of the evidence might convince you otherwise.

Native Americans of the region regarded this creature as a fact of life and celebrated its presence in art and ritual. In the winter of 1991, reports from a remote area of eastern Oregon's Blue Mountains told of more than 60 miles of tracks left in the snow by a large five-toed creature. Scientists on the scene were of the opinion that the pattern of the prints and the gait could not have been faked. A similar conclusion was reached in 1982 about a plaster cast of footprints taken from the same mountain range. A Washington State University professor detected humanlike whorls on the toe portions of the prints, which he said showed that the tracks had to have been made by a large hominid.

Reports and evidence of actual encounters abound in Pacific Northwest annals, compelling the U.S. Army Corps of Engineers to list the animal as an indigenous species, accompanied by a detailed anatomical description. Skamania County, Washington, whose southern border is the Columbia River shoreline, declared the harming of these creatures a gross misdemeanor punishable by a year in jail and a $1,000 fine.

The unwavering belief in Bigfoot and the Native American insistence that it's a living entity have naturally met with skepticism. But considering that stories about black-and-white bears roaming the alpine hinterlands of China persisted for centuries until the 1936 discovery of pandas, there could be something new under the sun in the 21st century.

---

circumnavigates the lake, and ambitious hikers can continue another two miles to the top of Tom, Dick, and Harry Mountain, named for its three distinct, but not very characteristic, summits.

Find the trailhead at the footbridge one mile west of Government Camp on U.S. 26. Because of its popularity, try to do this hike on a weekday.

## Timberline Trail

More ambitious trekkers will take on the 40-mile **Timberline Trail**, a three- to five-day backpacking trip usually started at Timberline Lodge. If you undertake this loop, you'll finish up back at the lodge to cool off in the showers or swimming pool. While the alpine meadows on the Timberline Trail are beautiful, consult the rangers to see if the half-dozen creeks that must be forded en route are too high during the June-July snowmelt season.

With almost two dozen trails branching off the Timberline, opportunities for shorter day-trip loop hikes abound. Most of the main trail follows the base of the mountain near the timberline at elevations of 5,000 to 7,000 feet. On the northwest side, however, it drops to 3,000 feet and merges with the Pacific Crest Trail. This means that there's snow on the trail most of the year. Make the trip in the early fall to avoid the crowds; in July and August, the mountain meadows are ablaze with wildflowers.

Backpackers must camp at least 200 feet from water and 100 feet from any trail, mountain meadow, or obvious viewpoint.

## Buried Forest Overlook

An easy one-mile round-trip leads to the **Buried Forest Overlook,** which provides a dramatic view of the White River Canyon, where a thick forest was buried during one of the mountain's major eruptive periods 200 to 250 years ago. Superheated gases blew down giant trees like matchsticks, and in the next instant everything was buried underneath a mixture of water, ash, and mud. The forces of wind and water erosion have since exposed the remains of the Buried Forest. To get here, follow one of the trails behind Timberline Lodge up the mountain about 0.25 miles until you reach the Pacific Crest National Scenic Trail. Turn east (right) onto the Pacific Crest Trail and follow it another 0.25 miles or so to the overlook.

## Cloud Cap

The best way to get up close and personal with Mount Hood is with a visit to **Cloud Cap.** A beautiful old lodge (now closed) and the entrance to the Mount Hood Wilderness are on the north side of the volcano. To get there, take Highway 35 south of Hood River 24 miles to Cooper Spur Road. Drive past the ski area until you come to Cloud Cap at the end of a twisting, 10-mile gravel road. The road is passable only in summer months due to snow at that altitude. From here, hardy adventurers can rub elbows with glaciers, walking up Cooper Spur (a side ridge of Mount Hood) without climbing gear in late summer to almost 8,600 feet elevation.

## SKIING

Wherever you ski here, November-April, be sure to purchase and display a **Sno-Park** permit ($25 for the season, $9 for 3 consecutive days, $4 one-day). Most ski shops near the slopes sell them.

From Portland you can hear road and ski condition reports (6:30am, 7:30am, and 12:15pm Mon.-Fri. Dec.-Mar.) on KINK (101.9 FM). Log on to www.tripcheck.com or call 800/977-6368 for road conditions and traveler advisory information.

In addition to being the state's highest mountain, Mount Hood also boasts the most ski areas—five in all.

## Mount Hood Meadows

The mountain's largest and most varied ski area is **Mount Hood Meadows** (503/287-5438, ext. 182, or 800/754-4663, www.ski-hood.com, $82 adults full-day, $72 adults afternoon, $49 children, discounts online), with 2,150 acres of groomed slopes, terrain parks, six high-speed quads, and half a dozen slower lifts. Even with all the lifts, this place is so popular at times you might have to wait. Night skiing is also popular.

Meadows is located 10 miles from Government Camp on Highway 35. It's often sunny here on the east slope of the mountain when it's snowing and raining on the west side; call 503/227-7669 for a snow report and

cross-country skiing on Mount Hood

hours. Check the ski area's website for current information about bus transportation from Portland.

## Cooper Spur Ski Resort

A popular destination for families and beginners is **Cooper Spur Ski Resort** (541/352-7803, www.cooperspur.com, $36 adults, $30 seniors and ages 7-14). On the northeastern flank of the mountain, 24 miles south of Hood River on Highway 35, the location occasionally offers protection from storms and prevailing westerlies, yet has more than enough snow for a good time and is more affordable than the other Mount Hood resorts. However, the trails are only served by a slow double chairlift and a rope tow. Cross-country skiers appreciate the **Tilly Jane Trail.**

## Mount Hood SkiBowl

**Mount Hood SkiBowl** (503/658-4385, www.skibowl.com, $71-76 adults, $62-66 night skiing, $61-63 ages 15-17 full-day, $47-48 children 7-14 and seniors 65-70 afternoon) is only 53 miles from Portland on U.S. 26 and features the most extensive night skiing in the country. The upper bowl has some of the most challenging skiing and snowboarding to be found on the mountain. In summer, the complex turns into a summer adventure park for bungee jumping, an alpine slide, mountain biking, and much more.

## Timberline Ski Area

**Timberline Ski Area** (503/231-7979, snow report 503/222-2211, www.timberlinelodge.com, $66-72 ages 18-64 full-day, $58-62 afternoon, $56-59 ages 15-17 full-day, $48 children afternoon) is known for its high-elevation Palmer lift and its nearly year-round season. With the highest vertical drop of any ski area in Oregon (3,690 feet) as well as the highest elevation accessible by chairlift (8,600 feet), 50 percent of Timberline's ski runs are in the intermediate-level category. Timberline has the longest ski season in the nation.

Although you'll rarely find powder conditions at Timberline, the 41 runs are so well groomed that Timberline snow is easily navigable. The chairlifts (six in winter, two in summer) are mostly obscured by trees or topography, so you get a feeling of intimacy with the natural surroundings when you're schussing downhill. You can go up two lifts, enjoying a nearly two-mile-long run. The upper Palmer lift, highest on the mountain, is open late spring-fall, when conditions are safe for skiing on the Palmer glacier. The Magic Mile chair ($15 pp), directly below the Palmer, is open to the 7,000-foot level for sightseers as well as skiers.

Located 60 miles east of Portland on U.S. 26, the skiing starts where the trees end. To get here, go east of Government Camp on U.S. 26 and take Forest Road 50 for six miles. Check the resort's website for information about bus transportation.

## Summit Ski Area

A mile south of the Timberline turnoff on U.S. 26 is **Summit Ski Area** (503/272-0256, www.summitskiarea.com, $35 adults, $25 over age 60 or under age 12), the place for families, beginners, and people who just like to play in the snow. You can ski on beginners' slopes or rent an inner tube to barrel down the gently sloping surrounding hills. Several other good sliding hills are close by. To get to Summit, drive through the town of Government Camp off U.S. 26. Beyond the stores and concessions, you'll see a large parking lot on the left side of the road with a structure housing a burger joint and equipment rentals.

## Cross-Country Skiing

Across Highway 35 from the Mount Hood Meadows turnoff, **Teacup Lake** offers a great network of cross-country skiing trails that are maintained by a club that requests a small donation. Another popular trail that's easy after you get past the first long downhill goes to **Trillium Lake.** Find the Sno-Park for this trail about three miles east of Government Camp on U.S. 26.

Rent cross-country skis and get info about

current conditions in the town of Sandy at **Otto's** (38716 Pioneer Blvd., 503/668-5947).

## CLIMBING

Mount Hood (11,239 feet), the highest mountain in Oregon, has the additional distinction of being the second-most-climbed glacier-covered peak in the world. Nicknamed the Fujiyama of America, Mount Hood offers ascents that cater to everyone, from beginners to advanced climbers. Another similarity to its Japanese counterpart is that only a brief part of the year is safe for climbing, from May to mid- or late July.

Since the summer heat brings the threat of avalanche danger and falling rock hazards, the time of day that you depart is just as important as the time of year. Most expeditions set out in the wee hours of the morning when the snow is firm and rock danger is slighter. Although you won't get as much sleep, you will be able to enjoy beautiful sunrise scenery as you venture to the top.

Unless climbers are very experienced, it is best to go with a guide. All climbers should register at the kiosk by Timberline Lodge before climbing and check out after the climb. While the climb looks like just a few miles on the map, it takes 10 to 15 hours to make the trip from Timberline Lodge to the top and back. The four primary routes up Mount Hood—**Hogsback, Mazama, Wyeast,** and **Castle Crags**—are all technical climbs; there is no hiking trail to the summit. Having the right equipment means little if you don't know how to use it. That said, all climbers should rent a Mount Hood Locator Unit, or MLU, available at local climbing shops and at the Mount Hood Inn off of U.S. 26 in Government Camp.

Two-day guided climbs are offered by **Timberline Mountain Guides** (541/312-9242, www.timberlinemtguides.com, $645).

## ACCOMMODATIONS

Remember that Mount Hood is just over an hour from Portland, so you can always return to the city if you don't want to spend the night on the mountain.

### Timberline Lodge

Of all the lodgings on Mount Hood, one is nearly as archetypal as the mountain itself: ★ **Timberline Lodge** (27500 E. Timberline Rd., Government Camp, 503/622-7979 or 800/547-1406, www.timberlinelodge.com, $145-165 shared bath, $250-355 private bath). This massive log lodge, built during the Great Depression by craftspeople working with the Works Progress Administration, is one of the best examples of rustic Craftsman style in the world. Timberline gained even more fame when it was used as one of the settings for the 1983 film *The Shining* (walk by room 217 and recall "red rum" with a shiver of fright).

One of the many charms of Timberline is the individuality of each room, which ranges from bunk bed-equipped "chalet rooms," with a bath down the hall, to large fireplace suites. No matter how humble the room, it will have the lodge's signature hand-loomed curtains and handcrafted furniture. Guests also have access to a sauna and the year-round outdoor pool.

The lodge's lobby is a good place to visit even if you aren't a guest. The upstairs Ram's Head Bar is a classic spot for an après-ski or post-hike drink, and the **Cascade Dining Room** (7:30am-10:30am, 11:30am-2pm, 5:30pm-8pm Mon.-Thurs., 7:30am-10:30am, 11:30am-3pm, 5:30pm-8pm Fri.-Sun., $20-48) serves outstanding though pricey food.

Adventuresome groups of travelers should check out Timberline's **Silcox Hut** ($185-225 pp, includes dinner and breakfast), a spacious but cozy onetime skiers' warming hut perched up the mountain, beyond the main lodge, at 7,000 feet. The hut does have electricity, running water, and toilets, but with its stone walls and big timbers, it definitely has rustic charm. The hut can sleep up to 24 people, and beds are bunk-style, in six rooms. Guests reach the hut either by snowcat or the ski area's Magic Mile chairlift and have the option of skiing back down to the base area in the morning. The hut's host prepares a family-style dinner (typically something like lasagna) as well as breakfast. A minimum of 12 to 18 people is required to rent the hut, depending on the season and day of the week; it's also a popular spot for weddings.

## Government Camp and Vicinity

Also operated by Timberline Lodge, the **Lodge at Government Camp** (along the Government Camp loop, www.thelodgeat-governmentcamp.com, $225-275 Mon.-Fri., $295-395 Sat.-Sun., for up to 6 people, 2-night minimum) is a rather grand structure that offers eight condo units with two to four bedrooms. All units are fully furnished and have complete kitchens; guests have access to all facilities at Timberline Lodge.

More conventional lodgings are also available in Government Camp. The **Best Western Mount Hood Inn** (87450 E. Government Camp Loop, 503/272-3205 or 800/443-7777, www.mthoodinn.com, $130-165) is a good bet. If that's too expensive, the venerable **Huckleberry Inn** (88611 E. Government Camp Loop, 503/272-3325, www.huckleberry-inn.com, $90-160) has both standard guest rooms and a slightly funky bunk room that you can rent for a group of up to 14 people ($160).

A new and outsize condo development, **Collins Lake Resort** (88544 E. Government Camp Loop, 800/234-6288, www.collinslakeresort.com, $210-369 chalet doubles) is in the heart of Government Camp and offers chalets and multi-bedroom condos. Also part of the resort are the Grand Lodges, a separate development with two- and three-bedroom units with luxury furnishings. The resort offers a variety of pools and a sauna.

Speaking of housing large groups, cabins are a cost-effective way for groups of three or more to stay in beautiful surroundings near hiking trails, ski slopes, and other outdoor recreation. Some of the most popular and best-situated cabins on the mountain are those at **Summit Meadow** (503/272-3494, www.summitmeadow.com, $190-265 Mon.-Fri., $410-625 Sat.-Sun., 2-night minimum). The five cabins range from a cozy

one-bedroom with a sleeping loft to a large two-bedroom cabin with a loft that'll sleep you and nine friends. These cabins are located 1.5 miles south of Government Camp in a secluded setting in the national forest. The cabins are open year-round, but in the winter are accessible only by cross-country skiing or snowshoeing in, about 1.5 miles from the Sno-Park.

**Mount Hood Village** (65000 E. U.S. 26, Welches, 800/255-3069, cabins $72-189) is another good value. Although it is primarily an RV park, it also includes a cluster of wooden cabins, cottages, tiny houses, and yurts ($52-83) near the Salmon River. Close by the U.S. Forest Service information center and bookstore as well as the Ramona Falls trailhead, Cascade Streamwatch, and the Rendezvous Grill and Tap Room, the resort includes a fitness room and the Courtyard Cafe, which serves breakfast and lunch. Choose between basic "cabins in the woods" sleeping four and large "vacation cottages," with features like hot tubs and saunas.

**Mt. Hood Vacation Rentals** (24403 E. Welches Rd., Suite 104, 503/622-5688 or 800/635-5417, www.mthoodrentals.com) posts dozens of enticing offerings on its website, most located down the mountain around the Sandy River. These cabins come with all the amenities you'd find in a hotel and more, like firewood and kitchen implements. Rates vary by season. A typical summer rate for a 1,500-square-foot unit with several bedrooms sleeping six might be $250. Rates go as low as $160 for small units to over $500 for larger cabins sleeping more than a dozen. Many of these cabins enjoy secluded locations, and the rental office provides discounted lift tickets to several Mount Hood ski areas. Look for the rental office just west of the Hoodland shopping center. For more listings of cabins and property management companies, see www.mthood.info.

## Camping

Most of the following campgrounds are in **Mount Hood National Forest**

(503/668-1700, www.fs.fed.us); some accept reservations.

Set along the banks of the Salmon River is **Green Canyon** (Zigzag Ranger District, 65000 E. U.S. 26, Welches, 503/622-3191, May-mid-Sept., $20-22). Here you'll find 15 campsites for tents and RVs (maximum 22 feet), with picnic tables and grills, piped water, pit toilets, and firewood available seasonally. The Salmon River Trail is nearby, and a store and a café are about five miles away. To get there, go to Zigzag on U.S. 26 and take Salmon River Road (Forest Rd. 2618) for four miles to the campground.

Near the replica of the Barlow Road Tollgate is **Tollgate Campground** (late May-mid-Sept., $21-23). Along the banks of the Zigzag River, this campground has 15 sites for tents and RVs up to 16 feet. Because it's close to the Mount Hood Wilderness and many hiking trails, it's so popular that finding a campsite without a reservation on a summer weekend is next to impossible. To get here, take U.S. 26 one mile past Rhododendron.

Situated on the Clear Fork of the Sandy River, **McNeil Campground** (May-early Sept., $16-18) has a good view of Mount Hood. The campground has 34 sites for tents and RVs up to 22 feet, with picnic tables and grills, vault toilets, and firewood available. To reach the campground, turn onto Lolo Pass Road (County Rd. 18) at Zigzag and follow it for four miles. Turn right onto Forest Road 1825 and follow signs to the campground, about a mile farther.

A popular place for a night out in the woods is **Camp Creek** (reservations 877/444-6777, www.recreation.gov, late May-early Sept., $18-20). This campground has 25 sites for tents and RVs up to 22 feet, with piped water, picnic tables, and grills. Vault toilets and firewood are also available. Situated along Camp Creek not far from the Zigzag River, the campground has double campsites that two parties can share. To get here, go three miles east of Rhododendron on U.S. 26 and turn south to the campground.

About one mile down the road from

Timberline Lodge is **Alpine** (July-late Sept., $20-22). The high-elevation setting lives up to its name, with snow remaining on the ground until late in the summer in heavy snow years. There are 16 campsites for tents, plus piped water, picnic tables, and grills. In addition to easy access to summer skiing up at Mount Hood, the Pacific Crest Trail passes close to the camp.

Near the junction of U.S. 26 and Highway 35 is **Still Creek** (reservations 877/444-6777, www.recreation.gov, mid-June-late Sept., $21-23). Here you'll find 27 sites for tents and RVs (16 feet maximum) with picnic tables and grills. Piped water, pit toilets, and firewood are also available. The campground has many large trees and good fishing, and it is close to a pioneer cemetery and Trillium Lake. To reach this spot, drive past Government Camp to Forest Road 2650.

A good place for a base camp for those who like to canoe is at **Trillium Lake** (reservations 877/444-6777, www.recreation.gov, late May-late Sept., $20-45). Just 60 miles from Portland, the lake is a great place for city kids. If they're ages 13 and under, they don't need a fishing license and may keep up to 10 fish per day. Crayfish also prowl the lake bottom awaiting capture. Families appreciate the opportunity to cruise the lake in a canoe or some other nonmotorized craft. At night, a new amphitheater hosts campfire programs and nature talks. There are 57 sites for tents and RVs (maximum 40 feet), with picnic tables and grills. Piped water and flush toilets were installed recently; boat docking and launching facilities are nearby, but no motorized craft are permitted on the lake. To get here, take U.S. 26 two miles southeast of Government Camp, then turn right onto Forest Road 2656. Proceed one mile to the campground.

A spot that offers good fishing, swimming, and windsurfing is **Clear Lake** (reservations 877/444-6777, www.recreation.gov, late May-early Sept., $21). Here you'll find 28 tent and RV sites (32 feet maximum) with picnic tables and grills. Piped water, vault toilets, and firewood are also available. Boat docking and launching facilities are nearby, and motorized craft are allowed on the lake. To get here, go 11 miles southeast of Government Camp on U.S. 26, then a mile south on Forest Road 2630 to the campground.

A midsize county park called **Toll Bridge** (7360 Toll Bridge Rd., Parkdale, 541/352-6300, Apr.-Nov. and off-season weekends, weather permitting, $20-30) is 18 miles south of Hood River on Highway 35. This campground has 18 tent and 20 RV (maximum 20 feet) sites with electricity, piped water, sewer hookups, and picnic tables. Flush toilets, showers, firewood, a recreation hall, and a playground are also featured. Set along the banks of the Hood River, Toll Bridge includes bike trails, hiking trails, and tennis courts.

**Nottingham** (15 miles south of Parkdale) and **Sherwood** (11 miles south of Parkdale, Hood River Ranger District, 541/352-6002, Memorial Day-Labor Day, $15) both include basic amenities. Both are located on the east fork of the Hood River along Highway 35 and offer good hiking.

## FOOD

Far and away, the top dining choice on Mount Hood is the ★ **Cascade Dining Room** (Timberline Lodge, 27500 E. Timberline Rd., Government Camp, 503/622-0700, 7:30am-10:30am, 11:30am-2pm, and 5:30pm-8pm Mon.-Thurs., 7:30am-10:30am, 11:30am-3pm, and 5:30pm-8pm Fri.-Sun., dinner reservations advised, $20-48). As at most of the top Oregon restaurants, the chefs here prepare meals to showcase regional foods—in this case, often wild mushrooms from Mount Hood's forested slopes and huckleberries from its meadows. Even if a full dinner doesn't fit into your plans or your budget, lunch in this huge timbered dining room is a hearty treat—take a break from skiing for some polenta served with roasted vegetables or a salmon BLT.

Down the hill at the west end of Government Camp, find the **Mount Hood Brewing Company** (87304 E. Government Camp Loop, Government Camp, 503/272-0102, www.mthoodbrewing.com, 11am-10pm daily, $11-21). Sandwiches, pasta, chili, and design-your-own pizza can be washed down with microbrews (try Mount Hood's own oatmeal stout), espresso drinks, and local wines. Also in town, the **Huckleberry Inn** (88611 E. Government Camp Loop, Government Camp, 503/272-3325, www.huckleberry-inn.com, $6-14) deserves mention if only for its 24-hour, 7-day-a-week restaurant—and, you guessed it, wild huckleberry pie.

## INFORMATION

The **Zigzag Ranger District Visitor Information Center** (70220 E. U.S. 26, 503/622-3191, 7:45am-4:30pm daily) is staffed by U.S. Forest Service rangers who can provide information about local places of interest. This is really an excellent stop, even for people who travel up to the mountain quite often.

# The Willamette Valley

The Willamette Valley, the primary destination of the Oregon Trail pioneers, is one of the most productive agricultural areas in the world. Wineries abound, as do plant nurseries and U-pick berry fields. During the spring, the tulip and iris fields are beautiful, especially when (as is common) they're backed up by a rainbow.

The Willamette Valley is also the population nexus of Oregon, supporting 100 cities (including Portland) and 70 percent of the state's population. Nonetheless, once you get south of Portland's suburbs, you'll seldom have the feeling of being in a big metropolis. The broad Willamette Valley, 130 miles long and at some points nearly 60 miles wide, rolls out between the rugged Coast Range and the glaciered peaks of the Cascades. Along the way, the Willamette collects the waters of other large rivers, including the McKenzie, the Santiam, and the Yamhill. By the time it joins the Columbia, the Willamette is the 10th largest river in the United States.

## PLANNING YOUR TIME

Although the Willamette Valley runs only about 100 miles from Portland to Eugene, it's worth taking some time to explore the back roads and smaller towns off I-5. For starters, roam through the Willamette Valley's wine country. By spending the night along the way, you'll get to enjoy a dinner at one of the area's excellent restaurants. The greatest concentration of wineries is between Newberg and McMinnville in the North Willamette Valley Wine Country; however, clusters of wineries run the length of the valley. If hiking is more your focus, head to Silver Falls State Park, home to 10 large waterfalls and within striking distance of the Oregon Garden (an 80-acre botanical paradise) and lovely Mount Angel Abbey (a working monastery).

Because of its youthful energy and high-quality facilities, Eugene—home to the University of Oregon—is a good place to spend a day or two, both to experience the town and to explore the river valleys and west slopes of the Cascades that lie to its east.

**Previous:** springtime at the Wooden Shoe Bulb Company; Willakenzie Estate. **Above:** pinot noir grapes.

Look for ★ to find recommended
sights, activities, dining, and lodging.

# Highlights

★ **Carlton:** The area around Carlton in Yamhill County is a great place to tour some of the nation's top pinot noir and pinot gris wineries (page 150).

★ **McMinnville:** Wine country's largest town has charm to spare, excellent restaurants, and relatively inexpensive lodging (page 151).

★ **State Capitol:** The art alone in the Oregon capitol in Salem is worth the trip (page 160).

★ **Mount Angel Abbey:** This hilltop abbey is a good place for both quiet reflection and architectural tourism; the splendid library was designed by famed Finnish architect Alvar Aalto (page 169).

★ **Silver Falls State Park:** Aren't waterfalls what Oregon is all about? Here, a seven-mile trail passes 10 waterfalls (page 171).

★ **McKenzie River National Recreation Trail:** This 26-mile trail follows the McKenzie, with waterfalls cascading over lava rocks and lush green streamside vegetation (page 199).

★ **Mountain Biking in Oakridge:** In the hills just outside this working-class mill town, you'll find some of the state's best mountain biking (page 205).

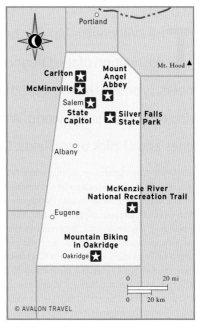

# The Willamette Valley

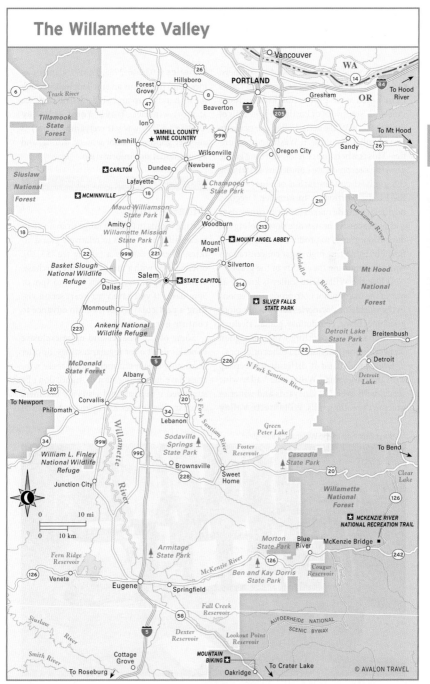

© AVALON TRAVEL

# Willamette Wine Country

Although wine is also produced in southern Oregon and the Columbia Gorge, the state's most noted wine production area includes vineyards southwest of Portland in the hills of the northern Willamette Valley, particularly in Yamhill and southern Washington counties. This is where the rich soil and long gentle growing season create conditions sustaining the greatest concentration of vineyards in the Pacific Northwest. In summer, Oregon's northern latitude makes for long, sunny days without excessive heat, while slow-cooling fall days allow grapes to produce a complexity of flavor by inhibiting high sugar concentrations while maintaining the acidity of the grape.

While the Willamette Valley is known as one of the major pinot noir-producing regions in the world, local wineries also put out pinot gris, pinot blanc, chardonnay, gamay, riesling, gewürztraminer, sparkling wine, sauvignon blanc, cabernet, merlot, and other offerings.

Even locals find it difficult to keep up with the burgeoning Willamette Valley wine scene, with over 700 vineyards and wineries gracing the rolling hills. **Willamette Valley Wineries** (503/646-2985, http://willamettewines.com) maintains an excellent website; look for its handy map and guide distributed free at most wineries. **Travel Yamhill Valley** (503/883-7770, www.travelyamhill.com) is another good source for winery, dining, and accommodations information.

## Wine-Tasting

Tasting rooms in Oregon range from no-frills makeshift back rooms to relatively grand affairs. There's usually a tasting fee ($5-20), often waived with a minimum wine purchase. Wineries are generally open 11am to 4pm or 5pm daily. If you have your heart set on visiting a particular winery, call in advance to confirm hours and details.

Some of the smaller and more exclusive wineries don't offer regular tastings, or offer them only by appointment. Since these wineries have no tasting staff on hand, don't be surprised if recreational visits are declined. Almost all wineries are open on Memorial

tasting pinot noir in the Willamette Valley

Day and Thanksgiving weekends, when thousands of people throng into the region to visit their favorite wineries.

Given the proximity of Portland, many folks visit the wine country as a day trip. To extend your stay, there are plenty of bed-and-breakfasts and a few hotels, including a luxurious resort.

## Wine Tours

Hiring a tour company has become an increasingly appealing and safer alternative for many wine enthusiasts than driving themselves. Several companies offer door-to-door service from Portland hotels. The well-established **Grape Escape Winery Tours** (503/283-3380, www.grapeescapetours.com) conducts a variety of private and semiprivate custom tours. **Eco Tours of Oregon** (503/245-1428, www.ecotours-of-oregon.com) offers van tours with Portland-area pickup and returns.

If you're already in the Willamette wine country, contact **Insiders Wine Tour** (503/791-0005, www.insiderswinetour.com), based in McMinnville. Thanks to their inside connections, you may get the chance to visit wineries not typically open to the public.

There are more exciting ways to tour wine country than in minivans. **Equestrian Wine Tours** (503/864-2336 or 866/864-5253, www.equestrianwinetours.com) provides horseback winery tours on Tennessee Walking horses. Hikers should consider the guided walking tours of Dundee-area wineries offered by **Oregon Dundee Hills Walking Wine Tours** (503/789-7629, markdartist@verizon.net). Want to see wine country from the air? Catch a ride on a hot-air balloon with the folks at **Vista Balloons** (503/625-7385 or 800/622-2309, www.vistaballoon.com, Apr.-Oct.).

## Getting Around

An unavoidable factor of Willamette Valley wine country: The traffic is often horrendous, particularly along Highway 99W, the valley's main drag. (The route is also patrolled heavily by police.) The only way to avoid the traffic is to steer clear of it as much as possible.

The tour described below is an alternate route, following four-lane U.S. 26 west from Portland to Forest Grove and into the heart of the wine country on back roads. To return to Portland without driving in 99W traffic, from Newberg, follow Highway 219 south across the Willamette River and turn left on McKay Road, passing near Champoeg State Park and the verdant fields of French Prairie, before joining I-5 at exit 278.

## FOREST GROVE AND GASTON

The northernmost reach of Willamette Valley wine country is in Forest Grove, about 20 minutes west of Portland off U.S. 26. Forest Grove is home to Pacific University, the oldest chartered university in the western United States, established in 1849.

### Wineries

**David Hill Winery** (46350 NW David Hill Rd., 503/992-8545, www.davidhillwinery.com) is a picturesque vineyard with a long history. The first wine grapes were planted here in the 19th century, and the vineyard produced award-winning wines until Prohibition. Part of the vineyards were replanted in the 1960s, making these some of the oldest pinot noir vines in the state.

**Montinore Estate** (3663 Dilley Rd., 503/359-5012, www.montinore.com) is just south and west of downtown Forest Grove. As at many Willamette Valley vineyards, the grapes are grown sustainably using biodynamic practices. Don't leave Forest Grove without stopping in at **Sake One** (820 Elm St., 503/357-7056, www.sakeone.com) to taste the local sake and tour the brewery. The sakes, made from California rice, range from the traditional Momokawa line of robust rice wines to the milky coconut-scented Pearl and the clean-tasting, slightly fruity Asian pear sake.

Seven miles south of Forest Grove on Highway 47, the tiny town of Gaston is home to **Elk Cove Vineyard** (27751 NW Olson

Rd., 503/985-7760, http://elkcove.com), one of the oldest and most respected operations in the area. Elk Cove's tasting room is especially lovely, and the pinot gris is one of the region's best.

## Food and Accommodations

One of the McMenamin brothers' largest projects is the **Grand Lodge** (3505 Pacific Ave., Forest Grove, 503/992-3442, www.mcmenamins.com), a hotel, brewpub, and entertainment center on 13 acres of lawns and gardens that was converted from a vast Masonic and Eastern Star retirement complex built in 1922. The Grand Lodge includes four bars and restaurants, a movie theater, a 10-hole disc golf course, and 77 hotel rooms. Guest rooms are a mix of European-style shared baths ($65-125) or rooms with private baths ($115-145). The entire establishment is rich with the McMenamins' signature funkiness; it's a fun place to stay if you appreciate old-fashioned atmosphere in an updated, but not utterly transformed, hotel.

## YAMHILL

In the Chahalem Mountains east of Yamhill is the small **Ribbon Ridge American Viticulture Area,** one of Oregon's most heralded wine regions and home to some of the state's top-rated wines.

## Wineries

From Yamhill, head east on Highway 240 to find the hillside vineyards of **Willakenzie Estate** (19143 NE Laughlin Rd., 503/662-3280, www.willakenzie.com). In a beautiful rural setting, the winery's three-level gravity-fed design (a tradition in Burgundy) ensures gentle handling of the wine. Along with several estate-grown pinot noirs, the tasting room pours lush pinot gris, pinot blanc, and gamay noir. Top-flight pinot noir is the specialty at highly recommended **Penner-Ash Wine Cellars** (15771 NE Ribbon Ridge Rd., 503/554-5545, www.pennerash.com). Atypical for the region, wines made from viognier and syrah grapes are also featured. One of Oregon's pioneer

wineries, **Adelsheim Vineyard** (16800 NE Calkins Lane, 503/538-3652, www.adelsheim.com) was established in 1971 and produces a range of single-vineyard pinot noir wines as well as excellent chardonnay, pinot gris, and rarely encountered auxerrois wines.

## ★ CARLTON

South on Highway 47, Carlton is a quiet, picturesque farm village with 18 wine-tasting rooms within a stroll of each other, plus good restaurants.

## Wineries

Just north of Carlton, the cooperative **Carlton Winemakers Studio** (801 N. Scott St., 503/852-6100, www.winemakersstudio.com) houses 14 boutique wineries, including Andrew Rich, Hamacher, and Bachelder. The studio helps up-and-coming winemakers by providing space and support. Sharing the same access road, **Cana's Feast** (750 W. Lincoln St., 503/852-0002, www.canasfeastwinery.com) focuses on Mediterranean grape varietals, including sangiovese, barbera, nebbiolo, and primitivo. Occasional weekend meals are served on the winery's grape-shaded veranda during summer and early fall; call to inquire.

In Carlton's old rail station is **Ken Wright Cellars** (120 N. Pine St., 503/852-7010, www.kenwrightcellars.com), with six vineyard-specific pinot noir bottlings. Wright also makes a delicious Bordeaux-style Claret from eastern Washington fruit under the Tyrus Evan label. In a handsome old brick storefront, **Scott Paul Wines** (128 S Pine St., 503/852-7300, http://scottpaul.com) specializes in elegant French-style pinot noir.

From Carlton, leave Highway 47 and travel the back roads. Follow Main Street east from downtown; it eventually turns into Hendricks Road and passes through lovely rolling hills lush with vineyards on the way to Newberg. Stop at **Lemelson Vineyards** (12020 NE Stag Hollow Rd., 503/852-6619, www.lemelsonvineyards.com, 11am-4pm Thurs.-Mon.) to taste outstanding organic pinot noir and pinot gris wines.

## Food

A great place for country-style French food is **Cuvée** (214 W. Main St., 503/852-6555, www.cuveedining.net, 5:30pm-9pm Wed.-Sat., 5pm-8pm Sun., $21-27). French standards include *coquilles* Saint-Jacques; make sure to check out the sautéed oysters with horseradish sauce as an appetizer. Three-course fixed-price dinners ($30, reservations advised) are offered Wednesday, Thursday, and Sunday nights.

For a lighter meal, head to **The Horse Radish** (211 W. Main St., 503/852-6656, www.thehorseradish.com, noon-3pm Sun.-Thurs., noon-10pm Fri.-Sat., $6-12), a deli with good soups and sandwiches, plus a large selection of cheese—perfect for a picnic. A phalanx of local wines is available by the glass or bottle, and you'll find live music on weekend evenings.

## Accommodations

Within easy walking distance to tasting rooms and restaurants in downtown Carlton, the **Carlton Inn** (648 W. Main St., 503/852-7506, www.thecarltoninn.com, $170-200) is a charming B&B in a 1915 arts and crafts-style home. Each of the four guest rooms has a private bath.

Nearby, the ★ **Abbey Road Farm B&B** (10501 NE Abbey Rd., 503/852-6278, www.abbeyroadfarm.com, $235) has elegant rooms located in—no joke—converted grain silos. This upscale B&B (think fine art and 600-thread-count sheets) is nicely appointed; the 82-acre Abbey Road Farm has cherry orchards, goats, llamas, donkeys, and gardens; guests can ask about assisting with farm chores. In the interest of your own relaxation, there are no phones or TVs. In addition to the B&B rooms, the farm also rents a three-bedroom, two-bath home with a full kitchen ($375, 2-night minimum).

## LAFAYETTE

While cruising the wine country, antiques collectors can pull off Highway 99 in the town of Lafayette to visit **Lafayette Schoolhouse Antiques** (748 Hwy. 99W, 503/864-2720, 10am-5pm daily), where Oregon's largest antiques market can be found in the old schoolhouse, mill, and auditorium. Imagine 10,000 square feet of antiques spread over three floors in a 1910 building, with an antique furniture showcase next door.

Just north of Lafayette, wine-tasters can enjoy the beautiful tasting room and one of the most panoramic views in the valley at **Anne Amie Vineyards** (6580 NE Mineral Springs Rd., 503/864-2991, http://anneamie.com), where you'll also find top-notch pinot noir, pinot blanc, and pinot gris.

## ★ McMINNVILLE

By far the largest town in the wine country, with a population of some 33,000, McMinnville is also one of the most appealing. Though surrounded by grim big-box development, the charming turn-of-the-20th-century downtown is lined with excellent restaurants, wine bars, boutique shopping, and a superlative organic grocery and health food store. McMinnville makes a great spot to spend the night; there are a wide range of lodging choices and enough fine restaurants to tempt diners into lingering on another night just to sample another good meal.

Another compelling reason to visit McMinnville is the **Evergreen Aviation and Space Museum** (500 NE Capt. Michael King Smith Way, 503/434-4180, www.evergreenmuseum.org, 9am-5pm daily, $27 adults, $24 seniors, $19 ages 5-16), just off Highway 18 south of McMinnville, a massive complex of two separate museums. The Aviation Museum houses the *Spruce Goose,* the giant wooden seaplane built for billionaire Howard Hughes in the 1940s. (The plane, which Hughes called a "flying boat," flew only once, for approximately one minute.) In addition to the *Goose,* the museum houses many other aircraft, including funky hand-built planes, bombers, and large cargo planes. Next to this vast hangar is yet another complex home to the Space Museum, which celebrates the history of space exploration and travel. In addition, you'll find an **IMAX theater** (tickets $11 adults, $10 seniors, $9 ages 5-16), a number of dining options, and a wine-tasting room.

As if this weren't enough, the enormous 70,000-square-foot **Wings and Waves Water Park** (10am-6pm Mon.-Fri., 10am-7pm Sat.-Sun. summer, 11am-7pm Fri., 10am-6pm Sat.-Sun. winter, museum only $10, museum and water park $20 under 42 inches tall, $29 over 42 inches) features a children's museum focusing on hydrology and the power of water plus 10 waterslides. You can't miss it; it's the building with a Boeing 747 on its roof.

## Wineries

McMinnville offers several wine-tasting rooms and a brewpub right in town, in addition to those found in the surrounding hills. Third Street is the main street downtown, lined with trees and lots of wine-tasting action. A good place to start is the **Willamette Valley Wine Center** (300 NE 3rd St., 503/883-9012, www.wvv.com, 11am-6pm Mon.-Wed., 11am-8:30pm Thurs., 11am-7pm Sat., noon-6pm Sun.), operated by Willamette Valley Vineyards, which offers wine-tasting and sales; there are always a few bottles from guest wineries around the valley available to sample along with Willamette Valley Vineyards wines.

More than almost any other winemaker, David Lett of **Eyrie Vineyards** (935 NE 10th St., 503/472-6315, www.eyrievineyards.com, noon-5pm daily) was responsible for shepherding Oregon's fledgling wine industry. Eyrie started up in 1966 and produced the Willamette Valley's first pinot noir and chardonnay as well as the first pinot gris in the United States. The winery, set in an industrial area, is a bit hard to find, but well worth the effort to taste some of the most refined of all Oregon wines.

**Yamhill Valley Vineyards** (16250 Oldsville Rd., 503/843-3100, http://yamhill.com, 11am-5pm daily) is set amid an oak grove on a 200-acre estate, southwest of McMinnville off Highway 18, and features a balcony overlooking the vineyard. This winery's first release, a 1983 pinot noir, distinguished itself at a 1985 tasting of French and Oregon vintages held in New York City. Since then, the winery has been a leader in producing high-quality pinot noir as well as riesling and pinot gris.

## Entertainment and Events
### BREWPUBS

A major eating and entertainment anchor on 3rd Street is the **Hotel Oregon** (310 NE Evans St., 503/472-8427 or 800/472-8427, www.mcmenamins.com, 7am-11pm Sun.-Wed., 7am-midnight Thurs., 7am-1am Fri.-Sat., $8-17), McMinnville's outpost of the local McMenamins microbrew chain. In addition to the bar and dining room (characteristically decorated with over-the-top panache), there are many other quirky spaces in which to eat and drink. Stop in at the famous rooftop bar or the cellar bar (usually only open on weekends) when the hotel features live music—sometimes several bands at once in different venues. The pub grub isn't sophisticated (burgers, pizza, sandwiches), but when accompanied by a pint of McMenamins ale, it's hard not to enjoy yourself.

Another brewpub is on the east end of downtown in a former rail warehouse. **Golden Valley Brewery** (980 E 4th St., 503/472-2739, www.goldenvalleybrewery.com, 11am-10pm Mon.-Thurs., 11am-11pm Fri.-Sat., 11am-9pm Sun., $9-17) offers beef from the owner's own Angus herd, vegetables from the kitchen garden, and most everything else made in-house. The menu features soup, salads, and sandwiches, and the quality of the food is high; craft brews are also excellent.

### FESTIVALS AND EVENTS

McMinnville's biggest annual event is the mid-May **UFO Festival,** a McMenamins-sponsored event that began as a way to honor a 1950 UFO sighting by two McMinnville residents. Along with guest speakers, expect to see lots of elaborate costumes, a parade, and music.

Oregon's top wine festival is the annual

You'll find good food in McMinnville.

**International Pinot Noir Celebration** (503/472-8964 or 800/775-4762, www.ipnc. org). More than 70 U.S. and international pinot noir producers are on hand for symposia, tastings, and winery tours. More than 50 chefs prepare wine-focused meals, many held at invitation-only winery events. The three-day festival takes place at the end of July on the Linfield College campus in McMinnville. While the cost of registration ($1,295) is prohibitive for all but the most serious oenophiles, tickets to the final tasting can be purchased separately ($125). Register well in advance; this event always sells out.

## Food

For variety and quality, McMinnville has the best and liveliest dining scene in the Willamette Valley wine country, much of it centered on the pleasant, leafy downtown area on 3rd Street. Be aware that many of the top restaurants are closed on Monday.

If you're looking to provision a picnic or pick up some healthy snacks, **Harvest Fresh Grocery** (251 NE 3rd St., 503/472-5740, 8am-8pm Mon.-Fri., 8am-7pm Sat., 10am-7pm Sun.) is a well-stocked natural foods store with a deli and salad bar. Get your coconut macaroon fix at **Red Fox Bakery** (328 NE Evans St., 503/434-5098, http://redfoxbakery.com, 7am-4pm Mon.-Sat.); they also serve good sandwiches and breakfast pastries.

A good spot for breakfast or lunch is **Community Plate** (315 NE 3rd St., 503/687-1902, www.communityplate.com, 7:30am-3:30pm daily, $5-12), which combines old-school diner cooking with an intense commitment to local and sustainable ingredients. Celebrate the local with a filbert butter and jam sandwich. The top spot for breakfast is **Crescent Café** (526 NE 3rd St., 503/435-2655, www.crescentcafeonthird.com, 7am-2pm Mon.-Fri., 8am-2pm Sat.-Sun., $6-12), a busy family-owned restaurant that elevates breakfast favorites to a new level of excellence.

The commitment to local farmers and producers is sharply in focus at chef-owner Eric Bechard's much-lauded restaurant ★ **Thistle** (228 NE Evans St., 503/472-9623, www.thistlerestaurant.com, 5:30pm-close Tues.-Sat., $24-27), where the daily-changing menu features the bounty of farms, pastures, and waters within a 45-mile radius of the restaurant. It's easy to sample a number of dishes on the chalkboard menu. An evening's choice may include gnocchi with fava beans, morels, tomato, and watercress, or salmon with sweet peppers, fennel, and green olives. The wine list is divided between local and French wines.

For decades, ★ **Nick's Italian Cafe** (521 3rd St., 503/434-4471, http://nicksitaliancafe. com, 5pm-9pm Mon.-Sat., $15-28), had the well-deserved reputation as the best restaurant in wine country, with a wine list that was both extensive and distinctive. Now under second-generation ownership and with a new, fresher approach to Italian food, Nick's is better than ever, with house-made pasta such as lasagna with Dungeness crab, wild mushrooms, and pine nuts, and main courses such as calamari, clams, and sea scallops in leek and potato broth.

A top choice for a casual meal is ★ **La Rambla** (238 NE 3rd St., 503/435-2126, www.laramblaonthird.com, 11:30am-2:30pm and 5pm-9 Mon.-Thurs., 11:30am-2:30pm and 5pm-10 Fri., 11:30am-10pm Sat., 11:30am-9pm Sun., tapas $4-16), an excellent Spanish restaurant that invites you to graze through a series of tapas and small plates. Feast on paella (small $19, large $32) or an assortment of traditional Spanish *raciones*. The wood-paneled candlelit dining room is flanked by a long copper bar, a perfect spot for a romantic dinner.

Traditional French provincial cooking is available at **Bistro Maison** (729 NE 3rd St., 503/474-1888, www.bistromaison.com, 11:30am-2pm and 5:30pm-9pm Wed.-Thurs., 11:30am-2pm and 5pm-9pm Fri., 5pm-9pm Sat., noon-7pm Sun., $18-27), a charming farmhouse-like restaurant that serves delicious standards such as coq au vin, duck confit, and steak tartare, plus a selection of specials that match more up-to-date preparations with local ingredients.

## Accommodations

McMinnville has the largest selection of lodging choices in wine country. If the high price of plush inns and B&Bs has you looking for a standard motel, this is the place to go.

For inexpensive lodgings, reserve a room at McMinnville's **Motel 6** (2065 SW Hwy. 99 W., 503/472-9493, $74-95), with an outdoor pool. Step up to the **GuestHouse Vineyard Inn** (2035 S. Hwy. 99W, 503/472-4900, www.guesthouseintl.com, $90-130), a pet-friendly place with breakfast included and an indoor pool and hot tub. Another standard hotel that's a good bet if you're traveling with a dog is the **Comfort Inn** (2520 SE Stratus Ave., 503/472-1700, www.comfortinn.com, $117-155). **Red Lion Inn and Suites** (2535 NE Cumulus Ave., 503/472-1500, www.redlion.com, $74-149) has spacious, well-furnished rooms with an indoor pool.

If you're in McMinnville to enjoy the restaurants and nightlife on 3rd Street, you should stay downtown. McMenamins' **Hotel Oregon** (310 NE Evans St., 503/472-8427 or 800/472-8427, www.mcmenamins.com, $110-190) has the McMenamins spirit of fun, funky art, and good food and drink. Built in 1905, Hotel Oregon has snug, updated guest rooms (some with private baths, most with shared baths, no TVs), and an outdoor rooftop bar, making this a winner for travelers looking for a relaxed good time. If traveling with a group of friends, inquire about the five rooms that share a private interior patio. Pets are permitted in a few of the rooms.

The top lodging in downtown McMinnville is the ★ **3rd Street Flats** (219 NE Cowls St., 503/857-6248, www.thirdstreetflats.com, $200-280 for 2, discounts for week-plus stays), with 11 units in two locations at the center of town. Four are above a historic 1885 bank building, the rest in a converted Odd Fellows Lodge. Each unit is designed by a different local decorator and filled with regional art; all have full kitchens and living rooms, and the larger units have separate dining rooms. The showcase is the corner Retreat flat, with a fireplace and 750 square feet of living space. These highly original units (some sleep up to six) are perfect for cooks, as well as friends traveling together. The folks behind 3rd Street Flats are building Atticus Hotel, a modern luxury hotel, in downtown McMinnville, due to open in summer 2018.

A short drive from McMinnville is the **Youngberg Hill Vineyards and Inn** (10660 SW Youngberg Hill Rd., 503/472-2727, www.youngberghill.com, $199-399), set atop a range of hills carpeted with vineyards. Excellent views take in the Coast Range, Mount Jefferson, Mount Hood, and the Willamette Valley, as seen from the rooms or from the covered decks that surround the inn. The eight rooms are large and nicely furnished; guests are treated to a wine-tasting of estate-grown wines plus a multicourse breakfast.

## DUNDEE

At one time, Dundee was noted mostly for its filberts (known to most of the world as hazelnuts) and the roadside Dundee Nut House.

Now the town is famous for the abundance of wineries in the hills above town. Some of Oregon's top-rated wines are grown in the Dundee Hills American Viticulture Area, but drive around—you'll still see filbert orchards.

No one would characterize Dundee as a charming town, mostly because busy Highway 99W funnels an incredible amount of traffic right through its heart. But with good restaurants and some excellent lodging options, Dundee offers many reasons to pull off the road and explore.

## Wineries

Midway between Newberg and Dundee is **Duck Pond Cellars** (23145 Hwy. 99W, 503/538-3199, www.duckpondcellars.com), which produces wines from both Oregon and Washington grapes. If you're a price-driven wine shopper, note that this is the place to pick up some less expensive wine.

Downtown Dundee may not seem to be much more than an intersection, but look more carefully and you'll see a number of wineries and tasting rooms scattered along the road. A favorite stop is **Dobbs Family Estate** (240 SE 5th St., 503/538-1141, www.dobbsfamilyestate.com), where winemaker Joe Dobbs crafts high-end vintages on the Dobbs Family label and delicious entry-level wines on the Wine by Joe label.

Located in an old farmhouse, the **Argyle Winery** (691 Hwy. 99W, 503/538-8520, www.argylewinery.com) tasting room is the place to sample sparkling wine good enough to have graced President Bill Clinton's White House table (and a certain travel writer's wedding reception). It is the state's leading producer of sparkling wine in the tradition of champagne. At the center of Dundee is the **Ponzi Wine Bar** (100 SW 7th St., 503/554-1500, http://ponziwines.com), where you can taste a selection of wines from Ponzi Vineyards, one of Oregon's oldest and most respected wineries (the actual vineyards are west of Portland). A number of other small wineries are also represented here, and you can order a sandwich or snack to accompany your wine. If you're

growing weary of the subtle and nuanced wines of the Willamette Valley and long for hearty, heavier wines, stop at **Zerba Cellars** (810 Hwy. 99 W., 503/537-9463, www.zerbacellars.com). This tasting room in downtown Dundee is an outpost of the Zerba winery near Walla Walla, Washington, and offers tastings of their Rhône-style wines as well as delicious sangiovese.

Though the tasting room is new (and spectacular), the vineyards at **Winderlea Wine Co.** (8905 NE Worden Hill Rd., 503/554-5900, http://winderlea.com) date from the 1970s and produce some of the region's most compelling wines. **Lange Estate Winery and Vineyards** (18380 NE Buena Vista Dr., 503/538-6476, www.langewinery.com) is an excellent place to try handcrafted pinot noir, chardonnay, or pinot gris. If you want a behind-the-scenes experience, private tours and tastings ($40 pp) are available.

**Sokol Blosser Winery** (5000 Sokol Blosser Lane, 503/864-2282, www.sokolblosser.com), two miles south of Dundee (follow the signs), is another of Oregon's pioneer wineries. Its strikingly beautiful tasting room is perched on top of a hillside planted with grapes. In addition to acclaimed pinot noir, the chardonnay and pinot noir rosé are especially recommended.

On the southern flanks of the Dundee Hills is another clutch of notable vineyards. **Domaine Drouhin** (6750 Breyman Orchards Rd., 503/864-2700, www.domainedrouhin.com/en, 11am-4pm daily) is the Oregon outpost of France's famed Drouhin family, making excellent pinot noirs in the Burgundy style. Multiple-award-winning **Domaine Serene** (6555 NE Hilltop Lane, 503/864-4600, www.domaineserene.com) is one of Oregon's top producers of ultra-premium wines: This is a must-sip for any serious wine lover. The winery's new Club House tasting room is modeled on the owner's château in France.

## Food

One of the wine country's top restaurants, intimate ★ **Tina's** (760 Hwy. 99W,

503/538-8880, www.tinasdundee.com, 5pm-9pm daily, $24-40) is right on the main drag in Dundee; look for a small red structure across from the Dundee fire station. Tina's uses the freshest Oregon ingredients to create simple yet elegant fare like the pan-fried oysters or beef short ribs braised in chocolate-red wine sauce. In what can only be interpreted as a good sign, it is common to see local winemakers hanging out at the tiny bar, sampling vintages from the wide-ranging wine list.

Affiliated with Ponzi Vineyards, **Dundee Bistro** (100-A SW 7th St., 503/554-1650, http://dundeebistro.com, 11:30am-9pm daily, $14-30) is a reliable spot for top-notch but not overly expensive food. The emphasis is on fresh and regional cooking, including delicious pizza, house-made pasta, and main courses such as smoked pork and corn risotto. The wine list is both tempting and reasonably priced.

**Red Hills Provincial Dining** (276 Hwy. 99W, Dundee, 503/538-8224, www.redhillsdining.com, 5pm-9pm Tues.-Sat., 5pm-8pm Sun., $24-32) is a cozy, charm-filled restaurant that uses fresh local ingredients to create award-winning French- and Italian-inspired food.

At the false-fronted **Red Hills Market** (155 SW 7th St., 971/832-8414, www.redhillmarket.com, 7am-8pm daily, $5-14), you can load up a picnic basket with tasty sandwiches, buy local wine and artisanal cheese, or settle in for a delicious, casual meal. Wood-fired pizzas are a menu stronghold, but there's also the veggie-laden breakfast bowl, with bacon, eggs, cheese, and spinach. Upstairs, find a wine-tasting room and a cooking school.

In tiny Dayton, six miles south of Dundee off Highway 18, the ★ **Joel Palmer House** (600 Ferry St., 503/864-2995, www.joelpalmerhouse.com, 4:30pm-9:30pm Tues.-Sat., reservations advised, $20-37) is considered one of Oregon's finest restaurants and historic homes—it's on the Oregon and the National Historic Registers and is top-rated by such publications as *Wine Spectator*. Many dishes include wild mushrooms. Indulge your

The Red Hills Market makes a good lunch stop in Dundee.

passion for mushrooms with the $99 five-course Mushroom Madness dinner (must be ordered by everyone at your table).

## Accommodations

Although it's right in the busy center of Dundee, the 20-room **Inn at Red Hills** (1410 N. Hwy. 99W, 503/538-7666, www.innatredhills.com, $189-259) is a gracious and relaxing place to stay. There is a good restaurant on the main floor and other excellent dining choices within walking distance.

Just up the road from Sokol Blosser, at the crest of the Dundee Hills, **Wine Country Farm Cellars** (6855 Breyman Orchards Rd., 503/864-3446 or 800/261-3446, www.winecountryfarm.com, $170-220) combines wine-growing with homey bed-and-breakfast accommodations. Views stretch from Salem to Mount Jefferson over miles of vineyards. Watch the pinot noir grow, take a hike, get a massage, or ride horseback to neighboring wineries. Guest rooms all have private baths and wireless Internet. While not the last word in upscale luxury, Wine Country Farm is noted for its friendly welcome and relaxed farm-like atmosphere.

The area's top lodging choice is the nine-room ★ **Black Walnut Inn** (9600 NE Worden Hill Rd., 503/429-4114 or 866/429-4114, www.blackwalnut-inn.com, $379-619), a villa-like complex that looks like it's been transported from Tuscany. The rooms are large and comfortable, most with wondrous views across the vineyards to Willamette Valley. Rates include a multicourse breakfast and an afternoon of appetizers and wine-tasting.

The **Dundee Manor** (8380 NE Worden Hill Rd., 888/262-1133 or 503/554-1945, www.dundeemanor.com, $259-279, 2-night minimum) is a gracious B&B set in a large 1908 arts and crafts mansion at the center of 4.5 wooded acres above Dundee. The four guest rooms, all with private baths, have decor based on a different continent, with tip-top furnishings and amenities. The central location puts you in walking distance of seven wineries.

About halfway between Dundee and McMinnville, on the outskirts of Dayton, it's impossible to miss the **Vintages RV Resort** (16205 SE Kreder Rd., 971/267-2130, www.the-vintages.com, $110-125), a campground full of classic Airstreams and other nicely renovated older RVs, all equipped with comfy beds and fine linens as well as an outdoor grill and other basic cooking facilities. Cruiser bikes come with every trailer rental, and it's an easy ride into Dayton or to nearby wineries.

## NEWBERG

Busy Highway 99W runs through the heart of Newberg, and the suburbs to the east are an unattractive sprawl. But Newberg is central to many wineries and home to the luxurious Allison Inn and Spa, one of the most impressive hotels in Oregon.

### Wineries

The old redbrick downtown offers a number of tasting rooms, including the outstanding **Chehalem Vineyards** (106 S. Center St., 503/538-4700, www.chehalemwines.com). Chehalem produces estate pinot noir from three different American viticulture areas, giving you a chance to taste different terroirs side by side. Also good here are rieslings and an unusual gamay-pinot noir blend.

Two miles east of Newberg is another wine country pioneer, **Rex Hill Vineyards** (30835 Hwy. 99W, 503/538-0666 or 800/739-4455,

Stay in a nicely refurbished trailer at Vintages RV Resort, just outside Dayton.

www.rexhill.com), with excellent pinot noir and chardonnay. The tasting room is itself worth a visit; fashioned from an old prune-and nut-drying shed, it now features Persian rugs, antiques, and a stone fireplace, all set in the midst of lovely gardens. Although generally not available for tasting, Rex Hill's popular and reasonably priced **A to Z Wineworks** line is sold here.

Like most Willamette Valley wineries, **Bergström Wines** (18215 NE Calkins Lane, 503/544-0468, www.bergstromwines.com) is a family-run business, crafting pinot noir and chardonnay from the grapes grown in their five vineyards. The tasting room is northwest of town, just south of Bald Peak.

## Food

Defining itself as a "neighborhood kitchen," **Recipe Part Deux** (602 E. 1st St., 503/487-6853, www.recipepartdeux.com, 4pm-9pm Tues.-Sat., $18-29) is a friendly bistro focusing on local and seasonal ingredients prepared with rustic, handmade aplomb.

A quiet block off busy Main Street, the **Painted Lady** (201 S. College St., 503/538-3850, www.thepaintedladyrestaurant.com, 5pm-10pm Wed.-Sun., tasting menu $105) is a highly regarded bastion of multicourse fine dining with a menu featuring the best of local farms. Located in an elegant Victorian home, the restaurant's seasonally changing menu features such delicacies as roasted rabbit roulade with morels or foie gras with apple butter and red-onion jam. In winter, Wednesday evenings are part of the Experimental Dinner Series, where the chefs make one-of-a-kind dinners based on the freshest of produce.

It's worth searching out **Subterra** (1505 Portland Rd., 503/538-6060, www.subterrarestaurant.com, 11:30am-close daily, $21-27), a wine cellar restaurant tucked behind Mike's Pharmacy and underneath the Dark Horse Wine Bar, for dinners ranging from "adult mac and cheese BLT" to seared scallops served on brussels sprout slaw. Of course, local wines are given the spotlight and can be enjoyed with small plates as well as entrées.

The beautifully furnished **Jory Restaurant** (Allison Inn, 2525 Allison Lane, 503/554-2525 or 877/294-2525, www.theallison.com, 6:30am-10:30am, 11:30am-2pm, and 5:30pm-9pm Mon.-Sat., 9am-2pm and 5:30pm-9pm Sun., $37-45) offers sweeping views of wine country plus elegant preparations of hearty regional cuisine. Local and seasonal specialties include salmon, lamb, venison, and wild mushrooms. It's entertaining to sit at the kitchen bar and watch the chefs in action. Or book the Chef's Table in the kitchen itself, where the chef will prepare a special dinner for up to 10 lucky diners. The wine list offers many rare and acclaimed bottles from both Oregon and France.

## Accommodations

If wine country B&Bs aren't your style, the **Best Western Newberg Inn** (2211 Portland Rd., 503/537-3000, www.bestwestern.com, $107-145) offers an indoor pool and hot tub in addition to well-appointed rooms.

The wine country's most opulent place to stay is the ★ **Allison Inn** (2525 Allison Lane, 503/554-2525 or 877/294-2525, www.theallison.com, $420-675), one of the finest hotels in all of Oregon. Set amid five acres of pinot noir vineyards, the Allison is a monumental structure of stone and wood, with sweeping wine-country views from its many terraces and balconies. Each spacious guest room has a gas fireplace, soaking tub, large flat-screen TV, bay window seats, private terrace or balcony, and beautiful furnishings and art, all from local artists. Facilities are top-notch and include Jory Restaurant, a casually elegant dining room with a noted wine list. The lounge features live music on weekend evenings. Perhaps most impressive is the 15,000-square-foot spa and fitness center, with indoor pool, steam room, and sauna. With its Gold LEED certification, the Allison is easy on the earth.

In the midst of 10 acres of gardens and fields, **Le Puy Wine Country Inn** (20300 NE Hwy. 240, 503/554-9528, www.lepuy-inn.com, $265-385, 2-night minimum) offers eight guest suites from a hillside perch above the trees—it's a wonderful place for a walk or bike ride. The name *Champoeg* means "field of roots" in Chinook, referring to the camas coveted by Native Americans, who boiled it to accompany the traditional salmon feast.

This park commemorates the site of the 1843 vote to break free from British and Hudson's Bay Company rule and establish a pro-American provisional government in the Oregon country. At the time, Champoeg was the center of settlement in the Willamette Valley, and the smattering of settlers here were almost exactly evenly split between newly arrived Americans and British and French Canadian former employees of the Hudson's Bay Company.

In addition to a visitors center, the grounds contain several historic buildings, including the Old Butteville Jail (1850) and a one-room schoolhouse. The **Newell Pioneer Village** (503/678-5537, http://newellpioneervillage.com, 11am-3pm Fri.-Sun. Mar.-Oct., $6 adults, $5 seniors, $3 children) centers on a replica of a 1852 house, which showcases Native American artifacts and a collection of inaugural gowns worn by the wives of Oregon governors. Also on the grounds are a historic schoolhouse and jail. The **Pioneer Mothers Memorial Cabin** replicates the dwellings in the Willamette Valley circa 1850. In addition to the historical exhibits, Champoeg features a botanical garden of native plants as well as four miles of hiking and biking trails beginning in the Riverside day-use area and heading to the historic Butteville Store, now an ice cream parlor.

To reach Champoeg State Heritage Area, take I-5's exit 278 and follow a rural route five miles to the park visitors center. The 568-acre park is equidistant from Portland and Salem along the Willamette River.

If you enjoy Champoeg and its mix of history and pastoral scenery, consider touring the **French Prairie Loop**, a 40-mile byway that passes through idyllic farmland and takes in a number of towns founded by the French Canadian traders, such as St. Paul, Donald,

Champoeg State Park has trails along the Willamette River.

Chehalem Valley, three miles northwest of Newberg. Each of the rooms is individually decorated; all have private baths, while some have balconies or patios. The upscale amenities and location in the country make it a romantic getaway.

## CHAMPOEG STATE HERITAGE AREA

Much of Oregon's early history played out on the fertile banks of the Willamette River between present-day Portland and Salem. Settlers made a break from the British Hudson's Bay Company and established an American-style provisional government. Along the banks of the Willamette River, just southeast of Newberg on Highway 219, is **Champoeg** (pronounced sham-POO-ee or sham-POO-eck; 503/678-1251, www.oregonstateparks.org, visitors center 9am-5pm daily, $5 day-use), often touted as the birthplace of Oregon. Far more than just a historic site, Champoeg is a beautiful park with broad meadows dominated by massive oak and Butteville. St. Paul is known for the Fourth of July **St. Paul Rodeo** (www.stpaulrodeo.com), which includes a fireworks display, a barbecue, and an art auction. French Canadian trappers from the Hudson's Bay Company started settling here in the 1820s and 1830s, establishing the first farms and villages in the Willamette Valley. This is an especially popular route for **bicyclists,** as the route is largely flat and traffic is light. Pick up a map and brochure at the Champoeg State Park visitors center.

## Camping

**Champoeg State Heritage Area** (503/678-1251 or 800/452-5687, www.oregonstateparks. org, $19 tents, $28-31 RVs, $42-52 yurts or cabins) has year-round camping and is one of the few campgrounds within easy driving distance (25 miles) of Portland. Add beautiful Willamette River frontage and prime bike-riding on the nearby country roads, and you might consider this the consummate budget alternative to a night in the city or a pricey wine country B&B.

# Salem

The used-car lots and fast-food outlets encountered on the way into Salem (pop. 167,000) contrast with the inspiring murals and displays in the capitol, where it is comforting to be reminded of Oregon's pioneer tradition and legacy of progressive legislation. Downtown Salem has had a bit of a renaissance in recent years; after visiting the capitol, walk a few blocks west past lovely old buildings, shops, and restaurants toward the Willamette River.

## SIGHTS
### ★ State Capitol

If visiting the **State Capitol** (900 NE Court St., 503/986-1388, www.oregonlegislature. gov, 8am-5pm Mon.-Fri., free) strikes you as the kind of excursion best reserved for a first-grade class trip, you're in for a pleasant surprise. The art deco-style capitol building is filled with attractive murals, paintings, and sculptures of seminal events in the state's history. The capitol is located on Court Street between West Summer and East Summer Streets, just north of Willamette University.

Atop the capitol dome is a gold-leafed bronze statue of a bearded ax-wielding pioneer. Massive marble sculptures flank the main entrance—*Covered Wagons* on the west side, *Lewis and Clark Led by Sacagawea* on the east. Maps of the Oregon Trail and the

route of Lewis and Clark are visible on the backs of the statues. The symbolism is sustained after you enter the double glass doors to the rotunda. Your eyes will immediately be drawn to a bronze state seal, eight feet in diameter and set into the floor, which juxtaposes an eagle in flight, a sailing ship, a covered wagon, and forests. The 33 marble steps beyond the cordoned-off emblem lead up to the House and Senate chambers and symbolize Oregon's place as the 33rd state to enter the Union. Four large murals adorning the rose travertine walls of the rotunda illustrate the settlement and growth of Oregon: Robert Gray sailing into the Columbia estuary in 1792; Lewis and Clark at Celilo Falls in 1805; the first European women to cross the continent being welcomed by Dr. John McLoughlin in 1836; and the first wagon train on the Oregon Trail in 1843. The best part of the capitol is the legislative chambers, up the sweeping marble staircases.

Near the ceiling in the Senate and House chambers are friezes depicting an honor roll of people who influenced the growth and settlement of Oregon. Included are President Thomas Jefferson, who sanctioned the Lewis and Clark expedition, and Thomas Condon, native son and naturalist extraordinaire. In both legislative chambers, look for forestry, agricultural, and fishing symbols woven into the carpets; murals about the coming of statehood are behind the speakers' rostrums.

If you don't want to roam independently, free half-hour-long building **tours** (10:30am, 11:30am, 1:30pm, and 2:30pm Mon.-Fri. Jan.-Nov.) are given.

A tower at the top of the capitol building gives a superlative view of the valley and surrounding Cascade peaks, worth the 121-step climb from the fourth floor. Tower tours (10am, 11am, 1pm, and 2pm Mon.-Fri. June-early Sept., closed when the temperature reaches 90°F) are given. Also worth a look is the ongoing exhibit of outstanding Oregon artists in the governor's ceremonial office upstairs. Downstairs is a café where visitors can eavesdrop on legislators and lobbyists. On the west side of the building (Court St. entrance) is an indoor visitors information kiosk.

To get to the Oregon State Capitol from I-5, take exit 253 to Highway 22 west. Take the exit for "Willamette University-State Offices" and follow the signs for "12th Street-State Offices." Turn left onto Court Street.

## Willamette University

**Willamette University** (900 State St., 503/370-6300, www.willamette.edu), just south of the Capitol Mall, is the oldest institution of higher learning west of the Mississippi. It began as the Oregon Institute in 1842, a school that Methodist missionary Jason Lee founded to instill Christian values among the settlers. Over the years, Willamette University has turned out its share of Oregon politicos, including longtime senators Mark Hatfield and Bob Packwood. It also has to be among the prettiest campuses in the nation.

The exceptionally good **Hallie Ford Museum of Art** (700 State St., 503/370-6855, www.willamette.edu, 10am-5pm Tues.-Sat., 1pm-5pm Sun., $6 adults, $4 age 55 and over, $3 educators and students, free to all on Tues.) features Native American baskets and a third-century Buddhist bas-relief from Pakistan. East Asian pieces are also prominent. High-caliber contemporary work is exhibited on a rotating basis.

## Willamette Heritage Center

Just east of Willamette University, a complex of historic buildings along an old millstream make up the **Willamette Heritage Center** (1313 Mill St. SE, 503/585-7012, www.willametteheritage.org, 10am-5pm Mon.-Sat., $8 adults, $7 seniors, $5 students, $4 ages 6-17). Its centerpiece is the reconstructed Thomas Kay Woolen Mill. The oldest frame house in

Families picnic and play in the fountains on the Capitol Mall.

# Salem

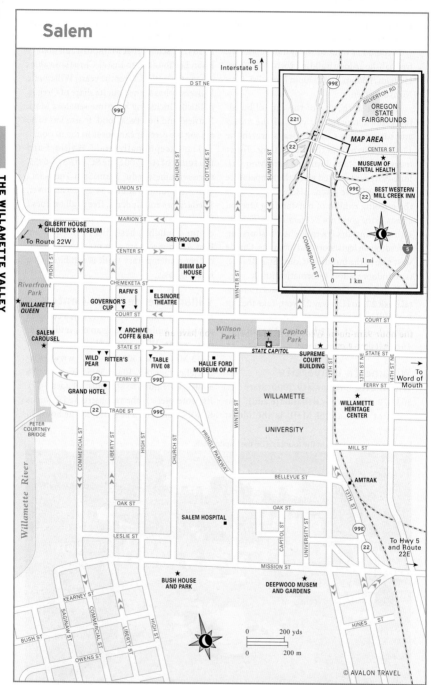

To Interstate 5

D ST NE

99E

**MAP AREA**

99E

SILVERTON RD

OREGON STATE FAIRGROUNDS

221

22

CENTER ST

MUSEUM OF MENTAL HEALTH

99E

22

BEST WESTERN MILL CREEK INN

COMMERCIAL ST

5

0        1 mi
0        1 km

CHURCH ST

COTTAGE ST

SUMMER ST

UNION ST

MARION ST

★ GILBERT HOUSE CHILDREN'S MUSEUM

To Route 22W

CENTER ST

FRONT ST

Riverfront Park

GREYHOUND

BIBIM BAP HOUSE

WINTER ST

CHEMEKETA ST

RAFN'S

GOVERNOR'S CUP

ELSINORE THEATRE

★ WILLAMETTE QUEEN

ARCHIVE COFFE & BAR

COURT ST

Willson Park

Capitol Park

COURT ST

SALEM CAROUSEL ★

STATE ST

STATE CAPITOL

SUPREME COURT BUILDING

STATE ST

STATE ST NE

WILD PEAR

RITTER'S

TABLE FIVE 08

HALLIE FORD MUSEUM OF ART

12TH ST

13TH ST

14TH ST NE

22

99E

FERRY ST

To Word of Mouth

GRAND HOTEL

22

TRADE ST

99E

WILLAMETTE UNIVERSITY

WILLAMETTE HERITAGE CENTER

PETER COURTNEY BRIDGE

COMMERCIAL ST

LIBERTY ST

HIGH ST

CHURCH ST

PRINGLE PARKWAY

WINTER ST

MILL ST

Willamette River

BELLEVUE ST

AMTRAK

OAK ST

OAK ST

CAPITOL ST

UNIVERSITY ST

13TH ST

99E

LESLIE ST

SALEM HOSPITAL

22

To Hwy 5 and Route 22E

MISSION ST

BUSH HOUSE AND PARK ★

★ DEEPWOOD MUSEM AND GARDENS

KEARNEY ST

SAGINAW ST

COMMERCIAL ST

LIBERTY ST

HIGH ST

HINES ST

BUSH ST

OWENS ST

0        200 yds
0        200 m

© AVALON TRAVEL

the Pacific Northwest and water turbines converting fleece into wool fabric are interesting, and the local fiber arts guild uses the building for classes. Several historic homes, including the 1841 Jason Lee House and a Methodist Parsonage, which were part of a mission to the Native Americans, have been moved to this site. Also on the museum campus, you'll find a free-to-visit hand bookbinder, a wool shop, and a gallery.

To get to the museum from I-5, exit at Highway 22, go west on Mission Street for two miles to the 13th Street overpass, turn north onto 12th Street, and go west on Mill Street. If you arrive by rail, Mission Mill is within walking distance of the Amtrak station.

## Deepwood Museum and Gardens

The **Deepwood Museum** (1116 Mission St. SE, 503/363-1825, http://deepwoodmuseum. org, gardens dawn-dusk daily, house tours on the hour 9am-noon Wed.-Mon. May-Sept., noon-3pm Wed.-Sat. Oct.-Apr., $6 adults, $5 seniors, $4 students, $3 ages 6-15) features tours of an elegant 1894 Queen Anne-style home with hand-carved woodwork, gorgeous stained-glass windows, and a well-marked nature trail. Tours are family-friendly and include an optional scavenger hunt. English formal gardens here were designed in the 1930s by the Pacific Northwest's first female-owned landscape architecture firm; the Pringle Creek Trail's native flora and the public greenhouse's tropical plants are also worth visiting. Parking (12th St. and Lee St.) is near the greenhouse.

## Bush House and Park

**Bush House Museum** (600 Mission St. SE, 503/363-4714, http://salemart.org, tours on the hour 1pm-4pm Wed.-Sun. Mar.-mid-Dec., $6 adults, $5 seniors, $4 students, $3 ages 6-15) is located in 90-acre **Bush Pasture Park** off Mission, High, and Bush Streets. This 1877 Victorian with many original furnishings is the former home of pioneer banker and newspaper publisher Asahel Bush, who once wrote

about his competitor, "There's not a brothel in the land that would not have been disgraced by the presence of *The Oregonian.*" Even if you're not big on house tours, the Italian marble fireplaces and elegant walnut-and-mahogany staircase are worth a look. Besides being a sylvan retreat for trail walkers and picnickers, the Bush Pasture Park is home to the **Bush Barn Art Center** (541/581-2228, 10am-5pm Tues.-Fri., noon-5pm Sat.-Sun., free). Next to the Bush House, this center features two galleries with monthly exhibits and a classy gift shop. To get there from I-5, take exit 253 and drive two miles west on Highway 22 (Mission St.). Turn south on High Street and enter the park on Bush Street, one block south of Madison.

## Oregon State Hospital Museum of Mental Health

If you've seen the movie made from Ken Kesey's *One Flew Over the Cuckoo's Nest,* you have an idea of what the **Oregon State Hospital Museum of Mental Health** (2600 Center St. NE, 971/599-1674, http://oshmuseum.org, noon-4pm Tues.-Sat., $5 adults, $4 seniors and students, free under age 10) is like—the movie was filmed in this imposing brick building, which started accepting patients in 1883. Patients were confined to the hospital both voluntarily and by commitment, and their ailments ranged from alcoholism to "women's problems," dementia, and "mania." Exhibits trace the history of the hospital, with placards focusing on individual patients or staff members, and look at conditions that patients were treated for, treatments offered (including straitjackets, lobotomies, ice baths, and sterilization, and those more progressive and humane), life on the ward, and the *Cuckoo's Nest* movie. The most moving display is a memorial a short walk downhill from the museum, where the unclaimed cremains of patients who died at the hospital are housed.

## Riverfront Park

Downtown Salem is bordered to the west by the Willamette River, and **Riverfront Park** is a good place for a stroll, a riverboat excursion, or a ride on the **Salem Carousel** (101 Front St. NE, 503/540-0374, www.salemcarousel.org, 10am-7pm Mon.-Sat., 11am-6pm Sun. June-Sept., 10am-6pm Mon.-Thurs., 10am-7pm Fri.-Sat., 11am-5pm Sun. Oct.-May, $1.50). Although featuring an old-world style, it's no antique—it was built in the late 1990s—and the carousel horses were hand-carved by volunteers.

Along the river near the carousel is the *Willamette Queen* (200 Water St. NE, 503/371-1103, www.willamettequeen.com), a stern-wheeler that cruises the Willamette year-round. Lunch cruises (noon-1pm Wed.-Sun., $28 adults, $18 ages 4-11) are offered, along with less expensive one-hour afternoon cruises (2pm Wed.-Sun., $12 adults, $6 ages 4-11) and allow you to eat at a restaurant downtown, a short walk away. Dinner and Sunday brunch cruises are also offered. This is a good way to get a decent look at the river and, if you're lucky, some of its wildlife.

The **Gilbert House Children's Museum** (116 Marion St. NE, 503/371-3631, www.acgilbert.org, 10am-5pm Sun.-Fri., 10am-7pm Sat., $8 ages 3-59, $6 seniors, $4 children ages 1-2) inspired by A. C. Gilbert, a Salem native whose many inventions included the Gilbert Chemistry Set and the Erector Set, is a cheerful cluster of restored Victorians with hands-on activities incorporating art, music, drama, science, nature, and outdoor play. If you don't have participatory inclinations, you can still enjoy fascinating exhibits like the one dedicated to A. C. Gilbert, whose Olympian athletic exploits and proficiency as a world-class magician were overshadowed by his inventions.

## Enchanted Forest

Seven miles south of Salem off I-5 on exit 248 is the **Enchanted Forest** (8462 Enchanted Way, Turner, 503/371-4242, www.enchantedforest.com, 10am-5pm or 6pm daily Mar. 15-31; 10am-5pm or 6pm Sat.-Sun. Apr., 10am-6pm or 7pm daily May-Labor Day; 10am-5pm or 6pm Sat.-Sun. Sept., $12.50

adults, $11 seniors and ages 3-12, rides $1-4 extra), one man's answer to Walt Disney. In the 1960s, an enterprising Oregonian single-handedly built a false-front Western town, a haunted house, and many more attractions here. You can visit the old woman who lived in the shoe, the seven dwarfs' cottage, or Alice in Wonderland's rabbit hole. It's a little dated, but still popular with kids. Hours vary; check the website if you are going to be visiting 5pm-6pm.

## Gardens

**Schreiner's Iris Gardens** (3625 NE Quinaby Rd., 503/393-3232, www.schreinersgardens.com, 8am-dusk daily) is one of the world's largest iris growers; visit mid-May through the first week of June to take in the peak blossom seasons. Schreiner's is seven miles north of Salem next to I-5.

## Wine and Beer

Some of Oregon's best wine is produced within a few miles of the State Capitol. **St. Innocent Winery** (5657 Zena Rd. NW, 503/378-1526, www.stinnocentwine.com, 11am-5pm daily) is just a few miles from downtown and is known for its good pinot noir and sustainable farming. In the same neighborhood, **Witness Tree Vineyard** (7111 Spring Valley Rd. NW, 503/585-7874, www.witnesstreevineyard.com, 11am-5pm Tues.-Sun. May-Oct.), named for an ancient oak that towers over this lovely vineyard, is a small producer of top-notch pinot noir and chardonnay.

Due west of Salem, you'll find **Firesteed Cellars** (2200 N. Hwy. 99W, Rickreall, 503/623-8683, www.firesteed.com, 11am-5pm daily), with some of the region's most affordable (but still delicious) wines, and **Eola Hills Wine Cellars** (501 S. Hwy. 99W, Rickreall, 503/623-2405, www.eolahillswinery.com, 10am-5pm daily), one of the area's pioneering wineries, which has many vineyard holdings and reasonably priced wine.

A few miles south of town, just off I-5, **Willamette Valley Vineyards** (8800 Enchanted Way SE, Turner, 503/588-9463 or 800/344-9463, www.wvv.com, 11am-6pm Sat.-Wed., 11am-8pm Thurs.-Fri.) is one of the state's largest wineries, with great views and a classy tasting room. Free tours (2pm daily) are given, and by-appointment private tours ($20) include a private tasting and cheese tray.

South of Salem, about seven miles southeast of the town of Independence, thoughts turn to beer. Stop by **Rogue Farms Hopyard** (3590 Wigrich Rd., Independence, 503/838-9813, www.rogue.com, 11am-9pm daily) to watch the hops grow, taste beer, and grab a meal made from farm crops. Seven varieties of hops, as well as pumpkins and other crops, grow here by the Willamette River. Farm tours are offered by request; it's best to call ahead to make sure someone is available to guide you.

## SPORTS AND RECREATION
### Bicycling

Although Salem is still developing its cycling infrastructure, there are more and more bike lanes and some fun places to ride away from traffic. The best news is the trail through Riverfront Park and over the no-car Peter Courtney Bridge to **Minto-Brown Island Park** (2200 Minto Island Rd. SE), a large natural park with 29 miles of interconnected trails through wooded and more open areas with good birding and an off-leash dog area. (You can also drive to Minto-Brown, but it's more fun to bike.) Another bridge from Riverfront Park, the **Union Street Railroad Bicycle and Pedestrian Bridge** crosses the Willamette River to link Riverfront Park and the downtown area with Wallace Marine Park on the west side of the river.

## ENTERTAINMENT AND EVENTS

Salem's recreational mix belies its reputation for being a town dedicated to legislation and little else. The **Elsinore Theatre** (170 High St. SE, 503/375-3574, www.elsinoretheatre.com) is a nicely restored vintage theater and downtown cultural venue that features music and dance performances and classic films as well as live theater. Other local venues include the L. B. Day Amphitheater at the fairgrounds, which hosts big-name acts; brewpubs featuring live music; and Salem Riverfront Park, which hosts summertime concerts.

Five miles west of downtown, the **Pentacle Theatre** (324 52nd Ave. NW, 503/364-7121, www.pentacletheatre.org) hosts an award-winning eight-play season.

The Peter Courtney Bridge leads pedestrians and cyclists from Riverfront Park to Minto-Brown Island Park.

The **Salem Art Association** (600 Mission St., 503/581-2228, http://salemart.org) puts on the mid-July **Salem Art Fair and Festival,** with 200 artists, performing arts, food, children's activities, a five-kilometer run, an Oregon authors table, wine and cheese tasting, and art technique demonstrations.

The **Oregon State Fair** (2330 NE 17th St., 971/701-6573, www.oregonstatefair.org. $8 adults, $6 ages 6-12, $1 over age 64, free under age 5, parking $5, cash only) is an annual celebration held in Salem during the 12 days prior to Labor Day. Here you can admire prize-winning cattle, sheep, quilts, and marijuana plants; enjoy carnival rides; watch dogs jump from a dock; get your tongue pierced; or attend a concert. The best way to get here from I-5 is via exits 253 or 258; signs point the way. Carnival rides are expensive; concerts are usually free with admission but cost $20 and up for reserved seats.

## ACCOMMODATIONS

Salem's lodgings are largely mid-range chain hotels clustered near I-5. The choice spot to stay is the downtown ★ **Grand Hotel** (201 Liberty St. SE, 503/540-7800, http://grand-hotelsalem.com, $179-199), an elegant hotel and conference center with large, nicely furnished guest rooms, a good restaurant, and proximity to the capitol and downtown restaurants.

A good bet that's close to the freeway on the south side of town is the **Best Western Mill Creek Inn** (3125 Ryan Dr. SE, 503/585-3332, www.bestwestern.com/millcreekinn, $179-225), with large rooms and a pool and hot tub, plus a free shuttle service to the Salem Airport and Amtrak station as well as included breakfast at a nearby Denny's. Take the Mission Street exit (exit 253) from I-5.

If you don't mind staying a little north of town, the **Hopewell House B&B** (22350 Hopewell Rd. NW, 503/868-7848, www. hopewellbb.com, $149-169, with breakfast $179-199) is a good place to relax in a newer B&B; cottages include kitchens and hot tubs in a rural setting.

Don't eat too many corn dogs before boarding the rides at the Oregon State Fair.

## FOOD

Downtown Salem is looking good these days, and its restaurants are better than ever.

### Classic American

★ **Word of Mouth** (140 17th St. NE, 503/930-4285, www.wordofsalem.com, 7am-3pm Wed.-Sun., $8-14), located in an old house east of the capitol and Willamette University, is known for its delicious breakfasts, where corned beef hash is the signature dish and the crème brûlée french toast a local favorite.

An extremely popular downtown spot is **Wild Pear** (372 State St., 503/378-7515, www. wildpearcatering.com, 10:30am-6:30pm Mon.-Sat., $9-16), a lunchtime restaurant with a good selection of sandwiches and salads. Lunches are large, but you might still consider adding an order of white-truffle sweet potato fries with mustard aioli.

Stop in at **Ritter's** (102 Liberty St. NE, 503/339-7928, www.ritterseatery.com, 8am-8pm Mon.-Wed., 8am-10pm Thurs.-Sat.,

$7-15) for breakfast or a casual lunch or dinner. The brother-and-sister Ritters take advantage of the excellent Willamette Valley produce, cheese, and wine. The pastrami sandwich on marbled rye is a standout.

**Rafns'** (479 Court St. NE, 503/580-2936, www.rafns.com, 5pm-9pm Tues.-Sat., $22-32) celebrates its ties to local farmers, serving seasonal food and local wines. Although the decor is unfussy, Rafns' is a good bet for a special dinner, with tasty options for vegetarians and vegans. Omnivores may choose the *caldeirada,* a flavorful Portuguese seafood stew.

**Table Five 08** (508 State St., 503/581-5508, http://tablefive08.com, 11am-10pm Mon.-Thurs., 11am-11pm Fri., 4pm-11pm Sat., $11-30) is a good pick for a slightly more formal, though far from stuffy, lunch or dinner. Try the halibut with charred corn and bacon for a special summertime treat. Vegetarians and vegans have many choices, including roasted eggplant with smoked farro. If you're not up for a big meal, stop in for happy hour or small plates at the bar.

## Asian

**Bibim Bap House** (635 Chemeketa St. NE, 503/585-1530, www.happybibimbaphouse.com, 11am-9pm Mon.-Sat., $10-17) serves traditional Korean rice bowls topped with veggies, spicy *gochujang* chili pepper paste, and a fried egg and meat. The menu includes Chinese-style dishes and sushi, but go for the Korean dishes.

## Mexican

Among Salem's many Mexican restaurants, a local favorite is **Hacienda Real** (3690 Commercial St. SE, 503/540-5537, www.lahaciendarealoregon.com, noon-10pm Tues.-Thurs., 11am-11pm Fri.-Mon., $10-23), known for homemade tortillas and Jalisco-style food. This location is south of downtown; there are a couple of other locations around town.

## Coffee

The downtown **Governor's Cup** (471 Court St. NE, 503/581-9675, www.thegovcup.com, 6am-11pm Mon.-Thurs., 6am-midnight Fri., 7am-midnight Sat., 7am-11pm Sun.) is a friendly coffee shop that attracts everybody from high school kids to retirees; it turns into a bar in the evening. Friday nights bring live music.

Salem's hip hang out at the **Archive Coffee and Bar** (102 Liberty St. NE, www.archivecoffeeandbar.com, 7am-midnight daily). During the day, order coffee or "coffee cocktails" (such as espresso with orgeat and black walnut bitters). In the evening, limited food service ($3-15) and boozy cocktail offerings ramp up.

## INFORMATION

The **Travel Salem Visitor Information Center** (181 High St. NE, 503/581-4325 or 800/874-7012, www.travelsalem.com, 9am-5pm Mon.-Fri., 10am-4pm Sat.) is downtown.

The Salem *Statesman Journal* (www.statesmanjournal.com) is sold throughout the Willamette Valley, central coast, and central Oregon. The newspaper's Weekend section features entertainment listings and reviews every Friday covering the week to come. Although these listings focus on Salem, considerable attention is also given to events throughout the Willamette Valley, central Oregon, and the coast.

## GETTING THERE AND AROUND

Salem's State, Court, and Center Streets run east-west; Commercial and Liberty Streets run north-south, as do numbered streets. There are a profusion of one-way streets and thoroughfares that end abruptly. One point of reference is that Commercial Street runs north-south along the Willamette River on the western edge of town.

Salem provides a lot of ways to get in and out of town. **Greyhound** (450 NE Church St., 503/362-2428) runs about five buses a day through Salem. The **Amtrak Station** (500 13th St. SE, 503/588-1551) is across from Willamette University and is close to Mission Mill Museum. The **Salem Airport**

(SLE, 503/588-6314) is a few miles east of downtown. A shuttle to Portland Airport is run by **Hut Shuttle** (503/364-4444, www. hutshuttle.com, $36 one-way).

Mass-transit bus service in town is run by **Salem Area Mass Transit** (Cherriots, 216 High St., 503/588-2877, www.cherriots. org, $1.60). Terminals are in front of the courthouse. Uber and Lyft both operate in Salem.

# Vicinity of Salem

## SILVERTON

Silverton, located in the foothills of the Cascades about 10 miles east of Salem, is a thriving small town with a major attraction—the Oregon Garden—right out its back door and a lovely waterfall-studded state park just a few miles farther. Don't rush past downtown Silverton; it's worth spending at least a few minutes wandering past or through the antiques shops and checking out the murals on downtown buildings.

The big annual event in Silverton is **Homer Davenport Days** (503/873-5615, http://homerdavenport.com), usually held the first weekend in August, when locals enjoy crafts, food, music, and the spectacle of neighbors racing furniture down Main Street. Davenport was a nationally famous cartoonist in the 1930s and a Silverton favorite son. Most of the action takes place at **Coolidge-McClain Park** (300 Coolidge St.).

### Oregon Garden

The **Oregon Garden** (879 W. Main St., 503/874-8100 or 877/674-2733, www.oregongarden.org, 9am-6pm daily May-Sept., 10am-4pm daily Oct.-Apr., $14 adults, $12 seniors, $11 ages 12-17, $8 ages 5-11) offers 20 different specialty gardens on 80 verdant acres, designed by a dream team of landscape architects with the backing of the state's dynamic nursery industry, among Oregon's most important agricultural products. A lovely hotel and spa make an overnight visit an attractive option.

There are some innovative parts of the gardens, such as the wetlands section, using treated wastewater from Silverton that travels through a series of terraced ponds and wetland plants to a holding tank; from there it is used to irrigate the entire garden. A garden of medicinal plants and a garden with a train running through it are also fun.

An attraction that makes the trip to the gardens worthwhile for architecture buffs is **Gordon House** (869 W. Main St., Silverton, 503/874-6006, www.thegordonhouse.org, tours noon, 1pm, and 2pm daily, reservations required, $20 adults, free children with adults), a Frank Lloyd Wright-designed home located within the Oregon Garden complex. The house was moved to its current spot when the original property was sold and the new owners planned to demolish the house and rebuild to suit their own tastes. The modestly sized house is an example of Wright's populist Usonian style and has beautiful western red cedar trim, many built-in drawers and cabinets, and lots of natural light. Terraces bring the outdoors in, and low ceilings in the bedrooms create a sense of retreat. Docents lead tours; this is the only way to see the inside of the house.

### Food and Accommodations

A perfect spot for breakfast or lunch is **Gather** (200 E. Main St., 503/874-4888, http://gather.cafe, 8am-3pm daily, $9-13), a friendly up-to-date diner with fantastic omelets, cinnamon roll pancakes, and a breakfast sandwich worth getting up early for. Downtown Silverton's ★ **Silver Grille** (206 E. Main St., 503/873-8000, www.silvergrille. com, 5pm-9:30pm Wed.-Sun., $16-29) has a big reputation among locals in the greater Salem area as *the* restaurant for casual fine

# Willamette Bird Sanctuaries

The federal government established several bird sanctuaries between Salem and Eugene in the mid-1960s because of the encroachment of urbanization and agriculture on the winter habitat of the dusky Canada goose, which now comes to **Baskett Slough National Wildlife Refuge** (NWR) west of Salem, **Ankeny NWR** southwest of Salem, and **Finley NWR** south of Corvallis each October after summering in Alaska's Copper River Delta. Forest, cropland, and riparian environments attract hummingbirds, swans, geese, sandhill cranes, ducks, egrets, herons, plovers, sandpipers, hawks and other raptors, wrens, woodpeckers, and dozens of other avian species. Migrating waterfowl begin showing up in the Willamette Valley in mid-October. By mid-March, large numbers of Canada geese, tundra swans, and a variety of ducks descend on the refuge. Visit the Portland Audubon website (http://audubonportland.org) or the refuge websites (www.fws.gov) for information on birds and wildlife; serious birders can download the eBird app or visit http://ebird.org for the most detailed info.

Some refuge trails are closed in winter. A hike that can be enjoyed any time of year is Finley NWR's one-mile **Woodpecker Loop.** Forests of oak and Douglas fir as well as a mixed deciduous grove combine with marshes to provide a wide range of habitats. Look for the pileated woodpeckers in the deciduous forest. Take Highway 99W from Corvallis to Refuge Road, and look for the footpath on the right after driving three miles.

Ankeny NWR is located 12 miles south of Salem off I-5's exit 243, and Baskett Slough NWR is northwest of Rickreall on Highway 22. Visit fall through spring for the best chance to see ducks, geese, swans, and raptors.

dining, where local produce and wines create a seasonal Willamette Valley cuisine that's both innovative and classic.

The ★ **Oregon Garden Resort** (895 W. Main St., 503/874-2500, www.oregongarden-resort.com, $160-200) is a great base for exploring this part of the Willamette Valley. The resort includes a restaurant, a lounge, and a spa; small six-unit buildings tucked behind the main lodge house the guest rooms, decorated in a way that's pretty and upscale but not too designer-slick, with private patios or balconies and gas fireplaces; some are pet-friendly. Many packages and deals are offered; during the off-season, this can be an affordable getaway.

In town, the **Silverton Inn and Suites** (310 N. Water St., 503/873-1000, www.silvertoninnandsuites.com, $119-199), a once-lackluster motel, has been transformed into a stylish suite hotel with kitchenettes in many guest rooms. Another good option in the heart of Silverton is the **Birdwood Inn B&B** (511 S. Water St., 503/873-3247, www.birdwoodbandb.com, $100-125, no breakfast),

with two bedrooms that have private baths and a separate cottage. The gardens at the Birdwood are a special delight.

## MOUNT ANGEL

Mount Angel's location an hour south of Portland makes it an excellent day trip. Take exit 272 for "Woodburn" off I-5 and follow the blue "Silver Falls" tour route signs. If you're approaching the Mount Angel Abbey from Salem off I-5, take the exit for "Chemawa" and follow the signs.

### ★ Mount Angel Abbey

Four miles northwest of Silverton off Highway 214 and high above the rest of the Willamette Valley is **Mount Angel Abbey** (1 Abbey Dr., Benedict, 503/845-3345, www.mountangelabbey.org). The abbey is perched above the faux-Bavarian town of Mount Angel; as you drive there you'll pass the neo-Gothic St. Mary's Church, which is staffed by abbey monks.

The Benedictine abbey sits on a 300-foot hill overlooking cropland and Cascade vistas. From the bluff, look northward to Mount

Hood, Mount St. Helens, Mount Adams, and, according to local monks, on clear days you can see Mount Rainier. The abbey **library,** designed by the famous Finnish architect Alvar Aalto, is an architectural highlight, with beautiful light and modern lines. The texts, especially those housed in the Rare Book Room, are pretty amazing. Also worth checking out are the display cases in the lobby; the exhibits are invariably interesting.

While at Mount Angel Abbey, visit its eccentric **museum** (9am-5pm Tues.-Sun., free), tucked in a basement to the side of the main church (get a map from the librarian). Displays include religious artifacts such as a crown of thorns, a world-class hairball, and a huge collection of taxidermy, including an eight-legged calf.

The abbey's late-July **Bach Festival** features professional musicians in an idyllic setting; call for tickets months in advance (503/845-3064).

Meditative retreats can be arranged at the abbey's **retreat house** (503/845-3025, www.mountangelabbey.org, $84 s, includes meals). Arrival days are Monday-Saturday. Although the accommodations are ascetic, the peace of the surroundings and the beauty of the monks' rituals deepen personal reflections.

## Wooden Shoe Bulb Company

Plant nurseries abound in the area. A visit to the **Wooden Shoe Tulip Farm** (33814 S. Meridian Rd., Woodburn, 541/634-2243, www.woodenshoe.com, $5 pp or $20 per car Sat.-Sun. during the tulip festival) in late March through May will colorfully illustrate Oregon's rites of spring. Take I-5's exit 271 and follow Highway 214 east. It will become Highway 211 to Molalla; turn right at the flashing yellow light onto Meridian Road and go two miles to the tulip fields. Afterward, you can head south through the town of Monitor and reach Mount Angel via a delightful rural route.

## Recreation and Events

**Bicyclists** relish the foothills and farmland around Mount Angel. Lowland hop fields and filbert orchards give way to Christmas tree farms in the hills. This region is known as well for its crop of red fescue, a type of grass seed grown almost nowhere outside the northern Willamette Valley.

### Events

The town of Mount Angel's holds a big **Oktoberfest** (541/845-9440) in mid-September, when folks flock here to enjoy the

Mount Angel Abbey is perched on a hill above the Willamette Valley.

North Falls is one of the most impressive of the 10 waterfalls at Silver Falls State Park.

*Weingarten,* the beer garden, the oompah-pah of traditional German music, art displays, yodeling, and street dancing amid beautiful surroundings. The biggest attraction of all, however, is the food: stuffed cabbage leaves, strudels, and an array of sausages.

## ★ SILVER FALLS STATE PARK

With 10 major waterfalls, nearly 30 miles of trails, and over 9,000 acres of woodlands (much of it temperate rainforest), **Silver Falls State Park** (22024 Silver Falls Hwy., Sublimity, 26 miles east of Salem, 503/873-8681, ext. 31, www.oregonstateparks.org, $5 day-use) was considered for national park status in the 1920s, but was rejected because parts of the land had been clear-cut. Much of the park's infrastructure was created by the Civilian Conservation Corps (CCC) during the 1930s using the rustic stone and log construction typical of national parks. Visit the South Falls Lodge, which now houses

interpretive displays and a café; nearby, find a viewpoint and the trailhead to South Falls.

### Hiking

The **Trail of Ten Falls** is a seven-mile loop linking the falls; the canyon half of the loop, where the falls are, is more interesting and has a few steep sections. The highlights are 177-foot **South Falls** and 136-foot **North Falls;** in both cases, trails run behind the falls. The rim half of the trail is easy but not so scenic; leashed dogs are allowed on this section, but not on the canyon section. Bikers and equestrians have their own specially designated trails.

If you don't want to hike the whole loop, a shorter loop starts at the North Falls parking area. North Falls itself is just a short (but steep) hike from the parking area; South Falls is easily reached from the large parking area at South Falls Lodge, a couple of miles south of the North Falls parking lot.

### Camping

**Silver Falls State Park's campground** (22024 Silver Falls Hwy., Sublimity, 503/873-8681, www.oregonstateparks.org, www.reserveamerica.com, $19-28 campsites, $41-51 cabins) is in a wooded setting, with relatively private sites separated into tent and RV loops. Large groups (up to 75 people) can rent dormitory-style bunkhouses, called "ranches" ($200, extra fees for more than 25 guests). Tent sites are open May-October; an RV campground loop and one of the "ranches" are open year-round. In addition to hiking, swimming, and biking, there are stables near the park's entrance and a horse camp.

## OPAL CREEK

The old-growth forests and emerald pools of Opal Creek, which includes a grove of 1,000-year-old 250-foot red cedar, has been called the most intact low-elevation old-growth ecosystem on the West Coast.

To reach Opal Creek from I-5, take Highway 22 for 22 miles east to Mehama. At a flashing yellow light, turn left off Highway

22 onto North Fork Road and continue 20 miles (it becomes gravel Forest Rd. 2209) and veer left, uphill, at the Y intersection. About six miles past the "Willamette National Forest" sign, a locked gate will bar your car from proceeding farther down Forest Road 2209. Park and follow the trail to a large wooden map displaying various hiking options. Dogs must be on leashes. (Before you get to the locked gate, there's a turn-off for **Three Pools,** a lovely and extremely crowded swimming hole.)

While old-growth trees abound not far from the Opal Creek parking lot, cross over to the south side of the North Fork of the Little Santiam River (indicated by trailside signs). Here you can take in the placid Opal Pool, a small aquamarine catch-basin at the base of a cascade that cuts through limestone. Located about 3.5 miles from the parking lot over gently rolling terrain, Opal Pool is the perfect day-hike destination.

The **Opal Creek Ancient Forest Center** (503/892-2782, www.opalcreek.org) is an environmental education center (broadly defined, including a workshop on forest mixology) three miles east of the trailhead with a few cabins for rent ($225-375; bring your own linens; no dogs; access is on foot only) and meals (dinner $18 adults, $9 children). A Bureau of Land Management campground, **Elkhorn Valley** (503/897-2406, www.blm. gov/or, mid-May-Labor Day, $14) is a good place to camp and stage a day trip to Opal Creek. To reach the campground, drive 24 miles east from Salem on Highway 22 and turn north on the North Fork Road. Continue 8.5 miles to the campground.

## DETROIT LAKE

It's a Salem tradition to take to the hills via Highway 22 along the North Santiam River to enjoy the fishing and camping at Detroit Lake. This large and busy 400-foot-deep reservoir is known for its boating, waterskiing, swimming, and fishing for rainbow trout, landlocked chinook, and kokanee. Boat rentals are available at the marina. Because the reservoir was built for water storage, during drought years it can be drawn down enough to make recreation unappealing.

### Camping

Although most Detroit Lake campers stay at the amenity-rich but busy **Detroit Lake State Recreation Area** (503/854-3346, www.oregonstateparks.org, www.reserveamerica.com, $19-29) on the lake's north shore, the remoter south-shore U.S. Forest Service campground at **Cove Creek** (Blowout Rd., 503/854-3366, reservations www.recreation.gov, $22) is more peaceful, though with flush toilets and showers, still not a wilderness experience.

## BREITENBUSH HOT SPRINGS

**Breitenbush Hot Springs Retreat and Conference Center** (503/854-3320, www. breitenbush.com) offers natural hot springs, trails forested with old growth, and a wide variety of programs aimed at healing body, mind, and spirit. Music, storytelling, yoga, and vegetarian meals are also part of the Breitenbush experience. Sweat lodge ceremonies are offered once a month. Although many visitors come to Breitenbush to take part in an organized workshop, it's also possible to come on your own for a personal retreat. Know before you go that most hot springs bathers go naked and that cell phones do not work here.

Cabins ($93-121 pp shared bath, $113-142 pp private bath) are Spartan but have electricity and heat. Bring your own linens or rent them ($18). Rates include three vegetarian meals daily and use of the facilities and waters. Single visitors may sometimes be assigned a cabin-mate unless they specify otherwise and pay extra. Large tents on platforms (June-Oct., $82-90) are also available, or you can camp in your own tent ($67-75 pp). Day use of the hot springs and other facilities ($18-32) is possible; it's essential to call and reserve in advance, even if you're just coming for a daytime visit. Individual all-you-can-eat lunches or dinners ($15) are available for daytime visitors. Bring your own caffeine if that's something you require; do not bring alcoholic beverages or marijuana.

On-site you'll find the Spotted Owl Trail near the entrance of the Breitenbush parking lot. Near Breitenbush are the remarkable natural areas Breitenbush Gorge, Opal Creek, Bull of the Woods, and Jefferson Park; for more information, contact the Detroit Ranger Station (503/854-3366).

To get to Breitenbush from Salem, take Highway 22 to the town of Detroit. Turn at the lone gas station onto Forest Road 46 and drive 10 miles, then take a right over the bridge across Breitenbush River. Follow the signs, taking every left turn after the bridge, to the Breitenbush parking lot.

On the way up Forest Road 46 from Detroit to Breitenbush Hot Springs, you will pass a number of U.S. Forest Service campgrounds. **Breitenbush Campground** (10 miles northeast of Detroit, 503/854-3366, www. fs.usda.gov, www.recreation.gov, May-Sept., $16) is less than two miles from Breitenbush Resort and is a good spot for campers who want to visit the hot springs without staying at the resort itself. Nearby, the Breitenbush River has good fishing.

## OLALLIE LAKE

To the east of Breitenbush, Olallie Lake is one of the nicest camping and hiking getaways in the area, with superb views of Mount Jefferson from the lake. The lake has a small **resort** (www.olallielakeresort.com) that offers cabins and yurts of varying sizes (usually July-Sept., $65-110) with woodstoves and outhouses and rents rowboats and canoes. Camp at the adjacent **Paul Dennis campground** ($15). Olallie Lake is along the Pacific Crest Trail, and there are hiking trails galore, many leading to other small lakes. In the early summer, wildflowers are an attraction; late in summer, this is a great place to pick wild huckleberries. The season up here is short—snows usually keep the resort closed until July.

From the Detroit area, head north and east on Forest Road 46, then turn right on rough gravel Forest Road 4220 and follow it 13 miles to the lake.

## MOUNT JEFFERSON

Mount Jefferson, Oregon's second-highest peak at 10,495 feet, dominates the Oregon Cascades horizon between Mount Hood to the north and the Three Sisters to the south—though, unlike Mount Hood, Mount Jefferson is rarely visible from the west.

Mount Jefferson is 12 miles east of Detroit. Take Highway 22 and turn left, following Forest Road 2243 (Whitewater Creek Rd.) 7.5 miles to the Whitewater Creek trailhead. From there, it's an easy 4.5-mile hike to **Jefferson Park.** This northern base of the mountain features many lakes and, in early summer, wildflowers. The alpine meadows are full of purple and yellow lupine and red Indian paintbrush in July.

Above Jefferson Park, the ascent of the dormant volcano's cone is a precarious endeavor and should only be attempted by truly experienced climbers. You'll reach the bottom of Whitewater Glacier at 7,000 feet. Thereafter, climbing routes steepen to 45 degrees, and snow and rock ridges crumble when touched. Near the top, the rocks aren't solid enough to allow the use of ropes; going down is even more dangerous than going up. Even if you head up the more sedate south face, you can expect difficulties due to the instability of the final 400 feet of rock on the pinnacle.

The mosquitoes in Jefferson Park are bloodthirsty, so bring insect repellent in summer. On occasion the area is so crowded with day-use visitors and folks trekking the nearby Pacific Crest Trail that Jefferson Park seems more like a city park than a mountain wilderness. The sight of Mount Jefferson in alpenglow at sunset or shrouded in moonlight will make you forget the intrusions of humans and insects alike.

# Corvallis

The name *Corvallis* refers to the city's pastoral setting in "the heart of the valley." But just as much as its physical setting, it's the culture of Oregon State University that defines the town.

Although Corvallis isn't a huge tourism destination, its beauty, tranquility, and central location make it a good base from which to explore the bird sanctuaries, the Coast Range, and nearby wineries and farmland. It's an especially appealing base for bike rides. Streets have wide bike lanes, and scenic routes for cyclists parallel the Willamette and Marys Rivers.

## SIGHTS

The beautiful parklike campus of **Oregon State University** (OSU, follow signs to Jefferson Ave. or Monroe Ave., 541/737-1000, http://oregonstate.edu), an 1868 land grant institution, is a major hub of activity in town and a good place to take a walk or attend a university-sponsored lecture or musical event. But even more intriguing is the thriving turn-of-the-20th-century downtown, filled with locally owned shops, pubs and restaurants, and a splendid path along the Willamette River. A number of restaurants face onto a riverfront park. The 1888 Benton County Courthouse, the oldest still operating in the state, dominates the downtown skyline.

A good place to start a downtown walk is around 2nd Street and Jackson Avenue. The **Historic Homes Trolley Tour** (541/757-1544, 1pm Sat. July-Aug., call to reserve, $5) leaves from this corner. This corner is also the hub of Wednesday- and Saturday-morning farmers markets.

## WINERIES

Located less than 10 miles southwest of Corvallis off Highway 99W is **Tyee Wine Cellars** (26335 Greenberry Rd., Corvallis, 541/753-8754, www.tyeewine.com, noon-5pm Fri.-Sun. Apr.-Dec.). Pinot gris, pinot noir, and gewürztraminer are featured. After wine-tasting, you can enjoy a picnic on the grounds of this historic farm site or walk a 1.5-mile loop to beaver ponds. Several other wineries are also located in the area and are easy to visit by bike from Corvallis; see http://heartofwillamette.com.

Corvallis, located in a rich agricultural area, has a good farmers market.

Peavy Arboretum, just north of Corvallis, is a good place for a walk in the woods.

Snow, an infrequent visitor to most Coast Range slopes, can often be found here in winter, even at lower elevations. In fact, the road is sometimes impassable without tire chains from late fall until early spring. A Sno-Park permit is required for day use November 15 to April 15.

Closer to town, the **McDonald Experimental Forest,** which includes **Peavy Arboretum** (541/737-6702, 8692 NW Peavy Arboretum Rd.), eight miles north of Corvallis on Highway 99W, serves primarily as a research forest for the university's Forestry Department. The arboretum's Woodland Trail is a good place to start; bikes and horses are also permitted on logging roads and trails in the areas of the McDonald Forest outside the arboretum boundaries. This is a good place to come when your dog needs a run.

Find good info about local trails at http://therighttrail.org or pick up a trail map ($7) at local stores.

## SPORTS AND RECREATION
### Hiking

**Marys Peak** (541/750-7000, www. fs.usda. gov, parking $5) is 16 miles southwest of Corvallis. Follow Highway 34 west to the road's Coast Range Summit (1,230 feet); turn north onto Forest Road 30 and drive 10 miles to a parking area. A 0.7-mile hike across the meadow leads to the 4,097-foot summit, offering perspectives on Mounts Hood and Jefferson, the Three Sisters to the east, and the Pacific Ocean to the west.

A biome unique to the Coast Range exists up here, with such flora as alpine phlox, bear grass, Pacific iris, Indian paintbrush, and the blue-green noble fir. Exceptionally large species of this fragrant tree grow on the Meadowedge Trail, which connects to a primitive campground (16 sites, no water, May-Oct., $10), also accessible from the road, two miles below the summit. It's part of a nine-mile network of trails around the upper slopes of the mountain.

### Biking

Corvallis has an excellent network of bike paths and on-street bike lanes. It's easy to bike anywhere in town in a few minutes, and the wide path along the downtown riverfront is a good place for kids or nervous cyclists to start out. More confident cyclists can begin in downtown Corvallis and ride eight miles on back roads to Philomath. Low-traffic back roads also lead to Alsea Falls, 30 miles southwest of town, where several mountain bike trails exist, and more are being developed.

Mountain bikers can pedal to the west edge of town to Bald Hill Park, where six miles of trails offer a few routes to the summit. The McDonald Forest, a few miles north and west of town, offers many miles of old logging roads and trails open to bikes; Lewisburg Saddle is a popular destination here.

Rent a bike or stop in for ride recommendations and a bike map at **Peak Sports** (135 NW 2nd St., 541/754-6444, www.peaksportscorvallis.com).

# Willamette Water Trail

How about seeing the Willamette Valley from the river? An outing on the **Willamette Water Trail** (http://willamettewatertrail.org) can be as simple as an afternoon paddle from Peoria to Corvallis or as involved as a weeklong camping expedition. Be prepared to pull out the binoculars and the camera repeatedly, and to settle into a quiet profound enough to make you forget that I-5 is nearby. In addition to the helpful Willamette Water Trail website, you'll find essential information on access points, campsites, and river hazards in a series of waterproof maps, available on the website.

The vessels of choice for Willamette River paddle trips are canoes and sea kayaks, available for rent at the following locations:

- **Alder Creek** (200 NE Tomahawk Dr., Portland, 503/285-0464, http://aldercreek.com)

- **Portland Kayak Company** (6600 SW Macadam Ave., Portland, 503/459-4050, www.portlandkayak.com)

- **Next Adventure** (704 SE Washington St., Portland, 503/233-0706, http://nextadventure.net)

- **eNRG Kayaking** (1701 Clackamette Dr., Oregon City, 503/772-1122, http://enrgkayaking.com)

- **Peak Sports** (207 NW 2nd St., Corvallis, 541/754-6444, www.peaksportscorvallis.com)

- **Oregon Paddle Sports** (520 Commercial Ave., Eugene, 541/505-9020, www.oregonpaddlesports.com)

- **REI** (locations in Portland, Tualatin, Salem, and Eugene; www.rei.com)

Put in at one of the many parks along the way. Although many paddlers set up their own vehicle

## Spectator Sports

The **OSU Beavers** (www.osubeavers.com) dominate the sports scene in Corvallis. In fact, unless you're a fan, you might want to avoid town if the Beavs are playing the University of Oregon Ducks; these teams have a rowdy rivalry.

## ENTERTAINMENT AND EVENTS

This university town has no shortage of drinking establishments, including six excellent brewpubs in the downtown area. A step up (well, all the way to the rooftop) is **Sky High Brewing** (160 NW Jackson Ave., 541/207-3277, http://skyhighbrewing.com, 11am-11pm Sun.-Wed., 11am-midnight Thurs.-Sat., rooftop from 4pm daily), a family-friendly pub with good food and great views of town and the river.

**Block 15** (300 SW Jefferson Ave., 541/758-2077, http://block15.com, 11am-11pm Sun.-Thurs., 11am-1am Fri.-Sat.), a brewpub with a strong emphasis on doing business sustainably, is a pleasant low-key place to hang out and enjoy hop-forward ales and sour and wild-yeast beers. Its sister pub, **Les Caves** (308 SW 3rd St., 541/286-4471, www.biercaves.com, 4pm-midnight Tues.-Thurs., 4pm-1am Fri., 9am-1am Sat.-Sun.) has a wide range of beers from all over the world and pretty good food (though it seems to be best known for its bier bread pretzels).

The **Majestic Theatre** (115 SW 2nd St., 541/766-6976, www.majestic.org), a restored 1913 vaudeville house, is a lovely place to watch a play or catch a concert. Close by is the excellent **Grassroots Books and Music** (227 SW 2nd St., 541/754-7558, www.grassrootsbookstore.com). The **Corvallis Fall Festival** (541/752-9655, www.corvallisfallfestival.org), a vibrant gathering of artists and craftspeople and a block of food concessions, including an Oregon wine garden, shuttles, if you're renting a canoe or kayak, ask at the rental shop about shuttle services. **River Trail Shuttle** (541/228-4084, www.rivertrailshuttle.com) runs shuttles ($30-130) based in Eugene.

If you decide you want to paddle some portion of the 187 river miles of the Willamette between Eugene and Portland with an outfitter, consider signing up for the mid-August event **Paddle Oregon** (www.paddleoregon.org, $789). Meals, side trips, yoga, and nightly entertainment round out the trip, which is run by Willamette Riverkeeper, a nonprofit organization dedicated to protecting and restoring the river.

Although the Willamette is generally regarded as an easy river to paddle, certain precautions are necessary. Paddlers must be able to read the river for hazards, maneuver in a current, self-rescue if capsized, and dress appropriately to avoid hypothermia. Hone your skills by taking a class from Alder Creek, eNRG Kayaking, Next Adventure, Oregon Paddle Sports, or Portland Kayak Company.

Children 12 and under must wear a personal floatation device. Paddlers should be aware that DUI laws apply on the river.

access point for Willamette Water Trail at Champoeg State Park

takes over Central Park the fourth weekend in September.

## FOOD

A great place to start your day is at **The Beanery** (500 SW 2nd St., 541/753-7442, 6am-8pm Sun.-Thurs. 6am-9pm Fri.-Sat.), a coffee shop that has long been the pulse of this old hippie community. You'll find good coffee, pastries, and live music on weekend evenings. The local favorite breakfast spot is **New Morning Bakery** (219 SW 2nd St., 541/754-0181, 7am-9pm Mon.-Sat., 8am-8pm Sun., breakfast $5-8), with excellent bread and pastries plus fresh-baked quiche and breakfast burritos. Lunch and dinner menus feature soups, salads, sandwiches, and pasta.

The riverfront stretch of downtown is home to several good restaurants. The hottest restaurant in Corvallis for a fine dining experience is ★ **del Alma** (136 SW Washington Ave., 541/753-2222, http://delalmarestaurant.com, 5pm-9:30pm Mon.-Thurs., 5pm-10pm Fri.-Sat., $19-36), serving "New Latin cuisine" inspired by food from Latin America, the Caribbean, and Spain. From barbecued pork tacos to tapas such as *albondigas* and rockfish ceviche, the menu has something to please everyone.

**Big River Restaurant and Bar** (101 N. Jackson St., 541/757-0694, www.bigriverrest.com, 11am-9:30pm Mon.-Thurs., 11am-10:30pm Fri., 10am-2pm and 4pm-10:30pm Sat., 4pm-9pm Sun., $12-22) is a lively, hip restaurant with Pacific Northwest cuisine and a farm-to-table sensibility. Big River also incorporates an on-site bakery and the more casual adjacent **101 Eat & Drink** (www.101atbigriver.com, 4:30pm-10pm Mon.-Thurs., 4:30pm-11pm Fri.-Sat.), with a cocktail bar atmosphere and salads, sandwiches, and pizza.

**Koriander** (215 SW 3rd St., 541/286-4157, 11am-9pm Mon.-Sat., $11-29) is an excellent spot for spicy Asian fusion dishes, most based on Korean cuisine. In addition to typical Korean standards like bibimbap (rice, eggs and vegetables) you'll find pad thai and udon noodle soup, plus locally made gelato.

Near the university, **Bombs Away Cafe** (2527 Monroe St., 541/757-7221, www.bombsawaycafe.com, 11am-midnight Mon.-Fri., 5pm-midnight Sat., $7-13) is a busy restaurant with colorful murals on the walls, frequent live music, and lines of lunchtime hopefuls anxious to sample Mexican-style food made with the freshest ingredients and organic produce. A gluten-free menu is available.

It doesn't get much fresher or more local than lunch at **Gathering Together Farm** (25159 Grange Hall Rd., Philomath, 541/929-4270, www.gatheringtogetherfarm.com, 11am-2pm Tues.-Wed., 11am-2pm and 5:30pm-9pm Thurs.-Fri., 9am-2pm and 5:30pm-9pm Sat., lunch $10, dinner $15-20), an organic farm five miles west of Corvallis. Lunches are the mainstay of this farm kitchen, where nearly everything is made by hand and grown on the farm; during the winter, when produce is harder to come by, it might include a house-made sausage with sauerkraut, potatoes, and carrots.

Nearby Albany has an unexpected outpost of fine dining. ★ **Sybaris Bistro** (442 1st Ave. W., 541/928-8157, http://sybarisbistro.com, 5pm-8pm Tues.-Thurs., 5pm-9pm Fri.-Sat., $18-30) is one of the top restaurants in the state, specializing in creative American cooking featuring the fresh bounty of local farms and waters. An appetizer of cured halibut and potato fritters is served with green tomato relish; pan-roasted pheasant breast is cooked with herbs.

Corvallis also has a **farmers market** (1st St. and Jackson Ave., 9am-1pm Wed. and Sat. mid-Apr.-mid-Nov.), held along the river.

## ACCOMMODATIONS

Hotel rates can vary dramatically in Corvallis, depending on what's going on at the university. Of the older and less expensive lodging options in the city center, the **Rodeway Inn**

**Willamette River** (345 NW 2nd St., 541/752-9601, www.rodewayinn.com, $64-90) is decidedly basic but has a good location downtown and near the river. Pets are permitted. The rooms at the **University Inn** (350 SW 4th St., 541/636-9416, www.universityinncorvallis.com, $61-75) are much nicer than this motor court's faded exterior would indicate, and you're just steps from downtown dining and nightlife.

A prime place to stay downtown along the river is the ★ **Holiday Inn Express** (781 NE 2nd St., 541/752-0800 or 800/315-2621, www.hiexpress.com, $177-200). From here, it's an easy and pleasant walk to downtown riverfront restaurants; get a river-view guest room and perhaps you'll see an eagle flying upriver early in the morning.

The **Hilton Garden Inn** (2500 SW Western Blvd., 541/752-5000 or 800/445-8667, www.hiltongardeninn.com, $195-222) is practically part of the OSU campus; it's located near the Reser football stadium, the Gill Coliseum basketball arena, and the OSU Conference Center. It's a comfortable hotel with good amenities.

If you want to get out into the countryside, consider a farm stay at the **Leaping Lamb** (20368 Honey Grove Rd., Alsea, 541/487-4966 or 877/820-6132, http://leapinglambfarm.com, 2-night minimum weekends, $250), where a private two-bedroom cabin, with cooking facilities and basic breakfast items supplied, is perfect for families; a farmhouse that sleeps four is also available. It's well situated for hikes into the nearby forest or for just communing with farm animals. The farm is on the way to the coast, 17 miles southwest of Philomath, near Alsea on Highway 34.

## Camping

Camping in this part of the Willamette Valley can be delightful, especially in late spring and early autumn. **Marys Peak Campground** (541/750-7000, www.fs.usda.gov, mid-May-Oct., $10) is 19 miles from town, off Highway 34. The final stretch of road to this spot is unsuitable for trailers. RV campers can stay at **Benton Oaks** (110 SW 53rd St., 541/766-6259, $25 tents, summer only; $40 RVs, year-round), immediately adjacent to the county fairgrounds. Reservations are required and rates are higher on OSU football weekends.

## INFORMATION

The **Corvallis Visitor's Information Center** (420 NW 2nd St., 541/757-1544 or 800/334-8118, http://visitcorvallis.com) maintains a good website. To catch up on local events, read the *Corvallis Gazette Times*

(www.gtconnect.com). **KOAC** (550 AM) is the public radio station.

## GETTING THERE AND AROUND

**Greyhound** (153 NW 4th St., 541/757-1797) operates daily with routes north and south. **Lincoln County Transit** (www.co.lincoln. or.us) runs one bus daily between Corvallis and Newport on the coast. **Amtrak** (110 W. 10th St., 541/928-0885) makes a stop in nearby Albany. **Corvallis Transit** (5th St. and Monroe Ave., 541/757-6988, Mon.-Sat., free within Corvallis) is the city bus company.

# Eugene

Oregon's third-largest city and home to the University of Oregon, Eugene (pop. 166,000) belongs on the itinerary of anyone who wants to experience a laid-back Pacific Northwest version of urban sophistication and active pursuits in a beautiful natural setting. The Willamette River curves around the northwest quarter of the community, and from an elevated perch you can see the Coast and Cascade Ranges beckoning you to beach and mountain playgrounds little more than an hour away.

In town, the world-renowned Bach Festival and other big-time cultural events are showcased in the acoustically excellent Hult Center. The University of Oregon campus provides another forum for the best in art and academe, while its Hayward Field track has been the site of the U.S. Olympic Trials several times. Outdoor gatherings such as the Saturday Market and Oregon Country Fair bring the community together for home-grown edibles, arts, and crafts. But it doesn't take an organized festival to draw the townsfolk outside. Even during persistent winter rains, locals can be seen jogging, bicycling, and gardening.

Eugene's labor, environmental, and human services organizations have labored with quiet

effectiveness for several decades, giving the town a distinct lefty touch with worker-owned collectives, a wheelchair-friendly cityscape, preserved ancient forests, and wetlands protected against industrial pollution.

## SIGHTS

Two major areas of interest to visitors are immediately south of the Willamette River. The University of Oregon campus, in Eugene's southeast quadrant, and the downtown (bounded by 5th Ave., 10th Ave., Charnelton St., and High St.) are only a five-minute drive or a two-mile walk from each other. Another excellent place to stroll, run, or cycle with the locals, Alton Baker Park, is just across the river from downtown and the university.

### Skinner Butte

A good place to get oriented in Eugene, visually as well as historically, is **Skinner Butte.** If you look north from almost anywhere downtown, you'll see this landmark. A park fronting the Willamette River is located at the butte's northern base. This riverfront site served as a dock for pioneer sternwheelers and was where founding father Eugene Skinner ran a ferry service for farmers living north of the river. The town tried to become a major shipping port, but the upper Willamette was uncharted and too shallow.

From downtown, head north on High Street, which becomes Cheshire Avenue as it curves to the left. Take a left onto Skinner Butte Loop and follow it to the top. You can also get here by traveling north on Lincoln Street to Skinner Butte Loop or by walking up from the south side, which takes about 15 minutes. The indigenous Kalapuyas people used this promontory for ceremonial dances. On a clear day you can still see the Cascade and Coast Ranges as well as pockets of greenery throughout the city. You can also spot another good reference point in your orientation, **Spencer Butte,** looming above the southern hills five miles away. If you've come equipped with ropes and harnesses, visit the basalt columns in the climbing area on the west face of the butte (near W. 2nd Ave. and Lincoln St.).

The 1888 Queen Anne-style **Shelton McMurphey-Johnson House** (303 Willamette St., 541/484-0808, www.smjhouse. org, 10am-1pm Tues.-Fri., 1pm-4pm Sat.-Sun., $6 adults, $5 students and seniors, $3 under age 13), on the lower south slope of Skinner Butte, is a museum of Victorian-era life and the most eye-catching of some 2,000 designated historic properties in the city.

## Owen Rose Garden

Near the base of Skinner Butte and along the banks of the Willamette, the 400 varieties of roses at the **Owen Rose Garden** (300 N. Jefferson St., 541/682-4800, daily) peak in June and bloom until fall. Along with 4,500 roses and magnolia blossoms in spring, tremendous old cherry and oak trees also command attention. To get here from I-5, take I-105 west and follow the "West Eugene" exit. Turn right at the bottom of the ramp onto Madison Street and follow it north toward the Willamette River. One block to the right is Jefferson Street and the entrance to the rose garden. A more pleasant approach is on foot, via the riverside bike path. From downtown, walk or bike east on 4th Avenue, cut down to the river at the Eugene Water & Electric Board building, and turn left onto the bike path. From the other side of the river, walk behind the Valley River Inn (ask at the front desk for directions) until you get to the footbridge. On the other side of the river, loop back in the direction of the hotel for about 0.5 miles until you arrive at the rose garden.

The Owen Rose Garden is a good place for a quiet stroll.

## Fifth Street Public Market

The past and the present happily coexist a few blocks from the butte's south flank at the **Fifth Street Public Market** (296 E. 5th Ave., www.5stmarket.com), an old-time feed mill converted into an atrium complex. This once-rustic structure houses an impressive collection of specialty stores and restaurants surrounding an open-air courtyard that is a favorite haunt of sun worshippers, people-watchers, and street performers. The market is an excellent spot for meals and snacks, as the complex and adjoining streets offer choices for both casual and fine dining.

## Eugene Saturday Market

For a more freewheeling version of the public market, explore the crafts, food, and street performances at the **Saturday Market** (8th Ave. and Oak St., 541/686-8885, www.eugene-saturdaymarket.org, 10am-5pm Sat. Apr.-mid-Nov.); the good vibes and creative spirit of the community are in ample evidence. The market moves indoors to the **Lane County Fairgrounds** (13th Ave. and Jefferson St.) to become the Holiday Market (Sat.-Sun.) from the weekend before Thanksgiving through Christmas Eve.

The small **farmers market** (9am-3pm Sat. Apr.-mid-Nov., 10am-3pm Tues. May-Oct.) that sets up across 8th Avenue from the crafts area is a good place to get fresh produce.

## Hult Center for the Performing Arts

The **Hult Center for the Performing Arts** (1 Eugene Center, Willamette St. between 6th Ave. and 7th Ave., 541/687-5000, www.hultcenter.org) stands at the center of Eugene and is one of the state's most prominent performing arts centers and worth a look for its aesthetics alone, from the frog and troll statues that greet you at the 6th Avenue entrance to the high-ceilinged interior bedecked with masks.

Hult Center's nine resident companies are showcased beneath interlocking acoustic panels on the domed ceiling and walls of the 2,500-seat **Silva Concert Hall** (which resembles a giant upside-down pastel-colored Easter basket), and the venue is home to the Oregon Bach Festival. The **Jacobs Gallery** exhibits local artwork, providing another feast for the eyes. Even the bath tile is done up in a visually pleasing theatrical motif.

## University of Oregon Campus

From downtown, head a few blocks south to 13th Avenue, then east to the **University of Oregon campus** (visitor information at Oregon Hall, Agate St. and 13th Ave., 541/346-3111, www.uoregon.edu). Car traffic is restricted on 13th Avenue in the heart of the campus; skirt to the edges to find parking lots or on-street metered parking. The campus is bounded by Franklin Boulevard, 11th and 18th Avenues, and Alder and Moss Streets. The university has an enrollment of over 20,000 and beautiful grounds graced by architecturally inviting buildings dating back to the school's creation in the 1870s, as well as 500 varieties of trees. The campus has often been selected by Hollywood to portray the ivy-covered halls of academe, most notably in the comedy *Animal House.*

**Deady Hall,** the oldest building on campus, was built in 1876. Also noteworthy are two museums: the **Jordan Schnitzer Museum of Art** and the **Natural History Museum.** Free **campus tours** are geared toward prospective students (sign up at www.uoregon.edu). If you're a casual visitor, pick up the map or download the campus app and set your own pace, or join a 3.7-mile running tour (8:30am 1st and 3rd Fri. of the month) of the trails surrounding the campus.

Across from the Schnitzer Museum is the **Knight Library.** Many buildings on campus are named for the Knight family, thanks to Nike cofounder Phil Knight's generosity toward his alma mater. Toward the eastern edge of the campus, Agate Street is dominated by **Hayward Field,** which regularly hosts championship meets and Olympic trials. Built in 1919 for football, it has been used by the track program since 1921. The Bowerman Building,

# Eugene

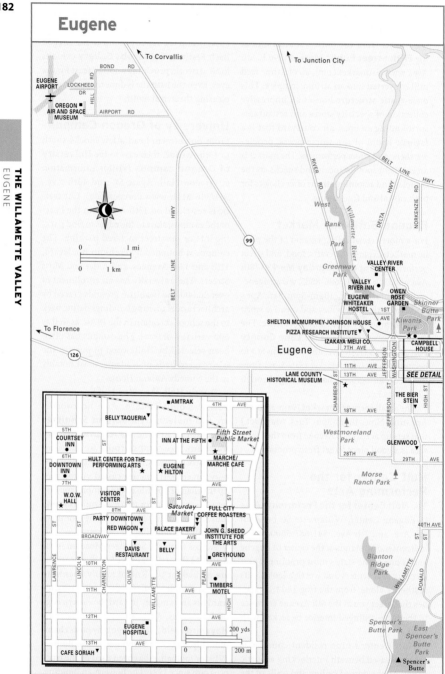

To Corvallis

To Junction City

EUGENE AIRPORT

BOND RD

LOCKHEED DR

HILL RD

OREGON AIR AND SPACE MUSEUM

AIRPORT RD

BELT LINE HWY

RIVER RD

DELTA HWY

NORKENZIE RD

BELT LINE HWY

HWY 99

West Bank Park

Willamette River

Greenway Park

VALLEY RIVER CENTER

VALLEY RIVER INN

EUGENE WHITEAKER HOSTEL

OWEN ROSE GARDEN

1ST AVE

Skinner Butte Park

SHELTON MCMURPHEY-JOHNSON HOUSE

PIZZA RESEARCH INSTITUTE

Kiwanis Park

CAMPBELL HOUSE

IZAKAYA MEIJI CO.

7TH AVE

Eugene

WASHINGTON

JEFFERSON

SEE DETAIL

11TH AVE

13TH AVE

LANE COUNTY HISTORICAL MUSEUM

CHAMBERS ST

18TH AVE

JEFFERSON ST

THE BIER STEIN

HIGH ST

To Florence

126

Westmoreland Park

28TH AVE

GLENWOOD

29TH AVE

Morse Ranch Park

0  1 mi
0  1 km

AMTRAK

BELLY TAQUERIA

5TH

COURTSEY INN

4TH AVE

AVE

Fifth Street Public Market

INN AT THE FIFTH

6TH

DOWNTOWN INN

HULT CENTER FOR THE PERFORMING ARTS

EUGENE HILTON

MARCHÉ/ MARCHÉ CAFÉ

7TH

W.O.W. HALL

VISITOR CENTER

8TH AVE

Saturday Market

FULL CITY COFFEE ROASTERS

AVE

PARTY DOWNTOWN RED WAGON

PALACE BAKERY

BROADWAY

DAVIS RESTAURANT

BELLY

JOHN G. SHEDD INSTITUTE FOR THE ARTS

AVE

GREYHOUND

LAWRENCE

LINCOLN

10TH

CHARNELTON

OLIVE

WILLAMETTE

OAK

PEARL

HIGH

AVE

TIMBERS MOTEL

11TH

AVE

12TH

AVE

EUGENE HOSPITAL

0  200 yds
0  200 m

13TH

AVE

CAFE SORIAH

40TH AVE

Blanton Ridge Park

WILLAMETTE ST

DONALD

Spencer's Butte Park

East Spencer's Butte Park

Spencer's Butte

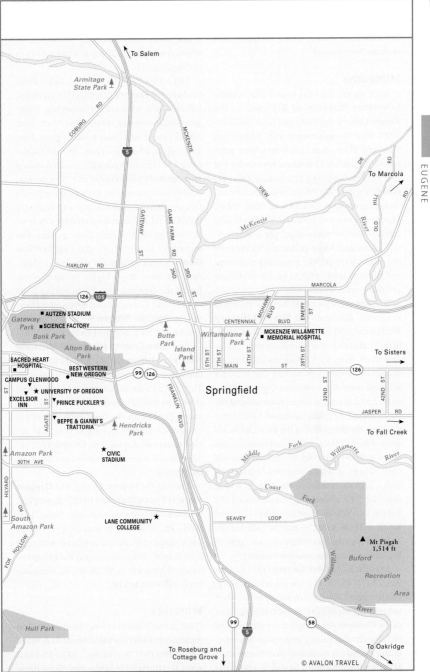

To Salem

Armitage
State Park

COBURG RD

MCKENZIE

VIEW

McKenzie

DR

7TH HILL RD

OLD RD

To Marcola

River

GATEWAY ST

GAME FARM RD

HARLOW RD

2ND ST

3RD ST

MARCOLA

126 105

■ AUTZEN STADIUM

Gateway
Park

■ SCIENCE FACTORY

Bank Park

CENTENNIAL

MOHAWK BLVD

EMERY ST

Alton Baker
Park

Butte
Park

Willamalane
Park

■ McKENZIE WILLAMETTE
MEMORIAL HOSPITAL

To Sisters

SACRED HEART ■
HOSPITAL

Island
Park

BEST WESTERN
NEW OREGON

99 126

5TH ST

7TH ST

14TH ST

28TH ST

ST

126

32ND ST

42ND ST

CAMPUS GLENWOOD
ST
EXCELSIOR ▼ ★ UNIVERSITY OF OREGON
INN ▼ PRINCE PUCKLER'S

FRANKLIN BLVD

MAIN

JASPER RD

Springfield

To Fall Creek

AGATE ST

■ BEPPE & GIANNI'S
TRATTORIA

Hendricks
Park

Amazon Park
30TH AVE

★ CIVIC
STADIUM

Middle

Fork

Willamette

River

HILYARD RD

Coast

Fork

South
Amazon Park

★ LANE COMMUNITY
COLLEGE

SEAVEY LOOP

▲ Mt Pisgah
1,514 ft

FOX HOLLOW

Willamette

Buford

Recreation

Area

River

Hull Park

99 5

To Roseburg and
Cottage Grove

58

To Oakridge

© AVALON TRAVEL

on the northwest edge of the track, houses locker rooms, memorabilia, and the university's International Institute for Sport and Human Performance.

## Museums

A must on any campus tour is the **Jordan Schnitzer Museum of Art** (next to the Knight Library, 1430 Johnson Lane, 541/346-3027, http://jsma.uoregon.edu, 11am-5pm Tues. and Thurs.-Sun., 11am-8pm Wed. year-round, $5 adults, $3 seniors, free under age 19). This museum is a real gem, with a surprisingly good collection of contemporary art, including works by Chuck Close, Mark Tobey, Morris Graves, and many Pacific Northwest artists. Another major highlight is a nationally renowned Asian collection (don't miss the jade carvings); the revolving paintings and photography exhibits on the first floor are also usually worthwhile.

The university's other notable museum is entirely different: The **Natural History Museum** (1680 E. 15th Ave., 541/346-3024, http://natural-history.uoregon.edu, 11am-5pm Tues.-Sun., $5, $3 students and seniors) showcases Oregon's prehistory and includes artifacts from digs in eastern Oregon as well as bird and mammal fossils from around the state, including many collected by Thomas Condon, the discoverer of the John Day Fossil Beds. There's also a set of sagebrush sandals dated at 9,350 years old, 15-million-year-old shell fossils, a whale vertebra, mammoth tusks, and an excellent collection of Arctic material. The museum is tucked behind the Knight Law School; to get here from Hayward Field on Agate Street, go east on 15th Avenue and look for a fish sculpture on your right, in front of an attractive wooden building.

**Maude Kerns Art Center** (1910 E. 15th Ave., 541/345-1571, www.mkartcenter.org, 10am-5:30pm Mon.-Fri., noon-4pm Sat. when exhibits are on display, donation) is just east of the University of Oregon campus. Set in an old church, this gallery and visual arts community center is dedicated to contemporary art of nationally known as well as regionally

prominent artists. This gallery and others downtown are the focal points of a **gallery walk** (Lane Arts Council, 541/485-2278, www.lanearts.org, 5:30pm-8:30pm 1st Fri. of the month).

Just across the river in Alton Baker Park, the **Science Factory** (2300 Leo Harris Pkwy., 541/682-7888, www.sciencefactory.org, 10am-4pm daily summer, 10am-4pm Wed.-Sun. school year, closed home football game days, $5 exhibits, $5 planetarium, $8 both) is designed to stimulate scientific understanding and curiosity in everyday life. The permanent exhibits are similar to those at Portland's Oregon Museum of Science and Industry (OMSI) and are complemented by a new set of traveling exhibits every three months. The museum's planetarium, the **Exploration Dome** (check website for showtimes 11am-3pm Sat.-Sun., $5) is highly recommended. Reach the complex from I-5 by taking I-105 west to the Coburg Road exit and following the signs for "Autzen Stadium" (look for Centennial Blvd. and the Leo Harris Pkwy.).

The **Lane County Historical Museum** (740 W. 13th Ave., 541/682-4242, www.lanecountyhistoricalsociety.org, 10am-4pm Tues.-Sat., $5 adults, $3 seniors, $1 children) is next to the fairgrounds. Just look for the steam donkey on the front lawn. There are other 19th-century logging vehicles and period rooms on display. The Oregon Trail exhibits and the rotating exhibits are the most interesting.

Close to the Eugene Airport, the **Oregon Air and Space Museum** (90377 Boeing Dr., 541/461-1101, www.oasm.info, noon-4pm Wed.-Sat., $7 adults, $6 seniors, $3 children) has vintage aircraft and artifacts. Although it's nowhere near as dazzling as the Evergreen Aviation Museum in McMinnville, aerospace buffs will want to visit.

## Wineries

Head to the Whiteaker neighborhood to find the winery of **Territorial Vineyards & Wine Company** (907 W. 3rd Ave., 541/684-9463, www.territorialvineyards.com, 5pm-10pm

Wed.-Sat.), where you can sample pinot noir, pinot gris, and riesling. Although the grapes are grown out toward the Coast Range, the wine is made here in a former coffee warehouse.

**Silvan Ridge Winery** (27012 Briggs Hill Rd., 541/345-1945, www.silvanridge. com, noon-5pm daily), 15 miles southwest of downtown near Crow, is a perfect place to spend a summer afternoon. Drive west on 11th Avenue, turn left on Bertelson Road, then right on Spencer Creek Road. A left down Briggs Hill Road takes you to the tasting room on a hillside overlooking a valley. The ride out is a favorite of local bicyclists, some of whom continue on into the Coast Range via Vaughan Road. While at the vineyard, ask to sample Hinman's award-winning gewürztraminer; the pinot gris is also delightful.

The lavish state-of-the-art **King Estate Winery** (80854 Territorial Hwy., 541/942-9874, www.kingestate.com, 11am-9pm Mon.-Fri., 10am-9pm Sat.-Sun.) is set on 820 acres and resembles a European château. Production focuses on organically grown pinot gris and pinot noir. You can also sit down to a meal at the well-regarded restaurant (541/685-5189, 11am-9pm Mon.-Fri., 10am-9pm Sat.-Sun., reservations advised, dinner $18-38). To reach the winery from Eugene, take I-5 South to exit 182 for "Creswell," and turn west on Oregon Avenue (which becomes Camas Swale Rd. and then Ham Rd.) to Territorial Highway. Turn left onto Territorial Highway and follow it about 2.5 miles to King Estate.

## SPORTS AND RECREATION

Eugene's identity is rooted in its reputation as "Tracktown USA" and also in its superlative Parks and Recreation Department, miles of bike paths and on-street bike lanes, and back-country cycling minutes from downtown.

The **Ruth Bascom Riverbank Trail System** comprises more than 20 miles of paths accessible to bikes and pedestrians along both banks of the Willamette River. Pedal, walk, or jog to the Owen Rose Garden, the bird-rich wetlands at Delta Ponds, the Valley River Inn, and Alton Baker Park (including the Science Factory and Autzen Stadium); the University of Oregon and downtown are just off the path. Five bike-pedestrian bridges cross the river and trailside signs abound, so it's easy to tailor a loop to your own ambitions. Access the trail from downtown by heading east on 8th Avenue to the river.

the restaurant at King Estate Winery

Connect with Eugene's track heritage by running **Pre's Trail,** on the north side of the Willamette River east of Alton Baker Park. A good route from the university is to head north on Agate Street, cross Franklin Boulevard, and cross the Willamette on a footbridge that takes bikers, hikers, and joggers to Pre's Trail, the Willamette River Bike Trail, Autzen Stadium, and other facilities found along the Willamette River Greenway.

Some of the best urban **rock climbing** to be found anywhere is at the Columns, a basalt cliff located on public land against the west side of Skinner Butte in downtown Eugene. Limited parking is available at the Columns, but it's more enjoyable to ride a bike here by following the road rimming the butte. Climbing is free.

## Parks

If you're looking for what makes Eugene *Eugene,* try visiting the city's parks. Go for a swim in the indoor pools at **Echo Hollow Park** (1560 Echo Hollow Rd., 541/682-5525) or **Sheldon Park** (2445 Willakenzie Rd., 541/682-5314); drop-in visitors pay a few dollars.

### ★ ALTON BAKER PARK

Just across the Willamette River from downtown, the 400-acre **Alton Baker Park** is home to a world-class running trail, the Science Factory and its adjoining planetarium, gardens, ponds, picnic areas, a canoe canal, and part of a cool scale model of the solar system (the sun and inner planets are here; Pluto, whether or not it's an actual planet, is 3.66 miles to the northwest, along the bike path). The western part of the park is more developed; to the east, it includes the 237-acre Whilamut Natural Area.

The four-mile **Pre's Trail** runs along the Willamette River east of Alton Baker Park. Named after runner Steve Prefontaine, whose world-record times and finishing kicks used to rock the Hayward Field grandstands before his untimely death in a car accident in 1975, this soft path meanders along the river and connects to the network of trails along the Willamette.

Reach Alton Baker Park from downtown by taking the Ferry Street Bridge and turning right just after crossing the river; if you're on foot or bike, the Peter DeFazio bike bridge is near the Ferry Street Bridge and is an easy walk from the Fifth Street Market area. From the university area, walk or bike across the Autzen Bike Bridge to the park.

### HENDRICKS PARK

About two miles southeast of the campus on a forested ridgeline is **Hendricks Park** (Summit Ave. and Skyline Blvd., 541/682-4800), home to 850 naturally occurring rhododendrons and azaleas and about 10,000 hybrids. There are several routes to the park, the easiest being to turn from Fairmount Boulevard onto Summit Drive. Two parking lots accommodate cars—one near the picnic area of stoves and tables, the other at the upper entrance on Sunset Boulevard. The rhododendron gardens are in their glory during May, and even though the display declines by late June, it's always a great place to stroll. Gorgeous views of the city can be enjoyed from the west end of the garden.

### RIDGELINE TRAIL

The South Hills **Ridgeline Trail** is only minutes south of downtown Eugene and offers wildlife-watching opportunities and more species of fern than perhaps any other single spot in Oregon. In addition, old-growth Douglas fir and the lovely and increasingly hard-to-find calypso orchid grow here. The trail is seldom steep and has some spectacular views of the city through clearings. A steep and often muddy spur trail leads up to Spencer Butte. The Ridgeline Trail can be reached from several points, including Dillard Road; near the corner of Fox Hollow and Christenson Roads; near Willamette Street and 52nd Avenue; off Blanton Road near 40th Avenue; and the Spencer Butte parking area.

# Hiking Kentucky Falls

Picturesque **Kentucky Falls** (www.fs.usda.gov/siuslaw) is in an old-growth forest on the upper slopes of the Coast Range. From Eugene, drive 33 miles west on Highway 126 to the Whittaker Creek Recreation Area on the south side of the road, six miles west of the Walton Store and post office. The route to Kentucky Falls winds through the clear-cut lower slopes of 3,700-foot-high **Roman Nose Mountain.**

From Whittaker Creek Recreation Area, drive 1.6 miles south and make a right turn. After 1.5 miles, bear left on Dunn Ridge Road. After about seven miles the pavement ends, and you'll turn left on Knowles Creek Road; go 2.7 miles. Make a right onto Forest Road 23 (gravel) and proceed 1.6 miles until you make a right onto Forest Road 919. Continue for 2.6 miles to the Kentucky Falls trailhead, marked by a sign on the left side of the road. An old-growth Douglas fir forest on gently rolling hills for the first 0.5 miles gives way to a steep descent into a lush canyon. The upper waterfall is visible a little less than a mile down the trail. Continue another 1.4 miles from the upper falls to an observation deck overlooking Lower Kentucky Falls, a 100-foot-high twin waterfall. On your drive back to Highway 126, retrace your route carefully to avoid veering off on a hair-raising spur route to Mapleton.

## SPENCER BUTTE

The view is great from the highest point in Eugene, 2,052-foot **Spencer Butte.** On a clear day you can see all the way up to Mount Hood, and you look down on Eugene-Springfield, with Fern Ridge Reservoir in the northwest. Beyond the reservoir you can sometimes see Marys Peak. Other Cascade Mountains sometimes visible from the butte include Mount Jefferson, Mount Washington, the Three Sisters, and Mount Bachelor.

Allow an hour to hike to the summit; be sure to take water. The main parking lot for Spencer Butte is on Willamette Street. Just drive south on Willamette Street until you see the signs on the left side of the road. There's also parking on Fox Hollow Road.

## MOUNT PISGAH ARBORETUM

The **Mount Pisgah Arboretum** (Buford Park, 34901 Frank Parrish Rd., 541/747-3817, www.mountpisgaharboretum.com, parking $4) features seven miles of trails that pass through a number of different habitats. The arboretum at the end of Seavey Loop Road sponsors such events as a fall fair dedicated to area mushrooms and a spring wildflower show and plant sale (dates vary). Reach Mount Pisgah by following East 30th Avenue from Eugene past Lane Community College to the I-5 interchange. Cross the bridge over the interstate, turn left, and take the next right onto Seavey Loop Road. You'll cross the Coast Fork of the Willamette River and then turn left onto a gravel road (look for the "Mount Pisgah" signs) that leads to the trailhead; the arboretum is just beyond the parking lot.

Other trails skirt the arboretum and climb (steeply) to the top of the 1,514-foot peak. A summit monument honors author Ken Kesey's son and other members of the University of Oregon wrestling team who perished in a van accident (the celebrated author lived two miles east, in Pleasant Hill). This memorial consists of a sculpture with a relief map depicting the mountains, rivers, towns, and other landmarks in the Eugene area. Supporting the map are three five-sided bronze columns upon which the geologic history of Oregon over the past 200 million years is portrayed, using images of more than 300 fossil specimens.

## FERN RIDGE LAKE

Reservoirs beyond downtown Eugene provide a wide range of recreation. The one closest to town is **Fern Ridge Lake** (25950 Richardson Park Rd., Junction City, 541/688-8147). This lake was formed when the Long Tom River was dammed in 1941, and its southeast shore was designated a wildlife refuge in 1979. Visitors can camp, picnic, swim, water-ski, sail, fish, or watch wildlife.

To reach the lake, drive 10 miles west of downtown Eugene on West 11th Avenue (Hwy. 126) toward Veneta, or take Clear Lake Road off Highway 99W. The lake is drained in winter to allow for flood control, but the resulting marsh and refuge provide wildlife habitat. The wildlife area is closed from January to March 15 to protect wintering birds.

## Biking

Eugene and Springfield together boast 120 miles of on-street bike lanes, limited-access streets, and off-street bikeways. The two cities collaborate to publish a free bicycle map; find it online at www.eugene-or.gov. Especially appealing and easy to get to is the **Ruth Bascom Willamette River Bike Trail.**

Rent a bike from **Paul's Bicycle Way of Life** (556 Charnelton St., 541/344-4105, http://bicycleway.com, 9am-7pm Mon.-Fri., 10am-5pm Sat.-Sun.). Another local bike business is **Bike Friday** (3364 W. 11th Ave., 541/687-0487 or 800/777-0258, www.bikefriday.com, 9am-5:30pm Mon.-Fri.), known for elegant custom-made folding bicycles.

## Water Sports

Alton Baker Park, along the Willamette River, and the Millrace Canal, which parallels the river for three or four miles, provide an escape from Eugene's main downtown thoroughfares. The canal is easily accessed from the university campus by crossing Franklin Boulevard. During the summer, **Northwest Canoe Tour** (100 Day Island Rd., 541/579-8990, http://canoetour.org, 11am-5pm daily, $12 per hour) rents canoes, kayaks, and stand-up paddleboards in Alton Baker Park.

## Golf

Of the many courses in Lane County, **Tokatee** (54947 Hwy. 126, Blue River, 541/822-3220 or 800/452-6376, www.tokatee.com, Feb.-mid-Nov., $55 for 18 holes) is the best. To get here, drive 47 miles east of Eugene on the McKenzie Highway (Hwy. 126). The 18 holes are set in a mountainous landscape patrolled by elk and other forest creatures in the shadow of the Three Sisters.

## Spectator Sports

Each spring, the University of Oregon track

It's worth climbing Mount Pisgah to see the memorial at the top.

team, a perennial contender for the status of best in the nation, holds meets at **Hayward Field** (Agate St. and 15th Ave.). This site has also hosted such world-class events as the NCAA Finals and the U.S. Olympic Trials.

Fall means University of Oregon Ducks football at **Autzen Stadium** (Martin Luther King Blvd. on Day Island). To get here, head north on Ferry Street; just after crossing the Willamette River, take a hard right on Martin Luther King Jr. Boulevard. Expect traffic. In summer, the **Eugene Emeralds** (541/342-5367), a farm team for the Chicago Cubs, play baseball at **PK Park** (2760 Martin Luther King Jr. Blvd.) right behind Autzen Stadium.

## ENTERTAINMENT AND EVENTS

To keep up with Eugene's multifaceted entertainment offerings see the alternative *Eugene Weekly* (http://eugeneweekly.com) and the daily *Eugene Register Guard* (www.registerguard.com); both papers have good online events listings. Check with the **University of Oregon ticket office** (541/346-4461, http://tickets.uoregon.edu) for athletic event and concert information. Cutting-edge theater can be enjoyed at **Oregon Contemporary Theatre** (194 W. Broadway, 541/465-1506, www.octheatre.org).

### Nightlife
#### BREWPUBS
Wander down Oak Alley to find **Falling Sky Brewing** (1334 Oak Alley, 541/505-7096, www.fallingskybrewing.com, 11am-11pm Mon.-Thurs., 11am-midnight Fri., 10am-midnight Sat., 10am-11pm Sun., $9-15) and snack on warm pretzel sticks or dig into a Cuban-style pork sandwich. Even when the weather's marginal, the covered and heated outdoor patio is a good place to sip one of the brews (which include a root beer). If you're in the Whiteaker neighborhood, stop by **Falling Sky's Delicatessen** (790 Blair Blvd., 541/653-9167, 11am-11pm Sun.-Thurs., 11am-midnight Fri.-Sat.) for a beer and a pastrami sandwich.

Between downtown and the university, find a couple of good places to drink beer. **16 Tons Taphouse** (265 E. 13th Ave., 541/345-2003, http://sixteentons.biz, noon-11pm Mon.-Sat.,) is an easygoing beer shop and pub with nearly 20 taps dispensing a rotating selection of some of the state's best beers. The **Bier Stein** (1591 Willamette St., 541/485-2437, http://thebierstein.com, 11am-midnight Mon.-Sat., noon-10pm Sun.) has 20 taps and a warehouse-size refrigerated case filled with beers and ciders from around the world.

Find more excellent beer at the **Oakshire Brewing Public House** (207 Madison St., 541/688-4555, http://oakbrew.com, 11am-10pm daily). The brewers started out with an amber, added an IPA and some seasonal brews, and now offer a changing menu of single-batch brews such as a Belgian-style strong wit or a double IPA (with 100-plus international bitterness units, or IBUs, for hopheads). Oakshire's food offerings are minimal, but customers are welcome to bring their own food to the pub.

By now, **Ninkasi Brewing Company** (272 Van Buren St., 541/344-2739, http://ninkasibrewing.com, noon-9pm Sun.-Wed., noon-10pm Thurs.-Sat.), which has made some of Oregon's best beer in the Whiteaker area since 2007, is a neighborhood institution. The ancient Sumerian goddess of fermentation surely casts a fond eye on Total Domination IPA, as do the locals and visitors who gather at the tasting room. The focus is on beer, not food, but there's always a food cart posted outside the tasting room, and the neighborhood is flush with restaurants.

Head north of town to find the intensely locavore **Agrarian Ales** (31115 W. Crossroads Lane, 541/510-4897, 3pm-9pm Fri.-Sat., noon-9pm Sun.). Not only do they grow all of their own hops, but the fields here also produce herbs and fruit that flavor the Agrarian beers and sodas. It's an easy-going, kid- and dog-friendly place to spend a couple of hours.

#### CANNABIS
Not surprisingly, it's easy to find a dispensary in Eugene. In the Whiteaker neighborhood,

ask the helpful budtenders at **Twenty After Four Wellness** (420 Blair Blvd., 541/393-6820, www.twentyafterfour.com, 10am-10pm daily) about products to fit your needs or desires; they're particularly good resources for using cannabis to manage pain.

North of the university, near the river, **Eugene OG** (2045 Franklin Blvd., 541/505-7575, www.eugeneog.com, 10am-10pm daily) is another professionally run dispensary with a wide selection of flowers, concentrates, and edibles. Also near the university, **Jamaica Joel's** (37 W. 13th Ave., 541/505-8293, www.jamaicajoels.com, 10am-10pm daily) is a friendly, homey dispensary with a laid-back tropical-Rasta vibe, free coffee, and lots of community spirit.

## LIVE MUSIC

The best spot in town for frenetic dancing is the **W.O.W. Hall** (291 W. 8th Ave., 541/687-2746, www.wowhall.org). This old Woodmen of the World meeting hall has remained a monument to Oregon's activist past in labor history (well, sort of, anyway: Its unofficial motto is now "Fighting to save rock & roll since 1975"). The W.O.W.'s floating hardwood dance floor and good acoustics allow it to rise above its junior high school gym ambience, and it hosts some surprisingly famous rock and blues performers. In any case, this all-ages venue is probably the most crowded and features an interesting cross-section of Eugenians. Beer and wine are served downstairs.

Local bands and national acts, including comedians, play at the **McDonald Theatre** (1010 Willamette St., 541/345-4442, www.mcdonaldtheatre.com), built in 1925 and now owned by the Kesey family, who work to maintain the old-fashioned ambience.

The **John G. Shedd Institute for the Arts** (868 High St., 541/687-6526, www.theshedd.org) brings in some really fun music (think Buckwheat Zydeco, or Steve Martin playing his banjo) and offers a wide variety of programs, including a performing arts company, a cultural arts center, and a community music school.

Big concerts occasionally take place within the cavernous enclaves of **Autzen Stadium** (2727 Leo Harris Pkwy., 541/346-4461, www.goducks.com), the home field to the Oregon Ducks football team. Near the Science Factory in Alton Baker Park, the **Cuthbert Amphitheater** (541/762-8099, www.thecuthbert.com) is a slightly more intimate 5,000-seat outdoor theater; this is where you might go to see the Shins or Michael Franti and Spearhead.

For more sedate listening, the **Hult Center** (E. 6th Ave. and Willamette St., 541/682-5000, www.hultcenter.org) is next door to the Hilton. The Eugene Symphony and other estimable local groups such as the Eugene Concert Choir perform here, along with a wide-ranging array of headliners from the world of music and comedy. This is also where most of the Bach Festival concerts occur.

Several clubs are clustered within a two-block area around West Broadway and Olive Street: the "Barmuda Triangle." The venerable **HorseHead** (99 W. Broadway, 541/683-3154, 11:30am-2:30am daily) has just about everything except live music—pool tables, darts, a pinball machine, and barbecue. **Cowfish** (62 W. Broadway, 541/683-6319, 10:30am-2:15am daily) is a dance club with an easygoing atmosphere and a large roster of DJs. **Jameson's** (115 W. Broadway, 541/485-9913, http://jamesonsbareugene.com, 4pm-2:30am daily) is classy but not overly fussy, with a retro-lounge feel. Here you'll also find Eugene's only queer bar, the always-inclusive **The Wayward Lamb** (150 W. Broadway, 541/654-5106, 4pm-midnight Sun.-Tues., 4pm-2am Wed.-Thurs., 2pm-2:30am Fri.-Sat.).

A downtown spot that's good for relaxing or socializing throughout the day is the **Barn Light** (924 Willamette St., 458/205-8914, 7am-midnight Mon.-Wed., 7am-2am Thurs.-Fri., 8am-2am Sat., 8am-10pm Sun.), a coffee shop and bar full of friendly hipsters.

Out in the Whiteaker neighborhood, **Sam Bond's Garage** (407 Blair Blvd., 541/421-6603, www.sambonds.com, 4pm-2:15am daily) has weekly bluegrass jams as well as microbrews and a menu of vegetarian pub grub.

## Festivals and Events

There is a lot happening in this south Willamette Valley hub of culture and athletics. Several events—particularly the Eugene Marathon, the Oregon Bach Festival, and the Oregon Country Fair—best impart the cultural flavor of the area.

The **Oregon Bach Festival** (541/346-5666 and 800/457-1486, www.oregonbachfestival.com) takes place over two weeks late June-early July and features a sparkling array of internationally renowned opera and symphonic virtuosos. Festivalgoers can choose from more than two dozen concerts (some are also performed in Portland, Ashland, and Bend), with musical styles ranging from the baroque era to the 20th century. The centerpieces of the festival, however, are Bach works such as the *St. Matthew Passion,* numerous cantatas, and the Brandenburg concertos. Performances take place in the Hult Center and the Beall Concert Hall at the University of Oregon Music School. Free events, including "Let's Talk with the Conductor," mini concerts, and lectures also take place at these venues during the festival.

A **gallery walk** (Lane Arts Council, 541/485-2278, www.lanearts.org, 5:30pm-8:30pm 1st Fri. of the month) the first Friday of every month lets culture vultures enjoy open house exhibitions all over town.

Late April brings runners to town for the **Eugene Marathon** (877/345-2230, www.eugenemarathon.com), which has a relatively flat course, starting and finishing at Hayward Field.

Appealing to lowbrow and highbrow alike is **Art and the Vineyard** (www.artandthevineyard.org, $10 adults, $5 ages 6-14), which generally takes place over the Fourth of July weekend in Alton Baker Park. This event brings together art, music, and wine with over 100 artists booths and the offerings of a dozen vineyards, accompanied by live jazz, country, blues, and folk as well as food concessions.

## FOOD

Eating out in Eugene has long been a delight, thanks to the staggering array of locally made gourmet products and organic foods available from local farms, ranches, and the nearby Pacific.

### Fifth Street Public Market Area

The northern edge of downtown Eugene is dominated by the **Fifth Street Public Market,** a renovated market building that houses a number of restaurants, including a large food court with five food purveyors to choose from. The three-story, internal courtyard is overflowing with art and greenery, making a pleasant spot for a casual meal.

Since it opened in 1997, ★ **Marché** (296 E. 5th Ave., 541/342-3612, www.marcherestaurant.com, 8am-11pm Sun.-Thurs., 8am-midnight Fri.-Sat., dinner entrées $20-36) has set the standard for fine dining in Eugene. In the ground-floor southwest corner of the Fifth Street Public Market, it is as close to a French bistro as you'll find, with a French-inflected emphasis on fresh local produce and meat. The atmosphere is crisp but not fussy, and if you sit in the bar, you can enjoy a not-too-expensive evening with drinks and casual fare such as steak frites ($19).

For a more casual take on Marché's food, head upstairs in the Fifth Street Market to **Marché Provisions** (296 E. 5th Ave., 541/743-0660, 7am-8pm daily, www.marcheprovisions.com, light meal $8-17), where the food spans the hours from late breakfast to early dinner with quiche, tasty open-face sandwiches, soups, salads, and dessert.

A few blocks west, near the train station, **Belly Taqueria** (454 Willamette Ave., 541/687-8226, www.eatbelly.com, 5pm-9pm Mon.-Thurs., 5pm-10pm Fri.-Sat., tacos $3-6, entrées $10-14) is high-end for a taqueria, with good cocktails and seasonal specials such as tacos filled with braised octopus and pork belly.

Northeast of Fifth Street Market, right off the Ruth Bascom bike path, find a French

# Oregon Country Fair

Don't expect to see livestock displays and prize-winning jelly. This is a place where body paint, feathers, man kilts, tie-dye, and good-natured frivolity rule. Like a giant street fair, with artisans, food, and music, albeit in a beautiful wooded setting along the Long Tom River about 13 miles west of Eugene, for the craftspeople, musicians, jugglers, and volunteers it's a celebration of life outside the edges of corporate America, a way of maintaining an alternative identity. This other world is pretty wide-ranging, including old hippies, circus performers, mystics, masseuses, musicians, fairies, community activists, and people dressed as trees. It's also very welcoming—especially to kids, elders, and the "alter-abled."

Shake off the everyday world at the Oregon Country Fair.

The crafts are high quality, and there's no better place to shop for a tie-dyed T-shirt. The best part are the performances, along the wooded paths and on the 18 stages, which include **Shady Grove,** a quiet venue for acoustic music; the **Daredevil Stage,** hosting contemporary New Vaudeville stars and other rollicking performers; and the **Main Stage,** which hosts the big acts. Don't miss the Fighting Instruments of Karma Marching Chamber Band-Orchestra parading through the fair or playing on **Stage Left;** various permutations of the band have been rocking the joint with everything from Sousa marches to Bollywood dance tunes for over 40 years.

The **Oregon Country Fair** (541/343-4298, www.oregoncountryfair.org, 11am-7pm Fri.-Sun. the weekend after July 4, $24-30, $70 for 3 days) is near Veneta on Highway 126. Tickets must be purchased in advance at a Safeway store or through **Tickets West** (800/992-8499, http://ticketswest.rdln.com).

Due to the popularity of this event, which attracts more than 50,000 attendees, the best way to get here is to take the free shuttle from Eugene's Valley River Mall or the downtown Eugene bus station. Bus service usually begins at about 10:30am, with the last departure from the fair site at 7pm. On-site parking is open 10am-6pm but is limited; expect a long walk from your car to the gate. Parking costs $15 at the gate, slightly less when reserved in advance.

touch (or French Canadian, if you go for the poutine) at ★ **Rye** (444 E. 3rd Ave., 541/653-8509, http://ryeon3rd.com, 11:30am-2pm and 5pm-9pm Mon.-Thurs., 11:30am-2pm and 5pm-10pm Fri., 5pm-10pm Sat., $16-26), which is also known for excellent cocktails and casual classy ambiance, including a dog-friendly patio.

## Central Downtown Area

**Full City Coffee Roasters** (842 Pearl St., 541/344-0475, www.full-city.com, 5:30am-6pm Mon.-Fri., 6:30am-6pm Sat., 7am-5pm Sun.) is locally noted for its coffee; pick up a muffin or a sandwich to accompany it at the adjacent **Palace Bakery** (844 Pearl St., 541/484-2435, 7am-5pm Mon.-Sat., 8am-noon Sun.).

**Belly** (30 E. Broadway, 541/683-5896, www.eatbelly.com, 11am-3:30pm Mon.-Sat. and 5pm-9:30pm Tues.-Thurs., 5pm-10:30pm Fri.-Sat., $16-19), in a noisy, consciously hip downtown location, offers country French cooking at dinner and an Asian-fusion lunch menu. In the evening, sample house-made charcuterie, confit, and other meaty dishes.

At the southwestern edge of downtown, **Cafe Soriah** (384 W. 13th Ave., 541/342-4410, http://cafesoriah.com, 11:30am-2pm and 5pm-10pm Wed.-Fri., 5pm-10pm Sat.-Tues., $17-34) is a popular choice for a romantic dinner. Both its patio for summer outdoor dining and its bar offer great ambience, but the Mediterranean-Middle Eastern cuisine is the real attraction. Moussaka as well as chicken or lamb with sautéed vegetables stand out.

Classy and inviting, **The Davis Restaurant & Bar** (94 W. Broadway, 541/485-1124, www.davisrestaurant.com, 11am-10pm Mon.-Thurs., 11am-2am Fri., 4pm-2am Sat., $9-24) has a broad selection of tempting starters, such as BLT *gougère* sliders. Most salads and main courses are available as small plates or dinner portions, making it fun to graze through a variety of dishes. Braised pork shoulder is served with ramps and wild mushroom demi-glace, and grilled quail comes with fig *agrodolce* sauce. At night, a young stylish crowd gathers for drinks and live music.

Scratch the ice cream itch at **Red Wagon Creamery** (55 W. Broadway, 541/485-1124, http://redwagoncreamery.com, 11am-10pm Sun.-Wed., noon-11pm Thurs.-Sat., $3-6). Although the menu only features a few flavors, from Not So Plain Jane vanilla to seasonal flavors such as fennel-thyme, it's all delicious and made here at Oregon's smallest dairy.

Tucked behind Red Wagon, find **Party Downtown** (64 W. 8th Alley, 541/345-8228, http://partyeugene.com, 5pm-9pm Sun.-Thurs., 5pm-10pm Fri.-Sat., $12-35), a food cart-turned-restaurant with a few Southern touches (fried chicken brined in sweet tea) that uses nearly 100 percent local and organic ingredients. Splurge on the $35 tasting menu, which is served family-style for the whole table, or keep it low-key with burgers and jo-jo potatoes.

## University Campus Area

The eateries on the campus periphery are a cut above those found in most college towns, and even the on-campus offerings are pretty good. One such campus food court, **Fresh**

**Marketcafé** (Global Scholars Hall, 541/346-4277, 10am-10pm daily, $5-12), is behind the Natural History Museum and offers pastas, sushi and bento, rice bowls, salads, smoothies, and coffee.

Start the day at **Campus Glenwood** (1340 Alder St., 541/687-0355, www.glenwood-restaurants.com, 7am-9pm daily, $7-17) or at the south-side **Glenwood** (2588 Willamette St., 541/687-8201, 6:30am-9pm Mon.-Fri., 7am-9pm Sat.-Sun., $6-15). Although both restaurants are open for three meals a day, breakfast is what keeps people coming back. Be prepared for a wait on weekend mornings.

In the shadow of the campus, the **Excelsior Inn Ristorante** (754 E. 13th Ave., 541/485-1206, www.excelsiorinn.com, 7am-10am and 11:30am-9pm Mon.-Thurs., 7am-10am and 11:30am-10pm Fri., 8am-10am and 4pm-10pm Sat., 8am-2pm and 4pm-9pm Sun., $26-38) is an elegant restaurant in a charming old home. The Italian menu might include ravioli filled with Dungeness crab and buttered leeks or grilled prawns with red-pepper risotto. Many ingredients are grown at the restaurant's farm south of town. Although the Excelsior is close to campus, it draws an older crowd; when you see students here, they're often with their parents, who may be staying in the inn upstairs.

Behind Hayward Field, find top-notch ice cream at **Prince Puckler's** (1605 E. 19th Ave., 541/344-4418, noon-11pm daily, $3-7), a Eugene institution since 1975. Although President Barack Obama went for the mint chocolate chip when he visited, our favorite is the Velvet Hammer shake with Mexican chocolate and espresso.

## South of Downtown

After a weekend morning run at Amazon Park, head to **Hideaway Bakery** (3377 E. Amazon Dr., 541/868-1982, 7am-6pm daily, $6-9) for pastries, a breakfast sandwich, or a slice of wood-oven pizza. This popular bakery, tucked behind the venerable Mazzi's Italian restaurant, has a great patio and delicious sweet and savory treats.

Dinner on the outside deck at **Beppe & Gianni's Trattoria** (1646 E. 19th Ave., 541/683-6661, http://beppeandgiannis.net, 5pm-9pm Sun.-Thurs., 5pm-10pm Sat.-Sun., $16-26) is one of Eugene's coveted summertime dining experiences. The menu features homemade pastas with light northern Italian cream- or olive oil-based sauces graced by fresh vegetables, meats, or fish. Try the *cappelli di vescovo* (bishop hats)—pasta stuffed with Swiss chard, prosciutto, and cheese in a brown-butter sage sauce.

### Whiteaker Neighborhood

Just west of the center city is Blair Boulevard and the agreeably funky Whiteaker neighborhood, where a restaurant row has developed with places that are mostly easy on the pocketbook and offer an interesting variety of cuisines.

**Wandering Goat** (268 Madison St., 541/344-5161, www.wanderinggoat.com, 6am-11pm Mon.-Fri., 7am-11pm Sat.-Sun.) is Eugene's top coffee shop, with discerning hip baristas serving coffee from beans roasted in the back room, music many evenings, good baked goods (many vegan), homemade chai, and beer.

One of the neighborhood highlights is the **Pizza Research Institute** (PRI, 530 Blair Blvd., 541/343-1307, www.pripizza.com, 5pm-9:30pm Wed.-Sun., small pizza $18), which has the most innovative pizza in town. In this case, innovation equals excellence—try the chef's choice, which is invariably tasty and has ingredients arranged to form a mandala. PRI, which serves only veggie pies, has a friendly, spunky feel that's thoroughly Eugenian.

Chill out at ★ **Izakaya Meiji Company** (345 Van Buren St., 541/545-8804, http://izakayameiji.com, 5pm-1am daily, $4-13) with good Japanese-inspired small plates and a cocktail. Later in the evening, it's more of a bar scene, with lots of late-night ramen.

If you need a treat to start the day, make it through the afternoon, or cap off a restaurant dinner, visit **Sweet Life Patisserie** (755 Monroe St., 541/683-5676, http://sweetlifedesserts.com, 7am-11pm Mon.-Fri., 8am-11pm Sat.-Sun.), where a hazelnut fig tartlet might just do the trick. Gluten-free and vegan options abound.

## ACCOMMODATIONS

Although there are abundant chain hotels at the I-5 exits, these lodgings are miles from the fun and bustle of downtown Eugene. Luckily, the campus and downtown neighborhoods

Wandering Goat serves some of Eugene's best coffee.

offer lots of choices for motels within walking distance of the Eugene scene. Expect prices to jump during football and back-to-school weekends.

## Under $50

The **Eugene Whiteaker International Hostels** (970 W. 3rd Ave., 541/343-3335, http://eugenehostel.org, $35-55) offer inexpensive lodging in dorms or private rooms in two older homes converted into well-run hostels in the funky, convenient Whiteaker neighborhood, just west of downtown.

## $50-100

A few older but well-kept motor court hotels have convenient locations in downtown Eugene. **Downtown Inn** (361 W. 7th Ave., 541/345-8739 or 800/648-4366, http://downtowninn.com, $99-135) is an accessible bargain. If you don't expect luxury, you'll enjoy the 1950s ambience of this classic motel.

The **Timbers Motel** (1015 Pearl St., 541/343-3345 or 800/643-4167, www.timbersmotel.net, $99-109) is one of our longtime downtown Eugene favorites; we like to bunk in the tiny timber-topped budget room. Dogs under 40 pounds can join you here for $40.

## $100-150

Another older but well-kept motor court hotel downtown, the **Courtesy Inn** (345 W. 6th Ave., 541/345-3391 or 888/259-8481, www.courtesyinneugene.com, $109) is a good bet; it's a couple of blocks from the Hult Center and within easy walking distance of restaurants.

The **Best Western New Oregon** (1655 Franklin Blvd., 541/683-3669, www.bestwestern.com, $122-144) is a good choice for visiting parents of university students or for folks in town to attend a sporting or cultural event. It's right across the street from the Registration Office and dormitories. Although the hotel is on a busy street, it backs up to the riverside millrace, and riverside paths lead to a footbridge to Alton Baker Park.

An excellent standard motel is the **Valley River Inn** (1000 Valley River Way, Valley River Center, 541/743-1000, www.valleyriverinn.com, $105-181, check website for discounts). Don't be deterred by its location away from downtown behind a giant shopping mall; the Willamette River is in back of the inn, which provides easy access to the riverside trail network. In fact, it's easier to get downtown along the bike path than it is to drive. The inn is pet-friendly, and the riverside path makes for delightful dog walks. A decent restaurant, a crackling fire in the lobby, and pool and spa facilities add to the allure. If it's in your budget, pony up an extra $40-50 for a riverside room—the view is worth it.

The **Campbell House** (252 Pearl St., 541/343-1119, www.campbellhouse.com, $109-199, breakfast included) is a 19-room Victorian mansion in the historic east Skinner Butte neighborhood. Proximity to the Fifth Street Market and the river, as well as the sophistication of a European-style B&B complete with a dinner restaurant, makes this antique-filled 1892 gem a good lodging choice. Note that the least expensive rooms are quite small.

The upstairs of a popular eatery just a block from campus, the **Excelsior Inn** (754 E. 13th Ave., 541/485-1206, www.excelsiorinn.com, $135-300, includes breakfast) offers 14 elegant bed-and-breakfast guest rooms featuring antiques, cherry furniture, marble tile, and fresh-cut flowers. An elevator makes the rooms wheelchair accessible.

## $150-200

At the center of downtown, the **Eugene Hilton** (66 E. 6th Ave., 541/342-2000, www3.hilton.com, $170-278, parking $15) has a great location right across the street from the Hult Center and within easy walking distance of the city's best restaurants. It sometimes has good weekend rates.

## $200-250

Eugene proves that it can be a little bit glamorous with ★ **Inn at the 5th** (205 E. 6th Ave., 541/743-4099, www.innat5th.com,

# Covered Bridges Scenic Bikeway

The town of Cottage Grove, 20 miles south of Eugene, is known for its six **covered bridges** (www.cgchamber.com) and as being the gateway to the Bohemia mining district, the site of old abandoned mines. The 14.1-mile **Row River Trail** is a rails-to-trails route that follows the paved-over tracks of an old mining train from Cottage Grove to Culp Creek—perfect for mountain biking, birding, and mushroom hunting (especially after the first fall rains). A longer bike route that includes the Row River Trail, the **Covered Bridges Scenic Bikeway** (http://rideoregonride. com), starts in Cottage Grove and runs 38 relatively flat miles past the six covered bridges and around Dorena Lake.

If you're looking for campsites in covered-bridge country, try the lakeside **Baker Bay County Park** (35635 Shoreview Dr., Dorena, 541/682-2000, www.lanecounty.org, mid-Apr.-mid-Oct., $20, plus $10 reservation fee). Take I-5 south to Mosby Creek Road (take the Cottage Grove exit), turn left, then left again on Row River Road, and then take the right fork. It's about 18 miles from Eugene.

$220-585). This boutique hotel is the place to stay for a romantic weekend or when you want to feel pampered. Of course, this being Oregon, the luxury is all sustainable: The giant wood-slab table in the lobby was taken from an 80-year-old bigleaf maple that was sacrificed to build the hotel; pieces of the tree are featured in rooms throughout. With room service by next-door Marché restaurant and a spa on the ground floor, it's easy to hole up at the inn, but bikes are available in case you want to cruise the riverside trails.

## Camping

**Richardson County Park** (25950 Richardson Park Rd., Junction City, 541/935-2005, www.lanecounty.org, Apr.-mid-Oct., $35, some sites higher) has sites with hookups on the shores of Fern Ridge Reservoir six miles northwest of Eugene; take Clear Lake Road off Highway 99 to its intersection with Territorial Road.

During Oregon Country Fair, many campgrounds spring up on private and public land near the fair site in Veneta; find a list at www.oregoncountryfair.org. **Zumwalt Park** (29652 Jeans Rd., Veneta, 541/935-2335, $35) is a private RV campground and marina 12 miles west of Eugene convenient to the Oregon Country Fair. Many spots are

occupied by long-term residents, and it's a well-kept place with a nice lakeside location.

## INFORMATION AND SERVICES

Find info about Eugene, the Cascades, and the coast at one of **Travel Lane County's** (www.eugenecascadescoast.org) two locations: downtown (754 Olive St., 800/547-5445) or just off I-5 in Springfield (3312 Gateway St., 541/484-5307 or 800/547-5445). The Springfield location is better if you're looking for info on outdoor activities.

The **Smith Family Bookstore** (768 E. 13th Ave., 541/345-1651; 525 Willamette St., 541/343-4717, www.smithfamilybookstore. com) purveys an excellent collection of used books. **Tsunami Books** (2585 Willamette St., 541/345-8986, www.tsunamibooks.org) is a local favorite for books and in-store events.

The main local public radio station, **KLCC** (89.7 FM), is an NPR affiliate with news and music programming ranging from new wave jazz to blues. The University of Oregon station **KWAX** (91.1 FM) provides continuous classical music.

*Eugene Weekly* (1251 Lincoln St., 541/484-0519, www.eugeneweekly.com) has the best entertainment listings in Eugene. At the beginning of each season, the magazine's Chow edition will point you in the direction of Eugene's hot restaurants. This publication is available free at commercial establishments all over town.

## GETTING THERE AND AROUND

If you're in your own car or on a bike, remember the campus is in the southeastern part of town; 1st Avenue parallels the Willamette River; and Willamette Street divides the city east and west. Navigation is complicated by many one-way roads and dead ends. Look for alleyways that allow through traffic to avoid getting stuck.

**Amtrak** (5th Ave. and Willamette St., 541/344-6265, www.amtrak.com) offers three different transport options. The Los Angeles-to-Seattle Coast Starlight links Eugene to major West Coast hubs. Two daily Cascades trains (www.amtrakcascades.com) link Eugene to Portland and Seattle, with connections to Vancouver, British Columbia. In addition, Amtrak runs bus service each day to Portland and the northern Oregon coast.

**Greyhound** (9th Ave. and Pearl St., 800/231-2222) buses travel south to San Francisco or north to Portland several times daily from Eugene. Within Eugene, **Lane Transit District** (541/687-5555, www.ltd. org, $1.75) has canopied pavilions displaying the bus timetables downtown. All buses are equipped with bike racks.

The **Eugene Airport** (EUG, 541/682-5430, www.eugene-or.gov/airport) is a 20-minute drive northwest from downtown—get on the Delta Highway from Washington Street and follow the signs. United, Alaska, American, Allegiant, and Delta operate flights. There is no city bus service to the airport. **OmniShuttle** (541/461-7959, www. omnishuttle.com, $27.50 from downtown) provides door-to-door shuttle service between the airport and points in Lane County. **Oregon Taxi** (541/434-8294) can also take you where you need to go (airport runs go for about $25). **Rental car companies** Avis, Budget, Hertz, and Enterprise have kiosks at the airport.

# The McKenzie River Highway

From I-5 near Eugene, reach the scenic McKenzie River Highway by taking Highway 126 east. Just past Springfield, where the four lanes become two, the McKenzie River Recreation Area begins. For the next 60 miles, you'll see beautiful views of the bluegreen McKenzie River with heavily forested mountains, waterfalls, jet-black lava beds, and snowcapped peaks as a backdrop.

The first 15 miles of the McKenzie River Highway pass through apple, cherry, and filbert orchards, Christmas tree farms, and berry patches. The Leaburg Dam signals the middle section of the McKenzie; six dams provide power, irrigation, and what the Army Corps of Engineers calls "fish enhancement." A favorite haunt of fishing enthusiasts, the mellow waters of the middle McKenzie teem with trout, steelhead, and

salmon. Mild white-water rafting and drift boat fishing are popular here, and local guides and outfitters are ready to help you float your expeditions.

The McKenzie River National Recreation Trail and other lovely trails feature waterfalls, mountain lakes, or lava formations a short trek from the road. In addition to the myriad recreational opportunities, hot springs, abundant accommodations, and a relative dearth of crowds characterize the western slopes of the Cascades.

## SIGHTS
### Aufderheide National Scenic Byway

The 58-mile **Aufderheide Drive** links Highway 126 to Highway 58 near Oakridge. You'll find the Aufderheide turnoff (Forest

Rd. 19) at mile marker 45.9 about five miles east of Blue River. The road winds along the south fork of the McKenzie River, crests the pass, and then follows the north fork of the middle fork of the Willamette River down to Oakridge and Highway 58. Sights along the way include the Delta Old-Growth Grove Nature Trail, Terwilliger (a.k.a. Cougar) Hot Springs, the Willamette River Gorge, and the Westfir covered bridge. The Aufderheide makes a spectacular, though difficult, bicycle ride; it's also a popular motorcycle route.

## Terwilliger (Cougar) Hot Springs

If you'd like to try soaking in hot springs in a natural setting, head for **Terwilliger Hot Springs**—also called **Cougar Hot Springs** ($6 pp day-use, sunrise-sunset daily)—in a forested canyon at the end of a 0.25-mile trail. Hot water bubbles out of the earth at 116°F and flows down through a series of log and stone pools, each a few degrees cooler than the previous one. The local custom is to forgo clothing.

To get here, take the Aufderheide Drive from Highway 126 south toward Cougar Reservoir. The trailhead for the hot springs on the west (right) side of the road is marked by a sign just past mile marker 7. You can park in a large lot on the east side of the road about 500 feet past the trailhead, alongside the reservoir. Parking along the road within a mile of the trailhead is prohibited and enforced sunset-sunrise.

The pools can be overcrowded on weekends, and despite the easygoing tranquil soaking experience, they can occasionally attract an unsavory crowd. Women traveling alone may want to scrutinize the scene before taking the plunge. If it's too warm for hot springs, consider swimming in the lagoon below the hot springs trail. From the pay station, it's a short hike in, and a steep descent along a path to the swimming hole.

## Proxy Falls

To get to **Proxy Falls,** follow the old McKenzie Pass road (Hwy. 242, 35-foot vehicle limit, closed in winter) from the new McKenzie Pass highway (Hwy. 126) for 10 miles. The 1.5-mile loop trail, on the south side of the road, leads to a spectacular pair of waterfalls, Upper and Lower Proxy Falls.

From the large bulletin board at the trailhead, a small arrow points to the right. However, that will be the longer route, and

Most bathers shed their clothes at Terwilliger (Cougar) Hot Springs.

it also requires hiking over sharp stones for part of the way. Going to the left at the bulletin board leads you to the trail, which is a shorter and easier route. Take a left at the trailhead for an easy 0.5-mile walk to Upper Proxy. Take a left at the first fork in the trail (marked by a sign) to Upper Proxy Falls.

Now that you've seen Upper Proxy Falls from the bottom up, check out Lower Proxy Falls from the top down. Go back to the fork in the trail and take a left. In less than 0.5 miles, you will suddenly be on a ridge looking across a valley at Lower Proxy Falls. The hike back to the trailhead passes over a lava field, so wear shoes that can withstand the sharp rocks.

## Dee Wright Observatory

The **Dee Wright Observatory** (57600 McKenzie Hwy./Hwy. 242, 541/822-3381, closed for winter at the first sign of snow), built in the early 1930s as a Civilian Conservation Corps (CCC) project, is at McKenzie Pass about halfway between Highway 126 and Sisters. The tower windows line up with views of Mount Jefferson, Mount Washington, and two of the Three Sisters, as well as the 8-mile-long, 0.5-mile-wide lava flow that bubbled out of nearby Yapoah less than 3,000 years ago. On a clear day, you can even see the tip of Mount Hood.

The 0.5-mile Lava River Trail next to the observatory offers a fine foray into the surrounding hills of rolling black rock. Note that on Highway 242, vehicle length is restricted to a maximum of 35 feet.

## Koosah Falls

**Koosah Falls** is about 20 miles from McKenzie Bridge on Highway 126. The visitor facilities here provide wheelchair access and excellent views of this impressive 70-foot-high waterfall on the McKenzie. If you look carefully, you can see many small springs flowing from crevices in the basalt at the base of the waterfall. The blue water may have inspired the name Koosah, which comes from the Chinook word for "sky."

## Sahalie Falls

**Sahalie Falls** is only 0.5 miles east from McKenzie Bridge on Highway 126 from Koosah Falls. From McKenzie Bridge, travel east on Highway 126 to Forest Road 2672. Follow Forest Road 2672 to Forest Road 655. Follow Forest Road 655 to the Sahalie Falls Day-Use Area. The result of a lava dam from the Cascade Range's not-so-distant volcanic past, the river tumbles 100 feet into a green canyon. This is the highest waterfall on the McKenzie River—*sahalie* means "high" in the Chinook language.

## Clear Lake

Just north of Sahalie and Koosah Falls and east of Highway 126 is **Clear Lake,** which forms the headwaters of the McKenzie River. The best way to appreciate this lake, which is indeed remarkably clear, is in a canoe, so that you can paddle out to the northern end of the lake and look down to see the 3,000-year-old underwater forest that was submerged when lava flows dammed the water. A campground and a resort are at the lake; the resort rents out canoes.

## SPORTS AND RECREATION

### Hiking

#### DELTA OLD-GROWTH GROVE NATURE TRAIL

Find the 0.5-mile loop **Delta Old-Growth Grove Natural Trail** through an old-growth ecosystem on the west side of the Aufderheide Byway not far from Highway 126. In addition to 650-year-old conifers, you'll see other layers of life, from shrubs and ground cover plants to fish and other wildlife. Many plant species are clearly marked along the trail.

#### ★ McKENZIE RIVER NATIONAL RECREATION TRAIL

The **McKenzie River National Recreation Trail** (Trail 3507) runs for 26.5 miles and is extremely popular with mountain bikers as well as hikers. It starts just east of the small town of McKenzie Bridge and continues to the Old Santiam Wagon Road, about three miles south of the junction of Highway 126 and U.S. 20. But don't let the long distance scare you; there are enough access points to let you design treks of three, five, eight, or more miles. Each section of the footpath has its own charms; the following are highlights.

Start at the top of the McKenzie River Trail at the Old Santiam Wagon Road. Completed in the early 1860s, this was the first link of the route from the mid-Willamette Valley to central and eastern Oregon. Way stations were established a day's journey apart to assist the pioneers along their weary way. Although most of these primitive establishments are no more, some of the historic buildings have survived. There isn't much left of the Old Santiam Wagon Road either, as much of it was destroyed with the construction of Highway 126. However, a seven-mile stretch remains from Highway 126 through the rugged lava country to the Pacific Crest Trail. A short walk on this former road to the promised land helps you to appreciate both the hardiness of the pioneers and the comforts of modern travel.

From the Old Santiam Wagon Road, the McKenzie River Trail surveys many remarkable volcanic formations. Lava flows over the last few thousand years have built dams, created waterfalls, and even buried the river altogether. Koosah and Sahalie Falls were also created by lava dams, and the view of these white-water cascades from the McKenzie River Trail is very different from the version accessible from the highway. Another interesting sight is the Tamolitch Valley, where the McKenzie gradually sinks beneath the porous lava, disappearing altogether until it reemerges three miles later at cobalt-colored Tamolitch Pool (often called the Blue Pool). This area is accessible only on the National Recreation Trail.

If possible, arrange your McKenzie outing with friends and run a two-car shuttle; **McKenzie River Mountain Resort** (541/822-6272, www.rivermountainresort. com) operates a shuttle service. Also keep in mind that hikes starting at the upper end of the trail take advantage of the descending elevation. Mountain bikes are allowed on all sections of the McKenzie River Trail; McKenzie River Mountain Resort also has a bike shuttle service.

## ROBINSON LAKE TRAIL

The 0.25-mile **Robinson Lake Trail** takes you to a heart-shaped lake with fishing and swimming. To get there, take Highway 126 about 16 miles east of McKenzie Bridge and turn right onto Robinson Lake Road. Be on the lookout for logging trucks and rocks on the gravel road. Follow the signs marked Forest Road 2664. At the junction, drive straight onto the red pumice road (Forest Rd. 2664) and continue until you reach the parking lot. It takes about 10 minutes to drive the four miles. The easy hiking trail is in good condition; the left fork takes you to the middle shore of Robinson Lake. The shallow lake warms up considerably during the summer, making a swim all the more inviting.

## Mountain Biking

In the upper sections of the McKenzie, most of the usable trails gain elevation rapidly due to the steep terrain and make for challenging biking. The most popular route is the **McKenzie River Trail.** Contact the **McKenzie River Ranger District** (503/822-3381) for information. **McKenzie River Mountain Resort** (541/822-6272, www. rivermountainresort.com) has bikes for rent and runs a shuttle service for trail users.

## Rafting

The McKenzie River becomes navigable at the Olallie campground, about 11 miles east of McKenzie Bridge. Between the Olallie campground and the town of Blue River, there are seven public boat launches, including at Paradise and McKenzie Bridge campgrounds. Expect to encounter Class II and III rapids along the Upper McKenzie. Many local outfitters can guide you down the river.

May to September, **McKenzie River Adventures** (541/822-3806 or 800/832-5858, www.mckenzieriveradventures.com) has half-day (3 hours, $60 adults), full-day (6 hours, $100, includes lunch), and two-day white-water rafting trips that range 7 to 18 miles and take in some Class II and III rapids. Reservations are recommended. **Oregon Whitewater Adventures** (39620 Deerhorn Rd., Springfield, 541/746-5422 or 800/820-7238, www.oregonwhitewater.com) has similar trips. All necessary gear and transportation back to your car are provided.

## Fishing

It is crowded, but the scenic beauty and the chance to bag a five-trout limit brings anglers to one of the state's best trout streams. Unless you can get a drift boat, access is limited. On weekends, drift boats and rafters vie for space. You can cast worms or spinners, though you're better off using flies when you're fishing off a boat for rainbow trout (Apr.-Oct.). Anglers might want to book a trip with **Helfrich Outfitters** (541/741-1905 or 800/507-9889, www.helfrichoutfitter.com, full-day $470 for 2). Consult the **Oregon Outfitters and Guides Directory** (www.ogpa.org) for other local guides. The best pools tend to be west of Blue River, but it's harder to get to them because of private landholdings. The **Department of Fish and Wildlife** (503/947-6000, www.dfw.state.or.us) can explain the rules and regulations before you go fishing.

## Golf

**Tokatee Golf Club** (54947 Hwy. 126, Blue River, 541/822-3220 or 800/452-6376, www.tokatee.com, Feb.-mid-Nov., $55 for 18 holes) is one of the Pacific Northwest's most beautiful courses and worth planning a vacation around. Good for all levels of experience, every hole has its own challenge. No houses are on the fairways to obstruct the knockout views of the forested mountains and the Three Sisters Wilderness.

## FOOD

Restaurants aren't a big deal out here—most overnight visitors are camping or renting cabins with cooking facilities. Just west of McKenzie Bridge, you can find decent food at **Takoda's** (91806 Mill Creek Rd., 541/822-1153, www.takodasrainbow.com, 8am-9pm daily, $9-16), next to Harbick's Country Store, for pizza, a burger, or a visit to the salad bar. During the summer, there's outside seating in a garden area. A few miles to the east, the **McKenzie General Store** (91837 Taylor Rd., 541/822-3221, www.mckenziegeneralstore.com, 7am-9pm Sun.-Thurs., 7am-10pm Fri.-Sat.) is an outwardly rustic high-end market with bulk foods, snacks, wine, cheese, and local produce. They also have beer on tap and kombucha, which you can drink out back with food from the **Obsidian Grill** (54771 McKenzie River Hwy.), a food cart serving good sandwiches and tacos.

## ACCOMMODATIONS

A great place for families (including pets) and those who want to get away from the noise of the McKenzie Highway is the **Wayfarer Resort** (46725 Goodpasture Rd., Vida, 541/896-3613, www.wayfarerresort.com, $115-355), featuring over a dozen cabins on the McKenzie and glacier-fed Marten Creek, east of Vida. Accommodating up to eight, the cabins have porches with barbecues overlooking the water, full kitchens, and lots of wood paneling. Two larger units that sleep eight are equipped with all major amenities. Children can enjoy fishing privileges in the resort's private trout pond, while the folks play on the resort's tennis court. In the summer, advance reservations are a must for this popular retreat.

The riverside **Eagle Rock Lodge** (49198 McKenzie Hwy., Vida, 541/822-3630, www.eaglerocklodge.com, $130-240) is one of the more elegant places to stay along the McKenzie. The large 1947 house has five very comfortable rooms, and there are three suites in the carriage house, with beautiful gardens and places to lounge outside. Guests can order dinner in advance from the lodge's personal chef ($45), a nice option, since there aren't many restaurants in the area.

**Heaven's Gate Cottages** (50055 McKenzie Hwy., Vida, 541/896-3855, www. heavensgaterivercottages.com) offers housekeeping cabins ($160) and a six-bedroom lodge ($500) right on the McKenzie River; the cabins are sandwiched between the highway and the river. One cabin is right over a good fishing hole, and night lights illuminate the rapids. These cabins may be old, small, and semi-rustic, but their riverside location helps overcome these issues. Note that although the address for Heaven's Gate is in Vida, the cabins are much closer to Blue River.

The former Blue River ranger station, which sits above the highway away from the river, has been repurposed as the lodge for the **McKenzie River Mountain Resort** (51668 Blue River Dr., Blue River, 541/822-6272, www.rivermountainresort.com, $100-170). The vacation cabins used to house the rangers. This is a popular base for mountain bikers riding the McKenzie River Trail; the resort offers shuttle service. It's common for groups to rent the entire lodge.

Although **Harbick's Country Inn** (54791 Hwy. 126, Blue River, 541/822-3805, www. harbicks-country-inn.com, $75-115) may not be as charming as some of the other lodgings along the McKenzie—it's basically a motel—it's a friendly place and within walking distance of one of the finest public golf courses in the country, Tokatee, and has a good restaurant next door. It's also popular—reserve in advance.

The ★ **Cedarwood Lodge** (56535 McKenzie Hwy./Hwy. 126, McKenzie Bridge, 541/822-3351, www.cedarwoodlodge.com, Apr.-Oct., $130-185) is tucked away in a grove of old cedars just outside the town of McKenzie Bridge. The lodge has nine vacation housekeeping cottages with fully equipped kitchens, baths (with showers), fireplaces (wood provided), and portable barbecues. This is a

sweet place to spend a couple of nights, particularly in those units with decks on the river.

The spacious and attractive cabins at ★ **Inn at the Bridge** (56393 McKenzie Hwy., McKenzie Bridge, 541/822-6006, www. mckenzie-river-cabins.com, year-round, $199) look like they are part of the landscape but were built in 2006 and are fully modern, with two bedrooms, full kitchens, river-rock fireplaces, two baths, and a back porch overlooking the river.

**Belknap Lodge and Hot Springs** (59296 Belknap Springs Rd., McKenzie Bridge, 541/822-3512, www.belknaphotsprings.com, $25-425) offers lodge rooms ($110-185 d), cabins (some pet-friendly, $135-425), camping ($30-40), and access to two hot-spring swimming pools. The lodge rooms have bathtubs plumbed with hot-spring water. The main attraction on the property is Belknap Springs: The piping-hot water runs into a swimming pool on the south bank of the McKenzie. Nonguests can use the pool for an hour ($8) or all day ($15).The pool closes at 9pm. If you forget your towel, you can rent one.

## Camping

The following campgrounds ($12-22) are under the jurisdiction of the Willamette National Forest's **McKenzie Ranger District** (541/822-3381, www.fs.usda.gov/Willamette, reservations 877/444-6777, www.recreation. gov). Many are along the beautiful McKenzie River National Recreation Trail, a prime location halfway between Eugene and Bend that helps make the area a popular vacation spot during the summer; reservations should be made at least five days in advance. All of these campgrounds have drinking water, vault toilets, and picnic tables.

Several choice campgrounds are south of the McKenzie Highway, off the Aufderheide Highway; these places are convenient to Cougar Reservoir and Terwilliger Hot Springs. **Delta** campground is closest to the McKenzie Highway, less than a mile south and about a mile north of the Aufderheide, along-side the river amid old-growth trees. Busy **Slide Creek** campground is on the east bank of Cougar Reservoir and has a boat ramp and swimming area. A few miles south of the reservoir along the South Fork of the McKenzie, **French Pete** and **Frissell Crossing** campgrounds are both quiet.

A half mile west of McKenzie Bridge on Highway 126 is the 20-site riverside **McKenzie Bridge Campground,** with a boat launch. About three miles east of McKenzie Bridge on Highway 126 is **Paradise Campground.** Although there are 64 tent and RV (up to 40 feet) campsites, only half of the sites are in premium riverside locations. The summer trout fishing here can be good. **Olallie Campground** is on the banks of the McKenzie River, 11 miles east of McKenzie Bridge on Highway 126; boating, fishing, and hiking are some of the nearby attractions.

On the south shore of lovely Clear Lake, 19 miles northeast of McKenzie Bridge on Highway 126, is **Coldwater Cove Campground** (mid-May-mid-Oct.). A county-run cabin resort, **Clear Lake Resort** (541/967-3917, www.linnparks.com) is adjacent to the campground and has a store, a summer-only café, and rustic cabins (bring cooking utensils and bedding, $70-135), as well as boat docks, launches, and rowboat rentals. No powerboats are permitted on the lake. The road to the resort closes at the end of September; guests can hike in to rustic cabins during the winter.

A handful of small campgrounds dot Highway 242, the old McKenzie Pass road, but none have piped water.

## INFORMATION

Read the local news online at **McKenzie River Reflections** (www.mckenzieriverreflectionsnewspaper.com). Wilderness permits, camping, hiking, and mountain biking information are available from the **McKenzie River Ranger District** (57600 McKenzie Hwy., McKenzie Bridge, 541/822-3381, www.fs.usda.gov).

## GETTING THERE

Amazingly, travelers without cars can get to the McKenzie National Recreation Trail from Eugene via **Lane Transit District** (541/687-5555, www.ltd.org, $1.75). The route 91 bus starts in Springfield at Thurston station (which has frequent bus connections to downtown Eugene) and heads up the McKenzie River Highway. The bus is equipped to carry a couple of bikes. The terminus point is the McKenzie River Ranger Station at McKenzie Bridge.

# Oakridge and the Upper Willamette River

Halfway between Eugene and the Cascades' summit on Highway 58 is Oakridge (pop. 3,200). Historically a timber town, mountain biking now helps to support this small community tucked away in a foothill valley of the Cascades. Over 100 nearby lakes and streams provide trout fishing. A short drive southeast of town, near Willamette Pass, are two central Oregon gems: Waldo Lake and Odell Lake.

## SIGHTS
### Westfir Covered Bridge
A short distance from Oakridge on the paved Aufderheide National Scenic Byway is the **Westfir Covered Bridge,** which has the distinction of being the longest covered bridge in Oregon (180 feet) and features a separate pedestrian walkway. You can get a photo-worthy view of the bridge from the road as you approach the nearby town of Westfir.

### Salt Creek Falls
About 20 miles southeast of Oakridge, just west of Willamette Pass on the way to Odell Lake on Highway 58, **Salt Creek Falls** forms the headwaters of the Willamette River. Shortly after the turnoff from the south side of the highway, take the right fork in the road and head down to the parking area (NW Forest Pass required). The short walk to the viewing area of the 286-foot-high cascade provides a great photo opportunity. Trails access both the top and the bottom of the waterfall.

### McCredie Hot Springs
**McCredie Hot Springs** is 10 miles southeast of Oakridge on Highway 58 near mile marker 45. A short walk down to Salt Creek brings you to a small hot spring adjacent to the river. This location allows you to enjoy the rush of simultaneously hot and cold water. Depending on how you position yourself, you can take a bath

at any temperature you choose—be careful, as there are some extremely hot spots. Because it's so close to the road this place is often busy; many visitors bathe nude here.

## SPORTS AND RECREATION
### Hiking
#### FALL CREEK NATIONAL RECREATION TRAIL
The 14-mile hiker-only **Fall Creek National Recreation Trail,** about 30 miles southeast of Eugene, is ideal for short day hikes or longer expeditions; there are several entry points along the way. Another plus is the low elevation of the trail, which makes it accessible year-round. Strolling through the wilderness, you will pass many deep pools, white-water rapids, and over a dozen small streams.

To get here, take Highway 58 about 15 miles to Lowell, then go north for two miles to the covered bridge at Unity Junction. Take a right onto Forest Road 18 (Fall Creek Rd.), and stay to the left of the reservoir. Follow the road for 11 miles to Dolly Varden Campground, where the trail starts. There are five campgrounds en route and three other spur trails that merge into the Fall Creek Trail. Bedrock Campground is a particularly popular spot for swimming.

#### LARISON CREEK TRAIL
The **Larison Creek Trail** (Trail 3646), shared by hikers and mountain bikers, is less than 10 minutes south of Oakridge. Multicolored mosses cover the valley floor, and its walls emulate a brush-stroked backdrop amid stands of old-growth fir. Further contrast is supplied by waterfalls and swimming holes. The mild grade and low elevation of this 6.3-mile trail make it accessible year-round. To get here, take Highway 58 to Oakridge. Turn onto

Salt Creek Falls

Kitson Springs County Road and proceed for 0.5 miles. Turn right on Forest Road 21 and follow it three miles to the trailhead, which you'll find on the right side of the road.

### ★ Mountain Biking

Mountain biking has become incredibly popular in the Oakridge area, which is not surprising given that there are an estimated 350 miles of single-track within an hour's drive of town. Find information and detailed trail descriptions at www.mtbikeoakridge.com.

Novice bikers and families can start with the 12-mile-long **Salmon Creek Trail,** which originates in town and heads along generally flat terrain to Salmon Creek Falls. Also just outside town, starting at Greenwaters Park near the fish hatchery, **Larison Rock** is a thrilling, technical five-mile downhill ride. Then, unless you've arranged a car shuttle, it's a bit of a slog back to the start. An easier but longer route back follows Forest Road 2102. The nearly 30-mile-long **Middle Fork River Trail** is a good bet for experienced mountain

bikers who want to test their stamina. It starts at the Sand Prairie campground south of town and heads south and east along the Middle Fork of the Willamette River.

Oakridge hosts a three-day **mountain bike festival** (503/968-8870, www.mtbikeoakridge.com, mid-July, $409) with guided rides of the area's trails, meals, demo bikes, beer, and camping. Road cyclists needn't avoid Oakridge; the **Aufderheide National Scenic Byway** is an excellent low-traffic paved road along the North Fork of the Willamette River.

## FOOD

If there are mountain bikers, there must be beer nearby. Find both at the **Brewers Union Local 180** (48329 E. 1st St., 541/782-2024, www.brewersunion.com, noon-9pm Sun.-Wed., noon-10pm Thurs., noon-11pm Fri.-Sat. summer, noon-8pm Sun.-Tues. and Thurs., noon-10pm Fri.-Sat. winter, $12-16), a family-friendly British-style public house where it's as easy to settle in with a cup of tea as with a pint of ale. Read a book or play pool. Just a block away, find stronger spirits at the **Deep Woods Distillery** (48217 E. 1st St., 541/968-4623, call for hours), a tiny start-up featuring Fir of the Doug, a grain alcohol flavored with Douglas fir tips.

Fuel up for the day's activities with a bagel from **Lion Mountain Bakery** (47781 Hwy. 58, 541/782-5797, 8am-noon Tues., 8am-4pm Wed.-Fri., 8am-3pm Sun.), located in the Cascade Event Center (an old general store); if you're passing through at lunchtime, the soup here is homemade.

**Lee's Gourmet Garden** (47670 Hwy. 58, 541/782-2155, 11am-9pm Tues.-Sun., $7-12) is better than your average small-town Chinese restaurant. The owner used to be martial artist and actor Jackie Chan's personal chef and brings a nice touch and a few special dishes to a pretty standard Chinese American menu.

## ACCOMMODATIONS

There are some reasonable lodging options in the area. The bike-friendly **Oakridge Lodge**

**and Guest House** (48175 E. 1st St., 541/782-4000, www.oakridge-lodge.com, Apr.-mid-Nov., $50 pp dorm, $115-125 private room) is housed in an old Masonic lodge with a shared bunkroom, four private rooms with a bath down the hall, and a good B&B-style breakfast, even for bunk dwellers. The lodge also serves wood-fired pizza and salads for dinner (5pm-9pm Fri.-Sun., $9-14), not included in room rates.

The **Bluewolf Motel** (47465 Hwy. 58, 541/782-5884, www.bluewolfmotel.com, $59-69) is a small, simple motel with microwaves and fridges. It's pet-friendly and has pleasant spacious grounds, including the Wolf Den, an outdoor kitchen with a gas grill, piped water, and seating.

In the former office building of Hines Lumber Company in Westfir, across the street from the covered bridge, is the **Westfir Lodge** (47365 1st St., Westfir, 541/782-3103, www.westfirlodge.com, $90-140). The building has been tastefully converted into seven guest rooms with private baths across the hall.

## INFORMATION

The **Oakridge-Westfir Chamber of Commerce** (48248 Hwy. 58, Oakridge, 541/782-4146, www.oakridgechamber.com) has a small visitors center in the rest area on the east side of town. Additional information on biking, hiking, camping, and the Aufderheide National Scenic Byway can be obtained from the **Middle Fork Ranger Station** (46375 Hwy. 58, Westfir, 541/782-2283, www.fs.usda.gov/willamette).

# North Coast

Look for ★ to find recommended sights, activities, dining, and lodging.

# Highlights

★ **Columbia River Maritime Museum:** One of Oregon's top museums tells the story of seafaring on the Columbia River (page 216).

★ **Fort Clatsop National Memorial:** This replica of Lewis and Clark's 1805-1806 winter camp offers a fascinating glimpse into frontier life (page 218).

★ **Haystack Rock:** This soaring sea stack on Cannon Beach is home to thousands of seabirds (page 243).

★ **Saddle Mountain State Natural Area:** This knobby mountain rises high above the northern coast, with a hiking trail leading through unusual plantlife on the way to an eye-popping vista (page 244).

★ **Cape Lookout Hikes:** Go for the great views of rocks and surf, the chance of seeing a whale, or to totally immerse yourself in the foggy coastal atmosphere (page 267).

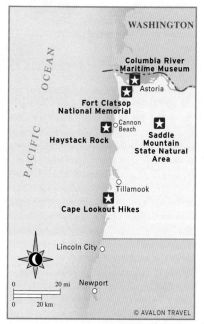

The enchanting north coast—from the mouth of the Columbia River south to Lincoln City—is little more than an hour's drive from the Portland metro area. It's the most popular part of Oregon's Pacific shoreline. Still, apart from the weekend crush at Cannon Beach and Seaside, there's more than enough elbow room for everyone.

Overlooking the Columbia River as it flows into the Pacific, the former shipping and fishing center of Astoria is fast rediscovering its own potential, with a lively arts scene, adventurous cuisine, and fine hotels and B&Bs hosting overnighters. Its long-idle waterfront is busy again with tourist attractions—most notably the Columbia River Maritime Museum, one of the best museums in Oregon.

West of Astoria, at Oregon's far northwestern tip, where the mighty Columbia River meets the Pacific, visitors to Fort Stevens State Park can inspect the skeleton of a century-old shipwreck and a military fort active from the Civil War to World War II, as well as revel in miles of sandy beaches. Fort Clatsop National Memorial, part of Lewis and Clark National Historical Park, includes a recreation of the Corps of Discovery's winter 1805-1806 quarters—a must-stop for Lewis and Clark buffs.

Cannon Beach and Seaside are two extremely popular resort towns that are polar opposites of one another. Cannon Beach, an enclave of tastefully weathered cedar-shingled architecture, is chockablock with art galleries, boutiques, and upscale lodgings and restaurants. A few miles north, Seaside is Oregon's quintessential family-friendly beach resort, with a long boardwalk, candy and gift shops, and noisy game arcades.

Just south of Cannon Beach, Oswald West State Park is a gem protecting old-growth forest and handsome little pocket beaches—as well as, some believe, a Spanish pirate treasure buried on Neahkahnie Mountain. Beyond Neahkahnie's cliff-top viewpoints along U.S. 101, the Nehalem Bay area attracts anglers, crabbers, and kayakers, as well as discriminating diners who come from far and wide to enjoy surprisingly sophisticated cuisine.

**Previous:** Haystack Rock; Ecola State Park. **Above:** Cape Meares Lighthouse.

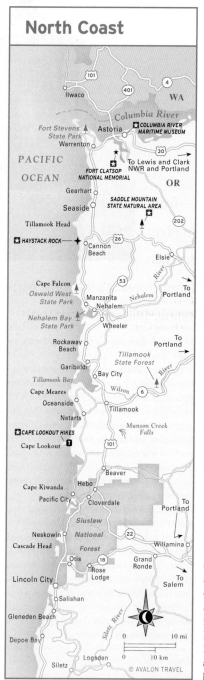

# North Coast

Tillamook County, home to more cows than people, is synonymous with delicious dairy products—cheese and ice cream in particular. It's no surprise that Tillamook's biggest visitor attraction is cheese-related. More than a million people a year come to the Tillamook Cheese Factory to view the cheese-making operations and sample the excellent results. The Tillamook Air Museum is another popular diversion, housing an outstanding collection of vintage and modern aircraft in gargantuan Hangar B, the largest wooden structure in the world. Tillamook Bay, fed by five rivers, yields oysters and crabs, while the active Garibaldi charter fleet targets salmon, halibut, and tuna in the offshore waters.

South of Tillamook, the Coast Highway wends inland through lush pastureland to Neskowin. It's a pleasant enough stretch, but the Three Capes Scenic Loop, a 35-mile scenic coastal detour, is a more attractive, if time-consuming, option. The spectacular views and bird-watching from Capes Meares and Lookout are the highlights of this beautiful drive. At Pacific City, at the southern end of the Three Capes Loop, commercial anglers launch their dories right off the sandy beach and through the surf in the lee of Cape Kiwanda and mammoth Haystack Rock—a sight not seen anywhere else on the West Coast. Just north of Lincoln City, Cascade Head beckons hikers to explore its rare prairie headlands ecosystem.

## PLANNING YOUR TIME

Although most Oregonians have a favorite beach town that they'll visit for weekends and summer vacations, if this is your grand tour of the Oregon coast, plan to spend a few days exploring the northern coast's beaches and towns. If you're interested in history, architecture, or ship-watching, spend a night in **Astoria**—it's one of our favorite coastal cities, even though it's several miles from the Pacific Ocean. If you can't wait to walk on Pacific beaches, head to **Cannon Beach** (for a more upscale stay) or **Seaside** (which the kids will love) and begin your trip there. By driving from north to south, you'll be able to pull off the highway more easily into beach access areas. Campers might want to reserve a space at Nehalem Bay State Park, near the small laid-back town of **Manzanita,** a few miles south of Cannon Beach; Manzanita is also a good place to rent a beach house for a weekend. Aside from the near-mandatory stop at the Tillamook Cheese Factory, you'll probably want to skip the town of Tillamook and head to the **Three Capes Loop,** where a night in Pacific City offers easy access to Cape Kiwanda as well as comfy lodgings and a good brewpub. On your way south to the central coast, or to the Highway 18 route back through the Willamette Valley wine country to Portland, do stop for a hike at **Cascade Head.**

# Astoria and Vicinity

The mouth of the mighty Columbia River, with its abundance of natural resources, was long a home for Native Americans; artifacts found in the area suggest that people have been living along the river for at least 8,000 years. Early European explorers and settlers also found the river and its bays to be propitious as a trading and fishing center. Astoria's dramatic location and deep history continue to attract new settlers and travelers drawn to the area's potent allure.

Astoria (pop. about 10,000) is the oldest permanent U.S. settlement west of the Rockies, and its glory days are preserved by museums, historical exhibits, and pastel-colored Victorian homes weathered by the sea air. Hollywood has chosen Astoria's picturesque neighborhoods to simulate an idealized all-American town, most notably in the cult classic *The Goonies.*

What sets Astoria apart from other destinations on the northern Oregon coast is that it's a real city, not a waterfront town made over into a resort. While the decline in the logging and fishing industries dealt the city many economic blows in the late 20th century, there's plenty of pluck left in this old dowager, and her best years may be yet to come as a thriving haven for artists and free spirits.

Astoria has many charms: Colorful Victorian mansions and historic buildings downtown are undergoing restoration, cruise ships are calling, fine restaurants are multiplying, a lively arts scene is booming, and there's new life along the waterfront, anchored by the excellent Columbia River Maritime Museum.

## History
The Clatsop people, a Chinook-speaking group, lived in this area for thousands of years before Astoria's written history began. When Lewis and Clark arrived in 1805, the Clatsops numbered about 400 people, living in three villages on the south side of the Columbia River, but their steady decline began soon after contact with whites.

The region was first chronicled by Don Bruno de Heceta, a Spanish explorer who sailed near the Columbia's mouth in August 1775. He named it the Bay of the Assumption of Our Lady, but the strong current prevented his ship from entering. American presence on the Columbia began with Captain Robert Gray's discovery of the river in May 1792, which he named after his fur-trading ship, *Columbia Rediviva.*

Thereafter, Lewis and Clark's famous expedition of 1803-1806, with its winter encampment at Fort Clatsop, south of present-day Astoria, helped incorporate the Pacific Northwest as part of a new nation. In 1811, John Jacob Astor's agents built Fort Astoria on a hillside in what would eventually grow into Astoria—the first American settlement west of the Rockies. The trading post was occupied by the British between 1813 and 1818, and the settlement was renamed Fort George.

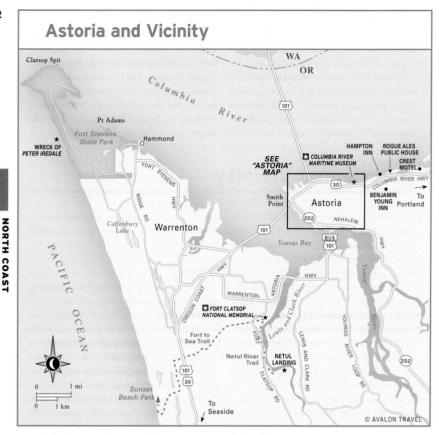

# Astoria and Vicinity

Real development began in the 1840s as settlers begin pouring in from the Oregon Trail. During the Civil War, Fort Stevens was built at the mouth of the Columbia to guard against a Confederate naval incursion.

Commerce grew with the export of lumber and foodstuffs to gold rush-era San Francisco and Asia. Salmon canneries became the mainstay of Astoria's economy during the 1870s, helping it grow into Oregon's second-largest city—and a notorious shanghaiing port, where young men, often drunk, were kidnapped from bars to serve as unwilling sailors on commercial and military ships. From that time through the early 1900s, the dominant immigrants to the Astoria area were Scandinavian, and with the addition of these seafaring folk, logging, fishing, and

shipbuilding coaxed the population up to 20,000 by World War II.

Some believe that the port city at the mouth of the Columbia might have grown to rival San Francisco or Seattle had it not been for the setback of a devastating fire in 1922. In the early morning hours of December 8, a pool hall on Commercial Street caught fire; the flames spread rapidly among the wooden buildings, many supported on wooden pilings, in Astoria's business district. By daybreak, more than 200 businesses in a 32-block area had been reduced to ashes. The downtown was rebuilt in the ensuing years, largely in brick and stone, but the devastation changed the fate of Astoria.

Near the end of World War II, a Japanese submarine's shelling of Fort Stevens made it the only fortification on U.S. soil to have sustained an attack in a world war. After the war, the region's fortunes ebbed and flowed with its resource-based economy. In an attempt to supplement that economy with tourism, the State Highway Division began constructing the Astoria-Megler Bridge in 1962 to connect Oregon and Washington.

## Orientation

The waters surrounding Astoria define the town as much as the steep hills it's built on. Along its northern side, the mighty Columbia, four miles wide, is a mega aquatic highway carrying a steady flow of traffic, from small pleasure boats to massive cargo ships a quarter-mile long. Soaring high over the river is an engineering marvel that's impossible to miss from most locations in town. At just over four miles long, the Astoria-Megler Bridge is the longest bridge in Oregon and the longest bridge of its type (cantilever through-truss) in the nation. When it opened in 1966, the bridge provided the final link in the 1,625-mile-long U.S. 101 along the Pacific coast.

On Astoria's south side, Young's River, flowing down from the Coast Range, broadens into Young's Bay, separating Astoria from its neighbor Warrenton to the southwest. A few miles to the west, the Columbia River finally meets the Pacific, 1,243 miles from its headwaters in British Columbia. Where the tremendous outflow (averaging 118 million gallons per minute) of the River of the West encounters the ocean tides, conditions can be treacherous, and the sometimes-monstrous waves around the bar have claimed more than 2,000 vessels over the years. This river's mouth could well be the biggest widow-maker on the high seas, earning it the title "Graveyard of the Pacific." Lewis and Clark referred to it as "that seven-shouldered horror" in a journal entry from the winter of 1805-1806.

Any visitor to Astoria should consider crossing the Astoria-Megler Bridge to visit the extreme southwest corner of Washington

State. Here the sands and soil carried by the Columbia create a 20-mile-long sand spit called the Long Beach Peninsula. Some of the West Coast's most succulent oysters grow in Willapa Bay, the body of water created by this finger of sand. Historic beach communities plus numerous Lewis and Clark sites also reward visitors to this charming enclave.

## SIGHTS

After getting a bird's-eye view from the Astoria Column, you might want to take a closer look at Astoria on foot. The town is home to dozens of beautifully restored 19th-century and early-20th-century houses.

Here's a suggested route: From the Flavel House Museum at 8th Street and Duane Street, start walking south on 8th Street and turn left on Franklin Avenue. Continue east to 11th Street, then detour south one block on 11th Street to Grand Avenue; head east on Grand, north on 12th Street, and back to Franklin, continuing your eastward trek. Walk to 17th Street, then south again to Grand, double back on Grand two blocks to 15th Street, then walk north on 15th to Exchange Street and east on Exchange to 17th, where you'll be just two blocks from the Columbia River Maritime Museum. This route takes you past 74 historical buildings and sites.

One of Astoria's most impressive sights is the commanding vista of the **Astoria-Megler Bridge.** To get there from the Flavel House Museum, head south uphill on 8th Street and turn right (west) on Franklin Avenue. Follow Franklin six blocks until it turns into Skyline Avenue. After one block, turn onto West Grand Avenue, which hugs the ridge. For the ultimate perch directly over the bridge, turn off W. Grand to follow Lincoln Street north downhill to Alameda Ave. where you're eye-to-eye with the bridge's soaring span.

### Astoria Column

The best introduction to Astoria and environs is undoubtedly the 360-degree panorama

**NORTH COAST**
ASTORIA AND VICINITY

from atop the 125-foot-tall **Astoria Column** (2199 Coxcomb Dr., 503/325-2963, www.astoriacolumn.org, dawn-dusk daily, $1 for parking) on Coxcomb Hill, the highest point in town. Patterned after Trajan's Column in Rome, the reinforced-concrete tower was built in 1926 as a joint project of the Great Northern Railway and the descendants of John Jacob Astor to commemorate the westward sweep of discovery and migration. The graffito frieze spiraling up the exterior illustrates Robert Gray's 1792 discovery of the Columbia River, the establishment of American claims to the Northwest Territory, the arrival of the Great Northern Railway, and other scenes of the history of the Pacific Northwest. The vista from the surrounding hilltop park is impressive enough, but for the ultimate experience, the climb up 164 steps to the tower's top is worth the effort.

If you have kids in tow, stop by the tiny gift shop to buy a balsa-wood glider. Lofting a wooden airplane from the top of the tower is an Astoria tradition.

Get to the Astoria Column from downtown by following 16th Street south (uphill) to Jerome Avenue. Turn west (right) one block and continue up 15th Street to the park entrance on Coxcomb Drive.

## The Waterfront

While most of Astoria's waterfront is lined with warehouses and docks, the **River Walk** will get you front-row views of the river. The River Walk provides paved riverside passage for pedestrians and cyclists along a five-mile stretch between the Port of Astoria and the community of Alderbrook, at the eastern fringe of Astoria.

An excellent way to cover some of the same ground, accompanied by commentary on sights and local history, is by taking a 50-minute ride on Old 300, the **Astoria Riverfront Trolley** (503/325-6311, www.old300.org, weather permitting daily Memorial Day-Labor Day, noon-6pm Fri.-Sun. fall and spring, $1 per ride or $2 all day), which runs on Astoria's original train tracks alongside the River Walk as far east as the East Mooring Basin. Trolley shelters are at nine stops along the route; you can also flag it down anywhere along the way by waving a dollar bill. The lovingly restored 1913 trolley originally served San Antonio and later ran between Portland and Lake Oswego in the 1980s.

Toward the eastern end of the River Walk, at Pier 39, the **Hanthorn Cannery** (100 39th St., 9am-6pm daily, free) is a rather informal but fascinating museum housed in an old

the Astoria waterfront

# Astoria

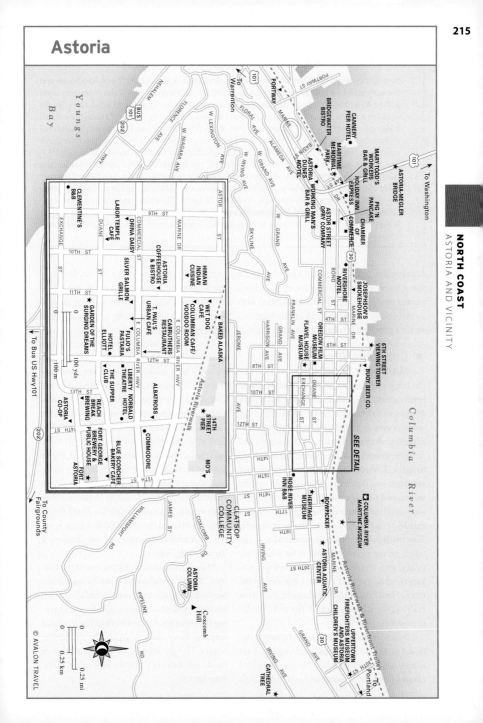

Youngs Bay

To Warrenton

To Washington

101

BUS 101 202

PORTWAY ST

PORTWAY MARINE

NETHANEM

FLORENCE AVE

NIAGARA AVE

IRVING AVE

GRAND AVE

FLORAL AVE

W LEXINGTON AVE

W IRVING AVE

W GRAND AVE

W NIAGARA AVE

ALAMEDA AVE

W LEXINGTON

SKYLINE AVE

ASTOR ST

MARINE DR

BRIDGEWATER BISTRO

CANNERY PIER HOTEL

MARITIME MEMORIAL PARK

BASIN

ASTORIA DUNES MOTEL

WORKING MAN'S BAR & GRILL

MARY TODD'S WORKERS BAR & GRILL

PIG 'N PANCAKE

HOLIDAY INN EXPRESS

CHAMBER OF COMMERCE

ASTOR STREET OPRY COMPANY

101

ASTORIA-MEGLER BRIDGE

To Washington

30

RIVERSHORE MOTEL

JOSEPHSON'S SMOKEHOUSE

6TH STREET VIEWING TOWER

BUOY BEER CO.

Columbia River

COMMERCIAL ST

BOND ST

FRANKLIN AVE

GRAND AVE

HARRISON AVE

4TH ST

6TH ST

8TH ST

10TH ST

12TH ST

MARINE DR

OREGON FILM MUSEUM

FLAVEL HOUSE MUSEUM

EXCHANGE ST

DUANE ST

SEE DETAIL

14TH ST

15TH ST

16TH ST

17TH ST

18TH ST

20TH ST

JAMES ST

IRVING AVE

GRAND AVE

ROSE RIVER INN B&B

HERITAGE MUSEUM

BOWPICKER

COLUMBIA RIVER MARITIME MUSEUM

CLATSOP COMMUNITY COLLEGE

ASTORIA AQUATIC CENTER

Astoria Riverwalk & Riverfront Trolley

UPPERTOWN FIREFIGHTERS MUSEUM AND ASTORIA CHILDREN'S MUSEUM

To Portland

30

CATHEDRAL TREE

ASTORIA COLUMN

Coxcomb Hill

COXCOMB DR

WILLIAMSPORT RD

PIPELINE RD

JAMES ST

To County Fairgrounds

To Bus US Hwy101

202

HWY

## Detail inset

CLEMENTINE'S B&B

LABOR TEMPLE CAFÉ

DRINA DAISY

SILVER SALMON GRILLE

ASTORIA COFFEEHOUSE & BISTRO

HIMANI INDIAN CUISINE

WET DOG CAFÉ

COLUMBIAN CAFÉ/ VOODOO ROOM

T. PAUL'S URBAN CAFÉ

CARRUTHERS RESTAURANT

FULIO'S PASTARIA

HOTEL ELLIOTT

THE SUPPER CLUB

LIBERTY THEATRE

NORBLAD HOTEL

ALBATROSS

ASTORIA CO-OP

REACH BREAK BREWING

FORT GEORGE BREWERY & PUBLIC HOUSE

BLUE SCORCHER BAKERY CAFÉ

FORT ASTORIA

COMMODORE

GARDEN OF THE SURGING DREAMS

BAKED ALASKA

14TH STREET PIER

MO'S

Astoria Riverwalk

9TH ST

10TH ST

11TH ST

12TH ST

13TH ST

14TH ST

15TH ST

COMMERCIAL ST

DUANE ST

EXCHANGE ST

MARINE DR

ASTOR ST

JEROME AVE

E COLUMBIA RIVER HWY

ASTORIA RIVER HWY

0    100 yds

0    100 m

0    0.25 mi

0    0.25 km

© AVALON TRAVEL

# Astoria Goes to the Movies

In recent decades, the Victorian homes and ocean view in Astoria's hillside neighborhoods and the surrounding maritime settings have provided the backdrop for such fanciful modern sagas as *Free Willy I* and *II, Kindergarten Cop, Teenage Mutant Ninja Turtles III, Short Circuit, Come See the Paradise,* and *The Goonies.* The last movie, a cult favorite shot in 1985, concerns a gang of local kids hunting for pirate's treasure; happy memories of the movie continue to attract a steady stream of visitors looking for the locations used in the film. More recently, films shot in Astoria have gravitated toward horror, including *The Ring Two* and *Cthulhu,* a film based on the horror novels of H. P. Lovecraft. A guide to movie locations is available at the Oregon Welcome Center in Astoria, the Heritage Museum, Flavel House Museum, and the Warrenton Visitors Center. Stop by the **Oregon Film Museum** (732 Duane St., 503/325-2203, www.oregonfilmmuseum.org, 10am-5pm daily May-Sept., 11am-4pm daily Oct.,-Apr., $6 adults, $2 ages 6-17), which ostensibly celebrates the various films shot in Oregon, but is mostly a paean to all things Goonie. The museum is housed in the old Clatsop County Jail (from 1914), which famously starred in *The Goonies* jailbreak scene.

Bumble Bee tuna cannery. Exhibits include some lovely old wooden boats, eye-catching photos, and canning equipment. There's also a coffee shop and a brewpub at this location, so it's a good place to take a break.

## ★ Columbia River Maritime Museum

On the waterfront a few blocks east of downtown Astoria, the **Columbia River Maritime Museum** (1792 Marine Dr., 503/325-2323, www.crmm.org, 9:30am-5pm daily, closed Thanksgiving and Christmas, $14 adults, $12 seniors, $5 ages 6-17, free under age 6) is hard to miss. The roof of the 44,000-square-foot museum simulates the curvature of cresting waves, and the gigantic 25,000-pound anchor out front is also impossible to ignore. What's inside surpasses this eye-catching facade. The introductory film is excellent and intense, giving a good glimpse of the jobs of bar pilots, who climb aboard huge ships to navigate them across the Columbia Bar and up the river. Floor-to-ceiling windows in the Great Hall allow visitors to watch the river traffic in comfort.

Historic boats, scale models, exquisitely detailed miniatures of ships, paintings, and artifacts recount times when Native American canoes plied the Columbia; Lewis and Clark camped on the Columbia's shores; and dramatic shipwrecks occurred on its bar. Local lighthouses, the evolution of boat design, scrimshaw, and harpoons are the focus of other exhibits here.

The museum also now houses two of three cannons that gave nearby Cannon Beach its name. These early-19th-century cannons, from the USS *Shark,* which met its end on the Columbia River Bar in 1846, were set adrift and washed up some 30 miles south of the Columbia's mouth, near Cannon Beach. The first of the cannons was discovered in 1894, and the last two were found in 2008. All were studied at Texas A&M University for a number of years, and two are now on display in Astoria's Columbia Maritime Museum, along with an officer's sword from the *Shark* found in the 1970s, and the Shark Rock, a large boulder into which survivors of the shipwreck carved their names.

Museum admission lets you board the 128-foot lightship *Columbia,* now permanently berthed alongside the museum building. This vessel served as a floating lighthouse, marking the entrance to the mouth of the river and helping many ships navigate the dangerous waters. The gift shop has a great collection of books on Astoria's history and other maritime topics.

## Heritage Museum and Research Library

The Clatsop County Historical Society operates three worthwhile historic destinations in Astoria, and if you're planning on visiting the Heritage Museum, the Oregon Film Museum, and the Flavel House museum, you should consider the three-in-one tickets ($12 adults, $10 seniors, $5 ages 6-17) available at any of the locations.

The **Heritage Museum** (1618 Exchange St., 503/325-2203, www.cumtux.org, 10am-5pm daily May-Sept., 11am-4pm daily Oct.-Apr., $6 adults, $5 seniors, $2 ages 6-12) is housed in a handsome neoclassical building that was originally Astoria's city hall. It has several galleries filled with antiques, tools, vintage photographs, and archives chronicling various aspects of life in Clatsop County. The museum's centerpiece exhibit concentrates on the culture of the local Clatsop and Chinook peoples, from before European contact up to the present day. Other exhibits highlight natural history, geology, early immigrants and settlers in the region, and the development of commerce in such fields as fishing, fish packing, logging, and lumber. The **research library** is open to the public.

## Flavel House Museum

Captain George Flavel, Astoria's first millionaire, amassed a fortune in the mid-19th century through his Columbia Bar piloting monopoly, and later expanded his empire through shipping, banking, and real estate. Between 1884 and 1886 he had a home built in the center of Astoria overlooking the Columbia River, now the **Flavel House Museum** (441 8th St., 503/325-2203, 10am-5pm daily May-Sept., 11am-4pm daily Oct.-Apr., $6 adults, $5 seniors and students, $2 ages 6-17, free under age 6), where he retired with his wife and two daughters. From its fourth-story cupola, Flavel could watch the comings and goings of his sailing fleet.

When the Clatsop County Historical Society assumed stewardship in 1951, the mansion was slated for demolition, to be paved over as a parking lot for the adjacent courthouse. Fortunately, thanks to the efforts of the historical society and many volunteers, the house still stands today at the corner of 8th and Duane Streets. The splendidly extravagant Queen Anne mansion reflects the rich style and elegance of the late Victorian era and the lives of Astoria's most prominent family.

The property encompasses a full city block. With its intricate woodwork inside and out, period furnishings, and art, along with its extravagantly rendered gables, cornices, and porches, the Flavel House ranks with the Carson Mansion in Eureka, California, as a Victorian showplace. The Carriage House, on the southwest corner of the property, serves as an orientation center for visitors with exhibits, an interpretive video, and a museum store.

## Garden of the Surging Dreams

A small garden and outdoor art display, **Garden of the Surging Dreams** (11th St. and Duane St.) commemorates Astoria's Chinese heritage. At the center is a pavilion with nine stone columns ornately carved with dragons. The garden's east facade is a finely worked metal screen with quotations from Chinese pioneers. This park is the first feature in the repurposing of an underutilized downtown parking lot into the Astoria Heritage Square, which in time will also feature an amphitheater and an open-air market.

## Fort Astoria

In a tiny park at the corner of 15th and Exchange Streets, a reproduction of a rough-hewn log blockhouse and a mural commemorate the spot where Astoria began, when John Jacob Astor's fur traders originally constructed a small fort in 1811. It's worth a quick stop for buffs of early Pacific Northwest history.

## Lewis and Clark National Wildlife Refuge

Six miles east of Astoria in the Burnside area is the **Twilight Creek Eagle Sanctuary.** To get there, drive seven miles east of town on U.S.

30 and turn left at Burnside. A viewing platform on the left, 0.5 miles later, overlooks the 35,000 acres of mudflats, tidal marshes, and islands (which Lewis and Clark called "Seal Islands") of the **Lewis and Clark National Wildlife Refuge.** Bald eagles live here year-round, and the area provides wintering and resting habitat for waterfowl, shorebirds, and songbirds. Beavers, raccoons, weasels, mink, muskrats, and river otters live on the islands; harbor seals and California sea lions feed in the rich estuary waters and use the sandbars and mudflats as haul-out sites at low tide.

## ★ Fort Clatsop National Memorial

In November 1805, after a journey of nearly 19 months and 4,000 miles, the Lewis and Clark expedition reached the mouth of the Columbia River, where they decided to winter. They chose a thickly forested rise alongside the Netul River (now the Lewis and Clark River), a few miles south of present-day Astoria, for their campsite. There, the Corps of Discovery quickly set about felling trees and building two parallel rows of cabins, joined by a gated palisade. The finished compound measured about 50 feet on each side. The party of 33 people, including an enslaved African American man and a Native American woman and her baby, moved into the seven small rooms on Christmas Eve and named their stockade Fort Clatsop, for the nearby Native American people.

The winter of 1805-1806 was cold, wet, rainy, and generally miserable. Of the 106 days spent at the site, it rained on all but 12. The January 18, 1806, journal entry of expedition member Private Joseph Whitehouse was typical of the comments recorded during the stay: "It rained hard all last night, & still continued the same this morning. It continued Raining during the whole of this day."

While at Fort Clatsop, the men stored up meat and other supplies, sewed moccasins and new garments, and traded with local indigenous people, all the while coping with the constant damp conditions, illness and injuries, and merciless plagues of fleas. As soon as the weather permitted, on March 23, 1806, they finally departed on their homeward journey to St. Louis.

Within a few years the elements had erased all traces of Fort Clatsop, and its exact location was lost. In 1955, local history buffs took their best guess and built a replica of the fort based on the notes and sketches of Captain Clark. In 1999, an anthropologist discovered

Fort Clatsop National Memorial

# The Long Beach Peninsula

If you've come as far as Astoria, at the edge of the continent and at the mouth of the Columbia River, you should consider crossing the soaring Astoria-Megler Bridge to explore sights on the Columbia's northern shore. There are both scenic and historical reasons to visit this remote corner of Washington State. The Lewis and Clark National and State Historical Parks aggregation includes a number of sites just across from Astoria in Washington, notably **Cape Disappointment State Park,** with a newly expanded Lewis and Clark Interpretive Center.

The **Long Beach Peninsula,** the thin sand spit just north of the mouth of the Columbia River, claims to have the world's longest beach. With 28 unbroken miles of beach, the boast has to be taken seriously. Like Seaside in Oregon, beach resorts at Seaview and Long Beach have a long pedigree, dating from the 1880s, when Portland families journeyed down the Columbia River by steamboat to summer at the coast. The bay side of the Long Beach sand spit creates **Willapa Bay,** known to oyster-lovers around the country for the excellent bivalves that grow in this shallow inlet, which is fed by six pristine rivers. Most of Willapa Bay is protected as a national wildlife refuge, and it's an excellent bird-watching site. **Oysterville,** a tiny village along the bay, stands largely unchanged since the 1880s, and the entire town has been placed on the National Register of Historic Places. The tip of the peninsula is preserved as 807-acre **Leadbetter Point State Park,** with informal hiking trails along both sandy beaches and the reedy bay.

a 148-year-old map identifying the location of Lewis and Clark's winter encampment, and as it turns out, the reproduction is sited close to the original. In 2005 this replica of Fort Clatsop burned, and a new replica, built mostly by volunteers using period tools, was reopened in 2006. Compared to the previous one, this new Fort Clatsop is a more authentic replica of the actual fort that housed the intrepid Corps of Discovery.

Today, in addition to the log replica of the fort, a well-equipped visitors center, museum, and other attractions make **Fort Clatsop Visitors Center and Fort Clatsop Replica** (92343 Fort Clatsop Rd., 503/861-2471, www. nps.gov/lewi, 9am-6pm daily mid-June-Labor Day, 9am-5pm daily Labor Day-mid-June, $5 adults, free under age 16) a must-stop for anyone interested in this pivotal chapter of American history. The expedition's story is nicely narrated here with displays, artifacts, slides, and films, but the summertime "living history" reenactments are the main reason to come. Paths lead through the grove of old-growth Sitka spruce, with interpretive placards identifying native plants. A short walk from the fort leads to the riverside, where dugout canoes are modeled on those used by

the corps while in this area. In addition, the 6.5-mile **Fort to Sea Trail** follows the general route blazed by Captain Clark from the fort through dunes and forests to the Pacific at Sunset Beach.

The winter of 1805-1806 put a premium on wilderness survival skills, some of which are exhibited here by rangers in costume. You may see the demonstrations of flintlock rifles, tanning of hides, making of buckskin clothing and moccasins, and the molding of tallow candles and lead bullets. In addition, Rangers also lead guided hikes along the river.

This 1,500-acre park sits six miles southwest of Astoria and three miles east of U.S. 101 on the Lewis and Clark River. To get there from Astoria, take Marine Drive and head west across Young's Bay to Warrenton. On the south side of the bay, look for signs for the Fort Clatsop turnoff; turn left off the Coast Highway about a mile after the bridge and follow the signs to Fort Clatsop.

## Fort Stevens State Park

Ten miles west of Astoria, in the far northwest corner of the state, the Civil War-era outpost of **Fort Stevens** (100 Peter Iredale Rd., Hammond, 503/861-3170, ext. 21, or

800/551-6949, www.oregonstateparks.org, $5 day-use for historic military area and Coffenbury Lake, $22 tent camping, $32-34 RV camping, $48-58 yurt, $90 cabin) was one of three military installations (the others were Forts Canby and Columbia in Washington) built to safeguard the mouth of the Columbia River. Established shortly before the Confederates surrendered on April 9, 1865, Fort Stevens served for 84 years, until just after the end of World War II. Today, the remaining fortifications and other buildings are preserved, along with 3,700 acres of woodland, lakes, wetlands, miles of sand beaches, and three miles of Columbia River frontage.

Although Fort Stevens did not see action in the Civil War, it sustained an attack in a later conflict. On June 21, 1942, a Japanese submarine fired 17 shells on the gun emplacements at Battery Russell, making it the only U.S. fortification in the 48 states to be bombed by a foreign power since the War of 1812. No damage was incurred, and the Army didn't return fire. Shortly after World War II, the fort was deactivated and the armaments removed.

Today, the site features a **Military Museum** (503/861-2000 or 503/861-2000, http://visitftstevens.com, 10am-6pm daily June-Sept., 10am-4pm daily Oct.-May) with old photos, weapons exhibits, and maps, as well as seven different batteries (fortications) and other structures left over from almost a century of service. Climbing to the commander's station for a scenic view of the Columbia River and South Jetty are popular visitor activities. The massive gun batteries, built of weathered gray concrete and rusting iron, eerily silent amid the thick woodlands, also invite exploration; small children should be closely supervised, as there are steep stairways, high ledges, and other hazards.

During the summer months, guided tours of the underground **Battery Mishler** (11am and 1pm daily, $5) and a narrated tour (12:30 and 2:30pm Mon.-Thurs., 11am, 12:30pm, 2:30pm, and 4pm Fri.-Sat. May-Sept., $4) of the fort's 37 acres on a two-ton U.S. Army truck are also available. Summer programs include Civil War reenactments and archaeological digs.

Nine miles of bike trails and five miles of hiking trails link the historic area to the rest of the park and provide access to Battery Russell and the 1906 wreck of the British schooner *Peter Iredale.* You can also bike to the campground one mile south of the Military Museum.

Parking is available at four lots about a mile from one another at the foot of the dunes. The beach runs north to the Columbia River, where excellent surf fishing, bird-watching, and a view of the mouth of the river await. South of the campground (east of the *Peter Iredale*) is a self-guided nature trail around part of the two-mile shoreline of **Coffenbury Lake.** The lake also has two swimming beaches with bathhouses and fishing for trout and perch.

To get to Fort Stevens State Park from U.S. 101, drive west on Harbor Street through Warrenton on Highway 104 (Ft. Stevens Hwy.) to the suburb of Hammond and follow the signs to Fort Stevens Historic Area and Military Museum.

## SPORTS AND RECREATION
### Hiking

An in-town hike that's not too strenuous begins at 28th and Irving Streets, meandering up the hill to the Astoria Column. If you drive to the trailhead, park along 28th Street. It's about a one-mile walk to the top. En route is the **Cathedral Tree,** an old-growth fir with a sort of Gothic arch formed at its roots.

The **Oregon Coast Trail** starts (or ends) at Clatsop Spit, at the north end of **Fort Stevens State Park** (100 Peter Iredale Rd., Hammond, 503/861-1671 or 800/551-6949, www.oregonstateparks.org, $5 day-use). The most northerly stretch extends south along the beach for 14 miles to Gearhart. It's a flat, easy walk, and your journey could well be highlighted by a sighting of the endangered silverspot butterfly, a small orange butterfly with silvery spots on the undersides of its wings.

# The *Peter Iredale*

the remains of the 1906 wreck *Peter Iredale,* Fort Stevens State Park

One of the best known of the hundreds of ships wrecked on the Oregon coast over the centuries is the British schooner *Peter Iredale.* This 278-foot four-master, fashioned of steel plates on an iron frame, was built in Liverpool in 1890 and came to its untimely end on the beach south of Clatsop Spit on October 25, 1906. En route from Mexico to pick up a load of wheat on the Columbia River, the vessel ran aground during high seas and a northwesterly squall. All hands were rescued, and with little damage to the hull, hopes initially ran high that the ship could be towed back to sea and salvaged. That effort proved fruitless, and eventually the ship was written off as a total loss. Today, over a century later, the remains of her rusting skeleton protrude from the sands of Fort Stevens State Park as a familiar sight to most who have traveled the north coast. Signs within Fort Stevens State Park lead the way to a parking area close to the wreck.

You might also encounter cars on the beach. This section of shoreline, inexplicably, is the longest stretch of coastline open to motor vehicles in Oregon. Call the **State Parks and Recreation Division** (800/551-6949) for an up-to-date report on trail conditions before starting out.

Fort Stevens State Park has nine miles of hiking trails through woods, wetlands, and dunes. One popular hike here is the two-mile loop around **Coffenbury Lake.**

In 2005, as part of the expansion of Lewis and Clark National Historical Park, the **Fort to Sea Trail** was created to link Fort Clatsop to the Pacific. The 6.5-mile trail follows the route through forest, fields, and dunes that

the corps traveled as they explored and traded along the Pacific coast.

The Fort to Sea Trail starts from the visitors center at Fort Clatsop. The first 1.5 miles involve a gentle climb past many trees blown down in a big 2007 storm to the Clatsop Ridge, where on a clear day you can see through the trees to the Pacific Ocean. The ridge makes a fine destination for a short hike, but the really beautiful part of the trail is the hikers-only (no dogs) stretch from the overlook to the beach, where you'll pass through deep woods and forested pastures dotted with small lakes. The trail passes a tunnel underneath U.S. 101 and continues through dunes to the Sunset Beach-Fort to

# Lewis and Clark National Historical Park

On November 2, 2004, President George W. Bush signed a bill into law to create the 59th national park in the United States. The Lewis and Clark National and State Historical Parks honor explorers Meriwether Lewis and William Clark, whose journey in 1804-1806 paved the way for the U.S. settlement of the West. The park focuses on the sites at the mouth of the Columbia River, where the Corps of Discovery spent the famously wet winter of 1805.

The park is somewhat unusual in that it is essentially a rebranding of current national park facilities and a federalization of current state parks. The new park includes a dozen sites linked to Lewis and Clark exploration, campsites, and lore. One of these, **Fort Clatsop National Memorial,** south of Astoria and where the Corps actually spent the winter, was already operated by the National Park Service, while **Cape Disappointment State Park** (formerly Fort Canby State Park), on the Washington side of the Columbia, remains a Washington state park but is managed by the national park entity.

Besides these two existing facilities, units of the new national park include the **Fort to Sea Trail,** a path linking Fort Clatsop to the Pacific; **Clarks Dismal Nitch,** a notoriously wet campsite near the Washington base of the Astoria-Megler Bridge; **Station Camp,** another improvident campsite for the Corps; the **Salt Works** in Seaside, where the Corps boiled seawater to make salt; **Netul Landing,** the canoe launch area used by Lewis and Clark near Fort Clatsop; and a **memorial to Thomas Jefferson** yet to be constructed on the grounds of Cape Disappointment State Park.

The new national park also encompasses the existing **Fort Columbia State Park** in Washington, which preserves a turn-of-the-20th-century military encampment, and **Fort Stevens, Sunset Beach,** and **Ecola State Parks** in Oregon.

The national park designation changes little for these once-disparate sites, at least for the moment. Fort Clatsop has been expanded to 1,500 acres, and the **Lewis and Clark Interpretive Center** at Fort Disappointment State Park was revamped. Visitors will mostly notice new and consistent signage throughout the park units. Ranger-guided hikes and living-history reenactors promise to bring to life the famous, often very wet, events that took place here over 200 years ago.

Sea Trail parking lot. From there, a one-mile path leads to the beach.

Unless you plan to return along the trail—which makes for a long day's hike—you'll need to arrange a pickup.

## Bicycling

You don't need a fancy bike to pedal the River Walk; rent a hefty cruiser from **Bikes and Beyond** (1089 Marine Dr., 503/325-2961, www.bikesandbeyond.com, 10am-6pm Mon.-Fri., 10am-5pm Sat., 11am-4pm Sun.). This friendly little shop also caters to bicycle travelers.

## Fishing Charters

More than any other industry, commercial fishing has dominated Astoria throughout its history. Salmon canneries lined the waterfront at the turn of the 20th century. In the modern era, commercial fishing has turned to tuna, sole, lingcod, rockfish, flounder, and other bottom fish. If it's not enough to watch these commercial operations from the dock, try joining a charter.

**Tiki Charters** (350 Industry St., 503/325-7818, www.tikicharter.com, $120 pp per day) will take you out for salmon, halibut, bottom fish, and sturgeon, depending on the season. Trips depart from the dock just off Industry Drive near the West Mooring Basin. Given the retail price of fresh salmon, you could theoretically pay for a charter trip by landing a single fish. **Gale Force Guides** (trips depart from Warrenton, 503/861-1494, www.galeforceguides.com, $120 pp per day) takes sport anglers fishing for salmon in either salt- or freshwater, depending on the season. Sturgeon and crabbing trips are also offered.

On your own, go after trout, bass, catfish, steelhead, and sturgeon in freshwater lakes, streams, and rivers. Lingcod, rockfish, surfperch, and other bottom fish can be pursued off jetties, or along ocean beaches.

## Diving and Kayaking
**Astoria Scuba** (on Pier 39, 503/325-2502, www.astoriascuba.com, 9am-6pm daily) offers diving lessons and kayak rentals for $25 for half a day.

## Zip-Lining
Explore the Northwest forests and lakes on the eight zip-line tours at **High Life Adventures** (92111 High Life Rd., Warrenton, $99 over age 15, $69 under age 16), five miles south of Astoria off U.S. 101. The tours soar above a 30-acre preserve of freshwater dune-trapped lakes and coastal forests. The Maple zip line even offers participants a chance to take a dunk in the lake.

## Water Parks
The **Astoria Aquatic Center** (20th St. and Marine Dr., 503/325-7027, www.astoriaaparks.com, 5am-7pm Mon.-Fri., 9am-4pm Sat., 11am-4pm Sun., $7.50 adults, $5.50 ages 2-17, $18 families) houses four pools, including a 100-foot waterslide with a 20-foot drop and a lazy-river current; a six-lane 25-yard lap pool; an adult hydro-spa pool; a kiddie wading pool; locker rooms; and a variety of fitness equipment.

## ENTERTAINMENT AND EVENTS
For the lowdown on all the happenings in and around Astoria, get your hands on a copy of *Hipfish*, Astoria's spirited monthly tabloid, distributed free all over town.

## Nightlife
### BREWPUBS
Astoria's oldest brewpub, the **Wet Dog Cafe & Brewery** (144 11th St., 503/325-6975, www.

wetdogcafe.com, 11am-9pm Sun.-Thurs., 11am-10pm Fri.-Sat., $9-20) is home to the Astoria Brewing Company, maker of excellent handcrafted microbrews, with a full bar available. The café is housed in a cavernous remodeled former waterfront warehouse, with good views of the river. The food is good basic pub grub: fish-and-chips, burgers (including seafood burgers), sandwiches, and salads.

The **Rogue Ales Public House** (100 39th St., 503/325-5964, 11am-9pm Sun.-Thurs., 11am-10 Fri.-Sat., $9-22) is east of downtown in the Hanthorn Pier development. The pub is set inside a wood-plank structure atop a former cannery pier and offers excellent ales, plus burgers, pizza, and sandwiches. It's hard to get more Astorian than this. For beer snobs, the place to go is **Fort George Brewery and Public House** (1483 Duane St., 503/325-7468, www.fortgeorgebrewery.com, 11am-11pm Mon.-Sat., noon-11pm Sun., $7-12), whose powerful ales have won it a reputation as one of Oregon's top breweries. The regular pub grub is basic, but the pizzas served on the pub's second floor are excellent. There's free live music every Sunday evening. In an old fish-processing warehouse right on the edge of the river is **Buoy Beer Company** (1 8th St., 503/325-4540, www.buoybeer.com, 11am-10pm Sun.-Thurs., 11am-11pm Fri.-Sat., $10-26), with good beer and an ambitious menu that includes chicken romesco sandwiches, petrale sole with herbed caper sauce, and ribeye steaks with gnocchi.

Opened in 2017, **Reach Break Brewing** (1343 Duane St., 503/468-0743, noon-8pm Sun.-Mon. and Thurs., noon-9pm Fri.-Sat.) has developed a delicious selection of wild yeast-powered sour beers as well as light *saisons* and more traditional Northwest IPAs. Reach Break doesn't have its own kitchen; instead, it relies on a clutch of food carts ($8-13) parked outside to feed the hungry crowds, with both outdoor and indoor seating.

### BARS
Befitting of a vintage fishing port, Astoria has lots of old bars and watering holes. As

a tribute to Astoria's scrappy spirit, explore some of the city's classic bars. The **Portway** (422 W. Marine Dr., 503/325-2651) is the oldest bar in the oldest American settlement west of the Rockies. The present building dates from 1923, and it's loaded with character and characters. Directly under the bridge, **Mary Todd's Workers Bar and Grill** (281 W. Marine Dr., 503/338-7291) is a classic old bar with a notable drink special: the Yucca. Also try the marvelously crispy onion rings. **Phyllis & Bob's Labor Temple Café & Bar** (939 Duane St., 503/325-0801) is the oldest communal union hall in the Pacific Northwest and is not to be missed. The clientele is a mix of longtime union activists, 20-something artists, and rowdy young sailors, making for some interesting dynamics. The **Voodoo Room** (1114 Marine Dr., 503/325-2233, www.columbianvoodoo.com) is a dark and cluttered bar with hipsters, cocktails, and occasional live music.

## The Arts

The handsome **Liberty Theatre** (1203 Commercial St., 503/325-5922, http://libertyastoria.org), whose colonnaded facades along Commercial and 12th Streets converge at the corner box office, is a vibrant symbol of Astoria's ongoing rejuvenation. The ornate Mediterranean-style building in the heart of downtown began its life in 1925 as a venue for silent films, vaudeville acts, and lectures. The theater continued as a first-run movie house, but after decades of neglect this grande dame was badly showing her age, and it looked as though the Liberty would eventually meet the sad wrecking-ball fate of so many fine old movie palaces. Fortunately, though, a nonprofit organization undertook efforts to restore the theater to its original elegance and equip it to be a state-of-the-art performing arts center. The Liberty currently hosts concerts, recitals, theater, and other events, including the Astoria Music Festival.

Astoria's long-running *Shanghaied in Astoria* (122 W. Bond St., 503/325-6104, www.shanghaiedinastoria.com, evening Thurs.-Sat. mid-July-mid-Sept., $13-21), based on the town's dubious distinction as a notorious shanghai port during the late 1800s, is a good old-fashioned melodrama. Chase scenes, bar fights, and a liberal sprinkling of Scandinavian jokes will have you laughing in between applauding the hero and booing the villain. Performed with

The Liberty Theatre, a former movie palace, is a great place to catch musical performances.

gusto by the Astor Street Opry Company, the show has been running since 1985, and has spawned a number of related shows: a "junior" *Shanghaied in Astoria* for kids, a once-yearly drag version, and the holiday season *Scrooged in Astoria.* Check the website for a growing roster of entertainment, including children's theater productions in March and April and other off-season productions from this lively troupe of thespians.

## Cinema

The **Columbian Theater** (1102 Marine Dr., 503/325-3516, www.columbianvoodoo.com, usually 7pm, $4, $2 under age 13) sits adjacent to the Columbian Cafe and screens the big movies you may have missed a month earlier in their first run. Enjoy beer, wine, cocktails, pizza, and other munchies while you watch. **Astoria Gateway Cinema** (1875 Marine Dr., 503/338-6575) is a modern movie multiplex, showing the usual stuff, where you can pass an afternoon trying to forget the often dismal weather.

## Festivals and Events
### FISHER POETS GATHERING

Modeled after Elko, Nevada's popular Cowboy Poets Gathering, the **Fisher Poets Gathering** (www.fisherpoets.org) provides a forum in which men and women involved in the fishing and other maritime industries share their poems, stories, songs, and artwork in a convivial seaport setting. The annual late-February event, which dates back to 1998, draws writers and artists from up and down the Pacific coast and farther afield for readings, art shows, concerts, book signings, workshops, films, a silent auction, and other activities at pubs, galleries, theaters, and other venues around town. Participation isn't limited to fisherfolk but extends to anyone with a connection to maritime activity. Themes range from the rigors (and humor) of life on the water to environmental issues. Admission ($15) covers all events for the weekend. For more details and a full schedule, check the website.

## ASTORIA-WARRENTON CRAB AND SEAFOOD FESTIVAL

The **Astoria-Warrenton Crab and Seafood Festival** (Clatsop County Fairgrounds, 92937 Walluski Loop, 503/325-6311 or 800/875-6807, http://astoriacrabfest. com, 4pm-9pm Fri., 10am-8pm Sat., 11am-4pm Sun., $5-10 adults, $3-5 ages 5-12), held the last weekend in April, is a hugely popular event that brings in crowds from miles around. Scores of booths feature a cornucopia of seafood and other eats, regional beers and Oregon wines, and arts and crafts. Activities include continuous entertainment, crab races, a petting zoo, and activities for kids. A traditional crab dinner caps off the evening. To get to the fairgrounds from Astoria, take Highway 202 for 4.5 miles to Walluski Loop and watch for signs. Parking is limited at the fairgrounds. It's smart to take the frequent shuttle that transports folks between the fairgrounds and park-and-ride lots, downtown, the Port of Astoria, and local hotels and campgrounds.

## ASTORIA MUSIC FESTIVAL
A three-week classical music showcase, the **Astoria Music Festival** (1271 Commercial St., 503/325-9896, http://astoriamusicfestival. org) brings top-ranked classical musicians to the northern Oregon coast. Since its beginning in 2002, the festival has quickly grown in stature and now features three different operatic performances (usually in concert) and numerous symphonic and chamber performances each year. Most events are in the small, acoustically splendid Liberty Theater or the Astoria Performing Arts Center (Franklin and 16th St.).

## SCANDINAVIAN MIDSUMMER FESTIVAL
The legacy of the thousands of Scandinavians who arrived to work in area mills and canneries in the late 19th and early 20th centuries is still strong in Astoria. For many locals, the summer's biggest event is the **Scandinavian Midsummer Festival** (503/325-6311, www.

astoriascanfest.com, $8 adults, $3 ages 6-12), which usually takes place Friday through Sunday on the third weekend of June. Local Danes, Finns, Icelanders, Norwegians, and Swedes come together to celebrate their heritage; visitors and musicians from the old countries keep the festivities authentic. Costumed dancers weave around a flowered midsummer pole (a fertility rite), burn a bonfire to destroy evil spirits, and have tugs-of-war pitting Scandinavian nationalities against each other. Food, dancing, crafts, musical concerts, and a parade bring the whole town out to the Clatsop County Fairgrounds on Walluski Loop, just off Highway 202.

### ASTORIA REGATTA WEEK

A tradition since 1894, **Astoria Regatta Week** is considered the Pacific Northwest's longest-running festival. Held on the waterfront in mid-August, the five-day event kicks off with the regatta queen's coronation and reception. Attractions include live entertainment, a grand street parade, historic home tours, ship tours and boat rides, sailboat and dragon boat races, a classic car show, a salmon barbecue, arts and crafts, food booths, a beer garden, and a twilight boat parade. For details and a schedule, contact the **Astoria Regatta Association** (503/325-6311 or 800/875-6807, http://astoriaregatta.com).

## SHOPPING

On Sundays between Mother's Day weekend to early October, follow local tradition and take a leisurely stroll up and down 12th Street between Marine Drive and Exchange Street for the **Astoria Sunday Market** (10am-3pm), where vendors offer farm-fresh produce, plants, crafts, and specialty foods.

A local store worth noting is **Finnware** (1116 Commercial St., 503/325-5720, www.finnware.com, 10am-5pm Mon.-Sat., 11am-4pm Sun.), which stocks Scandinavian crystal and glassware, jewelry, books, and kitchen tools. This is a store that takes its Finnish roots seriously.

## Art Galleries

Astoria has a well-deserved reputation as an art center, with many downtown storefronts now serving as art galleries. Not to miss is **RiverSea Gallery** (1160 Commercial St., 503/325-1270, http://riverseagallery.squarespace.com, 11am-5:30pm Mon.-Sat., 11am-4pm Sun.), with a large and varied selection of work by local painters, glass artists, jewelry makers, and craftspeople. For a more quixotic art scene, go to **Imogen Gallery** (240 11th St., 503/325-1566, http://imogengallery.com, 11am-5pm Mon.-Tues. and Thurs.-Sat., 11am-4pm Sun.), dedicated to contemporary and conceptual art by local artists. **Lightbox Photographic Gallery** (1045 Marine Dr., 503/468-0238, http://lightbox-photographic.com, 11am-5pm Tues.-Sat.) is the region's gallery for fine art photography. A special stop is **Ratz and Company** (260 10th St., 503/325-2035, www.ratzandcompany.com), which shows the work of Dave McMacken, an artist and graphic designer who was responsible for some of the great album covers of the 1970s and 1980s (think Frank Zappa). He now creates beautifully rendered, slightly unnerving images depicting the Pacific Northwest, though the incredible range of his commercial art is also available for sale at the gallery.

The second Saturday of each month is the **Astoria Art Walk** (5pm-9pm), when most galleries and shops in downtown stay open late.

## Bookstores

Several bookstores in town invite serious browsing, buying, and intellectual stimulation. **Lucy's Books** (348 12th St., 503/325-4210, 10am-5:30pm Tues.-Sat., 11am-3pm Sun.) is a small but bighearted locally owned bookshop with an emphasis on Pacific Northwest regional subjects. On the next block, **Godfather's Books and Espresso** (1108 Commercial St., 503/325-8143, 8am-8pm Mon.-Sat., 9am-6pm Sun.) sells a mix of new and used books and has a case of excellent antique maps and prints depicting the Columbia River and north coast.

# FOOD

In addition to the restaurants and cafés listed here, you'll find do-it-yourself options at local markets. Established in 1920 in a false-front clapboard building near the waterfront, **Josephson's Smokehouse** (106 Marine Dr., 503/325-2190, www.josephsons.com, 9am-6pm Mon.-Sat.) is Oregon's most esteemed purveyor of gourmet smoked fish, producing Scandinavian cold-smoked salmon without dyes or preservatives. On foggy days, there's nothing finer than a cup of Josephson's thick clam chowder. A good stop for fresh produce, health food, and deli items is the **Astoria Co-op** (355 Exchange St., 503/325-0027, 8am-8pm daily). To shop the daily catch, which can include Dungeness crab, wild salmon, halibut, albacore tuna, sardines, sole, and rockfish, go to **Warrenton Deep Sea Fish Market** (45 NE Harbor Place, Warrenton, 503/861-3911, 9am-5:30pm Mon.-Sat., 10am-4pm Sun.). They carry the largest selection of locally caught fish in the area, and you'll find a variety of smoked fish and seafood here as well.

Astoria also features a number of food carts—there is a pod at 13th and Duane Streets (in front of a handy brewpub for drinks) and another at Duane and 14th Streets. Most notable is **Bowpicker Fish and Chips,** with really good fish-and-chips served out of a converted boat near the corner of Duane and 17th Streets. You can also browse the fresh options at **Astoria's Sunday Market** (12th St. between Marine Dr. and Exchange St.).

## Pacific Northwest Cuisine

As widely appreciated as it is small, the **Columbian Cafe** (1114 Marine Dr., 503/325-2233, http://columbianvoodoo.com, 8am-2pm Mon.-Fri., 9am-2pm Sat.-Sun., $7-12) is an Astoria institution. The menu changes according to the season and the chef's whim (be daring and order the "chef's mercy") but generally includes a good selection of pastas, chilies, crepes, and fresh catch of the day, and always a selection of homemade garlic, jalapeño, and red-pepper jellies. Breakfast is a highlight here. If this is your first visit to the Columbian Cafe, don't let the tiny, slightly seedy-looking venue put you off. Expect to be here for a while; the Columbian is not a fast-food dining experience.

Another good restaurant with an inspiring motto ("Eat well, laugh often, and love much") is the easygoing **T. Paul's Urban Cafe** (1119 Commercial St., 503/338-5133, http://tpaulsurbancafe.com, 11am-9pm Mon.-Thurs., 11am-10pm Fri.-Sat., $9-24). The menu of hip

Bowpicker Fish and Chips

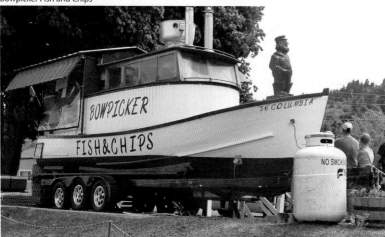

diner food with fresh Pacific Northwest twists includes towering turkey sandwiches, bay shrimp ceviche, Caribbean jerk quesadillas, prawn pasta, and clam chowder. Quesadillas are the specialty, with about a dozen innovative varieties served. T. Paul's has a second downtown location, ★ **The Supper Club** (360 12th St., 503/325-2545, http://tpaulssupperclub.com, 11am-9pm Mon.-Thurs., 11am-10pm Fri.-Sat., $12-32) with a wide-ranging menu, a rather swank dining room, and some of the most reliably delicious food in Astoria. Top choices are pasta dishes, burgers, salads, and fresh seafood. The tiny bar is the perfect spot for a cocktail.

A cross between a steampunk cocktail lounge and a restaurant, the **Albatross** (225 14th St., 503/741-3091, 5pm-11pm Tues.-Thurs., 5pm-midnight Fri.-Sat., $8-20) has excellent craft cocktails and brief menu of sandwiches and small plates, along with a few nightly dinner specials, all based on locally sourced food. The oysters (from Netarts Bay) on the half shell are excellent, and if you find slow-braised duck leg with morel mushrooms, asparagus, and brown butter grits as a special, order it.

## Seafood

One of Astoria's more notable restaurants is **Silver Salmon Grille** (1105 Commercial St., 503/338-6640, www.silversalmongrille.com,11am-9pm Sun.-Thurs., 11am-10pm Fri.-Sat., $13-32), for fine dining in an atmosphere that's somewhat formal but not starchy. The menu is broad, but stick to the fresh and local seafood dishes and you'll be happy. If the excellent razor clams are offered, order them; if fresh silver (a.k.a. chinook) salmon is on the menu, grab it, as the quality of salmon at the mouth of the Columbia is remarkable. The bar here is one of the nicest in downtown Astoria, and it's a favorite of locals out on the town.

Settle in for some excellent seafood at **Bridgewater Bistro** (20 Basin St., 503/235-6777, http://bridgewaterbistro.com, 11:30am-close Mon.-Sat., 11am-close Sun., $12-26), where you can graze on tapas (small plates menu 3pm-5pm) or order regular-size or smaller entrées. The soaring ceiling and riverside setting of the historic building next to the Cannery Pier Hotel are almost as compelling as the food. At the end of 12th Street, directly overlooking the Columbia, **Baked Alaska** (1 12th St., 503/325-7414, www.bakedak.com, 11am-9pm Sun.-Thurs., 11am-10am Fri.-Sat., $18-32) is a restaurant with many things going on at once. It features a bar and pizzeria, plus a dining room with big Columbia River vistas that offers a selection of small and large plates with modern international inflections. Seared sea scallops are served with maple butternut squash puree, while prawn and Dungeness crab spaghettini comes with dried cherries and pistachios. But about that name—yes, you can get classic baked Alaska here. The views rival the food, particularly in summer, when there's deck seating.

It took a while for **Mo's** (101 15th St., 971/704-1750, www.moschowder.com, 11am-10pm daily, $6-17), the wildly popular coastal restaurant chain, to reach Astoria, but here it is. Though dining here is hardly a culinary adventure, the fish is fresh and tasty, and it's hard not to enjoy yourself when you're eating good fish-and-chips and enjoying a local brew from this perch above the Columbia River.

## Eastern European

There aren't a lot of Bosnian restaurants around, and the **Drina Daisy** (915 Commercial St., 503/338-2912, www.drinadaisy.com, 11am-3pm and 4:30pm-8pm Wed.-Sun., $11-23) is worth a stop to sample foods from an unfamiliar part of the world. The cuisine, which promises "a taste of Sarajevo," is a cross between Greek and Central European cooking. You can't go wrong with the appetizers or salads, many of which come with smoked sausages and phyllo-wrapped goodies.

## International

With the classiest dining room in Astoria, **Carruthers Restaurant** (1198 Commercial St., 503/975-5305, 4pm-10pm Tues.-Thurs.,

4pm-11pm Fri.-Sat., $18-29) is also on the city's busiest corner. The food is focused on local seafood and other regional products, and prepared with a global flair. You'll find seafood paella, Thai dumplings, and lamb loin with confit vegetables. While the food can be uneven, this is a great spot for cocktails and appetizers.

## Italian

For Astoria's top Italian food, go to **Fulio's Pastaria** (1149 Commercial St., 503/325-9001, www.fulios.com, 11am-close daily, $11-30) with excellent pasta, Tuscan-style steaks, and a good wine list in a lively and convivial dining room.

## Indian

★ **Himani Indian Cuisine** (1044 Marine Dr., 503/325-8171, www.himaniic.com, lunch buffet 11am-3pm Sun.-Fri., dinner 5pm-9pm Sat.-Thurs. $9-20) serves a wide selection of Indian cuisine, with a specialty in southern Indian fare such as tandoori dishes (including tandoori salmon) and masala *dosa*. The naan breads are equally delicious. The buffet ($12) is available Monday-Friday for lunch and all day Sunday. Himani also serves food from its original stall at the Astoria Sunday Market. No alcohol is served.

## Breakfast

A good, if rather standard, choice for families with kids, the Astoria outlet of **Pig 'N Pancake** (146 W. Bond St., 503/325-3144, 6am-9pm Sun.-Thurs., 6am-10pm Fri.-Sat., breakfast and lunch $7-10, dinner $10-18), a small north-coast chain (others are in Seaside and Cannon Beach), excels at big, filling breakfasts at reasonable prices. The specialty is homemade pancakes and waffles, available in a dozen variations, including potato pancakes, Swedish pancakes (thin and crispy with lingonberries), pecan-filled pancakes, and, of course, pigs in a blanket.

## Bakeries and Cafés

Stop by the ★ **Astoria Coffeehouse and Bistro** (243 11th St., 503/325-1787, http://astoriacoffeehouse.com, 7am-9pm Sun., 7am-10pm Mon.-Thurs., 7am-11pm Fri.-Sat., $13-22) for fresh breakfast pastries and coffee, salads and sandwiches, and home-cooked regional fare. It's an airy, friendly place to sit and read the paper, or to enjoy cocktails and local seafood specialties late in the evening. This is the kind of place that makes everything from scratch, including slow-roasted turkey, corned beef, cakes, and even the ketchup, apple butter, and ice cream. All this, and it's a fun and lively place for a cocktail at night too.

At the collectively run ★ **Blue Scorcher Bakery Cafe** (1493 Duane St., 503/338-7473, www.bluescorcher.coop, 8am-4pm daily, $6-12), the motto is "joyful work, delicious food, and strong community," and it's all true. Settle in with a tasty veggie sandwich (if the tempeh Reuben is on the menu, don't turn up your nose) and watch the Astorians—any one of whom would make an excellent new friend—come and go. A personal favorite are cardamom almond rolls, an old-fashioned Swedish treat that's perfect with a cup of coffee on a brisk morning. A wide variety of freshly prepared seasonal dishes also appears, from nettle soup in spring to pumpkin-black bean chili in the fall. A range of gluten-free pastries are offered on Friday. If it's all too healthy and wholesome for you, there's a brewpub next door.

## ACCOMMODATIONS

The prices noted are for high season (summer) double-occupancy rooms. Rates fall by as much as half off-season. Also note that Astoria has many festival weekends, and on those occasions, rooms can be limited and prices high. In summer, plan your trip to avoid weekends if you're trying to save on lodging costs.

### $50-100

Astoria's ★ **Commodore** (258 14th St., 503/325-4747, http://commodoreastoria.com, $99-199) has simple but stylishly decorated rooms in a renovated downtown hotel.

The least expensive rooms ("cabins") are just sleeping chambers with a sink and a flat-screen TV and DVD player, with shared toilets and handsome tiled showers at the end of the hallway. Suite rooms are larger and include a private bath. The Commodore is popular with hip young travelers, especially its coffee shop on the ground floor. Be aware that the Commodore is on a busy downtown corner, so if traffic noise will bother you, bring earplugs.

Another vintage Astoria hotel made over into hip lodgings is the **Norblad Hotel and Hostel** (443 14th St., 503/325-6989, http://norbladhotel.com, $34 hostel beds, $79-119 rooms and suites). Owned by the same local team that runs the Commodore, the Norblad has the same youthful, stylish vibe, with crisply designed "Euro-style" rooms, nearly all with baths down the hall. For the price, you can't beat the quality and the downtown location, though budget travelers looking for a real hostel experience might be disappointed with the perfunctory shared kitchen and lounge areas (though dozens of restaurants and pubs are just steps away).

Astoria has several motels that offer basic but clean rooms. Except on summer weekends, the following should have rooms available without reservations. For basic motor court rooms, check out the **Atomic Motel** (131 W. Marine Dr., www.astoriamotel.com, $89-105), a vintage motel that's been updated with clean, unfussy rooms with a 1950s vibe. On the eastern edge of Astoria, the **Crest Motel** (5366 Leif Erickson Dr./U.S. 30, 503/325-3141 or 800/421-3141, www.astoriacrestmotel.com, $99-149 depending on views) offers cliffside river views, a coin-operated laundry, a whirlpool set in a gazebo overlooking the river, and pet-friendly rooms with no extra fees. About 0.5 miles east of the Astoria-Megler Bridge, the **Rivershore Motel** (59 W. Marine Dr., 503/325-2921, www.astoriarivershoremotel.com, $90-105) has 43 rooms with coffeemakers, microwaves, fridges, and Internet access. Some rooms include kitchens.

## $100-150

The **Astoria Riverwalk Inn** (400 Industry St., 503/325-2013, $147-329), right above the west marina, has many rooms with balconies over the harbor. The higher-priced rooms are decorated in a classy, subdued style while others are bold and energetic. All come with great views and free breakfast.

**Clementine's Bed and Breakfast** (847 Exchange St., 800/521-6801, www.clementines-bb.com, 2-night minimum, $98-176), a handsome two-story 1888 home built in the Italianate style, stands in good company across the street from the Flavel House and is itself on Astoria's Historic Homes Walking Tour. From the gardens around the house come the fresh flowers that accent the guest rooms and common areas and the herbs that spice the delicious gourmet breakfasts. There are five rooms in the main house, all with feather beds and private baths; upper-story rooms have private balconies with river views.

In addition to these guest rooms, two spacious sunny suites are available in the **Moose Temple Lodge** ($249-299 for up to 4), adjacent to the main house. Built in 1850, this is one of the oldest extant buildings in Astoria; it was the Moose Temple from 1900 to 1940 and later served as a Mormon church. Renovated with skylights, wood floors, fireplaces, small kitchens, and several beds, these suites are ideal for families or groups. Pets are welcome.

A couple of blocks away from busy downtown streets, the **Rose River Inn B&B** (1510 Franklin Ave., 503/325-7175, www.roseriverinn.com, $115-160) offers two river-view suites and three guest rooms in a large, cheerfully painted Victorian, decorated with European antiques and art and surrounded by a neatly tended garden. Each room includes a claw-foot tub.

## $150-200

Stay right downtown in the beautifully renovated ★ **Hotel Elliott** (357 12th St., 877/378-1924, www.hotelelliott.com, $189-289), a small boutique hotel that's an easy walk from good restaurants and the river. The Elliott first opened in 1924, and its current incarnation has preserved much of the original charm of its Craftsman-era details, including the mahogany-clad lobby, handcrafted cabinetry, and wood and marble fireplaces. An original banner painted across the hotel's north side proudly proclaims "Hotel Elliott—Wonderful Beds." The new Elliott has made a point of living up to this claim, with goose-down pillows, luxurious 440-thread-count Egyptian cotton sheets, feather beds, and top-of-the-line mattresses to ensure a memorable slumber. In addition to standard rooms, the Elliott has a variety of suites, including the five-room Presidential Suite with access to a rooftop garden. The rooftop is open to all and is a fine place to enjoy a glass of wine and the sunset.

The **Benjamin Young Inn** (3652 Duane St., 503/325-6172, www.benjaminyounginn.com, $150-175) is an elegant 1888 Queen Anne-style mansion with four large guest rooms, all with private baths and great river views. The inn is in the eastern part of Astoria, away from the hubbub of downtown.

You can't top the views at the **Holiday Inn Express Hotel & Suites** (204 W. Marine Dr., 503/325-6222 or 888/898-6222, www.astoriahie.com, $173-283), directly under the Astoria-Megler Bridge. Guest rooms have a fridge, a microwave, a coffeemaker, a high-speed Internet connection, a flat-screen TV, and a DVD player. Facilities include an indoor pool, a breakfast bar, a business center, and an exercise room. Pets are welcome with a $20 fee.

### Over $200

★ **Cannery Pier Hotel** (10 Basin St., 503/325-4996 or 888/325-4996, www.canner ypierhotel.com, $309-399) is a modern luxury hotel on the former site of a historic cannery, jutting 600 feet out into the Columbia below the Astoria-Megler Bridge. The opulently furnished rooms have dramatic views, even from the shower; all rooms have balconies, fireplaces, and beautiful hardwood floors.

Complimentary continental breakfast is included in the rates, as are hors d'oeuvres and wine in the afternoon. There's also a day spa in the hotel, plus a Finnish sauna, a fitness room, and a hot tub.

**Hampton Inn & Suites Astoria** (201 39th St., 503/325-8888, $202-236) is located east of downtown near Pier 39, so not really within walking distance of the city center. However, the Astoria Waterfront Trolley passes directly in front of the hotel, and you can ride it downtown and back during its operating season. The rooms are spacious and nicely furnished, facing directly onto the river. Amenities include a pool and a business center, plus an included breakfast.

### Camping

Families flock to **Fort Stevens State Park** (100 Peter Iredale Rd., Hammond, reservations 800/452-5687, www.oregonstateparks.org, year-round, $22 tent camping, $32-34 RV camping, $48-58 yurts, $90 cabins). With over 500 sites, the campground is the largest in the state park system, and it's incredibly popular. The park's many amenities and attractions make it the perfect base camp from which to take advantage of the region.

Across the road from the state park, **Astoria Warrenton Seaside KOA** (1100 NW Ridge Rd., Hammond, 503/861-2606 or 800/562-8506, www.astoriakoa.com, $29 tents, $50 RVs with electric, $59 RVs with full hookups, cabins from $73, $10 resort fee) is another sprawling campground. Amenities include an indoor pool and hot tub, a pancake breakfast, a game room, miniature golf, and bike rentals.

## INFORMATION AND SERVICES

The **Astoria Chamber of Commerce** (111 W. Marine Dr., 503/325-6311 or 800/875-6807, www.travelastoria.com, 8am-6pm daily May-Sept., 9am-5pm Mon.-Fri. Oct.-Apr.) operates the Oregon Welcome Center at its offices, providing an abundance of brochures and maps for visitors to Astoria and other destinations on the north Oregon coast and southwest Washington.

With 10,000 people, Astoria is the largest city and the media hub of the north coast. The local newspaper, the *Daily Astorian* (www.dailyastorian.com), is sold around town and worth a look. The free monthly *Hipfish* is a publication in the great tradition of the alternative press of the 1960s. Whether you agree with its take on regional politics or not, the thoughtful and lively articles and complete entertainment listings will enhance your visit to the north coast.

Throughout the north coast, **KMUN** (91.9 FM in Astoria and Seaside, 89.5 FM in Cannon Beach) is a public radio station with excellent community-based programming. Folk, classical, jazz, and rock music, public affairs, radio drama, literature readings, children's bedtime stories, and National Public Radio news will keep your dial set on this frequency. A sister station, KCPB, broadcasts classical music in addition to NPR news.

The **Astoria Post Office** is located in the Federal Building (750 Commercial St.).

Useful numbers to know include the **county sheriff** (503/225-2061), the **Coast Guard** (2285 Airport Rd., Warrenton, 503/861-6220), and **Columbia Memorial Hospital** (2111 Exchange St., Astoria, 503/325-4321).

## GETTING THERE AND AROUND

**Amtrak Thruway Motorcoach Service** (800/USA-RAIL—800/872-7245, www.amtrak.com) runs two buses daily between the north coast and Portland Union Station. Board the coach in Astoria at the downtown transit center (9th St. and Astor St.). The bus also stops at Cannon Beach, Seaside, and Warrenton.

Car rentals are available from **Enterprise** (644 W. Marine Dr., 503/325-6500). For visitors willing to let go of their cars for a while, the Sunset Empire Transportation District, better known as **The Bus** (503/861-RIDE—503/861-7433 or 800/776-6406, www.ridethebus.org), provides reasonably frequent transportation around Astoria and along the coast to Warrenton, Gearhart, Seaside, and Cannon Beach.

# Seaside and Gearhart

Seaside is Oregon's quintessential, and oldest, family beach resort. The beach is long and flat, sheltered by a scenic headland, with lifeguards on duty during the summer months, beachside playground equipment, and a boardwalk winding through the dunes. Ice cream parlors, game arcades, eateries, and gift shops crowd shoulder to shoulder along the main drag, Broadway. The aromas of cotton candy and french fries lend a heady incense to the salt air, and the clatter of bumper cars and other amusements can induce sensory overload. Atlantic City it's not—thank goodness—but on a crowded summer day the town evokes the feeling of a carnival midway by the sea. During spring break, when Pacific Northwest high school and college students arrive, the

town's population of 6,200 can quadruple almost overnight.

Neighboring Gearhart, a mainly residential community (pop. 1,100) just to the north, has a few lodgings away from the bustle of Seaside as well as a venerable 18-hole golf course.

Located along the Necanicum River, in the shadow of majestic Tillamook Head, Seaside has attracted tourists since the early 1870s, when transportation magnate Ben Holladay sensed the potential for a resort hotel near the water. But better transportation was needed to get customers to the place. At that time, the way to get to Seaside was first by boat from Portland down the Columbia River to Skipanon (now Warrenton), and from there by carriage south to Seaside. To speed the connection, Holladay later constructed a railroad line from Skipanon to Seaside.

To escape Portland's summer heat, families in the late 19th century would make the boat and railroad journey to spend their summer in Seaside. Most men would go back to Portland to work during the week, returning to the coast on Friday to visit the family. Every weekend the families would gather at the railroad station to greet the men, then see them off again for the trip back to Portland. It wasn't long before the train became known as the "Daddy Train." As roads between Portland and the coast were constructed, the car took over, and the railroad carried its last dad in 1939.

## SIGHTS
### The Promenade and Broadway

Sightseeing in Seaside means bustling up and down Broadway and strolling leisurely along the Prom. This three-mile-long concrete walkway, extending from Avenue U north to 12th Avenue, was initially constructed in 1908 to protect ocean properties from the waves. A pleasant walk alongside the beach, the boardwalk offers a fine vantage point from which to contemplate the sand, surf, frolicking beach lovers, and the massive contours of 1,200-foot-high Tillamook Head to the south. The Prom is also popular for jogging, bicycle and surrey riding, and in-line skating.

Midway along the Prom is the **Turnaround,** a concrete-and-brick traffic circle that is the western terminus of Broadway. A bronze statue of Lewis and Clark gazing ever seaward proclaims this point the end of the trail for their expedition, though in fact they explored a bit farther south, beyond Tillamook Head. Eight blocks south of the Turnaround, between Beach Drive and the Prom, is a replica of the Lewis and Clark salt cairn.

Heading east from the Turnaround, Broadway runs 0.5 miles to Roosevelt Avenue (U.S. 101) through a dizzying gamut of tourist attractions, arcades, restaurants, and bars. Along Broadway, in a four-block area west of U.S. 101 and bordered by the Necanicum River, 1st Avenue, and Avenue A, you'll find some fancy Victorian frame houses, a few of the old buildings that survived the 1912 fire that destroyed much of the town.

Today, the most notable sight in this busy section of Seaside is the enormous $73.3 million WorldMark Seaside time-share condo development containing nearly 300 units. Condos in this outsize structure aren't

The Turnaround is midway along Seaside's Promenade.

# Seaside and Gearhart

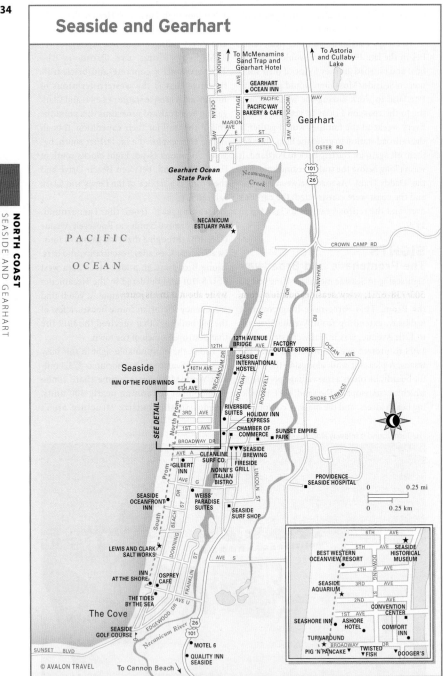

To McMenamins
Sand Trap and
Gearhart Hotel

To Astoria
and Cullaby
Lake

MARION AVE

OCEAN AVE

COTTAGE

MARION AVE

E ST

F ST

G ST

GEARHART
OCEAN INN

PACIFIC

PACIFIC WAY
BAKERY & CAFE

WAY

WOODLAND AVE

Gearhart

OSTER RD

101
26

PACIFIC

OCEAN

Gearhart Ocean
State Park

Neawanna Creek

CROWN CAMP RD

NECANICUM
ESTUARY PARK ★

WAHANNA RD

NECANICUM DR

DR

OCEAN AVE

12TH

12TH AVENUE
BRIDGE

12TH AVE

FACTORY
OUTLET STORES

Seaside

10TH AVE

SEASIDE
INTERNATIONAL
HOSTEL

ROOSEVELT

HOLLADAY

SHORE TERRACE

INN OF THE FOUR WINDS

6TH AVE

North Prom

3RD AVE

1ST AVE

BROADWAY DR

RIVERSIDE
SUITES

HOLIDAY INN
EXPRESS

CHAMBER OF
COMMERCE

SUNSET EMPIRE
PARK

LINCOLN ST

AVE A

CLEANLINE
SURF CO.

SEASIDE
BREWING

FIRESIDE
GRILL

PROVIDENCE
SEASIDE HOSPITAL

SEE DETAIL

Prom

GILBERT
INN

AVE G

NONNI'S
ITALIAN
BISTRO

0        0.25 mi

0        0.25 km

SEASIDE
OCEANFRONT
INN

South Prom

BEACH ST

DOWNING

FRANKLIN ST

WEISS'
PARADISE
SUITES

AVE S

SEASIDE
SURF SHOP

LEWIS AND CLARK
SALT WORKS

INN
AT THE SHORE

OSPREY
CAFE

THE TIDES
BY THE SEA

AVE U

The Cove

EDGEWOOD DR

Necanicum River

26

SEASIDE
GOLF COURSE

101

SUNSET   BLVD

© AVALON TRAVEL

To Cannon Beach

MOTEL 6

QUALITY INN
SEASIDE

6TH AVE

5TH AVE

SEASIDE
HISTORICAL
MUSEUM ★

BEST WESTERN
OCEANVIEW RESORT

4TH AVE

DOWNING

SEASIDE
AQUARIUM ★

3RD AVE

S

2ND AVE

CONVENTION
CENTER

1ST AVE

SEASHORE INN

ASHORE
HOTEL

COMFORT
INN

TURNAROUND ★

BROADWAY

DR

PIG 'N PANCAKE

TWISTED
FISH

DOOGER'S

available for rent directly from WorldMark, though vacation property rental companies can handle sublets.

## Seaside Historical Society Museum

If you tire of Broadway and the beach is too cold and wet, make your way to the **Seaside Historical Society Museum** (570 Necanicum Dr., 503/738-7065, www.seaside-museum.org, 10am-3pm Mon.-Sat., $3 adults, $2 seniors, $1 students), housed in a classic seaside cottage six blocks north of Broadway, where Clatsop artifacts and exhibits on early tourism in Seaside impart more of a sense of history than anything else in town.

## Seaside Aquarium

Right on the Prom north of the Turnaround is the **Seaside Aquarium** (200 N. Promenade, 503/738-6211, www.seasideaquarium.com, 9am-7pm daily Mar.-Oct., 9am-5pm daily Wed.-Sun. Nov.-Feb., $8 adults, $6.75 seniors, $4 ages 6-13). It's not quite the Oregon Coast Aquarium (find that in Newport), but if you're not going to make it that far south, it's an okay introduction to sealife for young children. Back in the era of the Daddy Train, this place served as a natatorium, but was converted to its current use in 1937. Today the pool is filled with raucously barking seals. In addition, a hundred species of marinelife here include 20-ray sea stars, crabs, ferocious-looking wolf eels and moray eels, and octopuses.

## Lewis and Clark Salt Works

Near the south end of the Prom at Lewis and Clark Way are the reconstructed salt works of Lewis and Clark. While camped at Fort Clatsop during the winter of 1805-1806, the captains sent a detachment south to find a place suitable for rendering salt from seawater. Their supply was nearly exhausted, and the precious commodity was a necessity for preserving and seasoning their food on the expedition's return journey. At the south end of present-day Seaside, five men built a cairn-like stone oven near a settlement of the Clatsop and Killamox people and set about boiling seawater nonstop for seven weeks to produce 3.5 bushels (about 314 pounds) of salt for the trip back east.

## SPORTS AND RECREATION
### Hiking

From the south end of Seaside, walk in the footsteps of Lewis and Clark on an exhilarating hike over Tillamook Head. In January 1806, neighboring Native Americans told of a beached whale lying several miles south of their encampment. William Clark and a few companions, including Sacajawea, set off in an attempt to find it and trade for blubber and whale oil, which fueled the expedition's lanterns. Climbing Tillamook Head from the north, the party crested the promontory. Clark was moved enough by the view to later write about it in his journal:

I beheld the grandest and most pleasing prospect which my eyes ever surveyed. Immediately in front of us is the ocean breaking in fury. To this boisterous scene the Columbia with its tributaries and studded on both sides with the Chinook and Clatsop villages forms a charming contrast, while beneath our feet are stretched the rich prairies.

Today, you can experience the view that so impressed Clark on the **Tillamook Head National Recreation Trail,** which runs seven miles through Ecola State Park. Prior to setting out, you could arrange to have a friend drive south to Indian Beach to pick you up at the end of this three- to five-hour trek; or you can be picked up another mile south at the Ecola Point parking lot just north of Cannon Beach. As you head up the forested trail on the north side of Tillamook Head, look back over the Seaside town site. In about 20 minutes, you'll be gazing down at the ocean from cliffs 1,000 feet above. A few hours later, you'll hike down onto Indian Beach.

To get to the trailhead from Seaside, drive south, following Avenue U past the golf course to Edgewood Street, and turn left;

continue until you reach the parking lot at the end of the road.

## Bicycling

Seaside has a bumper crop of places that rent bicycles, skates, and surreys, all for similar rates, starting at around $10 per hour for a bike. The **Prom Bike Shop** (622 12th Ave., 503/738-8251, http://prombikeshop.com, 10:30am-5:30pm daily summer, noon-5pm Thurs.-Mon. fall-spring) is a full-service bike shop. Rent cruisers, surreys, mopeds, and novelty bikes at **Wheel Fun Rentals** (151 Ave. A, 503/738-7212, 11am-7pm Mon.-Thurs., 11am-8pm Fri., 10am-8pm Sat., 10am-7pm Sun.), with four locations in Seaside, this one closest to the Boardwalk.

## Wildlife-Watching

Bird-watchers gather at **Necanicum Estuary Park,** at the 1900 block of North Holladay Drive across the street from Seaside High School. Local students have built a viewing platform, stairs to the beach, a boardwalk, and interpretive signs. Great blue and green herons and numerous migratory bird species flock to the grassy marshes and slow tidal waters near the mouth of the Necanicum River. During the fall and winter, buffleheads and mergansers shelter in the estuary, while in summer the waters are often thronged with pelicans. Occasionally Roosevelt elk, black-tailed deer, river otters, beavers, mink, and muskrats can also be sighted.

## Boating and Fishing

Just because you're smack-dab in the middle of a family resort town doesn't mean you can't enjoy some of nature's bounty: Anglers can reel in trout, salmon, and steelhead from the Necanicum River right in the center of downtown. The **12th Avenue Bridge** is a popular spot for fishing and crabbing.

**Cullaby Lake,** on the east side of U.S. 101 about four miles north of Gearhart, offers fishing for crappies, bluegills, perch, catfish, and largemouth bass. At 88 acres, Cullaby is the largest of the many lakes on the Clatsop

Seaside is a good spot to test-drive a surrey.

Plains. Two parks on the lake, **Carnahan Park** and **Cullaby Lake County Park,** have boat ramps, picnic areas, and other facilities. Cullaby is the only practical place to water-ski in the area.

**Sunset Beach Park,** 0.5 miles west of U.S. 101 on Neacoxie Lake (also known as Sunset Lake), has a boat ramp, picnic tables, and a playground. Anglers come for warm-water fish species, plus the rainbow trout stocked in the spring. From Astoria, drive south 10 miles on U.S. 101 and turn west on Sunset Beach Road.

At **Quatat Park** (503/440-1548), beside the Necanicum River in downtown Seaside, rent kayaks, canoes, and pedal boats for exploring the waterway.

## Surfing

The best surfing spot in the Seaside area is the beach just south of town, simply referred to as **The Cove,** directly north of Tillamook Head and reached from parking areas along Sunset Boulevard. While prevailing winds

the Seaside Brewing Company

Sea. Gearhart boasts a quieter beach than Seaside's, although the water is every bit as cool. Warm-blooded swimmers can head to the facilities at **Sunset Empire Park** (1140 E. Broadway, Seaside, 503/738-3311, daily), which includes three pools, waterslides, a 15-person hot tub, and fitness equipment.

## Golf

Golfers can escape to public courses south of Seaside and north in the small town of Gearhart. At **Seaside Golf Club** (451 Ave. U, 503/738-5261), greens fees start at $15-17 for nine holes. The **Highlands at Gearhart** (1 Highland Rd., Gearhart, 503/738-5248, www.highlandsgolfgearhart.com, $19 for nine holes) is another public nine-hole course, with ocean views from most holes. The British-links-style course at **Gearhart Golf Links** (1157 N. Marion St., Gearhart, 503/738-3538, www.gearhartgolflinks.com, $85 for 18 holes in summer) was established in 1892, making it Oregon's oldest, and one of the oldest west of the Mississippi River. A multiyear restoration of the course, completed in 2015, returned the links to their original character.

## ENTERTAINMENT AND EVENTS

Seaside predates any other town on the Oregon coast as a place built with good times in mind. A zoo and racetrack were among Seaside's first structures, and arcades are still thriving near the foot of Broadway. **Cannes Cinema** (U.S. 101 at 12th Ave.) is a five-screen multiplex showing first-run films.

The **Seaside Brewing Company** (851 Broadway, 503/717-5451, http://seaside-brewery.com, 11:30am-10pm daily, $10-13) makes great ales and has a handsome location in Seaside's old 1914 city hall and jail. Expect burgers, sandwiches, and pizza. At the Gearhart Golf Links, the old clubhouse now houses **McMenamins Sand Trap Pub** (1157 N. Marion Ave., 503/717-8150, 7am-11pm Sun.-Thurs., 7am-1am Fri.-Sat., $7-27); it has been decorated with the McMenamins'

favor winter surfing rather than summer, this is in fact a popular destination year-round. Local surfers can be impatient with beginners, so this probably isn't a good spot for novices.

**Seaside Surf Shop** (1116 S. Roosevelt Dr., 503/717-1110, www.seasidesurfshop.com, 10am-6pm Mon.-Fri., 9am-6pm Sat., 9am-5pm Sun.) and **Cleanline Surf Co.** (60 N. Roosevelt Dr., 503/738-2061, www.cleanlinesurf.com, 9am-6pm daily) rent and sell surfboards as well as wetsuits, boots, and flippers; Cleanline Surf also offers instruction. **Northwest Women's Surf Camps** (503/440-5782, www.nwwomenssurfcamps.com) will give you a bit of land training (the camp includes yoga to get you limbered up and in the right frame of mind) and then accompany you into the waves.

## Swimming

Despite the lifeguard on duty in summer, swimming at Seaside's beach isn't exactly comfortable, unless you're used to the North trademark whimsical artwork and serves the local chain's decent (not great, but always edible) upscale pub food. Free live music is featured in the pub most Friday evenings, open to all ages.

The annual **Oregon Dixieland Jubilee** (800/738-6894, www.jazzseaside.com) takes place at the end of February. This event has been gaining momentum for some 35 years and appeals to fans of Dixieland and traditional jazz. The town celebrates the **Fourth of July** with a parade, a picnic and social at the Seaside Historical Society Museum (570 Necanicum Dr.), and a big fireworks show on the beach.

In early September, **Wheels and Waves** (503/717-1914) brings over 500 classic hot rods and custom cars (1962 and earlier, please) to downtown and the **Civic and Convention Center** (1st Ave. at Necanicum Dr.).

## SHOPPING

Seaside is a shopping hub not only for its own population but also for Cannon Beach, which oddly doesn't even have a real grocery store, let alone a shopping mall. A number of shopping centers line U.S. 101 as it passes through Seaside; the **Seaside Factory Outlet Center** (1111 N. Roosevelt Dr., 503/717-1603) has 25 discount stores, including outlets for Eddie Bauer, Nike, and Pendleton.

## FOOD

While a stroll down Broadway might have you thinking that cotton candy, corn dogs, and saltwater taffy are the staples of Seaside cuisine, several eateries here can satisfy more refined palates as well. But there's no disputing the fact that Seaside, despite being one of Oregon's most popular Pacific-front towns, is not a mecca of fine dining.

### Seafood

**Dooger's** (505 Broadway, 503/738-3773, http://doogersseafood.com, 11am-9pm daily, $11-20), which also has an outlet in Cannon Beach, is a popular Broadway mainstay known for its clam chowder. Although it's kind of a frumpy-looking place, it serves good seafood. Local clams and oysters, fresh Dungeness crab legs, sautéed shrimp, and marionberry cobbler are also the basis of Dooger's reputation.

Right in the heart of busy Broadway, **Twisted Fish** (311 Broadway, 503/738-3467, www.twistedfishsteakhouse.com, 11am-10pm daily, $10-30) is a Pacific Northwest-style steakhouse, with hand-cut steaks, fresh fish and seafood, pasta, and Mediterranean-inflected dishes such as chicken and prawn *piccata*. All bread and desserts are made in-house; in the lounge, you'll find karaoke and dancing on weekend evenings.

### Classic American

If you're traveling with kids, you'll almost inevitably end up eating at **Pig 'N Pancake** (323 Broadway, 503/738-7243, 6am-8pm Sun.-Thurs., 6am-9pm Fri.-Sat., breakfast and lunch $7-10, dinner $10-18), where the Swedish pancakes and crab-and-cheese omelets are tops at breakfast, and the Frisbee-size cinnamon rolls will launch your blood sugar to new heights.

A top choice for home-style American fare is **Firehouse Grill** (841 Broadway, 503/717-5502, www.firehousegrillseaside.net, 8am-3pm Mon. and Thurs.-Sat., 8am-2pm Sun., $8-14), where classic breakfasts feature biscuits and gravy and chicken-fried steak, and lunch focuses on burgers.

An excellent destination for breakfast and brunch is the **Osprey Café** (2281 Beach Dr., 503/739-7054, 7:30am-3pm Thurs.-Tues., $9-13) with breakfast all day (classic American egg dishes plus Mexican fare and Indonesian *nasi goreng* as well), and sandwiches for lunch. The Osprey is south of downtown, near the end of the Boardwalk, near some of Seaside's more affordable hotels.

Should the frenetic ambience of Seaside on a holiday weekend begin to wear thin, try Gearhart's ★ **Pacific Way Bakery and Cafe** (601 Pacific Way, Gearhart, 503/738-0245, www.pacificwaybakery-cafe.com, bakery 7am-1pm Thurs.-Mon., restaurant 11am-3:30pm and 5pm-9pm Thurs.-Mon., dinner $10-30, dinner reservations recommended). Pasta, crusty pizzas, and seafood dishes (including thick seafood cioppino) as well as Dungeness crab sandwiches with aioli pop up at lunch and dinner. Rib-eye steak and local razor clams are other frequent dinnertime highlights in the surprisingly urbane little café hidden behind a rustic old storefront. In the morning, the bakery side of the operation is *the* place to be for coffee and pastries.

### Italian

The menu at **Nonni's Italian Bistro** (831 Broadway, 503/738-4264, 3pm-9pm Thurs.-Mon., $11-29) extends from meatball sandwiches to crab- and salmon-rich cioppino, with a selection of pasta dishes in between. This small and popular restaurant fills up fast, so call ahead for reservations.

## ACCOMMODATIONS

Whatever your price range, you'll have to reserve ahead for a room in Seaside during the summer and on weekends and holidays (especially spring break). If you do, chances are you'll be able to find the specs you're looking for, given the area's array of lodgings and over 1,800 hotel rooms. The **Seaside Visitors Bureau** (www.seasideor.com) has a helpful website with comprehensive listings and a handy booking engine for last-minute rooms.

Generally speaking, there are three lodging areas in Seaside. First, there are several modern motels along busy U.S. 101, about eight blocks from the beach. If you're just passing through or waited too long to call for reservations, these offer inexpensive rooms, but little in the way of beachside charm. A second grouping of hotels is in the center of Seaside, along the Necanicum River. These have a quieter riverside setting but still aren't beachfront (though you won't have to cross U.S. 101 to get to the beach). Finally, there are numerous hotels that face directly onto the beach or are just a short stumble to the strand. Even here, there's quite a difference in price between rooms that face the beach and those that face the parking lot.

### Under $50

The cheapest place in town is the quite nice **Seaside International Hostel** (930 N. Holladay Dr., 503/738-7911 or 888/994-0001, www.seasidehostel.net, dorm-style bunk $35 pp, private rooms $79-99), with special touches such as morning meditation and exercise classes. Unlike many hostels, it doesn't close down during the day, and there's no curfew at night. There's an espresso bar on-site, and the Necanicum River runs through the backyard. Close by is the Necanicum Estuary Park.

### $50-100

**Motel 6** (2369 S. Roosevelt Dr., 503/738-6269 or 800/466-8356, $70-90), on U.S. 101 about 0.5 miles south of Broadway, isn't near the sand but does offer reasonably priced rooms.

### $100-150

There's a clutch of motels south of the Broadway-Prom axis that offer easy beach access at fair prices—and a much quieter beachfront experience than in the town center. **The Tides by the Sea** (2316 Beach Dr., 503/738-6317 or 800/548-2846, www.thetidesbythesea.com, $138-252) is a well-located older motel that has converted its large guest rooms and cottages into condos. About a quarter of the units face onto the Prom, but those that don't are just seconds away from the beach. If you can live without an ocean view, you'll save a bundle here. Each of the units is different, but most have kitchens and fireplaces. In high season, there is a two-night minimum stay.

The rooms at **Seashore Inn** (60 N. Promenade, 503/738-6368 or 888/738-6368, www.seashoreinnor.com, $139-229) are right in the thick of it along the Promenade. Half the guest rooms face the beach, but half don't. These rooms are just steps from the beach but are a fraction of the cost of rooms on the other side of the building. All guest rooms have microwaves and mini-fridges, and some have full kitchens and balconies. There's also an indoor pool in case the weather turns foul.

In the center of Seaside, with balconies over the Necanicum River, the **Holiday Inn Express & Suites Seaside Convention Center** (34 Holladay Dr., 503/717-8000, $143-218) has an indoor pool and spa and rooms with fridges, microwaves, coffeemakers, and CD and DVD players. Rates include a complimentary breakfast bar.

Farther north, the **Tradewinds Condo Hotel** (1022 N. Promenade, 503/738-9468, www.seaside-tradewinds.com, $144-164) doesn't look like much from the outside, but the rooms are very nice and represent some of the best values in Seaside, particularly off-season, when room prices can drop by half. All the rooms are individually decorated and come in different configurations, from studios with kitchenettes to one-bedroom condos with full kitchens and living areas. Book well in advance: This is a popular spot.

Well south of the bustling Broadway scene, the **Inn at the Shore** (2275 S. Promenade, 503/738-3113 or 800/713-9914, www.innat-theshore.com, $119-239) has nicely appointed rooms, each with a gas fireplace, a balcony, a wet bar, a microwave, a coffeemaker, a fridge, a flat-screen TV, and a VCR/DVD player. The less expensive rooms don't have ocean views, but the beach is just steps away.

Out along U.S. 101, on the southern edge of town, **Quality Inn Seaside** (2455 S. Roosevelt Dr., 503/738-7666 or 866/482-7666, www.qualityinnseaside.com, $143-167), isn't particularly close to the beach but has free breakfast pancakes, free high-speed Internet, and a fitness room.

## $150-200

Just north of the Necanicum River's mouth, Gearhart offers a respite from the bustle of Seaside. The ★ **Gearhart Ocean Inn** (67 N. Cottage St., Gearhart, 503/738-7373, www.gearhartoceaninn.com, $170-250) offers a choice of 12 New England-style wooden cottages with comforters, wicker chairs, and throw rugs, and the beaches are a short walk away. The two-story deluxe units have kitchens and hardwood floors. Pets are allowed in some units. Especially during the off-season, this spruced-up old motor court is one of the best values on the north coast.

While motels dominate the lodging scene in Seaside, a few B&Bs and small inns offer an alternative. The **Gilbert Inn** (341 Beach Dr., 503/738-9770 or 800/410-9770, www.gilbertinn.com, $179-189) is a well-preserved 1892 Queen Anne just a block south of Broadway and a block from the beach. Period furnishings adorn the 11 guest rooms, which all have private baths, down comforters, and other nice touches (though this seems like a classic B&B, no breakfast is served). The third-floor "Garret" sleeps up to four in a queen and two twin beds, with ocean views from the dormer window. All guests must be 18 or older.

A charmingly refurbished lodging just three short blocks from the beach, ★ **Weiss' Paradise Suites** (741 S. Downing St., 503/738-6691 or 800/738-6691, www.seaside-suites.com, $149-169) is south of the Broadway action but offers homey, upgraded units with lots of extras, including full kitchens, decks, two TVs, free DVDs, and robes. If you're looking for a cottage rental, ask about the two vacation houses available from this proprietor.

The four-story shingle-sided **Seaside Oceanfront Inn** (581 S. Promenade, 503/319-3300 or 800/772-7766, http://theseasideinn.com, $169-349) stands right on the beach, with its north gable skewered by a clock tower. Each of the 14 guest rooms is decorated in a unique theme. Most have a spectacular ocean view, and pets are permitted in certain rooms. The on-site restaurant is very good. In addition, this operation also rents Beach Drive Suites, newly renovated two-bedroom condos at a beachside location south of the main hotel.

Seaside's most stylish rooms are at the ★ **Inn of the Four Winds** (820 N. Promenade, 503/738-9524 or 800/818-9524, www.innofthefourwinds.com, $179-329). This 14-room boutique hotel has comfortable rooms furnished with taste and panache. Each guest room has a microwave, a coffeemaker, a fridge, an MP3 player, a gas fireplace, and a deck or balcony with an ocean view. Best of all, the inn faces directly onto the beach eight blocks north of the frenetic Broadway strip.

If you're looking for a hotel with character, consider **Ashore Hotel** (125 Oceanway, 503/568-7506, $173-226), an older motorcourt hotel that's been renovated with a hip, urban industrial vibe. All the rooms are dog-friendly, and there's a small café and bar where you can find craft cocktails, hand-forged snacks, and local brews.

Just four miles north of Seaside at the sleepy town of Gearhart is the ★ **Gearhart Hotel** (1157 N. Marion Ave., Gearhart, 503/717-8159 or 855/846-7583, $150-180), a boutique hotel developed out of the historic Gearhart Golf Links clubhouse by the McMenamins local chain of hotels and breweries. It has all the trademark comfortable funkiness of other McMenamins properties, with the added benefits of sitting on the oldest golf course in Oregon and Pacific beaches just across the street. Rooms have en suite baths, and there's a lively pub on the main floor.

### Over $200

**Best Western Oceanview Resort** (414 N. Promenade, 503/738-3264 or 800/234-8439, www.oceanviewresort.com, $219-289) is a large hotel right on the beach near the center of town. Amenities include an on-site restaurant and lounge, a heated pool, and a spa; the majority of rooms face the ocean.

In the center of Seaside, right on the Necanicum River, the **Rivertides Suites** (102 N. Holladay Dr., 877/871-8433, www.rivertidesuites.com, $215-240) offers some of the most upscale accommodations in Seaside. All rooms have balconies, full kitchens, fine linens, and jetted tubs, plus free breakfast, an indoor pool and hot tub, an exercise room, and great views from the rooftop viewing deck. In addition to the entry-level studio suites, there are also one- and two-bedroom suites.

### Vacation Rentals

A good option for many travelers is one of the several dozen vacation rentals. Options range from tiny cottages for less than $100 per night (minimum stays are often required, especially in summer) to large homes that can host groups of 10 or 12. Check with the **Seaside Visitors Bureau** (7 N. Roosevelt St., 503/738-3097 or 888/306-2326, www.seasideor.com, 8am-5pm daily), or contact one of the rental agencies: **Beachhouse Vacation Rentals** (503/738-9068, www.beachhouse1.com), **Oceanside Vacation Rentals** (503/738-7767 or 800/840-7764, www.oceanside1.com), or **Northwind Vacation Rentals** (503/738-5532 or 866/738-5532, www.northwindrentals.com).

### Camping

One mile south of Seaside in a lush green meadow is **Circle Creek RV Park and Campground** (85658 U.S. 101, 503/738-6070, http://circlecreekrv.com, RVs $50). The campground offers showers, a small store, picnic tables, and fire rings, but no tent camping.

## INFORMATION AND SERVICES

The **Seaside Visitors Bureau** (7 N. Roosevelt St., 503/738-3097 or 888/306-2326, www.seasideor.com) is open 8am-5pm daily. **Providence Seaside Hospital** (725 S. Wahanna Rd., 503/717-7000) has 24-hour service and an emergency room.

## GETTING THERE

Sunset Empire Transportation District operates **The Bus** (503/861-RIDE—503/861-7433 or 800/776-6406, www.ridethebus.org), serving Cannon Beach, Seaside, Astoria-Warrenton, and points between. **Amtrak** (800/872-7245, www.amtrak.com) buses pass through twice daily on their run between Portland and Astoria.

# Cannon Beach and Vicinity

In 1846, the USS *Shark* met its end on the Columbia River Bar. The ship broke apart, and a section of deck bearing cannons and an iron capstan drifted south, finally in 1894 washing ashore south of the current city limits at Arch Cape. And so this town got its name, which it adopted in 1922. In the winter of 2008, during an especially low tide, two additional cannons were revealed. After a thorough study by historians and archivists at Texas A&M University, the cannons are now on display at Astoria's Columbia Maritime Museum.

In 1873, stagecoach and railroad tycoon Ben Holladay helped create Oregon's first coastal tourist mecca, Seaside, while ignoring its attractive neighbor in the shadow of Haystack Rock. In the 20th century, Cannon Beach evolved into a bohemian alternative to the hustle and bustle of the family-oriented resort scene to the north. Before the recent era of development, this place was a quaint backwater attracting laid-back artists, summer-home residents, and the overflow from Seaside.

Today, the low-key charm and atmosphere conducive to artistic expression have in some part been quashed by development and the attendant massive visitor influx and price increases. While such vital signs as a first-rate theater, a good bookstore, cheek-by-jowl art galleries, and fine restaurants are still in ample evidence, your view of them from the other side of the street might be blocked by a convoy of Winnebagos.

Nonetheless, the broad three-mile stretch of beach dominated by the impressive monolith of Haystack Rock still provides a contemplative experience. And if you're patient and resourceful enough to find a space for your wheels (try the free municipal lot one block east of the main street), the finest gallery-hopping, crafts, and shopping on the coast await. Wood shingles and understated earth tones dominate the architecture of tastefully rendered galleries, bookstores, and bistros. The city is small enough for strolling, and its location, removed from U.S. 101, spares it the kind of traffic blight seen on the main drags of other coastal tourist towns.

Cannon Beach is a popular summer getaway.

# Cannon Beach

## SIGHTS
### ★ Haystack Rock

**Haystack Rock** looms large above the long, broad beach. This is the third-tallest sea stack in the state, measuring 235 feet tall. As part of the Oregon Islands National Wildlife Refuge, it has wilderness status and is off-limits to climbing. Puffins and other seabirds nest on its steep faces, and intertidal organisms thrive in the tide pools around the base. The surrounding tide pools, within a radius of 300 yards from the base of the monolith, are designated a "marine garden"; they are open to exploration, but with strict no-collecting (of anything) and no-harassment (of any living organisms) protections in effect. Flanking the monolith are two rock formations known as the Needles. These spires had two other counterparts at the turn of the 20th century that have gradually been leveled by weathering and erosion. Old-timers will tell you that the government dynamited a trail to the top of Haystack in 1968 to keep people off this bird rookery. It also reduced the number of intrepid hikers trapped on the rock at high tide.

Volunteers from the **Haystack Rock Awareness Program** (503/436-1581) are often on the beach with displays, spotting scopes, and answers to many of your questions. Spend some time chatting with these folks, but don't forget to listen to the beach's own distinctive voices. You can't miss the cacophony of seabirds at sunset and, if you listen closely, the winter phenomenon of "singing sands" created by wind blowing over the beach.

Beach access is available at the west end of any public east-west street. From downtown, Harrison Street works well; south of downtown, Tolovana Beach Wayside has a large parking area and easy beach access.

## Cannon Beach History Center
Permanent exhibits at the small **Cannon Beach History Center** (1387 S. Spruce St., 503/436-9301, www.cbhistory.org, 11am-5pm Wed.-Mon., free) chronicle the town's timeline, from prehistory to the modern expansion

of tourism and recreation. The original eponymous cannon (the one found in 1894) from the ill-fated *Shark* is also on display here.

## Ecola State Park

**Ecola State Park** (off U.S. 101, 800/551-6949, www.oregonstateparks.org, $5 day-use) is two miles north of Cannon Beach. Thick conifer forests line the access road to Ecola Point. This forested cliff has many trails leading down to the water. The view south takes in Haystack Rock and the overlapping peaks of the Coast Range extending to Neahkahnie Mountain. This is one of the most photographed views on the coast. Out to sea, the sight of sea lions basking on surf-drenched rocks (mid-Apr.-July) or migrating gray whales (Dec. and Mar.) and orcas (May) are seasonal highlights.

From Ecola Point, trails lead north to horseshoe-shaped **Indian Beach,** a favorite with surfers. Some prefer to drive the steep, narrow road down to Indian Beach as a prelude to hiking up Tillamook Head, considered by Lewis and Clark the region's most beautiful viewpoint. The 2.5-mile Clatsop Loop Trail begins and ends at Indian Beach and climbs through Sitka spruce to a viewpoint. Ambitious hikers can do the first half of the loop, then continue another four miles north to Seaside.

The name Ecola means "whale" in Chinook and was first used as a place-name by William Clark, referring to a creek in the area. Lewis and Clark journals note a 105-foot beached whale found somewhere within present-day Ecola Park's southern border at Crescent Beach. This area represents the southernmost extent of Lewis and Clark's coastal Oregon travels.

## ★ Saddle Mountain State Natural Area

A good reason to head east from Cannon Beach is the hike up 3,283-foot Saddle Mountain at **Saddle Mountain State Natural Area** (off U.S. 26, 800/551-6949, www.oregonstateparks.org). On a clear day, hikers can see some 50 miles of the Oregon

and Washington coastlines, including the Columbia River. Also possible are spectacular views of Mounts Rainier, St. Helens, and Hood, and miles of clear-cuts. On the upper part of the trail, plant species that pushed south from Alaska and Canada during the last ice age still thrive. The cool, moist climate here keeps them from dying out as they did at lower elevations. Some early blooms include pink coast fawn lily, monkeyflower, wild rose, wood violet, bleeding heart, oxalis, Indian paintbrush, and trillium. Cable handrails provide safety on the narrow final 0.25-mile trail to the summit.

To get to the trailhead, take U.S. 26 from its junction with U.S. 101 for 10 miles and turn left on the prominently signed Saddle Mountain Road. (Although it's paved, this road is not suitable for RVs or wide-bodied vehicles.) After seven twisting miles, you'll come to the trailhead of the highest peak in this part of the Coast Range. The trail itself is steep, gaining more than 1,600 feet in 2.5 miles. Wet conditions can make the going difficult (allow four hours round-trip) and the scenery en route is not always exceptional unless you look down for the lovely May-August wildflower display; the view from the top is worth the climb.

The campground ($11) at Saddle Mountain is tiny and rustic and offers a secluded option for campers not attracted to the busy family scene at nearby Fort Stevens State Park.

## Beaches

Stunning beaches don't end with Cannon Beach. Sandy expanses stretch seven miles south to the Arch Cape tunnel on U.S. 101, indicating the entrance to Oswald West State Park. Several of these beaches are reached via state park waysides. As you head south, views of **Hug Point State Recreation Site** (off U.S. 101, 800/551-6949, www.oregonstateparks.org, free) and pristine beaches will have you ready to pull over. In summer, this can be a good escape from the crowds at Cannon Beach. Time your visit to coincide with low tide, when all manner of marinelife will be exposed in tidal pools. Also at low tide, you may see remains of an 800-foot-long Model T-size road blasted into the base of Hug Point, an early precursor to U.S. 101. The cliffs are gouged with caves and crevasses that also invite exploring, but be mindful of the tides so that you don't find yourself stranded. Hug Point got its name in the days when stagecoaches used the beach as highways; they had to dash between the waves, hugging the jutting headland to get around.

## SPORTS AND RECREATION
### Bicycling
**Family Fun Cycles** (1160 S. Hemlock, Cannon Beach, 503/436-2247, 10am-6pm Thurs.-Tues., $10-17 per 90 minutes) rents all manner of bikes, including mountain bikes, road bikes, beach cruisers, and three-wheeled recumbent "fun cycles," which zip up and down the hard-packed sand when the tide is out.

### Horseback Riding
**Sea Ranch Stables** (415 Old U.S. 101, 503/436-2815, 9am-4:30pm daily mid-June-Labor Day, 9am-4:30pm Sat.-Sun. mid-May-mid-June, $80-140), at the north entrance to Cannon Beach off U.S. 101, offers a number of one- to two-hour guided rides, including sunset rides. Rides to Haystack Rock start at 9am, before the beach gets crowded.

### Surfing
The area around Cannon Beach has several good surfing beaches. The most popular, and the best bet for beginners, is **Short Sands Beach,** at the end of the trail to the beach at Oswald West State Park, south of Arch Cape. It's a bit of a hike down to the beach, but the sheltered cove is a great place to spend the day, even if you're just bobbing around in the waves.

Another good spot for somewhat more advanced surfers (and surf kayakers) is **Indian Beach** at **Ecola State Park** (off U.S. 101, 800/551-6949, www.oregonstateparks.org,

$5 day-use). Rent a board and wetsuit at **Cleanline Surf** (171 Sunset Blvd., 503/436-9726, 10am-6pm Sun.-Fri., 9am-6pm Sat.).

## ENTERTAINMENT AND EVENTS
Going strong since 1972, the **Coaster Theatre Playhouse** (108 N. Hemlock St., 503/436-1242, www.coastertheatre.com, $20-25) stages a varied bill of musicals, dramas, mysteries, comedies, concerts, and other entertainment. It's open year-round in a building that started in the 1920s as a skating rink-turned-silent movie house.

### Brewpubs
**Bill's Tavern** (188 N. Hemlock St., 503/436-2202, 11:30am-10pm daily, bar open later, $7-13), once a legendary watering hole, is now a more traditional brewpub. Sweet thick onion rings, good fries, one-third-pound burgers, sautéed prawns, and grilled oysters are on the menu.

Farther south near Tolovana, the **Warren House Pub** (3301 S. Hemlock St., 503/436-1130, 11:30am-1am daily, $7-14) serves local beers from Bill's Tavern, but in an English pub setting. The menu includes good smoked ribs, burgers, and seafood; in summer the backyard beer garden is a lovely spot to relax. Kids are allowed on the restaurant side of the pub.

The **Public Coast Brewing Co.** (264 3rd St., 503/436-0285, http://publiccoastbrewing.com, noon-9pm Thurs.-Mon., $11-23) is a block away from busy downtown Cannon Beach, but this spacious brewpub offers good food and excellent beers at good prices. The food specialty is build-your-own burgers, but you can also find fish tacos and three kinds of fish-and-chips. A dozen beers (plus a house-brewed root beer) are usually on tap, including a "beast" of an IPA.

### Festivals and Events
The half-dozen or so other sand-sculpting contests that take place on the Oregon coast pale in comparison to Cannon Beach's annual **Sandcastle Day** (503/436-2623, late

June, call to confirm dates). In 1964 a tsunami washed out a bridge, and the isolated residents of Cannon Beach organized the first contest as a way to amuse their children. Now in its sixth decade, this is the state's oldest and most prestigious competition of its kind. Tens of thousands of spectators show up to watch 1,000-plus competitors fashion their sculptures with the aid of buckets, shovels, squirt guns, and any natural material found on the beach. The resulting sculptures are often amazingly complex and inventive. This event is free to spectators, but entrants pay a fee. Recent winners included Egyptian pyramids and a gigantic sea turtle. This collapsible art show usually coincides with the lowest-tide Saturday in June and takes place north of Haystack Rock. Building begins in the early morning; winners are announced at noon. The American Legion serves a big breakfast buffet ($7 adults, $5 ages 6-12) at 1216 South Hemlock Street, open to all.

Writers, singers, composers, painters, and sculptors take over the town for the **Stormy Weather Arts Festival** (503/436-2623), usually held the first weekend of November. Events include music in the streets, plays, a Saturday afternoon Art Walk, and the Quick Draw, in which artists have one hour to paint, complete, and frame a piece while the audience watches. The art is then sold by auction.

Beginning in July, the city park (Spruce St. and 2nd St.) hosts **Concerts in the Park** (5pm-7pm Sun.), a series of jazz, rhythm and blues, and popular music at the bandstand.

## SHOPPING

Besides the beach, much of the attraction of Cannon Beach is window shopping up and down Hemlock Street, which, in addition to galleries, is lined with clothing stores, gift shops, and other boutiques. Cannon Beach supports a fine kite store, **Once Upon a Breeze** (240 N. Spruce St., 503/436-1112) and one of the better bookstores on the coast, the **Cannon Beach Book Company** (130 N. Hemlock St., 503/436-1301, http://cannonbeachbooks.com, 11am-6pm Mon.-Fri.,

10:30am-6pm Sat.-Sun.); it's the place to pick up regional titles or a good novel (lots of mysteries) for that rainy weekend.

## Art Galleries

Cannon Beach has long attracted artists and artisans, and here art lovers and shoppers will find nearly two dozen galleries and shops with high-quality works. Most of the Cannon Beach galleries and boutiques are concentrated along Hemlock Street, where you can hardly swing a Winsor & Newton No. 12 hog-bristle brush without hitting one. Not surprisingly, the seashore itself is the subject and inspiration of many works you'll see here, with Haystack Rock frequently depicted in various media. The **Cannon Beach Information Center** (201 E. 2nd St., 503/436-2623, www.cannonbeach.org, 11am-5pm Mon.-Sat., 10am-4pm Sun.) has a guide to all the galleries in town, or you can just stroll and discover them for yourself.

At the north end of town, **Northwest by Northwest Gallery** (232 N. Spruce St., 503/436-0741, www.nwbynwgallery.com, 11am-6pm daily) showcases photography, painting, sculpture, and ceramics and glass by noted regional artists. **White Bird Gallery** (251 N. Hemlock St., 503/436-2681, www.whitebirdgallery.com, 11am-5pm daily, call for winter hours), founded in 1971 and one of Cannon Beach's oldest galleries, casts a wide net with paintings, sculpture, prints, photography, glass, ceramics, and jewelry. Nearby, the **Bronze Coast Gallery** (224 N. Hemlock St., 503/436-1055, www.bronzecoastgallery.com, 10am-6pm daily) shows both traditional Western bronzes and innovative bronze works and paintings that may appeal to those who aren't crazy about traditional Western art. In midtown, **Icefire Glassworks** (116 Gower St., 503/436-2359, 10am-5pm Thurs.-Mon.) is a working glass studio where you can watch glassblowers and artists shape their work and then shop for unique pieces in the gallery.

**DragonFire Gallery** (123 S. Hemlock St., 503/436-1533, www.dragonfirestudio.com, 10am-5pm daily) shows the work of a wide variety of artists; on Saturday afternoons throughout the summer, everyone is invited to come and meet gallery artists.

## FOOD

If you're on a budget, keep dining prices down at the **Mariner Market** (139 N. Hemlock St., 503/436-2442, 8am-9pm daily), a dimly lit old grocery that's fully stocked with fresh meat, fruit, vegetables, and deli items.

### Pacific Northwest Cuisine

Whether or not you're staying at the **Stephanie Inn** (2740 S. Pacific St., 503/436-2221 or 855/977-2444, www.stephanie-inn.com, 5pm-9pm daily, $45-50), you are welcome to join guests in the dining room for creative Pacific Northwest cuisine (reservations required for nonguests). The atmosphere boasts mountain views, open wood beams, and a river-rock fireplace. Since guests get first shot at tables, those staying elsewhere should reserve well ahead of time.

For a much more casual dining experience, go to **Sweet Basil's Cafe** (271 N. Hemlock St., 503/436-1539, www.cafesweetbasils.com, 11am-10pm Wed.-Sun., $12-21), a tiny restaurant whose commitment is "natural, organic, wild" international fare, with an emphasis on Cajun and Creole cuisine in the evening. At lunch, enjoy mostly vegetarian sandwiches and salads. In the evening, linger in the wine bar, where you have a choice of tapas-style dishes such as a wild prawn martini with banana chili salsa, chicken and sausage gumbo, or crab-stuffed portobello mushrooms.

Formerly a bakery open only during the day, ★ **Harding Trading Company** (277 Beaver St., 503/739-2693, 4pm-9pm Wed.-Mon., $19-30) is now open as an evening fine-dining restaurant. The chef-owners bring careful finesse to their mostly French- and Italian-style cooking, which is dominated by the freshest Northwest ingredients. The mushroom *tarte,* with puff pastry, sherry, tarragon, and leeks, is outstanding, and the line-caught halibut with pea sauce is delicate and commanding at the same time. As you'd expect, desserts are masterful.

### Seafood

Hankering for some authentic West Coast chowder? Head to **Dooger's Seafood and Grill** (1371 S. Hemlock St., 503/436-2225, 8am-9pm daily, dinner $12-45) for seafood that's always fresh and delicious. Don't overlook Dooger's for breakfast—during crab season (mostly winter-spring), the crab benedict

the Harding Trading Company

is a real treat. **Mo's at Tolovana** (195 Warren Way, Tolovana Park, 503/436-1111, www. moschowder.com, 11am-8pm Sun.-Thurs., 11am-9pm Fri., 8am-9pm Sat., $3-16) has great views; although its clam chowder is locally famous, the mostly traditional, but very fresh, fried food is not the big draw (although it's very good).

In the fishing business since 1977, **Ecola Seafoods** (208 N. Spruce St., 503/436-9130, 10am-9pm daily summer, 10am-6pm daily winter) features fresh-catch Dungeness crab and bay shrimp cocktails, as well as a decent clam chowder ($5). Or sample the smoked salmon and enjoy a big selection of fish-and-chips ($11-17). You'll find it across from the public parking lots and information center.

## Classic American

The local **Pig 'N Pancake** (223 S. Hemlock St., 503/436-2851, 7am-3pm daily, $6-15) has large picture windows overlooking a leafy ravine. Choose from 35 breakfast dishes, served anytime, including homemade pancakes (which are very good and extremely popular—expect to wait). For lunch, try the soups, chowder, or halibut and chips.

Check out the wood-paneled skylighted **Lazy Susan Cafe** (126 N. Hemlock St., 503/436-2816, www.lazy-susan-cafe.com, 8am-3pm Sun.-Mon. and Wed.-Thurs., $7-13) for a great breakfast (waffles are a specialty) or satisfying lunch (salads are good).

If all you need is excellent coffee and delicious fresh baked goods, go to **Sea Level Bakery** (3116 S Hemlock, 503/436-4254, 7:30am-3pm Mon.-Thurs., 7:30am-5pm Fri., 7am-5pm Sat.-Sun., $4-12), where you'll find great bread for picnics, plus pastries and lunches that include a charcuterie plate, soups, quiche, and sandwiches.

Somewhat oddly, few of Cannon Beach's top restaurants have a view of the beach, so if excellent vistas of Haystack Rock and breaking waves are important to you, call to reserve a table at **The Wayfarer** (1190 Pacific Dr., 503/436-1108, www.wayfarer-restaurant. com, 8am-9pm daily, dinner $21-42), tucked

above a beach entrance at Gower Street. The food, which is quite good but not as memorable as the views, features classic steak and seafood main courses. The lounge here is a good spot for a drink.

## Italian

The pizza at **Pizza a'Fetta** (231 N. Hemlock St., 503/436-0333, 11am-8pm Sun.-Thurs., 11am-9pm Fri.-Sat., slices $3-4, whole pies $20-33) is Cannon Beach's best, with a selection of to-go slices available at a takeout window. Or crowd into the always-busy dining room for your choice of pies, salads, minestrone soup, and Oregon microbrew beer and Italian wines.

Cozy and refined, ★ **The Bistro** (263 N. Hemlock St., 503/436-2661, 4pm-9pm Wed.-Sun., $20-25) is tucked back in a maze of shops and gardens in downtown Cannon Beach. This longtime favorite restaurant has a new chef-owner, and the menu reflects international flavors, while the atmosphere remains charmingly country French. The cioppino seafood stew is a wonderful blend of Pacific Northwest fish and shellfish prepared with Asian zest, and the locally sourced pork chops, served with goat milk polenta and Italian *agrodolce* sauce, are out of this world. The dining room is truly tiny and the food superlative, so reservations are mandatory.

**Castaways Tini Tiki Hut** (316 N. Fir St., 503/436-4444, 5pm-9pm Wed.-Sun., $22-29) describes its cooking as global, but many of the best dishes spring from Creole or New Orleans traditions. Several dishes are based on local seafood, such as Caribbean curried prawns and Bahamian crusted mahimahi. This is a busy spot, also popular for exotic cocktails.

## Mediterranean

★ **Newman's at 988** (988 S. Hemlock St., 503/436-1151, www.newmansat988.com, 5:30pm-9pm Tues.-Sat. Oct. 16-June, 5:30pm-9pm daily July-Oct. 15, $19-26) is a good special-occasion restaurant in a tiny house, with an elegant atmosphere and excellent food. The chef-owner takes great pride in using fresh local ingredients to prepare seasonal menus with French and Italian influences, featuring such dishes as seared duck breast with foie gras and truffle oil or grilled portabella mushroom with spinach, tomato, gorgonzola, and carrot juice.

While it's not a traditional restaurant, the **EVOO Cannon Beach Cooking School** (188 S. Hemlock, 503/436-8555, http://evoo. biz, cooking classes 6pm-9pm daily, $119-149 pp) is one of Cannon Beach's favorite "dinner theaters," where a small group of guests watch their meals cooked before their eyes. Dinners focus on seasonal ingredients and include a starter plus a three-course dinner, dessert, and one glass of wine. You don't need to help prepare the food, though special "hands on" dinners are offered occasionally. Check the website for occasional mid-day lunch classes.

### Irish

The **Irish Table** (1235 S. Hemlock St., 503/436-0708, 5:30pm-9pm Fri.-Tues., $11-22) makes the most of the Pacific Northwest bounty and hearty Irish cooking traditions, including meat pastries, grilled salmon, braised mussels, and variations on local lamb, including Irish lamb stew. The bar offers a wide selection of Scotch and Irish whiskies, plus Irish ales.

## ACCOMMODATIONS

Cannon Beach is very popular in summer. Make reservations as early as possible in the spring to even get a room. By Memorial Day weekend, many of the most popular spots will be completely booked for the summer and early fall. Plan well ahead if you have your heart set on staying here in July and August. On the other hand, prices drop by as much as half for midweek off-season stays.

### $50-100

There aren't many inexpensive lodging options in Cannon Beach, but "mountain-view" rooms at the enormous **Tolovana Inn** (3400 S. Hemlock St., 503/436-2211 or 800/333-8890, www.tolovanainn.com, minimum stay in summer, $89-129 mountain view, $154-279 ocean view) hotel complex at the southern end of the Cannon Beach sprawl offer a good location at a fairly reasonable price. To make up for the rather cookie-cutter design and furnishings, you'll get a swimming pool, a spa, and a sauna, a number of restaurants sharing the same parking lots, and the beach right out the front door. Most oceanfront rooms have private patios or balconies; one- and two-bedroom suites are also available.

### $100-150

About a minute's walk to the beach, with friendly management and a great vibe, the **Blue Gull Inn** (632 S. Hemlock St., 503/436-2714 or 800/507-2714, www.bluegullinn.net, 2-night minimum in summer, $109-209) offers a choice between a beach house or less expensive motel units that come with housekeeping facilities. The modern cottages have in-room whirlpool tubs, fireplaces, and full kitchens. Cottages for larger groups are also available.

The **McBee Cottages** (888 S. Hemlock St., 503/436-0247 or 800/238-4107, www. mcbeecottages.com, $104-194) is a 1940s-era motel with semidetached units that have been nicely renovated. The rooms are simple, but the McBee is nonetheless a favorite of many visitors looking for cozy accommodations, and it's just a minute from the beach and within walking distance of downtown. McBee accepts pets in several of its homey cottages.

For more homey atmosphere, try the **Argonauta Inn** or **The Waves Motel,** which share an office (188 W. 2nd St., 503/436-2205 or 800/822-2468, www.thewavescannonbeach. com). The Argonauta ($149-289) is made up of four houses in the middle of downtown and has five furnished units just 150 feet from the beach. A cluster of six beachfront buildings makes up The Waves ($149-285), with units to fit the needs of families, couples, or larger groups. These are not cookie-cutter units, but the kind of individual lodgings you'd expect in Oregon.

The **Cannon Beach Hotel** (1116 Hemlock St., 503/436-1392 or 800/238-4107, www.cannonbeachhotel.com, $134-239) is a converted 1910 loggers' boardinghouse with 30 rooms and a small café and restaurant on the premises. The most expensive rooms have fireplaces, whirlpools, and partial ocean views. Meals are available in the restaurant adjacent to the lobby.

Just a few minutes' walk from downtown, **Ecola Creek Lodge** (208 E. 5th St., 503/436-2776 or 800/873-2749, www.ecolacreeklodge.com, $136-213) is a Cape Cod-style inn with 22 unique units set in four buildings. Accommodations range from simple queen-bed studios to two-bedroom suites. Special features include stained glass, lawns, fountains, flower gardens, and a lily pond. Les Shirley Park and Ecola Creek separate the lodge from the beach.

## Over $200

The ★ **Surfsand Resort** (148 W. Gower St., 503/436-2274 or 800/547-6100, www.surfsand.com, $239-349) offers a great combination of location and amenities, with Haystack Rock right out the door and spacious, nicely furnished suites. The resort has an indoor pool and spa and on-site massage services; pets are permitted in some rooms. The popular Wayfarer Restaurant is adjacent.

The handsome **Inn at Cannon Beach** (3215 S. Hemlock St., 503/436-9085 or 800/321-6304, www.atcannonbeach.com, minimum stay in summer, $245-289) has large and stylish cottage-like rooms in a beautifully landscaped garden setting with a courtyard pond, just a block from the beach. All guest rooms include a gas fireplace, a fridge, a microwave, a coffeemaker, and a TV/DVD combo; some rooms can accommodate pets.

The small all-suites **Lighthouse Inn** (963 S. Hemlock St., 866/265-1686 or 503/463-2929, www.cblighthouseinn.com, $205-240) offers eight attractive king and queen suites, some with full kitchens. The suites are quite spacious and nicely furnished, and all have

balconies or patios, a separate bedroom, a dining area, a fridge, a fireplace, and other extras. The beach is just a block away.

The fabulously expensive (for Oregon) ★ **Stephanie Inn** (2740 S. Pacific St., 503/436-2221 or 800/633-3466, www.stephanie-inn.com, $559-639) offers attentive B&B-style service (breakfast buffet and evening wine gathering included), attention to detail, and luxury-level rooms with a low-key, not-too-fussy Oregonian touch. All guest rooms have balconies, fireplaces, wet bars, jetted tubs, fine linens, and all the extras you'd expect in an upscale resort hotel, including a fine-dining restaurant. The Stephanie is a romantic, adult-focused inn; children under 12 are not permitted.

The **Ocean Lodge** (2864 S. Pacific Dr., 503/436-2241 or 888/777-4047, www.theoceanlodge.com, $259-359) feels like a long-established beach getaway, though in fact it opened in 2002. The high-end furnishings also give a clue that despite its venerable design, this rambling lodge isn't soaked in tradition. Rooms all have balconies, fireplaces, microwaves, and fridges. Lower-cost rooms don't have ocean views, though all are just steps from the beach.

For a more private experience just steps from the ocean, the **White Heron Lodge** (356 N. Spruce St., 503/436-2205 or 800/822-2468, www.thewavescannonbeach.com, 3-night minimum stay in summer, $349) comprises six fully furnished oceanfront one-bedroom suites with a wall bed in the living room, so all can sleep up to four. Each of the suites looks directly out on the Pacific. Wide sandy beaches and spacious front lawns make it a great location for families, especially those with small children. Located on a residential dead-end street, the lodge is only one block from downtown Cannon Beach.

Three miles south of Cannon Beach in quiet Arch Cape, the **Arch Cape Inn** (31970 E. Ocean Lane, 503/436-2800 or 800/436-2848, www.archcapeinn.com, $209-349) is a bit over-the-top in its turreted castle-like design, but it is supremely luxurious. Although it's not on the beach, it's an easy walk, and several rooms have good ocean views.

## Vacation Rentals

Several local property management companies offer a large selection of furnished rentals, ranging from grand oceanfront homes to quaint secluded cottages. **Cannon Beach Property Management** (3188 S. Hemlock St., 503/436-2021 or 877/386-3402, www.cbpm.com) and **Cannon Beach Vacation Rentals** (P.O. Box 723, Cannon Beach 97110, 866/436-0940, www.visitcb.com) both have good websites. During the summer, many beach houses are only available for weekly rentals.

## Camping

Camping offers easier access to Cannon Beach's natural wonders at a bargain price. Although camping is not permitted on the beach or in Cannon Beach city parks, there are plenty of options for RV, tent, and outdoor enthusiasts.

Unlike most private campgrounds, the small family-run **Wright's for Camping** (334 Reservoir Rd., 503/436-2347, www.wrightsforcamping.com, $36-40) is geared toward tent campers. It's just east of U.S. 101 and has 20 sites with picnic tables and fire rings as well as restrooms and a laundry. Wright's is wheelchair accessible; leashed pets are allowed.

For a more pampered RV-only experience, check out the **RV Resort at Cannon Beach** (345 Elk Creek Rd., 503/436-2231 or 800/847-2231, www.cbrvresort.com, $52). Open year-round, the RV Resort has 100 full hookups, an indoor pool and spa, free cable TV, an on-site convenience store, a laundry facility, restrooms, and a meeting room.

Roughly 20 miles east of Cannon Beach off U.S. 26 is **Saddle Mountain State Natural Area** (800/551-6949, www.oregonstateparks.org, Mar.-Oct., $11 tents), which offers 10 first-come, first-served tent camping sites at the base of 3,283-foot Saddle Mountain, one of the highest peaks in Oregon's Coast Range. This more primitive and remote campground (although there are flush toilets and piped water, in addition to picnic tables and fire pits) might just be the tonic if you're weary of the crowds along the beach.

## INFORMATION AND SERVICES

The chamber of commerce operates the **Cannon Beach Information Center** (201 E. 2nd St., 503/436-2623, www.cannonbeach.org, 11am-5pm Mon.-Sat., 10am-4pm Sun.). This facility is close to the public restrooms (2nd St. and Spruce St.) and basketball and tennis courts.

**Providence North Coast Clinic** (171 N. Larch St., 503/717-7000) offers medical care and minor emergency services. It's located in Sandpiper Square behind the stores on the main drag.

## GETTING THERE AND AROUND

From U.S. 101, there's a choice of four entrances to the beach loop (also known as U.S. 101 Alternate, a section of the old Oregon Coast Highway) to take you into town. As you wade into the town's shops, galleries, and restaurants, the beach loop becomes Hemlock Street, the main drag of Cannon Beach. Sunset Empire Transportation District operates **The Bus** (503/861-RIDE—503/861-7433 or 800/776-6406, www.ridethebus.org), which serves Cannon Beach, Seaside, Astoria-Warrenton, and points between. **Parking** can be hard to come by, especially on weekends, but you'll find public lots south of town at Tolovana Park and in town at Hemlock at 1st Streets and on 2nd Street.

The **Cannon Beach Shuttle** (10am-6pm daily, longer hours in summer, $1) runs every half-hour on a 6.5-mile loop, from Les Shirley Park on the north end of town to Tolovana Park.

**Amtrak Thruway Motorcoach Service** (800/USA-RAIL—800/872-7245, www.amtrak.com) runs two buses daily between Portland Union Station and Cannon Beach, continuing on to Seaside and Astoria. The bus stops at 1088 South Hemlock Street, across the street from the Cannon Beach Mercantile store.

# Nehalem Bay Area

## MANZANITA AND VICINITY

Just south of Arch Cape, Neahkahnie Mountain towers nearly 1,700 feet up from the edge of the sea. U.S. 101 climbs up and over its shoulder to an elevation of 700 feet, and the vistas from a half-dozen pullouts (the highest along the Oregon coast) are spectacular—but do try to keep your eyes on the snaking road until you've parked your car.

This stretch of the highway, built by the Works Progress Administration in the 1930s, was constructed by blasting a roadbed from the rock face and buttressing it with stonework walls on the precarious cliffs. The fainthearted or acrophobic certainly couldn't have lasted long on this job. The handiwork of these road builders and masons can be admired at several pullouts, along with the breathtaking vistas of Manzanita Beach and Nehalem Spit, stretching some 20 miles south to Cape Meares. Much of Neahkahnie Mountain and its rugged coastline are preserved in Oswald West State Park, one of the state's finest.

Immediately to the south, huddled along an expansive curve of beach at the foot of Neahkahnie Mountain, quiet Manzanita (pop. 700) makes a pleasant stop for lunch or for the weekend. When adjacent coastal areas are fogbound, the seven-mile-long Manzanita Beach often enjoys sunshine because of the shelter of Neahkahnie Mountain. As one of the few towns along the north Oregon coast that's not located directly on U.S. 101, Manzanita feels more peaceful and secluded than most others; like Cannon Beach, it's also a relatively wealthy and stylish town.

Just two miles south of Manzanita on U.S. 101, tiny Nehalem occupies just a few blocks along U.S. 101 on the north bank of the Nehalem River. It's a lovely location with a few Old West-style storefronts. Sizable runs of spring and fall chinook salmon and winter steelhead make this a popular destination for anglers.

### Oswald West State Park

Most of Neahkahnie Mountain and the prominent headlands of Cape Falcon are encompassed within the 2,500-acre gem of **Oswald**

The wide beach at Manzanita is good for horseback riding.

West State Park (off U.S. 101, 800/551-6949, www.oregonstateparks.org). Whether or not you believe in the stories of lost pirate wealth buried somewhere on the mountain, there is real treasure today for all who venture here in search of the intangible currency of extraordinary natural beauty. The state park bears the name of Governor Oswald West, whose farsighted 1913 beach bill was instrumental in protecting Oregon's virgin shoreline.

Several hiking trails weave through the park, including the 13 miles of the Oregon Coast Trail linking Arch Cape to the north with Manzanita. From the main parking lot on the east side of U.S. 101, a 0.5-mile trail follows Short Sands Creek to Short Sands Beach, a relatively sheltered beach that's popular with surfers year-round. Rainforests of hemlock, cedar, and gigantic Sitka spruce crowd the secluded boulder-strewn shoreline. From Short Sands Beach, hike north on the three-mile old-growth-lined Cape Falcon Trail to spectacular views.

From the trail to the beach, it's also possible to turn south and hike to Neahkahnie Mountain (4 miles one-way) with some stiff climbing. Shave about 1.3 miles off the hike by starting a mile south of the main Oswald West parking lot, where there's an access road to the Neahkahnie Mountain Summit Trail on the east side of the highway. It's not well marked; look for a subdivision on the golf course to the west. Drive up the gravel road 0.25 miles to the trailhead parking lot and begin a moderately difficult 1.5-mile ascent. Allow about 45 minutes to get to the top. The summit view south to Cape Meares and east to the Nehalem Valley ranks as one of the finest on the coast.

Visitors who remember camping among the old-growth trees at Oswald West should treasure the memory. Due to the instability of the ancient trees, the campground remains closed.

## Food

House renters, budget diners, and picnickers can take advantage of the excellent produce and impressive (for a coastal market) grocery section at Manzanita Grocery & Deli (193 Laneda Ave., 503/368-5362, 8am-8pm daily). One block away, Mother Nature's Natural Foods Store (298 Laneda Ave., 503/368-5316, 10am-7pm Mon.-Sat.) stocks natural groceries, coffees and teas, bulk foods, wine, and beer.

Stop at Manzanita News & Espresso (500 Laneda Ave., 503/368-7450, 7:00am-5pm daily, $2-5) for a coffee, pastry, and magazine (there are lots to choose from, and the selection is anything but generic).

The local bakery, Bread and Ocean (154 Laneda Ave., 503/368-5823, 7:30am-2pm Wed.-Sat., 8am-2pm Sun., $4-11), makes sandwiches as well as cinnamon rolls. The local favorite for hefty traditional breakfasts is Big Wave Cafe (822 Laneda Ave., 503/368-9283, 8am-8pm Sun.-Thurs., 8am-9pm Fri.-Sat., $7-18), where you'll find Makin' Waves eggs Benedict, dressed with spinach and chipotle hollandaise sauce.

Left Coast Siesta (288 Laneda Ave., 503/368-7997, 11:30am-8pm Tues.-Sat., noon-7pm Sun. summer, 11:30am-8pm Wed.-Sat., noon-7pm Sun. winter, $6-11) specializes in design-your-own burritos, the perfect takeout for a beach lunch or dinner. Options include spicy beef, spicy chicken, tequila-lime chicken, or black beans to fill a selection of flavored tortillas. It also serves tacos and enchiladas. And if you like it *caliente,* this is the place for you: Left Coast Siesta stocks a hot-sauce bar with 200-plus different types of the hot stuff, many available to purchase by the jar.

Just a couple of blocks from the beach, Marzano's (60 Laneda Ave., 503/368-3663, 4pm-8:30pm Thurs.-Mon., large pies mostly $20-25) serves the area's best slices of gourmet pizza. The roasted vegetable pizza is recommended, and the smoked prosciutto with aged montegrappa cheese is another winner.

For relaxed fine dining, the best option is Neah-Kah-Nie Bistro (519 Laneda Ave., 503/368-2722, www.nknbistro.com, 5pm-9pm Tues.-Sun., $16-27), a small dining room serving local seafood and meats with up-to-date continental preparations. True cod is pan-seared and served with lemon butter over Parmesan and asparagus risotto, while grilled pork chops come with dates and blue cheese crumbles.

**Blackbird** (503 Laneda Ave., 503/368-7708, http://blackbirdmanzanita.com, 5pm-9pm Thurs. and Sun.-Mon., 5pm-10pm Fri.-Sat., $18-29) is a classy fine-dining restaurant with inventive ways of preparing local produce, fish, and meats. The lamb burger is excellent, Brussels sprouts with lemon, almonds and Parmesan are deliciously decadent, and you can't go wrong with flat-iron steak served with duck-fat fingerling potatoes and red wine jus.

## Accommodations

Manzanita is a small town without an abundance of lodgings. Advance reservations are a must, especially in summer, and many accommodations require two- or three-night stays during the high season and on some holidays. A good alternative to motels for families here are the rentals available from the several property management agencies in town. Among these is **Manzanita Beach Getaway** (503/368-2929 or 855/368-2929, www.manzanitabeachgetaway.com), with fully furnished homes to rent, running $110-259 per night, most require weekly rentals in July and August.

If you're looking for a quiet retreat, the cedar-clad **Inn at Manzanita** (67 Laneda Ave., 503/368-6754, www.innatmanzanita.com, $179-225) is set in a Japanese-accented garden just a short walk from the beach. Each of its 14 wood-paneled guest rooms features a gas fireplace and a two-person tub; most rooms have a balcony, offering glimpses through the evergreens of the nearby beach. Fresh flowers daily, robes, and other amenities help you feel pampered. Despite being in the middle of town near restaurants and the beach, a feeling of luxurious seclusion prevails.

The remodeled **Ocean Inn** (32 Laneda Ave., 866/3687701 or 503/368-7701, www. oceaninnatmanzanita.com, $154-224) has 10 large and comfortable condo-like rooms (most with full kitchens); several have wood stoves, and two have patios. Most rooms have ocean views, and the beach is just moments away.

Six blocks from the beach, the spacious, stylish, and airy cabins of ★ **Coast Cabins** (635 Laneda Ave., 503/368-7113, www.coast-cabins.com, 2-night minimum stay summer and weekends, $225-465) comfortably sleep two, though some are designed for up to four people and offer kitchenettes or full kitchens, satellite TV, and goose-down pillows and comforters. The Coast Cabins folks also rent out a few sophisticated one- and two-bedroom condos in downtown Manzanita.

For a more standard motel experience, the **Sunset Surf** (248 Ocean Rd., 503/368-5224 or 800/243-8035, www.sunsetsurfocean.com, $74-165) offers guest rooms (many with kitchens) in three oceanfront units that share an outdoor pool. Although rooms are basic, the setting is great.

Another upgraded older motel, the **Spindrift Inn** (114 Laneda Ave., 503/368-1001 or 877/368-1001, www.spindrift-inn.com, $150-165) has rooms that are nicer than the rather plain exterior. It's a short walk to the beach.

## Camping

Just south of Manzanita and occupying the entire sandy appendage of Nehalem Spit is scenic, sprawling **Nehalem Bay State Park** (800/452-5687, www.oregonstateparks.org, year-round, $29 tents, $32 RVs, $47 yurts, $5 day-use for noncampers), a favorite with bikers, beachcombers, anglers, horse owners, and pilots (yes, there's a little airstrip and a fly-in campsite). Sandwiched between the bay and a beautiful four-mile beach stretching from Manzanita to the mouth of the Nehalem River is a vast campground with hot showers. Sites are a little bit close together, with few trees to screen the neighbors; dunes separate campers from the ocean. As big as this park is, it does fill up in summer, so reservations (www.reserveamerica.com) are advised, especially in

July and August. To get there, turn south at Bayshore Junction just before U.S. 101 heads east into the town of Nehalem.

## WHEELER

Wheeler (pop. 393) is a little town flanking the Nehalem River where most accommodations are low-cost efficiencies for visiting fisherfolk, but the 10 guest rooms of the **Wheeler on the Bay Lodge and Marina** (580 Marine Dr., 503/368-5858 or 800/469-3204, www.wheeleronthebay.com, $110-164), on U.S. 101 on the shore of Nehalem Bay, have more appeal. These are anything but cookie-cutter rooms and are clean and appealing. Most guest rooms have at least partial bay views, and several have jetted tubs. There's also a video store, kayak rentals, and on-site massage services, and they can help arrange fishing charters.

Rooms at **The Old Wheeler Hotel** (495 U.S. 101, 503/368-6000 or 877/653-4683, www.oldwheelerhotel.com, $119-178), a 1920s landmark across the road from the bay, may remind you of your great-aunt's guest room. They're old-fashioned in a down-to-earth way. Although all guest rooms have private baths, some baths are down the hall from their rooms.

In a tiny cottage just off the main drag, the ★ **Rising Star Cafe** (92 Rorvik St., 503/368-3990, www.risingstarcafe.net, 2pm-8pm Wed.-Sat., 10am-2pm Sun., $13-26, cash only) is a sweet spot for excellent pasta, sandwiches, and chowder—some of the best on the coast. There are only seven tables in this popular restaurant, so call ahead for reservations. The food can be good here (the North Coast cioppino and rib-eye steak with wild mushrooms are recommended), and the atmosphere is comfortable and friendly.

Though not yet open at press time, the **Salmonberry Saloon** (380 Marine Dr., 503/368-7636, www.salmonberrysaloon. com) has a coveted spot right on the Nehalem River and promises good food and drinks in addition to eye-popping views above a river marina.

Between Wheeler and Rockaway Beach is the **Jetty Fishery** (27550 U.S. 101 N., 503/368-5746, www.jettyfishery.com), a combo fishing camp and fresh fish shop where you have the choice of renting a boat and going crabbing near the mouth of the Nehalem River, or buying a just-cooked fresh crab to take out or eat right there at picnic tables on the pier. This isn't a fancy spot, but it sure is authentic.

## ROCKAWAY BEACH

This town of 1,400 was established as a summer resort in the 1920s by Portlanders who wanted a coastal getaway. And so it remains today—a quiet spot without much going on besides walks on the seven miles of sandy beach, a **Kite Festival** in mid-May, and an **Arts and Crafts Fair** in mid-August. Shallow **Lake Lytle,** on the east side of the highway, offers spring and early summer fishing for trout, bass, and crappie. While the town of Rockaway is singularly unattractive from U.S. 101—a lengthy stretch of tacky shops, modest motels, and big new condos—the beach is quite nice, anchored at the south by the impressive Twin Rocks formation. The **Visitor Information Center** (503/355-8108, www.rockawaybeach.net), lodged in a bright red caboose in the center of town, can fill you in on other goings-on.

### Food

**Cow Belle Cafe** (194 U.S. 101 S., 503/355-2441, 8am-2pm Mon.-Sat., 8am-noon Sun., $8-14) is a local favorite for breakfast. The biscuits and gravy here are renowned, as is the bovine-rich decor. The **Offshore Grill and Coffeehouse** (122 U.S. 101 N., 503/355-3005, 9am-5pm Mon., 8am-9pm Wed.-Thurs., 7am-9pm Fri., 7am-9pm Sat.-Sun., $14-25) is one of the classier dining places in town (don't worry, flip-flops and a sweatshirt will get you by), bringing well-prepared comfort food to Rockaway Beach. The menu extends from grilled meatloaf to orange-glazed duck breast and also usually includes local seafood and fish in interesting preparations (clams with gnocchi). Breakfasts are excellent.

## Accommodations

Rockaway's motels are basic and family-oriented; if you are planning in advance, take a moment to check out the beach houses and condos available for rent on the **chamber of commerce website** (www.rockaway-beach.net).

The following motels are on the ocean side of busy U.S. 101, which dominates this long string bean of a town. **Surfside Resort Motel** (101 NW 11th St., 503/355-2312 or 800/243-7786, www.surfsideocean.com, $94-154 with no ocean view, $139-181 ocean view)

is a large beachfront complex with an indoor pool. Some guest rooms with kitchens are available. **Silver Sands Oceanfront Resort** (215 S. Pacific Ave., 503/355-2206 or 800/457-8972, www.oregonsilversands.com, $116-166) is also right on the beach, with fairly basic rooms (some kitchenettes), an indoor pool and hot tub, and a sauna.

About a mile south of town, **Twin Rocks Motel** (7925 Minehaha St., 503/355-2391 or 877/355-2391, www.twinrocksmotel.net, $204-229) is a small cluster of dog-friendly two-bedroom oceanfront cottages. If you're looking for a simple, quiet getaway with family or a couple of friends, this might be your place.

# Tillamook Bay

## GARIBALDI

Tillamook Bay's commercial fishing fleet is concentrated in this little port town (pop. 970) near the north end of the bay. Garibaldi, named in 1879 by the local postmaster for the Italian patriot, is a fish-processing center: Crabs, shrimp, fresh salmon, lingcod, and bottom fish (halibut, cabezon, rockfish, and sea perch) are the specialties. At the marina, **Garibaldi Cannery** (606 Commercial Dr., 503/322-3344, 9am-6pm Mon.-Thurs., 7am-6pm Fri.-Sun. summer, call for winter hours, $5-12) and **The Spot** (304 Mooring Basin, 503/322-0080, 9am-5pm daily, $8-15) get crab, fish, and other seafood right off the boats, so the selection is both low-priced and fresh. If you want it fresher, you'll have to catch it yourself.

In addition to dock fishing, guide and charter services offer salmon and halibut fishing, bird-watching, and whale-watching excursions. North of Garibaldi on U.S. 101, the bay entrance is a good place to see brown pelicans, harlequin ducks, oystercatchers, and guillemots. The Miami River marsh, south of town, is a bird-watching paradise at low tide, when ducks and shorebirds hunt for food.

## Garibaldi Maritime Museum

The small but interesting **Garibaldi Maritime Museum** (112 Garibaldi Ave., 503/322-8411, http://garibaldimuseum.org, 10am-4pm Thurs.-Mon. Apr.-Nov., $4 adults, $3 seniors, $4 ages 11-18) retells the history of this longtime fishing village. It also focuses on the late-18th-century sailing world and the British sea captain Robert Gray and his historical vessels, the *Lady Washington* and the *Columbia Rediviva,* which explored the Pacific Northwest in 1787 and 1792. Among the museum displays are models of these ships, an eight-foot-tall reproduction of the *Columbia* figurehead, a half model of the *Columbia* showing how the ship was provisioned for long voyages, as well as reproductions of period musical instruments and typical sailors' clothing.

## Oregon Coast Explorer Trains

The **Oregon Coast Scenic Railroad** (503/842-8206, www.oregoncoastscenic.org, basic tours $20 adults, $19 seniors, $12 ages 3-10) operates a number of rail excursions on a train pulled by a 1910 Heisler Locomotive Works steam engine between Garibaldi and

Rockaway Beach. The basic tour is 1.5 hours round-trip; trains depart Garibaldi at 10am, noon, and 2pm, with opportunities to board in Rockaway Beach at 11am and 1pm. The train operates weekends only mid-May–mid-June and late September, and daily mid-June–Labor Day as well as assorted holidays throughout the year. Dinner trains are also offered.

## Fishing

The town's fishing and crabbing piers attract visitors looking to catch their own. Rent fishing boats, crab traps, and other gear at the **Garibaldi Marina** (302 Mooring Basin Rd., 503/322-3312, www.garibaldimarina.com).

The **Miami River** and **Kilchis River,** which empty into Tillamook Bay south of Garibaldi, get the state's only two significant runs of chum salmon, a species much more common from Washington northward. There's a catch-and-release season for them mid-September to mid-November. Both rivers also get runs of spring chinook and are open for steelhead most of the year.

Several charter companies have offices at the marina. **Garibaldi Charters** (607 Garibaldi Ave., 503/322-0007, www.garibaldicharters.com) offers fishing excursions. A full day of light-tackle bottom fishing runs about $105, with guided bay crabbing ($65 pp), salmon ($200) and tuna ($325) fishing also offered, and wildlife-viewing or whale-watching trips (Mar.-Apr., $40 pp). One-hour bay tours (late May-early Aug. and mid-Sept.-Oct., $40) are also offered.

## Food

One of the joys of eating on the Oregon coast is getting really good fish-and-chips from rough-edged dives on the docks. In Garibaldi, the **Fisherman's Korner Restaurant** (306 Mooring Basin, 503/322-2033, 7:30am-8pm Thurs.-Mon., $6-15) is right on the wharf and offers absolutely fresh fish-and-chips and excellent clam chowder. Breakfasts here are massive—meant for hungry sailors.

If you're looking for pub grub, a good choice is **Ghost Hole Public House** (409 Garibaldi Ave., 503/322-2723, 11am-2:30am daily, $6-15), with good burgers and sandwiches and a friendly vibe.

Just north of Garibaldi, **Pirate's Cove Restaurant** (14170 U.S. 101 N., 503/322-2092, http://piratesonline.biz, 8am-9pm Mon.-Sat., noon-8pm Sun., dinner $10-30) is one of the better restaurants between Manzanita and Lincoln City, with a dramatic vista of the

This is The Spot to buy fresh seafood in Garibaldi.

# Bayocean Spit

Bayocean Spit

At the western entrance to Tillamook Bay, a long narrow spit of land reaches north from Cape Meares nearly all the way to Garibaldi. Although today it's a good place for a long and sandy flat hike, it was once developed as the town of Bayocean, promoted as "the Atlantic City of the West." In the early 1900s, two real estate developers, enchanted by the great views of the ocean, built a grand resort hotel on the spit and began selling lots. A giant natatorium—a heated, saltwater surf pool—was built in 1914. Initially, the only access was by boat or ferry; in 1928, a road was built from Tillamook.

The town that grew on the four-mile-long spit was thriving when the inevitable erosion began to chip away at the peninsula. Houses slipped into the sea, and by the late 1930s, most residents had packed up and left. By 1939 the natatorium had been swallowed up. Since the early 1990s, the spit has been managed for protection and preservation of its ecosystem, which is dominated by beach grass and Scotch broom.

To reach Bayocean Spit from Tillamook, head west on the Three Capes Scenic Loop (3rd St. from downtown Tillamook) and travel three miles to the "Bayocean Spit" sign. Turn right and follow a gravel road 1.5 miles to the parking area.

mouth of Tillamook Bay. Try the local oysters and razor clams. Lunches are a better deal than the rather expensive dinners.

Four miles south at the little enclave of Bay City is another temple to seafood. **Pacific Oyster** (5150 Oyster Bay Dr., 503/377-2323, 9am-8pm daily, $5-16) is mostly an oyster-processing center, but it's also an excellent spot for a few oyster shooters or a quick meal. Although there are a variety of seafood choices, the main draw is the oysters, which are both a meal and entertainment here. As

you eat, you can watch the oyster shuckers in action next door, as the dining area overlooks the oyster-processing area.

## Accommodations and Camping

If you want to wake up on the docks, spend the night at **Harbor View Inn** (302 S. 7th St., 503/322-3251, www.harborviewfun.com, $85-110), a motel popular with fishers and sports enthusiasts. A more standard motel is the **Garibaldi House Inn** (502 Garibaldi Ave.,

503/322-3338 or 877/322-6489, www.garibaldihouse.com, $149-199), which offers pleasant rooms as well as an indoor pool, a hot tub, a sauna, and a fitness room; it includes a hot breakfast.

Both tent and RV campers are welcome at **Barview Jetty County Park** (503/322-3522, reservations accepted, $15-32), a large campground in the tiny community of Barview (2.5 miles north of Garibaldi) with easy access to the beach forming the north side of Tillamook Bay. Most of the sites are for tents, with a section reserved for hikers and cyclists; hot showers are a welcome amenity.

# TILLAMOOK

Without much sun or surf, what could possibly draw enough visitors to the town of Tillamook (pop. 4,500) to make it one of Oregon's top three tourism attractions? Superficially speaking, cheese factories and a World War II blimp hangar, in a town flanked by mudflats and rain-soaked dairy country, shouldn't pull in more than a million tourists per year. But they do. And after a drive down U.S. 101 or along the scenic Three Capes Loop, you too will be mysteriously drawn to the huge white, blue, and gold building proffering bite-size samples of cheddar, not to mention ice cream.

Tillamook County is home to more than 26,000 cows, which easily outnumber the county's human population. They're the foundation of the Tillamook County Creamery Association's famous cheddar cheese and other dairy products, which generate about $654 million in annual sales—dwarfing the region's other important contributors to the local economy, fishing and oyster farming.

In 1940-1942, partially in response to a Japanese submarine firing on Fort Stevens in Astoria, the U.S. Navy built two blimp hangars south of town, the two largest wooden structures ever built, according to *Guinness World Records*. One of five naval air stations on the Pacific coast, the Tillamook blimp guard patrolled the waters from Northern California to Washington's San Juan Islands and escorted ships into Puget Sound. While all kinds of blimp stories abound in Tillamook bars, only one wartime encounter has been documented. Declassified records confirm that blimps were involved in the sinking of what was believed to be two Japanese submarines off Cape Meares. In late May 1943, two of the high-flying craft, assisted by U.S. Navy subchasers and destroyers, dropped several depth charges on the submarines, which are still lying on the ocean floor.

Until 1946, when the station was decommissioned, the naval presence here created a boomtown. Bars and businesses flourished, and civilian jobs were easy to come by. After the war years, Tillamook County returned to the economic trinity of "trees, cheese, and ocean breeze" that has sustained the region to the present day.

## Tillamook Cheese Factory

With over a million visitors a year, the **Tillamook Cheese Factory** (4175 U.S. 101 N., 503/815-1300, www.tillamook.com/cheese-factory, 8am-6pm daily Labor Day-mid-June, 8am-8pm daily summer, free) is far and away the county's biggest draw. The plant welcomes visitors with a reproduction of the *Morningstar,* the schooner that transported locally made butter and cheese in the late 1800s and now adorns the label of every Tillamook product. The quaint vessel symbolizing Tillamook cheese-making's humble beginnings stands in contrast to the technology and sophistication that go into making this world-famous lunchbox staple today.

Note that the longtime visitors center, built in 1985 to accommodate 600,000 visitors per year, is being replaced with a new and larger facility. The new 38,500-square-foot visitors center is scheduled to open in 2018 and will better accommodate the roughly 1.5 million visitors who now stop by annually. In the meantime, a temporary visitors center—with food, ice cream, and merchandise—is open on an adjacent section of the property.

In the early 1900s, the Tillamook County

Creamery Association absorbed smaller operations; the modern plant opened in 1949. Today, Tillamook produces tens of millions of pounds of cheese annually, including monterey jack, swiss, and multiple variations of the award-winning cheddar. Pepperoni, butter, cheese soup, milk, and other products are also available.

## Blue Heron French Cheese Company

A quarter-million people per year visit Tillamook County's *second*-most-popular attraction, **Blue Heron French Cheese Company** (2001 Blue Heron Dr., 503/842-8282, www.blueheronoregon.com, 8am-7pm daily Memorial Day-June, 8am-8pm daily July-Labor Day, 8am-6pm daily Labor Day-Memorial Day, free, $6-16), a mile south of the Tillamook Cheese Factory. Housed in a large white barn, Blue Heron is famous for its brie-style cheese (though it's not produced on-site). In addition to cheeses and other gourmet foods, the shop sells gift baskets; over 120 varieties of Oregon wines are available in the wine-tasting room. A deli serves lunches of homemade soups and salads. For kids, there's a petting farm with the usual barnyard suspects.

## Tillamook Air Museum

South of town off U.S. 101, you can't possibly miss the enormous Quonset hut-like building east of the highway. The world-class aircraft collection of the **Tillamook Air Museum** (6030 Hangar Rd., 503/842-1130, www.tillamookair.com, 10am-5pm daily, $9.75 adults, $8.75 seniors, $6.50 ages 7-16, $2.75 ages 1-6) is housed in and around Hangar B of the decommissioned Tillamook Naval Air Station. At 1,072 feet long, 206 feet wide, and 192 feet high, it's the largest wooden structure in the world, and it's worth the price of admission just to experience the enormity of it. During World War II, this and another gargantuan hangar on the site (which burned down in 1992) sheltered eight K-class blimps, each 242 feet long.

Inside the seven-acre structure, you can learn about the role the big blimps played during wartime, as well as how they are used today. In addition, there's a collection of World War II fighter planes (many one-of-a-kind models) and photos and artifacts from the naval air station days. Check out the cyclo-crane, a combination blimp, plane, and helicopter. This was devised in the 1980s to aid in remote logging operations; it ended up an $8 million bust.

the Tillamook Air Museum

To get here from downtown, take U.S. 101 south two miles, make a left at the flashing yellow light, and follow the signs.

## Tillamook County Pioneer Museum

East of the highway in the heart of downtown, **Tillamook County Pioneer Museum** (2106 2nd St., 503/842-4553, www.tcpm.org, 10am-4pm Tues.-Sun., $4 adults, $3 seniors, $1 ages 7-10) is famous for its taxidermy exhibits as well as memorabilia from pioneer households. Particularly intriguing are hunks of ancient beeswax with odd inscriptions recovered from near Neahkahnie Mountain, which are thought to be remnants from 18th-century shipwrecks. The old courtroom on the second floor has one of the best displays of natural history in the state. There are many beautiful dioramas, plus shells, insects, and nests. The Beals Memorial Room houses a large rock, mineral, and fossil collection.

## Latimer Quilt and Textile Center

The collection at the **Latimer Quilt and Textile Center** (2105 Wilson River Loop Rd., 503/842-8622, www.latimerquiltandtextile. com, 10am-5pm Mon.-Sat., noon-4pm Sun. Apr.-Oct., 10am-4pm Tues.-Sat. Nov.-Mar., $4 over age 12, $3 seniors, free under age 13) includes quilts from the 1850s to the present as well as looms, spinning wheels, and a variety of woven items. On Friday, you can see weavers at work; lessons can be arranged by calling ahead. The center, housed in a restored school, is just south and east of the cheese factory.

## Munson Creek Falls

The highest waterfall in the Oregon Coast Range is lovely **Munson Creek Falls,** which drops 266 feet over mossy cliffs surrounded by an old-growth forest. A steep 0.25-mile trail leads to the base of the falls, while another, slightly longer trail leads to a higher viewpoint; wooden walkways clinging to the cliff lead to a small viewing platform. This is a spectacle in all seasons, but in winter the falls pour down with greater fury.

To reach the falls, drive seven miles south of Tillamook, turn east from U.S. 101 on Munson Creek Road, and then drive 1.5 miles on a well-signed but very narrow and bumpy dirt access road that leads to the parking lot. Note that motor homes and trailers cannot get into the park; the lot is too small.

## Tillamook State Forest

A series of intense forest fires in the 1930s and 1940s burned vast amounts of land in the northern Coast Range. Most of this land was owned by private timber companies, who walked away from the seemingly worthless "Tillamook Burn," leaving property rights to revert to the counties, who then handed the land over to the state. A massive replanting effort ensued, and in 1973 the Tillamook Burn became the **Tillamook State Forest.** In 2006 the **Tillamook Forest Center** (45500 Wilson River Hwy., 503/815-6800 or 866/930-4646, www.tillamookforestcenter.org, 10am-5pm daily Memorial Day-Labor Day, reduced hours spring and fall, closed winter, free) opened in a soaring timbered building in the middle of the now-lush forest. Stop in to see the short movie about the area's history; the vivid fire scenes are a bit frightening—a sensation that's enhanced when the smell of smoke is released into the auditorium. Don't leave without walking out through the center's back door, crossing the footbridge, and taking at least a short hike, where you'll see an assortment of native wildflowers, shrubs, and trees. If you head west from the bridge, Wilson Falls is about two miles away.

If a short hike outside the Forest Center leaves you hankering for more, head east along Highway 6 to the Kings Mountain trailhead. On a clear day (ha!), there are good views from the top. Several more trails start at the summit of the Coast Range. The campgrounds along Highway 6, including Jones Creek, which is right next to the Tillamook Forest Center, are popular with off-road vehicle drivers, who have their own trail network back in the hills.

# The Lost Treasure of Neahkahnie Mountain

Is there pirate gold on Neahkahnie Mountain? Local Native American legends tell of Spanish pirates burying a treasure here. One story relates that the crew of a shipwrecked Manila galleon salvaged its cargo of gold and beeswax (a valuable commodity in trade with Asia) by burying it in the side of the mountain. To deter local people from going to the site, the pirates killed a man and buried him on top of the cargo. While this account, taken from Native American histories, has never been substantiated, a piece of crudely inscribed beeswax retrieved from the Neah-kahnie region, carbon-dated to 1500-1700 and on display at the **Tillamook County Pioneer Museum,** keeps speculation alive.

Further intrigue was added by the 1993 discovery of an ancient wooden rigging block. Found in the mud at the mouth of the Nehalem River, it was determined by a Spanish maritime expert to have been from a Manila galleon during that same time period. Lewis and Clark's 1805 reports of an indigenous Chinook person with red hair, and similar accounts from the Vancouver Expedition's 1792 encounter with a redheaded indigenous man who claimed his late father had been a shipwrecked Spanish sailor, would tend to corroborate the shipwreck and treasure stories passed down in oral histories.

## Entertainment and Events

In recent years, Tillamook has substantially upped its game in terms of brewpubs. For sour-beer geeks, the most notable tasting room is **de Garde Brewing** (6000 Blimp Blvd., 503/815-1635, www.degardebrewing. com, 3pm-7pm Thurs.-Fri., 11am-7pm Sat., 11am-5pm Sun., no minors or pets), one of Oregon's most notable wild-yeast breweries (note that these unusual beers will not please everyone). The only place to taste de Gard's wild beers on tap is at the brewery, just across from the air museum, and it's the best place to buy the brewery's limited selection of bottled beer.

A couple of blocks west of downtown is the new **Pelican Brewing Company Pub** (1708 1st St., 503/842-7007, 11am-10pm Sun.-Thurs., 11am-11pm Fri.-Sat., $12-16), where you'll find the bottling plant for popular Pelican beers, plus a pub that offers burgers, fish-and-chips, tacos, and other pub favorites. The tap room overlooks the brewery's 50,000-barrels-per-year production facility. If you'd like to check on how it's all done, ask about tours.

## Hiking

The Tillamook State Forest offers plenty of recreational opportunities. From a distance, the forest seems like a tree plantation, but hidden waterfalls, old railroad trestles from the days of logging trains, and moss-covered oaks in the Salmonberry River Canyon will convince you otherwise. Bird-watchers and mushroom pickers can easily penetrate this thicket, thanks to 1,000 miles of maintained roads and old railroad grades.

Two challenging trails off Highway 6, **Kings Mountain** (25 miles east of Tillamook) and **Elk Mountain** (28 miles east of Tillamook) climb through lands affected by the Tillamook Burn, but with scenic views throughout. Thanks to salvage logging in the wake of the disaster and subsequent replanting, myriad trails crisscross forests of Douglas and noble fir, hemlock, and red alder. Stop at the visitors center for maps and trail descriptions.

## Wildlife-Viewing

Bird-watchers flock to Tillamook Bay June to November to view pelicans, sandpipers, tufted puffins, blue herons, and a variety of shorebirds. Prime time is before high tide, but step lively, because this waterway was originally called "quicksand bay."

## Fishing

Among Oregon anglers, Tillamook County is known for its steelhead and salmon. Motorists along U.S. 101 can tell the fall chinook run has arrived when fishing boats cluster outside the Tillamook Bay entrance at Garibaldi. As the season wears on, the fish—affectionately called "hogs" because they sometimes weigh in at more than 50 pounds—make their way inland up the five coastal rivers—the Trask, Wilson, Tillamook, Kilchis, and Miami—that flow into Tillamook Bay. At their peak, the runs create such competition for favorite holes that the process of sparring for them is jocularly referred to as "combat fishing," as fishing boats anchor up gunwale to gunwale to form a fish-stopping palisade called a "hogline." Smokehouses and gas stations dot the outer reaches of the bay to cater to this fall influx.

## Golf

The par-69 **Alderbrook Golf Course** (7300 Alderbrook Rd., 5 miles south of Tillamook, 503/842-6413, www.alderbrookgolfcourse.com, 7am-dusk daily, $34-38 for 18 holes) is one of the Oregon coast's oldest courses (dating from 1924), featuring 5,965 yards of golf from the back tees.

## Food

To sample the county's freshest produce, visit the **Tillamook Farmers Market** (2nd St. and Laurel Ave., Sat. mid-June-late Sept.) in downtown Tillamook.

As part of the rebuilding of the Tillamook Cheese Factory visitors center, its café will be expanded. Check it out when it reopens in 2018. The deli at the **Blue Heron French Cheese Company** (2001 Blue Heron Dr., 503/842-8282, www.blueheronoregon.com, 11am-6pm daily) fixes sandwiches, soups, and salads; in polls conducted by the local paper, this is a locals' favorite lunch spot. On the west side of U.S. 101, between the two cheese meccas, lunchtime do-it-yourselfers might check the locally raised and cured meat and smoked salmon at **Debbie D's Sausage Factory** (503/842-2622).

In downtown Tillamook, attempts to open fine-dining restaurants have faltered in recent years. There are a number of vintage cafés to check out, and **Fat Dog Pizza** (116 Main St., 503/354-2283, 11:30am-9pm Sun.-Thurs., 11:30am-10pm Fri.-Sat., $15) is worth a stop. Pizzas feature house-made dough (the Fat Dog Special is for meat lovers), and the submarine sandwiches, called Zeppelins in honor of Tillamook's dirigible history, are tasty.

Tillamook is more an agricultural town than a coastal resort, so **Rodeo Steak House and Grill** (2015 1st St., 503/842-8288, http://rodeosteakhouseandgrill.com, noon-9pm Sun.-Wed., noon-10pm Thurs.-Sat., $9-30) is right at home. Lighter appetites will find salads, sandwiches, wraps, and an array of burgers (the Snake Bit Burger comes with jalapeño slices, pepper jack cheese, and chipotle mayo), while hungry travelers can enjoy excellent prime rib, grilled ribs, and steaks.

Some of the best food in Tillamook is found at food trucks. Most are just north of downtown along U.S. 101. The selection of Mexican food is especially large. **La Mexicana** (2203 3rd St., 503/842-2101, 11am-9pm daily, $8-21) is the town's best Mexican restaurant, housed in a vintage home on the edge of downtown. Going way beyond tacos and burritos, La Mexicana prepares local fish and seafood with south-of-the-border zest and finesse.

Take your time to savor a cup of tea at **La Tea Da Tea Room** (904 Main Ave., 503/842-5447, 9am-5pm Tues.-Sat. summer, 11am-4pm Tues.-Sat. winter, high tea $29). Go for the full high tea or settle for scones, soup, salads, home-made baked sweets, or little tea sandwiches.

## Accommodations

Most travelers seem to pass through Tillamook on their way to someplace else, and there are plenty of chain motels available all along the busy U.S. 101 strip north of town. A good local choice along this strip is **Ashley Inn** (1722 N. Makinster Rd., 503/842-7599 or 800/299-4817, www.ashleyinntillamook.

com, $100-165), close to the cheese factory. Rooms have a fridge, a microwave, an iron and ironing board, a coffeemaker, and cable TV. Amenities include an indoor pool, a sauna, and a hot tub, and continental breakfast is included.

## Information

The **Tillamook Chamber of Commerce** (208 Main Ave., 503/842-7525, www.tillamookchamber.org, 9am-5pm Mon.-Fri.) can help you with any business-related question about Tillamook and vicinity.

## Getting There and Around

The **Tillamook County Transportation District** (503/815-8283, www.nworegon-transit.org) offers public bus transportation around Tillamook County, and also runs a couple of buses of interest to travelers. The district offers twice-daily buses north to and from Cannon Beach, with service to points north, including Astoria, and also four buses a day south to and from Lincoln City. It also runs two buses a day to and from the Greyhound station in Portland ($15). The Tillamook Transit Center is at 2nd and Laurel Streets.

# Three Capes Scenic Loop

The Three Capes Scenic Loop, a 35-mile byway off U.S. 101 between Tillamook and Pacific City, stays close to the ocean, which U.S. 101 does not. And although the beauty of Capes Meares, Lookout, and Kiwanda certainly justifies leaving the main highway, it would be an overstatement to portray this drive as a thrill-a-minute detour on the order of the south coast's Boardman State Park or the central coast's Otter Crest Loop. Instead of fronting the ocean, the road connecting the capes winds mostly through dairy country, small beach towns, and second-growth forest. What's special here are the three capes themselves, and unless you get out of the car and walk on the trails, you'll miss the aesthetic appeal and distinctiveness of each headland's ecosystem. The wave-battered bluffs of Cape Kiwanda, the precipitous overlooks along the Cape Lookout Highway, and the curious Octopus Tree at Cape Meares are the perfect antidotes to the inland towns along this stretch of U.S. 101. The majority of the Three Capes lodging and dining options are clustered in Netarts and Oceanside and at the other end in Pacific City. In between, it's mostly sand dunes, isolated beaches, rainforest, and pasture. To reach the Three Capes Scenic Loop from the north, turn west at Tillamook and follow signs to Cape Meares. From the south, follow signs north of Neskowin to Pacific City.

## CAPE MEARES STATE SCENIC VIEWPOINT

With stunning views, picnic tables, a newly restored lighthouse, and a uniquely contorted tree a short walk from the parking lot, **Cape Meares State Scenic Viewpoint** is the most effortless site to visit on the Three Capes Loop. It was named for English navigator John Meares, who mapped many points along this coast in a 1788 voyage. The famed **Octopus Tree** is less than 0.25 miles up a forested hill. The tentacle-like extensions of this Sitka spruce have also been compared to candelabra arms.

The 45-foot diameter of its base supports five-foot-thick trunks, each of which is large enough to be a single tree. Scientists have propounded several theories for the cause of its unusual shape, including everything from wind and weather to insects damaging the spruce when it was young. A Native American legend about the spruce contends that it was shaped this way so that the branches could hold the canoes of a chief's dead family. Supposedly, the bodies were buried near the tree. This was a traditional practice among the

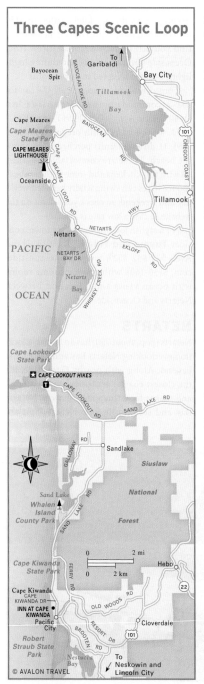

## Three Capes Scenic Loop

To Garibaldi

Bayocean Spit

Bay City

Tillamook Bay

Cape Meares
Cape Meares State Park
**CAPE MEARES LIGHTHOUSE**

Oceanside

Tillamook

Netarts

**PACIFIC**

NETARTS BAY DR

Netarts Bay

**OCEAN**

Cape Lookout State Park

**CAPE LOOKOUT HIKES**

SAND LAKE RD

Sandlake

Siuslaw

Sand Lake
Whalen Island
County Park

National

Forest

0        2 mi
0        2 km

Cape Kiwanda State Park

Hebo

Cape Kiwanda
**INN AT CAPE KIWANDA**
Pacific City

Cloverdale

Robert Straub Park

Nestucca Bay

To Neskowin and Lincoln City

© AVALON TRAVEL

BAYOCEAN DIKE RD
BAYOCEAN RD
101 OREGON COAST HWY
CAPE MEARES LOOP RD
NETARTS HWY
EKLOFF RD
WHISKEY CREEK RD
CAPE LOOKOUT RD
GALLOWAY RD
SAND LAKE RD
FERRY RD
OLD WOODS RD
RESORT DR
BROOTEN RD
CAPE KIWANDA DR
22
101

indigenous people of the area, who referred to species formed thusly as "council trees."

Beyond the tree you can look south at Oceanside and Three Arch Rocks Wildlife Refuge. The sweep of Pacific shore and offshore monoliths makes a fitting beginning (or finale, if you're driving from the south) to your sojourn along the Three Capes Scenic Loop. Also be sure to stroll the short paved trail down to the lighthouse, which begins at the parking lot and provides dramatic views of an offshore wildlife refuge, **Cape Meares Rocks.** Bring binoculars to see tufted puffins, pelagic cormorants, seals, and sea lions. The landward portion of the refuge protects rare old-growth evergreens.

The restored interior of **Cape Meares Lighthouse** (503/842-2244, 11am-4pm daily Apr.-Oct., free) was built in 1890. This beacon was replaced as a functioning light in 1963 by the automated facility behind it, and it now houses a gift shop. A free tour is occasionally offered by volunteers, who might tell you about how the lighthouse was built here by mistake and perhaps offer a peek into the prismatic Fresnel lenses.

## OCEANSIDE

The road between Cape Meares and Netarts heads into the beach house community of Oceanside (pop. about 340). Many of the homes are built into the cliff overlooking the ocean, Sausalito-style. This maze of steep, narrow streets reaches its apex atop Maxwell Point. You can peer several hundred feet down at **Three Arch Rocks Wildlife Refuge** (www.fws.gov), part-time home to one of the continent's largest and most varied collections of shorebirds. A herd of sea lions also populates this trio of sea stacks from time to time.

### Food and Accommodations

A popular draw for hungry Three Capes travelers, ★ **Roseanna's Oceanside Cafe** (1490 Pacific Ave. NW, 503/842-7351, www.roseannascafe.com, 11am-8pm Mon. and Thurs.-Fri., 10am-8pm Sat.-Sun. summer, call for winter hours, $11-26) garners high marks from just about everyone. At first, the weather-beaten cedar-shake exterior might lead you to expect an old general store, as indeed it was decades ago. Once you're inside, however, the ornate decor leaves little doubt that this place takes its new identity seriously. From an elevated perch above the breakers, you'll be treated to expertly prepared local oysters, fresh salmon, a bevy of chicken dishes, and interesting pastas, such as gorgonzola and pear with penne noodles. Save room for blackberry cobbler; order it warm so the Tillamook Vanilla Bean ice cream on top melts down the sides, and watch the waves over a long cup of coffee.

**Blue Agate Cafe** (1610 Pacific Ave., 503/815-2596, 9am-2pm Mon.-Thurs., 9am-9pm Fri.-Sat., 8am-8pm Sun., $7-15), is a happening little eatery in the center of Oceanside with fun breakfasts (try the Dungeness crab scramble), sandwiches, pasta, and excellent fish tacos.

There aren't many lodging options in Oceanside. While low prices and a window on the water can be found at **Ocean Front Cabins** (1610 Pacific Ave., 503/842-6081 or 888/845-8470, www.oceanfrontcabins.com, $70-155), the older, smallish guest rooms here might give upscale travelers pause. Nonetheless, for as little as $70 for a

sleeping unit without a kitchenette—or $130 for a two-bed room with a full kitchen—you'll find yourself literally a stone's throw from Oceanside's beachcombing and dining highlights. Pets are accepted in some cabins.

Considerably more upscale are the condo-like accommodations at **Oceanside Inn** (1440 Pacific Ave., 503/842-2961 or 800/347-2972, www.oceansideinn-oregon.com, $99-589), 11 different units perched right above the beach. These are comfortable lodgings, all with full kitchens and some with two bedrooms. Rates can swing wildly between weekday and weekend, so check your dates on the website in case a low rate is available.

For a stylish lodging outside of town, consider **Thyme and Tide B&B** (5015 Grand Ave., 503/842-5527, www.thyme-and-tide.com, $150-160), with two handsome rooms with ocean views and a location between Netarts and Oceanside.

## NETARTS

Netarts (pop. about 750) has an enviable location overlooking Netarts Bay and the Pacific beyond. Along with nearby Oceanside, it's the closest coastal settlement to Tillamook and makes for a fine quiet getaway. Netarts Bay and seven-mile-long Netarts Spit are

Three Arch Rocks Wildlife Refuge at Oceanside

popular with clam diggers and crabbers, who can launch boats from Netarts Landing at the northeast corner of the bay. **Netarts Bay RV Park and Marina** (2260 Bilyeu St., 503/842-7774) and **Big Spruce RV Park** (4850 Netarts Hwy. W., 503/842-7443) rent out motorboats and crabbing supplies.

## Food and Accommodations

The view of Cape Lookout is tops at **The Schooner** (2065 Netarts Bay Rd., 503/842-4988, www.theschooner.net, 11:30am-8pm Mon.-Thurs., 11:30am-9pm Fri.-Sat., 9am-8pm Sun. $10-25), and the food is a nice surprise also. Stop by for some steamer clams, fresh oysters, or tasty wood-fired pizza.

The **Terimore** (5105 Crab Ave., 503/842-4623 or 800/635-1821, www.terimoremotel.com, motel rooms $78-121, cabins $89-150) is situated a short walk from the water at the north end of Netarts Bay. Other than some units with fireplaces and kitchens, there are few frills, but for fair rates you'll find yourself close to the water, within easy driving distance of the Cape Lookout Trail, and a beach walk away from Roseanna's, the best restaurant on the Three Capes Scenic Loop.

## CAPE LOOKOUT STATE PARK

One of the scenic highlights of the Three Capes route, **Cape Lookout State Park** (off U.S. 101, www.oregonstateparks.org, $5 day-use) juts out nearly a mile from the mainland, like a finger pointing out to sea. The cliffs along the south side of the cape rise 800 feet from the Pacific's pounding waves. The best way to take in the vista and the thrill of the location is on foot.

### ★ Hiking

Hiking to the end of mile-wide Cape Lookout is one of the top coastal hikes in Oregon. The trail begins either at the campground, where it climbs 2.5 miles up to a ridgetop trailhead with a parking lot, or from the Three Capes road at a well-signed trailhead. An orientation map at the trailhead details the options. The main 2.5-mile trail out to the end, along the narrowing finger of land, can give hikers the impression that they're on the prow of a giant ship suspended 500 feet above the ocean on all sides. Here, more than anywhere else on the Oregon coast, you get the sense of being on the edge of the continent. Giant spruce, western red cedars, and hemlocks surround the gently hilly trail to the tip of the cape. In March, Cape Lookout is a popular vantage point for whale-watching. June through August, a bevy of wildflowers and birds further enhance the rolling terrain en route to the tip of this headland, and in late summer red huckleberries line the path.

Halfway to the overlook, there are views north to Cape Meares over the Netarts sand spit. Even if you settle for a mere 15-minute stroll down the trail, you can look southward beyond Haystack Rock to Cascade Head. Right about where the trees open up, look for a bronze plaque commemorating the crash of a World War II plane and nearly a dozen casualties, which is embedded in the rock wall bordering the right-hand (north) side of the trail at eye level. If you're unable to take this hike, two unmarked turnouts along the Three Capes road between the sand dunes and Cape Lookout parking lot let you survey the terrain south to Cape Kiwanda. Don't be surprised if you see hang gliders and paragliders.

Another popular trail in the state park heads north from the campground through a variety of estuarine habitats along the sand spit separating Netarts Bay from the Pacific. It's a popular site for agate hunters, clammers, and crabbers.

### Camping

At the southern end of Netarts Spit is the state park's **campground and beach extension** (13000 Whiskey Creek Rd. W., information 503/842-4981, reservations 800/452-5687, www.reserveamerica.com, $5-7), which also encompasses the entire cape and the seven-mile-long Netarts Spit within its boundaries. The campground has 173 tent sites ($21) and 38 full-hookup sites ($33), as well as 13 yurts

($47), three cabins (with baths, a kitchen, and a TV/video player, $88-98), and a hiker-biker camp ($6); discounts apply October-April. Some yurts accept pets ($10). Amenities include showers, flush toilets, and evening programs. Reservations and a deposit are almost always required at this popular campground.

South of Cape Lookout, the terrain suddenly changes. Extensive sand dunes surrounding the Sand Lake Estuary suddenly appear, drowning the forest in sand. The dunes and beach attract squadrons of dune buggy enthusiasts. Camping is available year-round at **Sand Beach Campground** (Galloway Rd., 5 miles south of Cape Lookout, 503/392-3161 or 877/444-6777, reservations www.recreation.gov, $16), a part of the Siuslaw National Forest, which has basic sites for tents and RVs. This dramatic area is also popular with hikers.

## PACIFIC CITY AND CAPE KIWANDA

As you approach the shore in Pacific City, the sight of **Haystack Rock** will immediately grab your attention. At 327 feet, this sea stack is nearly 100 feet taller than the similarly named rock in Cannon Beach. Standing a mile offshore, this monolith has a brooding, enigmatic quality that constantly draws the eye. Look closely, and you'll understand why some folks call it Teacup Rock.

The tawny sandstone escarpment of Cape Kiwanda juts half a mile out to sea from Pacific City and frames the north end of the beach. In storm-tossed waters, this cape is the undisputed king, if you go by coffee table books and calendar photos. While other sandstone promontories on the north coast have been ground into sandy beaches by the pounding surf, it's been theorized that Kiwanda has endured thanks to the buffer of Haystack Rock. In any case, hang gliding aficionados are glad the cape is here. They scale its shoulders and set themselves aloft off the north face to glide above the beach and dunes.

The small town of Pacific City, with about 1,000 residents, is at the base of Cape Kiwanda. It attracts growing numbers of vacationers and retirees, but remains true to its 19th-century origins as a working fishing village. In addition to the knockout seascapes and recreation, if you come here at the right time of day, you may be treated to a unique spectacle—the launch or return of the **dory fleet.**

It's a tradition dating back to the 1920s, when gillnetting was banned on the Nestucca River to protect the dwindling salmon runs. To retain their livelihood, commercial fishers began to haul flat-bottomed double-ended dories down to the beach on horse-drawn wagons, then row out through the surf to fish. These days, trucks and trailers get the boats to and from the beach, and outboard motors have replaced oar power, enabling the dories to get 50 miles out to sea. If you come around 6am, you can watch them taking off. The fleet's late-afternoon return attracts a crowd that arrives to see the dory operators skidding their craft as far as possible up the beach to the waiting boat trailers. Others meet the dories to buy salmon and tuna.

In mid-July, **Dory Days** celebrate the area's fleet. The three-day fete includes craft and food booths, a pancake breakfast, a fishing derby, and other activities. For more information, call the **chamber of commerce** (503/965-6161). If you want to join the anglers for a summertime ocean fishing trip on a dory, contact **Haystack Fishing** (888/965-7555), across from the beach near the Inn at Cape Kiwanda. Four- to six-hour salmon and bottom fishing trips start at $200 per person.

In addition, the Pacific City area is besieged by surfers, who enjoy some of the longest waves on the Oregon coast. **Robert Straub State Park,** just south of town, offers access to Nestucca Bay and to the dunes and a long uninterrupted stretch of beach. Pacific City surfers should use *extreme* caution when the dories are returning to the beach.

### Food

A popular and well-known Pacific City hangout is the ★ **Pelican Pub and Brewery**

(33180 Cape Kiwanda Dr., 503/965-7007, 8am-10am Sun.-Thurs., 8am-11pm Fri.-Sat., $6-23). Set in a most enviable spot right on the beach opposite Cape Kiwanda and Haystack Rock, this place boasts the best coastal view of any brewpub in Oregon. Buttermilk-beer pancakes, dory-caught fish-and-chips, pizzas, "shark bites," tasty chili, and IPA-poached salmon are some of the standouts. The pub's brews, including Tsunami Stout, Doryman's Dark Ale, India Pelican Ale, and MacPelican's Scottish Style Ale, have garnered stacks of awards.

**Delicate Palate Bistro** (35280 Brooten Rd., 503/965-6464, www.delicatepalate.com, 5pm-close Wed.-Sun., $28-36) is a classy little place where the chef brings a deft touch to classics—think pan-seared wild salmon with balsamic blood orange reduction sauce or bouillabaisse made with a coconut curry broth and served with soba noodles—and the meals are backed up by an excellent wine list (or a long martini menu, if you prefer). The deck, which overlooks the local airstrip, is open for dining when weather allows.

Also on Brooten Road toward the north end of town, find the ★ **Grateful Bread Bakery** (34085 Brooten Rd., 503/965-7337, www.gratefulbreadbakery.com, 8am-9pm Thurs.-Mon., dinners $15-21), where the challah bread, carrot cake, marionberry strudel, and other homemade baked goods deserve special mention. The breakfast and lunch menu ($9-13) offers a range of tasty pancakes, scrambles and omelets served with oven-roasted spuds at great prices. Lunch sandwiches, quesadillas and rice bowls include a wide range of vegetarian options. This well-loved bakery just started serving dinner as well, when you'll find dory-caught blackened rockfish with fresh fruit salsa, shrimp with spicy peppers, and sirloin steak with horseradish rosemary butter.

## Accommodations

The nicest motel on the Three Capes Scenic Loop is the large ★ **Inn at Cape Kiwanda** (33105 Cape Kiwanda Dr., 503/965-6366 or 888/965-7001, www.yourlittlebeachtown.com/inn, $269-329). All rooms face a beautiful beach and Cape Kiwanda's giant sand dune. If it's too rainy to go outside, fireplaces and spacious well-appointed rooms make for great storm-watching. Whirlpool tub rooms are available, and pets are permitted in some rooms.

## Camping

About 4.5 miles north of Pacific City on the Three Capes Loop Road, the **Clay Meyers Natural Area at Whalen Island** (4.5 miles north of Pacific City on Sandlake Rd., 503/965-6085, www.co.tillamook.or.us, $10-15) has a small campground run by Tillamook County. It's an open, sandy spot with a boat launch and flush toilets; nearby hiking trails traverse wetlands and provide a great look at the coastal Sand Lake Estuary.

# Neskowin and Cascade Head

## NESKOWIN

The tiny vacation village of Neskowin (rhymes with "let's go in," pop. 170) has a quiet appeal based on a beautiful beach and a golf course in the shadow of 1,500-foot-high Cascade Head. It's the polar opposite of busy Lincoln City, 15 miles south. There's not much to do here but relax on the uncrowded beach and enjoy the views of Cascade Head and the dark beauty of **Proposal Rock,** a stony, forested hillock that stands right at the edge of the surf, with Neskowin Creek curving around it. The feature was named by Neskowin's first postmistress, whose daughter received a marriage proposal nearby. Neskowin has a reputation as a beach town for old-money, in-the-know Portland families.

The sleepy town has only one art gallery, and it's a good one. **Hawk Creek Gallery** (48460 U.S. 101 S., 503/392-3879, www.hawkcreekgallery.com, 11am-5pm daily summer, 11am-5pm Sat.-Sun. spring and fall) is the studio and showroom for the works of painter Michael Schlicting, who exhibits his work internationally but has made the Hawk Creek Gallery his home base since 1978.

**Neskowin Marsh Golf Course** (48405 Hawk St., 503/392-3377, $18 for nine holes) has streams and water hazards adding a challenge to most of the nine greens.

### Food

Waits can be long at the tiny **Hawk Creek Cafe** (4505 Salem Ave., 503/392-3838, 9am-9pm daily, call for winter hours, $15-29), particularly at breakfast, but the food is worth it. Count on filling omelets for breakfast; sandwiches (about $10), burgers, and wood-fired pizza ($16-18) for lunch; and grilled fish and steaks for dinner. Hidden behind the general store is **Beach Club Bistro** (48880 Hwy 101 S., 503/392-3035, http://beachclubbistro.com, 4pm-8pm Wed.-Sun., $17-30), a friendly spot with a selection of small plates for grazing, and such main courses as crab and Parmesan ravioli with seared scallops and prawns if you're looking for serious dining.

Hawk Creek leads to the secluded beach at Neskowin.

## Accommodations

**Proposal Rock Inn** (48988 U.S. 101 S., 503/392-3115, www.proposalrockneskowin. com, rooms $82-157, suites $139-278) backs up on Hawk Creek and commands a fine view of the beach and the eponymous rock. Two-room ocean-view suites with a full kitchen fetch higher prices than the standard no-view guest rooms, but all are right on the beach.

The nine two-bedroom condo units at **The Chelan** (48750 Breakers Blvd., 503/392-3270, www.rentoregoncoast.com, $125-278) are comfier than the boxy stucco exterior suggests, with fireplaces, kitchens, views, and direct access to the beach.

## CASCADE HEAD
### Cascade Head Scenic Research Area

About 10 miles north of Lincoln City, the 11,890-acre Cascade Head Experimental Forest was set aside in 1934 for scientific study of typical coastal Sitka spruce and western hemlock forests found along the Oregon coast. In 1974, Congress established the 9,670-acre **Cascade Head Scenic Research Area** (www.fsl.orst.edu/chef), which includes the western half of the forest, several prairie headlands, and the Salmon River estuary. In 1980, the entire area was designated a biosphere reserve as part of the United Nations Biosphere Reserve system.

The headlands, reaching as high as 1,800 feet, are unusual for their extensive prairies still dominated by native grasses: red fescue, wild rye, and Pacific reedgrass. The Nechesney people, who inhabited the area as long as 12,000 years ago, purposely burned forest tracts around Cascade Head, probably to provide browse for deer and to reduce the possibility of larger uncontrollable blazes. These human-made alterations are complemented by the inherent dryness of south-facing slopes, which receive increased exposure to the sun. In contrast to these grasslands, the northern part of the headland is the domain of giant spruces and firs because it catches the brunt of the heavy rainfalls and lingering fogs.

Endemic wildflowers include coastal paintbrush, goldenrod, streambank lupine, rare hairy checkermallow, and blue violet, a plant critical to the survival of the Oregon silverspot butterfly, a threatened species found in only six locations. Deer, elk, coyotes, snowshoe hare, and the Pacific giant salamander find refuge here, while bald eagles, great horned owls, and peregrine falcons may be seen hunting above the grassy slopes. Today, in addition to its biological importance, the area is a mecca for some 6,000 hikers annually, and for anglers who target the salmon and steelhead runs on the Salmon River.

On the north side of the Salmon River, turn west from U.S. 101 onto **Three Rocks Road** for a scenic driving detour on the south side of Cascade Head. The paved road curves about 2.5 miles above the wetlands and widening channel of the Salmon River estuary, passes Savage Road, and ends at a parking area and boat launch at Knight County Park. From the park, the road turns to gravel and narrows (not suitable for RVs or trailers), and continues about another 0.5 miles to its end at a spectacular overlook across the estuary.

### HIKING

Cascade Head offers some outstanding scenic hikes, with rainforest pathways and wildflower meadows giving way to dramatic ocean views.

A short but brisk hike to the top of the headland on a **Nature Conservancy trail** begins near Knight County Park. Leave your car at the park and walk 0.5 miles up Savage Road to the trailhead. It's 1.7 miles one-way, with 1,100 feet of elevation gain. No dogs or bicycles are allowed on the trail, which is open year-round.

Two trails are accessible from Cascade Head Road (Forest Rd. 1861), a gravel road open seasonally (July 16-Dec. 31) that heads west off U.S. 101 about three miles north of Three Rocks Road, near the highway summit of Cascade Head. Travel this road four miles west of U.S. 101 to the **Hart's Cove Trailhead.** The first part of the trail runs through arching red alder treetops and 250-year-old Sitka spruces with five-foot diameters. The understory of mosses and ferns is nourished by 100-inch rainfalls. Next, the trail emerges into open grasslands. The five-mile round-trip hike loses 900 feet in elevation on its way to an oceanfront meadow overlooking Hart's Cove, where the barking of sea lions might greet you. This trail can have plenty of mud, so boots are recommended as you tromp through the rainforest.

An easier trail accessible from Cascade Head Road heads to a viewpoint on the Nature Conservancy's preserve. (Again, no dogs or bikes are allowed on Nature Conservancy land.) The one-mile trail starts about 3.5 miles west of U.S. 101 and heads to a big meadow and an ocean overlook. It's possible to continue from the overlook, heading downhill to join up with the lower Nature Conservancy trail described above.

The **Cascade Head Trail** runs six miles roughly parallel to the highway, with a south trailhead near the intersection of Three Rocks Road and U.S. 101 and a north trailhead at Falls Creek, on U.S. 101 about one mile south of Neskowin. It passes through old-growth forest and is entirely inland, without the spectacular ocean views of other trails in the area.

## Sitka Center for Art and Ecology

The region in the shadow of Cascade Head can be explored in even greater depth thanks to the **Sitka Center for Art and Ecology** (56605 Sitka Dr., Otis, 541/994-5485, www.sitkacenter.org, 8:30am-4:30pm Mon.-Fri.), located off Savage Road on the south side of the headland. Workshops (May-Sept.) are offered, focusing on art and nature, with an emphasis on the strong relationship between the two. Experts in everything from local plant communities to the baskets of the Siletz people conduct outdoor workshops on the grounds of Cascade Head Ranch. Classes can last from a couple of days to a week, and fees vary accordingly.

# Central Coast

Look for ★ to find recommended
sights, activities, dining, and lodging.

# Highlights

★ **Oregon Coast Aquarium:** Explore the life of Oregon's shores and the ocean at this excellent aquarium (page 292).

★ **Yaquina Head Outstanding Natural Area:** A soaring lighthouse stands above a tide-pool-studded inlet at this small park, the quintessence of the Oregon coast (page 296).

★ **Whale-Watching:** *Thar she blows!* Newport is a great departure point for gray whale-watching tours (page 298).

★ **Cape Perpetua:** One of the most dramatic natural areas along the Oregon coast, Cape Perpetua is a top spot for hiking and exploring tide pools (page 307).

★ **Heceta Head Lighthouse and Devil's Elbow:** Climb to the top of this whitewashed lighthouse for wonderful views—or stay in the lighthouse keeper's house, now a B&B (page 312).

★ **Sea Lion Caves:** Take an elevator ride down to the caves at cliff's bottom to get a close look at the Steller sea lion rookery (page 312).

★ **John Dellenback Trail:** Explore 400-foot dunes in the Oregon Dunes National Recreation Area. It's like trekking the Sahara (page 323).

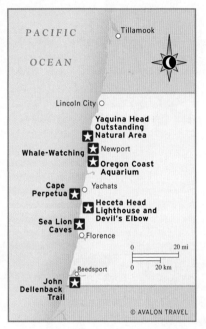

Oregon's central coast, from Lincoln City to Reedsport and Winchester Bay, embraces such contrasts that it's difficult to generalize about the region.

In the north, Lincoln City's dense mix of lodgings and shopping, combined with its Native American casinos, generates the coast's worst traffic jams, especially on holidays and weekends. The sprawling town isn't everyone's first choice for a quiet getaway, but it's a long-time favorite with families. Depoe Bay—built around the world's smallest navigable natural harbor—is headquarters for the coast's busiest whale-watching fleet, and one of its largest and most sprawling condo developments.

A necklace of small state parks adorns the shore every couple of miles all the way from southern Lincoln City southward; inland, the Siuslaw National Forest safeguards several wilderness areas and groves of rare old-growth coastal forest, beckoning hikers to explore the primeval landscapes. Just north of Newport, Yaquina Head Outstanding Natural Area offers excellent vantage points for up-close whale-watching and bird-watching, plus tide pools accessible to wheelchair users.

The bustling harbor at Newport is home to the state's largest commercial fishing fleet and second-largest recreational fleet, which runs charters year-round for rockfish and seasonally for salmon, tuna, and halibut. Newport also boasts the state-of-the-art Oregon Coast Aquarium, former residence of Keiko the beloved orca, and the bohemian resort community of Nye Beach, which has been attracting visitors since the 19th century.

Just south of Yachats, the panoramic view from Cape Perpetua can, on a clear day, extend 75 miles in each direction. Down at sea level, the tide pools here are some of the most fascinating on the coast. At Sea Lion Caves, a touristy but unique experience between Yachats and Florence, the world's largest sea cave is the only mainland rookery of Steller sea lions in the lower 48 states. Close by, photographers spend more time trying to capture the perfect image of Heceta Head Lighthouse than any other sight along the entire coast.

## PLANNING YOUR TIME

It's easy to spend a few days exploring the central coast. Although Lincoln City has

**Previous:** Ona Beach; giant spruce tree at Cape Perpetua. **Above:** wayside south of Yachats.

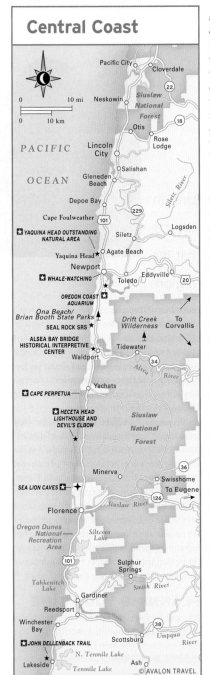

# Central Coast

0    10 mi
0    10 km

PACIFIC

OCEAN

Pacific City
Cloverdale
22
Neskowin    Siuslaw
National
Forest
Otis    18
Rose
Lincoln    Lodge
City
Salishan
Gleneden
Beach    Siletz River
Depoe Bay
Cape Foulweather    229
101    Logsden
★ YAQUINA HEAD OUTSTANDING    Siletz
NATURAL AREA
Yaquina Head ★ ○ Agate Beach
Newport
★ WHALE-WATCHING    Toledo    Eddyville
★    20
OREGON COAST ★
AQUARIUM
Ona Beach/    Drift Creek    To
Brian Booth State Parks    Wilderness    Corvallis
SEAL ROCK SRS ★
ALSEA BAY BRIDGE    Tidewater
HISTORICAL INTERPRETIVE
CENTER ★    34
Waldport
Alsea River
Yachats
★ CAPE PERPETUA
★ HECETA HEAD    Siuslaw
LIGHTHOUSE AND    National
DEVIL'S ELBOW    Forest
★
Minerva    36
○ Swisshome
SEA LION CAVES ★ +    To Eugene
126
Florence ○    Siuslaw River
Oregon Dunes    Siltcoos
National    Lake
Recreation
Area
101
Sulphur
Springs
Tahkenitch    Smith River
Lake
Gardiner
Reedsport
Winchester    38
Bay
★ JOHN DELLENBACK TRAIL    Scottsburg    Umpqua
River
N. Tenmile Lake
Lakeside ○    Ash
Tenmile Lake    © AVALON TRAVEL

abundant hotel rooms and is a good fallback during busy times of the year, tiny **Depoe Bay** is a great place to spend a night, perhaps with an early rise to take a fishing or whale-watching trip. And though **Newport** is a big city by Oregon coast standards, it's definitely worth spending a couple of nights here. In fact, if you're looking for a base for central coast explorations, Newport is well situated to visit sites from Lincoln City down to Florence. While in Newport, you may simply want to poke around the Nye Beach and Bayfront neighborhoods, beachcomb on Agate Beach, and check out the tide pools and lighthouse at the Yaquina Head Outstanding Natural Area; or you might decide to devote a day to the Oregon Coast Aquarium and the nearby Oregon State University Hatfield Marine Science Center.

Personally, when we have the opportunity to plunk down at the coast for a long week-end, we almost always head to **Yachats** to enjoy the low-key atmosphere, the incredible natural beauty, and the good restaurants of this tiny town. If you are touring the coast, we think it (and the incredible Cape Perpetua coastline just south) is worth a full day and night of your time.

**Florence** is a short hop from Yachats and is a good alternative if you'd rather stay in a slightly larger town with a lively Old Town and easy access to the north end of the Oregon Dunes National Recreation Area, a fantastic landscape of dazzling white-sand mountains and jewel lakes stretched along nearly 50 miles of shoreline.

Although anglers may want to stay at **Winchester Bay,** for most coast travelers this little town is a good stop for fish-and-chips, but not an overnight destination. Nearby, **Reedsport** is in the heart of the dune country and a good place to camp while exploring the dunes, but it does not have a huge wealth of fancy hotels and restaurants.

# Lincoln City

Back in 1964, five burgs that straddled seven miles of beachfront between Siletz Bay and the Salmon River came together and incorporated as Lincoln City. In commemoration, a 14-foot bronze statue of President Abraham Lincoln was donated to the city by an Illinois sculptor. *The Lank Lawyer Reading in His Saddle While His Horse Grazes* originally occupied a city park; today the statue stands in a nondescript lot at NE 22nd Street and Quay Avenue. Look for the sign on U.S. 101 near the Dairy Queen.

In the following decades, what were discrete towns have grown and melded into an uninterrupted conurbation with a population of about 8,000 (which can balloon to 30,000 on a busy weekend). While the resulting sprawl and heavy traffic on U.S. 101 can be maddening at times, once you get off the highway, Lincoln City has some charming neighborhoods (check out the Taft area at the south end of town); wide sandy beaches; superlative wildlife-viewing around Siletz Bay; the large, freshwater Devils Lake; and two Native American casinos. Add prime kite-flying, some of the coast's better restaurants, and bibliophilic and antiquing haunts, and it's clear that there's more to the area than the pull of saltwater taffy and outlet malls.

## SIGHTS AND RECREATION
### Lincoln City Beach

Lincoln City boasts seven uninterrupted miles of sandy beach. From Siletz Bay north to Road's End State Recreation Area, there are more than a dozen access points. You can head west from U.S. 101 on just about any side street to get there, though high coastal bluffs lining the north-central portion of town may mean a climb down (and back up) long flights of stairs cut into the cliff. For something approaching solitude on a crowded day, follow Logan Road west from the highway near the north end of town to **Road's End State Recreation Area;** tide pools and a secluded cove add to the allure. This stretch is also popular with windsurfers.

Tide pool explorers should also check out the **rock formations** at SW 11th Street (Canyon Drive Park), NW 15th Street, and SW 32nd Street.

The **D River Wayside,** a small park on the beach in more or less the middle of town, is a state park property where you can watch what locals claim is the "world's shortest river" empty into the ocean. Flowing just 120 feet from its source, Devils Lake, to its mouth at the Pacific, it's short, all right; despite its unspectacular appearance, it was a cause célèbre when *Guinness World Records* withdrew the D's claim to fame in favor of a Montana waterway, the Roe. Local schoolkids rallied to the D's defense with an amended measurement, but the Roe, at a mere 53 feet long, carries the *Guinness* imprimatur as the shortest river. In addition to seeing the D River flow from "D" Lake into "D" ocean, you can fly a kite on the beach. It's one of the easier beach access points between stretches of high motel-topped bluffs, so it can get a little crowded.

Another convenient beach access is off SW 51st Street at the south end of town, just before **Siletz Bay.** A large parking area here in what's known as the Taft District stands beside the driftwood-strewn shore of the bay, where you can often see a group of harbor seals chasing their dinner or coming in for a closer look at you. It's a short walk to the ocean.

Time was when it was common for storms and currents to wash up that ultimate beachcomber's prize—**glass fishing floats**—on the Oregon coast. Lincoln City improves the beachcomber's odds with its Finders Keepers program, in which the city distributes nearly 3,000 glass floats along its beaches mid-October-Memorial Day. Handcrafted by Pacific

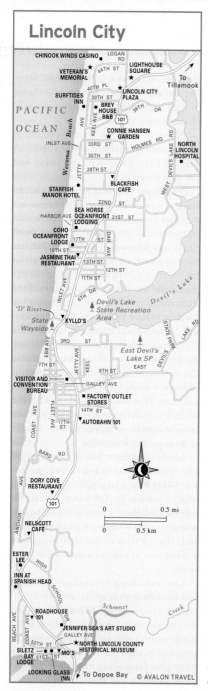

## Lincoln City

CHINOOK WINDS CASINO
LOGAN RD

VETERAN'S MEMORIAL
44TH ST
LIGHTHOUSE SQUARE

40TH PL
LINCOLN CITY PLAZA

SURFTIDES INN
39TH ST

To Tillamook

PACIFIC
OCEAN

KEEL AVE
Wecoma Beach
AVE

BREY HOUSE B&B
101
36TH DR

CONNIE HANSEN GARDEN

INLET AVE
33RD ST
HOLMES RD
NORTH LINCOLN HOSPITAL

JETTY
30TH ST

28TH ST

STARFISH MANOR HOTEL
BLACKFISH CAFE

22ND ST

HARBOR AVE
SEA HORSE OCEANFRONT LODGING
21ST ST

COHO OCEANFRONT LODGE
17TH ST
OAR AVE

15TH ST

JASMINE THAI RESTAURANT
13TH ST

12TH ST

11TH ST

INLET AVE
6TH DR
Devil's Lake State Recreation Area
Devil's Lake

'D' River
State Wayside
KYLLO'S

EBB AVE
3RD ST
JETTY AVE
KEEL
East Devil's Lake SP EAST
STATE PARK RD
DEVILS

7TH ST
8TH ST

VISITOR AND CONVENTION BUREAU
GALLEY AVE
LAKE RD

FLEET AVE
FACTORY OUTLET STORES

COAST AVE
14TH ST
17TH ST
AUTOBAHN 101

BARD RD

N

DORY COVE RESTAURANT
101

ANCHOR AVE
NELSCOTT CAFE

0         0.5 mi
0         0.5 km

ESTER LEE
HIGH

INN AT SPANISH HEAD
SCHOOL

BEACH AVE
COAST AVE
ROADHOUSE 101
Schooner Creek

JENNIFER SEA'S ART STUDIO
GALLEY AVE

SILETZ BAY LODGE
50TH ST
NORTH LINCOLN COUNTY HISTORICAL MUSEUM
MO'S
51ST ST

LOOKING GLASS INN
To Depoe Bay
36TH
© AVALON TRAVEL

Northwest glass artists, each of the colorful floats is signed and numbered and placed by volunteers on the beaches above the high-tide line. If you find one, it's yours to keep; you can call or stop in at the visitors center for a certificate and information about the artist who created it.

## Devils Lake

Devils Lake, just east of the highway, is the recreation center of Lincoln City. In addition to windsurfing and hydroplaning, you can fish here—the lake is stocked with hatchery trout, and there's also a population of wild coho salmon (catch-and-release only) as well as lampreys. There's good bird-watching on and around this shallow 678-acre lake, which attracts flocks of migratory geese, ducks, and other waterfowl. Species to look for include canvasbacks, Canada geese, widgeons, gadwalls, grebes, and mallards. Bald eagles and ospreys nest in the trees bordering the lake.

The lake takes its name from a local Native American legend. The story goes that when Siletz warriors paddled a canoe across the lake one moonlit night, a tentacled beast erupted from the still water and pulled the men under. It's said that boaters today who cross the moon's reflection in the middle of the lake tempt the same fate, but the lake's devil has remained silent for years.

Of the five access points, East Devils Lake Road off U.S. 101 northeast of town offers a scenic route around the lake's east side before rejoining U.S. 101 near the day-use portion of the state park at the south end of the lake. To reach the camping area of **Devils Lake State Recreation Area,** take NE 6th Drive east from U.S. 101, about 0.25 miles north of the D River. The day-use area has a boat ramp, and there's a moorage dock across the lake adjacent to the campground.

Mountain bikes, canoes, fishing boats, and Jet Skis can be rented at **Blue Heron Landing** (4006 W. Devils Lake Rd., 541/994-4708, www.blueheronlanding.net, 9am-7pm daily).

# The Legacy of Ken Kesey

Two miles south of Lincoln City, you'll come to the turnoff for Highway 229 along the Siletz River. If you drive down the north side of the river about 1.25 miles, on the opposite shore you'll notice a showy Victorian-ish house. It was constructed for the movie version of *Sometimes a Great Notion*. The 1971 film, a so-so adaptation of Ken Kesey's memorable novel, starred Paul Newman, Lee Remick, Henry Fonda, and Michael Sarrazin. The plot concerns the never-say-die spirit of an antiunion timber baron, his not-always-supportive family, and life in the mythical Coast Range logging community of Wakonda. A huge porch once fronted the riverbank, heavily reinforced against the elements. It was taken down in the decade after the movie was made, but it lives on in the pages of the book. Much of the movie was shot in this area, with café scenes taking place at Mo's on Newport's bay front. Other scenes were shot near Florence.

## Drift Creek Falls

Although it requires a drive inland, it's worth heading about 10 miles east to hike **Drift Creek Falls** (503/392-3161, $5 NW Forest Pass to park). The relatively easy but steadily downhill 1.5-mile trail passes through a forest with mostly second growth, a little old growth, lots of big stumps, and an understory of lovely native plants, and it leads to a dramatic 240-foot-high suspension bridge overlooking the 75-foot falls. The bridge, built in 1998, is as much an attraction as the falls—it sways a little bit as you walk out to view the falls. From the bridge, the trail continues another 0.25 miles to the base of the falls.

From Highway 18, turn south at Rose Lodge onto Bear Creek Road (which becomes Forest Road 17) and follow it for about nine miles. At the fork with Schooner Creek Road, go left (uphill); a rustic sign notes that it's the way to "Drift Creek Camp."

From U.S. 101, turn east onto Drift Creek Road (at the south end of Lincoln City), then south onto South Drift Creek Road and east onto Forest Road 17. Follow Forest Road 17 for about 10 miles.

## Siletz River

The **Siletz Bay National Wildlife Refuge** preserves coastal estuaries and wetlands on either side of U.S. 101 at the south end of Lincoln City. The skeleton trees here are reminders of times when the salt marsh was diked to provide pasture for dairy cows. Now these snags are used by red-tailed hawks, bald eagles, and other birds of prey. The wetlands provide habitat for great blue herons, egrets, and other waterbirds.

During the summer, refuge rangers lead a small number of **paddle trips** along the Siletz estuaries. Trips are free, but participants must register well beforehand (541/270-0610) and provide their own canoe or kayak. **Siletz Moorage** (82 Siletz Hwy., 541/996-3671) rents kayaks ($25 for 4 hours) from its location on the north bank of the river just east of the highway.

## Casinos

One of the biggest draws in town is the **Chinook Winds Casino** (1777 NW 44th St., 541/996-5825 or 888/244-6665, www.chinookwindscasino.com, 24 hours daily), operated by the Confederated Tribes of Siletz Indians, near the north end of town. In addition to slots, blackjack, poker, keno, bingo, craps, and roulette, the casino has two on-site restaurants and a busy schedule of big-name (or formerly big-name) entertainment.

About 25 miles east of Lincoln City is the state's number-one visitor attraction, **Spirit Mountain Casino** (21700 SW Salmon River Hwy., Grand Ronde, 800/760-7977, http://spiritmountain.com, 24 hours daily), operated by the Confederated Tribes of Grand Ronde. Games of chance include slots, craps, blackjack, poker, keno, and bingo. No matter what you think of the casino, it should be noted that the Grand Ronde people have done a great job at getting their tribal status officially reinstated after the U.S. government terminated it in 1954, leaving it with not much more than the tribal cemetery and a shed. They have amassed land and established a community fund that is a substantial supporter of nonprofit organizations in Oregon; 6 percent of the casino's proceeds go into this charitable fund.

## North Lincoln County Historical Museum

The modest **North Lincoln County Historical Museum** (4907 SW U.S. 101, 541/996-6614, www.northlincolncountyhistoricalmuseum.org, noon-5pm Wed.-Sun. June-Sept., noon-5pm Wed.-Sat. Oct.-Dec. 14 and Feb.-May, free) tells the story of this area through exhibits of old-time logging machinery, homesteading tools, fishing, military life, and Native American history. A highlight is the great collection of Japanese glass fishing floats.

## Connie Hansen Garden

Tucked into the neighborhood between busy U.S. 101 and the beach, the **Connie Hansen Garden** (1931 NW 33rd St., 541/994-6338, www.conniehansengarden.com, dawn-dusk daily, free) is a great example of a coastal rainforest garden. The late Connie Hansen bought the land because its dampness seemed well suited to growing irises, her favorite plants, but she soon expanded her vision, working with the site's ecology and her own artistic talents to create a horticultural showcase. Guided tours are available for a small fee with advance notice, and there's a gift shop (10am-2pm Fri.-Sun. and Tues. Mar.-mid-Dec.).

## Glass Art

Spend a rainy day learning to blow a glass float or paperweight at the **Jennifer Sears Art Studio** (4821 SW U.S. 101, 541/996-2569, www.jennifersearsglassart.com, 10am-6pm daily, classes $65-185, reservations required). Kids ages eight and older may participate with

parental supervision. Wear closed-toe shoes, and no fleece!

About four miles south of town, near Salishan, you can watch the glass blowers at **Alder House** (611 Immonen Rd., 541/994-6485, www.alderhouse.com, 10am-5pm daily May-Oct.) and buy floats, paperweights, or other glass creations at reasonable prices. Call ahead to confirm opening hours.

## Golf

The area's most prestigious golf resort is seven miles south of Lincoln City at Gleneden Beach. **Salishan Spa and Golf Resort** (7760 N. U.S. 101, Gleneden Beach, 541/764-3632 or 800/890-8037, www.salishan.com, $89-119 for 18 holes) is an award-winning 18-hole course set in the foothills of the Coast Range and bordered by Siletz Bay and the sea. This challenging 6,470-yard, par-71 championship layout course was redesigned by Oregon golf superstar Peter Jacobsen and includes stunning ocean views. Keep in mind that this is a Scottish links course, where the roughs are really rough.

The 18-hole **Chinook Winds Golf Resort** (3245 NE 50th St., 541/994-8442, http://chinookwindscasino.com, $35-40 for 18 holes) is set in hilly (and frequently windy) terrain amidst towering coastal mountains on the edge of Lincoln City. This course is another venture of the Chinook Winds Casino, operated by the Confederated Tribes of Siletz Indians. The golf course spans just 5,000 yards, with men's par 65 and women's 72.

# ENTERTAINMENT AND EVENTS
## Brewpubs

The **Lighthouse Brew Pub** (4157 U.S. 101 N., 541/994-7238, 11am-10pm Sun.-Thurs., 11am-11pm Fri.-Sat., $9-20) is a welcome rehash of the successful McMenamins formula. Just look for a lighthouse replica in a parking lot on the northwest side of U.S. 101 across from McDonald's. Pizza, burgers, sandwiches, and salads can be washed down with

McMenamins' own ales as well as hard cider and wine.

The venerable **Roadhouse 101** (4649 SW U.S. 101, 541/994-7729, www.roadhouse101. com, 11:30am-9pm Sun.-Thurs., 11:30am-midnight Fri.-Sat., $8-20) has added Rusty Truck Brewing to its already rockin' establishment, with a selection of house-made ales and a "south of the border" lager. The Roadhouse features hearty American-style food, frequent live music, and a lively crowd ready to party.

## The Arts

Lincoln City's homegrown theater company, **Theatre West** (3536 SE U.S. 101, 541/994-5663, www.theatrewest.com), stages half a dozen productions each year, with an emphasis on comedies, musicals, and drama. Visit the website for a list of current plays and their synopses.

Housed within the renovated Gleneden Brick and Tile Factory, five miles south of Lincoln City in Gleneden Beach, **Eden Hall** (6645 Gleneden Beach Loop Rd., 541/764-3826 performance info, 541/764-3825 restaurant, www.sidedoorcafe.com) stages live theater and hosts an impressively eclectic roster of regional and touring musicians. This spacious, airy warehouse has an excellent sound system and is a wonderful place to take in a concert, with an emphasis on jazz, folk, and blues. Enjoy lunch or dinner at the adjacent Side Door Café. At Eden Hall, catch the **Gleneden Harvest Market** (11am-4pm Thurs. May-Sept.) with produce, meat, and food from local farms in addition to arts and crafts.

## Cinema

Catch first-run flicks at the **Bijou Theatre** (1624 NE U.S. 101, 541/994-8255), an old-time movie house dating back to the 1930s—making it a rare old survivor around here. The six-screen **Regal Cinemas** (3755 SE High School Dr., 541/994-7649), just east of U.S. 101 in the south end of town, is its modern competitor.

## Festivals and Events

Lincoln City calls itself the kite capital of the world, pointing to its position midway between the pole and the equator, which gives the area predictable wind patterns. The town holds not one but two kite fiestas at the D River Wayside each year. The summer **Kite Festival** (541/994-3070 or 800/452-2151) takes place the last weekend in June; the fall festival is held the second weekend in October. The event is famous for giant spin socks, some as long as 150 feet.

# SHOPPING

To sample the work of area artists, check out the **Ryan Gallery** (4270 N. U.S. 101, 541/994-5391, www.ryanartgallery.com, 10am-5pm daily). **Artists' Co-Op Gallery** (620 NW U.S. 101, 541/557-8000, 10am-5pm daily) represents the work of some 40 artists and craftspeople in the Lincoln City area.

South of town at Salishan, the **Lawrence Gallery** (7755 U.S. 101 N., 541/764-2318, www.lawrencegallery.net, 10am-6pm daily) is high-end and has an eclectic selection of art by regional artists.

With some 65 shops, the **Tanger Outlet Center** (1500 SE East Devils Lake Rd., 541/996-5000), near the south end of town, is the largest outlet mall on the Oregon coast and has become something of a regional destination. Shops here include the ones you'd expect—Coach, Chico's, Eddie Bauer—plus the Oregon-based **Pendleton Woolen Mills** (541/994-2496, www.pendleton-usa. com).

**Northwest Winds** (130 SE U.S. 101, 541/994-1004) sells and repairs kites just across the highway from the D River Wayside, Lincoln City's kite-flying hub.

# FOOD

Lincoln City offers many dining options, most of them busy and family-focused. There are several fine dining and ethnic options, however, and the general quality of food is high.

## Pacific Northwest Cuisine

Some of coastal Oregon's top dining experiences are found just south of Lincoln City. The reasonable prices at the Salishan Lodge's **Sun Room Restaurant** (7760 N. U.S. 101, Gleneden Beach, www.salishan.com, 7am-9pm daily, $11-28) are a welcome surprise. This casual restaurant might be less elaborate and half the price of Salishan's signature **Samphire** (5pm-9:30pm daily, 3-course tasting menu $59), but its cuisine comes from the same kitchen. The specialties are local seafood, meat and game. The wine list here is one of the largest in the state, and if you plan ahead, you can arrange for your meal to be served in the resort's wine cellar.

The ★ **Blackfish Cafe** (2733 NW U.S. 101, 541/996-1007, www.blackfishcafe.com, 11:30am-close Wed.-Mon., $12-28) is a great find. Presided over by former Salishan Resort executive chef Rob Pounding, who has longstanding relationships with local farmers, anglers, and mushroom foragers, the Blackfish Cafe is dedicated to fairly priced and delicious regional cooking. The emphasis is on what's fresh, homegrown, and creative, such as grilled Willamette Valley pork brisket rubbed with coriander and cumin and troll-caught chinook salmon with fennel-lime butter. There is no shortage of humbler fare, either, such as the self-proclaimed best clam chowder on the coast, Pacific City dory-caught fish-and-chips, and amazing fish tacos.

The **Bay House** (5911 SW U.S. 101, 541/996-3222, www.thebayhouse.org, 5pm-9pm Wed.-Sun., $27-40) combines oceanfront views with exquisite Pacific Northwest cuisine. Moscovy duck breast is served with parsnip-nutmeg puree and bing cherry demi-glace. A $76 five-course tasting menu is available, but must be ordered by everyone at the table. For a more casual and less expensive light dinner, eat from the small plates menu in the lounge; the three-course $25 menu is a great deal. In either dining area, oenophiles will want to look at the wine list, praised by *Wine Spectator*.

A half-mile south of Salishan (five miles equidistant from Depoe Bay and Lincoln City) is a Gleneden Beach eatery with considerable appeal. The **Side Door Café** (6675 Gleneden Beach Loop, 541/764-3825, www.sidedoorcafe.com, 11am-9pm Wed.-Mon., $20-31) combines a gourmet restaurant with a musical venue. The airy yet cozy-feeling dining room features a menu where honey mustard and herb-rubbed salmon with marionberry glaze exemplifies the offerings.

## Seafood

If coastal restaurants are eating a hole in your wallet, there's always tried-and-true **Mo's** (860 SW 51st St., 541/996-2535, www.moschowder.com, 10:30am-9pm daily, $10-18). As at all Mo's locations, the view is great, and the seafood more than serviceable.

The chowder is a little tastier at the **Dory Cove Restaurant** (2981 SW U.S. 101, 541/557-4000, www.dorycove.com, 8am-8pm Sun.-Thurs., 8am-9pm Fri.-Sat., $5-23), but the views from this simple restaurant are out onto the highway. Rest assured that the focus is on the food—good old-fashioned deep-fried and sautéed seafood main courses (halibut fish-and-chips are recommended) and homemade pies.

**Kyllo's Seafood Grill** (1110 NW 1st Court, 541/994-3179, www.kyllosrestaurant.com, 11:30am-8:30pm Sun.-Thurs., 11:30am-9pm Fri.-Sat., $9-25) specializes in broiled, sautéed, and baked seafood, plus excellent pasta, sandwiches, and homemade desserts served with Oregon microbrews and wines. The restaurant is visible from U.S. 101 right in the middle of Lincoln City as you drive by the D River Wayside. With views of the water on all sides, this restaurant is a good place to linger, though waits can be long in the evening since no reservations are taken.

## Classic American

If you're en route to the wine country or the Willamette Valley or just want a respite from coastal traffic, a place that appeals to everybody is ★ **Otis Cafe** (1259 Salmon River

Hwy., 541/994-2813, www.otiscafe.com, 7am-8pm daily, $5-18), at the Otis Junction on Highway 18, five miles northeast of Lincoln City. Innovative variations on American road food have earned the Otis a devoted following (stop by to read the enthusiastic review by a satisfied *New York Times* reporter). Long waits on the porch are the rule on weekend mornings, though it's worth it for thick-crusted molasses bread, buttermilk waffles, and hash browns under a crust of melted Rogue Valley white cheddar. Even if it's not mealtime, stop in for a slice of outstanding pie.

Two Native American gaming casinos are located within 25 miles of one another and offer dining alternatives to the coast-bound traveler. Both **Chinook Winds** (1777 NW 44th St., 541/966-5825 or 888/244-6665), and **Spirit Mountain** (21700 SW Salmon River Hwy., Grand Ronde, 800/760-7977), about 25 miles east of Lincoln City on Highway 22 in Grand Ronde, have many dining options. Each offers generous full buffets for breakfast, lunch, and dinner daily, and both have full-service fine dining restaurants offering moderate to expensive ($18-35) prices. Both casinos have nightly buffets ($15-20). Chinook Winds' ocean views are also worth noting. Both casinos have outlets for 24-hour dining.

If you're looking for the perfect homey spot for a traditional breakfast, head to the **Nelscott Café** (3237 SW U.S. 101, 541/994-6100, 9am-3pm Thurs.-Mon., $6-12). The breakfast standards such as omelets and French toast are well prepared, and there are good burgers and sandwiches for lunch. This is a small place and can get busy on weekends.

## Asian

**Jasmine Thai Restaurant** (1437 NW U.S. 101, 541/994-2022, 11am-3pm and 4:30pm-9pm Mon.-Sat., noon-9pm Sun., $9-14) serves well-prepared traditional Thai cuisine. An extensive menu includes a number of seafood specialties, as well as daily specials that take advantage of seasonal vegetables and other local produce.

In the outlet mall, **Momiji** (1500 SE Devils Lake Rd., 541/996-8886, 10am-9pm daily, sushi rolls $4-17) offers both Chinese and Japanese cooking, but the reason this restaurant is so popular is the excellent sushi rolls and sashimi. You're welcome to watch at the bar as the sushi is made, eat family-style in the restaurant, or get your order to go.

## German

If gluey Oregon clam chowder is wrecking your appetite, perhaps you're ready for **Autobahn 101** (1512 SE U.S. 101, 541/614-1811, 11:30am-11pm Sun.-Tues. and Thurs., 11:30am-2pm Fri.-Sat., $10-14), a German pub with seven German beers on tap and a big menu of Teutonic bar food. Check out the schnitzel dinners and the house-made *weisswurst* (white sausage) with sauerkraut.

## ACCOMMODATIONS

Lincoln City has more hotel rooms than any other coastal Oregon city. There are plenty to choose from, and many are similar—basic hotel rooms within walking distance of the beach. However, there are some distinctions. Unless severely constrained by budget, one would not purposefully choose to stay on the east side of U.S. 101, necessitating an unpleasant fording of that great vehicular river just to walk to the beach, so, with one exception (Salishan), all the following hotels are on the beach side of the highway. Also, just because a hotel is newer doesn't mean that it's preferred over older models. Many vintage hotels and motels have the best locations, and their slightly worn-in atmosphere is perfect for a summer holiday. For one-stop room shopping, the local visitors association **Central Oregon Coast** (www.oregoncoast.org) has a booking service with good rates.

### $100-150

The **Ester Lee** (3803 SW U.S. 101, 541/996-3606 or 888/996-3606, www.esterlee.com, $116-139) is a decades-old family motel complex, with some cottages and motel units on a bluff above miles of beachfront. All rooms have ocean views and fireplaces; some have kitchens and hot tubs. Pets are allowed in some of the cottage units, most of which have kitchens and fireplaces. It's not a fancy place, but it's clean and pleasant, with a great location and a good value.

The **Siletz Bay Lodge** (1012 SW 51st St., 541/996-6111 or 888/430-2100, http://siletzbaylodgelincolncity.com, $128-148), on the north end of Siletz Bay on a driftwood-strewn beach, is a family-friendly and wheelchair-accessible (with elevators) lodging in a location ideal for bird-watching and viewing seals. About half of the standard rooms of this older hotel have balconies, with delightful views of the bay and the sunset over Salishan Spit. In-room amenities include microwaves, fridges, and coffeemakers, and a continental breakfast is offered.

A small oceanfront luxury hotel near the popular D River Wayside, the **Shearwater Inn** (120 NW Inlet Court, 541/994-4121 or 800/869-8069, www.theshearwaterinn.com, $149-199) offers 30 units with balconies and gas fireplaces. Guests meet in the lobby every afternoon to sample Oregon wine. The hotel provides concierge and massage services and a continental breakfast, and accepts pets. The building is also wheelchair accessible.

On the bluff above the beach, with fine views and easy access to the sand, **Seahorse Oceanfront Lodging** (2039 NW Harbor Dr., 541/994-2101 or 800/662-2101, www.seahorsemotel.com, $145-249) has a dizzying selection of lodging options, from simple motel rooms to cottages, houses, and two- and three-bedroom units, all in an extensive and quiet oceanfront compound. While it's a bit hard to generalize, most rooms have kitchens, some have fireplaces, and all guests are welcome at the breakfast bar, indoor pool, and outdoor hot tub, which overlooks the beach. There are a handful of discounted partial or no-view rooms available. This friendly and venerable operation is one of the reasons Lincoln City is so popular with families.

Another good spot on the north end of Siletz Bay in Lincoln City's historic Taft area is the **Looking Glass Inn** (861 SW 51 St., 541/996-3996 or 800/843-4940, www.lookingglass-inn.com, $129-159), an attractive place that would be quiet and tucked away if it weren't for the busy Mo's restaurant just across the road. Most rooms have kitchenettes, and most are dog-friendly.

Close to the beach at the north end of town, **Brey House B&B** (3725 NW Keel Ave., 541/994-7123, www.breyhouse.com, $114-164) is one of the oldest bed-and-breakfasts on the Oregon coast. The B&B is a three-story Cape Cod-style home built in 1940 with four bedrooms, all with private baths and entrances. The excellent breakfast is served in a light-filled room overlooking the ocean. Rooms are for adults only.

## $150-200

A landmark that has had a recent makeover is the **Surftides Inn** (2945 NW Jetty Ave., 541/994-2191 or 800/452-2159, www.surftidesinn.com, $159-249), a large complex hugging the beach at the northern edge of Lincoln City. All of the oceanfront guest rooms have balconies, and most have fireplaces. All rooms include a small fridge, microwave oven, and coffeemaker, as well as cable TV with a DVD player. The inn has an indoor pool, a decent restaurant, a lounge, and meeting rooms. Prices vary by view; ask about partial- or no-view rooms, which are up to 30 percent cheaper. Pets are accepted in some rooms.

A longtime Lincoln City motel, the **Coho Oceanfront Lodge** (1635 NW Harbor Ave., 541/994-3684 or 800/848-7006, www.thecoholodge.com, $185-235), has undergone a multimillion-dollar renovation; guest rooms have a sleek and sophisticated modern look; a new guestroom wing opened in 2016. A DVD library, indoor pool, hot tub, and sauna are available for guests to use; pets are allowed in some rooms.

## Over $200

If you've been fantasizing about rolling out of bed, slipping on your robe, and walking out—coffee in hand—onto a semiprivate stretch of beach, then the **Inn at Spanish Head** (4009 SW U.S. 101, 541/996-2161 or 800/452-8127, www.spanishhead.com, $229-359) may be your best bet. Oregon's only resort hotel right on the beach, the inn takes its place—large and looming—against the backdrop of rugged cliffs. Whether a suite, studio, or bedroom unit, every room has an ocean view. On-site amenities include Fathoms, the 10th-floor restaurant-bar, a fireplace lounge, meeting rooms, a heated outdoor pool, saunas, a spa, and an exercise room.

More a small boutique hotel than the sprawling motel complex that typifies Lincoln City, ★ **Starfish Manor Hotel** (2735 NW Inlet Ave., 541/996-9300 or 800/972-6155, www.onthebeachfront.com, $229-399) has just 17 oceanfront guest rooms and suites perched above the beach. All units have large ocean-view whirlpool tubs, fireplaces, oceanfront decks, kitchenettes, tasteful furnishings, and fine linens. Some units have two bedrooms. The Starfish is in a quiet part of town, perfect for a romantic getaway. The folks who own the Starfish have three other small boutique hotels with condo-like accommodations and similar prices; see the Starfish website.

When asked to choose *the* place to stay on the Oregon coast, many Oregonians would select the ★ **Salishan Spa & Golf Resort** (7760 N. U.S. 101, Gleneden Beach, 541/764-3600 or 800/452-2300, www.salishan.com, $219-418), a few miles south of Lincoln City.

While there are distant Siletz Bay views, Salishan isn't a beachfront resort, but most folks quickly learn to appreciate the peace of the forest and the golf course. This paradigm shift is facilitated by art and landscape architecture that convey the vision of John Gray, who built Salishan and such other Pacific Northwest properties as Skamania Lodge (on the Washington side of the Columbia Gorge) and Sunriver (south of Bend) from native materials with respect for the surrounding environment.

Even if you don't stay here, the grounds and facilities are worth a look. The art gallery is free and features works by top Oregon artists; also check out master woodcarver Leroy Setziol's bas-relief panels in the dining room. In addition to the recreational and aesthetic appeal of the resort, the dining room contributes to Salishan's lofty reputation. The forested trails behind the golf course showcase the rainforest foothills of the Coast Range and the waterfowl near Siletz Bay. Across the street, the Salishan Marketplace features first-rate galleries, a café, and clothing boutiques.

Lodging at Salishan Spa & Golf Resort is designed to meld into the landscape.

In high season, Salishan attracts well-heeled nature lovers, corporate expense-account clientele, folks enjoying a special occasion, and serious golfers. You'll also find everyday folks and seminar attendees on winter weekend specials at half the summertime rates. Ask about multiday packages for big savings on your room rate.

### Vacation Rentals

To rent vacation homes throughout Lincoln County, contact the **Lincoln City Visitor and Convention Bureau** (800/452-2151, www.oregoncoast.org), or try **Meredith Lodging** (541/996-2955 or 800/224-7660, www.meredithlodging.com), which features a selection of vacation home rentals.

### Camping

**Devils Lake State Recreation Area** (1452 NE 6th St., information 541/994-2002, reservations 800/452-5687, www.reserveamerica.com, $21 tents, $31-33 RVs, $47 yurts, $6 hiker-biker) is the main public campground in Lincoln City, with 54 tent sites, 28 RV sites with full hookups, 10 yurts, and a hiker-biker camp. This campground is right in town, just off U.S. 101 at the northeast end, so it's hardly a quiet wilderness retreat, but it does provide easy access to swimming or boating on Devils Lake.

The **Salmon River RV Park** (6029 Salmon River Hwy., 541/994-3116, www.salmonriverrvp.com, $20 tents, $20-30 RVs) is a good spot for anglers; it's on the Salmon River near the town of Otis. The **Lincoln City KOA** (5298 NE Park Lane, 541/994-2961 or 800/562-3316, http://koa.com, $32 tents, $43-46 RVs, $70 cabins) is also just a little ways inland, near the northeast corner of Devils Lake. At the south end of town, **Coyote Rock** (1676 Siletz Hwy., 541/996-6824, www.coyote-rock.com, $21 tents, $27-38 RVs, $46 cabins) has a nice setting where the Siletz River meets its bay. All of these campgrounds, including the state park, have showers.

## INFORMATION

The **Lincoln City Visitors Center** (540 NE U.S. 101, 541/994-3302 or 800/452-2151, www.oregoncoast.org, 10am-4pm Mon.-Sat.) has a website that's full of helpful information.

The **Central Oregon Coast Association** (541/265-2064 or 800/767-2064, www.coast-visitor.com) also maintains a useful website with details on Lincoln City and the rest of coastal Lincoln County.

## GETTING THERE AND AROUND

**Lincoln County Transit** (541/265-4900, www.co.lincoln.or.us/transit) buses stop in town for service Monday-Saturday. The line goes as far south as Yachats and does not run on major holidays. The county also offers five daily buses to and from Lincoln City and the joint Salem Greyhound and Amtrak station.

Peak traffic times in Lincoln City can result in 25,000 cars a day crawling through town. As an alternative to rush hour on U.S. 101, you could try detouring on NE West Devils Lake Road or NE East Devils Lake Road, which bypass the worst congestion.

# Depoe Bay

With its dramatic keyhole harbor—claimed to be the world's smallest natural harbor—Depoe Bay has long been a popular tourist destination. At least since the establishment of the town: for all intents and purposes, the town didn't really exist until the completion of the Roosevelt Highway (now U.S. 101) in 1927, which opened the area up to car travelers. Prior to that time, the area had been occupied mainly by a few Siletz people. One worked at the U.S. Army depot and called himself Charlie Depot. The town was named after him, eventually taking on the current spelling.

Regardless of what you think of the busy commercial strip and the enormous time-share resort along the highway, the scenic appeal of Depoe's location is impossible to ignore. The rocky outer bay, flanked by headlands to the north and south, is pierced by a narrow channel through the basalt cliffs leading to the inner harbor. It's home to an active sportfishing fleet as well as the whale-watching charters that have earned Depoe Bay its distinction as the whale-watching capital of the state. Depoe Bay's harbor was scenic enough to be selected as the site from which Jack Nicholson commandeered a yacht for his mental-patient crew in the classic 1975 film *One Flew Over the Cuckoo's Nest*.

## SIGHTS AND RECREATION

### The Bayfront and Harbor

Depoe Bay is situated along a truly beautiful coastline that cannot be fully appreciated from the highway. A quarter-mile-long seawall and promenade invite a stroll. For a panorama of the harbor, continue along the sidewalks across the gracefully arching concrete bridge, designed by Conde McCullough and built in 1927. Other photogenic perspectives are offered from residential streets west of U.S. 101; try Ellingson Street, south of the bridge, and Sunset Street, at the north end of the bay. Two "spouting horns," natural blowholes in the rocks north of the harbor entrance, can send plumes of spray 60 feet into the air when the tide and waves are right.

East of the bridge is Depoe Bay's claim to international fame, the world's smallest navigable natural harbor. This boat basin is also exceptional because it's a harbor within a harbor. This topography is the result of wave action cutting into a fissure in the basalt cliffs over eons, finally creating a 50-foot passageway leading to a six-acre inland lagoon. In addition to whale-watching, folks congregate on the bridge between the ocean and the harbor to watch boats maneuver into the enclosure.

### Whale Watching Center

Stop in at the **Whale Watching Center** (119 SW U.S. 101, 541/765-3304, www.oregonstateparks.org, 10am-4pm daily summer, 10am-4pm Wed.-Sun. winter, free) where volunteers can help you spot whales and answer your questions about them. The center, right on the seawall, is an ideal viewing spot. Peak viewing times are mid-December-January, when whales are migrating south; late March-early June, when they're traveling north (mothers and babies generally come later in the season); and mid-July-early November, when resident whales feed off the coast. The least likely times to see whales from the central Oregon coast are mid-November-mid-December and mid-January-mid-March.

### Whale, Sea Life & Shark Museum

The private **Whale, Sea Life & Shark Museum** (234 S. U.S. 101, 541/912-6734, www.oregonwhales.com, 10am-4pm daily summer, 10am-4pm Sat.-Sun. winter, $5 adults, $3 ages 4-10) on the harbor side of the highway, 100 feet south of the bridge, is run in conjunction with the business Whale Research

Eco Excursions, which offers whale-watching tours in Zodiac craft. The museum, which is free with a whale-watching trip, features models of marine mammals, a large collection of shark jaws, and lots of photos of whales.

## Boiler Bay State Scenic Viewpoint

Boiler Bay, half a mile north of Depoe Bay, is so named because of the boiler left from the 1910 wreck of the *J. Marhoffer*. The ship caught fire three miles offshore and drifted into the bay. The remains of the boiler are visible at low tide. This rock-rimmed bay is a favorite spot for rock fishing, birding, and whale-watching. A trail leads down to some excellent tide pools.

## Whale Cove

This picturesque bay 1.5 miles south of Depoe Bay has been scooped out of the sandstone bluffs. The tranquility of this calendar photo come to life is deceptive. There's considerable evidence to suggest that this tiny embayment—and not California's Marin County—was the site of Francis Drake's 1579 landing, but the jury is still out. During Prohibition, bootleggers used the protected cove as a clandestine port.

**Rocky Creek State Scenic Viewpoint** (800/551-6949, www.oregonstateparks.org) overlooks Whale Cove. There are picnic tables, and it's a good spot for whale-watching, but there's no beach access.

## Otter Crest Loop

The rocky bluffs of this coastal stretch take on an even more dramatic aspect as you leave the highway at the **Otter Crest Loop,** a winding three-mile section of the old Coast Highway, two miles south of Depoe Bay. The northernmost part of the loop, down as far as Cape Foulweather, is one-way southbound, with a generous bike lane.

From atop **Cape Foulweather,** the visibility can extend 40 miles on a clear day. The view south to Yaquina Head and its lighthouse is a photographer's fantasy of headlands, coves, and offshore monoliths. Bronze plaques in the parking lot tell of Captain Cook naming the 500-foot-high headland during a bout with storm-tossed seas on March 7, 1778.

**The Lookout** (milepost 131.5, U.S. 101, 541/765-2270, http://oregonstateparks.org, 9am-5pm daily, free), a longtime gift shop on the north side of the promontory, is now operated by Oregon State Parks. The

the Whale Watching Center at Depoe Bay

# Drake's Lost Harbor?

In 1996 the media exploded with stories raising the possibility that the tiny hamlet of Whale Cove, 1.5 miles south of Depoe Bay, could supplant Plymouth Rock as the birthplace of a nation. Rotting timbers from what is theorized to have been a stockade built by Francis Drake in 1579 were unearthed in an area where stories have long circulated that the English privateer made landfall.

Over the years, these notions have been fueled by several tantalizing pieces of evidence: an unsigned ship's log from Drake's voyage in a museum in England that identified 44 degrees north latitude—the same as Whale Cove—as a landing site; an English shilling dating from 1560 found on the central Oregon coast in 1982; a photo from the 1930s showing a local resident with a distinctly English sword he unearthed; and a ship's cutlass found in Newport in the early 19th century bearing the markings of a 16th-century English arsenal. Moreover, excavations of a nearby Native American village thought to have been buried in 1600 turned up brass items, blades, and Venetian beads.

An amateur British historian, Bob Ward, makes a compelling case for Whale Cove as the place where Drake spent five weeks in the summer of 1579. In his flagship *Golden Hynde,* the only one of his five-ship fleet to survive the stormy straits around Cape Horn, Drake harassed Spanish settlements throughout Latin America and plundered Spanish ships wherever he met them. Sailing west from Mexico on its return to England via the Cape of Good Hope, the treasure-laden *Golden Hynde* was beset by storms, and Drake had to retreat to land to make repairs. Conventional history has held that he made landfall around San Francisco, most likely on the Marin County coast.

Ward, however, believes that Drake continued his voyage farther north and sailed into the Strait of Juan de Fuca, thinking he had found the fabled Northwest Passage. Turning around before he realized his mistake, Drake then headed south down the Washington and Oregon coasts, where he found a sandy cove in which to drop anchor and make repairs before the long journey home.

On Drake's return to England after four years at sea, news of his exploits were suppressed. Queen Elizabeth confiscated the logs and charts, and it would be 10 years before an official account of the voyage would be published. Then, Drake's New Albion was described as being around 38 degrees north latitude (in northern California), in an attempt, Ward believes, to fool the Spanish into thinking the Northwest Passage was much farther south.

After Elizabeth's death in 1603, however, new charts began to appear that placed the landing site much farther north, and early 17th-century charts show a small shallow bay labeled Novus Albionis (New Albion) that is an uncannily accurate depiction of Whale Cove.

Since the initial blizzard of publicity, there has been no final word from the archaeologists and historians involved in corroborating these claims. Because most history books have placed New Albion, Drake's fabled lost settlement, near San Francisco, researchers will not be too quick to claim otherwise without definitive research.

---

million-dollar view from inside the shop is easily one of the most spectacular windows on the ocean to be found anywhere.

A mile south, in the hamlet of **Otter Rock,** you'll find another of the Oregon coast's several diabolically named natural features, the **Devil's Punchbowl.** The urn-like sandstone formation, filled with swirling water, has been sculpted by centuries of waves flooding into what had been a cave until its roof collapsed. The inexorable process continues today, thanks to the ebb and flow of the Pacific through two openings in the cauldron wall. A state park viewpoint gives you a ringside seat for this frothy confrontation between rock and tide. When the water recedes, you can see purple sea urchins and starfish in the tide pools of the **Marine Gardens** 100 feet to the north.

To the south of the Punchbowl vantage point are picnic tables and a wooden walkway down to the beach. Close by in tiny Otter Rock, you'll find a small restaurant called **Mo's** (122 1st St., 541/765-2442, 11am-3pm daily Mar.-Sept., $4-16). Next door, the **Flying Dutchman Winery** (915 1st St., 541/765-2553, 11am-5pm daily) makes limited batches of handcrafted wines from grapes grown in southern Oregon and the Willamette Valley (grapes won't ripen on the coast).

Back on U.S. 101, a mile's drive south brings you to Beverly Beach State Park.

## Fishing and Whale-Watching Charters

With the ocean minutes from Depoe Bay's port, catching a salmon or seeing a whale is possible as soon as you leave the harbor.

Carrie Newell, a marine biologist and whale researcher, offers whale-watching tours with her company **Whale Research Eco Excursions** (234 S. U.S. 101, 541/912-6734, www.oregonwhales.com, 1.5 hours $40, 2 hours $50) in inflatable Zodiac craft, which hold just six passengers. Carrie and her team offer insights into the local ecosystem and the life cycles of the local gray whales. Three-hour crabbing and sightseeing tours ($85) are also offered.

Most charter operators here also offer both fishing and whale-watching excursions. Bottom-fishing trips average $80 for a five-hour run; salmon fishing (available only when salmon season is open) are about $130 for a seven- or eight-hour day; tuna and halibut fishing trips are available in season.

Both the following outfitters offer charter fishing trips in addition to whale-watching cruises. **Dockside Charters** (541/765-2545 or 800/733-8915, http://docksidedepoebay.com) offers one-hour whale-watching trips ($20 adults) aboard its 50-foot excursion boat. **Tradewinds Charters** (541/765-2345 or 800/445-8730, www.tradewindscharters.com) hosts one- and two-hour trips (Dec.-May, $20-35 adults).

## Surfing

If you're itching to actually get into the water and catch a few waves, the beach at **Otter Rock,** a few miles south of Depoe Bay, is a good place to surf. Park in the lot at Devil's Punchbowl and walk down the long flight of steps to the beach, which is relatively protected and has a large area where beginners tend to hang out. There's also a section that gets bigger waves and better surfers.

## ENTERTAINMENT AND EVENTS

The **Horn Public House and Brewery** (110 SE U.S. 101, 541/765-2261, http://thehorn.pub, 11am-8pm Wed.-Thurs. and Sun.,11am-9pm Fri.-Sat.) offers a dozen brews on tap. From the second-story dining room, you'll have great views of the harbor and the boats negotiating the narrow passage to the Pacific. The menu offers typical pub grub and good Chicago-style pizza ($11-24).

The **Depoe Bay Classic Wooden Boat Show, Crab Feed, and Ducky Derby** is held the third weekend in April. Several dozen wooden craft, both restored and newly constructed vessels, including kayaks, skiffs, dinghies, and larger fishing boats, are displayed in the harbor and the adjacent Depoe Bay City Park. Rowing races, boatbuilding workshops, crab races, and other activities are scheduled. The big Crab Feed (11am-5pm Sat., 11am-3pm Sun., $12-18) sees some 2,000 pounds of crab plus side dishes devoured at the Community Hall. The Ducky Derby is a raffle in which you purchase "tickets" in the form of rubber duckies that race down the harbor's feeder stream vying for prizes. For more information, contact the **Depoe Bay Chamber of Commerce** (223 SW U.S. 101, 541/765-2889 or 877/485-8348, www.depoebaychamber.org).

The **Fleet of Flowers** happens each Memorial Day in the harbor to honor those lost at sea and in military service. Thousands come to witness a blanket of blossoms cast upon the waters.

The **Depoe Bay Salmon Bake** ($25-27 adults, $10-12 children) takes place on the third Saturday of September (10am-5pm) at Depoe Bay City Park, flanking the rear of the boat basin. Some 3,000 pounds of fresh ocean fish are caught, cooked Native American-style on alder stakes over an open fire, and served with all the trimmings, to be savored to the accompaniment of live entertainment. It always seems to rain on the day of this event, but that's life on the Oregon coast.

## FOOD

Of Depoe Bay's several restaurants, **Tidal Raves** (279 NW U.S. 101, 541/765-2995, www.tidalraves.com, 11am-9pm daily, $12-25) has the best combination of flavor, views, and casual ambience. A number of seafood dishes take on an Asian twist, such as Thai red curry barbecued shrimp. A pasta dish features crab, shrimp, lingcod, snapper, and more on a bed of linguine with your choice of sauce. The Dungeness crab mac and cheese is also noteworthy.

★ **Restaurant Beck** (2345 S. U.S. 101, 541/765-3220, http://restaurantbeck.com, 5pm-9pm daily, $27-30), in the Whale Cove Inn south of town, is Depoe Bay's only really elegant restaurant. It has a great view and excellent food, much of which originates on nearby farms and waters. Be prepared to experiment: Pork belly confit and pickled sea beans are paired with miso ice cream; king salmon is served with popcorn, corn puree, and beet tops. Seasonal ingredients figure prominently; in June, Rainier cherries pair with ancho chilies atop a lamb loin.

## ACCOMMODATIONS

Lodgings in popular Depoe Bay require advance reservations on most weekends and holidays.

The **Inn at Arch Rock** (70 NW Sunset St., 541/765-2560 or 800/767-1835, www.innatarchrock.com, $99-309) is a cluster of white clapboard buildings that overlook Depoe Bay from a cliff-top perch at the north end of town. Most rooms have ocean views and are in the $150-200 range; a no-view room goes for much less. Pets are permitted in several rooms.

**Depoe Bay Inn** (235 SE Bay View Ave., 541/765-2322 or 800/228-0448, www.depoebayinn.com, $119-198), a small inn overlooking the harbor, has the distinct advantage of being distant from busy U.S. 101. Perched above the marina and the Coast Guard station, this homey inn with recently updated rooms affords views of sea otters, ducks, and geese while the whale-watching and fishing boats come and go. All rooms have a harbor view; rates include a hot breakfast. Small pets are allowed with prior approval. The dining room is open for dinner Wednesday to Saturday.

The ★ **Channel House** (35 Ellingson St., 541/765-2140 or 800/447-2140, www.channelhouse.com, rooms $140-295) features both standard B&B rooms and spacious suites boasting expansive views of the ocean, private decks with outdoor whirlpool tubs in most rooms, fireplaces, plush robes, and other amenities. This bluff-top B&B (there isn't a beach below, just miles of ocean and surrounding cliffs) may not look prepossessing from the outside, but inside, the place is all windows and angles—imagine *Architectural Digest* in a nautical theme. This is one of the best places on the Oregon coast to commune with whales, passing boats, winter storms, and the setting sun. A continental breakfast with tasty baked goods in an ocean-side dining area is included in the rates.

About a mile south of town, perched above scenic Whale Cove, find the boxy new **Whale Cove Inn** (2345 S. U.S. 101, 541/765-4300 or 800/628-3409, www.whalecoveinn.com, $475-850), a small boutique hotel that's a sister hotel to the Channel House. Here you can lounge in the hot tub on your private deck or on the Tempur-Pedic mattress in your bedroom alcove. All accommodations are in spacious suites; the top-end suites sleep six. Fine dining is available in the inn's Restaurant Beck. This is as high-end as the Oregon coast gets; kids 16 and older are welcome, but pets are not.

About three miles south of Depoe Bay, at one of the most scenic spots on the central coast, is the **Inn at Otter Crest** (301 Otter Crest Loop, Otter Rock, 541/765-2111 or 800/452-2101, www.innatottercrest.com,

$140-230), a large condo resort perched near the sandstone bluffs at the ocean's edge. Hotel rooms have a king or two queen beds, a fridge, a coffeemaker, and a private deck with picture windows. Studios have a queen Murphy bed or a regular bed, a full kitchen, a fireplace, and a dining area; larger one- and two-bedroom suites are also available. The least expensive rooms have a forest view.

The **Surfrider Resort** (3115 NW U.S. 101, 541/764-2311 or 800/662-2378, www.choicehotels.com, $170-199) is a few miles north of Depoe Bay on picturesque Fogarty Creek's rockbound coast. Oceanfront suites and rooms have decks; some feature whirlpool tubs, kitchens, and fireplaces. The good restaurant, the indoor pool, and the fitness center are also noteworthy.

## INFORMATION

On the east side of the highway, opposite the seawall, the **Depoe Bay Chamber of Commerce** (223 SW U.S. 101, 541/765-2889 or 877/485-8348, www.depoebaychamber.org) offers literature about the town and the central coast in general.

## GETTING THERE

On weekdays and Saturday, **Lincoln County Transit** (541/265-4900, www.co.lincoln.or.us/transit) runs buses, four times daily, north to Lincoln City and south to Yachats.

# Newport

In January 1852, a storm grounded the schooner *Juliet* near Yaquina (pronounced yah-KWIN-nah) Bay, where her captain and crew were stranded for two months. When they finally made their way inland to the Willamette Valley, they reported their discovery of an abundance of tiny sweet-tasting oysters in the bay. Within a decade, commercial oyster farms were established—the first major impetus to growth and settlement in Newport. The tasty morsels, a Pacific Northwest species called Olympias, that delighted diners in San Francisco and at New York City's Waldorf-Astoria Hotel were almost harvested to extinction, but the oyster industry continued by introducing Japanese species. Dedicated oyster farmers have recently reestablished Olympias in Oregon waters. They can now be found in select restaurants around the state. They are often called Olys and have a snappy, briny flavor.

In 2011, Newport (pop. 10,000) became the National Oceanic and Atmospheric Administration's Pacific Marine Operations Center, managing a fleet of research ships. During the summer, these ships are usually out at sea conducting oceanographic research, but when they're in port, the large white vessels are easy to spot in the harbor.

The port also bustles with the activity of Oregon's largest commercial fishing fleet and second-largest recreational fleet. Factories to process *surimi* (a fish paste popular in Japan) and whiting have provided jobs, and a state-of-the-art aquarium that once housed Keiko the whale (from the movie *Free Willy*) brings in the tourists. Wildlife observation facilities and access to tidal pools north of town at Yaquina Head make this park a highlight of the coast. The shops, galleries, and restaurants along Newport's historic bay front, together with the Performing Arts Center and quieter charm of Nye Beach, keep up a tourism tradition that goes back to when this town was the "honeymoon capital of Oregon."

## SIGHTS
### ★ Oregon Coast Aquarium

There are 6,000 miles of water between the Oregon coast and Japan—the largest stretch of open ocean on earth. You can hear our side of the story at the **Oregon Coast Aquarium** (2820 SE Ferry Slip Rd., 541/867-3474, www.aquarium.org, 10am-6pm daily

# Newport

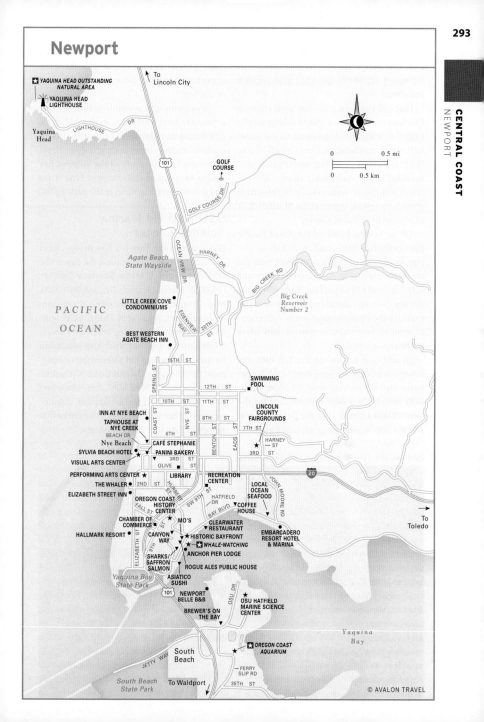

YAQUINA HEAD OUTSTANDING NATURAL AREA
YAQUINA HEAD LIGHTHOUSE
Yaquina Head

To Lincoln City

LIGHTHOUSE DR

101

GOLF COURSE

GOLF COURSE DR

OCEAN VIEW DR

HARNEY DR

BIG CREEK RD

Big Creek Reservoir Number 2

Agate Beach State Wayside

PACIFIC OCEAN

LITTLE CREEK COVE CONDOMINIUMS

EDENVIEW WAY

20TH ST

BEST WESTERN AGATE BEACH INN

15TH ST

SPRING ST

12TH ST

SWIMMING POOL

10TH ST

11TH ST

8TH ST

LINCOLN COUNTY FAIRGROUNDS

7TH ST

INN AT NYE BEACH
TAPHOUSE AT NYE CREEK

COAST ST

NYE ST

6TH ST

BENTON ST

EADS ST

HARNEY ST

BEACH DR
Nye Beach
SYLVIA BEACH HOTEL
VISUAL ARTS CENTER

CAFÉ STEPHANIE
PANINI BAKERY

3RD ST

3RD ST

OLIVE ST

PERFORMING ARTS CENTER
THE WHALER
ELIZABETH STREET INN

2ND ST

HURBERT ST

LIBRARY

RECREATION CENTER

LOCAL OCEAN SEAFOOD

JOHN MOORE RD

I-20

To Toledo

FALL ST

HATFIELD DR

SW 9TH

BAY BLVD

COFFEE HOUSE

OREGON COAST HISTORY CENTER

CHAMBER OF COMMERCE
HALLMARK RESORT

9TH ST

ELIZABETH ST

MO'S
CANYON WAY

CLEARWATER RESTAURANT

HISTORIC BAYFRONT
WHALE-WATCHING

EMBARCADERO RESORT HOTEL & MARINA

SHARKS/ SAFFRON SALMON

ANCHOR PIER LODGE

ROGUE ALES PUBLIC HOUSE

ASIATICO SUSHI

101

Yaquina Bay State Park

NEWPORT BELLE B&B

BREWER'S ON THE BAY

OSU DR

OSU HATFIELD MARINE SCIENCE CENTER

Yaquina Bay

South Beach

JETTY WAY

OREGON COAST AQUARIUM

FERRY SLIP RD

35TH ST

South Beach State Park

To Waldport

0      0.5 mi
0      0.5 km

© AVALON TRAVEL

Memorial Day-Labor Day, 10am-5pm daily Labor Day-Memorial Day, closed Christmas Day, $23 adults, $19 seniors and ages 13-17, $15 ages 3-12), one of the state's most popular attractions.

One of the gems of the aquarium is Passages of the Deep, a 200-foot-long acrylic tunnel offering 360-degree underwater views in three diverse habitats, from Orford Reef to Halibut Flats to Open Sea, where you're surrounded by free-swimming sharks. The jellyfish exhibit is a surprising highlight; it showcases several dozen kinds of jellyfish in an almost psychedelic display.

Of the several hundred species of Pacific Northwest fish, birds, and mammals on display in the rest of the facility, don't miss the sea otters, wolf eel, leopard sharks, lion's mane jellyfish, and tufted puffins. Kids will enjoy the sea cave with simulated wave action and a resident octopus. Simulations of indigenous ecosystems help visitors immerse themselves in the region's biology.

In addition to the regular exhibits, the aquarium offers hour-long Behind the Scenes tours (age 6 and over only, 12:30pm daily, $15), which show how keepers care for the over 15,000 animals that live here. The seal and sea lion "kisses" program (age 8 and over only, 2pm Sat.-Sun., $35) offers the chance to be involved in an animal training session and Q&A with an animal keeper, plus the selfie opportunity of a lifetime: a smooch with a seal or sea lion.

Advance tickets, available online, are recommended on weekends, major holidays, and during the summer. The facility also includes a couple eateries and a gift shop. To get here from U.S. 101 south of the Yaquina Bay Bridge, turn east on OSU Drive or 32nd Street and follow Ferry Slip Road to the parking lot.

## OSU Hatfield Marine Science Center

Just south of the Yaquina Bay Bridge, head east on the road that parallels the bay to the **OSU Hatfield Marine Science Center** (2030 SE Marine Science Dr., 541/867-0100, http://hmsc.oregonstate.edu, 10am-5pm daily summer, 10am-4pm Thurs.-Mon. winter, 10am-4pm daily spring and winter break, $5 donation). This research and education facility is a low-key but interesting complement to the nearby Oregon Coast Aquarium. The center has a "hands-on" area, where you can experience the feel of starfish, anemones, and other sea creatures, plus tanks that represent different sea ecosystems. The back

Passages of the Deep at the Oregon Coast Aquarium

hallway has educational dioramas, and a theater shows marine science films throughout the day. Perhaps the biggest thrill is watching the octopus eat—it's fed at 1pm each Monday, Thursday, and Saturday.

## Oregon Coast History Center

Lincoln County Historical Society has two facilities in Newport. For a glimpse into the rich past of Lincoln County, stop at the **Burrows House** (545 SW 9th St., 541/265-7509, http://oregoncoasthistory.org, 11am-4pm Thurs.-Sun. $5 donation), which incorporates a Queen Anne-style former boardinghouse, built in 1895, and the adjacent Log Cabin Museum. It's a half-block east of the chamber of commerce on U.S. 101. The logging, farming, pioneer life, and maritime exhibits (particularly Newport shipwrecks) are interesting, but the Siletz baskets and other Native American artifacts steal the show.

Here you can learn the heartbreaking story of the hardships—forced displacement, inadequate housing, insufficient food, and poor medical facilities—that plagued the diverse Native American groups that made up the Confederated Siletz Reservation.

The historical society also runs the **Pacific Maritime & Heritage Center** (333 SE Bay Blvd., 11am-4pm Thurs.-Sun. $5 adults, free under age 12), which occupies a huge old mansion overlooking the Bayfront. Local residents have donated everything from ships' wheels to vintage surfboards to this museum, which is worth visiting for the setting and the building alone.

## Bayfront District

Newport's Old Town Bayfront District can be easy to miss if you're not alert. At the north end of the Yaquina Bay Bridge, look for the signs pointing off U.S. 101 that lead down the hill to Bay Boulevard, the Bayfront's main drag. Alternatively, turn southeast off the highway a few blocks north onto Hurbert Street; it runs into Canyon Way, which ends at Bay Boulevard. On summer weekends, forget about parking anywhere near here unless you arrive early. Spots close by the boulevard can often be found, however, along Canyon Way, the hillside access route to downtown.

Until 1936, ferries shuttled people and vehicles to and from Newport's waterfront. With the completion of the Yaquina Bay Bridge that year, however, traffic bypassed the Old Town area. Commerce and development moved to the highway corridor, and the Bayfront faded in importance. Within the last couple of decades, the pendulum has swung back, and the Bayfront District is now one of Newport's prime attractions, with some of its best restaurants and watering holes, shopping, and tourist facilities.

One of the first things that'll strike you about the Bayfront today is that it's still a working neighborhood, not a sanitized recreation of a real seaport. Chowder houses, galleries, and shops stand shoulder to shoulder with fish-processing plants and canneries, and the air is filled with the cries of fishmongers and the barking of sea lions and harbor seals. On the waterfront, sport anglers step off charter boats with their catches, and vessels laden with everything from wood products to whale-watching tourists ply the bay. Unfortunately, the severe catch limits and cost of equipment make this less of a working port every year.

## Yaquina Bay State Recreation Site

In 1871 a lighthouse was built here on a bluff overlooking the mouth of Yaquina Bay, and the lighthouse keeper, his wife, and seven children moved into the two-story wood-frame structure. It soon became apparent, however, that the location was not ideal, as the light could not be seen by ships approaching the harbor from the north. The station was abandoned after just three years once the nearby light at Yaquina Head was completed. The building was slated for demolition in 1934, when local residents formed the Lincoln County Historical Society to preserve it. In 1997 the government decided to turn Yaquina Bay's beacon back on.

Today, the handsome restored structure and surrounding grounds make up **Yaquina Bay State Recreation Site** (541/574-3129 or 800/551-6949, www.oregonstateparks.org, lighthouse hours noon-4pm daily, free), in a beautiful location at the north end of the Yaquina Bay Bridge. The last wooden lighthouse on the Oregon coast is also the oldest building in Newport. The living quarters, replete with period furnishings, are open to the public. Ask the volunteers about the resident ghost.

From the parking area, you have an excellent photo op of the bay and the bridge. The park is a good place to have a picnic, or you can descend the trails to the beach and dig for razor clams or hunt for agates and petrified wood.

## Nye Beach

The 1890s-era tourism boom that came to Newport's Bayfront spilled over into Nye Beach. In 1891, the city built a wooden sidewalk connecting the two neighborhoods, and soon "summer people" were filling the cedar cottages. In the next century, thanks to an improved river-and-land route from Corvallis, health faddists (who came for hot seawater baths in the sanatorium) and honeymooners soon joined the mix.

A mile north from the Bayfront, to the west of U.S. 101 (look for signs on the highway), this onetime favorite retreat for wealthy Portlanders has undergone a revival in recent years. Rough times and rougher weather had reduced luxurious beach houses here to a cluster of weather-beaten shacks until a performing arts center went up in 1988. On the heels of the development of this first-rate cultural facility, the conversion of a 1910 hotel into a kind of literary hostel encouraged other restorations and plenty of new construction. Culture vultures, beach lovers, and people-watchers now flock to Nye Beach, which feels a world away from the Coast Highway commercial strip just a few blocks to the east.

Yaquina Head Lighthouse

## ★ Yaquina Head Outstanding Natural Area

Five miles north of Newport, rocky Yaquina Head juts out to sea. Tools dating back 5,000 years have been unearthed at Yaquina Head. Many were made from elk and deer antlers and bone, as well as stone. Clam and mussel shells from middens in the area evidence a diet rich in shellfish for the area's ancient inhabitants.

Today, much of the headland is encompassed in the **Yaquina Head Outstanding Natural Area** (750 NW Lighthouse Dr., 541/574-3100, www.blm.gov, $7 per vehicle), managed by the federal Bureau of Land Management. "Outstanding" is indeed the word for this place. Where the pounding ocean meets the land in a series of cliffs and tide pools, a visitor could easily spend several hours exploring all the site has to offer.

At its outer tip stands **Yaquina Head Lighthouse** (guided tours 10am-4pm Thurs.-Tues. July-Aug., weather permitting), the coast's

# Agate Hunting

Hunting for agates after winter storms is a passion at several Oregon beaches, particularly around Newport. Deep in the earth, metals, oxides, and silicates fused together to create this type of quartz. Red, amber, blue, and other tones sometimes form stripes or spots in the translucent rocks. One of the best places to find these treasures is on the beach near the Best Western Agate Beach Hotel, not surprisingly called Agate Beach. Nearby Moolack Beach and the beach at Seal Rock, north of Waldport, as well as area estuaries and streambeds, are spots more worth a look October to May.

tallest beacon. In the early 1870s, materials intended for construction of a lighthouse several miles north at Otter Crest were mistakenly delivered here. The 93-foot tower began operation in 1873, replacing the poorly located lighthouse south of here, at the mouth of Newport's harbor. When tours are offered, walk up the 114 cast-iron steps for a spectacular panorama of the headland and surrounding coast.

Below, an observation deck provides views of seals, sea lions, gray whales, and seabirds. Of the half-dozen varieties of pelagic birds that cluster on Colony Rock—a large monolith in the shallows 200 yards offshore—the tufted puffin is the most colorful. It's sometimes called a sea parrot because of its large yellow-orange bill. Puffins arrive here in April and are most visible early in the day on the rock's grassy patches. The most ubiquitous species are common murres, pigeon guillemots, and cormorants. The murre's white breast and belly contrast with its darker bill and elongated back. The guillemot resembles a pigeon, with white wing patches and bright red webbed feet, while the cormorant looks like a prehistoric pelican.

Down a flight of steps from the observation area is Cobble Beach, covered with surprisingly round stones. At low tides, the tide pools at Cobble Beach are teeming with sea stars, purple urchins, anemones, and hermit crabs.

On the way to the lighthouse, the large **Interpretive Center** (541/574-3116, 9:30am-5pm daily summer, 10am-5pm daily fall and spring, 10am-4pm daily winter) features exhibits on local ecosystems, Native American culture, and historical artifacts such as a 19th-century lighthouse keeper's journal. Other highlights include a life-size replica of the Fresnel lens that shines from the top of the nearby lighthouse, statues of birds and harbor seals, and information on tide pool inhabitants.

## Beaches

The beach at **Yaquina Bay State Recreation Site** (541/574-3129 or 800/551-6949, www.oregonstateparks.org) is accessible via a trail from the bluff-top parking area. This is a popular spot for clam digging and agate hunting. There's also easy beach access from the Nye Beach neighborhood, with a large parking lot at the end of NW Beach Street. Two miles south of the Yaquina Bay Bridge, **South Beach State Park** (541/867-4715 or 800/551-6949, www.oregonstateparks.org) draws beachcombers, anglers, campers, and picnickers to its miles of broad, sandy beach.

North of town along U.S. 101, **Agate Beach** is a wide swath of coastline famed for its agate-hunting opportunities and its views of nearby Yaquina Head. In addition to the semiprecious stones, the contemplative appeal of Agate Beach inspired no less a figure than Ernest Bloch, the noted Swiss composer, who lived here from 1940 until his death in 1959. Famed violinist Yehudi Menuhin spoke of Bloch and the locale thusly: "Agate Beach is a wild forlorn stretch of coastline looking down upon waves coming in all the way from Asia to break on the shore, a place which suited the grandeur and intensity of Bloch's character."

**Moolack Beach,** two miles north of Yaquina Head, is a favorite with kite flyers and agate hunters. **Beverly Beach,** 1.5 miles farther north, is a place where 20-million-year-old fossils have been found in the sandstone cliffs above the shore. Beverly Beach also attracts waders, unique for Oregon's chilly waters. Offshore sandbars temper the waves and the weather, so it's not as rough or as cold as many coastal locales. This long stretch of sand (panoramic photos are best taken from Yaquina Head Lighthouse looking north) is connected via an under-highway passage to a large state park campground.

# SPORTS AND RECREATION
## Fishing

Newport is one of the top spots on the coast for charter fishing, and opportunities abound at the home port of Oregon's second-largest recreational fleet. Bottom fishing (year-round), tuna fishing (Aug.-Oct.), crabbing (year-round), and salmon and halibut fishing (seasonal) are all possible. Typical rates are $75 for a half-day and $125 for a full day of bottom fishing, $130 for an eight-hour chinook salmon outing, $225 for 12 hours of tuna fishing, and $195 for an all-day halibut charter.

**Newport Marina Store and Charters** (2212 OSU Dr., South Beach, 541/867-4470, www.nmscharters.com) offers two-hour whale-watching trips ($30 adults). Two other local operators with similar trips and prices are **Newport Tradewinds** (653 SW Bay Blvd., 541/265-2101 or 800/676-7819, www. newporttradewinds.com) and **Captain's Reel Charters** (343 SW Bay Blvd., 541/265-7441 or 800/865-7441, www.captainsreel. com). In addition to a full menu of fishing excursions, these Newport operators also offer whale-watching charters.

For those who prefer to take matters into their own hands, the clamming and Dungeness crabbing are superlative in Yaquina Bay. If you haven't done this before, local tackle shops, such as the Newport Marina Store in South Beach, rent crab pots or rings and offer instruction. The best time to dig clams is at extremely low tide. At that time, look for clammers grabbing up cockles in the shallows of the bay. Tide tables are available from the chamber of commerce and many local businesses; they're also easy to find online.

## Golf

The public course closest to Newport is nine-hole **Agate Beach Golf Course** (4100 North Coast Hwy., 541/265-7331, www.agatebeachgolf.net, year-round, $36 for 18 holes), just north of town. The views of Yaquina Head alone are worth a visit.

## ★ Whale-Watching

The best company on the coast in terms of state-of-the-art equipment and natural history interpretation is **Marine Discovery Tours** (345 SW Bay Blvd., 541/265-6200 or 800/903-2628, www.marinediscovery.com, $40 adults, $25 ages 4-12). The two-hour SeaLife tour is narrated by naturalist guides and includes, depending on the time of year, whale-, seal-, and bird-watching, an oyster-bed tour, estuary and ocean exploration, and a harbor tour. The 65-foot *Discovery* features video cameras that magnify the fascinating interplay between smaller life-forms, but the real attractions can be appreciated by the naked eye. Landlubbers will especially relish the full crab pots pulled up from the deep and the resident pod of whales often visible north of Yaquina Bay off Yaquina Head.

During the prime whale-watching weeks of late December and late March, trained volunteers from Whale Watching Spoken Here (an Oregon Parks and Recreation Department program) staff the **Don A. Davis City Kiosk** in Nye Beach to answer questions and help you spot whales.

# ENTERTAINMENT AND EVENTS

In the Bayfront District, **Mariner Square** (250 SW Bay Blvd., 541/265-2206, 10am-7pm July-Aug., 10am-5pm June and Sept., usually 10am-4pm Oct.-May, $15 per attraction adults, $8 ages 5-12, three-in-one tickets $25 adults, $15 ages 5-12) is a complex of three attractions that mostly appeal to kids: **Ripley's Believe It or Not!, The Waxworks,** and the **Undersea Gardens.**

## Brewpubs

**Rogue Ales Public House** (748 SW Bay Blvd., 541/265-3188, 11am-midnight Sun.-Thurs., 11am-1am Fri.-Sat., $7-15) is a lively pub along the bay in Old Town with 35 taps and outdoor seating. In addition to pouring some of Oregon's finest ales, the public house serves seafood salads, shrimp-melt sandwiches, pizza, fish-and-chips, and seasonal fish dishes. Besides the renowned Rogue ales, there's Rogue's draft root beer—a creamy concoction laced with honey and vanilla. Another Rogue Ales brewery, called **Brewers on the Bay** (2320 OSU Dr., 541/867-3660, 11am-9pm Sun.-Thurs., 11am-10pm Fri.-Sat., $7-15), is a pub and brewery complex across Yaquina Bay, near the Oregon Coast Aquarium. This is where the actual brewing is now done; tours (3pm daily) are available.

Rogue's third local outlet is the **Rogue House of Spirits** (2122 Marine Science Dr., 541/867-3670, 2pm-9pm Sun.-Thurs., 2pm-10pm Fri.-Sat.), a distillery pub that produces rum, gin, vodka, and whiskey. The menu here is less extensive than at Rogue's brewpubs and features excellent cheese from Central Point, Oregon's Rogue Creamery. Minors are not allowed.

The **Taphouse at Nye Creek** (515 NW Coast St., 541/272-5545, http://taphouseat-nye.com, 11am-10pm Sun.-Thurs., 11am-11pm Fri.-Sat.) offers 30 beers, wines, and ciders on tap, plus a full bar, right in the thick of things in the Nye Beach neighborhood. The wood-fired pizzas here are recommended: for a dollar more, you can get truffled fries with your burger or salmon caprese sandwich.

## The Arts

Overlooking the sea in Nye Beach, the **Newport Performing Arts Center** (777 W. Olive St., 541/265-2787, www.coastarts.org), the central coast's largest performance venue, hosts local and national entertainment in the 400-seat Alice Silverman Theatre and the smaller Studio Theatre. At the same address is the **Oregon Coast Council for the Arts,** which puts out a free monthly newsletter and has ticket information on the center venues. It also has updates on the **Newport Visual Arts Center** (777 NW Beach Dr., 541/265-6540), right above the beach two blocks north at the Nye Beach turnaround. Two floors and two galleries—**Runyan Gallery** (11am-5pm Tues.-Sun.) and the **Upstairs Gallery** (noon-4pm Tues.-Sat.)—offer art education programs and exhibition space for paintings, sculpture, and other works, often with a maritime theme. All exhibits are free.

## Cinema

In addition to its impressive schedule of music, dance, drama, and other arts, the Performing Arts Center screens a series of imported and art films—the ones you probably won't find at the multiplex **Newport Cinema** (5836 N. Coast Hwy., 541/265-2111).

## Festivals and Events

The biggest bash (and one of the largest events of its kind in the country) is late February's **Newport Seafood and Wine Festival** (541/265-8801 or 800/262-7844, www.seafoodandwine.com, $8-22), which features dozens of food booths and scores of Oregon wineries serving up palate pleasers, along with music and crafts, at the **South Beach Marina** (across Yaquina Bay from the Bayfront). A huge tent joins the exhibition hall, wherein festivalgoers wash down delights from the deep with Oregon vintages. The event is open only to the 21-and-over crowd.

The second event of note is **Loyalty Days and Sea Fair** (541/961-1466, free) in early May. What began during the Depression as the Crab Festival, intended to stimulate the market for Dungeness crab, was recast during the depths of the Red Scare of the 1950s as a public expression of patriotism. Although that aspect still undergirds the events, it's really just a big community party stretching over four days, with carnival rides, veterans events, bike races, and a parade.

## FOOD

This is a town for serious diners—folks who know good food and don't mind paying a tad more for it. It's also the kind of place where wharf-side vendors supply fresh fish on the cheap. Mid-May through October, you can pick up the freshest garden produce the area has to offer, plus baked goods, honey, and other delectables, at the Lincoln County Small Farmers Association's **Saturday Farmers Market,** held in the parking area of the **Newport City Hall** (U.S. 101 and Angle St., 9am-1pm Sat. May-Oct.).

About seven miles east of the Bayfront, the **Oregon Oyster Farms** (6878 Yaquina Bay Rd., 541/265-5078, www.oregonoyster.com, 9am-5pm daily) is the only remaining commercial outlet for Yaquina Bay oysters. Visitors are welcome to observe the farming and processing of these succulent shellfish. Try oysters on the half-shell, or sample smoked oysters on a stick. To get there, follow Bay Boulevard east six miles from the Embarcadero Resort.

### Bakeries and Cafés

Down along the Bayfront is a wonderful breakfast haunt, the **Coffee House** (156 SW Bay Blvd., 541/265-6263, www.thecoffeehousenewport.com, 7am-2pm daily, $6-16). Scones, muffins, and such creative brunch fare as a wild mushroom omelet, crab cakes florentine, various crepes, meat pasties, and oysters lightly breaded with Japanese panko breadcrumbs are complemented by well-made espresso drinks. In fair weather, the outside deck is a relaxing spot for soaking up some rays while you gaze out on the harbor.

In the Nye Beach neighborhood, a charming spot for breakfast (including a good breakfast burrito) and sandwiches is **Café Stephanie** (411 Coast St., 541/265-8082, 7:30am-2pm daily, $6-11), a bustling cubbyhole with friendly service. Here both breakfast and lunch are served during open hours; consider starting your day with a bowl of smoked salmon chowder.

Nearby, the tiny ★ **Panini Bakery** (232 NW Coast St., 541/265-5033, 7am-7pm daily, sandwiches $5-12) is a great spot for a chocolate panini, a ginger scone, a slice of pizza, and the local vibe. It's the best bakery in town and has a few tables.

### Seafood

If you're hankering for a broad selection of fresh local seafood but don't need a fancy dining room to enjoy it in, ★ **Local Ocean Seafoods** (213 SE Bay Blvd., 541/574-7959, http://localocean.net, 11am-9pm Sun.-Thurs., 11am-9:30pm Fri.-Sat., $6-28) is the place for you. Part fish market, part seafood grill, this bright and bustling restaurant spotlights sustainably caught, impeccably fresh fish and offers a lively atmosphere; now there's a second-story dining area. Each item in the fish case is identified by name, where it was caught, how it was harvested, and who caught it. The menu items change depending on what's fresh, and though you can count on great fish-and-chips here, you may want to step up to the albacore tuna mignon or the fishwives seafood stew, with crab, shrimp, clams, and scallops.

Right on the bay front, with windows overlooking the active fishing port, ★ **Saffron Salmon** (859 SW Bay Blvd., 541/265-8921, http://saffronsalmon.com, 5pm-8:30pm Mon.-Tues. and Thurs., 11:30am-2:30pm and 5pm-8:30pm Fri.-Sun., $12-26) is one of Newport's finest choices for expertly prepared, sophisticated seafood. As you'd expect, the specialty is fresh wild salmon, grilled and served with shiitake mushrooms and white truffle crema, while calamari are sautéed with olive oil and red cabbage. There's also the option of prime-grade steaks and rack of lamb.

Also in the old-town harbor area, **Sharks Seafood Bar & Steamer Co.** (852 SW Bay Blvd., 541/574-0590, http://sharksseafoodbar.com, 4pm-9pm Sun.-Wed., 4pm-9:30pm Fri.-Sat., $10-25) specializes in steamed seafood.

But don't worry—this isn't tasteless health food. The Catalina bouillabaisse packs a wallop, with 1.5 pounds of seafood in every spice-filled bowl. You'll also find a savory seafood gumbo, oyster stew, and a mix of stewed and sautéed fish called a pan roast. Fresh fish gets the steam treatment—in season, try halibut, salmon, and rockfish steamed and served with the chef's special sauces. Sharks is a fun, quirky place; the proprietors provide not just dinner, but a show. Sidle up to the bar in front of the cooking area to watch the chef in action.

The Newport Bayfront is where Mohava Niemi first opened the original **Mo's** (622 SW Bay Blvd., 541/265-2979, www.moschowder.com, 11am-9pm Mon.-Thurs., 11am-10pm Fri.-Sun., $4-16) in 1946. When word got out about the good food and low prices, Mo's small, homey place soon had more business than it could handle. In response to the overflow, **Mo's Annex** (657 SW Bay Blvd., 541/265-7512, 11am-3pm Sun.-Fri., 11am-7pm Sat., $4-16) was created across the street. While both establishments feature old-fashioned favorites, such as oyster stew, fried fish, and peanut butter cream pie, the Annex bay windows have the best view.

With three tiers of seating, one of them outdoors, right above Newport's fishing docks, ★ **Clearwater Restaurant** (325 Bay Blvd, 541/272-5551, www.clearwaterrestaurant.com, 11am-9pm Mon.-Thurs. 11am-10pm Fri., 9am-10pm Sat., 9am-9pm Sun., $16-38) offers postcard views along with upscale dining. Fresh local seafood leads the menu, such as baked halibut with mango papaya salsa. You'll also find a selection of burgers and beef and lamb dishes.

There are ample opportunities to buy fresh fish or crab along the bay front in Newport. About half a mile south of the bridge, the **South Beach Fish Market** (3640 S. U.S. 101, 541/867-6800, 7am-7pm daily, $8-12) sells fresh fish, cooked and uncooked; 90 percent of what it sells comes from the Newport fishing fleet. It's a good place for the family to stop for fish-and-chips after a visit to the aquarium.

## Asian

With both indoor and outdoor seating at a prime harbor-front location, **Asiatico Waterfront Fusion Sushi** (875 SW Bay Blvd., 541/265-8387, 11:30am-2pm and 4pm-8:30pm Sun.-Thurs., 11:30am-2pm and 4pm-9pm Fri.-Sat., $11-30) serves up Newport's freshest fish and seafood in a variety of rolls, sushi, *nigiri,* and sashimi. Add in a compelling cocktail menu and you've found a great spot to experience Newport's legendary seafood.

# ACCOMMODATIONS
## $100-150

For location, you can't beat **The Whaler** (155 SW Elizabeth St., 541/265-9261 or 800/433-9444, www.whalernewport.com, $139-189). Each of the 73 rooms has a view, and some have fireplaces, wet bars, and private balconies. Guests can use the pool and exercise facilities; continental breakfast is served. Dogs are permitted in some guest rooms.

Stay right above the Bayfront harbor at **Anchor Pier Lodge** (345 SW Bay Blvd., 541/265-7829, www.marinediscovery.com, $125-199), up a long flight of stairs from street level, where you'll truly be living "above the store" (there's a gift shop down below). The rooms are simple, with wood-plank floors, but tastefully and individually decorated. Although the Bayfront can be a little noisy with carousing people and sea lions, the inn provides earplugs. Rooms that overlook the bay have balconies; they're the ones to go for.

The **Best Western Plus Agate Beach Inn** (3019 N. Coast Hwy., 541/265-9411 or 800/547-3310, www.newportbestwestern.com, $145-195) is a tall oceanfront hotel with a fine view overlooking Yaquina Head Lighthouse and Agate Beach. The rooms are comfortable standard-issue hotel rooms, and although it's a little bit of a hike down to the beach, it is one of Newport's best beaches. A sports bar and a restaurant are on-site. Pets are permitted in some guest rooms.

North of town and above a great stretch of beach, the **Moolack Shores Motel** (8835 N. U.S. 101, 541/265-2326, http://moolackshores.

com, $105-159) is a quiet spot, even though its parking area is just off the highway. The rooms are individually decorated and more than a little bit quirky, but most have good ocean views, and the beach is just down a long flight of wooden stairs from the motel.

The ★ **Sylvia Beach Hotel** (267 NW Cliff St., 541/265-5428, www.sylviabeach-hotel.com, $135-250), a favorite of many Oregonians, combines the camaraderie of a hostel with the intimate charm of a bed-and-breakfast. Built in the era when the Corvallis-to-Yaquina Bay train and seven-seater Studebaker touring cars from Portland ferried the summer folks to Nye Beach, the hotel and its National Historic Landmark designation and literary theme have attracted an enthusiastic following. The 21 guest rooms, named after different authors, are furnished with decor evocative of each respective literary legacy. The Edgar Allan Poe Room, for instance, has a pendulum guillotine blade and stuffed ravens, while the Agatha Christie Room drops such clues as shoes underneath the curtains and capsules marked "Poison" in the medicine cabinet.

Most of the rooms ("best-sellers") run $170, with several oceanfront suites ("classics") featuring a fireplace and a deck going for $235. "Novels" go for $135 (no ocean view, but still quite charming). All rates include a full breakfast and reflect double occupancy. At breakfast, you have a choice of entrées and share a table with eight other guests, so misanthropes beware. Reservations are required for dinner in the hotel's Tables of Content, where a fixed-price family-style dinner is served at 7pm daily. No smoking, pets, or radios are allowed on the premises, and small children are discouraged.

## $150-200

The **Hallmark Resort** (744 SW Elizabeth St., 541/265-2600 or 888/448-4449, www.hall-markinns.com, $189-239) is a large hotel complex sitting atop the Newport bluffs, looking westward over the Pacific and miles of sandy beach. Of the many modern hotels that share this vista, the Hallmark is one of the nicest,

with large, well-maintained guest rooms. Facilities include an indoor pool, a spa, and a restaurant. Many guest rooms are pet-friendly.

You may not find any riverboat gamblers aboard the **Newport Belle Bed & Breakfast** (2126 SE OSU Dr., 541/867-6290, www.new-portbelle.com, mid-Feb.-Sept., $165-175), a sternwheeler designed as a floating inn, but this 97-foot-long B&B moored on the H Dock of the Newport Marina evokes the ambience of the sternwheeler heyday. Choose from five generous staterooms, each with its own personality and private bath. Most have fabulous vistas of the bustling marina and bridge area. In the evening, guests can retire to their staterooms, enjoy the open afterdeck, or socialize in the main salon, where a gourmet breakfast is served every morning. Children and smoking are not permitted; pets are allowed in one room. Soft-soled shoes are required.

The **Embarcadero Resort** (1000 SE Bay Blvd., 541/265-8521 or 800/547-4779, www.embarcadero-resort.com, $180-250) is bay-front but not beachfront; it overlooks Yaquina Bay and the soaring bay bridge, arguably one of the best views in Oregon. The Embarcadero has an assortment of suites and townhouses (including many timeshare units) with full kitchens and fireplaces. Facilities include an indoor pool, a sauna, two outdoor hot tubs, a restaurant and bar, a private dock, and boat rentals.

If you want to get away from it all, **Little Creek Cove Condominiums** (3641 NW Oceanview Dr., 541/265-8587 or 800/294-8025, www.littlecreekcove.com, $159-259) is a small condo resort that might be what you're looking for. Little Creek Cove resort is two miles north of Newport, perched just above an isolated stretch of beach. You have a choice of studio, one-, and two-bedroom units, each with a private deck, full kitchen, and fireplace.

## Over $200

**Elizabeth Street Inn** (232 SW Elizabeth St., 541/265-9400 or 877/265-9400, www.eliza-bethstreetinn.com, $210-260), in the Nye Beach neighborhood, sits on a bluff overlooking the ocean. All of the spacious rooms in this newer property face the ocean and have private balconies. They come fully equipped with fireplaces, fridges, microwaves, and coffeemakers. Guests also get a complimentary continental breakfast and have use of the indoor pool, spa, and fitness room. Pets are permitted in some rooms.

At the center of Nye Beach dining and arts activities, the **Inn at Nye Beach** (729 NW Coast St., 541/265-2477, www.innatnyebeach.com, $200-254) is a stylish and comfortable new hotel just steps from Pacific beaches. Rooms have gas fireplaces and balconies or patios, and guests share a beach-view infinity hot tub and deck, with nightly bonfires on the beach. Contact the inn to learn about one- and two-bedroom condos that are part of the same development.

## Camping

The campgrounds at Beverly Beach State Park and South Beach State Park are among the most popular on the Oregon coast. Their proximity to Newport, the absence of other camping in the area, and the special features of each explain their appeal.

**Beverly Beach State Park** (information 541/265-9278 or 800/452-5687, reservations 800/452-5687, www.reserveamerica.com, $21 tents, $31-33 RVs, $47-57 yurts, $6 hiker-biker) is huge multiple-loop campground set seven miles north of Newport on the east side of the highway in a mossy glade. A pedestrian tunnel passes under the highway and leads to a long, wide beach that is, unfortunately, directly bordered by the road. Devil's Punchbowl and Otter Crest are one and two miles up the highway, respectively.

It's just a hop over the sand dunes to the beach at **South Beach State Park** (information 541/867-4715 or 800/551-6949, reservations 800/452-5687, www.reserveamerica.com, $21 tents, $31 RVs, $47-57 yurts, $6 hiker-biker), just south of the Yaquina Bay Bridge. The long beach has opportunities for fishing, agate hunting, windsurfing (for experts), horseback riding, and hiking; sign up in advance (541/867-6500) for kayak tours of nearby Beaver Creek.

# INFORMATION

The **Greater Newport Chamber of Commerce** (555 SW U.S. 101, 541/265-8801 or 800/262-7844, http://newportchamber.org, 8:30am-5pm Mon.-Fri.) has lots of literature, but the most helpful website for visitors is the chamber's visitors website (http://discovernewport.com).

A public radio station, **KLCO,** a local repeater station for Eugene's KLCC, is heard on your dial at 90.5 FM. The **Newport Public Library** (541/265-2153, 10am-9pm Mon.-Wed., 10am-6pm Thurs.-Sat., noon-5pm Sun.) is at 35 NW Nye Street. The **post office** (310 SW 2nd St., 541/265-5542) is one block west of the highway.

**Samaritan Pacific Communities Hospital** (930 SW Abbey St., 541/265-2244) is the central coast's only major hospital.

## GETTING THERE AND AROUND

**Lincoln County Transit** (541/265-4900, www.co.lincoln.or.us/transit) runs buses, several times daily Monday-Saturday, north to Lincoln City and south to Yachats, with numerous stops en route through Newport. In addition, the county also offers the Coast to Valley Express, a four-times-daily bus service to and from Corvallis (with Greyhound) and Albany (with Greyhound and Amtrak) in the Willamette Valley.

A **shuttle bus** (http://discovernewport.com, 8am-5:30pm daily) travels up and down the length of Newport on streets just east and west of U.S. 101, going as far south as the Newport Business Plaza in South Beach and north to NE 73rd Street. The wheelchair-accessible bus is equipped with a bike rack. It's free for those with a pass from their Newport hotel and $1 for others. The route is not straightforward; it helps to have a map and schedule (www.newportchamber.org).

Newport's car rental agency of choice is **Enterprise Rent-A-Car** (533 E. Olive St., 541/574-1999).

# Waldport and Vicinity

Originally a stronghold of the Alsea Native Americans, Waldport also has had incarnations as a gold rush town, salmon-canning center, and lumber port. This town of about 2,000, whose name means "forest port" in German, is pretty quiet today, with a nondescript main drag that gives no hint of the surrounding beaches and prime fishing and crabbing spots. Waldport provides a low-cost alternative to the big-name destinations; you won't have to fight for a parking spot or make reservations months in advance.

## SIGHTS AND RECREATION
### Ona Beach State Park
Beaver Creek flows into the ocean at **Ona Beach State Park** (800/551-6949, day-use only). A 0.25-mile trail starts at the parking area and crosses a footbridge over the creek before landing at a fine stretch of beach.

### Brian Booth State Park
**Beaver Creek State Natural Area** runs through **Brian Booth State Park**

(541/563-6413, visitors center 10am-4pm daily June-Aug., noon-4pm daily Sept.-May); the visitors center is two miles east of Ona Beach, up Beaver Creek Road. This coastal wetland area has good paddling on ranger-led kayak tours (http://store.oregonstateparks.org, 8:30am Thurs.-Mon. July-Aug., reservations required, $20) and wildlife-watching, both from the creek and from a viewing blind that's just a short walk from the road. If you're not prepared to paddle, a seven-mile network of hiking trails starts near the visitors center.

### Seal Rock State Recreation Site
Four miles north of Waldport, **Seal Rock** (800/551-6949, day-use only) attracts beachcombers and agate hunters as well as folks who come to explore the tide pools and observe the seals on offshore rocks. The park's name derives from a seal-shaped rock in the cluster of interesting formations in the tidewater. The picnic area is set in a shady area behind the sandy beach. During Christmas and spring breaks, the volunteers of Whale Watching

A short trail leads to rarely crowded Ona Beach.

Spoken Here are on hand to help visitors spot passing grays from 10am to 1pm.

## Alsea Bay Bridge Historical Interpretive Center

The small museum and visitors center known as the **Alsea Bay Bridge Historical Interpretive Center** (620 NW Spring St., 541/563-2133 www.oregonstateparks.org, 9am-4pm Tues.-Sat. free), operated by the Oregon Parks and Recreation Department and Waldport Chamber of Commerce, stands along the highway on the south side of the river. Exhibits here tell the story of how the sleek 1991 bridge replaced the aging Conde McCullough span across the bay, which has since been demolished. Displays about transportation methods along the central coast since the 1800s, information on the Alsea Native American people, and a telescope trained on the seals and waterfowl on the bay are worth a quick stop. On summer weekends, Oregon Parks and Recreation gives clamming and crabbing demonstrations (locations and times vary according to the tides; see the website for a calendar).

## Drift Creek Wilderness

Seven miles east of Waldport are the nearly 5,800 acres of the **Drift Creek Wilderness,** which protects the Coast Range's largest remaining stands of old-growth rainforest. Here you can see giant Sitka spruce and western hemlock hundreds of years old, nourished by up to 120 inches of rain per year. These trees are the "climax forest" in the Douglas fir ecosystem. They seldom reach old-growth status because the timber industry tends to replant fir seedlings after logging operations. The forest provides habitat for spotted owls along with bald eagles, Roosevelt elk, and black bears. Drift Creek sustains wild runs of chinook, steelhead, and coho salmon, which come up the Alsea River.

Steep ridges and their drainages, as well as small meadows, make up the topography, which is accessed via a couple of hiking trails. The trailhead closest to Waldport is the 3.5-mile **Harris Ranch Trail,** which descends 1,200 feet to a meadow near Drift Creek. The local access to Harris Ranch Trail and the conjoining Horse Creek Trail is via Highway 34; turn north off 34 at the Alsea River crossing, seven miles east of Waldport. Here, pick up Risely Creek Road (Forest Rd. 3446) and Forest Road 346 to the trailhead.

## Fishing

Waldport's recreational raison d'être is fishing. World-class clamming and Dungeness crabbing in Alsea Bay and the Alsea River's salmon, steelhead, and cutthroat trout runs account for a high percentage of visits to the area. Before commercial fishing on the river was shut down in 1957, as much as 137,000 pounds of chinook were netted in a season. The wild fall chinook run remains healthy and starts up in late August. Catch-and-release for sea-run cutthroats starts in mid-August, while steelhead are in the river December to March. Crabbers without boats can take advantage of the Port of Waldport docks. **Dock of the Bay Marina** (1245 NE Mill St., 541/563-2003) rents and sells crabbing and fishing supplies and can guide you to the best spots.

## FOOD

Dining options in Waldport are limited. We recommend heading about 10 miles south to Yachats for dinner. If you just need a loaf of artisanal bread or a pastry and time it right, **Pacific Sourdough** (740 NE Mill St., 541/563-3044, 10am-3pm Thurs. and Sat.) is the place to go. The bakers sell their bread to several restaurants in Yachats.

## ACCOMMODATIONS

Midway between Waldport and Yachats, the **Terry-a-While Motel** (7160 SW U.S. 101, 541/563-3377, www.terry-a-while.com, 3-night minimum summer, 2 nights winter, no pets, $70-200) has simple guest rooms that range in style from modern to vintage and in size from basic budget motel size to two-bedroom units with kitchens. Although the guest rooms are not extravagantly furnished, they all have decks with nice views and easy access to the beach.

The vintage **Cape Cod Cottages** (4150 SW U.S. 101, 541/563-2106, www.capecod-cottagesonline.com, $99-235) offer one- and two-bedroom oceanfront units with complete kitchens, fireplaces, spectacular views, and private decks. The least expensive units are basic motel rooms with no decks. A three-night minimum stay is required in summer.

The historic **Cliff House** (1450 Adahi Rd., 541/563-2506, www.cliffhouseoregon.com, $125-225) may appear rustic, but in fact this is a lovingly restored historic home, and the location can't be beat. Four guest rooms, some with whirlpools, are decorated with antiques; even the woodstoves are period. No pets are allowed, and children are best left home with the grandparents or a sitter.

### Camping

Two campgrounds sit about four miles south of Waldport on U.S. 101 along the beach. **Beachside State Park** (information 541/563-3220, reservations 800/452-5687, www.reserveamerica.com, $21 tents, $31 RVs, $47 yurts, $57 pet-friendly yurt) is between the beach and the highway (some sites get highway noise) not far from Alsea Bay and the Alsea River. This is a paradise for rock fishers, surfcasters, clammers, and crabbers. Beachside fills up fast, so reserve early for space Memorial Day-Labor Day.

Half a mile south of Beachside, the Siuslaw National Forest's **Tillicum Beach** (877/444-6777, www.recreation.gov, reservations strongly advised in summer, $26 tents, $33 RVs with electricity) is set right along the ocean. U.S. Forest Service roads from here

access Coast Range fishing streams. You'll also appreciate the strip of vegetation blocking the cool evening winds that whip up off the ocean.

Should Beachside and Tillicum be filled to overflowing, you might want to set up a base camp in the Coast Range along Highway 34—especially if you have fishing or hiking in the Drift Creek Wilderness in mind. Just go east of Waldport 17 miles on Highway 34 to the Siuslaw National Forest's **Blackberry Campground** (reservations 877/444-6777, www.recreation.gov, $24). The 33 sites are open year-round; most are right on the river. A boat ramp, flush toilets, and piped water are on-site.

## INFORMATION

The Waldport Chamber of Commerce operates a **visitors center** (620 NW Spring St., 541/563-2133, www.waldport-chamber.com, 9am-4pm Tues.-Sat.) in the Alsea Bay Bridge Historical Interpretive Center, just south of the river. The **Siuslaw National Forest-Waldport Ranger Station** (1130 Forestry Lane, 541/563-8400) can provide information on area camping and hiking, including the trails in the Drift Creek Wilderness.

## GETTING THERE

Highway 34 runs east from Waldport, following the Alsea River for several miles before veering northeast to Corvallis, about 65 miles away. This is one of the prettiest (and slowest) routes between the coast and the Willamette Valley.

The **Lincoln County Transit** (541/265-4900, www.co.lincoln.or.us/transit) buses run four times a day Monday-Saturday between Yachats and Newport.

# Yachats and Cape Perpetua

Yachats (pronounced YAH-hots) is derived from an Alsea word meaning "dark waters at the foot of the mountain." The phrase aptly describes the location of this picturesque resort village of 700 people, clustered on the hillsides and coastal shelf beside the Yachats River mouth in the shadow of Cape Perpetua. Word of mouth has helped to spread the popularity of Yachats as a place for a quiet getaway and a base for enjoying the 2,700-acre Cape Perpetua Scenic Area and nearby beaches.

## SIGHTS AND RECREATION
### ★ Cape Perpetua

The most notable sight near Yachats, indeed on the whole central coast, is the view from 803-foot-high Cape Perpetua. The name derives from Captain Cook's sighting of the promontory on March 7, 1778, St. Perpetua's Day. The road to the top of the cape affords 150 miles of north-to-south visibility from the top of the headland. On a clear day, you can also see nearly 40 miles out to sea.

Prior to hiking the 23 miles of foot trails or driving to the top of the cape, stop off at the **Cape Perpetua Visitors Center** (541/547-3289, 9:30am-4:30pm mid-June-Aug., 10am-4pm daily Sept.-mid-June, Northwest Forest Pass or $5 per car), three miles south of Yachats on the east side of the highway. A picture window framing a bird's-eye view of rockbound coast, along with exhibits on forestry, marinelife, and monster storms, provide an introduction to the region. Stick around to watch the excellent 15-minute film about Oregon's intertidal biome. During the summer, rangers give talks and lead hikes; call for the schedule.

### HIKING

Pick up a map or pamphlet about such trails as Cummins Creek, Giant Spruce, and Restless Waters, as well as directions for the drive (or stiff hike) to the summit of the cape, from which you can take the 0.25-mile **Whispering Spruce Trail** through the grounds of a former World War II Coast Guard lookout built by the Civilian Conservation Corps (CCC) in 1933. The southern views from the crest take

Cape Perpetua

in the highway and headlands as far south as Coos Bay. Halfway along the path, you'll come to a Works Progress Administration-built rock hut called the West Shelter, which makes a lofty perch for whale-watching. Beyond this ridgetop aerie, the curtain of trees parts to reveal fantastic views of the shoreline between Yachats and Cape Foulweather.

To begin your auto ascent, from the visitors center drive 100 yards north on U.S. 101 and look for the steep, winding spur road (Forest Rd. 55) on the right. As you climb, you'll notice large Sitka spruce trees abutting the road. Halfway up the two-mile route, you'll come to a Y in the road. Take a hard left and follow the road another mile to the top of Cape Perpetua. If you miss the left turn and go straight ahead, you'll soon find yourself on a 22-mile loop through the Coast Range to Yachats. Along the way, placards annotate forest ecology.

If you'd rather hike to the top of the cape, the awe-inspiring 1.5-mile **Saint Perpetua Trail** from the Cape Perpetua visitors center to the summit is of moderate difficulty, gaining 600 feet in elevation. En route, placards explain the role of wind, erosion, and fire in forest succession in this mixed-conifer ecosystem.

The actual cape is only half the attraction at Cape Perpetua. At least as fascinating are the rocky coast and its tide pools, churns, and spouting horns of water. Just north of the turnoff for the top of Cape Perpetua (Forest Rd. 55) and U.S. 101 is the turnout for **Devil's Churn,** on the west side of the highway. Here the tides have cut a deep fissure in a basalt embankment on the shore. You can observe the action from a vertigo-inducing overlook high above or take the easy switchbacking trail down to the water's edge. While watching the white-water torrents in this foaming cistern, beware of "sneaker waves," particularly if you venture beyond the boundaries of the **Trail of the Restless Waters.** The highlights here are the spouting horns and acres of tide pools. All along this stretch of the coast, many trees appear to be leaning away from the ocean, as if bent by storms. This illusion is caused by

salt-laden westerlies drying out and killing the buds on the exposed side of the tree, leaving growth only on the leeward branches.

Another hike from the Cape Perpetua visitors center goes down to a geological blowhole (called a spouting horn), where seawater is funneled between rocks and explodes into spray. This is the **Captain Cook Trail,** which runs six miles through a dense wind-carved forest and the remains of an old CCC camp under U.S. 101 to an ancient lava deposit on the shore. Given enough wave action, water bubbles up through fissures in the basalt. There are also Native American shell middens built up from 300 to 2,000 years ago in the area.

## State Parks and Coastal Waysides

In this part of the coast, state parks and viewpoints abound with attractions. There's so much to see here that keeping your eyes on the road in this heavily traveled section is a challenge.

A mile north of Yachats, **Smelt Sands State Recreation Site** gives access to tide pools and the 0.75-mile **804 Trail**, which follows the rocky shore north to a broad, sandy beach, where it continues along the beach all the way north to Waldport (about seven miles). To the south, the 804 Trail cuts across the Adobe Lodge's lawn and passes a residential area on the way to the **Yachats State Recreation Area.** An alternate route to the wave-battered recreation area is from 2nd Street in downtown Yachats.

On the south bank of the Yachats River is a short but beautiful beach loop off U.S. 101 (going south, look for the "Beach Access" sign). The road runs between the landscaped grounds of beach houses and resorts on one side and the foamy sea on the other. A wide beach, tide pools, and blowholes on the bank by the river's mouth are a special treat.

A mile south of Cape Perpetua, **Neptune State Park** has a beautiful beach and is near the 9,300-acre **Cummins Creek Wilderness** east of U.S. 101. Just north of Neptune Park, Forest Road 1050 leads east to the Cummins

Creek Trailhead. Half a mile south, gravel Forest Road 1051 can take you to a point where a moderately difficult 2.5-mile hike leads to Cummins Ridge Trailhead. This pathway has some of the last remaining coastal old-growth Sitka spruce stands. Get maps and detailed directions for these and other area trails at the Cape Perpetua visitors center.

Close by, there's a chance to explore tide pools and sometimes observe harbor seals at **Strawberry Hill.** Scenic shorelines can also be found in the next few miles farther south at **Stonesfield Beach State Recreation Site** and **Muriel O. Ponsler State Scenic Viewpoint.**

## ENTERTAINMENT AND EVENTS

The little village of Yachats seems to be busy with some festival or other event just about every weekend. For a full schedule, see the local chamber of commerce website (www.yachats.org). What follows are some highlights.

In late March, the chamber-sponsored **Original Yachats Arts and Crafts Fair** (Yachats Commons, U.S. 101 and W. 4th St., 541/547-3530 or 800/929-0477, free) exhibits the work of some 75 Pacific Northwest artists and artisans.

Yachats pulls out all the stops for the **Fourth of July.** Events include the short and silly La De Da Parade at noon, a pie and ice cream social, lots of live music, and a fireworks show on the bay when darkness falls.

Fall is mushroom season on the coast, and the **Yachats Village Mushroom Fest** (541/547-3530 or 800/929-0477), held the third weekend in October, showcases the native mushrooms that abound in these temperate rainforests. Activities over the weekend include the fungi feasts, mushroom cooking and growing lessons, talks on forest ecology, and guided mushroom walks.

## SHOPPING

Yachats has long been a center for artists and bohemians, and for proof of this you need go no farther than **Earthworks Gallery** (2222 U.S. 101 N., 541/547-4300, http://earthworks-galleries.net, 10am-5pm daily). This excellent gallery displays the work of local painters, glass artists, and jewelers, as well as high-quality crafts. **Touchstone Gallery** (2118 U.S. 101 N., 541/547-4121, 10am-5pm daily) is another gallery with unique Pacific Northwest arts and crafts.

## FOOD

For a town its size, Yachats has particularly good restaurant choices. Start the day at **Green Salmon Bakery and Cafe** (220 U.S. 101, 541/547-3077, www.thegreensalmon.com, 7:30am-2:30pm daily, $3-12) for fresh breads and good pastries plus soup and sandwiches for lunch. Lines can be long and slow-moving at the counter, so come equipped with patience; the upside is that you'll probably be waiting with a bunch of friendly locals.

Stop by ★ **Yachats Brewing** (348 U.S. 101 N., 541/547-3884, http://yachatsbrewing.com, 11:30am-9pm Mon.-Thurs., 11:30am-10pm Fri.-Sat., 10am-7pm Sun., $10-16) for a pint or a meal. The beer, including a sour made from local salal berries, is perfect after a hike or beach walk, and the food, including many fermented veggie dishes, is some of the best, and certainly most creative, in town.

The carefully restored but easygoing and family-friendly **Drift Inn Pub** (124 U.S. 101 N., 541/547-4477, http://the-drift-inn.com, 8am-10pm daily summer, 8am-9pm daily winter, $12-32) offers seafood dishes, big salads, fish-and-chips, and other well-prepared pub grub in a relaxed atmosphere. There's often really good live music here, making this a lively spot whether you're here to eat or to quaff a pint or two. If you never want to leave, rooms are available for rent ($80-150) upstairs.

If you are looking for the classic fresh seafood experience, go to tiny **Luna Sea Fish House** (153 NW U.S. 101, 541/547-4794, www.lunaseafishhouse.com, 8am-9pm daily summer, 8am-8pm daily winter, $10-17), a seafood restaurant owned by a local fisherman. Don't let the simple decor put you off; the food here is *good*. Using local ingredients, and particularly locally caught (not farmed) fish, Luna Sea offers superlative fish-and-chips and fish tacos. Breakfast omelets are also top-notch.

**Heidi's** (84 Beach St., 541/547-4409, 5pm-8pm Wed.-Sun., $17-22) is a quintessential Yachats business. This tiny Italian café serves brick oven-baked pizza and homey Italian comfort food, including cioppino and butternut squash lasagna, in a modest little space that fronts the bay. Everything is homemade and served with charm and care. Takeout and dinner delivery are also available.

The simply decorated bay-view **Ona Restaurant** (131 U.S. 101 N., 541/547-6627, www.onarestaurant.com, 4pm-8:30pm Mon.-Fri., 11am-8:30pm Sat.-Sun. winter, 11am-8:30pm daily summer, $12-37) serves grilled seafood, meatloaf, steak, and fresh pasta. For appetizers, you can choose between oysters, shrimp, clams, and crab cakes. Ona has a good happy hour (4pm-6pm Sun.-Thurs.), which is a good time to check out its offerings without emptying your wallet.

On a bluff overlooking Smelt Sands Beach is the glass-enclosed **Adobe Resort** (1555 U.S. 101 N., 541/547-3141, 8am-2:30pm and 5pm-9pm Mon.-Sat., 9am-1pm and 5pm-9pm Sun., $16-27). Two side-by-side semicircular dining rooms, with windows on the crashing surf, are a great place to start the day for breakfast or end it with a romantic evening meal, with such favorites as grilled oysters and steaks. Ask about the loft, where elevated coastal views provide photo ops; this is the perfect place to nurse a drink. A Sunday champagne brunch ($20) is served.

## ACCOMMODATIONS
### $50-100

Facing onto the beach loop south of town, the **Yachats Inn** (331 U.S. 101, 541/547-3456 or 888/270-3456, www.yachatsinn.com, $94-150) offers basic summer shelter with unfussy rooms that have little decks and TVs but no phones, though some have kitchens and fireplaces. There's great access to the beach. Suites with full kitchens and fireplaces are newer, but they are set back from the beach and don't permit dogs. An indoor pool overlooks the beach.

For those looking for budget prices close to the center of town, try **Rock Park Cottages** (431 W. 2nd St., 541/547-3214, www.sweethomerentals.com, $50-95), adjacent to Yachats State Recreation Area. Consisting of five rustic cottages arranged around a courtyard, Rock Park has to be one of the better bargains on

Enjoy a beer and a plate of pickled veggies at Yachats Brewing.

the coast. The kitchens are well equipped, and the vintage cottages couldn't be better located.

Set back from U.S. 101 with a short walk to the beach, the **Dublin House Motel** (251 W. 7th St., 541/547-3703 or 866/922-4287, www.dublinhousemotel.com, $84-114) offers standard motel rooms and ocean views, each room having a microwave, a fridge, a coffeemaker, and cable TV; some kitchen units are also available. The indoor heated pool is especially nice in the winter months.

## $100-150

A little north of the town center, the imposing **Adobe Resort** (155 U.S. 101 N., 541/547-3141, www.adoberesort.com, $175 ocean view, $135 hillside view) overlooks Smelt Sands Beach. Although the Adobe isn't what you'd call luxurious, it is one of the few full-service resorts in the area, with an on-site restaurant. All units have fridges, microwaves, satellite TV, DVD players, and a phone with voice mail. Pets are accepted in some guest rooms. Two-bedroom hot tub suites are 1,400 square feet and have all the comforts of a small home.

The **Fireside Motel** (1881 U.S. 101, 541/547-3636 or 800/336-3573, www.firesidemotel.com, $119-189) is known for its pet-friendly policies. The more expensive rooms have fireplaces, balconies, and views of tide pools; the cheaper rooms are pretty basic, but you're still located right next to a beachside trail.

**Deane's Oceanfront Lodge** (7365 U.S. 101, 541/547-3321, www.deaneslodge.com, $109-155) is about halfway between Yachats and Waldport. The rooms are well-kept but not fancy; the least expensive don't share the great ocean views afforded by the top-end rooms. Pets are permitted in some rooms.

## Over $200

A mile north of Yachats, above a thrust of wave-pounded tide pools, ★ **Overleaf Lodge** (2055 U.S. 101, 541/547-4880 or 800/338-0507, www.overleaflodge.com, $221-515) offers the nicest rooms in the Yachats area. Most guest rooms have balconies, hot tubs, and fireplaces, and all have fantastic

views. Rates include a breakfast buffet plus access to a fitness area. A 3,000-square-foot spa has treatment rooms, steam rooms, and saunas, plus ocean-view hot tubs. Adjacent to the lodge are six cottages ($295-445) tucked into the forest. With two to four bedrooms, these charming units with Craftsman-style decor have full kitchens and everything a family or small group will need for a great beach vacation.

## Vacation Rentals

If you'd rather settle into a house, check out **Yachats Village Rentals** (541/547-3501 or 888/288-5077, www.97498.com), which offers a varied stable of vacation homes ($140-350) for long- or short-term rental.

## Camping

Set along Cape Creek in the Cape Perpetua Scenic Area, the Forest Service's **Cape Perpetua Campground** (reservations 877/444-6777, www.recreation.gov, May-Sept., $24), with 38 sites for tents, trailers, or motor homes up to 22 feet long, is a great base for exploring the wonderful Cape Perpetua area. Trails run from the campground to the top of the cape and to the beach. Flush toilets and piped water are available.

## INFORMATION

The **Yachats Area Chamber of Commerce** (241 U.S. 101, 541/547-3530 or 800/929-0477, www.yachats.org, 10am-5:30pm daily mid-Mar.-Sept., Fri.-Sun. Oct.-mid-Mar.) has a central location on the highway (next to Clark's Market) and enthusiastic staff. Ask them about fishing, rockhounding, bird-watching, and beachcombing in the area.

## GETTING THERE

The bus stop is also in the parking lot of the **bead shop** (U.S. 101 and W. 3rd St.). Here you can catch **Lincoln County Transit** buses (541/265-4900, www.co.lincoln.or.us/transit), which run four times a day Monday-Saturday between Yachats and Newport, with a link to Lincoln City.

# Florence and Vicinity

If you study the map of the central Oregon coast, you'll see that Florence is oriented along the Siuslaw River; a spit of dunes reaches up from the south, barring quick access from downtown to the ocean. But don't dismiss this riverfront town for its lack of oceanfront real estate: The views onto the river are plenty scenic, and Old Town is charming and easy to navigate on foot.

## SIGHTS

If first and last impressions are enduring, Florence is truly memorable. A short way to the north of town, U.S. 101 passes over Heceta Head, with great views onto the lighthouse there. As you leave the city to the south, a graceful bridge over the Siuslaw ushers you away.

The Siuslaw River Bridge is an impressive example of Conde McCullough's Works Progress Administration-built spans. The Egyptian obelisks and art deco styling of McCullough's designs are complemented by the views to the west of the coruscating sand dunes. To the east, the riverside panorama of Florence's Old Town beckons for further investigation.

Old Town itself is a tasteful restoration, with all manner of shops and restaurants and an inviting boardwalk along the river. The quickest access to the beach and dunes is south of the bridge via South Jetty Road.

### ★ Heceta Head Lighthouse and Devil's Elbow

Twelve miles north of Florence, **Heceta Head Lighthouse** (541/547-3416, www.oregonstateparks.org, tours 11am-3pm daily summer, 11am-2pm daily winter, $5 day-use) is dramatically situated above a lovely cove at the mouth of Cape Creek and wedged into the flanks of 1,000-foot-high Heceta Head. The whitewashed lighthouse was completed in 1894 and beautifully restored in 2013; it's

still in use, beaming the strongest light on the Oregon coast from its perch 205 feet above the pounding surf. A little below the lighthouse is Heceta House, where the lighthouse keepers used to live. Today, it serves both as a **gift shop** (11am-6pm daily Memorial Day-Sept.) and the **Heceta Head Lighthouse B&B** (92072 U.S. 101, 541/547-3696 or 866/547-3696, www.hecetalighthouse.com, $215-355). An easy 0.5-mile trail leads up from the lighthouse's picnic and parking area to the tower; a trail network stretches 7 miles. Other than the day-use fee, admission and tours are free.

Just south of the lighthouse, the graceful arc of Conde McCullough's Cape Creek Bridge spans a chasm more than 200 feet deep. From the lighthouse parking lot, a trail leads down to where Cape Creek meets the beach at **Devil's Elbow State Park.** Be conscious of tides here if you climb along the rocks adjoining the beach.

Heceta Head is said to be the most photographed lighthouse in the country; that may be difficult to verify, but it's impossible to quibble with the magnificent sight of the gleaming white tower and outbuildings on the headland, particularly when viewed from a set of highway pullouts just south of the bridge. The vistas from the lighthouse and network of trails on the headland are no less dramatic: See murres, tufted puffins, and other seabirds as well as sea lions on the rock islands below; bald eagles soaring overhead; and in spring, northbound female gray whales and their calves as they pass close to shore. A trail leading to the north side of Heceta Head offers views to Cape Perpetua, 10 miles to the north.

### ★ Sea Lion Caves

Eleven miles north of Florence, you can descend into a massive sea cave to observe the only U.S. mainland rookery of Steller sea lions (*Eumetopias jubatus*). **Sea Lion Caves** (91560 U.S. 101, 541/547-3111, www.sealioncaves.

com, 9am-5pm daily, closed Thanksgiving and Christmas, $14 adults, $13 seniors, $8 ages 5-12, free under age 5) is home to a herd that averages 200 individuals, although the numbers change from season to season. These animals occupy the cave during the fall and winter, which are thus the prime times to visit. The Steller sea lions you'll see at those times are cows, yearlings, and immature bulls. In spring and summer, they breed and raise their young on the rock ledges just outside the cave. In addition, California sea lions (*Zalophus californianus*), common all along the Pacific coast, are found at Sea Lion Caves from late fall to early spring.

Enter Sea Lion Caves through the gift shop on U.S. 101. A steep downhill walk reveals stunning perspectives of the coastal cliffs as well as several kinds of gulls and cormorants that nest here. The final leg of the descent is by an elevator that drops an additional 208 feet. After stepping off the lift into the cave, your eyes adjust to the gloomy subterranean light, and you'll see sea lions on the rock shelves amid the surging water inside the enormous cave. Flash photography is forbidden, so study your camera's settings if you want to take pictures inside. You have a better chance of seeing these animals inside during

fall and winter. A set of stairs leads up to a view of Heceta Head Lighthouse through an opening in the cave.

Steller sea lions were referred to as *lobos marinos* (sea wolves) in early Spanish mariners' accounts of their 16th-century West Coast voyages, and their doglike yelps might explain why. You'll notice several shades of color in the herd, which has to do with the progressive lightening of their coats with age. Males sometimes weigh more than a ton, and dominate the scene with macho posturings to scare off rivals for harems of as many as two dozen cows. Their protection as an endangered species enrages many commercial anglers, who claim that the sea lions take a significant bite out of fishing revenues by preying on salmon. In any case, the close-up view of these huge sea mammals in the cavernous enclaves of their natural habitat should not be missed—despite an odor not unlike sweat-soaked sneakers.

If you can't observe the animals to your satisfaction in the cave, or if you want a free look from a distance, go 0.25 miles north of the concession entrance to the "rockwork" turnout, where the herd sometimes populates the rocky ledges several hundred feet below. It's also a good place to snap a shot of the

Observe the only U.S. mainland rookery of Steller sea lions at Sea Lion Caves.

picturesque Heceta Head Lighthouse across the cove to the north from the turnout.

## Darlingtonia Botanical Gardens

Three miles north up the Coast Highway from Florence, in an area noted for dune access and freshwater lakes, are the **Darlingtonia Botanical Gardens** (east side of U.S. 101, 5 miles north of Florence, 800/551-6949, www.oregonstateparks.org, free). In a sylvan grove of spruce and alder is a series of wooden platforms that guide you through a bog where carnivorous *Darlingtonia californica* plants thrive. Shaped like a serpent's head, the *Darlingtonia* is variously referred to as the cobra orchid, cobra lily, or pitcher plant.

The plant produces a sweet smell that invites insects to crawl through an opening into a hollow chamber beneath the plant's hood. Inside, thin transparent "windows" allow light to shine inside the chamber, confusing the bug as to where the exit is. As the insect crawls around in search of an escape, downward-pointing hairs within the enclosure inhibit its movement to freedom. Eventually, the tired-out bug falls to the bottom of the stem, where it is digested. The plant needs the nutrients from the trapped insects to compensate for the lack of sustenance supplied by its small root system. If you still have an appetite after witnessing this carnage, you might want to enjoy lunch at one of the shaded picnic tables.

## Siuslaw Pioneer Museum

To fill yourself in on the early history of Florence and the Siuslaw River Valley and to get some notion of Native American and pioneer life, spend an hour or so at the **Siuslaw Pioneer Museum** (278 Maple St., 541/997-7884, www.siuslawpioneermuseum.com, noon-4pm daily May-Sept., noon-4pm Tues.-Sun. Feb.-Apr. and Oct.-Dec., $4 adults, free under age 17). You'll find it in Old Town in a renovated school building dating from 1905. Along with exhibits on early logging and farming, read an account of how the U.S.

government double-crossed the Siuslaw people, who sold their land to the feds and never received the promised recompense. The museum can also set you loose on a walking tour of historic Old Town buildings.

## Jessie M. Honeyman Memorial State Park

**Jessie M. Honeyman Memorial State Park** (84505 U.S. 101 S., information 541/997-3641, reservations 800/452-5687, Oregon Coast Passport or $5 day-use), three miles south of Florence, has a spectacular dune-scape and then some. Come here in May when the rhododendrons bloom along the short, sinuous road heading to the parking lot. A short walk west of the lot brings you to a 150-foot-high dune overlooking Cleawox Lake, which is a good place for a swim in the summer. From the top of this dune, look westward across the expanse of sand, marsh, and remnants of forest at the blue Pacific some two miles away. This is also a popular place to camp.

## South Jetty

The northern boundary of the Oregon Dunes National Recreation Area is at the **South Jetty** (Northwest Forest Pass or $5 parking), where the Siuslaw River flows into the Pacific Ocean. May-September and on all weekends and holidays, the beach at the South Jetty is closed to motor vehicles, and even though there are no marked trails, it's a great place to explore the dunes in near solitude. The road into the jetty has several staging areas for off-highway vehicles; during the summer months, the area south of the road is open to motor vehicles. South Jetty Road is 0.5 miles south of the Siuslaw River Bridge.

## SPORTS AND RECREATION

**Huckleberry picking** is an attraction just outside Florence. Some prime pickings are found about five miles north of Florence along the Sutton Creek Trail, which begins in the Sutton campground just off U.S. 101. During late summer or fall, these berries flourish below the dense canopy of shore pines.

## Hiking

You'll find incredibly scenic hiking in the area around **Carl G. Washburne State Park,** 14 miles north of Florence on U.S. 101. About a mile south of the park entrance, find the parking area for the **Hobbit Trail** on the east side of the highway. This salal-lined trail winds 0.4 miles through dense forest thickets of pine, fir, and rhododendrons to the secluded three-mile-long beach. From the same trailhead, another path takes off uphill to the **Heceta Head Lighthouse.** In its 1.75-mile run, the trail gains quite a bit of elevation and passes some outstanding viewpoints. Also starting at the same U.S. 101 parking area, the **China Creek Trail** (a.k.a. the Valley Trail) runs 1.7 miles on the east side of the highway through a series of elk meadows to the Washburne campground. If the parking area is full, head to the day-use lot across the highway from the campground, catch the Valley Trail near the campground entrance, and hike to the Hobbit and Heceta Head Trails.

Up the North Fork of the Siuslaw River is the **Pawn Old-Growth Trail,** a 0.5-mile pathway through 9-foot-thick, 275-foot-tall Douglas fir and hemlock trees that are several hundred years old. The trailhead, at the confluence of the North Fork of the Siuslaw and Taylor's Creek, is a good place to see salmon spawning in the fall and observe water ouzels (also called dippers). The trail follows the creek and offers interpretive placards along the way. At one point in the trail, visitors walk through fallen Douglas fir logs 21 feet in diameter. Placards explain the science of tree rings. From Florence, take Highway 126 east for one mile, then turn north onto Forest Road 5070 and take it 12 miles to Forest Road 5084; stay right and go another five miles to the trailhead.

An excellent and not terribly difficult introduction to dune hiking can be found about 10 miles south of Florence at the **Oregon Dunes Day-Use Area** ($5 day-use). The **Overlook Beach Trail** runs for about a mile from a viewing platform to the beach. Follow the blue-topped wooden posts that mark the trail through the sand. To turn this into a more strenuous 3.5-mile loop, continue one mile south along the beach, and head back inland (again following the posts) along the more rugged **Tahkenitch Creek Loop.** Find the turnoff from U.S. 101 near milepost 201.

Another good place to explore the dunes is along **Carter Dunes Trail** and **Taylor Dunes Trail.** Carter Dunes Trail starts near Carter Lake and heads west 1.5 miles to the beach. The first half of the mile-long Taylor Dunes Trail is wheelchair accessible; the trail passes some of the oldest (and gnarliest) conifers in the area. Both of these trails are good places to view wildlife, especially in the winter and spring, when the dunes take on wetland characteristics. The two trails link up, forming a Y rather than a loop. The turnoff for both trails is 7.5 miles south of Florence. Carter Lake also has a campground.

Hike the **Waxmyrtle Trail** along the Siltcoos River; the 1.5-mile trail travels along the estuary and ends up at the beach. The trail is closed March 15-September 15 to protect nesting snowy plover. This is a good spot for bird-watching. Find the trailhead near the Waxmyrtle campground about eight miles south of Florence at the Siltcoos Recreation Area.

## Dune Rides

Ride into the dunes with the folks from **Sand Dunes Frontier** (83960 U.S. 101, 541/997-3544, http://sanddunesfrontier.com, 9am-6pm daily summer, 10am-4pm Tues.-Sat. mid-Dec.-mid-Mar.). on 30-minute, 20-person dune buggy rides ($14 adults, $11 ages 4-11). Protective goggles are provided, along with a driver. At the same location, **Torex ATV Rentals** (541/997-5363, $50-300 per hour) rents vehicles for travel in specially designated areas within the Oregon Dunes National Recreation Area. Go in

# Dune Country: Florence to Coos Bay

a jumping-off point for trails in the Oregon Dunes, south of Florence

Even though the 47-mile stretch of U.S. 101 between Coos Bay and Florence does not overlook the ocean, your eyes will be drawn constantly westward to the largest and most extensive oceanfront dunes in the world.

How did they come to exist in a coastal topography otherwise dominated by rocky bluffs? A combination of factors created this landscape over the past 12,000 years, but the principal agents are the Coos, Siuslaw, and Umpqua Rivers. The sand and sediment transported to the sea by these waterways are deposited by waves on the flat, shallow beaches. Prevailing westerlies move the particulate matter exposed by the tide eastward up to several yards per year. Over the millennia, the dunes have grown huge, with some topping 500 feet.

Constantly on the move, the shifting sands have engulfed ancient forests, a fact occasionally corroborated by hikers as they stumble on the top of an exposed snag. The cross-section of sand-swept woodlands seen from U.S. 101 demonstrates that this inundation is still occurring. Nonetheless, the motorist gets the impression that the trees are winning the battle, because the dunes are only intermittently visible from the road.

the morning, when the sand tends to blow around less.

## Sandboarding

Dude, it's a natural! Wax up a board, strap it onto your bare feet, and carve your way down the dunes. On the outskirts of Florence, you can rent a board and try out the rails and jumps at **Sand Master Park** (5351 U.S. 101, 541/997-6006, www.sandmasterpark.com, 9am-7pm daily mid-June-mid-Sept., 10am-5pm Mon.-Tues. and Thurs.-Sat., noon-5pm Sun. Mar.-May and mid-Sept.-mid-Jan.,

board rentals $10-25, includes admission). If you're more of a do-it-yourselfer, a number of roadside shops rent sandboards, and the dunes are certainly plentiful.

## Horseback Riding

Riding across the dunes into the sunset on a trusty steed sounds like a fantasy, but you can do it thanks to **C&M Stables** (90241 U.S. 101, 541/997-7540, www.oregonhorse-backriding.com, 10am-5pm daily). Rates range $65-150 per person for trips of one to two hours, with discounts for larger parties.

The stables are open year-round and are located near 14 miles of horse trails that wind through the forest on a bluff above the beach. With beach rides, dune trail excursions, and sunset trips, there's something for everybody.

## Fishing

Oregon's largest coastal lake, 3,100-acre **Siltcoos Lake,** six miles south of Florence, offers excellent fishing and other recreation. The lake is stocked with rainbow trout in the spring, and steelhead, salmon (the lake is closed to coho fishing), and sea-run cutthroat trout move from the ocean into the lake via the short Siltcoos River in late summer and fall. But the real excitement here is the fishing for warm-water species, which are some of the best in the Pacific Northwest. Bluegill, crappie, yellow perch, and brown bullhead action is good through the summer, while fishing for largemouth bass can be good year-round. Access points include several public and private boat ramps on the lake, as well as a wheelchair-accessible fishing pier at Westlake Resort.

## Water Sports

Although only the hardiest swimmers go into the ocean without wetsuits, **Cleawox** and **Woahink Lakes** warm up sufficiently to make summertime swimming enjoyable. Cleawox, the smaller of the two, is especially well suited for swimming. A lodge (10am-5pm daily Memorial Day-Labor Day) by the swimming beach rents pedal boats, canoes, and kayaks. Both lakes are within Honeyman State Park (day-use $5 per vehicle), three miles south of Florence.

Surfers head to the beaches at South Jetty, where the waves are best when small—they can often become overwhelming and unsuitable for novices. Look for more protection from the wind at the mouth of the river.

South of Florence, in the Oregon Dunes National Recreation Area, the three-mile **Siltcoos River Canoe Trail** invites kayakers and canoeists to paddle among the dunes. Meandering two miles through dunes, forest,

and estuary, the Siltcoos is a gentle Class I paddle with no white water or rapids, although a small dam midway must be portaged. Wildlife that you may encounter along the way include mink, raccoons, otters, beavers, and even bears. In the estuary, sea lions and harbor seals are common. Rent a kayak from **Siltcoos Lake Resort** (82855 Fir St., Westlake, 541/999-6941, www.siltcooslakeresort.com, $45-55 per day).

## Golf

**Ocean Dunes Golf Links** (3345 Munsel Lake Rd., 541/997-3232, $48 for 18 holes), part of the Three Rivers Casino complex, lets you tee off with sand dunes (some more than 60 feet high) as a backdrop. The manicured 18-hole course has a driving range, a full pro shop, and equipment rentals on-site. For the ultimate in golfing by the dunes, however, try **Sandpines Golf Course** (1201 35th St., 541/997-1940, www.sandpines.com, $79 for 18 holes). To get there, go west off U.S. 101 on 35th Street. In May and June rhododendrons line this drive, which heads into dune country as you move toward the sea. Follow the signs until you see a water tower not far from the pro shop. A 7,190-yard par-72 course, Sandpines's layout features fairways lined with lakes, Douglas firs, and beach grass on gently undulating terrain; the inward nine holes are traditional links style. Coastal winds that kick up in the afternoon can figure prominently in your shot selection.

## ENTERTAINMENT AND EVENTS

For current information on Florence area events, contact the **Florence Chamber of Commerce** (541/997-3128, www.florence-chamber.com).

During the third weekend of May, Florence celebrates the **Rhododendron Festival,** coinciding with the blooming of these flowers, which proliferate in the area. It's a tradition that goes back to 1908, when the festival was started as a way to draw attention and commerce to the town. A parade, carnival, flower show, 5K "Rhody Run," and the crowning of Queen Rhododendra are highlights of the festivities. This is a popular event, attracting more than 15,000 visitors each year.

**Fourth of July** celebrations include live outdoor music and a barbecue in Old Town, along with a fireworks display over the river. Authors, publishers, and readers gather at the **Florence Festival of Books** (541/997-1994) at the Florence Events Center the last weekend of September. For general entertainment, the Coos, Lower Umpqua, and Siuslaw tribes run **Three Rivers Casino** (5647 Hwy. 126, 541/997-7529). Along with the slots and game tables, there's a hotel and golf course.

## FOOD

Many Florence restaurants are along the Old Town waterfront. Walk along Bay Street and discover dozens of dining options, from casual to upscale.

### Pacific Northwest Cuisine

The Oregon coast isn't really known for adventurous fine dining, but a handful of hip eateries are spicing up the scene. At the edge of Old Town, the ★ **Homegrown Public House** (294 Laurel St., 541/997-4886, www.

homegrownpub.com, 11am-8pm Tues.-Thurs., 11am-9pm Fri.-Sat., $9-21) is an easygoing place for a beer and a snack or a full meal. As the name implies, much of the food is locally grown or gathered (try the summer chanterelles if they're available) and seasonal. Around the corner from the main restaurant, **Homegrown Wildcrafters Deli** (249 Maple St., 541/997-5916, www.homegrownpub.com, 10:30am-4:30pm Fri.-Wed., $5-12) is a good place to grab a sandwich or salad to go.

### Seafood

No one will ever accuse the ★ **Waterfront Depot** (1252 Bay St., 541/902-9100, www.thewaterfrontdepot.com, 4pm-10pm daily, reservations recommended, $15-30) of lacking in personality; it's a friendly, bustling place with good views out onto the river and a delicious signature dish of crab-encrusted halibut; razor clams are also a treat. This historic structure was formerly the rail station at nearby Mapleton before it was barged down the Siuslaw River to its current riverfront location.

In Old Town, the local **Mo's** (1436 Bay St., 541/997-2185, www.moschowder.com, 11am-8pm Sun.-Thurs., 11am-9pm Fri.-Sat., $6-18) is the largest outlet of this famed Oregon

Shoot a few baskets before dinner at the Homegrown Public House.

chowder house, and its fresh fish, fast service, fair prices, and Siuslaw River frontage make it a good bet for a family meal.

## Mexican

It doesn't look like much from the front, but the best reason to seek out the **Traveler's Cove** (1362 Bay St., 541/997-6845, 9am-9pm daily, $9-22) is the lovely back patio, with tables directly over the river. The food is eclectic, with homemade clam chowder, tempting salads and sandwiches, and a number of Mexican dishes. Fresh Dungeness crab makes an appearance here with crab quiche, crab enchiladas, and "crabby" Caesar salad.

## Italian

A good place to take a break from chowder (though not necessarily seafood) is **La Pomodori Ristorante** (1415 7th St., 541/902-2525, www.lapomodori.com, 11:30am-2pm and 5pm-8pm Tues.-Fri., 5pm-8pm Sat., $15-24), an intimate northern Italian restaurant in a converted house. Specialties include fresh shrimp and halibut and pasta, as well as a pork chop stuffed with shrimp, pancetta, scallions, and tomatoes.

Down in Old Town, **1285 Restobar** (1285 Bay St., 541/902-8338, www.1285restobar. com, 11am-9pm daily, $9-17) is a lively trattoria with a focus on good seafood entrées; pizza is also a popular choice. During happy hour, have a seat at a sidewalk table and watch the action on Bay Street; the patio out back is more secluded.

## Coffee and Tea

Under the bridge in Old Town, **Siuslaw River Coffee Roasters** (1240 Bay St., 541/997-3443, www.coffeeoregon.com, 7am-5pm daily, $2-6) serves good coffee and pastries. There's a little deck out back overlooking the river, and lots of books, gifts, and hobnobbing inside.

If you're visiting on a rainy afternoon, a good place to while away the time is **Lovejoy's Tea Room** (129 Nopal St., 541/997-0502, http://lovejoysrestaurant.com, 11am-2:30pm Tues.-Fri., 8am-2:30pm Sat.,

$8-25), where you can share a pot of Earl Grey, dine on a Cornish pasty or sausage roll, or go for high tea service.

## Dessert

After dinner, have dessert at one of the two locations of **BJ's Ice Cream Parlor** (2930 U.S. 101; 1441 Bay St., 541/997-7286, 10am-11pm daily summer, 11am-10pm daily winter, $2-6). BJ's churns out hundreds of flavors, with 48 on display at any given time. Full fountain service, ice cream cakes, cheesecakes, gourmet frozen yogurt, and pies complement the cones and cups.

## ACCOMMODATIONS

Like just about everywhere else, there are budget motels on the main drag. We've selected a few with some character, but urge you to consider one of the local B&Bs. Unless otherwise noted, prices listed are for high-season doubles.

### $50-100

One of the best bargains in town is the **Lighthouse Inn** (155 U.S. 101, 541/997-3221 or 866/997-3221, http://lighthouseinn-florence.com, $89-145), a Cape Cod-style two-story motel on the highway close to the bridge and convenient to Old Town. With neatly kept but aging rooms decorated with bric-a-brac and other homey touches, it may give you the feeling that you're spending the night at your grandmother's house. A pet-friendly suite includes a kitchenette, and most rooms have microwaves and fridges. Most guest rooms also have a queen or king bed and sleep two; some are considered suites, with two rooms and a connecting bath, sleeping up to five guests. A few rooms are designated as pet-friendly.

If it's not important for you to be an easy walk from Old Town, consider staying three miles south of town at the charming and pet-friendly ★ **Park Motel** (85034 U.S. 101, 541/997-2634 or 800/392-0441, www.park-motelflorence.com, $99-135), a classic mom-and-pop place set well back from the highway in a stand of Douglas firs. The guest rooms are paneled in knotty pine and come in a variety of sizes and configurations, including a few cabins, making it a good place for families or groups of friends.

## $100-150

For a river experience, try the ★ **River House Inn** (1202 Bay St., 541/997-3933 or 888/824-2454, www.riverhouseflorence.com, $129-199). It's worth paying extra for a waterfront balcony ($169). This newer and attractive motel, which also has good views of the Siuslaw River Bridge, is just two blocks away from the heart of Old Town.

Just around the corner from Old Town and across the highway from the Lighthouse Inn, the pet-friendly **Old Town Inn** (170 U.S. 101 N., 541/997-7131 or 800/301-6494, www.old-town-inn.com, $124) provides guests with spacious rooms a short walk away from the river and Old Town. Although this motel is on U.S. 101, the guest rooms are fairly quiet.

## $150-200

★ **The Edwin K B&B** (1155 Bay St., 541/997-8360 or 800/833-9465, www.edwink.com, $165-190) has six guest rooms, all with private baths, as well as an apartment suite ($190-215). The Edwin K is just two blocks from Old Town, across the street from the Siuslaw River. River views, period antiques, and multicourse breakfasts with locally famous soufflés and home-baked breads served on fine china have established this gracious 1914 home as Florence's preeminent B&B. Add a private courtyard and waterfall in back, tea and sherry in the afternoon, and a restful atmosphere, and you'll understand the need to reserve well in advance.

At Heceta Beach, on the northern edge of Florence, **Driftwood Shores Resort** (88416 1st Ave., 541/997-8263 or 800/422-5091, www.driftwoodshores.com, $130-374) is unique among Florence lodgings in that it is ocean-side. It is also a huge complex and in a pretty isolated area, far from Old Town and restaurants (except the resort restaurant). All rooms face the ocean and have decks or patios, as well as microwaves and fridges; some suites have full kitchens.

## Over $200

Twelve miles north of Florence and just a short walk from Heceta Head Lighthouse is **Heceta Head Lighthouse B&B** (92072 U.S. 101, 541/547-3696 or 866/547-3696, www.hecetalighthouse.com, $215-355), built in 1893. It used to be the lighthouse keeper's home; today it's a B&B with antique furnishings and vintage photos, which help recreate the lives of the keepers of the flame. Among the six bedrooms, the two Mariners' rooms command the finest views. The current caretakers maintain a garden on the grounds, as did the actual lighthouse keepers of yesteryear, and they use some of the produce to turn out amazing seven-course breakfasts. The innkeepers are more likely to tell you about resident ghosts during breakfast than right before bedtime.

On the south bank of the river, just across the bridge from Old Town, the **Best Western Pier Point Inn** (85625 U.S. 101, 541/997-7191 or 800/435-6736, www.bwpierpointinn.com, $205-220) offers spacious rooms, great bay views, sand-dune hiking across the street, and a complimentary hot breakfast. Rates at this large and classy motel drop by about half in the off-season.

## Camping

There are excellent campgrounds around Florence, several with recreational opportunities comparable to those at the nearby Oregon Dunes National Recreation Area but with more varied scenery.

**Carl G. Washburne State Park** (93111 U.S. 101 N., information 541/547-3416, yurt reservations 800/452-5687, www.oregonstate-parks.org, year-round, $21 tents, $31-33 RVs, $46 yurts, $56 pet-friendly yurts, $5 hiker-biker) is popular with Oregonians because of its proximity to beaches, tide pools, Sea Lion Caves, and hiking trails. The seven walk-in tent sites are secluded, and the remaining 57 have electricity and water (some also have sewer hookups); like almost all state park campgrounds, there are showers. Reservations are not accepted for regular sites, but the park's two yurts can be reserved. It's 14 miles north of Florence on U.S. 101 and three miles past Sea Lion Caves, then one mile west on a park road. This state park offers a number of good hiking trails and, via the Hobbit Trail, three miles of relatively isolated beach.

Three miles south of Florence's McCullough Bridge and on both sides of U.S. 101 is **Honeyman State Park** (84505 U.S. 101 S., information 541/997-3641, reservations 800/452-5687, www.oregonstateparks.org, $21 tents, $31-33 RVs, $46 yurts, $56 pet-friendly yurts, $5 hiker-biker). This large and exceedingly popular campground gets crowded in the summer—reservations are a must—but it empties out enough during spring and autumn to make a stay here worthwhile. The park is popular with all-terrain vehicle (ATV) users, who camp in the H loop, where there's a two-mile ATV trail to the beach. Hiking from the campground to the beach is discouraged. In spring, pink rhododendrons line the highway and park roads.

If you're looking for something smaller and low-key, then two Siuslaw National Forest Service campgrounds just north of Florence might be the ticket. **Sutton Campground** (877/444-6777 or www.recreation.gov, regular sites $24, with electricity $29) is four miles north of Florence, and in addition to 80 campsites amid the dunes, it features a *Darlingtonia* bog and a hiking trail network. In high summer season, about a quarter of the sites can be reserved; the rest are available on a first-come, first-served basis.

Just another mile north is **Alder Dune Campground** (877/444-6777 or www.recreation.gov, $24) with two lakes with swimming beaches and trout fishing. Hiking trails lead out into the dunes and reach the Pacific beaches. During summer high season, all of the campground's 39 sites can be reserved. For more information on these campgrounds, contact the **Siuslaw National Forest** (541/271-6000, www.fs.fed.us).

## INFORMATION AND SERVICES

The **Florence Area Chamber of Commerce** (290 U.S. 101, 541/997-3128, www.florencechamber.com, 9am-5pm Mon.-Fri., 10am-2pm Sat.) is three blocks north of the Siuslaw River Bridge.

**Peace Harbor Hospital** (400 9th St., Florence, 541/997-8412) is open 24 hours daily, with a handful of specialists and an emergency room. The **post office** (770 Maple St., 541/997-2533), near the junction of Highway 126 and U.S. 101, is close to the library.

## GETTING THERE

**Pacific Crest Bus Lines** (541/344-6265, http://pacificcrestbuslines.com) offers bus service (Sun.-Fri.) between Coos Bay in the south and Eugene to the east. Eugene offers both Greyhound and Amtrak service, as well as air links to the rest of the country from Mahlon Sweet Field Airport (EUG).

# Reedsport and Winchester Bay

If you're going fishing or coming back from a dunes hike, you'll appreciate a clean low-priced motel room in Reedsport. Otherwise, this town of 5,000 people might seem like a strange mirage of cut-rate motels, taverns, and burger joints in the midst of the Oregon Dunes National Recreation Area. Reedsport is not a tourist town, to put it politely. But there's lots of fascinating recreation available in the Oregon Dunes NRA that encircles the town, and the Umpqua River is itself a destination for anglers.

Three miles southwest of Reedsport, Salmon Harbor Marina in **Winchester Bay,** a busy port for commercial sportfishing at the mouth of the Umpqua, has given the whole area new life in recent years, following hard times precipitated by the decline in timber revenues. In many ways, Winchester Bay is the more interesting destination of the two side-by-side towns, with its busy harbor and collage of waterfront bars and restaurants.

## SIGHTS
### Oregon Dunes

A great place to start your explorations is the **Oregon Dunes National Recreation Area Visitor Information Center** (885 U.S. 101, Reedsport, 541/271-6100, www.fs.usda.gov/siuslaw, 8am-4:30pm Mon.-Fri.), at the junction of the Coast Highway and Highway 38. In addition to the printed information on hiking, camping, and recreation, the Siuslaw Forest Service personnel are helpful. Note that a $5 day-use fee is charged per vehicle at most facilities and access points within the NRA. You can purchase an annual pass at the Dunes Visitors Center for $30.

Because the dunes are difficult to see from the highway in many places, the most commonly asked question in the visitors center is "Where are the dunes?" To answer that question for everybody, the National Forest Service

opened **Oregon Dunes Overlook** just south of Carter Lake, midway between Florence and Reedsport, at the point where the dunes come closest to U.S. 101. In addition to four levels of railing-enclosed platforms connected by wooden walkways, there are trails down to the sand. It's only about 0.25 miles to the dunes and then 1 mile through sand and wetlands to the beach.

You can hike a loop beginning where the sand gives way to willows. Bear right en route to the beach. Once there, walk south 1.5 miles. A wooden post marks where the trail resumes. It then traverses a footbridge going through trees onto sand, completing the loop. If you go in February, this loop has great bird-watching potential.

### Umpqua Discovery Center

In Reedsport's Old Town, on the south bank of the river, the **Umpqua Discovery Center** (409 Riverfront Way, 541/271-4816, www.umpquadiscoverycenter.com, 10am-5pm Mon.-Sat., noon-4pm Sun. June-Sept., 10am-4pm Mon.-Sat., noon-4pm Sun. Oct.-May, $8 adults, $4 ages 6-15) interprets the regional human and natural history through multimedia programs, dioramas, scale models, and helpful staff. The gift store is stuffed with local goodies. The boardwalk and observation tower give a good view of the broad lower reaches of the Umpqua.

### Dean Creek Elk Viewing Area

Three miles east of Reedsport and stretching three miles along the south side of Highway 38, the **Dean Creek Elk Viewing Area** (48819 Hwy. 38, Reedsport, www.blm.gov, 541/756-0100) provides parking areas and viewing platforms for observing the herd of some 120 wild Roosevelt elk that roam this 1,100-acre preserve. The elk move out of the forest to graze the preserve's marshy pastures, sometimes coming quite close to the highway.

The Umpqua Discovery Center is on the Reedsport waterfront.

Elk can reach 1,100 pounds at maturity, and the majestic rack on a fully grown bull can spread three feet across. Early mornings and just before dusk are the most promising times to look for them; during hot weather and storms, the elk tend to stay within the cover of the woods.

## Umpqua Lighthouse State Park

Less than one mile south of Winchester Bay is **Umpqua Lighthouse State Park** (460 Lighthouse Rd., Winchester Bay, 541/271-4118, www.oregonstateparks.org). Tour the red-capped 1894 **lighthouse** (1020 Lighthouse Rd., 541/271-4631, 10am-4:30pm daily May-Oct., 10am-4pm daily Nov.-Dec. and Mar.-Apr., lighthouse tours $5) or admire it from the roadside. Next door, in a former Coast Guard building, a **visitors center and museum** has marine and timber exhibits; this is also where tours begin. Directly opposite the lighthouse, overlooking the mouth of the Umpqua and oceanfront dunes, is a whale-watching platform with a plaque explaining where, when, and what to look for.

The main part of the state park, which includes a campground and Lake Marie, is a five-minute drive from the lighthouse itself. The lake has a swimming beach and is stocked with rainbow trout. A one-mile forest trail around the lake makes for an easy hike. A trail from the campground leads to the second-highest dunes in the United States (elev. 545 feet), west of Clear Lake.

## SPORTS AND RECREATION
### Hiking

There are three excellent state parks and a dozen Siuslaw National Forest Campgrounds within the **Oregon Dunes NRA.** Although joyriding in noisy dune buggies and other off-road vehicles doesn't lack devotees, the best way to appreciate the interface of ecosystems is on foot. Dunes exceeding 500 feet in height, wetland breeding grounds for waterfowl and other animals, evergreen forests, and deserted beaches can be encountered in a march to the sea. Numerous designated hiking trails, ranging from easy 0.5-mile loops to 6-mile round-trips, give visitors a chance to star in their own version of *Lawrence of Arabia*. The soundtrack is provided by over 200 species of birds—along with your heartbeat—as you scale these elephantine anthills. Deserted beaches and secret swimming holes are among the many rewards of the journey.

Before setting out, pick up the *Hiking Trails Recreation Opportunity Guide* from the **Oregon Dunes NRA Visitor Information Center** (885 U.S. 101, Reedsport, 541/271-6100, www.fs.usda.gov/siuslaw, 8am-4:30pm Mon.-Fri.). Carry plenty of water and dress in layers—there are hot spots in dune valleys and ocean breezes at higher elevations.

### ★ JOHN DELLENBACK TRAIL
This spectacular dunes landscape can be found 10.5 miles south of Reedsport and 0.25 miles south of the Eel Creek Campground

near Lakeside. After you emerge from a 0.5-mile hike through coastal evergreen forest, you'll be greeted by dunes 300 to 400 feet high. It's said that dunes near here can approach 500 feet high and one mile long after a windblown buildup. The trail, marked by blue-banded wooden posts, continues another 2.5 miles to the beach. Note that dune hiking can be a bit disorienting. If you lose the trail, climb to the top of the tallest dune and scan for the trail markers.

A shorter and easier one-mile loop trail leads through woodlands to the dunes for a quick introduction to this landscape.

### Skate Park

Near the south end of Reedsport in Lions Park is a world-class **skate park** (U.S. 101 and S. 22nd St.). Here you'll find a funnel-shaped full pipe and a 360-degree full loop, as well as many more approachable features.

### Fishing

Winchester Bay and the tidewater reaches of the lower Umpqua River are Oregon's top coastal sturgeon fishery and one of the best areas for striped bass, particularly near the mouth of the Smith River, which enters the Umpqua just east of Reedsport. The best action for the Umpqua's spring chinook tends to be inland, below Scottsburg. Fall chinook enter the bay from July to September. Other notable fisheries here are the huge runs of shad, which peak in May and June, and smallmouth bass offer action upstream from Reedsport. Crabbing and clamming are also popular and productive pastimes in Winchester Bay and the lower reaches of the river.

Fishing charter services operating in the area include **Living Waters** (541/584-2295, www.fishinglivingwaters.com) and **Winchester Bay Charters** (541/361-0180, www.winchesterbaycharters.com).

### Water Sports

Ten miles south of Reedsport, the sleepy resort town of **Lakeside** hosted visits from Bob Hope, Bing Crosby, and the Ink Spots, among other luminaries, back in its 1930s and 1940s heyday. Today, it's still a popular destination, primarily for its proximity to the sprawling, many-armed Tenmile and North Tenmile Lakes. These large, shallow lakes offer waterskiing and excellent fishing for stocked rainbow trout and warm-water species, including crappie, yellow perch, bluegill, and lunker largemouth bass, which can grow up to 10 pounds. A 0.25-mile channel connects the two lakes, and a county park on Tenmile Lake has a paved boat ramp, fishing docks, a sandy swimming beach, and a picnic area.

## ENTERTAINMENT AND EVENTS

Every June over Father's Day weekend, chainsaw sculptors compete for $10,000 in prizes as they transform pieces of raw western red cedar into grizzly bears, giant salmon, and other rustic works of art during the **Chainsaw Sculpture Championships** (www.odcsc.com) at the Rainbow Plaza in Old Town Reedsport, near North 2nd Street and Greenwood Avenue.

**Dunefest** (541/271-3495, http://dunefest.com) brings ATV riders to town for races, freestyle shows, a treasure hunt, and more at the end of July.

## FOOD

Seek not cuisine in Reedsport—standard American fare is the norm in this hardscrabble town. The best bets for seafood are the wharf-side restaurants in Winchester Bay.

### Reedsport

A popular diner on U.S. 101 is **Don's Main Street Restaurant** (2115 Winchester Ave., 541/271-2032, 8am-8pm daily, $7-10), with burgers, fried chicken, and a parlor serving local Umpqua ice cream. This is the local favorite place for pies.

The **Schooner Inn Café** (423 Riverfront Way, 541/271-3945, 10am-4pm Sun.-Wed., 10am-7pm Thurs.-Sat., $9-15), on the boardwalk next door to the Discovery Center, has a pleasant riverside patio and a good selection of delicious salads and sandwiches. It's a quiet spot for an alfresco lunch overlooking the Umpqua.

## Winchester Bay

For the best fresh seafood in the dune country, head down to the Salmon Harbor Marina at Winchester Bay, where there are a number of casual seafood restaurants within easy strolling distance.

Stop by **Sportsmen's Cannery and Smokehouse** (182 Bay Front Loop, 541/271-3293, shop 9am-5pm daily) to pick up cans of tuna. No kidding, it's worth the price and will make a great gift for the folks back home. While you're at this fish market, order an oyster shooter or shrimp cocktail and dine at a picnic table out front.

Another good bet for fresh seafood in an authentic, albeit indoor, dockside setting is **Fishpatrick's Crabby Cafe** (196 Bay Front Loop, 541/271-3474, 11am-3pm Sun. and Wed., 11am-8pm Thurs.-Sat., $8-25), which offers excellent fish-and-chips, crab, and fish sandwiches in a woodsy dining room.

## ACCOMMODATIONS

Just off U.S. 101 on the road to Winchester Bay, **Salmon Harbor Landing** (265 8th St., Winchester Bay, 541/271-3742, www.salmonharborlanding.com, $65-75) is a simple but clean and friendly motel. This is a good place to stay if you don't need fancy amenities yet enjoy a personal touch. Each room is individually decorated, with many of the owner's antiques featured.

Anglers, or anyone who'd rather be in a location off the main drag, should consider the **Winchester Bay Inn** (390 Broadway, Winchester Bay, 541/271-4871 or 800/246-1462, www.winbayinn.com, $79-160), just across from the docks. Guest rooms are basic but clean, and some include kitchens. Even though this is a large, sprawling complex, reserve ahead of time in fishing season. Pets are permitted in some guest rooms.

The **Best Western Plus Salbasgeon Inn**

(1400 U.S. 101, 541/271-4831 or 800/780-7234, $132-162) is Reedsport's largest and most full-service hotel, on U.S. 101 just south of the Umpqua River bridge. Amenities include an indoor pool, a fitness center, guest laundry, a hot tub, and breakfast included.

## Camping

Choices abound in this recreation-rich area. Just south of Winchester Bay is **Umpqua Lighthouse State Park** (460 Lighthouse Rd., Winchester Bay, information 541/271-4118, reservations 800/452-5687, www.oregonstateparks.org, $19-80). The campground alongside Lake Marie has firewood, flush toilets, showers, picnic tables, electricity, and piped water. The 20 RV sites go for $28; the 24 tent sites are $19; two basic yurts are $43; six deluxe yurts (with shower, small kitchen, fridge, microwave, and TV/DVD player) are $82; and two rustic cabins are $41. The lake offers fishing, boating, and swimming. Trails from the campground lead to the second-highest dunes in the United States (elev. 545 feet), west of Clear Lake.

**William A. Tugman State Park** (information 541/759-3604, reservations 800/452-5687, www.oregonstateparks.org, $24-26 tents or RVs, $46 yurts, $56 pet-friendly yurts) is eight miles south of Reedsport, in the heart of dune country. This larger campground, with 115 sites, sits on the west shore of Eel Lake, east of U.S. 101 across from the widest point of the dunes and two miles from the sea.

**Windy Cove Campground** (541/271-4138, www.co.douglas.or.us/parks) is a county park with 24 full-hookup sites ($25) and four other sites with electricity only ($17). Located on the south side of Salmon Harbor Drive across from the Winchester Bay marina, it has restrooms, picnic tables, grass, and paved site pads. No reservations are accepted. It is legal to drive your off-highway vehicle (OHV) from this campground directly to the dunes, but that requires a couple of miles' drive on the pavement.

About nine miles south of Reedsport, set along Eel Creek near Eel and Tenmile Lakes, is **Eel Creek Campground** (reservations 877/444-6777, www.recreation.gov, $22), a Siuslaw National Forest facility with 51 basic tent and RV sites; reservations are advised. The Umpqua Dunes Trail offers access to the dunes and the beach.

Eight miles north of Reedsport, the **Tahkenitch Campground** (reservations 877/444-6777, www.recreation.gov, mid-May-Sept., $22) is another Forest Service facility set among ancient Douglas firs and conveniently located near Tahkenitch and other lakes, dunes, and ocean beaches. A network of trails branch out through the dunes, along Tahkenitch Lake, and to the beach. Just a mile away, another Forest Service campground is **Tahkenitch Landing Campground** (reservations 877/444-6777, www.recreation.gov, year-round, $22), which doesn't have piped water. If you're coming to the dunes to ride ATVs and don't mind noise, consider spending the night at the all-in-one **Discovery Point Resort** (242 Discovery Point Lane, 541/271-3443, www.discoverypointresort. com, $18 tents, $34-37 RVs) near Winchester Bay. The resort offers OHV enthusiasts dune access and ATV rentals, and provides 60 RV spaces, tent sites, condos, and one- to three-bedroom cabins ($55-325). To get here from Reedsport, head two miles south on U.S. 101 to Winchester Bay, then turn right at Pelican Market onto Salmon Harbor Drive. Go one mile, and you'll see Discovery Point Resort on the left. Reservations are strongly advised.

## INFORMATION

The **Oregon Dunes NRA Visitor Information Center** (885 U.S. 101, Reedsport, 541/271-6100, www.fs.usda. gov/siuslaw) and **Reedsport Chamber of Commerce** (541/271-3495, www.reedsportcc. org) share a building at the junction of U.S. 101 and Highway 38, open 8am-4:30pm Monday-Friday year-round.

# South Coast

Look for ★ to find recommended
sights, activities, dining, and lodging.

# Highlights

★ **Shore Acres State Park:** The regal manor house is gone, but the formal gardens from a onetime private estate still thrive above an especially rugged stretch of beach (page 333).

★ **Bandon Dunes Golf Resort:** This links-style course on the coastal headlands is evocative of Scotland. There are four golf courses, each expertly designed in a gorgeous setting (page 348).

★ **Cape Blanco State Park and Hughes House:** This is the only lighthouse in Oregon that allows visitors into the lantern room, with its massive Fresnel lens (page 353).

★ **Humbug Mountain:** The three-mile trail to the top of Humbug Mountain passes a spectacular array of native plants. Even if the promised mountaintop view is shrouded in fog, it's a great hike (page 354).

★ **Cape Sebastian:** Hike up Cape Sebastian for a front-row seat for springtime whale-watching (page 358).

★ **Rogue River Jet-Boat Ride:** Even diehard paddlers won't regret succumbing to a jet-boat tour up the Rogue River. Boaters often get to see ospreys and eagles fishing along this stretch of river (page 359).

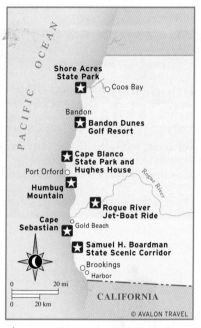

★ **Samuel H. Boardman State Scenic Corridor:** North of Brookings, the road winds hundreds of feet above the surf, allowing you to peer down at one of the most dramatic meetings of rock and tide in the world (page 368).

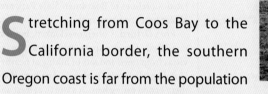

Stretching from Coos Bay to the California border, the southern Oregon coast is far from the population centers of Oregon's interior valleys, but amply rewards visitors who make the effort to get here. The foothills of the Klamath Mountains tumble down the narrow coastal plain and fall off in precipitous headlands at the ocean's edge. Close to shore, the waters are a rocky garden of sea stacks and islets that are home to uncounted flocks of pelagic birds. With half a dozen wild rivers slicing through the mountains to the sea, the south coast is famed for its outstanding salmon fishing, especially on charters from the harbors of Charleston, Gold Beach, Bandon, and Brookings.

In addition, the southern region is blessed with the fairest weather on the Oregon coast and generally gets the most sunshine, the least rain, and the warmest temperatures—attributes as appealing to visitors as to the area's many retirees and other transplants.

Scenic highlights of the south coast include the weather-beaten bluffs and formal gardens at Cape Arago and Shore Acres State Parks, the gorgeous scenery of Boardman and Harris Beach State Parks, and just about every inch of the drive between Brookings and Port Orford. Outstanding courses draw golfers to Bandon; some of the coast's top windsurfing and kiting are found near Cape Sebastian; and popular jet-boat tours run up the Rogue River from Gold Beach.

## PLANNING YOUR TIME

Plan to spend at least a day or two exploring the **Coos Bay-Bandon** region. Coos Bay is the only real city along the southern coast, and like Tillamook to the north, it's a gateway to some spectacular areas, but pretty workaday itself. Head west and south from town to explore the wonderful shoreline parks at Sunset Bay and Cape Arago.

Don't overlook the coastal wetlands, especially the coastal estuary at **South Slough National Estuarine Research Reserve,** south of Coos Bay. **Bandon Marsh National Wildlife Refuge** protects the largest remaining tract of salt marsh within

---

**Previous:** beach at the foot of Humbug Mountain; Cape Blanco Lighthouse. **Above:** Myers Creek Beach.

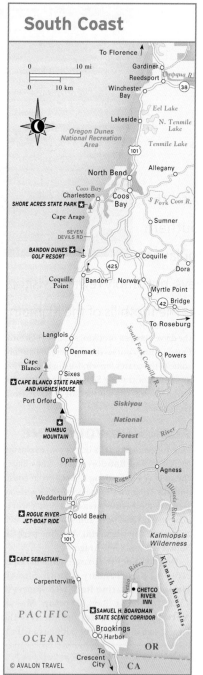

**South Coast**

0        10 mi

0        10 km

To Florence

Gardiner
Reedsport          Umpqua R.
Winchester          38
Bay

Eel Lake

Lakeside          N. Tenmile
Lake

Oregon Dunes          Tenmile Lake
National Recreation
Area          101

North Bend          Allegany

Coos Bay
Charleston          Coos          S Fork Coos R.
SHORE ACRES STATE PARK          Bay

Cape Arago          Sumner

SEVEN
DEVILS RD

BANDON DUNES
GOLF RESORT          Coquille

42S          Dora

Coquille          Bandon   Norway
Point          Myrtle Point
42   Bridge

To Roseburg

Langlois

Denmark          Powers

Cape
Blanco          Sixes

CAPE BLANCO STATE PARK
AND HUGHES HOUSE

Port Orford          Siskiyou

National

HUMBUG          Forest          River
MOUNTAIN

Ophir          Agness

Rogue          Illinois River

Wedderburn

ROGUE RIVER          Gold Beach
JET-BOAT RIDE

101          Kalmiopsis
Wilderness

CAPE SEBASTIAN

River          Klamath Mountains

Carpenterville          Chetco
CHETCO
RIVER
INN

SAMUEL H. BOARDMAN
STATE SCENIC CORRIDOR

PACIFIC          Brookings
Harbor          OR

OCEAN          To
Crescent          CA
© AVALON TRAVEL          City

the Coquille River estuary. Major habitats include undisturbed salt marsh, mudflat, Sitka spruce, and alder riparian communities, which provide resting and feeding areas for migratory waterfowl, shore and wading birds, and raptors.

Although **Bandon** is known for its world-class Bandon Dunes Golf Resort, the old downtown area still hums to counterculture vibes. Bandon's beachfront, along with the Coos Bay sand spit, the beaches on the western side of Humbug Mountain, and the isolated shorelines of Boardman State Park are choice beachcombing spots.

**Port Orford** is often overlooked, but it's one of our favorite spots, with great ocean vistas from town and lots of hiking at nearby Humbug Mountain. It also doesn't hurt that there's good eating here. It's worth at least an afternoon stop.

Jet-boat tours start in **Gold Beach** and head up the Rogue River, offering those with just a morning to spare the chance to explore stunning river vistas—and perhaps help deliver the mail. Between Gold Beach and Brookings, save some serious time to explore beaches sequestered between steep cliffs and pounding surf at the 11-mile-long **Boardman State Scenic Corridor.**

# Charleston, Coos Bay, and North Bend

The towns around the harbor of Coos Bay—Charleston, Coos Bay, and North Bend—refer to themselves collectively as the Bay Area. In contrast to its namesake in California, the Oregon version is not exactly the Athens of the coast. Nonetheless, visitors will be impressed by the area's beautiful beaches and three wonderfully scenic and historic state parks. Because much of this natural beauty is away from the industrialized core of the area and U.S. 101, it's easy to miss. All that many motorists see upon entering Coos Bay and North Bend on the Coast Highway are the dockside lumber mills and foreign vessels anchored at the onetime site of the world's largest lumber port.

The little town of Charleston to the southwest makes few pretenses of being anything other than what it really is—a bustling commercial fishing port. Processing plants here can or cold-pack tuna, salmon, crab, oysters, shrimp, and other kinds of seafood. The few restaurants and lodgings are good values, the Marine Life Center is worth a visit, and the area is the gateway to a trio of extraordinary state parks: Sunset Bay, Shore Acres, and Cape Arago.

To reach Charleston from points south, or to head south from town, take the slow but interesting **Seven Devils Road,** which has its southern terminus about three miles north of Bandon. This winding route runs 13 miles past forests, a few clear-cuts, and an estuarine preserve.

## SIGHTS

### Coos Bay Harbor

A good place to take in the bustling bay front is the **Coos Bay Boardwalk** (U.S. 101 and Anderson Ave.), where you can check out the oceangoing freighters, visit a restored tugboat, and learn of the harbor's history courtesy of interpretive placards. A 400-gallon saltwater aquarium holds fish and other marinelife of Coos Bay. This is the largest coastal harbor between San Francisco and Puget Sound.

### Coos History Museum

The expansive new **Coos History Museum** (1210 N. Front St., Coos Bay, 541/756-6320,

The Coos Bay Boardwalk is like an open-air museum.

# Coos Bay and North Bend

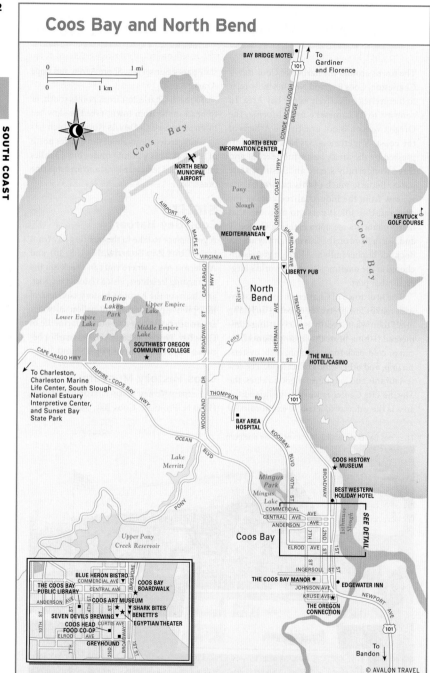

0     1 mi
0     1 km

BAY BRIDGE MOTEL

To Gardiner and Florence

101

CONDE MCCULLOUGH BRIDGE

Coos Bay

NORTH BEND INFORMATION CENTER

NORTH BEND MUNICIPAL AIRPORT

OREGON COAST HWY

SHERIDAN AVE

KENTUCK GOLF COURSE

Pony Slough

CAFE MEDITERRANEAN

VIRGINIA AVE

LIBERTY PUB

Coos Bay

North Bend

River

Pony

Empire Lakes Park

Upper Empire Lake

Lower Empire Lake

Middle Empire Lake

CAPE ARAGO HWY

MAPLE ST

AIRPORT AVE

CAPE ARAGO HWY

BROADWAY ST

SHERMAN AVE

TREMONT ST

SOUTHWEST OREGON COMMUNITY COLLEGE

NEWMARK ST

THE MILL HOTEL/CASINO

EMPIRE - COOS BAY HWY

To Charleston, Charleston Marine Life Center, South Slough National Estuary Interpretive Center, and Sunset Bay State Park

WOODLAND DR

THOMPSON RD

101

BAY AREA HOSPITAL

OCEAN BLVD

KOOSBAY BLVD

COOS HISTORY MUSEUM

Lake Merritt

PONY

Mingus Park

Mingus Lake

10TH ST

BROADWAY

BEST WESTERN HOLIDAY HOTEL

COMMERCIAL AVE

Coos Bay

CENTRAL AVE

ANDERSON AVE

7TH ST

2ND ST

1ST ST

Ishmuan Slough

SEE DETAIL

Upper Pony Creek Reservoir

ELROD AVE

INGERSOLL ST

THE COOS BAY MANOR

EDGEWATER INN

JOHNSON AVE

NEWPORT AVE

KRUSE AVE

THE OREGON CONNECTION

101

To Bandon

## Detail inset

BLUE HERON BISTRO

COMMERCIAL AVE

THE COOS BAY PUBLIC LIBRARY

CENTRAL AVE

COOS BAY BOARDWALK

BAYSHORE

ANDERSON AVE

COOS ART MUSEUM

SHARK BITES

4TH ST

SEVEN DEVILS BREWING

BENETTI'S

COOS HEAD FOOD CO-OP

CURTIS AVE

EGYPTIAN THEATER

10TH ST

7TH ST

ELROD AVE

2ND ST

1ST ST

BROADWAY

GREYHOUND

© AVALON TRAVEL

www.cooshistory.org, 10am-6pm Tues.-Sat., $7 adults, $6 AAA or AARP, $3 ages 5-17) right on the waterfront at the north end of Coos Bay, is worth a visit for its visually compelling exhibits. The cedar-lined Welcoming Gallery invokes the look of a Pacific Northwest plank house. A logging display features a giant rotating band saw, and in the fishing area, a boat seems to sail right out of a wall. After traveling around the area, visitors may want to take a close look at the Fresnel lens from the Cape Arago lighthouse or a section of the McCullough Bridge.

## Coos Art Museum

The **Coos Art Museum** (235 Anderson Ave., Coos Bay, 541/267-3901, www.coosart. org, 10am-4pm Tues.-Fri., 1pm-4pm Sat., $5 adults, $2 seniors and students), in downtown Coos Bay, is the Oregon coast's only art museum and features primarily 20th-century and contemporary works by American artists, including pieces by Robert Rauschenberg and Larry Rivers. Etchings, woodcuts, serigraphs, and other prints make up a large part of the permanent collection, which includes several of Janet Turner's richly detailed depictions of birds in natural settings. Don't miss the Prefontaine Room on the second floor of the museum. Photos, trophies, medals, and other memorabilia of native-son world-class runner Steve Prefontaine illustrate his credo: "I want to make something beautiful when I run."

In addition to the permanent collection, recurring events worth detouring for are the May-June juried show of artists from the Western states.

## Sunset Bay State Park

The Cape Arago Highway west of Charleston leads to some of the most dramatic beaches and interesting state parks on the coast. Among the several beaches on the road to Cape Arago, the strand at **Sunset Bay State Park** (13030 Cape Arago Hwy., information 541/888-4902, reservations 800/452-5687, www.oregonstateparks.org, camping $19-29, yurts $53) is the big attraction because its

sheltered shallow cove, encircled by sandstone bluffs, is warm and calm enough for swimming, a rarity in Oregon. Local legend tells that pirates hid out in this well-protected cove. In addition to swimmers, divers, surfers, kayakers, and boaters, many people come here to watch the sunset; the campground, just inland from the beach, is a good base for exploring the local parks.

A spectacular four-mile cliffside segment of the **Oregon Coast Trail** runs from Sunset Beach south to Cape Arago. Good views of **Cape Arago Lighthouse** across the water can be seen along this route. Listen for its unique foghorn. For a short hike, follow the signs from the mouth of Big Creek to the viewpoint overlooking Sunset Bay.

The Cape Arago Lighthouse is on Chief Island and was once linked to the mainland by a steel-truss bridge. For the local Coos people, Chief Island and the adjacent shoreline were a traditional burial ground, though after the building of the first lighthouse in 1866, the Coast Guard no longer allowed burials. However, the island continued to have sacred significance for the Coos. After the lighthouse was decommissioned in 2006, the ownership of island, the lighthouse, and adjacent shoreline was transferred to the Confederated Tribes of the Coos, Lower Umpqua, and Siuslaw Indians. The bridge to Chief Island has been removed, and the lighthouse and Chief Island are currently not open to the public.

## ★ Shore Acres State Park

Less than one mile south of Sunset Bay at **Shore Acres State Park** (541/888-3732, 8am-sunset year-round, no pets outside vehicles, Oregon Coast Passport or $5 per vehicle, free with camping receipt from Sunset Bay State Park), the grandeur of nature is complemented by human endeavor. The park is set on the grounds of lumber magnate and entrepreneur Louis J. Simpson's early-1900s mansion, which began as a summer home in 1906 and grew into a three-story mansion complete with an indoor heated swimming pool

## Coos Bay Shipwrecks

The *Captain Lincoln,* whose grounding on the treacherous North Spit of Coos Bay led to settlement of the area, would not be the last ship to meet its end on these dangerous shores. In 1910, the *Czarina* foundered in heavy seas on the bar; 24 people were killed in one of the worst shipwrecks on Oregon's south coast. The *Claremont* and the *Santa Clara* both wrecked on the bar in 1915, and the *Sujameco* grounded on Horsfall Beach in 1929. Although most of the ship was removed during salvage operations, iron projections can sometimes still be seen in the sand at low tide.

The most recent and infamous shipwreck here, though, was the February 4, 1999, grounding of the 640-foot wood-chip carrier *New Carissa,* on the North Spit. After the Coast Guard firebombed the freighter in an attempt to burn off the 150,000 gallons of fuel oil on board, the vessel broke into two parts. After weeks of failed attempts, the bow section was finally towed out to sea and sunk in 10,000 feet of water by a Navy torpedo. Most of the stern was finally removed, but a section of it remained mired in the sand on the North Spit, just beyond the surf, until 2008. During the shipwreck and months of salvage efforts, the hulk leaked some 70,000 gallons of oil, which killed an estimated 2,400 seabirds and destroyed oyster beds. See the ship's damaged propeller in front of the Coos History Museum.

and large ballroom. Originally a Christmas present to his wife, Shore Acres became the showplace of the Oregon coast, with formal and Japanese gardens eventually added to the 743-acre estate. After a 1921 fire, a second, larger (two stories high and 224 feet long) incarnation of Simpson's "shack by the beach" was built. Over the following years the building fell into disrepair; the house and grounds were ceded to the state in 1942. Because of the high cost of upkeep, the mansion had to be razed, but the gardens have been lovingly maintained.

The gardens are compelling attractions, but the headland's rim is more dramatic. Perched near the edge of the bluff, on the site formerly occupied by the mansion, a glass-enclosed observation shelter makes a perfect vantage point from which to watch for whales or marvel at the crashing waves. When there's a storm, the waves slam into the sandstone reefs and cliffs, hurling up tremendous fountains of spray. It's not uncommon to feel the spray atop the 75-foot promontory. The history of the Simpson family is really the history of the Bay Area, and their story is captioned beneath period photos in the observation gazebo and in the garden in a small enclosure at the west end of the floral displays.

In the seven acres of neatly tended gardens, set back from the sea, the international botanical bounty culled by Simpson clipper ships and schooners is still in its glory, complemented by award-winning roses, rhododendrons, tulips, and azaleas. A restored gardener's cottage with antique furnishings stands at the back of the formal gardens. It's open for special occasions and during the winter holidays. Also in the gardens, note the copper egret sculptures at the pond and the greenhouse for rare plants from warmer climes.

From Thanksgiving until New Year's, during the annual **Holiday Lights and Open House** (4pm-10pm daily), the gardens are decorated with 250,000 colored lights and other holiday touches. The gardener's cottage opens and serves free refreshments during this time.

If you bear right and follow the pond's contours toward the ocean, you'll come to the **Simpson Beach Trail.** Follow it north for cliffside views of the rock-studded shallows below. Southward, the trail goes downhill to a scene of exceptional beauty. From the vantage point of a small beach, you can watch waves crash into rocks with such force that the white spray appears to hang suspended in the air. Pursuits for the active traveler include exploring tide pools and caves as well as springtime swimming in a cove, formed by winter storms, on the south side of the beach.

## Cape Arago State Park

A little more than one mile south of Shore Acres is **Cape Arago State Park** (800/551-6949, day-use only, free), at the end of the Cape Arago Highway. Locals have made much of the fact that this was a possible landing site of the English explorer Sir Francis Drake in 1579, and put a plaque here commemorating him.

Beachcombers can make their own discoveries in the numerous tide pools, some of the best on the coast. The south cove trail (find it past the picnic shelter) runs down to a sandy beach and the better tide pools. The north cove trail leads to more tide pools, good spots for fishing, and views of the colonies of seals and sea lions at Shell Island, including the most northerly breeding colony of enormous elephant seals. Their huge pups when just a month old may already weigh 300 to 400 pounds. Note that the north trail closes from March 1 to June 30 to protect seal pups. The picnic tables on the headlands command beautiful ocean panoramas and are superbly placed for whale-watching.

## Charleston Marine Life Center

Right on the docks of this fishing town, and directly across the road from the University of Oregon's Institute of Marine Biology, the **Charleston Marine Life Center** (63466 Boat Basin Rd., Charleston, 541/888-2581, www.charlestonmarinelifecenter.com, 11am-5pm Wed.-Sat., $5 adults, $4 seniors or AAA) is smaller and more intimate than the Oregon Coast Aquarium in Newport. In fact, it's so intimate that a volunteer will introduce you to the nudibranchs and other invertebrates housed in aquariums, and encourage you to plunge a hand into a tide-pool-like touch tank. Most of the creatures here were brought in by local fisherfolk or marine biology students who'd finished their experiments. In addition to these up-close encounters with the local fauna, visitors can look at underwater images of various places along the Oregon coast (they vary widely!) and live video feeds from deep-ocean exploration in the Pacific.

## South Slough National Estuarine Research Reserve

Estuaries, where freshwater and saltwater interface, form some of the richest ecosystems on earth—capable of producing five times

Cape Arago State Park

more plant material than a cornfield of comparable size while supporting great numbers of fish, birds, and other wildlife. The South Slough of Coos Bay is the largest such web of life on the Oregon coast. The **South Slough National Estuarine Reserve Interpretive Center** (61907 Seven Devils Rd., 541/888-5558, www.oregon.gov/dsl/SS, 10am-4:30pm Tues.-Sat., free), four miles south of Charleston, will help you coordinate a canoe trip through the estuary.

The center looks out over several estuarine arms of Coos Bay. These vital wetlands nurture a variety of life-forms, detailed by the placards captioning the center's exhibits. Eight miles of trails and boardwalks (open daily) form a loop with many shorter options. The coastal ecosystem is introduced by the "10-minute trail" behind the interpretive center. The various conifers and the understory are clearly labeled along the gently sloping 0.5-mile loop. Branch trails lead down toward the water for an up-close view of the estuary. Down by the slough, you may see elk grazing in marshy meadows and bald eagles circling above, while *Homo sapiens* harvest oysters and shrimp in these waters.

### Whiskey Run Beach

Midway between Charleston and Bandon is the quiet beach at **Whiskey Run,** whose ore-bearing sands spread gold fever down the south coast in the early 1850s. As many as 2,000 miners worked here until a storm washed away the deposit. Other forms of beachcombing at Whiskey Run and on the beaches to the north are still thriving, however. Agate-hunting after a season of winter storms and clamming at low tide make these solitary shorelines ideal places to forget worldly concerns. To get there, turn west from the lightly traveled Seven Devils Road onto Whiskey Run Road and drive 1.5 miles to this county park. Just to the north, you'll find Seven Devils State Wayside. Vehicles are permitted on the beach at Whiskey Run (and not infrequently towed from it); Seven Devils is reserved for foot traffic.

### Horsfall Beach and the North Spit

On the spit north of North Bend, the Oregon Dunes taper down to wide sandy beaches and wetlands. **Horsfall Beach** is extremely popular with all-terrain vehicle (ATV) riders, but it's also a good place to enjoy nature. It's worth exploring on foot, especially in the winter, when storms can expose old shipwrecks.

### Myrtlewood

To see Oregon coast folk art in the making, visit the **Oregon Connection** (1125 S. 1st St., Coos Bay, 541/267-7804, www.oregonconnection.com, 9am-5pm Mon.-Sat., 10am-4pm Sun.), just off U.S. 101 at the south end of Coos Bay. The guided working factory tour (25 minutes, free) shows you how a myrtlewood log gets fashioned into bowls, clocks, tables, and other utensils. After you're done, the store is a delight, with Oregon gourmet foods and crafts supplementing the quality woodwork.

## SPORTS AND RECREATION

Take a walk with a naturalist from **Wavecrest Discoveries** (541/267-4027, http://wavecrest-discoveries.com) to explore forest trails, wetlands, or tide pools, and maybe even arrange for some clamming.

### Hiking

Although most hikers head to the coast, especially the four-mile stretch of the **Oregon Coast Trail** between Sunset Bay and Cape Arago, for a nice trail with spectacular views, it's also worth looking inland. Twenty-five miles northeast of Coos Bay in the Coast Range is **Golden and Silver Falls State Natural Area** (800/551-6949, www.oregonstateparks.org). Two spectacular waterfalls are showcased in this little-known gem of a park. To find your way from Coos Bay, look for the Allegany/Eastside exit from U.S. 101. Beyond the community of Allegany, continue up the East Fork of the Millicoma River to its junction with Glenn Creek, which ultimately

# The Myrtlewood Tree

When exploring the southern Oregon coast, you'll soon discover that myrtlewood is popular hereabouts—nearly every town has a myrtlewood factory or showroom that peddles bowls, sculpture, furniture, and other products fashioned from this rare and unusual wood.

Myrtlewood is a member of the Lauraceae family of small trees and is a relative of the camphor, bay, and sassafras trees. Like these trees, the leaves and wood of the tree have a pungent odor, not unlike bay leaves. The myrtlewood tree grows only in a small area of southern Oregon and northern California, and it is large enough to harvest only after 100 to 150 years of growth. The wood is highly patterned, with the grain forming erratic bands of differing color in a single block of wood.

Myrtlewood is particularly popular for turning into bowls—salad and serving bowls make a lovely gift or keepsake of a trip to coastal Oregon. However, the tree and its wood have been used for myriad other functional and decorative purposes for many years. Hudson's Bay Company trappers used myrtlewood leaves to brew tea as a remedy for chills. In 1869 the golden spike marking the completion of the nation's first transcontinental railroad (near Promontory, Utah) was driven into a highly polished myrtlewood tie. Novelist Jack London was so taken by the beauty of the wood's swirling grain that he ordered an entire suite of furniture.

During the Depression, the city of North Bend issued myrtlewood coins after the only bank in town failed. The coins ranged $0.50 to $10 in value and are still redeemable, although they are worth far more as collectors' items.

leads to the park. The narrow winding gravel roads make this half-hour trip unsuitable for a wide-body vehicle.

You can reach each waterfall by way of two 0.5-mile trails. The 100-foot cataracts lie about one mile apart, and although both are about the same height, each has a distinct character. For most of the year, Silver Falls is more visually arresting because it flows in a near semicircle around a knob near its top. During or just after the winter rains, however, the thunderous sound of Golden Falls makes it the more awe-inspiring of the two. Along the trails, look for the beautifully delicate maidenhair fern.

## Kayaking

From a canoe or sea kayak, as you pass tide flats, salt marshes, forested areas, and open water, you can really begin to grasp the richness of the estuarine habitat at the **South Slough National Estuarine Research Reserve** (541/888-5558, www.oregon.gov/dsl/SS). The estuary here has two main branches, offering plenty of territory for a day of exploration.

Although the waters are placid, they are strongly influenced by the tides—be sure to consult tide tables when you plan an outing. Wind can also affect your trip: Know that in the spring and summer, the prevailing winds are from the northwest; in the winter they're from the southwest. At all times of year, the wind blows hardest in the afternoon.

## Fishing

Spring chinook salmon, which sometimes exceed 30 pounds and are renowned as an unrivaled dining treat, offer prime fishing in Coos Bay. However, their population levels and fishing rules vary from year to year. Mid-August to November, Isthmus Slough sees a good return of fin-clipped hatchery cohos. In saltwater, chinook and coho are usually found in good numbers within a one- to two-mile radius of the mouth of Coos Bay from June to August, although the legal season varies; in 2016 and 2017, the southern Oregon coast was closed to salmon fishing due to crashes in fish populations returning to California's Klamath River.

Coos Bay is also one of the premier areas for crabbing and clamming. The Charleston Fishing Pier is a productive spot for crabs, while the best clamming spots are found along the bay side of the North Spit.

Fishing charters, bay cruises, whale-watching, and the like can be arranged through a number of charter outfits based at the Charleston Boat Basin. **Betty Kay Charters** (541/888-9021 or 800/752-6303, www.bettykaycharters.com) charges typical prices: $85 for 5 hours of rock fishing; $200 per person for 12 hours of tuna or halibut fishing.

### Surfing and Swimming

The best spot on the entire Oregon coast for swimming is **Sunset Bay State Park** (13030 Cape Arago Hwy., Coos Bay, 541/888-4902). The water is warm enough for most adults and gentle enough for most kids.

Surfing is best just northeast of Sunset Bay, at **Bastendorff Beach County Park** (63379 Bastendorff Beach Rd., Charleston, 541/888-5353). Rent a board in downtown Coos Bay at **Waxer's Surf & Skate** (240 S. Broadway, 541/266-9020, www.surfwaxers.com, 11am-6pm Mon.-Sat.).

### Golf

Tee up in a lovely setting at **Sunset Bay Golf Course** (11001 Cape Arago Hwy., Charleston, 541/888-9301, www.sunsetbaygolf.com, $20 Sat.-Sun., $18 Mon.-Fri.), a nine-holer close to Sunset Bay State Park.

## ENTERTAINMENT AND EVENTS

### Brewpubs

Spend an evening on the patio at **Seven Devils Brewing** (247 S. 2nd St., 541/808-3738, www.7devilsbrewery.com, 11am-10pm Sun.-Mon. and Wed.-Thurs., 11am-11pm Fri.-Sat., shorter hours in winter, $8-13), where the fire pit is a good place to get the local vibe and wash down an order of poutine fries with a hoppy Northwest-style ale.

### Casinos

Occupying the former bayside site of the Weyerhaeuser mill alongside U.S. 101 in North Bend, the **Mill Casino** (3201 Tremont Ave., North Bend, 541/756-8800 or 800/953-4800, www.themillcasino.com) is operated by the Coquille Indian Tribe. Open 24 hours daily, the casino offers blackjack, lots o' slots, poker, and bingo. A large hotel, lounge, and several restaurants are on-site.

### Festivals and Events

The first event of note in summer is the **Oregon Coast Music Festival**

Charleston marina

(541/267-0938, www.oregoncoastmusic.com), which runs for two weeks in mid-July and has been bringing music to the coast since 1978. Coos Bay is the central venue for these classical, jazz, pop, and world music concerts, but Bandon, North Bend, Charleston, and other neighboring burgs host some performances as well. Tickets to some events are free, with tickets to the majority of events under $25.

In late August, the ubiquitous Oregon blackberry is celebrated with the **Blackberry Arts Festival** (541/266-9706, blackberryartsfestival.com). Food and wine-tasting booths, a juried arts-and-crafts show, and entertainers fill the **Coos Bay Mall** (Central Ave. in downtown Coos Bay).

Polish up the spotting scope and head to the Oregon Institute of Marine Biology in Charleston during the last weekend of August or first weekend of September to see migratory shorebirds with the **Oregon Shorebird Festival** (541/867-4550). Guided trips on land and water are offered; a boat trip out to see albatross and other seldom-seen species that frequent the open ocean is a highlight. Other excursions visit the Bandon Marsh National Wildlife Refuge and Coos Bay to see plovers, loons, and a variety of other shorebirds.

In mid-September, perhaps the best-known Bay Area sports celebrity, Steve Prefontaine, is honored with a 10K race and two-mile walk in the annual **Prefontaine Memorial Run** (www.prefontainerun.com). Prefontaine was a world-class runner whose gutsy style of running and record performances made him a major sports personality until his premature death at age 24 in 1974. Many top-flight runners pay homage by taking part in the race. Events begin and end at the runner's alma mater, **Marshfield High School** (4th St. and Anderson Ave., Coos Bay).

## FOOD

Oregon's Bay Area has many eateries where your nutritional needs can be met, if not in fine style then at least at the right price. With a couple of notable exceptions, in both Coos Bay and North Bend, you won't find it easy to dine on seafood—in these hardworking towns, eating well seems to require heartier fare. For fresh seafood, you're advised to head to the docks in Charleston.

### Coos Bay

Nearly all the following are located along a two-block section of busy Broadway, which is the name given to southbound U.S. 101 as it passes through downtown Coos Bay. So just park the car and check out which of the following looks good.

One good spot for seafood in Coos Bay is ★ **SharkBites** (240 S. Broadway, 541/266-7582, www.sharkbitescafe.com, 11am-9pm Mon.-Thurs., 11am-9:30pm Fri.-Sat., $8-26), a hip little eatery with a droll sense of humor and good, freshly prepared food, with several local seafood options. A variety of wraps and sandwiches—including a tasty halibut burger—as well as pasta and fish tacos are favorites. Best of all, prices are fair and quality is high.

If you're visiting the waterfront boardwalk and feel the hankering for seafood, stop by **Fishermen's Seafood Market** (200 S. Bayshore Dr., 541/267-2722, http://fishermensseafoodmarket.com, 10:30am-7pm Mon.-Sat., $6-17), a boat anchored off the boardwalk that serves as a seafood store for a local fishing family, plus a casual spot for (mostly) carry-out seafood sandwiches, fish-and-chips, and chowder.

The **Blue Heron Bistro** (110 W. Commercial Ave., 541/267-3933, 11am-9pm Mon.-Fri., 9am-9pm Sat., 9am-8pm Sun., $17-25) is in the heart of downtown Coos Bay—with its Bavarian-style half-timbered exterior, you can't miss it. The specialty is traditional German cooking, such as sauerbraten, schnitzel, and sausages, although fresh salmon and seafood are also featured.

For delicious old-school Italian food, try the family-run **Benetti's** (290 S. Broadway, 541/267-6066, http://benettis.com, 4pm-9pm daily, $10-28). Choose between pasta dishes such as spaghetti with house-made meatballs, chicken parmigiana, or a grilled steak.

**Coos Head Food Co-Op** (353 S. 2nd St., 541/756-7264, 9am-7pm Mon.-Fri., 9am-6pm Sat., 10am-6pm Sun.) has the largest selection of certified organic produce and food on the south coast.

## North Bend

If you've had enough of the standard coastal fare, try ★ **Cafe Mediterranean** (1860 Union St., 541/756-2299, www.cafemediterranean.net, 11am-9pm Mon.-Fri., 5pm-9pm Sat., $9-19) for Middle Eastern-style Mediterranean food, including a locally famed lentil soup, in a friendly relaxed setting. This is a good spot for sharing a meze platter, a Greek salad, and some kebabs.

Stop by the **Liberty Pub** (2047 Sherman Ave., 541/756-2550, 4pm-10pm Wed.-Thurs., 4pm-11pm Fri.-Sat., 4pm-9pm Sat., $10-13), with a good selection on Northwestern beers on tap, tasty pizza, and music whenever possible. Half of the restaurant is family-friendly (minors are allowed).

The **Mill Casino** (3201 Tremont Ave., 541/756-8800 or 800/953-4800, www.themillcasino.com) has a total of five dining options, including the **Timbers Café** (6am-2:30am daily, $8-12), with breakfast all day and pre-made sandwiches. The more upscale **Plank House** (7am-2pm Mon.-Sat., 7am-2pm Sun., 4pm-9pm Sun.-Thurs., 4pm-10pm Fri.-Sat., $18-45) offers three meals daily in a waterfront dining room. At the **Saw Blade** (3pm-9pm Fri.-Sat., 10am-2pm Sun., 4pm-9pm Mon., $10-16), diners load up at a buffet.

## Charleston

You can't go too far wrong looking for a fresh seafood meal down at the docks—a number of casual restaurants and seafood vendors (some more like shacks) cluster here, including one spot where the crab cooker is always on. If you're an oyster lover, you'll certainly want to visit **Qualman's** (63218 Troller Rd., 541/888-3145, 10am-5:30pm Wed.-Sat.), which sells incredibly fresh oysters from its nearby beds. Just look for the signs on the north side of the Charleston Bridge on the east side of the highway.

Part sports bar, part seafood restaurant, ★ **Miller's at the Cove** (63346 Boat Basin Rd., 541/808-2904, 11am-midnight daily, $7-17) has seafood every bit as fresh as it should be. Don't expect anything fancy, but it's a good place for fish tacos. Kids are allowed until 9pm.

Close by, the classier **Portside** (63383 Kingfisher Rd., Charleston Boat Basin, 541/888-5544, www.portsidebythebay.com, 11:30am-11pm daily, $15-55) has a view of the water and a wide menu of rather old-fashioned seafood specialties.

The casual **High Tide Cafe** (91124 Cape Arago Hwy., 541/888-3664, 11am-8pm Wed.-Thurs. and Sun., 11am-9pm Fri.-Sat., $18-25) is a good place for seafood dinners such as cioppino, albacore tuna fish-and-chips, or a plate of pasta, including seafood pasta. If the weather's nice, sit outside, where there's a view of South Slough near its entrance to the bay.

For a coffee and a pastry, a breakfast burrito, a lunchtime sandwich, or a birthday cake, stop by **Crabby Cakes Bakery** (91120 Cape Arago Hwy., 541/888-3664, 8am-3pm Wed.-Thurs., 8am-5pm Fri.-Sun., $3-10), a sweet family-run spot for a snack or a meal.

## ACCOMMODATIONS AND CAMPING

Most of the lodgings in Coos Bay and North Bend stretch along busy U.S. 101, and most are of the mid-century motor-court variety, but the majority are well-maintained and represent good value. Another option is staying in Charleston, particularly if your destination includes local state parks, ocean beaches, or South Slough. Charleston lodgings are pretty basic, but you'll stay near the fishing marina, not the highway.

### Coos Bay

Close to downtown, the pet-friendly **Best Western Holiday Hotel** (411 N. Bayshore

Dr., 541/269-5111, www.bestwestern.com, $150) is an older but well-kept hotel within walking distance of city center restaurants with a pool, a hot tub, and a hot breakfast buffet.

**Coos Bay Manor** (955 5th St., 800/269-1224, www.coosbaymanor.com, $145-235, full breakfast included) is a grand high-ceilinged colonial-style home with eye-popping river views from the open-air second-floor breakfast balcony. The B&B's five spacious rooms have distinctive decor; two of the rooms can be combined to make a suite for families.

The waterfront **Edgewater Inn** (275 E. Johnson Ave., 541/267-0423 or 800/233-0423, www.theedgewaterinn.com, $120-125) is located off the highway facing the working waterfront. Room decor is a bit dated, but many rooms have good views, and the pet-friendly motel also offers fitness equipment, an indoor pool, a spa and sauna, and a light complimentary breakfast.

Northwest of the Bay Area—2.5 miles north of the McCullough Bridge—is the Trans-Pacific Parkway, a causeway west across the water leading to Coos Bay's North Spit and the south end of the Oregon Dunes National Recreation Area, with four **U.S. Forest Service campgrounds** (541/271-6000 or 877/444-6777, www.recreation.gov, year-round, $22-25) and expansive dunes that draw ATV enthusiasts. The main **Horsfall Campground** is popular with crowds of noisy ATVs and RVs. It's the only campground on the spit with showers. For more quiet and privacy, continue another mile on Horsfall Beach Road to **Bluebill Lake.** There isn't ATV dune access from this campground, and it tends to attract trekkers who use their feet to explore. Ask the campground hosts about area trails and the nearby oyster farm for the ultimate in campfire fare. Close by, **Horsfall Beach Campground** is in the dunes next to the beach. ATV access and beachcombing are popular activities. A half-mile away, **Wild Mare Horse Camp** has beach and dune access and a dozen primitive campsites, each with a single or double horse corral.

## North Bend

One of the best values in the area is **Bay Bridge Motel** (33 Coast Hwy., 541/765-3151, www.baybridgemotel.com, $70-110), a small, older motel just north of the McCullough Bridge, with good views of the bay from the higher-priced rooms.

**The Mill Hotel** (3201 Tremont Ave., 541/756-8800 or 800/953-4800, www.

Coos Bay Manor

themillcasino.com, $150-190) is just south of the Mill Casino along the waterfront in a new seven-story tower and a building that once housed a plywood mill. Owned and operated by the Coquille (pronounced ko-KWELL in the local dialect) Indian Tribe, the hotel seeks to express its owners' patrimony: The exterior of this three-story hotel is the same cedar that the Coquille people used to build their plank houses, and the fireplace in the lobby is made of Coquille River rocks. The canoe displayed behind the front desk was carved by Coquille community members and is part of an interpretive display that tells the story of the Coquille people. Guest rooms are nicely furnished, and waterfront views from the tower are especially dramatic. And, of course, all the pleasures of a modern casino are just a few feet away. In addition to gaming, the casino has a restaurant, shops, and a performance center.

## Charleston

There are a few basic motels in Charleston, but even better are the nearby campgrounds. The **Plainview Motel** (91904 Cape Arago Hwy., 541/888-5166 or 800/962-2815, www.stay-hereandplay.com, $89-150) is easy to spot—it's covered with colorful murals of sealife. If you'd like to catch your own dinner, the Plainview is a good base for clamming expeditions or fishing trips. This small older motel has rooms with kitchenettes, plus a cabin and a two-bedroom home.

If you want proximity to the area's parks, consider camping. Even though the crowds at **Sunset Bay State Park** (13030 Cape Arago Hwy., 541/888-4902 or 800/452-5687, reservations www.reserveamerica.com, $5-50) can make it seem like a trailer park in midsummer, the proximity of Oregon's only major swimming beach on the ocean keeps occupants of the 66 tent sites ($19) and 65 trailer sites ($26-29) happy. Yurts go for $43 each ($53 for a pet-friendly yurt), and primitive hiker-biker sites are $5 each. Facilities include the standard state park showers, and there is a boat launch at the north end of the beach. This site, three miles southwest of Charleston,

is popular with anglers, who can cast into the rocky intertidal area for cabezon and sea bass. It's also a good base camp for hikers.

**Bastendorff Beach County Park** (63379 Bastendorff Beach Rd., Charleston, 541/888-5353, www.co.coos.or.us, year-round, campsites $18-26, camping cabin $45) is a conveniently and beautifully located park two miles west of Charleston, just off the Cape Arago Highway. It has camping with RV and tent sites as well as cabins and some hiker-biker sites. The campground has drinking water, flush toilets, and hot showers ($2). Fishing, hiking, and a nice stretch of beach are the recreational attractions, plus there's a good playground for toddlers.

## INFORMATION AND SERVICES

The **Coos Bay Visitors Center** (50 E. Central Ave., Coos Bay, 541/269-0215 or 800/824-8486, www.oregonsadventurecoast.com, 9am-5pm Mon.-Fri., 11am-3pm Sat.-Sun.) is right downtown across from the Boardwalk. *The Coos Bay World* (www.theworldlink.com) is the largest daily paper on the south coast.

For health care and emergencies, the **Bay Area Hospital** (1775 Thompson Rd., Coos Bay, 541/269-8111), 0.5 miles west of U.S. 101 via Newmark Street, is the south coast's largest medical facility.

## GETTING THERE AND AROUND

Improvements to Highway 42 make it possible to get to and from Roseburg, 87 miles from Coos Bay, in less than two hours.

**Pacific Crest Bus Lines** (541/269-7183, http://highdesert-point.com) operates bus service Sunday-Friday between Coos Bay and Eugene via Reedsport and Florence. Eugene has Amtrak rail and regular Greyhound bus service, as well as an airport served by national carriers. **Coastal Express** buses (800/921-2871, www.currypublictransit.org), operated by Curry County Transport, run Monday to Friday between North Bend and Brookings to the south.

The **Southwest Oregon Regional Airport** (OTH, www.flyoth.com), at the north end of North Bend, offers scheduled flights to Portland and San Francisco. Public transportation in the Bay Area is limited; one bus line, **Coos County Area Transit** (541/267-7111, www.coostransit.org), makes a loop in Coos Bay and North Bend.

# Bandon and Vicinity

Between Coos Bay and Bandon, U.S. 101 veers inland through forests and bucolic farmland. The highway reencounters the Pacific at Bandon, near the mouth of the Coquille River. Bandon (pop. 3,000) is characterized by the style and grace of an earlier era, especially in Old Town, a picturesque collection of shops, galleries, and restaurants fronting onto a bustling waterfront.

Although logging, fishing, dairy products, and the harvest of cranberries have been the traditional mainstays of the local economy, in the early part of the 20th century Bandon also enjoyed its first tourism boom. In addition to being a summer retreat from the heat of the Willamette Valley, it was a port of call for thousands of San Francisco-to-Seattle steamship passengers. This era inspired such tourist venues as the Silver Spray dance hall and a natatorium with a saltwater pool. The golden age that began with the advent of large-scale steamship traffic in 1900, however, came to an abrupt end following a fire in 1936 that destroyed most of the town. The blaze was started by the easily ignitable gorse weed, imported from Ireland (as was the town's name) in the mid-1800s.

The facelift given Old Town decades later, and the subsequent tourist influx, conjured for many the image of the mythical phoenix rising from its ashes to fly again. Today, Bandon is a curious mixture of provincial backwater, destination golf resort, and artists' colony.

## SIGHTS

One of the appealing things about Bandon is that most of its attractions are within walking distance of each other. In addition, on the periphery of town is a varied array of things to see and do, including a beautiful stretch of beach just south of downtown.

### Old Town

Bandon's **Old Town** is a half-dozen blocks of shops, cafés, and galleries squeezed in between the harbor and a steep bluff. The renovated waterfront invites relaxed strolling, and crabbers and anglers pull in catches right off the city docks. The small commercial fleet based here pursues salmon and tuna offshore.

Preservation buffs should check out **Masonic Hall,** one of the few buildings to have survived Bandon's 1914 and 1936 blazes. A photo in the local historical museum shows the same building and surrounding structures circa 1914. The photo depicts boardwalks leading to a woolen mill, old storefronts, a theater, and the Bandon Popular Hotel and Restaurant, outside which a horse and buggy await. The scene today has changed dramatically—the Masonic Hall now houses a good shoe store, the **Cobbler's Bench** (110 2nd St., 541/347-9012, www.bandoncobblers-bench.com, 10am-6pm Mon.-Sat., 11am-5pm Sun.)—but an early-1900s charm still pervades the neighborhood.

Throughout Old Town are artists and artisans pursuing their crafts and selling their wares. The **2nd Street Gallery** (210 2nd St., 541/347-4133, http://secondstreetgallery.net, 11am-5:30pm daily) has a little of everything, from functional and art pottery to blown glass to paintings and sculptures. **WinterRiver Books and Gallery** (170 2nd St., 541/347-4111, www.winterriverbooks.com, 10am-6pm daily) has a wide-ranging assortment of travel titles, photo essays, and fiction that makes this the

# Bandon

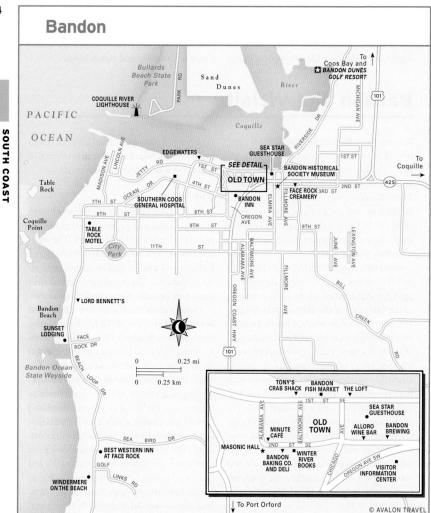

best bookstore on the south coast. Close by, the **Bandon Driftwood Museum** (130 Baltimore Ave., 541/347-3719, 9am-5:30pm Mon.-Sat., 10am-5pm Sun., free) shows off an interesting collection of natural sculptures, from gnarly root balls to whole tree trunks. It's housed at the **Big Wheel General Store,** where you'll also find the Fudge Factory and 24 flavors of homemade ice cream and butter fudge.

As you enter Old Town, you may spot a giant fish sculpture. Take a closer look; it's made of plastic beach debris. The **Washed Ashore Project** (http://washedashore.org) draws attention to the problem of plastic pollution; the **Harbortown Events Center** (325 2nd St. S.E., 541/329-0317, 11am-5pm Tues.-Sat.) hosts an exhibit of more beach litter art.

## Bandon Historical Society Museum

The captivating **Bandon Historical Society Museum** (270 Fillmore St., 541/347-2164,

# Bogged Down with Cranberries

From the vantage point of U.S. 101 between Port Orford and 10 miles north of Bandon, you'll notice what appears to be reddish-tinged ground in flood-irrigated fields. If you get closer, you'll see cranberries—small evergreen bushes that creep along the ground and send out runners that take root. Along the runners, upright branches six to eight inches long hold pink flowers and, later, deep-red fruit.

These berries are cultivated in bogs to satisfy their tremendous need for water and to protect them against insects and winter cold. Bandon leads Oregon in this crop, with an output ranking third in the nation. Oregon berries are often used in cranberry juice production because of their deep red pigment and high vitamin C content.

Fill up on cranberry confections at **Cranberry Sweets** (280 1st St. SE, Bandon, 541/347-9475 or 800/527-5748, 9:30am-5:30pm daily). For sale are confections ranging from cranberry fudge to cranberry truffles. Other shops in town, including the local grocery store, stock **Vincent Family** (www.vincentcranberries.com) dried cranberries or cranberry juice. Three generations of Vincents have been tending cranberry bogs; they're committed to making the business sustainable and are working toward organic certification for their berries.

http://bandonhistoricalmuseum.org, 10am-4pm daily June-Sept., 10am-4pm Mon.-Sat. Oct.-Dec. and Feb.-May, $3 adults, free for children), at the corner of U.S. 101 and Fillmore Street in Bandon's former city hall, traces the history of the Coquille people and their forebears. The chronology continues with the steamers and railroads that brought in white settlers. One room is devoted to Bandon's unofficial standing as the cranberry capital of Oregon. Black-and-white photos showing women stooping over in the bogs to harvest the ripe berries are captioned with such quips as this classic from an overseer: "I had 25 women picking for me, and I knew every one by her fanny." Color photos spanning five decades of Cranberry Festival princesses also adorn the walls.

Another room depicts Bandon's Resort Years, 1900 to 1931, when the town was called the "Playground of the Pacific." The most compelling exhibits in the museum deal with shipwrecks and the fires of 1914 and 1936.

## Scenic Beach Loop

U.S. 101 follows an inland path for more than 50 miles between Coos Bay and Port Orford, but you can leave the highway in Bandon and take the four-mile Beach Loop for a lovely seaside detour south of town. Several access roads lead west from the highway to Beach Loop Drive (County Rd. 29), each about 0.25 miles from the others. Most people begin the drive by heading west from Old Town on 1st Street along the Coquille. Another popular approach is from 11th Street, which leads to Coquille Point. The south end of the drive runs through the northern portion of **Bandon State Natural Area,** providing parking, beach access, and picnic tables.

The once-bucolic drive along the Beach Loop has changed a bit—trophy homes form pretty much the only view you have for the first mile or two. Still, there are state park parking areas that let you put the McMansions to your back and allow a look at the gorgeous ocean views or a trek down the bluff to a gorgeous beach.

Along this fine stretch of beach are rock formations with such evocative names as Table Rock, Elephant Rock, Garden of the Gods, and Cat and Kittens Rocks. The whole grouping of sea stacks (rocks eroded away from their original cliffs by the sea), included within the Oregon Islands National Wildlife Refuge, looks like a surrealist chess set cast upon the waters. The most eye-catching of all is **Face Rock,** a basalt monolith that resembles the face of a woman gazing skyward. A Native American legend says that she was a princess frozen by an evil sea spirit. Look for the Face Rock turnout 0.25 miles south of Coquille Point on the Beach Loop. Every few weeks, a volunteer group, Circles in the Sand (http://onepath.us), carves an elaborate labyrinth into the sand at the Face Rock beach; semi-organized mindfulness walks occur in the mornings when the labyrinth is intact.

Despite their scenic and recreational attractions, the beaches south of town can be surprisingly deserted, perhaps because of the long, steep trails up from the water along some parts. In any case, this dearth of people can make for great beachcombing. Agates, driftwood, and tide pools full of starfish and anemones are commonly encountered, along with bird-watching opportunities galore. Elephant Rock has a reputation as the Parthenon of puffins, while murres, oystercatchers, and other species proliferate on the other offshore formations.

### Bullards Beach State Park

Two miles north of Bandon, bordering the Coquille River estuary and more than four miles of beachfront, **Bullards Beach State Park** (541/347-2209 or 800/551-6949, www.oregonstateparks.org, most campsites $26-29) is a great place to fish, crab, bike, fly a kite, windsurf, picnic, or overnight in the large sheltered campground. The beach and lighthouse are reached via a scenic three-mile drive paralleling the Coquille River. Look for jasper and agates amid the heaps of driftwood on the shore. Equestrian trails and horse-camping facilities make this a popular destination for riders. The boat ramp gives anglers, kayakers, and canoeists access to the lower Coquille River and Bandon Marsh National Wildlife Refuge.

The riverside road going out to the Coquille's north jetty takes you through the dunes to the picturesque **Coquille River Lighthouse** (tours 11am-5pm daily mid-May-Sept., free), a squat tower with adjacent octagonal quarters. The last lighthouse built on the Oregon coast, it was completed in 1896, then abandoned in 1939 when the Coast Guard installed an automated light across the river. After years of neglect, the structure was restored in the late 1970s; its light is now solar-powered. Etchings of ships that made it across Bandon's treacherous bar—and some that didn't—greet you inside.

The Coquille River Lighthouse is just north of Bandon.

## West Coast Game Park

Seven miles south of Bandon is the **West Coast Game Park Safari** (46914 U.S. 101 S., 541/347-3106, www.westcoastgamepark-safari.com, 10am-5pm daily mid-June-Labor Day, call for hours fall-spring, $17.50 adults, $16.50 seniors, $10 ages 7-12, $7 ages 2-6), the self-proclaimed largest wild animal petting park in the country. There are 450 animals representing 75 different species, including tiger cubs, camels, zebras, monkeys, and snow leopards. Visitors may be surprised to see a lion and tiger caged together, or a fox and a raccoon sharing the same nursery. The park tries raising different species together and often finds that animals can live harmoniously with their natural enemies. Free-roaming animals include deer, peacocks, pygmy goats, and llamas. An elk refuge is another popular area of the park. Even if you're not with a child, the opportunity to pet a pup, a cub, or a kit can bring out the kid in you. The park is open year-round, but call during winter because the hours of operation are restricted.

## New River

In 1890, storm-blown sand blocked the outlet of Floras Lake (located south of Bandon), and flood water flowed into a low channel just east of a dune paralleling the beach, forming New River. The river runs north from the lake for nine miles, through a remote area with only a couple of roads leading to it and a trail along its length. Hikers and paddlers have the chance to see birds, animals, and plants that are otherwise rarely spotted. Some areas are set aside from March 15 to September 15 for nesting snowy plovers; check the information boards so you'll be sure to avoid these areas. A **nature center** (Croft Lake Lane, 541/756-0100, www.blm.gov, sunrise-sunset daily, free) located at Storm Ranch, two miles west of the highway and about 8.5 miles south of Bandon, is a good place to learn more about the area and access trails. The trail is also easy to reach at Floras Lake, west of the town of Langlois.

# SPORTS AND RECREATION

## Horseback Riding

**Bandon Beach Riding Stables** (2640 Beach Loop Rd., 541/347-3423, year-round, $50-70) is four miles south of Face Rock on the Beach Loop. Several beach rides are offered daily, plus sunset rides in the summer. Riders of all abilities are welcome, including those with disabilities. Reservations are advised.

## Wildlife-Viewing

Bird-watchers flock to the tidal salt marsh and the elevated observation deck of the **Bandon Marsh National Wildlife Refuge** (541/347-1470, www.fws.gov, sunrise-sunset daily), especially in the fall, to take in what may be the prime birding site on the coast. The extensive mudflats attract flocks of shorebirds, including red phalaropes, black-bellied plovers, long-billed curlews, and dunlins, as well as such strays from Asia as Mongolian plovers.

Reach Bandon Marsh by a short paddle across the river from the Bullards Beach State Park, or via Riverside Drive, which runs from Bandon to U.S. 101 on the south side of the Coquille River bridge. The refuge protects more than 700 precious acres of the Coquille estuary's remaining salt-marsh habitat along the southeastern side of the river. Migrating waterfowl, bald eagles, California brown pelicans, and other birds feast on the rich food sources. From U.S. 101 just north of Bandon, turn west onto Riverside Drive and continue for about one mile, where you'll reach the refuge.

## Fishing

The Coquille River runs 30 miles from its Siskiyou headwaters before meandering leisurely through Bandon. The north and south jetties are popular spots for perch and rockfish, while the city docks right in Old Town yield catches of perch and crab April-October and smelt July-September. The spring chinook run pales in comparison to those in the Rogue and Chetco Rivers to the south, but the fall runs of chinook (Sept.-Oct.) and coho (Oct.-Nov.) are strong and productive. Steelhead usually arrive in November, and the run gathers steam in January-February. A boat is necessary for the best steelhead and salmon water, but bank anglers can fish the mouth of Ferry Creek, just off Riverside Drive in Bandon. Fishing guides and gear can be arranged through **Bandon Bait & Tackle** (110 1st St., 541/347-3905, 6am-6pm daily), across from the boat basin. The shop also rents crab rings and other gear and can point you to productive spots for catching Dungeness crab. It's also not a bad place to grab a plate of fish-and-chips.

Just off the south end of Beach Loop Drive, 30-acre **Bradley Lake,** protected from ocean winds by high dunes, offers good trout fishing and a boat ramp. Each spring the lake is stocked with trophy rainbows, averaging five pounds, reared at the Bandon Fish Hatchery east of town.

### Golf

South of town, **Bandon Crossing Golf Course** (87530 Dew Valley Lane, 541/347-3232, www.bandoncrossings.com, $49-84 for 18 holes) is a forested, challenging, but fun course that's good for families, novices, and anyone looking for a less intense experience than at the Bandon Dunes Golf Resort.

### ★ BANDON DUNES GOLF RESORT

**Bandon Dunes Golf Resort** (57744 Round Lake Dr., 541/347-4380 or 800/742-0172, www.bandondunesgolf.com, May-Oct. greens fees $275 hotel guests, $325 nonguests, off-season $85-295, reduced rates for same-day 2nd round) has drawn accolades from the golf press and is by far the most spectacular place to golf in Oregon. The original Bandon Dunes course has 7 holes along the Pacific and unobstructed ocean views from all 18. Three other 18-hole courses, Pacific Dunes, Bandon Trails, and Old Macdonald (inspired by golf course architect C. B. Macdonald), give golfers a chance to stay for a few days and keep encountering new territory. Resort guests also have free access to the Punchbowl, an 18-hole

putting course, and Shorty's, a 9-hole par-3 practice course.

In addition to the main courses, the 13-hole par-3 Bandon Preserve course ($100 peak season, $50-75 off-season) starts at the top of a sand dune and works its way down to the beach. Proceeds from this course go to the Wild Rivers Coast Alliance, an organization that supports conservation, community, and the economy along the southern Oregon coast. To preserve the natural surroundings along the ocean bluffs, this Scottish links course doesn't allow carts (the only amenity missing), so you'll have to hire a caddie or schlep your own bag (a practice that is frowned upon here). A luxurious resort with Pacific views, attentive staff, and a fine restaurant are also available for those who come to worship in the south coast's Sistine Chapel of golf.

Golfers who have never played on the Oregon coast should come prepared for wind, especially in the afternoon. Oregon golfers may know about the wind, but we have a special piece of advice for you—dress up. This is a rather formal place, and you'll feel out of place in your baggy cargo shorts and faded polo shirt. The resort is one mile north of the Coquille River. November through April, Oregonians are admitted at the guest rate. Caddies expect at least $100 per bag.

## ENTERTAINMENT AND EVENTS

### Brewpubs

Although **Bandon Brewing** (395 2nd St. SE, 541/347-3911, www.bandonbrewingco.com, 11am-8pm Sun.-Thurs., 11am-10pm Fri.-Sat., $8-14) was brand new when we visited, and they were just getting going with the actual on-site brewing (imports from Coos Bay were on offer), this family- and dog-friendly pub with good wood-fired pizza and a friendly atmosphere was still a fun place to spend an evening.

### Festivals and Events

A parade, cardboard boat races, and ice cream and apple pie are highlights of Bandon's **Fourth of July** celebration; at dusk, fireworks are launched across the Coquille to burst above the river.

The biggest weekend of the year for Bandonians comes the second weekend in September, when the **Cranberry Festival** (541/347-9616, www.bandon.com) brings everyone together in Old Town for a parade, a crafts fair, tours of a cranberry farm, and the Bandon High Cranberry Bowl—in which the local footballers take on traditional rival Coquille High.

## FOOD

If you want an edible souvenir or gift, stop by the roadside stand **Misty Meadows Jams** (48053 U.S. 101 S., 541/347-2575, www.oregon-jam.com, 9am-5pm daily) for a wide variety of jams and jellies, including products incorporating Bandon cranberries. In addition to preserves, the shop sells olives and fruit-based barbecue sauce, syrup, honey, and salsa. Look here and in other shops in town for Vincent Family dried cranberries or cranberry juice, produced by three generations of Vincents.

### Face Rock Creamery

For over a century, Bandon was Oregon's "other" cheese-making center, and cheeses from the Bandon Cheddar Cheese Factory rivaled those of Tillamook until the operation closed in 2002. Cheese making returned to Bandon in 2013 with the opening of the **Face Rock Creamery** (680 2nd St. SE, 541/347-3233, www.facerockcreamery.com, 9am-7pm daily), just north of downtown Bandon on U.S. 101. Stop to watch cheese production and taste the many samples of cheese made from local milk (the Coquille River valley east of Bandon is lined with dairies). The creamery also sells a large selection of cheeses and gourmet food items from around the world—this is a good place to stock up for picnics—and it offers freshly made ice cream, deli sandwiches, and a wine bar as well.

### American

Head to the bustling **Minute Café** (145 2nd St., 541/347-2707, 5:30am-8pm Thurs.-Mon.,

5:30am-3pm Tues.-Wed., $6-14), where locals and visitors settle in with the morning paper, omelets, and pancakes. Later in the day, the menu features burgers, sandwiches, and chowder. For coffee and a tasty cinnamon roll, head across the street to the **Bandon Baking Co. and Deli** (160 2nd St., 541/347-9440, www.bandonbakingco.com, 8am-4pm Tues.-Sat. Feb.-Dec.).

### Italian

Although it's called a wine bar, ★ **Alloro Wine Bar** (375 2nd St., 541/347-1850, www.allorowinebar.com, 4pm-9pm daily Mar.-Dec., dinner $26-36) is the top choice in town for an Italian dinner. But don't come looking for basic spaghetti—the cuisine is much more upscale. Instead, expect smoked steelhead alfredo or Tuscan-style seafood stew. The food is excellent, and the pace is relaxed. The pasta is house-made, and most of the produce is local. If you don't want a full dinner, there's a small bar where you can taste a flight of wines and nibble on olives or Italian cheeses.

### Pacific Northwest Cuisine

From its second-floor perch above the harbor, ★ **The Loft** (315 1st St. SE, 541/329-0535, www.theloftofbandon.com, 5pm-9pm Tues.-Sun., $18-38) serves some of the best dinners—and best views—in town and with lovely views out. Abundant use is made of local produce, and there's always lots of good seafood on the menu. The dining room is fairly small, so reservations are a good idea.

Although the initial attraction may be the views of the Coquille River and lighthouse, the food is also very good at **Edgewater's** (480 1st St. NW, 541/347-8500, http://edgewaters.net, 11:30am-3pm and 5pm-9:30pm Fri.-Sun., 5pm-9:30pm Mon.-Thurs. June-Sept., 11:30am-3pm and 5pm-9:30pm Fri.-Sun., 5pm-9:30pm Tues.-Thurs. Oct.-May, $15-30). Fresh fish is a highlight here—go for the halibut if it's in season—but there are also plenty of steak and pasta dishes, including a rich and delicious farfalle with smoked salmon.

A longtime favorite on the Beach Loop,

Lord Bennett's (1695 Beach Loop Dr., 541/347-3663, http://lordbennett.com, 5pm-9pm daily, 10am-2pm Sun. $15-31) offers a dramatic ocean view. The food does justice to these surroundings with elegantly rendered pasta, steak, chicken, and seafood dishes. Jazz on selected evenings in the lounge adds a nice touch.

The Bandon Dunes Golf Resort (57744 Round Lake Dr., 541/347-4380 or 888/345-6008, www.bandondunesgolf.com) offers a number of dining options. In the main lodge is the Gallery (6am-10pm daily, $24-60), a good place to eat an excellent steak, and the many seasonal fish and seafood preparations are always noteworthy. If you're not staying at the resort, lunch ($9-14) is an interesting time to get a feel for the place and to enjoy the views out onto the Bandon Dunes course. If you're looking for a less formal atmosphere, check out the adjacent Tufted Puffin Lounge or the Bunker Bar downstairs, which has a gentlemen's club vibe; both serve snacks and light meals. Lunch and bar snacks have an Asian touch at the Trails End Clubhouse (6am-7pm daily, $10-14), in the Bandon Trails Clubhouse. In the evening, a good spot for an informal meal is McKee's Pub (2pm-midnight, $12-34), which has a Scottish country pub atmosphere, plus a wide-ranging menu that includes individual pizzas, burgers, steaks, and hearty favorites like meatloaf and fish-and-chips. In addition to a good selection of regional microbrews, in good weather McKee's also offers a marvelous outdoor patio fronting onto the course. In the Pacific Dunes Clubhouse is the Pacific Grill (6am-10pm daily, $24-38) for a dining-in-the-round experience. The menu ranges from burgers and sandwiches for lunch to sturgeon or pork for dinner.

## Seafood

If you're looking for inexpensive street food, check along 1st Street near the Old Town Marina, where Tony's Crab Shack (155 1st St., 541/347-2875, http://tonyscrabshack.com, 10:30am-7pm daily, $9-16) sells crab sandwiches, fish tacos, grilled salmon, steamer clams, and lots more. As the name implies, it's not really a sit-down place, though there are a few picnic tables on the dock.

Line up for your fish-and-chips to go at the Bandon Fish Market (249 1st St. SE, 541/347-4282, www.bandonfishmarket.com, 11am-7pm daily, $5-20). Though it's takeout only, a picnic table outside near the harbor is the place to enjoy it all, with a trip across the street to Cranberry Sweets (280 1st St. SE, 541/347-9475 or 800/527-5748, 9:30am-6pm Mon.-Sat., 9:30am-5pm Sun.) for dessert.

## ACCOMMODATIONS

For the best ocean views, often with nearby trails to the beach, look to the lodgings along the Beach Loop. If you want to be able to walk to dinner in Old Town, stay at one of the in-town locations. For the best of both worlds, bring a bike and cycle into town from a Beach Loop room. Bandon bills itself as America's storm-watching capital, and special packages are often available October to March.

### $50-100

Right in the heart of Old Town, the ★ Sea Star Guesthouse (370 1st St., 541/347-9632, www.seastarbandon.com, $80-125) has just six rooms. Four rooms are spacious, charming, and uniquely decorated, with skylights, wood-beam ceilings, a verdant courtyard, and views onto the harbor. The other two rooms are less expensive and a bit less spacious, but are some of the best deals in town.

On a bluff at the top of Beach Loop Road, find an assortment of motel rooms and small cottages at Table Rock Motel (840 Beach Loop Dr., 541/347-2700 or 800/457-9141, www.tablerockmotel.com, $70-175). The least expensive rooms are small, with no ocean views, but all are a short, steep walk away from one of the coast's prettiest beaches.

Farther down the Beach Loop is Sunset Lodging (1865 Beach Loop Rd., 541/347-2453 or 800/842-2407, www.sunsetmotel.com, $85-225), a motel complex with a variety of lodging types, including some that have been recently (and deservedly) remodeled. With some units built right into the cliff above a scenic beach, the view here is hard to beat. Nonetheless, the steep steps down the 80-foot-high bluff to the beach, the busy atmosphere, and the rusticity of the least expensive guest rooms might not be to everyone's liking.

## $100-150

Set on a bluff overlooking Old Town, the ★ **Bandon Inn** (355 U.S. 101, 541/347-4417 or 800/526-0209, www.bandoninn.com, $144-185) has spectacular views, comfortable rooms—all with balconies—and a path down to town. Pets are permitted in some rooms; a couple of suites ($259-279) are also available. This is a great spot to stay if you want the wining and dining of Old Town within walking distance.

A favorite place to stay on the Beach Loop is the older but refurbished **Windermere on the Beach** (3250 Beach Loop Rd., 541/347-3710, www.windermereonthebeach.com, $139-209), where baby-boomers can relive their childhood beach getaways in old-fashioned cottages or motel rooms (some with kitchens), situated on a bluff above a windswept beach. Housekeeping facilities and proximity to restaurants (Lord Bennett's) and the West Coast Game Park also make this an ideal family vacation spot.

## $150-200

Another popular place is the **Best Western Inn at Face Rock** (3225 Beach Loop Rd., 541/347-9441 or 800/638-3092, www.innatfacerock.com, $179-299). Part of its popularity has to do with the motel's location—set back from the road near the southern end of the Beach Loop, across the road from Bandon's coastline. Many of the modern well-appointed guest rooms have magnificent ocean views. The indoor pool, fitness room, whirlpool, and restaurant also make this an especially good choice for travelers looking for amenities. Some suites have fireplaces, kitchenettes, and private patios. There is a short path to the beach.

## Over $200

For avid golfers or those seeking upscale accommodations, amenities, and service, the **Bandon Dunes Golf Resort** (57744 Round Lake Dr., 541/347-4380 or 888/345-6008, www.bandondunesgolf.com, most rooms $220-430) is the place to stay. Lodging is in several different locations around the resort and includes single lodge or inn rooms in various sizes, two- or four-bedroom suites, and multiple-bedroom cottages (up to $1,900). View options vary from golf course and ocean views to dune and surrounding woods. Bandon Dunes is 5 minutes from Bandon, 1 mile north of the Coquille River, and 27 miles (30 minutes' drive) from the North Bend Airport, which is served by daily flights from Portland and Denver. Nongolfers can fish, take a meditative walk on the resort's labyrinth, or hike more wild trails.

## Vacation Rentals

Bandon is an easy place to spend a weekend, and there are several property management companies that can help you find a house to rent.

Many of the places offered by **Exclusive Property Management** (541/347-3790 or 800/527-5445, www.visitbandon.com) are large and quite upscale, with great locations and lovely interior design. It also rents a few more modest homes, so don't be afraid to call or check the website. **Bandon Beach Vacation Rentals** (54515 Beach Loop Rd., 541/347-4801 or 888/441-8030, www.bandonbeachrentals.com) has several reasonably priced units available, including one that'll sleep 10 people.

## Camping

**Bullards Beach State Park** (information 541/347-2209 or 800/551-6949, reservations 800/452-5687, www.oregonstateparks.org, $26-29, horse camp $19, yurts $43-53, hiker-biker $5) is a large and busy state park, with over 200 tightly packed campsites in a great location between the Coquille River and four miles of beach. To get here, drive north of town on U.S. 101 for about one mile; just past the bridge on the west side of the highway is the park entrance. The beach is reached via a scenic two-mile drive paralleling the Coquille River. Electricity, picnic tables, and grills are provided.

## INFORMATION AND SERVICES

The **Bandon Chamber of Commerce** (300 W. 2nd St., Bandon, 541/347-9616, www.bandon.com) in Old Town distributes a comprehensive guide and a large annotated pictographic map of the town.

**Southern Coos General Hospital** (900 11th St. SE, 541/347-2426) features an ocean view that is in itself therapeutic, as well as a 24-hour emergency room.

## GETTING THERE AND AROUND

North- and southbound **Coastal Express** (800/921-2871, www.currypublictransit.org) buses run Monday-Friday between North Bend and Brookings.

Between Bandon and Coos Bay, you can escape the tedium of U.S. 101's inland route by taking twisty-turning **Seven Devils Road** about three miles north of Bandon. This route runs 13 miles to **Charleston,** a fishing village that sits closer to the ocean than its larger neighbors to the northeast, Coos Bay and North Bend. En route, beaches, state parks, and an estuarine preserve make the drive interesting, although the miles of heavily logged mountainsides may take you aback.

# Port Orford and Vicinity

Port Orford marks the northernmost end of one of the most spectacular stretches of coastline in the United States. From Bandon, the highway runs inland; when it hits Port Orford, the road nearly runs into the Pacific. And what a splendid place to encounter the ocean: The beach is perfect for long treasure-hunting walks, and the bluffs just to the north are also fun to explore. A few miles north, blustery Cape Blanco is the westernmost point of the continental United States; a short distance south, Humbug Mountain rises almost directly from the ocean. All of these places are great for a quick ogle and a snapshot, but even better for hiking and exploring. Port Orford is a good base for all of that, with a wide range of accommodations and a few good places to eat.

## SIGHTS AND RECREATION

Port Orford has an ocean view from downtown that is arguably the most scenic of any town on the coast. A waterfront stroll lets you appreciate the cliffs and offshore sea stacks, as well as the unique sight of commercial fishing boats being hoisted by large cranes into and out of the harbor. With only a short jetty on its north side, Port Orford's harbor, the only open-water port in Oregon, is unprotected from southerly swells, so boats can't be safely moored on the water. When not in use, the fleet rests on wheeled trailer-like dollies near the foot of the pier.

A stroll or bike ride through town is a perfect way to visit Port Orford's impressive selection of galleries. These are, by and large, much different and far more interesting than the typical seaside-town collections of landscape paintings and sunset photos. Expect to find high-quality crafts, glass art, sculpture, and computer-generated art.

### Battle Rock Park

As you come into town on U.S. 101, it's hard to ignore enormous Battle Rock on the shoreline, the site of the 1851 conflict between local Native Americans and the first landing party of white colonists. If you can make your way through the driftwood and blackberry bushes surrounding its base, you can climb the short

# Port Orford Indian Wars

In 1850, the U.S. Congress passed the Oregon Donation Land Act, allowing white settlers to file claims on Native American land in western Oregon. This was news, of course, to the Native American nations of the region, who had not been consulted on the decision. William Tichenor, captain of the steamship *Gull*, hoping to exploit the new act, had ambitions to establish an outpost on the coast at what's now Port Orford. When Tichenor observed the hostility of the Quatomah band of the Tututni people in the tidewater, he put nine men ashore on an immense rock promontory fronting the beach because of its suitability as a defensive position. The Native Americans besieged the rock for two weeks before the colonists escaped under cover of night. Tichenor returned with a well-armed party of 70 men and succeeded in founding his settlement.

From this inauspicious beginning, Port Orford established itself as the first town site on the south coast. Shortly thereafter, the town became the site of the first fort established on the coast during the Rogue River Wars. This conflict started when gold miners and settlers came into Native American lands. As a result of the clashes, hundreds of local indigenous people were rounded up and sent to the Siletz Reservation near Lincoln City in 1856.

trail to the top for a heightened perspective on the rockbound coast that parallels the town. You'll also notice the east-west orientation of the harbor. Once you get to the top of the rock, don't think the battle is necessarily over. Bracing winds often chill you, and high tides can sometimes render this coastal finger of land an island. The rock is also the site of a fireworks display at the **Fourth of July Jubilee Celebration.**

Even if you're not up for a scramble on Battle Rock, do take the short path down to the beach, which is relatively sheltered from the wind and a good place for a walk. It's also a good spot for beachcombing, with agates and fishing floats being the prize finds.

If you'd rather do your scavenging inland, try searching the nearby foothills for the lost Port Orford meteorite. The meteorite was found in the 1860s by a government geologist, who estimated its weight at 22,000 tons. Unfortunately, he was unable to locate the meteorite when he returned for another look.

## Port Orford Heads State Park

Another shoreline scene, featuring a striking panorama from north to south, is up West 9th Street at **Port Orford Heads State Park** (541/332-6774, www.oregonstateparks.org, free). If you go down the cement trail to the

tip of the blustery headland, you look south to the mouth of Port Orford's harbor. To the north, many small rocks fill the water, along with boats trolling for salmon or checking crab pots. On clear days, visibility extends from Cape Blanco to Humbug Mountain.

Also here is the historic **Port Orford Lifeboat Station** (10am-3:30pm Wed.-Mon. Apr.-Oct., free), built by the Coast Guard in 1934 to provide rescue service to the southern Oregon coast. After it was decommissioned in 1970, the officers' quarters, the pleasingly proportioned crew barracks, and other outbuildings were converted into a museum depicting the work of the station. A trail leads down to Nellie's Cove, site of the former boathouse and launch ramp.

## ★ Cape Blanco State Park and Hughes House

Four miles north of Port Orford, west of U.S. 101, is **Cape Blanco,** whose remoteness gives you the feeling of being at the edge of the continent—as indeed you are here, at the westernmost point in Oregon. From the vantage of Cape Blanco, dark mountains rise behind you and the eaves of the forest overhang the tidewater. Below, driftwood and 100-foot-long bull kelp on slivers of black-sand beach fan out from both sides of this earthy red bluff.

Somehow, the Spaniards who sailed past it in 1603 viewed the cape as having a *blanco* (white) color. It has been theorized that perhaps they were referring to fossilized shells on the front of the cliff.

With its exposed location, Cape Blanco really takes it on the chin from Pacific storms. The vegetation along the five-mile state park road down to the beach attests to the severity of winter storms in the area. Gales of 100-mph winds (record winds have been clocked at 184 mph) and horizontal sheets of rain have given some of the usually massive Sitka spruces the appearance of bonsai trees. An understory of salmonberry and bracken fern help evoke the look of a southeast Alaskan forest.

Atop the weathered headland is Oregon's oldest, most westerly, and highest lighthouse in continuous use. Built in 1870, the beacon stands 256 feet above sea level and can be seen some 23 nautical miles out at sea. **Cape Blanco Lighthouse** (541/332-6774, 10am-3:30pm Wed.-Mon. Apr.-Oct., $2 adults) also holds the distinction of having had Oregon's first female lighthouse keeper, Mabel E. Bretherton, who assumed her duties in 1903. Tours of the facility include the chance to climb the 64 spiraling steps to the top. This is the only operational lighthouse in the state that allows visitors into the lantern room to view the working Fresnel lens.

Near Cape Blanco on a side road along the Sixes River is the **Hughes House** (541/332-0248, 10am-3:30pm Wed.-Mon. Apr.-Oct., free), a restored Victorian home built in 1898 for rancher and county commissioner Patrick Hughes. Owned and operated today by the state of Oregon, the house offers an intriguing glimpse of rural life on the coast over a century ago.

## ★ Humbug Mountain

Some people will tell you that 1,756-foot-high Humbug Mountain, six miles south of Port Orford on U.S. 101, is the highest mountain rising directly off the Oregon shoreline. Because the criteria for such a distinction vary as much as the tides, let's just say it's a special place. There's more than one version of how the peak, formerly called Sugarloaf Mountain, got its name. According to one, gold miners drawn here in the 1850s by tales of gold in the black sands nearby soon discovered that the rumored riches proved to be "humbug."

Once the site of Native American vision quests, Humbug Mountain now casts its shadow upon a state park campground surrounded by myrtles, alders, and maples. Just

Humbug Mountain

north is a breezy black-sand beach. A three-mile trail to the top of Humbug rewards hardy hikers with impressive vistas to the south of Nesika Beach and a chance to see wild rhododendrons 20 to 25 feet high. Rising above the rhodies and giant ferns are bigleaf maples, Port Orford cedars, and Douglas and grand firs. Access the trail from the campground or from a trailhead parking area off the highway near the south end of the park. In addition, the **Oregon Coast Trail,** which follows the beach south from Battle Rock, traverses the mountain and leads down its south side to the beach at Rocky Point.

## Prehistoric Gardens

What can we say about this unique roadside attraction, featuring a 25-foot-tall Formica-green *Tyrannosaurus rex* standing beside the parking lot? Is it kitsch, or is it educational? You decide. In any case, if you've got children in the car, unless they're sleeping or blindfolded, you're probably going to have to pull over. **Prehistoric Gardens** (36848 U.S. 101, 541/332-4463, www.prehistoricgardens.com, 9am-6pm daily summer, 10am-5pm daily spring and fall, call for winter hours, $12 adults, $10 over age 59, $8 ages 3-12), about 10 miles south of Port Orford, is the creation of E. V. Nelson, a sculptor and self-taught paleontologist who began fabricating life-size dinosaurs here back in 1953 and placing them amid the lush rainforest on the back of Humbug Mountain. Paths lead through the ferns, trees, and undergrowth to a towering brontosaurus, triceratops, and 20 other ferro-concrete replicas, painted in a dazzling palette of Fiestaware colors.

## Grassy Knob Wilderness

The **Grassy Knob Wilderness** (Siskiyou National Forest, Powers Ranger District, 541/439-6200, www.fs.usda.gov) encompasses 17,200 acres of steep, rugged terrain and protects rare stands of Port Orford cedar. The wood of this majestic fragrant tree is light, strong, and durable. Its use in planes during World War II and in Japanese construction has made it highly valued, but a fatal root fungus spread by logging trucks accounts for its rarity and astronomically high price. (As you travel around the area, you may notice the dead or dying cedars.) During World War II, Japanese submarines used Cape Blanco Lighthouse as an orientation mark to aim planes loaded with incendiary bombs at the Coast Range. The Japanese hoped to ignite forest fires that would destroy the region's Port Orford cedar trees, which were used to construct airplanes. Because of the perennial dampness, the results were negligible. A short (0.8-mile) but moderately difficult trail leads to the summit of Grassy Knob. To get here, follow U.S. 101 north of Port Orford about four miles, then go east on County Road 196 to Forest Road 5105, which ends at the trailhead.

## Bicycling

The **Wild Rivers Coast Scenic Bikeway** (rideoregonride.com) starts and ends in Port Orford, and over the course of 61 miles visits the Elk River, Cape Blanco State Park, Paradise Point, and Port Orford Heads State Park. It's easy to break this long ride down into shorter trips.

## Boating and Waterskiing

In the northwest part of town, drive west of the highway on 14th or 18th Streets to 90-acre **Garrison Lake** for boating, waterskiing, and fishing for stocked rainbow and cutthroat trout. **Buffington Memorial City Park,** at the end of 14th Street, has a dock for fishing or swimming, plus playing fields, tennis courts, picnic areas, hiking trails, and a horse arena. Half a mile north of the lake, look for agates on **Paradise Point Beach.**

## Fishing

The **Elk River,** which empties on the south side of Cape Blanco, and the **Sixes River,** which meets the sea north of the cape, are two popular streams for salmon and steelhead fishing. Chinook and steelhead begin to enter both rivers after the first good rains of fall arrive, usually in November. Private lands limit bank access, with the exception of a good stretch of the Sixes that runs through Cape Blanco State Park. The salmon season runs to the end of the year, and steelhead through the following March. **Lamm's Guide Service** (541/784-5145, www.umpquafishingguide. com) leads trips on both rivers.

## Surfing

The south-facing beach at **Battle Rock Beach,** in downtown Port Orford, can be okay for surfing during the winter, when northwesterly winds blow in. Otherwise, surfers tend to go about a mile south of town to the beach at **Hubbard Creek** (best in the spring). What these spots may lack in intensity, they make up for in scenery.

## Windsurfing and Kiteboarding

Between Port Orford and Bandon (just southwest of Langlois) is **Floras Lake,** one of the southern Oregon coast's two great windsurfing and kiteboarding spots (the other is south of Gold Beach at **Pistol River**). The lake, just barely inland from the beach, catches incredible breezes. **Floras Lake Windsurfing & Kiteboarding** (541/348-9912, www.floraslake.com) offers lessons and rentals; the proprietors also have a nice B&B just above the lake. It's 11 miles north of Port Orford, about four miles west of the highway on Floras Lake Loop Road. On the lake is **Boice Cope County Park,** which has basic tent and RV sites and a boat ramp. When the wind's not blowing (fat chance, though), explore the hiking trails from the campground to the beach. From Floras Lake north to Bandon is the most isolated beachfront on the Oregon coast—ideal for beachcombing. Follow the New River north from Floras Lake. Grasses, dunes, and shore pines usher you the 25 miles back to Bandon, and chances are good you won't see a soul.

## FOOD

Port Orford doesn't have a lot of restaurants, but there are a few good places to eat,

Winds rip at Pistol River, south of Gold Beach, attracting windsurfers and kiteboarders.

including two of the best fish-and-chips joints on the coast.

Make sure to visit Port Orford's docks, where **Griff's on the Dock** (303 Dock Rd., 541/332-8985, 10:30am-8pm Mon.-Sat., 10:30am-7:30pm Sun., $7-20), a weathered shack amid the boats and tackle shops, serves up excellent fish-and-chips. The fish here is as fresh as it gets, and the atmosphere, with crusty old anglers eating hot dogs and talking crabbing, is not your cookie-cutter idea of a fish-and-chips place.

There are more really good fish-and-chips up on the highway, where **The Crazy Norwegians** (259 6th St., 541/332-8601, 11am-8pm Tues.-Sun., $8-16) also serves tasty tuna melts, burgers, and chowder. It's a busy place, so expect to wait on a summer weekend.

The best views and most upscale dinners are at **Redfish** (517 Jefferson St., 541/366-2200, www.redfishportorford.com, 11am-9pm Mon.-Fri., 10am-3pm and 5pm-9pm Sat.-Sun., $15-38). There's always fresh fish, perhaps halibut served over Israeli couscous with béarnaise sauce. The food is a little hit-or-miss, but the setting is almost worth the price (come 4pm-6pm Mon.-Fri. happy hour). Adjoining the restaurant is an upscale gallery.

## ACCOMMODATIONS

With one notable exception, Port Orford is the kind of place where a room with a view will not break your budget.

### $50-100

Just south of town, the **Seacrest Motel** (44 U.S. 101 S., 541/332-3040, www.seacrestoregon.com, $60-91) features views of coastal cliffs and a garden from a quiet hillside on the east side of the highway. Pets are welcome at this older motel.

★ **Castaway-by-the-Sea** (545 W. 5th St., 541/332-4502, www.castawaybythesea.com, $85-165) features ocean and harbor views from high on a bluff, fireplaces, and housekeeping units, and it allows pets. In addition to the rather basic motel rooms, the Castaway has a two-bedroom lodge that'll sleep up to seven (from $185). The rates on the upper-end lodgings go down significantly in the off-season. It's said that Jack London once stayed in an earlier incarnation of this place.

### $150-200

North of Port Orford, the **Floras Lake House B&B** (92870 Boice Cope Rd., Langlois, 541/348-2573, www.floraslake.com, $175-195, includes breakfast) is perfectly suited for windsurfers or others who want to explore the beaches in this unpopulated area. The spacious light-filled house looks out onto Floras Lake and the ocean, and the proprietors also offer windsurfing and kiteboarding lessons.

### Over $200

Port Orford's serene luxury resort is ★ **Wildspring Guest Habitat** (92978 Cemetery Loop, www.wildspring.com, $298-328, including continental breakfast). The small (five-cabin) resort is in a forested setting on a bluff high above the highway (but totally secluded from it), with views of the ocean from the main lodge and hot tub. The cabins are beautifully and meticulously designed and furnished (including a fridge, a massage table, and Wi-Fi access in each cabin, but no telephones or TVs) and are as comfortable as they are perfect-looking. The main guest hall has a kitchen that's available to guests as long as it's not being used to prepare breakfast. The well-tended grounds include a labyrinth and several meditation nooks, but perhaps the best place to hang out is the slate-lined hot tub, which looks out over treetops to the ocean. It's a good idea to take binoculars, as Wildspring is a stop along the Oregon Coast Birding Trail. This is a good place for a romantic retreat or a solo contemplative getaway.

### Camping

**Humbug Mountain State Park** (541/332-6774, www.oregonstateparks.org, reservations 800/452-5687 or www.reserveamerica.com), six miles south of Port Orford on U.S. 101, features 62 tent sites ($17) and 32 electrical sites for RVs ($24), along with wind-protected sites reserved for hikers and bikers ($5). Flush toilets, showers, picnic tables, water, and firewood are available. A short trail leads under the highway to the beach; a longer one goes up Humbug Mountain.

Reach **Cape Blanco State Park** (39745 U.S. 101 S., information 541/332-6774, cabin reservations 800/452-5687, $22-24 tents or RVs, $17 horse camp, $5 hiker-biker, $41-51 rustic cabins) by driving four miles north of Port Orford on U.S. 101, then heading northwest on the park road that continues five miles beyond to the campground. Sites are nestled into salal hedges where they're largely protected from the wind; picnic tables, water, and showers are available. For horseback riders, there's a seven-mile trail and a huge open riding area; horses are also allowed on the beach. Only cabins can be reserved; regular sites are first-come, first-served.

**Boice Cope County Park** (92850 Boice Cope Rd., Langlois, general information

541/247-3386, reservations 541/373-1555, www.co.curry.or.us, $15-22), on the shore of Floras Lake, is a good base for windsurfers and kiteboarders. The area is known for its wind.

## INFORMATION AND SERVICES

Begin your travels at **Battle Rock Information Center** (Battle Rock Wayside, 541/332-4106, www.enjoyportorford.com, 10am-3pm daily), on the west side of U.S. 101. The people here are especially friendly and helpful.

## GETTING THERE

Curry County's **Coastal Express** buses (800/921-2871, www.currypublictransit.org) run up and down the south coast Monday-Friday between North Bend and the California border, including local service in Port Orford.

# Gold Beach and Vicinity

This town is one part of the coast where the action is definitely away from the ocean. To lure people from Oregon's superlative ocean shores, the Rogue estuary has been bestowed with many blessings. First, the gold-laden black sands were mined in the 1850s and 1860s. While this short-lived boom era gave Gold Beach its name, the arrival of Robert Hume, later known as the Salmon King of the Rogue, had greater historical significance. By the turn of the 20th century, Hume's canneries were shipping out some 16,000 cases of salmon per year and established the river's image as a leading salmon and steelhead stream. This reputation was later enhanced by outdoorsman and novelist Zane Grey in his *Rogue River Feud* and other writings. Over the years, Herbert Hoover, Winston Churchill, Ginger Rogers (who had a home on the Rogue), Clark Gable, Jack London, George H. W. Bush, and Jimmy Carter, among other notables, have come here to try their luck. During the last several decades, boat tours focusing on the abundant wildlife, scenic beauty, and fascinating lore of the region have hooked other sectors of the traveling public.

At the north end of town, just before the road gives way to Conde McCullough's elegant Patterson Bridge (illuminated at night by LED lights), the harbor comes into view on the left, full of salmon trawlers, jet boats, pelicans, and seals bobbing up and down. Across the bridge is **Wedderburn,** a baby sister to Gold Beach and named for the Scottish birthplace of Robert Hume.

## SIGHTS
### Beaches

The driftwood-strewn strand of **South Beach,** just south of Gold Beach's harbor, is convenient but only so-so. You'll find more exciting stretches both north and south of town. Two miles south, there's easy access to a nice beach and some tide-pooling at tiny **Buena Vista State Park,** at the mouth of Hunter Creek. Seven miles south of Gold Beach, there's more tide-pooling amid the camera-friendly basalt sea stacks at beautiful **Myers Creek Beach,** part of Pistol River State Park south of Cape Sebastian. The south side of Cape Sebastian and **Pistol River State Park,** a couple of miles farther south, are the best places on the Oregon coast for windsurfers to sail in the ocean. The beaches around Pistol River are also great places to find razor clams.

**Bailey Beach,** north of town between the Rogue River jetty and Otter Point, is a popular spot for razor clamming, and **Nesika Beach,** seven miles north of Gold Beach, is a good tide-pooling destination.

## ★ Cape Sebastian

Seven miles south of Gold Beach is **Cape Sebastian.** This spectacular windswept headland was named by explorer Sebastián Vizcaíno, who plied offshore waters here for Spain in 1602 along with Martín de Aguilar. At 720 feet above the sea, Cape Sebastian is the highest south coast overlook reachable by a paved public road. On a clear day, visibility extends 43 miles north to Humbug Mountain and 50 miles south to California. This is one of the best perches along the south coast for whale-watching. A trail zigzags through beautiful springtime wildflowers down the south side of the cape for about two miles until it reaches the sea. In April and May, Pacific paintbrushes, Douglas irises, orchids, and snow queens usher you along. In addition, Cape Sebastian supports a population of large-headed goldfields, a summer-blooming yellow daisy-like flower found only in coastal Curry County.

In 1942, a caretaker heard Japanese voices drifting across the water through the fog. When the mist lifted, he looked down from Cape Sebastian trail to see a surfaced submarine. This sighting, together with the Japanese bombing at Brookings and the incendiary balloon spotted over Cape Blanco, sent shock waves up the south coast. But the potential threat remained just that, and local anxiety eventually subsided.

## Museums and Books

At the **Curry County Historical Museum** (29419 S. Ellensburg Ave., 541/247-9396, www.curryhistory.com, 10am-4pm Tues.-Sat. Feb.-Dec., $2), the local historical society has assembled a small collection of exhibits. Particularly interesting are a realistic reconstruction of a miner's cabin, vintage photos, and Native American petroglyphs.

In the harbor area on the west side of U.S. 101, **Jerry's Rogue Jets** (29980 Harbor Way, 541/247-9737, 9am-6pm Mon.-Sat., 10am-5pm Sun. Sept.-June, 9am-9pm Mon.-Sat., 10am-9pm Sun. July-Aug., free) has assembled the best regional museum on the south coast in its gift shop. Centuries of natural and human history are depicted. Museum photos of early river runs—hauling freight, passengers, and

mail—can impart a sense of history to your trip upriver or up the road.

And although it's not exactly a museum, **Gold Beach Books** (29707 Ellensburg Ave., 541/247-2495, 7am-5:30pm Mon.-Sat., 8am-5pm Sun.) is an amazing treasure trove of mostly used and obscure books. Even on a nice day, it's hard to leave; on a rainy day, it's a place to grab a coffee from **Rachel's,** the in-house coffee shop, and settle in for a long browse.

## Scenic Drives

From U.S. 101, two miles south of town, you can pick up **Hunter's Creek Road,** which loops north through the forest, finally following the course of the Rogue back into Gold Beach along Jerry's Flat Road. The three-hour drive follows Hunter's Creek inland for several miles, passing several picnic areas and campgrounds.

Other roads less traveled include the old **Coast Highway,** which you can pick up near Pistol River and Brookings; the **Shasta Costa Road,** paralleling the Rogue from Gold Beach to Galice; and an unpaved summer-only road into the **Rogue Wilderness** from Agness (a town upriver on the Rogue) to Powers. Despite most of these routes being paved (except the last one), they are all narrow, winding, and not suitable for trailers or motor homes. Be sure to travel with a good map; don't just rely on your GPS.

## SPORTS AND RECREATION
### ★ Rogue River Jet-Boat Ride

The most popular way to take in the mighty Rogue is on a jet-boat ride from Gold Beach. It's an exciting and interesting look at the varied flora and fauna along the estuary as well as the changing moods of the river. Three different lengths of river tours are available. Most of the estimated 50,000 people per year who "do" the Rogue in this way take the 64-mile round-trip cruise. An 80-mile trip goes farther up the Rogue, and the most adventurous trip is the 104-mile excursion that enters the

Rogue River canyon. Meals are not included in the cost of the cruise, and you can either bring your own food or have a meal at one of the secluded fishing lodges upriver, where the tours stop for meal breaks. The pilot-commentators are often folks who have grown up on the river, and their evocations of the diverse ecosystems and Native American and gold-mining history can greatly enhance your enjoyment. Bears, otters, seals, and beavers may be sighted en route, and anglers may hold up a big keeper to show off. Ospreys, snowy egrets, eagles, mergansers, and kingfishers are also seen with regularity in this stopover for migratory waterfowl.

In the first part of the journey, idyllic riverside retreats dot the hillsides, breaking up stands of fir and hemlock. Myrtle, madrona, and impressive springtime wildflower groupings also vary the landscape. All of the jet-boat trips out of Gold Beach focus on the section of the Rogue protected by the government as a Wild and Scenic River. Only the longer trips take you into the pristine Rogue Wilderness, an area that motor launches from Grants Pass do not reach. The 13 miles of this wilderness you see from the boat have canyon walls rising 1,500 feet above you. Geologists say this part of the Klamath Mountains is composed of ancient islands and seafloor that collided with North America. To deal with the rapids upstream, smaller and faster boats are used to skim over the boulders with just six inches of water between hull and the rock surface.

The season runs from May to October 15. Remember that chill and fog near the mouth of the estuary usually give way to much warmer conditions upstream. These tour outfits have wool blankets available on cold days as well as complimentary hot beverages. Also keep in mind that the upriver lodges can be booked for overnight stays, and your trip may be resumed the following day.

Just south of the Rogue River Bridge, west of U.S. 101 on Harbor Way, is **Jerry's Rogue Jets** (29985 Harbor Way, 541/247-4571 or 800/451-3645, www.roguejets.com). Jerry's offers 64-mile ($50 adults, $25 ages 4-11), 80-mile ($70 adults, $35 ages 4-11), and 104-mile ($95 adults, $45 ages 4-11) trips. There are usually two departures for each trip daily: one in the morning and one near midday. This heavily patronized company is noted for personable, well-informed guides.

## Hiking

The 40-mile **Rogue River Trail** (www.blm.gov/or) offers lodge-to-lodge hiking, which

the Rogue River

means you need little more in your pack than the essentials. The lodges here are comfortably rustic, serve home-style food in copious portions, and run $130-310 for a double room. They are also comfortably spaced, so extended hiking is seldom a necessity.

Before you go, check with the **Gold Beach Ranger Station** (29279 Ellensburg Ave., 541/247-3600, www.fs.usda.gov/rogue-siskiyou, 8am-5pm Mon.-Fri.) on trail conditions and specific directions to the trailhead. Pick up the western end of the trail 35 miles east of Gold Beach, about 0.5 miles from Foster Bar, a popular boat landing. Park there and walk east and north on the paved road until you see signs on the left marking the Rogue River Trail. Go in spring before the hot weather and enjoy yellow Siskiyou irises and fragrant wild azaleas. The trail ends at Grave Creek, 27 miles northwest of Grants Pass. Be careful of rattlesnakes, and note that summers are extremely hot on the trail.

## Fishing

Fishing is a mighty big deal in Gold Beach, which has one of the highest concentrations of professional guides in the state. There's something to fish for just about year-round, but salmon and steelhead are the top quarry. When the spring chinook are running (Apr.-June), anglers will need to book guided trips well in advance to get a shot at them. Catches peak in May, though it's important to check in advance; if fish aren't plentiful enough, the season may be limited or closed. Summer steelhead and fall-run chinook usually arrive July-September, then it's hatchery coho September-November (sometimes as early as August). In December, the first of the winter steelhead make their appearance and continue into March.

The **Rogue Outdoor Store** (29865 Ellensburg Ave., 541/247-7142, 8am-6pm daily) is well stocked with fishing, camping, and other gear, and its staff can advise on where, when, and what to fish. Typical rates for guided salmon trips are $250-400 per person depending on the size of your group.

Contact the **Gold Beach Visitors Center** (541/247-7526 or 800/525-2334, www.visit-goldbeach.com) for a list of over two dozen licensed guides. **Fish Oregon** (541/347-6338, www.fishoregon.com) is a well-established guide service; **Sportfishing Oregon** (541/425-1318, www.sportfishingoregon.com) also guides salmon and steelhead fishing trips on a number of southern Oregon rivers.

## Windsurfing

Although beginners may want to hone their skills up north at Floras Lake, experienced windsurfers head out into the ocean near the debouchment of the **Pistol River.**

## ENTERTAINMENT AND EVENTS

The **Pistol River Wave Bash National Windsurfing Competition** (http://internationalwindsurfingtour.com) brings four days of competitive riding to Pistol River State Park each June. The **Curry County Fair** takes place at the **Event Center on the Beach** (29392 Ellensburg Ave., 541/247-4541, admission varies) in late July.

Since 1982, the **Pistol River Concert Association** (541/247-2848, www.pistolriver.com, $15 adults) has produced a top-notch **concert series,** encompassing bluegrass, folk, jazz, classical, and blues at the Pistol River Friendship Hall. Concerts are held roughly once a month throughout the year, and it's well worth fussing with your schedule in order to catch one. Past and present performers are a who's who of acoustic music, including Greg Brown, Mike Seeger, Peggy Seeger, Kevin Burke, Norman and Nancy Blake, Peter Rowan, and Tony Rice, to name a few. To get there from Gold Beach, take U.S. 101 for 10 miles south to the second Pistol River exit (Pistol River-Carpenterville), then take the first right. The Pistol River Friendship Hall is 0.5 miles ahead on the right.

## FOOD

Drive a mile up the south bank of the Rogue to eat breakfast in a relaxed riverfront setting at **Indian Creek Café** (94682 Jerry's Flat Rd., 541/247-0680, 5:30am-2pm daily, $8-12). In good weather, there's seating on a deck overlooking Indian Creek, which flows into the Rogue here. Omelets, pancakes, and other traditional breakfast items are well prepared; lunch is mostly burgers and sandwiches.

Locals recommend the **Port Hole Café** (29975 Harbor Way, 541/247-7411, http://portholecafe.com, 11am-9pm daily, $9-20), with bay and river views in the Cannery building at the port, for hearty portions of fish-and-chips, chowder, and homemade pies at decent prices. If you don't want to stop for a meal, pick up some fresh seafood or the best canned tuna you'll ever taste next door at **Fishermen Direct Seafoods** (29975 Harbor Way, 541/247-9494, 9am-5:30pm Mon.-Sat., 10am-2pm Sun.).

The squat, octagonal **Barnacle Bistro** (29805 Ellensburg Ave., 541/247-7799, www.barnaclebistro.com, 11:30am-8pm Mon.-Sun., $8-18) is a lively spot for light meals, offering sandwiches, burgers, and fish tacos. The salad greens are local and organically grown, and all the sauces and dressings are made in-house. This is also a good place to sample the local Arch Rock Brewing beer, which is also available in growlers at the **Arch Rock Brewing Company** (28779 Hunter Creek Loop, 541/248-0555, tasting room 11am-6pm Tues.-Fri., 11am-5pm Sat.-Sun. Mar.-Sept., 11am-6pm Tues.-Fri., 11am-5pm Sat. Oct.-Apr.).

The menu at **Spinner's Seafood, Steak and Chophouse** (29430 Ellensburg Ave., 541/247-5160, www.spinnersrestaurant.com, 4:30pm-9pm daily, $9-39) is wide-ranging and the dining room extremely pleasant. Look for fresh, well-prepared seafood and prime rib, along with choice beef and chops. A children's menu is available.

★ **Anna's By the Sea** (29672 Stewart St., at 3rd St., 541/247-2100, www.annasbythesea.com, 5pm-8pm Wed.-Sat., reservations recommended, $17-39), tucked into a residential neighborhood a couple of blocks east of busy Ellensburg Avenue, is a wonderfully quirky and intimate restaurant serving "nouvelle Canadian Prairie cuisine"—think Angus beef drizzled with black truffle oil or locally caught cod in a vegetable-based broth over dumplings. The chef-owner hates to make desserts; instead, enjoy an after-dinner drink (try an *eau de vie* from the excellent list of distilled fruit brandies) and some excellent homemade cheeses. Anna's is a tiny place—just 15 seats—so come early if you don't want to wait (in summer, there's more seating on the deck).

## ACCOMMODATIONS

As in most coastal towns, there is no shortage of places to stay along the main drag, Ellensburg Avenue (a.k.a. U.S. 101). In fact, Gold Beach offers the largest number and widest range of accommodations on the south coast, with intimate lodges overlooking the Rogue as popular as the oceanfront motels. A discount of 20 percent or more on rooms is usually available during winter, when 80-90 inches of rain can fall.

### $50-100

The best bet for a clean, inexpensive room is the **Wild Chinook Inn** (94200 Harlow St., 541/247-6675, http://chinookinn.com, $85-125), where you get no-frills accommodations in a motor court motel across from the fairgrounds. Rooms have Wi-Fi, a fridge, and a microwave; some full-kitchen units are available.

Don't turn up your nose at this **Motel 6** (94433 Jerry's Flat Rd., 541/247-4533 or 956/668-7829, $95-150); the location—perched above the Rogue River—is great, and the rooms are modern and comfy. Pets are permitted.

If you're looking for a simple place to spend a night or two and don't care about frills, the **Azalea Lodge** (29481 Ellensburg Ave., 541/247-6635 or 866/381-6635, www.azalealodge.biz, $95-195) is a good bet, with friendly owners and clean rooms. No pets are allowed; all guest rooms have fridges.

### $100-150

Though it's true that **Ireland's Rustic Lodges** (29330 Ellensburg Ave., office 29346

Ellensburg Ave., 541/247-7718, www.ireland-srusticlodges.com, cabins $119-149, lodge rooms $134-199) include vintage (and pretty rustic) cabins, it also offers somewhat more modern lodge rooms, condos, and beach houses. Many of the guest rooms have fireplaces, knotty-pine interiors, and distinctive decor. Best of all, the parklike grounds are lovingly landscaped with pine trees, flowers, and ocean views. A sandy beach is a short stroll to the west. There are 33 lodge units (some with kitchens), seven vintage but well-kept log cabins (recommended) that sleep up to five, houses that sleep as many as 11, and a cluster of outdoor hot tubs.

Another older but well-situated motel with beach access is the **Pacific Reef Hotel** (29362 Ellensburg Ave., 541/247-6658, www.pacificreefhotel.com, ocean-view $109-209, no view $99). Ocean-view rooms (some pet-friendly) have balconies with rocking chairs; during the evening, outdoor movies are projected onto a large screen.

## $150-200

For a more traditional oceanfront hotel, the **Gold Beach Resort** (29232 Ellensburg Ave., 541/247-7066 or 800/541-0947, www.gbresort.com, $150-170) offers nicely furnished ocean-view rooms, all with balconies. Also part of this large complex, with easy beach access, are one- and two-bedroom condos, all with fireplaces. Facilities include an indoor pool and a fitness center; a complimentary continental breakfast is available.

## Over $200

Three miles upriver from U.S. 101, the **Rogue River Lodge at Snag Patch** (94966 North Bank Rogue River Rd., 541/247-0101, www.rogueriverlodge.com, $225-280, including breakfast) is a small lodge perched above the Rogue, with a couple of standard rooms and a variety of kitchenette suites, including one with three bedrooms ($580). All rooms have private decks, most have river views, and the grounds are as beautiful as the classy rooms.

★ **Tu Tu Tun Resort** (96550 N. Bank Rogue River Rd., 541/247-6664 or 800/864-6357, http://tututun.com, rooms $290-385, suites $445-525, house $550-1,075) is the most luxurious place to stay on the southern Oregon coast, where lucky guests take in river views through the floor-to-ceiling windows, enjoy a good book from the lodge's library in front of the massive river-rock fireplace, and savor delicious Pacific Northwest cuisine. As you sit on your patio overlooking the water along with the resident bald eagles, only the sounds of an occasional passing boat may intrude upon your Rogue River reverie. Rooms are graciously furnished, but not overly fussy—why interfere with the stunning views? The lodge is seven miles up the Rogue River from Gold Beach.

This acclaimed retreat also offers a heated pool and other recreational facilities. A meal package ($75 pp) includes hors d'oeuvres, a gourmet four-course dinner, and breakfast; guests can also pay by the meal (dinner $60). Nonguests are welcome to dinner ($70) with reservations. Tu Tu Tun is not a secret, so reservations are required well in advance of your stay.

## Upriver Lodges

Several lodges on the Rogue, some accessible only by boat or via hiking trails, lure visitors deep into the Rogue interior. Jet-boat trips can drop you off for an overnight or longer stay. Advance reservations are essential.

Also accessible by road and boat, the authentically rustic **Lucas Lodge** (3904 Cougar Lane, Agness, 541/247-7443, www.lucaslodgeoregon.com, $50-100) is 32 miles east of Gold Beach. Some cabins here come equipped with kitchen options. Meals (daily May-mid-Oct., dinner $15-22) are served in the lodge—chicken, biscuits, and garden vegetables are standard fare. Reservations are required.

Accessible only by helicopter, boat, or on foot, the **Paradise Lodge** (541/842-2822 or 888/667-6483, www.paradise-lodge.com, May-Oct., $155-165 pp, $95 children, includes meals) attracts guests who want to immerse themselves in nature but still eat and sleep well. Electricity only operates during certain hours. A huge on-site garden provides ingredients for home-cooked meals.

Another backcountry lodge, the **Clay Hill Lodge** (541/859-3772, www.clayhilllodge.com, $165 pp, $100 children, includes meals), is accessible via raft (from upstream), jet boat, or on foot. On foot, it's about three hours (six miles) up from the trailhead near Foster Bar, east of Gold Beach.

## Camping

There are no public campgrounds along the coast between Humbug Mountain, just south of Port Orford, and Harris Beach, at the northern entrance to Brookings. But campsites east of town up the Rogue River provide wonderful spots to bed down for the night. Those taking the road along the Rogue should be alert for oncoming log trucks, raft transport vehicles, and other wide-body vehicles. In addition to the public campgrounds listed, there are *many* private RV resorts up the north bank of the Rogue.

**Foster Bar Campground** (Siskiyou National Forest, 541/247-6651, www.fs.usda.gov, year-round, flush toilets May-Oct., $10) is 30 miles east of Gold Beach on the south bank of the Rogue. Take Jerry's Flat Road east for 30 miles to the turnoff for Agness. Turn right on Illahe Agness Road and drive three miles to camp. Campsites here come equipped with drinking water, toilets, ADA-compliant facilities, picnic tables, fire rings, and a boat ramp. Sites are available on a first-come, first-served basis only. This is a popular spot from which to embark on an eight-mile inner-tube ride to Agness. It's also where rafters pull out, so the parking lot may be jam-packed. The rapids

are dangerous—wear a life jacket. You are also within walking distance of the trailhead of the Rogue River Trail.

**Lobster Creek Campground** (541/247-3600, www.fs.usda.gov, year-round, $10) is nine miles east of Gold Beach via Forest Road 33. This small campground with large grassy sites has flush toilets and drinking water. The Schrader old-growth trail is two miles from the campground via Forest Road 090. It is a gentle one-mile walk through a rare and majestic ecosystem. Also nearby is the world's largest myrtle tree.

## INFORMATION AND SERVICES

The **Gold Beach Visitors Center** (94080 Shirley Lane, 541/247-7526 or 800/525-2334, www.visitgoldbeach.com, 8am-4pm daily) has an excellent and informative website. The **Gold Beach Ranger Station** (29279 Ellensburg Ave., 541/247-3600, www.fs.usda.gov/rogue-siskiyou, 8am-5pm Mon.-Fri.) can provide information on camping and recreation in the district.

The **post office** (541/247-7610) is at the port on Harbor Way. A modern building houses the **public library** (94341 3rd St., 541/247-7246, 10am-7pm Mon.-Thurs., 10am-5pm Fri.-Sat.), one block east of the highway in the north end of town. **Curry General Hospital** (94220 4th St., Gold Beach, 541/247-6621) is the only hospital in the county.

## GETTING THERE

Curry County's **Coastal Express** (541/412-8806 or 800/921-2871, www.currypublictransit.org) buses run up and down the south coast Monday-Friday between North Bend and the California border, including local service in Gold Beach.

# Brookings-Harbor and Vicinity

Brookings and Harbor sit on a coastal plain overlooking the Pacific six miles north of the California border, split by U.S. 101 (Chetco Ave.) and the Chetco River. Flowing out of the Klamath Mountains east of town, the Chetco drains part of the nearby Siskiyou National Forest and the Kalmiopsis Wilderness, extensive tracts encompassing some of the wildest country in the Lower 48 and renowned for their rare flowers and trees. The Kalmiopsis Wilderness is named for a unique shrub, the *Kalmiopsis leachiana,* one of the oldest members of the heath family (Ericaceae) that grows nowhere else on earth.

Don't form your opinion of Brookings by simply driving down U.S. 101. Just make your way past the somewhat drab main drag to Samuel Boardman State Park north of town, where 11 of the most scenic miles of the Oregon coast await you. Or head down to the harbor to embark on a boating expedition, with some of the safest offshore navigation conditions in the region. Or drive up the Chetco River, where the fog that frequently drenches the coastline during the summer months burns away a couple of miles inland and hikers can find trails.

During winter, Brookings and its neighbor, Harbor, enjoy mild temperatures. Enough 60-70°F days occur during January and February in this south coast "banana belt" town that more than 50 species of flowering plants thrive—along with retirees, outdoor-sports lovers, and beachcombers. With two gorgeous state parks virtually inside the city and world-class salmon and steelhead fishing nearby, only the lavish winter rainfall, averaging over 73 inches a year, can cool the ardor of local outdoor enthusiasts. In the springtime, the area south of town is lush with lilies—it's the Easter lily capital of the world.

Note: Shortly after our 2017 visit, the massive Chetco Bar Fire broke out; at least 200 square miles had burned in the area, mostly northeast of Brookings, at press time. If you're planning travel into the national forest, especially the Kalmiopsis Wilderness Area, check conditions before you go. Fire damage may make travel less pleasant or impossible for a few years.

Brookings-Harbor

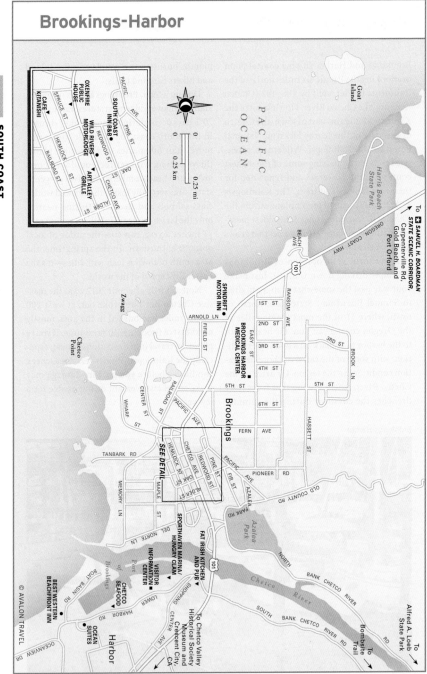

PACIFIC OCEAN

Goat Island

Harris Beach State Park

OREGON COAST HWY

To ✚ SAMUEL H. BOARDMAN
STATE SCENIC CORRIDOR,
Carpenterville Rd,
Gold Beach, and
Port Orford

BEACH AVE

101

Zwagg

Chetco Point

SPINDRIFT MOTOR INN

ARNOLD LN

FIFIELD ST

RAILROAD ST

PACIFIC AVE

CENTER ST

WHARF ST

TANBARK RD

MEMORY LN

1ST ST

2ND ST

3RD ST

4TH ST

5TH ST

6TH ST

FERN AVE

EASY ST

RANSOM AVE

3RD ST

5TH ST

BROOK LN

HASSETT ST

BROOKINGS HARBOR MEDICAL CENTER

Brookings

SEE DETAIL

PIONEER RD

PACIFIC AVE

FIR ST

AZALEA AVE

AZALEA PARK

PARK RD

OLD COUNTY RD

MAPLE ST

DEL NORTE LN

SPORTHAVEN MARINA/ HUNGRY CLAM

FAT IRISH KITCHEN AND PUB

VISITOR INFORMATION CENTER

CHETCO SEAFOOD

SHOPPING

LOWER HARBOR RD

BOAT BASIN RD

BEST WESTERN BEACHFRONT INN

OCEAN SUITES

OCEANVIEW DR

Harbor

Port of Brookings

101

To Chetco Valley Historical Society Museum and Crescent City, CA

CENTER AVE

NORTH BANK CHETCO RIVER

Chetco River

SOUTH BANK CHETCO RIVER RD

BANK CHETCO RIVER

To Alfred A. Loeb State Park

To Bombsite Trail

© AVALON TRAVEL

**Detail inset:**

PACIFIC AVE

PINE ST

SPRUCE ST

HEMLOCK ST

RAILROAD ST

REDWOOD ST

OAK ST

CHETCO AVE

ALDER ST

OXENFIRE PUBLIC HOUSE

CAFE KITANISHI

SOUTH COAST INN B&B

WILD RIVERS MOTORLODGE

ART ALLEY GRILLE

0    0 mi
0    0.25 mi
0    0.25 km

# Brookings: From Box Factory to Retirement Haven

What is now the shopping hub of rural Curry County started out in 1913 as a factory town for the Brookings Box Company. Owner J. L. Brookings hired the architect Bernard Maybeck (famous for designing the Palace of Fine Arts in San Francisco) to lay out the streets and design housing and community buildings for his mill workers. Maybeck drew up extensive plans for a model company town, but most of them were never realized; his central vision was eventually gutted when the state highway was laid through, rather than around, the town. Examples of Maybeck's craftsmanship can still be seen around Brookings, notably in the 1917 Craftsman-style residence (now the South Coast Inn B&B) he designed for lumber baron William Ward.

In the years that followed, the timber industry was augmented with fishing, horticulture, and tourism. Omitting for the moment the possibility that the offshore waters here were visited by Spanish explorer Juan Cabrillo (in 1542) and English explorer Sir Francis Drake (in 1579), the local event with the greatest historical significance was a Japanese aerial bombing on September 9, 1942, when a Japanese incendiary bomb scorched the treetops of Mount Emily, southeast of town, in one of only two documented wartime air-bombing missions against the U.S. mainland (the other occurred three weeks later near Port Orford). The resulting fires were quickly doused by the damp conditions, and no significant harm was done. A trail now leads to the bomb site.

Since the late 1980s, Brookings's greatest growth industry has been as a haven for retirees, and that population has been booming in recent years.

## SIGHTS

In Brookings, camellias bloom in December, and flowering plums add color the next month. Daffodils, grown commercially on the coastal plain south of Brookings, bloom in late January and into February. Magnolia shrubs, some early azaleas, and rhododendrons bloom in late winter. The area also produces 90 percent of the world's Easter lily crop.

**Azalea Park** (640 Old Country Rd.) is a quiet place just off the main drag to picnic and enjoy the flowers. This Works Progress Administration-built enclave features 20-foot-high azaleas (which are several hundred years old), hand-hewn myrtlewood picnic tables, an excellent playground, and a band shell that hosts summer concerts. Wild cherry and crab apple blooms, wild strawberry blossoms, and purple and red violets round out the bouquet. Butterflies, bees, and birds all seem to concur with locals that this array smells sweetest around graduation time in mid-June.

### Harris Beach State Park

At the northern limits of Brookings, **Harris Beach State Park** makes up for all the strip-mall architecture you'll find on Chetco Avenue. Besides its stunning views, this state park offers many incoming travelers from California their first chance to actually walk on the beach in Oregon. You can begin directly west of the park's campground, where a sandy beach strewn with boulders often becomes flooded with intertidal life and driftwood. The early morning hours, as the waves crash through a small tunnel in a massive rock onto the shoreline, are the best time to look for sponges, umbrella crabs, solitary corals, and sea stars. In addition to beachcombing, you can picnic at tables above the parking lot, loll about in the shallow waters of nearby Harris Creek, or cast in the surf for perch.

Offshore, **Bird Island** (also called Goat Island) is the largest island along the Oregon coast and the state's largest seabird rookery. This outpost of Oregon Islands National Wildlife Refuge dispatches squadrons of cormorants, pelicans, tufted puffins, and other waterfowl, which dive-bomb the incoming waves for food.

**Mill Beach** is the southernmost part of the Harris Beach area. Locals prefer the beach access from downtown, which is easy to miss. To get here, drive toward the ocean on Center Street in downtown Brookings, make a right at the plywood mill, and stop next to a small ballpark. An unimproved road leads to a hillock, from which trails take you down to a beach full of driftwood. Residents say that Japanese fishing floats occasionally roll up onto the beach after a storm.

### Chetco Valley Historical Society Museum

The **Chetco Valley Historical Society Museum** (5461 Museum Rd., 541/469-6651, www.chetcomuseum.org, 1pm-5pm Fri.-Sun. Memorial Day-Labor Day, donation), in the red-and-white Blake House, sits on a hill overlooking U.S. 101 two miles south of the Chetco River. The structure dates to 1857 and was used as a stagecoach way station and trading post before Abraham Lincoln was president. Oregon's largest Monterey cypress tree is located on the hill near the museum. The 130-foot-tall tree has a trunk diameter of more than 18 feet.

### ★ Samuel H. Boardman State Scenic Corridor

The stretch of highway from Brookings to Port Orford is known as the "fabulous 50 miles." Some consider the section of coastline just north of Brookings to be the most scenic in Oregon—and one of the most dramatic meetings of rock and tide in the world. The offshore rock formations and winding roadbed hundreds of feet above the surf invite comparison to Europe's Amalfi Drive. The "fabulous 50" sobriquet is perhaps most apt in the dozen miles directly north of Brookings, encompassed by **Samuel H. Boardman State Scenic Corridor.** You'll want to have a camera close at hand and a loose schedule when you make this drive, because you'll find it hard not to pull over again and again, as each photo opportunity seems to outdazzle the last. Of the 11 named viewpoints that have been cut into the highway's shoulder, the following are especially recommended

Arch Rock, Samuel H. Boardman State Scenic Corridor

(all viewpoints are marked by signs on the west side of U.S. 101 and are listed here from north to south).

Near the north end of Boardman State Park, a short walk down the hillside trail leads you to the **Arch Rock** viewpoint, where an immense boomerang-shaped basalt archway juts out of the water about a quarter mile offshore. This site has picnic tables within view of the monolith.

A few miles south, the sign for **Natural Bridges Cove** seems to front just a forested parking lot. However, the paved walkway at the south end of the lot leads to a spectacular overlook. Below, several rock archways frame an azure cove. This feature was created by the collapse of the entrance and exit of a sea cave. A steep trail through giant ferns and towering Sitka spruce and Douglas fir takes you down for a closer look. Thimbleberry (a sweet but seedy raspberry) is plentiful in late spring. As in similar forests on the south coast, it's important to stay on the trail. The rainforest-like biome is exceptionally fragile, and the

**Thomas Creek Bridge,** the highest bridge in Oregon (345 feet above the water) as well as the highest north of San Francisco, has been used as a silent star in many TV commercials. A parking lot at the south end of the bridge offers the best views.

**House Rock** was the site of a World War II air-raid sentry tower that sits hundreds of feet above whitecaps pounding the rock-strewn beaches. To the north, you'll see one of the highest cliffs on the coast, Cape Sebastian. A steep circuitous trail lined with salal goes down to the water. The path begins behind the Samuel Boardman monument on the west end of the parking lot. The sign to the highest viewpoint in Boardman State Park is easy to miss, but look for the turnout that precedes House Rock, called Cape Ferrelo (for Juan Cabrillo's navigator, who sailed up much of the West Coast in 1543).

Drive down to **Lone Ranch Beach,** where you can get down to water level with close-up views of offshore rocks.

## Carpenterville Road

The current roadbed of U.S. 101 was laid in southern Oregon in 1961. The previous coastal route still exists along **Carpenterville Road,** which can be picked up near Harris Beach. It comes out near the Pistol River, where it descends in a series of switchbacks. Its highest point is 1,700 feet above sea level at Burnt Hill. Views of the Siskiyous to the east and the Pacific panoramas to the west make the sometimes-rough road worth the effort. In clear weather, it's possible to look back toward the southeast at Mount Shasta between the ridgelines. This route is best appreciated going south, and it makes for a great 20-mile bike ride, with a long climb to 1,700 feet above sea level.

## Alfred A. Loeb State Park

Eight miles northeast of Brookings, on North Bank Chetco River Road (which follows the Chetco River), the **Alfred A. Loeb State Park** preserves 320 acres of old-growth myrtlewood, the state's largest grove. Many of these aromatic trees are much older than 200 years.

The 0.25-mile Riverview Trail passes numerous big trees to connect Loeb Park with the **Redwood Nature Trail.** This trail winds 1.2 miles through the northernmost stands of naturally occurring *Sequoia sempervirens.* This is Oregon's largest redwood grove and contains the state's largest specimens. Within the grove are several trees more than 500 years old, measuring 5 to 8 feet in diameter and towering more than 300 feet above the forest floor. One tree has a 33-foot girth and is estimated to exceed 800 years in age. When the south coast is foggy and cold on summer mornings, it's often warm and dry in upriver locations such as this one, inviting the possibility of swimming in the Chetco.

## Kalmiopsis Wilderness

The lure of untrammeled wilderness attracts intrepid hikers to the **Kalmiopsis Wilderness,** despite the summer's blazing heat and winter's torrential rains. In addition to enjoying the isolation of the wilderness, they come to take in the pink rhododendron-like blooms of *Kalmiopsis leachiana* (in June) and other rare flowers. The area is also home to such economically valued species as Port Orford cedar and, in the past, illegal marijuana grows. (Cannabis is a leading cash crop in this part of the state.) During the fall there's a lucrative mushroom harvest; take care not to encroach on pickers, who may be quite territorial.

In any case, the Forest Service prohibits plant collection *of any kind* to preserve the region's special botanical populations. These include the insect-eating *Darlingtonia* plant and the Brewer's weeping spruce. The forest canopy is composed largely of the more common Douglas fir, canyon live oak, madrona, and chinquapin. Stark peaks top this red-rock forest, whose understory is choked with blueberry, manzanita, and dense chaparral.

Many of this wilderness's rare species

survived the glacial epoch because the glaciers from that era left the area untouched. This, combined with the fact that the area was once an offshore island, has enabled the region's singular ecosystem to maintain its integrity through the millennia.

In summer 2002, the **Biscuit Fire** raged out of control for weeks, ravaging nearly half a million acres of southwestern Oregon, engulfing most of the Siskiyou National Forest and virtually all of the Kalmiopsis Wilderness. Shortly after our 2017 visit, the Chetco Bar Fire broke out in more or less the same area; this fire was still burning at press time.

Even if you don't have the slightest intention of hiking the Kalmiopsis, the scenic drive through the **Chetco Valley** is worth it. From Brookings, turn off U.S. 101 at the north end of the Chetco River Bridge. Follow this paved road upriver past Loeb State Park and continue along the river on County Roads 784 and 1376 until a narrow bridge crosses the Chetco. From here, turn right for 18 miles along Forest Roads 1909, 160, and 1917 to reach the Upper Chetco Trailhead (just past the Quail Prairie Lookout). The driving distance from Brookings is 31 miles. If you're not hiking into the wilderness, you can continue west on national forest road 1917 (portions are not paved), which will return you to the above-mentioned narrow bridge over the Chetco.

## Crissey Field State Recreation Area

**Crissey Field State Recreation Area** lies south of Brookings, almost to the California border, and is set along the Winchuck River. The park, which was added to the state park system in 2008, is a great place to watch birds, harbor seals, California sea lions, and other wildlife. A trail leads through a huge pile of driftwood logs to dunes that shelter native plants, tiny wetlands, and old-growth Sitka spruce trees. Crissey Field is also the site of a spacious **visitors center.** Incidentally, the park's name has nothing to do with the San Francisco park (that's Crissy); it's in the heart of the lily-growing area and is named for a lily bulb grower.

## HIKING
### Bombsite Trail

Brookings takes a peculiar pride in having been bombed by the Japanese during World War II. In 1942, two incendiary bombs were dropped about 16 miles east of town, on the slopes of Mount Emily. Although they were intended to start a fire, conditions were wet, and the small blaze that resulted was easily controlled. A sort of mutual respect eventually developed between the Japanese pilot who dropped the bomb and the town of Brookings. The pilot was a guest of honor at one Azalea Festival, and his family later presented the town with his samurai sword, which he wore during the bombing and throughout the war. The sword is now on exhibit at the local library (420 Alder St.).

The Mount Emily **Bombsite Trail,** 19 miles by road from town, commemorates the bombing. It's a two-mile stretch with redwoods near the beginning and fire-dependent species such as knobcone pine and manzanita along the way. To reach the trail, head eight miles east up South Bank Road and turn right onto Mount Emily Road. At the fork, turn onto Wheeler Creek Road and follow the signs.

### Oregon Redwoods Trail

In addition to the trail through redwood trees in Loeb Park, hikers can explore some not huge but still old-growth redwoods along the 1.7-mile **Oregon Redwoods Trail** southeast of town. The first 0.5 miles of the trail is wheelchair-accessible; a longer stretch leads downhill to a scattered collection of redwoods. Although redwoods here at the northern edge of their range aren't the monster trees that you see in California, this is a pretty trail.

Getting to this trailhead is half the fun of the hike. From U.S. 101, take the Winchuck River Road; turn right onto Forest Road 1101

the Oregon Redwoods Trail

Ave, 541/247-3600, 8:30am-12:30pm and 1:30pm-4:30pm) to see if the road to the Vulcan Lake trailhead is open and passable, because weather-related closures occasionally occur and the road can be in really rough condition.

To reach the trailhead from Brookings, turn east off U.S. 101 at the north end of the Chetco River Bridge, follow North Bank Road (County Rd. 784) and Forest Road 1376 along the Chetco River for six miles, and then turn right and follow Forest Road 1909 to its bumpy end. Driving distance from Brookings is 31 miles. Hikers should watch out for the three shiny leaves of poison oak, as well as for rattlesnakes, which are numerous. Black bears also populate the area, but their lack of contact with humans makes them shier than their Cascade counterparts. Note: The massive Chetco Bar Fire burned in this area in 2017; contact the U.S. Forest Service for news on closures.

and continue four miles up this narrow gravel road to the trailhead, which is 11 miles from town. It's best not to take a trailer or large RV on this road.

## Vulcan Lake Trail

A good introduction to the Kalmiopsis Wilderness is along the one-mile trail to **Vulcan Lake** at the foot of Vulcan Peak, which is the major jumping-off point for trails into the wilderness. The trail begins at Forest Road 1909 and takes off up the mountains past Pollywog Butte and Red Mountain Prairie. The open patches in the Douglas firs reveal a kaleidoscope of Pacific Ocean views and panoramas of the Chetco Valley and the Big Craggies. For the botanist in search of rare plants, however, the real show is on the trail; it's located in the area burned by the 2002 Biscuit Fire and shows the recovery since then. Despite steep spots, the walk from County Road 1909 to Vulcan Lake is not difficult. Before going, check with the **Gold Beach ranger station** (29279 Ellensburg

## SPORTS AND RECREATION

For some mellow fun in the sun, cruise down Easy Street, east off U.S. 101, to **Bud Cross City Park** for some tennis, a dip in the outdoor pool, or a visit to the skate park.

### Fishing

Fishing on the Chetco was once one of southern Oregon's best-kept secrets, but word has gotten out about the river's October run of huge chinook and its superlative influx of winter steelhead. The late-summer ocean salmon season out of Brookings may be the best in the Pacific Northwest. Boatless anglers can try their luck at the public fishing pier at the harbor and on the south jetty at the mouth of the Chetco. Chinook season generally runs mid-May-mid-September, but that's subject to change, so check the regulations.

Guided fishing trips for salmon, steelhead, and ocean bottom fish can be arranged through **Wild Rivers Fishing** (541/813-1082, www.wildriversfishing.com) or **Tidewind**

Sportfishing (16368 Lower Harbor Rd., 541/469-0337, www.tidewindsportfishing. com).

## Surfing, Boogie Boarding, and Kayaking

The best surfing is usually found at **Sporthaven Beach,** at the north end of the jetty in Harbor. Reach it by driving to the end of Boat Basin Road to the RV park. There's plenty of parking at the very end of the road. Even if the surf is not spectacular (it's usually best in the winter), it's a pretty mellow place for beginners, and as a fringe benefit, it can be a good spot to see whales during their springtime or December migrations.

Boogie boarders tend to favor **Harris Beach State Park.** From fall to spring, the waves are big and dangerous, and the water is cold. If you know what you're doing, come on in.

**South Coast Tours** (541/373-0487, www. southcoasttours.net) leads kayak tours in the ocean ($90) or Chtetco River ($75). The three- to four-mile trip heads out from the calm mouth of the Chetco at the boat basin into a fairly protected area of the ocean, making it accessible for even beginning sea kayakers. More advanced paddlers can join a paddle trip through arches and around islands in the more challenging waters off Samuel Boardman State Park (about 10 miles, $130). They also lead stand-up paddling tours into coves and around the natural arches (experience required, $110) as well as in the calmer waters of the Chetco estuary ($70).

If you'd rather rent a kayak and go at it yourself down the mostly mellow Chetco, head three miles up North Bank Road to the **Riverside Market** (98877 N. Bank Chetco Rd., 541/661-3213, www.chetcokayaks.com), where you can rent a kayak or stand-up paddleboard ($30-45 per day). They can also arrange a shuttle to pick you up downstream.

## Golf

The beautiful 18-hole public **Salmon Run Golf Course** (99040 South Bank Chetco River Rd., 541/469-4888, http://salmonrun. net, $40 for 18 holes) was designed with environmentally sensitive imperatives to enable wildlife to thrive. Whether it's the chance to see salmon (usually after the first rains in November) and steelhead spawning (January), black bears, elk, and wild turkeys, or just the opportunity to play a first-rate course, golfers shouldn't overlook this one. Beginner and intermediate players may find the executive nine-hole ($30) course ideal. This par-34 course within a course is located on the back nine holes and measures 1,310 yards. Your Oregon coastal golf pilgrimage can begin here, then hit Bandon Dunes, Sandpines (Florence), and Salishan (near Lincoln City).

# ENTERTAINMENT AND EVENTS

Brookings's big event is the **Azalea Festival** (541/469-3181 or 800/535-9469, Memorial Day weekend), which celebrates the local flower with carnival rides, street food, a fun run, and a parade. Most of the action is down at the harbor, which is thronged with vendors, food stands, music, and giant inflatables.

Like several other Oregon coast towns, Brookings puts its windy weather to good use with its annual **Southern Oregon Kite Festival** (www.southernoregonkite-festival.com), held the third weekend in July. Individuals and teams display their aerial skills at the port of Brookings-Harbor.

# FOOD

Brookings has a profusion of family-friendly, though unexciting, restaurants that serve large portions at a good value—this is not a fine-dining capital. For slightly more distinctive fare than the usual fast food and family-dining joints, check out the following places.

A coastal town is certainly a safe place to eat sushi. In Brookings, find it at **Cafe Kitanishi** (632 Hemlock St., 541/469-7864, www.cafekitanishi.com, lunch 11am-3pm Wed.-Fri., noon-3pm Sat., dinner 5pm-9pm

Thurs.-Sat., $9-28), which also serves bento boxes to go.

Down in the harbor area, you'll find a number of seafood shops. For fresh, traditional fish-and-chips, you can't miss at **Sporthaven Marina** (16374 Lower Harbor Rd., 541/469-3301, www.sporthavenmarina. com, 11am-6pm Sun.-Thurs., 11am-7pm Fri.-Sat., $6-15) with good clam chowder and fried seafood done up in traditional Oregon style. Yet more fresh fried seafood is ready for you at the adjacent **Hungry Clam** (16350 Lower Harbor Rd., 541/469-2526, www.hungryclam. com, 11am-7pm Sun.-Thurs., 9am-8pm Fri.-Sat., $9-17), with crab cake sliders, fresh tuna melts, crab cocktails, and a host of fried fish with slaw and chips.

More fish-and-chips, as well as burgers, salads, and a good selection of local beers, can be found near the entrance to the harbor at the fun and family-friendly **Fat Irish Kitchen & Pub** (16403 Lower Harbor Rd., no phone, www.fatirishpub.com, 11am-10pm Mon.-Thurs., 11am-midnight Fri.-Sat., 11am-9pm Sun., $10-17).

A pleasant surprise in downtown Brookings is the ★ **Oxenfre Public House** (631 Chetco Ave., 541/813-1985, www.oxenpub.com, 4pm-9pm daily dinner, bar until 11pm or later, $15-27), a self-proclaimed gastropub with a hip atmosphere and trendy meals such as Korean short-rib tacos with sesame cucumber relish and chili peanut slaw. There are also plenty of pub standards with tasty twists—have a late-night meal of Parmesan truffle fries and a Kobe beef frankfurter on pretzel bread, or hot pastrami on pretzel bread. Kids are welcome until 9pm.

Brookings's only real fine dining is at the intimate and charming **Art Alley Grille** (515 Chetco Ave., 541/469-0800, http://artalleygrill.com, 4:30pm-8:30pm Wed.-Sat., $15-30), a basement spot tucked downstairs from an art gallery. The menu is fairly wide-ranging, with items such as pork with house-made harissa and seared tuna steak with *ponzu* sauce and wasabi.

# ACCOMMODATIONS

Rooms in Brookings are generally rather expensive; there are more budget accommodations 29 miles north in Gold Beach. It's also harder to find pet-friendly lodgings here than in most other coastal towns.

## $50-100

Just north of the Chetco River Bridge, **Wild Rivers Motorlodge** (437 Chetco Ave., 541/469-5361, www.wildriversmotorlodge. com, $93-117) is the most attractive roadside budget motel in town. Rooms come with fridges and microwaves; some are pet-friendly.

The **Spindrift Motor Inn** (1215 Chetco Ave., 541/469-5345, $99) is a well-managed property and a decent value. However, its ambience is strictly roadside-budget, and it is a bit of a walk to the beach.

At the southern edge of the Brookings-Harbor stretch of U.S. 101, the **Harbor Inn Motel** (15991 U.S. 101 S., 541/469-3194 or 800/469-8444, www.harborinnmotel.com, $82) is not a bad place to land. It's nothing fancy, but it's pretty quiet and permits pets; all rooms have a fridge, a microwave, and Wi-Fi. If you head west from the stoplight at the motel, it's about a mile to the port of Harbor.

## $100-150

A coastal gem one block north of the highway, the ★ **South Coast Inn B&B** (516 Redwood St., Brookings, 541/469-5557 or 800/525-9273, www.southcoastinn.com, $119-159) is a 1917 Craftsman building and was once the home of lumber baron William Ward. Designed by famed architect Bernard Maybeck and situated in the heart of old Brookings just blocks away from the beach and shopping, this 4,000-square-foot B&B offers four guest rooms, a guest cottage, and an apartment. All rooms have TVs with video players (and access to the inn's video library), private baths, and other amenities. An indoor spa with a sauna and a hot tub and an included breakfast featuring a health-conscious menu are additional enticements to book space early. Ask the friendly innkeepers about other Maybeck structures in town.

Perhaps the best value in Brookings lodgings is **Ocean Suites Motel** (16045 Lower Harbor Rd., 541/469-4004 or 866/520-9768, www.oceansuitesmotel.com, $135), at the Harbor end of town. These really are suites—each has a full kitchen (especially nice to have if you buy fresh fish at the harbor) and a living room. No pets are allowed.

### $150-200

Stay up the river at **Mt. Emily Ranch B&B** (99847 South Bank Chetco Rd., 541/661-211134 or 541/469-3983, www.mtemily-ranch.com, $195), a large, newer log home with a comfortable level of rusticity. Because the B&B is several miles from town, you may want to settle in and eat dinner ($24) as well as breakfast here. This is a real ranch, and dinner may feature ranch-raised beef or organic veggies from the garden.

### Over $200

The best conventional hotel is south of the Chetco River in Harbor. The ★ **Best Western Beachfront Inn** (16008 Boat Basin Rd., Harbor, 541/469-7779, www.bestwestern. com, $230-250) sits right on the beach at the mouth of the Chetco River, just past the port and marina. All units feature private decks, microwaves, and fridges. Kitchenettes as well as suites with ocean-view hot tubs and an indoor pool are available. Pets are permitted on a very limited basis; call the hotel directly to plead your case.

## Camping

**Harris Beach State Park** (1655 U.S. 101, 541/469-2021, www.oregonstateparks.org, reservations 800/452-5687, www.reserveamerica.com, year-round, $20 tents, $30-32 RVs, $45-55 yurts, $5 hiker-biker), on an ocean-side bluff two miles north of town, has over 150 sites. Reservations are definitely necessary from Memorial Day to Labor Day. Flush toilets, electricity, water, sewer hookups, sanitary service, showers, firewood, and a playground are available. Whale-watching is particularly good here in January and May, and the birding is good year-round.

**Alfred A. Loeb State Park** (541/469-2021, www.oregonstateparks.org, campsites $22, cabins $40-50) is nine miles northeast of Brookings on North Bank Chetco River Road. There are 48 sites with electrical hookups for trailers and RVs (50 feet maximum) or tents as well as three cabins. Electricity,

The South Coast Inn B&B dates from 1917 and was designed by architect Bernard Maybeck.

piped water, and picnic tables are provided; flush toilets, showers, and firewood are available. The campground is in a fragrant and secluded myrtlewood grove on the east bank of the Chetco River. From here, the Riverview Trail takes hikers to the Siskiyou National Forest's Redwood Nature Trail, where nature lovers will marvel at 800-year-old redwood beauties. Although the cabins can be reserved (800/452-5687, www.reserveamerica.com), campsites are all first-come, first-served.

Beyond Loeb State Park is the more primitive dispersed camping at **Redwood Bar** (Gold Beach Ranger District, 541/247-3600, www.fs.usda.gov, mid-May-Sept., no water, $10). To get here, go up the North Bank Chetco River Road about seven miles. At Forest Road 376, turn northeast and drive six miles to the camping area. Redwood Bar is a popular place to hang out on the river; it's also on the main access route to the Kalmiopsis Wilderness, 20 miles away, and is a good spot for fishing during the winter steelhead run.

The Forest Service rents several cabins and fire lookouts ($40-50) for overnight stays; advance booking is required. Contact the **Gold Beach Ranger District** (541/247-3600, www.fs.usda.gov, reservations 877/444-6777, www.recreation.gov) for information about renting Packer's Cabin, Ludlum House, or the Quail Prairie Lookout.

## INFORMATION

Pull off the highway and talk to the friendly folks at the **Crissey Field Welcome Center** (16633 U.S. 101 S., 541/469-4117, 9am-5pm daily Apr.-Oct., 9am-4:30pm Mon.-Fri. Nov.-Mar.), where you can gather information and brochures about the coast and the rest of the state. The **Brookings-Harbor Visitors Center** (16358 Lower Harbor Rd., 541/813-2300, 9am-5pm daily) is down at the harbor. For additional information pertinent to Brookings and environs, the **Brookings-Harbor Chamber of Commerce** (16330 Lower Harbor Rd., Brookings, 541/469-3181, www.brookingsharborchamber.com) is also down at the harbor.

## GETTING THERE

It takes determination to get to Brookings using public transportation. Curry County's **Coastal Express** (800/921-2871, www.currypublictransit.org) buses run up and down the south coast Monday-Friday only between North Bend and the California border, including local service in Brookings. **Pacific Crest Bus Lines** (541/344-6265, http://pacificcrestbuslines.com) operates Sunday-Friday bus service between Coos Bay and Eugene via Reedsport and Florence. Eugene has Amtrak trains and regular Greyhound bus service, as well as an airport served by national carriers.

# Ashland and Southern Oregon

**W**hen Oregonians talk about southern Oregon, they usually mean the southwestern corner of the state, including the upper valleys of the Umpqua and Rogue Rivers, the spine of the southern Cascade Mountains, and east to Klamath Falls. The outstanding features of this region include world-class culture-fests at Ashland and Jacksonville, the dramatically beautiful Rogue and Umpqua Rivers, and more summer sun and heat than you would expect to find in Oregon.

It also includes Crater Lake National Park, Oregon's only national park, one of the most spectacular natural wonders in the United States. Driving up the desert slopes to the rim and then glimpsing the lake's startlingly blue water ringed by rock cliffs is a magnificent experience.

## PLANNING YOUR TIME

Ashland and the **Oregon Shakespeare Festival** are undeniably the largest draw in southern Oregon, although to make the most of this world-class theater festival, you must reserve seats and lodging well in advance.

Increasingly, southern Oregon is becoming a major center for wine production, and it's easy to add a bit of wine-tasting to your theater itinerary. We've included some of our favorites, and for a full listing of area wineries, the **Southern Oregon Wineries Association** (www.southernoregonwines. org) has a brochure and map.

Southern Oregon's other top destination is **Crater Lake National Park.** Even though a summer weekend visit to the park itself—which for most travelers involves driving the loop route around the rim of the caldera—can be hectic due to excessive traffic, the approaches to the park along the Rogue or Umpqua river valleys offer excellent opportunities for less-thronged outdoor recreation.

The larger cities of southern Oregon—Medford, Grants Pass, and Roseburg—are mostly utilitarian, with little to delay or seduce the traveler.

---

**Previous:** vineyards near Grants Pass; Crater Lake. **Above:** along the Watson Falls trail.

# Ashland and Southern Oregon

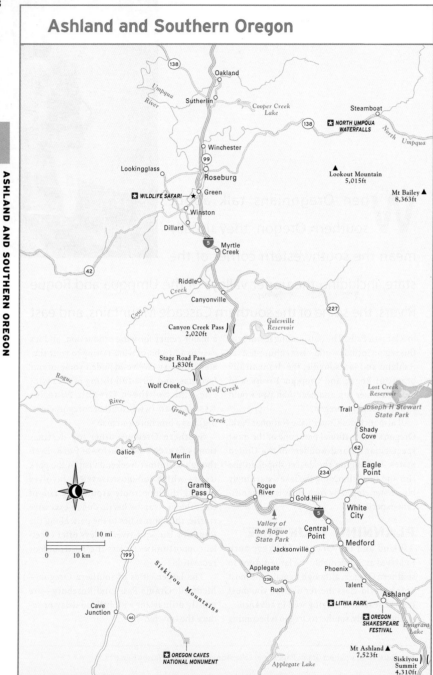

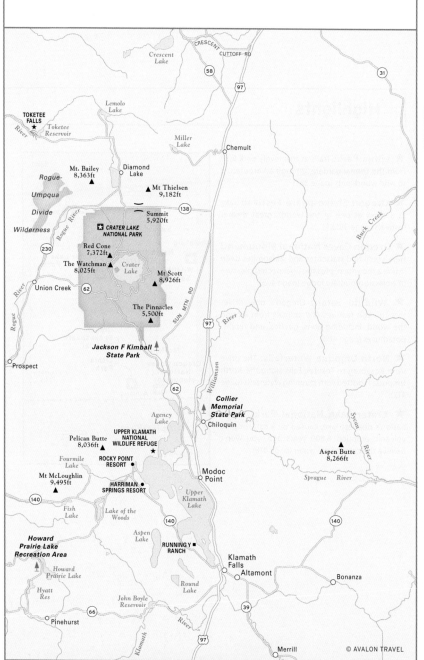

Crescent Lake

CRESCENT CUTTOFF RD

58

97

31

Lemolo Lake

Miller Lake

Chemult

TOKETEE FALLS
★

Toketee Reservoir

River

Mt. Bailey
8,363ft

Diamond Lake

Rogue
Umpqua
Divide
Wilderness

Rogue River

230

▲ Mt Thielsen
9,182ft

Summit
5,920ft

138

Buck Creek

★ CRATER LAKE
NATIONAL PARK

Red Cone
7,372ft ▲

The Watchman
8,025ft ▲

Crater Lake

▲ Mt Scott
8,926ft

Union Creek

62

The Pinnacles
5,500ft

SUN MTN RD

97

River

River

Prospect

Jackson F Kimball
State Park

62

Williamson

Collier
Memorial
State Park

Sycan River

Agency Lake

Chiloquin

Pelican Butte
8,036ft

UPPER KLAMATH
NATIONAL
WILDLIFE REFUGE
★

▲ Aspen Butte
8,266ft

Fourmile Lake

ROCKY POINT
RESORT ●

Modoc
Point

Sprague River

Mt McLoughlin
9,495ft ▲

HARRIMAN
SPRINGS RESORT ●

Upper
Klamath
Lake

140

Fish Lake

Lake of the
Woods

140

Howard
Prairie Lake
Recreation Area

Aspen Lake

RUNNING Y
RANCH ■

Klamath
Falls

Altamont

Bonanza

140

Howard
Prairie Lake

Hyatt
Res

John Boyle
Reservoir

Round
Lake

Pinehurst

66

River

39

Klamath

97

Merrill

© AVALON TRAVEL

# Highlights

★ **Lithia Park:** Trails at this lovely park lead from the formal gardens through an arboretum to wild woodlands (page 381).

★ **Oregon Shakespeare Festival:** Take in a show at one of the world's great theater festivals (page 385).

★ **Oregon Caves National Monument:** Here you'll find stalactites and stalagmites deep inside a mountain, plus the unexpected pleasure of a classic mountain lodge (page 405).

★ **Wildlife Safari:** Oregon's only drive-through zoo features 600 animals from around the world, including lions, giraffes, and hippopotamuses (page 408).

★ **North Umpqua Waterfalls:** The drive from Roseburg to Toketee Falls along the North Umpqua is dotted with stunning waterfalls (page 412).

★ **Crater Lake National Park:** At the nation's deepest lake, caused by a catastrophic volcanic eruption 6,600 years ago, you won't believe the color of the water (page 418).

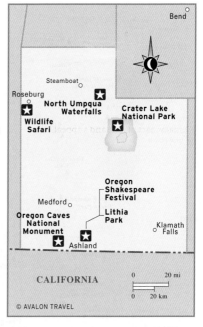

# Ashland

Few towns are as closely identified with theater as Ashland (pop. 21,000). Tickets to the renowned Oregon Shakespeare Festival are the coin of the realm here, with contemporary classics and off-off-Broadway shows joining productions by the Bard. You can immediately sense that this is not just another timber town by the Tudor-style McDonald's, vintage Victorian houses, and high-end clothing stores on Main Street.

Ashland's tourist economy is also sustained by its auspicious location equidistant to Portland and San Francisco. Closer to home, day trips to Crater Lake, Rogue River country, and the southern Oregon wineries have joined the tradition of "stay four days, see four plays" as a major part of Ashland's appeal.

## SIGHTS
### ★ Lithia Park

Ashland's centerpiece is 100-acre **Lithia Park** (340 S. Pioneer St.). Recognized as a National Historic Site, the park was designed by John McLaren, landscape architect of San Francisco's Golden Gate Park. It is set along Ashland Creek, where the Takelma people camped and where Ashland, Ohio, immigrants built the region's first flour mill in 1854.

The park owes its existence to Jesse Winburne, who made a fortune from New York City subway advertising and in the 1920s tried to develop a spa around Ashland's Lithia Springs, which he said rivaled the venerated waters of Saratoga Springs, New York. Although the spa never caught on due to the Great Depression, Winburne was nevertheless instrumental in landscaping Lithia Park and was responsible for piping the famously sulfurous Lithia water to the plaza fountains so all might enjoy its beneficial minerals.

Pick up a guide to the park's trails at the plaza's visitors center kiosk. Paths line both banks of Ashland Creek. Park on the west side (to the right as you face the park) or drive up scenic Winburne Way. The park is nicely landscaped in a naturalistic way. A good destination on a hot day is the swimming reservoir, 1.4 miles up the east bank.

The hub of the park in the summer is the band shell, where entertainment includes

Spend a hot summer afternoon relaxing in Lithia Park.

# Ashland

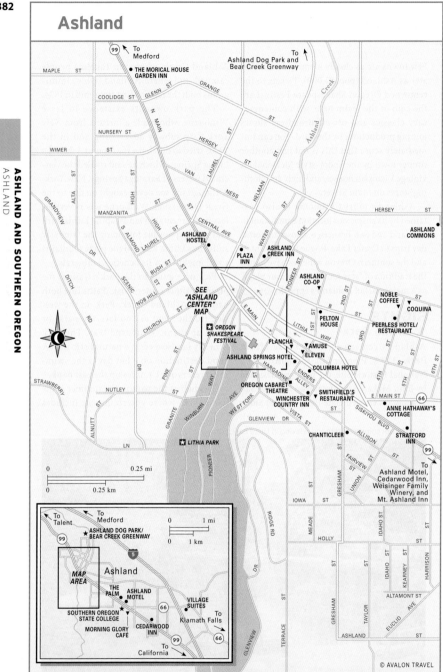

To Medford

To Ashland Dog Park and Bear Creek Greenway

MAPLE ST

THE MORICAL HOUSE GARDEN INN

COOLIDGE ST

GLENN ST

ORANGE

NURSERY ST

N MAIN

Creek

Ashland

WIMER ST

HERSEY

VAN

LAUREL

NESS

HELMAN

ST

HERSEY ST

MANZANITA

HIGH

CENTRAL AVE

WATER

OAK

ASHLAND COMMONS

ALTA ST

HIGH ST

LAUREL

ASHLAND HOSTEL

PLAZA INN

ASHLAND CREEK INN

GRANDVIEW

S ALMOND

BUSH ST

PIONEER ST

ASHLAND CO-OP

A ST

NOBLE COFFEE

ST

SCENIC DR

NOB HILL

SEE "ASHLAND CENTER" MAP

E MAIN

B ST

2ND ST

3RD ST

COQUINA

DITCH RD

CHURCH

LITHIA

PELTON HOUSE

1ST ST

WAY

PEERLESS HOTEL/ RESTAURANT

PINE ST

★ Oregon Shakespeare Festival

PLANCHA

AMUSE

C ST

4TH ST

5TH ST

6TH ST

STRAWBERRY

ELEVEN

ASHLAND SPRINGS HOTEL

HARGADINE

ENDERS ALLEY

COLUMBIA HOTEL

NUTLEY

GRANITE ST

OREGON CABARET THEATRE

AVE

WEST FORK

VISTA ST

SMITHFIELD'S RESTAURANT

E MAIN ST

66

WINBURN WAY

WINCHESTER COUNTRY INN

SISKIYOU BLVD

ANNE HATHAWAY'S COTTAGE

LN

GLENVIEW DR

CHANTICLEER

ALLISON

STRATFORD INN

★ LITHIA PARK

PIONEER

GRESHAM ST

FAIRVIEW ST

UNION ST

99

To Ashland Motel, Cedarwood Inn, Weisinger Family Winery, and Mt. Ashland Inn

0        0.25 mi

0        0.25 km

RIDGE RD

IOWA ST

MEADE ST

HOLLY

IDAHO ST

To Talent

To Medford

ASHLAND DOG PARK/ BEAR CREEK GREENWAY

99

5

0        1 mi

0        1 km

IDAHO ST

KEARNEY ST

HARRISON

ALTAMONT ST

MAP AREA

Ashland

THE PALM

ASHLAND MOTEL

GLENVIEW DR

GRESHAM

TAYLOR

EUCLID AVE

ASHLAND ST

SOUTHERN OREGON STATE COLLEGE

66

VILLAGE SUITES

To Klamath Falls

MORNING GLORY CAFE

CEDARWOOD INN

66

TERRACE ST

99

To California

© AVALON TRAVEL

musical and dance performances and alfresco movies. Children love to play at the playgrounds or feed the ducks in the ponds. **Dogs are not permitted** in the park.

## Museums and Galleries

There are over 30 retail galleries in Ashland. Check out www.ashlandgalleries.com for an online guide and map. Two favorites are the **Hanson Howard Gallery** (89 Oak St., 541/488-2562, www.hansonhowardgallery. com, 11am-5pm Tues.-Sat.), which features monthly exhibits of contemporary artists in a bright airy shop next to the Standing Stone brewpub, and the **Gallerie Karon** (500 A St., 541/482-9008, 10:30am-5pm Tues.-Sat.), with the works of 21 artists in an eclectic collection of sculpture, paintings, photography, and jewelry. It is located in a thriving commercial strip by the railroad tracks.

**Schneider Museum of Art** (Southern Oregon University campus, 1250 Siskiyou Blvd., 541/552-6245, http://sma.sou.edu, 10am-4pm Mon.-Sat., donation) features contemporary art by national and international artists. Ashland is also home to the **ScienceWorks Hands-On Museum** (1500 E. Main St., near Walker St., 541/482-6767, www.scienceworksmuseum.org, 10am-6pm daily Memorial Day-Labor Day, 10am-5pm Wed.-Sun. Labor Day-Memorial Day, $12 adults and teenagers, $10 seniors and ages 2-12, free under age 2), a hands-on museum that offers interactive exhibits, live performances, and activities.

## Wine-Tasting

The climate of southern Oregon is ideal for many Bordeaux varietals such as cabernet sauvignon, sauvignon blanc, and merlot. Though the area's largest concentration of wineries is in the nearby Applegate Valley, a handful are close to Ashland.

Just south of town is **Weisinger Family Winery** (3150 Siskiyou Blvd., 541/488-5989, www.weisingers.com, 11am-6pm daily May-Sept., 11am-5pm Wed.-Sun. Oct.-Apr.). The vineyard, which has received national and

Ashland Center

© AVALON TRAVEL

international awards, produces cabernet sauvignon, viognier, sauvignon blanc, and Italian varietals.

Just north of Ashland, **Paschal Winery** (1122 Suncrest Rd., Talent, 541/535-7957, www.paschalwinery.com, noon-6pm daily summer, call for winter hours) crafts refined viognier and a delicious red blend of tempranillo, sangiovese, and syrah called Civita Di Bagnoregio.

## SPORTS AND RECREATION

**Ashland Mountain Supply** (31 N. Main St., 541/488-2749, 11am-6pm Mon.-Tues., 10am-6pm Wed.-Sat., 11am-5pm Sun.) sells and rents outdoor recreation equipment.

### Golf

A few miles outside of Ashland on Highway 66 is **Oak Knoll Golf Course** (3070 Hwy. 66, 541/482-4311, www.oakknollgolf.org, $16 for 9 holes in summer), an affordable nine-hole municipal course.

### Hiking

If you want more than a trek through Lithia Park, the walk to the top of **Mount Ashland** is an easy one, with good views of the Siskiyou Mountains and 14,162-foot Mount Shasta in California. Bring a sweater even in warm weather, as it can get windy.

The **Pacific Crest Trail** crosses the Mount Ashland road about three miles past the ski area. By early July, the snow is mostly gone, and the wildflowers are abundant.

### Horseback Riding

Saddle up and head out for a trail ride with **City Slickers** (776 W. Valley View Rd., 541/951-4611, www.oregontrailrides.com, from $80). A variety of rides in and around Ashland are available, and horses and guides are experienced with beginning riders.

### Biking

One of the more popular local bike rides, the **Lithia Loop Mountain Bike Highway** (www.fs.usda.gov) is a strenuous 28-mile ride that starts and ends in Lithia Park, with a steep six-mile uphill stretch at the beginning and a screamingly steep seven-mile descent at the end. To avoid the steep ups and downs, you can drive to the top and ride the fairly level 15-mile stretch. The Lithia Loop may be closed during midsummer and fall when fire danger is high.

The **Siskiyou Crest Mountain Bike Highway** (www.fs.usda.gov) begins at the Mount Ashland ski area parking lot. The 31-mile round-trip ranges from moderate to difficult and affords incredible views of Mount Shasta. The route ends at Dutchman Peak, where you'll find one of the few cupola-style fire lookouts left in the Pacific Northwest. This particular lookout was built in 1927. Note that bicycles are not allowed on the nearby Pacific Crest Trail.

The 26-mile paved **Bear Creek Bike and Nature Trail** crisscrosses town before going down the valley to Medford along Bear Creek. The **Ashland Ranger District** (645 Washington St., 541/482-3333, www.fs.usda. gov) can provide directions and additional information about these and other mountain bike trails in the area.

### Skiing

Perched high atop the Siskiyou range and straddling the California-Oregon border is 7,523-foot **Mount Ashland** (541/482-2897, www.mtashland.com, adults $39 Mon.-Fri., $46 Sat.-Sun., $25 night, ages 7-12 $29 Mon.-Fri., $36 Sat.-Sun., $19 night). To get here, take the "Mount Ashland" exit off I-5 and follow the road eight miles uphill.

view of California's Mount Shasta from the Pacific Crest Trail near Mount Ashland

Skiers of all levels enjoy the 23 different runs, 100 miles of cross-country trails, and breathtaking vistas, and the vertical drop is 1,150 feet. Although climate change has brought some low-snow winters to Mount Ashland, it's a great place to ski when the snow allows. Don't forget to purchase your Oregon Sno-Park permit.

## Water Sports

**Jackson WellSprings** (2253 Hwy. 99 N., 541/482-3776, www.jacksonwellsprings.com, 8am-midnight daily Apr. 15-Oct. 14, 10am-midnight daily Oct. 15-Apr. 14, $10 adults, $8 seniors and students, $4 children, plus $5 insurance), a rather informal, decidedly hippie place, is two miles north of Ashland on the old highway and has a large naturally heated public swimming pool, a hot soaking pool, a sauna, and a steam room as well as private mineral baths. Clothing is optional after 8pm. The pool is closed Monday until the 6pm "ladies night."

**Meyer Memorial Pool** (Hunter Park, Homes Ave. and Hunter Court, 541/488-0313, summer) includes a wading pool and a large swimming pool. Six miles east of Ashland on Highway 66 is **Emigrant Reservoir** (541/776-7001, http://jacksoncountyor.org, parking $4). In addition to waterskiing, sailing, fishing, and swimming, there is a 270-foot twin flume waterslide (noon-6pm daily Memorial Day-Labor Day, 1.5-hour wristband $6 Mon.-Fri., $7 Sat.-Sun.).

## Outfitters

The **Adventure Center** (40 N. Main St., 541/488-2819 or 800/444-2819, www.raftingtours.com) offers half-day, full-day, and multiday fishing, rafting, and cycling trips for any size party. Rates include wetsuits and other gear, guides, and transportation from Ashland. Half-day rafting trips on the Rogue River (9:30am-2pm or 1:30pm-5:45pm, $75) include a snack; the longer white-water picnic trip (8am-4pm, $129) includes lunch. Rated one of the best floats in southern Oregon, the upper Klamath River trip (7:30am-5:30pm,

$135) includes all meals. The Adventure Center also rents bikes and leads easygoing bike rides on quiet paved roads.

# ENTERTAINMENT AND EVENTS
## Brewpubs

Bright, airy, and with a delightful back patio open in good weather, **Standing Stone Brewing Company** (101 Oak St., 541/482-2448, www.standingstonebrewing.com, 11am-midnight daily, $8-19) has one of the most pleasant dining rooms in Ashland. Not only are the beers tasty, the menu is also very broad, including soups, salads, burgers, wood-fired pizzas, and entrées verging on fine dining.

Tucked down near Ashland Creek, the **Caldera Tap House** (31 Water St., 541/482-4677, www.calderabrewing.com, 2pm-10pm Sun.-Tues., 2pm-11pm Wed.-Thurs., 2pm-midnight Fri.-Sat., $8-14) serves some of the best locally brewed beer along with fairly typical pub food and live music.

## Festivals and Events

Shakespeare isn't the only act in town. Local companies include the **Oregon Cabaret Theatre** (1st St. and Hargadine St., 541/488-2902, www.oregoncabaret.com), with musical revues in a club setting and Southern Oregon State College productions.

Ashland's biggest summertime event, aside from the Shakespeare Festival, is the **Fourth of July parade,** which is more of an exuberant and slightly wacky celebration of the community than a patriotic event.

TOP EXPERIENCE

★ **OREGON SHAKESPEARE FESTIVAL**
While Lithia Park is the heart of Ashland, Shakespeare is the soul of this community. The festival began when Angus Bowmer, an English professor at Ashland College, decided to celebrate Independence Day weekend in 1935 with a Shakespeare production.

The city leaders were so unsure of the reception it would get that they asked him to allow boxing matches on the stage during the day prior to the performance. By the time he retired as artistic director of the festival in 1971, his Fourth of July dream had grown into an internationally acclaimed theater company with three stages, one named in his honor.

Performances run from mid-February through late October or early November, though the famed outdoor **Elizabethan Theatre,** built on the site of Ashland's Chautauqua Dome and modeled after the Fortune Theatre of London circa 1600, is open in summer only. This is the largest of the festival's three theaters. While Shakespeare under the stars is incredibly romantic, it can also get cold after sunset; bring warm clothing. Curtain times run 8pm-8:30pm, with most shows ending around 11pm. This outdoor theater opens in early June and closes by mid-October.

The 600-seat **Angus Bowmer** is an indoor complex with excellent acoustics, computerized sound and lighting, and nary a bad seat in the house, and the 150-seat **Thomas Theatre** is where modern works and experimental productions are the norm. This theater is small enough to stage plays that might be overwhelmed by a larger venue.

In addition to the plays themselves, two other events are popular with theatergoers. **Backstage Tours** (10am Tues.-Sun., reservations required, high season $20) explore the history, design, and technology of all of the festival's repertory theaters, including the fascinating Elizabethan Stage. The regular tour is a walking tour and has six flights of stairs; call ahead to schedule a tour without stairs.

Catch the free **Green Show** on the plaza outside the Elizabethan Theatre. It begins at 6:45pm and features live music, lectures, performance, storytelling, and other entertainment. It ends just before 8pm, when the outdoor performance starts in the Elizabethan Theatre.

Tickets to the **Oregon Shakespeare Festival** (15 S. Pioneer St., Ashland, OR 97520, 541/482-4331 or 800/219-8161, www.osfashland.org, box office 9:30am-performance time Tues.-Sun., 9:30am-5pm Mon., closed holidays, $30-110) often sell out months in advance. All seats are reserved, and children under age six are not permitted.

If you are unable to get advance tickets, your best bet is to show up at the Shakespeare Plaza an hour or two before the show with a

Catch the nightly Green Show before evening plays start; it's free!

sign stating what show you want to see. If you are lucky, you will score tickets from someone with extras. Avoid bidding wars with other would-be theatergoers. Otherwise, be at the ticket window at 6pm; any available seats will be released at that time. There is no late seating.

## FOOD

Ashland's creative talents are not just confined to theatrical pursuits; some of Oregon's better restaurants can be found here. Even the humbler fare served in Ashland's unpretentious cafés and pubs can be memorable. The city has a 5 percent restaurant tax, a surcharge seen nowhere else in the Beaver State except Lincoln City.

Stock up on groceries or pick up a deli sandwich at the **Ashland Food Co-op** (237 N. 1st St., 541/482-2237, www.ashlandfood. coop, 7am-9pm daily).

### Pacific Northwest Cuisine

The restaurant at the historic Winchester Inn, **Alchemy** (35 S. 2nd St., 541/488-1115, www. alchemyashland.com, 5pm-8:30pm Sun.-Thurs., 5pm-9pm Fri.-Sat., dinner $23-36) serves sit-up-and-take-notice modern cuisine prepared with rarified techniques and ingredients. In the stately dining room, you can savor seared duck breast with prickly pear gastrique. The bar is a classy spot to enjoy a cocktail.

The ★ **Peerless Restaurant** (265 4th St., 541/488-6067, http://peerlessrestaurant. com, 5pm-9pm Tues.-Sat., $13-35) is part of a picturesque historic hotel complex; the garden is spectacular, so dine alfresco if possible. The impressive selection of small plates ($4-22) makes casual dining fun and exciting—start with lobster-stuffed potato skins. The menu also includes several burger options, which can keep the price of dinner from skyrocketing.

★ **Amuse** (15 N. 1st St., 541/488-9000, http://amuserestaurant.com, 5:30pm-9pm Tues.-Sun., $26-38) is Ashland's top French-via-Pacific Northwest restaurant, with a menu that changes weekly and features fresh local fruit, vegetables, and mushrooms as well as locally harvested fish. Expect such sophisticated dishes as crispy veal sweetbreads with pickled cherries and corn puree or black truffle-roasted game hen. Desserts ($10) are especially good. The back patio is shady and expansive.

Just down the road from Ashland is the absolutely unique **New Sammy's Cowboy Bistro** (2210 S. Pacific Hwy., 541/535-2779, www.newsammyscowboybistro.com, noon-1:30pm and 5pm-9pm Wed.-Sat., $18-30, 3-course prix fixe $50). The limited menu changes frequently, but expect delicious fish, rabbit, lamb, and charcuterie, locally sourced and cooked with French finesse. If the braised beef ribs are offered, by all means order them. The wine list has hundreds of choices. If possible, ask to be seated in the old dining room with cow wallpaper and just six tables in what was once a gas station. Call for winter hours; reservations are strongly advised.

Head down to Ashland Creek and search a bit to find the door to the ★ **Loft** (18 Calle Guanajuato, 541/482-1116, http://loftashland. com, 11:30am-2pm and 5:30pm-9pm daily, $16-32), a multistory brasserie with a patio overlooking the creek. The French-Oregonian menu features locally sourced food, including grilled king salmon served with gnocchi and pea shoot salad.

Classy but casual, **Coquina** (542 A St., 541/488-0521, www.coquinarestaurant.com, 5pm-10pm Tues.-Sat., $18-32) serves refined Pacific Northwest cuisine based on local, seasonal ingredients. This Railroad District restaurant features such tempting creations as seared duck breast with polenta and pickled wild mushrooms.

### Steak House

**Smithfields Restaurant and Bar** (36 S 2nd St., 541/488-9948, www.smithfieldsashland. com, 5pm-10pm Mon.-Fri., 10am-2:30pm and 5pm-10pm Sat.-Sun., $14-28) is the kind of nose-to-tail establishment where you'll find excellent house-made charcuterie and epic steaks as well as duck confit cassoulet, cider-braised pork belly, and a selection of meat-free salads. In good weather, ask for seating in the park-like back garden.

## Classic American

For Ashland's most popular breakfast café, head to **Morning Glory Restaurant** (1149 Siskiyou Blvd., 541/488-8636, www.greenleafrestaurant.com, 8am-1:30pm daily, $10-12) for delicious omelets, pancakes, and breakfast sandwiches. Lines on weekend mornings can be long.

The **Greenleaf Restaurant** (49 N. Main St., 541/482-2808, http://greenleafrestaurant.com, 8am-8pm daily, $9-20) is known for its reasonably priced veggie-forward food and for its lovely patio overlooking Lithia Creek.

## Bakeries and Cafés

Find Ashland's best coffee and a friendly place to hang out for a while at **Noble Coffee** (281 4th St., 541/488-3288, www.noblecoffeeroasting.com, 7am-4pm daily), in the hip railroad district. A friendly spot for pastries and desserts is **Mix Bakeshop** (57 N. Main St., 541/488-9885, www.mixashland.com, 7am-10pm Sun.-Thurs., 7am-10:30 Fri.-Sat.), with Direct Trade coffee, excellent ice cream, and a bohemian atmosphere.

## Asian

The **Thai Pepper** (84 Main St., 541/482-8058, http://thaipepperashland.com, 5pm-10pm Sun.-Thurs., 5pm-11pm Fri.-Sat., $15-19) has a lot to offer: Not only is the spicy, flavorful Southeast Asian cuisine well prepared and moderately priced, the dining room steps down into the steep gulch of Ashland Creek, offering a cool and quiet haven in the summer heat and one of the most pleasant patio dining areas in town.

For North Indian food, go to **Taj** (31 Water St., 541/488-5900, www.taj-indiancuisine.com, 11am-3pm and 5pm-9pm daily, $13-17), which has a number of vegetarian dishes, traditional curries, and tandoor specialties. At lunchtime, enjoy the buffet ($11).

## Pizza

Stop by **Martolli's** (38 E. Main St., 541/482-1918, www.martollis.com, 11am-9pm daily, $8-11 for personal pie); it's the best pizza in town, and the café is a cheery place with a Deadhead theme.

## Mexican

**Plancha** (165 E. Main St., 541/708-0883, www.planchamex.com, 11:30am-3pm and 4pm-9pm daily, $4-16) performs a great service by bringing bright, fresh, and affordable Mexican food to downtown Ashland. The menu offers a selection of tasty tacos, enchiladas, and *torta* sandwiches and other snacks. Best of all, Plancha has a fine collection of tequila to wash it all down, so the small dining room is usually full of high spirits.

## Wine Bars

If you're looking for a glass of wine or cocktail plus a delicious selection of snacks and entrées, try **Liquid Assets** (96 N. Main St., 541/482-9463, www.liquidassetswinebar.com, 4pm-10pm Mon.-Thurs., 4pm-midnight Fri.-Sat., small plates $4-16, entrées $14-26), with a good choice of cheeses and cured meats, plus tempting house specialties such as Dungeness crab cakes, warm chèvre salad, and roast lamb loin with chimichurri.

# ACCOMMODATIONS

Quoted rates are for June-September; expect prices to drop around one-third outside the summer high season. Look for chain motels at the freeway exits. If Ashland's prices seem too high, you can find less expensive rates in Medford, a 10-minute drive to the north.

The traditions of Britain are represented in Ashland not only by the Oregon Shakespeare Festival but also by the town's numerous bed-and-breakfasts, the most of any locale in the state. Many B&Bs require a two-night minimum stay during summer. **Stay Ashland** (800/944-0329, http://stayashland.com) can help you find quality B&B lodgings in town.

## Under $50

Offering dorm beds and a handful of private rooms, the Ashland Hostel (150 N. Main St., 541/482-9217, www.theashlandhostel.com, $31 pp dorm, $60-69 d private room with shared bath, $69-139 suite with private bath) is a two-story 1902 house near the Pacific Crest Trail, only three blocks from the Elizabethan Theatre and Lithia Park and two blocks from the Greyhound station. Reservations are essential, especially March-October. The hostel has a coin-op laundry.

A newer hostel, Ashland Commons (437 Williamson Way, 541/482-6753, www.ashlandcommons.com, $28 pp dorm, $50-85 pp private room), is a little farther from the downtown hub in a quiet residential neighborhood. Though it commonly accommodates school groups, it also offers individual hostel stays.

## $50-100

Moderately priced guest rooms are available from Cedarwood Inn (1801 Siskiyou Blvd., 541/488-2000 or 800/547-4141, www.ashlandcedarwoodinn.com, $80-125), with a pool and continental breakfast. Two-bedroom and kitchen units are also available.

The Ashland Motel (1145 Siskiyou Blvd., 541/482-2561 or 800/460-8858, www.ashlandmotel.com, $95-130) offers good value and clean, cheery, and basic pet-friendly guest rooms. All rooms have fridges and microwaves; there are two two-bedroom units and a small outdoor pool.

A dollar-wise choice with some charm is the Columbia Hotel (262½ E. Main St., 541/482-3726 or 800/718-2530, www.columbiahotel.com, $98-149), in the center of town. This well-kept 1910 hotel with a grand piano in the lobby has 24 rooms, most of which share baths.

## $100-150

The Pelton House B&B (228 B St., 541/488-7003 or 866/488-7003, www.peltonhouse.com, $125-355) is located in a historic Victorian just a few blocks from the Shakespeare Festival. Each of its seven rooms is themed, and two suites are available for families or groups. Guests have free use of an electric charging station.

The ★ Morical House Garden Inn (668 N. Main St., 541/482-2254, www.moricalhouse.com, $140-270) is a restored 1880s farmhouse with seven rooms and a guesthouse with three luxury suites, each with a picture-postcard view of Grizzly Mountain and the Siskiyou foothills. In season, the two acres of gardens provide organic produce for breakfast and habitat for birds and butterflies. It's sometimes hard to remember that you are only a few blocks away from downtown theaters and shopping.

## $150-200

If you want to stay in the center of Ashland, Best Western Bard's Inn Motel (132 N. Main St., 541/482-0049 or 800/533-9627, www.bardsinn.com, $166-225) is a good choice. Just across the Main Street bridge from downtown, the Bard's Inn is no more than five minutes' walk from the theaters. There are a number of buildings and room types, all nicely furnished and well maintained. Facilities include a streamside restaurant and bar.

Clean and meticulously maintained, the privately owned and operated Stratford Inn (555 Siskiyou Blvd., 541/488-2151 or 800/547-4741, http://stratfordinnashland.com, $185-199) is just five blocks from the theaters. All guest rooms have a fridge and there are a couple of kitchen suites. A guest laundry, ski lockers, an elaborate continental breakfast, and an indoor pool and whirlpool tub all contribute to the inn's high occupancy rate.

Rooms at ★ The Palm (1065 Siskiyou Blvd., 877/482-2635, www.palmcottages.com, $179-209), are in a well-maintained cottage-style motel in the midst of lovely gardens. A saline pool, a sundeck, and cabanas complete the oasis atmosphere. Pet-friendly rooms are sometimes available.

The 70-room Ashland Springs Hotel (212 E. Main St., 541/488-1700, www.

ashlandspringshotel.com, $189-289), a block from the Elizabethan Theatre, is first-class, with a grand ballroom, a bar to enjoy parlor games and musical entertainment, and English gardens evocative of another era. The handsome Lark restaurant offers regionally focused fine dining. Luxuriously appointed guest rooms aren't large but boast oversize windows highlighting nice views. Minimum stays may apply.

The historic ★ **Peerless Hotel** (243 4th St., 541/488-1082, www.peerlesshotel.com, $164-283) was established in 1900 for railroad travelers. The old hotel has been thoroughly modernized and converted into a boutique B&B-style hotel. One of the most distinctive places to stay in Ashland, the Peerless also offers a fine-dining restaurant and a location in the art gallery-rich Railroad District.

**Plaza Inn and Suites** (98 Central Ave., 541/488-8900 or 888/488-0358, www.plazainnashland.com, $169-279) is a large, modern hotel just below downtown and within easy walking distance of the theaters. Many of the rooms look onto a parklike courtyard that fronts Ashland Creek. Guest rooms are nicely appointed; many have balconies, and some allow pets. A breakfast buffet is included in the rates.

The ★ **Chanticleer Inn** (120 Gresham St., www.ashland-bed-breakfast.com, 541/482-1919, $180-215), Ashland's oldest B&B and still leading the way, has five romantic guest rooms and gourmet breakfasts. Dogs are permitted (with prior approval) in some of the rooms. There are round-the-clock refrigerator rights, complimentary wines and sherry, and a full cookie jar on the kitchen counter.

**Anne Hathaway's Cottage** (586 E. Main St., 541/488-1050, www.ashlandbandb.com, $195-215), four blocks from the theaters, was once a boardinghouse; the cottages across the street are part of this B&B complex. Kids and dogs are welcome.

Bathe in naturally occurring hot springs at the **Lithia Springs Inn** (2165 W. Jackson Rd., 541/482-7128 or 800/482-7128, www.ashlandinn.com, $169-259), a couple of miles from downtown amid four acres of gardens, far enough for real peace and quiet. The rooms, suites, and bungalows are stylishly modern, with bathwater fed from the hot springs. Most rooms have soaking tubs, and an on-site spa can provide treatments.

## Over $250

At the ★ **Ashland Creek Inn** (70 Water St., 541/482-3315, www.ashlandcreekinn.

Ashland is full of vintage B&Bs.

com, $295-450), you won't get any closer to Ashland Creek without getting wet. This small luxury-level inn is directly adjacent to the stream and has several guest rooms with cantilevered decks directly above the rushing water. Each of the 10 suites is uniquely decorated according to a theme—the Caribe, the Marrakech, the Edinburgh—and each offers complete kitchens, living rooms, private entrances, and decks. Best of all, this comfort and style are just moments from downtown shopping and the theaters.

Two blocks south of the theaters is the acclaimed **Winchester Country Inn** (35 S. 2nd St., 541/488-1113 or 800/972-4991, www.winchesterinn.com, $250-430, packages available), offering 19 guest rooms and suites with private baths and loads of personality. The individual attentiveness of the large staff recalls a traditional English country inn. Bay windows, private balconies, and exquisite English gardens add further distinction. Gourmet delicacies are featured at breakfast, and dinner and Sunday brunch are available in the inn's restaurant.

## Camping

**Emigrant Lake** (5505 Hwy. 66, 541/774-8183, http://jacksoncountyor.org/parks, $20 tent, $30 RV), a few miles east of Ashland, has RV and tent camping. South of town, **Mount Ashland** has a primitive campground (no water, free) about a mile past the ski resort.

On the northern edge of town, **Jackson WellSprings** (2253 Hwy. 99 N., 541/482-3776, http://jacksonwellsprings.com, tents $25 for 1 person, $15 per additional adult) has tent sites on a grassy tree-shaded lawn. It's highly informal, with a hippie vibe, and gets a bit of road noise. However, camping gets you admission to the pool, sauna, and steam room, and it's only a 10-minute drive from downtown.

## INFORMATION

**Ashland Visitor Information Center** (110 E. Main St., 541/482-3486, www.ashlandchamber.com, 9am-5pm Mon.-Fri.) offers brochures, play schedules, and other up-to-date information on happenings. The **Ashland-Siskiyou Visitors Center** (60 Lowe Rd., 541/488-1805, 9am-5pm daily May-Sept.), just off I-5 at exit 19, offers travel information on the whole state.

## GETTING THERE AND AROUND

United, Delta, Alaska, and Allegiant fly into **Rogue Valley-Medford Airport** (MFR, 1000 Terminal Loop Pkwy., Medford, 541/772-8068 or 800/882-7488, www.co.jackson.or.us), 15 miles north of Ashland. **Amtrak** (800/872-7245) has a station 70 miles east at Klamath Falls and 75 miles south at Dunsmuir, California. The **Southwest Point bus** (585 Siskiyou Blvd., 541/482-4495) stops at the Ashland Safeway on its route between Brookings and Klamath Falls; it also stops in Medford. The local bus service is **Rogue Valley Transportation** (541/779-2877, www.rvtd.org), with a line that runs to Medford with several stops in Ashland.

# Medford

Along with an economy based on agriculture and timber products, Medford (pop. 77,600) is a popular retirement center. Some of the enticements are proximity to Ashland's culture, Rogue Valley recreation, Cascade getaways, and rainfall totals that are half those recorded in the Willamette Valley. All that summer heat is good for fruit production—the Rogue River Valley around Medford is a major center for peach and pear production, and wine grapes are displacing dairy cows and berries on area farms.

## SIGHTS
### Table Rocks

About 10 miles northeast of Medford are two eye-catching basaltic buttes, **Upper and Lower Table Rocks.** They are composed of sandstone with erosion-resistant lava caps deposited during a massive Cascade eruption 4-5 million years ago. Wind and water have gradually undercut the sandstone. Stripped of its underpinnings, the heavy basalt on top of the eroded sandstone is pulled down by gravity, creating the nearly vertical slabs that we see today.

Water doesn't readily percolate through the lava. Small ponds collect on top of the butte, nurturing the wildflowers that flourish in early spring. The wildflower display reaches its zenith in April. A dozen species cover the rock-strewn flats in bright yellow and vivid purple.

The **Lower Table Rock** protects an area of special biological, geological, and historical value. Pacific madrone, white oak, manzanita, and ponderosa pine grow on the flank of the mountain; the crown is covered with grasses and wildflowers, including dwarf meadow foam, which grows nowhere else.

Hikers who take the 2.6-mile trail to the top of horseshoe-shaped Lower Table Rock should watch for batches of pale lavender fawn lilies peeking out from underneath the shelter of the scraggly scrub oaks on the way up the mountain. Walk over to the cliff's edge, past some of the Mima mounds or "patterned ground" that distinguishes the surface of the

The cliff-lined Table Rocks are preserves of unusual plant ecosystems.

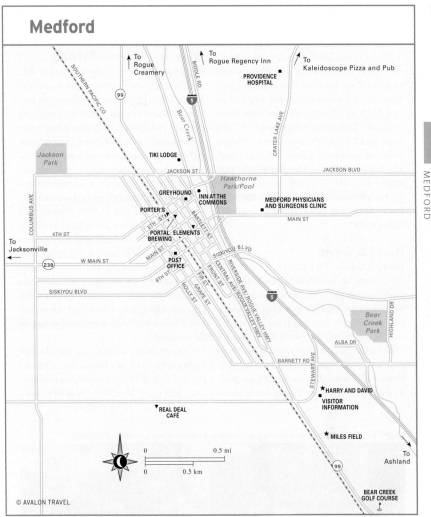

# Medford

To Rogue Creamery

To Rogue Regency Inn

To Kaleidoscope Pizza and Pub

PROVIDENCE HOSPITAL

SOUTHERN PACIFIC CO

BIDDLE RD

Bear Creek

CRATER LAKE AVE

99

5

Jackson Park

TIKI LODGE

JACKSON ST

Hawthorne Park/Pool

JACKSON BLVD

COLUMBUS AVE

GREYHOUND

INN AT THE COMMONS

MEDFORD PHYSICIANS AND SURGEONS CLINIC

PORTER'S

BARTLETT ST

MAIN ST

4TH ST

5TH ST

PORTAL ELEMENTS BREWING

To Jacksonville

238

W MAIN ST

MAIN ST

SISKIYOU BLVD

RIVERSIDE AVE ROGUE VALLEY HWY

CENTRAL AVE ROGUE VALLEY HWY

POST OFFICE

8TH ST

FRONT ST

HOLLY ST

FIR ST

GRAPE ST

SISKIYOU BLVD

5

Bear Creek Park

HIGHLAND DR

ALBA DR

BARNETT RD

STEWART AVE

REAL DEAL CAFÉ

HARRY AND DAVID

VISITOR INFORMATION

MILES FIELD

0      0.5 mi

0      0.5 km

To Ashland

99

BEAR CREEK GOLF COURSE

© AVALON TRAVEL

butte. How the mounds were formed is a matter of scientific debate. Some scientists believe they represent centuries of work by rodents; others think they are accumulated silt deposits; while still others maintain they were created by the action of the wind. However they got here, the mounds are the only soil banks on the mountain that support grasses, which are unable to grow on the lava. Lichens and mosses manage to grow on the lava, however, painting the dull black basalt with luxuriant green and fluorescent yellow during the wetter months.

The trail up **Upper Table Rock** is a little over one mile but can be muddy during the wet season. The trail affords wonderful vistas of the Rogue River and Sams Valley to the north. The ponds up here are smaller and fewer than those on Lower Table Rock, but the Mima mounds are more clearly defined. It's easy to get disoriented out here, with hundreds of acres to explore. The point where the trail heads back down the mountain is marked by two large trees, a ponderosa pine and a Douglas fir, accompanied by a smaller cedar.

To get to the Table Rocks, from I-5 take exit 33 for "Central Point" east about a mile to Table Rock Road and turn north (left). Continue 5.3 miles on Modoc Road, then turn north for 1.5 miles to Upper Table Rock. For Lower Table Rock, go eight miles on Table Rock Road, turn left (west) onto Wheeler Road and continue 0.5 miles to the trailhead. The **Bureau of Land Management** (3040 Biddle Rd., 541/770-2200, www.blm.gov/or) has additional information on the Table Rocks. **Dogs are prohibited** on the Table Rocks trails.

## Harry & David

**Harry & David** (1314 Center Dr., 541/776-2277, www.harryanddavid.com), the nation's leading purveyor of mail-order fruit, has a store just off I-5's exit 27 in the south part of Medford. Here you'll find fresh fruit and vegetables, rejects from Harry & David's Fruit-of-the-Month Club that are nearly as good as the mail-order fruit but too small or blemished to meet the company's high quality standards, jams and fruit spreads, and a really large selection of Oregon wines. The local visitors center is right next door.

## Wine and Cheese Tasting

**RoxyAnn Winery** (3285 Hillcrest Rd., 541/776-2315, www.roxyann.com, noon-7pm Mon.-Thurs., 11am-9pm Fri., 11am-7pm Sat.-Sun.) is one of the top wineries in southern Oregon, and conveniently the tasting room is immediately east of Medford in an old pear orchard. RoxyAnn makes particularly rich red wines—the claret and syrah are especially delicious. The tasting room is in an old barn, and it's the setting for music on Friday evenings.

**Kriselle Cellars** (12956 Modoc Rd., 541/830-8466, www.krisellecellars.com, 11am-5:30pm Wed.-Sun.) is about 12 miles north of Medford, with a stunning tasting room overlooking the Rogue Valley. The wines here are notable, particularly the French-style viognier and award-winning cabernet sauvignon. The tasting room also offers light meals, with wood-fired pizzas on the weekend.

Central Point is home to the **Rogue Creamery** (311 N. Front St., Central Point, 541/665-1155, www.roguecreamery.com, 9am-5pm Mon.-Fri., 9am-6pm Sat.,

Sample excellent blue cheese at the Rogue Creamery in Central Point, just north of Medford.

11am-5pm Sun.), which makes some of the best cheese in the Pacific Northwest, with a focus on blue cheese; the Caveman Blue is exceptionally rich. In the same block, taste wine at **Ledger David Cellars** (245 N. Front St., 541/664-2218, http://ledgerdavid.com) and chocolate at **Lillie Belle Farms** (211 N. Front St., 541/664-2815, www.lilliebellefarms.com).

## GOLF

**Eagle Point Golf Course** (100 Eagle Point Dr., Eagle Point, 541/826-8225, www.eaglepointgolf.com, $47 Mon.-Fri., $55 Sat.-Sun.) is arguably the finest course in the Rogue River Valley. Designed by Robert Trent Jones Jr., the course boasts enough character to challenge beginners and experts alike. Impressive views of Mount McLoughlin and Table Rocks add to the experience.

## ENTERTAINMENT AND EVENTS

### Brewpubs

Downtown also has a couple brewpubs of note. **Bricktowne Brewing Company** (44 S. Central Ave., 541/973-2377, www.bricktownebeer.com, 11am-10pm Mon.-Thurs., 11am-late Fri.-Sat., 11am-7pm Sun., $8-14) offers Big Northwest-style ales plus burgers, sandwiches, salads, and a friendly atmosphere.

Housed in a historic fire station, **Portal Brewing Company** (100 E. 6th St., 541/499-0804, http://portalbrewingco.com, 4pm-10pm Mon.-Fri., noon-10pm Sat., $6-10) offers good brews plus tasty food such as lamb *shawarma*, carrot soup, and pretzels.

### Festivals and Events

The **Jackson County Fair** (http://jacksoncountyfairmn.com) is held at the county fairgrounds (1 Penninger St., Central Point) just north of town the third weekend in July, with livestock competitions, midway rides, and musical entertainment.

The **Pear Blossom Festival** (http://pearblossomparade.org) takes place the second weekend in April, with arts and crafts exhibits, a parade, and a 10K run. The real attraction is the panorama of the pear orchards in bloom against the backdrop of snowcapped Mount McLoughlin. The parade and run take place downtown, and festivities continue at Commons blocks (N. Bartlett St. and 5th St.) with arts and crafts, food, music, and children's activities.

## FOOD

The local wine industry's recent boom has been the catalyst for a number of excellent new Medford restaurants. Start your morning with a delicious breakfast pastry at the **Buttercloud Bakery and Café** (310 Genessee St., 541/973-2336, www.buttercloudbakery.com, 7am-3pm Mon.-Sat., 8am-2pm Sun., biscuit sandwiches $5-9). In addition to scones and sticky buns, you'll find flaky breakfast sandwiches. The **Real Deal Café** (811 W. Stewart Ave., 541/770-5571, http://realdealcafe.com, 7am-2pm daily, breakfast $6-11) serves old-fashioned breakfasts and casual lunches. Everything is made from scratch at this friendly diner, and in good weather there is seating on a shady patio.

Medford's best pizza is at **Kaleidoscope Pizzeria and Pub** (3084 Crater Lake Hwy., www.kaleidoscopepizza.com, 541/779-7787, 11am-9pm Sun.-Thurs., 11am-10pm Fri.-Sat., small pizza $8-13), a bit north of town on Highway 62. In addition to traditional toppings, Kaleidoscope also features unusual pizza choices like chipotle steak and spicy Thai chicken. There's also a good selection of local microbrews.

**Jasper's Cafe** (2739 N. Pacific Hwy., 541/776-5307, http://jasperscafe.com, 11am-7pm Mon.-Thurs., 11am-8pm Fri.-Sat., 11am-6pm Sun., $5-11) has been a Medford tradition since 1976, and it aims to do just a few things well: making the best hamburgers and hot dogs in the region. Add a hand-scooped milk shake and you've got an authentic, delicious slice of Americana.

**Larks** (200 N. Riverside Ave., 541/774-4760, www.larksrestaurant.com, 11:30am-2pm Fri.-Mon. and 5pm-8pm Sun.-Thurs., 5pm-9pm Fri.-Sat., $24-35), the Medford outpost of an Ashland restaurant, has good farm-to-table dishes that take full advantage of the Rogue Valley's excellent produce.

For a traditional steak house atmosphere in Medford, go downtown to the old rail depot, where **Porters** (147 N. Front St., 541/857-1910, www.porterstrainstation.com, 5pm-9pm daily, $22-39) serves pasta, steaks, and plenty of local seafood options, including seared steelhead trout topped with Rogue Creamery blue cheese and pinot noir pear compote, or slow-cooked prime rib seasoned with rosemary and garlic.

One of the top places for an excellent relaxed meal is ★ **Elements** (101 E. Main St., 541/779-0135, http://elementsmedford.com, 4pm-midnight Sun.-Thurs., 4pm-1am Fri.-Sat., $7-15), a tapas and wine bar. The food is sophisticated, but the atmosphere is friendly, which makes dishes like ham-wrapped artichoke hearts, spare ribs with apricot cardamom glaze, and chorizo-stuffed dates all the more enjoyable.

★ **Bambu Asian Café and Wine Bar** (970 N. Phoenix Rd., 541/608-7545, www.tigerroll.com, 11:30am-2pm and 5pm-9pm Mon.-Thurs., 11:30am-2pm and 5pm-9:30pm Fri., 5pm-9:30pm Sat., $14-24), located in a shopping center on the southeast edge of town, features updated and reinterpreted pan-Asian cooking, with a mix of small and large plates that encourages sharing and exploring.

## ACCOMMODATIONS

Medford has no shortage of motel rooms, with national chains clustered near the interstate exits. The cluster of hotels at I-5's exit 27 is just 10 miles from Ashland and offers a good alternative if you can't find affordable rooms. Check hotel websites to find deals, since the differences in the hotels aren't great, and nearly all are near freeway exits.

You don't have to stay near the freeway, however. Just north of downtown on Highway 99 (N. Riverside Ave.) are a number of inexpensive, older, but well-maintained motels, including the basic but perfectly acceptable **Tiki Lodge** (509 N. Riverside Ave., 541/773-4579, www.tikilodgemotel.com, $72-92). The closest hotel to downtown is the ★ **Inn at the Commons** (200 N. Riverside Ave., 541/779-5811 or 866/779-5811, http://innatthecommons.com, $99-129), a full-service establishment that offers a breakfast buffet, airport shuttle service, an outdoor pool, access to a local health club, and the excellent Larks restaurant.

A number of new upscale hotels have been built in recent years a bit out of town but near I-5. One of the nicest is **Rogue Regency Inn** (2300 Biddle Rd., 541/770-1234 or 800/535-5805, www.rogueregency.com, $110-350) which offers an indoor pool and spa, a fitness center, a business center, a complimentary shuttle to the airport, and a bar and restaurant.

## INFORMATION

The **Medford Visitors and Convention Bureau** (1314 Center Dr., 800/469-6307, www.travelmedford.org, 9am-6pm daily) has all kinds of useful maps, directories, and information. Find its visitors center near the Harry & David store.

## GETTING THERE AND AROUND

A half-dozen buses dock daily at the **Greyhound station** (220 S. Front St., 541/779-2103) and travel along I-5. **Rogue Valley Transportation** (200 S. Front St., 541/779-2877, www.rvtd.org) shares the same station and runs buses (Mon.-Fri.) to nearby Jacksonville, Phoenix, White City, Talent, and Ashland. **5 Star Taxi** (541/245-5555) has 24-hour service in the Medford area.

**Rogue Valley-Medford Airport** (MFR, 1000 Terminal Loop Pkwy., 541/772-8068 or 800/882-7488, www.co.jackson.or.us) is the air hub for southern Oregon and is served by United, Delta, Alaska, and Allegiant.

# Jacksonville

Southern Oregon's pioneer past is vividly preserved in Jacksonville (pop. 2,800). Five miles west of Medford, cradled in the foothills of the Siskiyou Mountains, this small town retains an atmosphere of tranquil isolation. With more than 100 original wooden and brick buildings dating to the 1850s, it has been designated a National Historic Landmark District.

Between 1873 and 1884, three major fires reduced most of the original wooden buildings to ash, prompting merchants to use brick in the reconstruction. To protect them from the elements and the damp season, the porous bricks were painted; cast-iron shutters and door frames further reinforced the structures.

Today, Jacksonville paints a memorable picture of a Western town with its pretty surroundings and beautiful pioneer cemetery. On summer Saturdays there's often a chance to catch an exhibit or reenactment in the historic **Beekman House** (452 E. California St., 541/899-8118, www.historic-jacksonville.org). In addition, a renowned music festival, colorful pageants, and rich local folklore all pay tribute to Jacksonville's golden age.

## SIGHTS

Hop aboard the old-fashioned **Jacksonville Trolley** (541/899-8118, www.jacksonvilleoregon.org, $6 adults, $3 ages 6-12) and learn a bit about local history from a period-dressed guide. Tours (on the hour 10:30am-2:30pm daily June-Sept., 10:30am-2:30pm Fri.-Mon. May and Oct.) depart from the Visitor Information Center (C St. and N. Oregon St.).

On a hot afternoon, the hills of Jacksonville can seem pretty steep. Join up with **Segway of Jacksonville** (360 N. Oregon St., 541/899-5269, www.segwayof-jacksonville.com) and spend a few minutes mastering your wheeled steed before heading out on a two-hour guided tour (10am and 2pm Tues.-Sat., $75).

## Peter Britt Gardens

Swiss-born Peter Britt came to Jacksonville not long after gold was discovered in Rich Gulch in 1851. After trying his hand at prospecting, he redirected his efforts toward painting and photography. The latter became his specialty, and for nearly 50 years, he photographed the people, places, and events of southern Oregon (Britt was the first person to photograph Crater Lake).

Britt was also an accomplished horticulturalist and among the first vintners in southern Oregon, experimenting with several varieties of fruit and nut trees and keeping the first weather records of the region. Exploring the 4.5-acre **Britt Gardens** (S. 1st St. and W. Pine St.) is particularly pleasant in the spring when the wildflowers are in bloom and the mosses and ferns are green. Especially notable is the giant redwood tree on the garden's western edge, planted by Britt in 1862 to commemorate the birth of his first child, Emil.

## Wine-Tasting

Over 20 wineries are found near Jacksonville, many of them in the Applegate Valley, west of town. Four miles east of Jacksonville is **EdenVale Winery** (2310 Voorhies Rd., 541/512-2955, www.edenvalewines.com, 11am-6pm Mon.-Thurs., 11am-7pm Fri.-Sat., 11am-5pm Sun. summer, 11am-5pm Sun.-Thurs., 11am-6pm Fri.-Sat. winter), on the imposing Voorhies estate. EdenVale's most interesting wines are tempranillo, cabernet franc, chardonnay, and red blends. The tasting room also offers samples of wines from other small Rogue Valley vintners.

Rising like a Tuscan villa above rolling hills, upscale **Dancin Vineyards** (4477 S. Stage Rd., 541/245-1133, http://dancinvineyards.com, noon-8pm Thurs.-Sun.) combines the features of a top-notch winery and a restaurant. While Dancin makes outstanding pinot noir and chardonnay, the salads and wood-fired pizza served in a garden setting attract their own fans.

About eight miles southwest of Jacksonville in the Applegate Valley is **Valley View Winery** (1000 Upper Applegate Rd., 541/899-8468 or 800/781-9463, www.valleyviewwinery.com, 11am-5pm daily). While focused on the grape varieties of southern France, Valley View also makes tempranillo, pinot gris, and port. The Bordeaux-style blends are especially good.

With a tasting room that resembles a French villa, **Troon Vineyard** (1475 Kubli Rd., 541/846-9900, www.troonvineyard.com, 11am-5pm daily) offers zinfandel, cabernet sauvignon, merlot, syrah, and chardonnay, all grown based on organic principles, plus a red and white blend called Druid Fluid.

Though it's 14 miles south of Jacksonville, **Cowhorn Vineyard** (1665 Eastside Rd., 541/899-6876, 11am-4pm Thurs.-Sun.) is worth seeking out for its excellent Rhône-style wines, including delicious syrahs and a marsanne, roussane, and viognier blend to rival white Châteauneuf-du-Pape.

## ENTERTAINMENT AND EVENTS

The small classical **Peter Britt Music Festival** (Britt Pavilion, 1st St. and Fir St., 541/773-6077 or 800/882-7488, www.brittfest.org, late June-early Sept., general admission $25-90, concerts $45) began in 1962 on a grassy hillside amid majestic ponderosa pines near the site of the original Britt home. Today, the festival encompasses jazz, folk, country, bluegrass, rock, and dance, in addition to the original classical repertoire. Michael Franti, Judy Collins, the Avett Brothers, the Decemberists, and Dwight Yoakam are just a few of the artists who have performed here in recent years.

Reserved seats are available but are more expensive. Concertgoers often bring along blankets, small lawn chairs (allowed only in designated areas), and a picnic supper to enjoy along with entertainment on balmy summer evenings. You are allowed to bring your own wine or beer to some but not all concerts. Food, wine, and beer are sold in the pavilion for all concerts. Order your tickets well in advance: Like the Oregon Shakespeare Festival, some shows sell out months ahead, especially for the well-known performers.

The Applegate Valley is one of southern Oregon's top wine-tasting regions.

## FOOD

The **Jacksonville Inn** (175 E. California St., 541/899-1900 or 800/321-9344, www.jacksonvilleinn.com, 7am-10:30am and 5pm-10pm Mon.-Tues., 7am-10:30am, 11:30am-2pm, and 5pm-9pm Wed.-Sat., 7:30am-10am and 5pm-9pm Sun., reservations recommended, $21-38) offers steaks, seafood, and specialties of the inn, such as stuffed hazelnut chicken and prime rib, in a redbrick and velvet Victorian atmosphere. Vegetarian dishes are available. A cellar of over 2,000 wines enhances your dining experience. There's also a bistro menu after 4pm for lighter appetites, and lovely patio seating during the summer.

The **Bella Union Restaurant and Saloon** (170 W. California St., 541/899-1770, www.bellau.com, 11:30am-10pm Mon.-Sat., 10am-2pm and 10am-9pm Sun., $13-30) is another popular spot. Pizza, pasta, sandwiches, and steaks headline the menu. The patio behind the restaurant is a pleasant place to eat lunch or enjoy a beer. Also available are picnic boxes, a good choice if you're going to a Britt festival concert. Call in your order by 2pm before an evening performance. For the best Thai food in the valley, head for the **Thai House Restaurant** (215 W. California St., 541/899-3585, www.thaihousejville.com, 11:30am-2:30pm and 4pm-9pm Mon.-Fri., noon-9pm Sat., noon-8pm Sun., $13-16).

Ashland's outpost of contemporary fine dining is ★ **Gogi's Restaurant** (235 W. Main St., 541/899-8699, www.gogisrestaurant.com, 5pm-9pm Wed.-Sat., 10am-1pm and 5pm-9pm Sun., $26-37), where the dining room is warm and modern and the food is absolutely here and now. A salmon filet is served with red onion jam and strawberry balsamic syrup; a cider-brined pork chop comes with fresh corn polenta and bacon-apple compote.

Just north of downtown Jacksonville, the **Onyx Restaurant** (635 N. Oregon St., 541/702-2700, http://onyxjvilleor.wixsite.com, 4pm-9pm Tues.-Sat., $14-28) is a bustling gastropub in a former carriage house on the historic 3.1-acre Nunan estate. Dishes come in small, medium, or large sizes, so you can mix and match options such as beet salad with pickled egg and Humboldt Fog cheese, duck wing pad thai, and salmon doused with a caper and leek sauce.

## ACCOMMODATIONS

**Country House Inns** (541/899-2050, www.countryhouseinnsjacksonville.com) operates several lodging options in Jacksonville. The **Wine Country Inn** (830 N. 5th St., $149-209) is a well-maintained motel and the only place in town that deviates from the B&B model. Its exterior was designed to resemble historic stage stops along the route from Sacramento to Portland. The **McCully House Inn** (240 E. California St., $199-248) is a block from downtown, with a good restaurant on the premises. Built in 1861 in the classical revival style, this mansion has four beautifully appointed guest rooms with private baths.

The Craftsman-style **Touvelle House** (455 N. Oregon St., 541/899-3938 or 800/846-3992, www.touvellehouse.com, $130-199) offers five guest rooms and one suite, all with private baths. Out back, near the carriage house, is a heated swimming pool. Common areas include a library and large living room. A full breakfast is included; other goodies like fruit and cookies are available for snacking any time.

The **Jacksonville Inn** (175 E. California St., 541/899-1900 or 800/321-9344, www.jacksonvilleinn.com, $159-465, breakfast included), built in 1861, lies in the heart of the commercial historic district. In addition to eight air-conditioned guest rooms in the vintage hotel itself, all furnished with restored antiques and private baths, the inn also offers four deluxe cottages complete with antiques, fireplaces, and canopied king beds. The inn has an excellent dining room.

## INFORMATION

The **Jacksonville Chamber of Commerce** (185 N. Oregon St., 541/899-8118, http://jacksonvilleoregon.com, 10am-3pm daily May-Oct., 10am-3pm Mon.-Fri., 10am-1pm Sat. Nov.-Apr.) has the scoop on events and activities.

# Grants Pass

The banner across the main thoroughfare in town proudly proclaims: "It's the Climate." But while the 30-inches-per-year precipitation and 52°F mean temperature might be desirable, the true allure of Grants Pass (pop. 37,800) is the mighty Rogue River, which flows through the heart of this community. Outfitters in Grants Pass and the surrounding villages of Rogue River and Merlin specialize in fishing, float, and jet-boat trips. Riverside lodges, accessible by car, river, or footpath, yield remote relaxation in the shadow of the nearby mountains. Grants Pass also makes a good base for trips to Crater Lake and Oregon Caves.

The city itself has an active downtown area, with a large and dynamic **Farmers Market** (4th St. and F St., 9am-1pm Sat. mid-Mar.-Thanksgiving). On busy summer days, Grants Pass buzzes with high spirits and activity.

Don't miss the 18-foot-tall statue near I-5's exit 58 for "Grants Pass"; the *Caveman* welcomes travelers to Grants Pass.

## SIGHTS
### Palmerton Arboretum

Six miles down Highway 99 in the town of Rogue River is the **Palmerton Arboretum** (W. Evans Creek Rd., Rogue River, 541/776-7001, 8am-dusk, free). Originally a five-acre nursery, the arboretum features plant specimens from around the globe, including Japanese pines and Mediterranean cedars, in addition to redwoods and other trees native to the Pacific Northwest. While you're here, see **Skevington's Crossing,** a 200-foot-high swinging suspension bridge over Evans Creek that connects the arboretum to Anna Classick City Park.

### Wildlife Images Rehabilitation and Education Center

Originally a rehabilitation station for injured birds of prey, **Wildlife Images Rehabilitation and Education Center** (11845 Lower River Rd., 541/476-0222, www.wildlifeimages.org, 9am-5pm daily June-Aug., 9am-4pm daily Sept.-May, $12 adults, $10 seniors, $7 ages 4-13) has expanded into an outreach program to aid all kinds of injured or orphaned wildlife as well as to educate the public. Once the animals are well enough to survive in the wild, they are released. Tours (hourly 9am-4pm daily summer, every 2 hours 10am-2pm daily winter) last 1 to 1.5 hours; reservations are required. To get here from 6th Street downtown, head south, turn right onto G Street, continue to Upper River Road, and then turn onto Lower River Road.

### Oregon Vortex

About 10 miles south of Grants Pass on I-5 is the **House of Mystery** at the **Oregon Vortex** (4303 Sardine Creek Rd., Gold Hill, 541/855-1543, www.oregonvortex.com, 9am-4pm daily Mar.-May and Sept.-Oct., 9am-5pm daily June-Aug., $12.75 adults, $11.75 seniors, $9 ages 6-11). Called Forbidden Ground by the indigenous Rogue people because the place spooked their horses, it is actually in a repelling geomagnetic field where objects tend to move away from their center of alignment and lean in funny directions. For example, a ball at the end of a string does not hang straight up and down, and people seem taller when viewed from one side of the room as opposed to the other. It's truly a weird spot, and if nothing else, the drive through stands of madrone trees to the vortex is beautiful.

## SPORTS AND RECREATION
### Rafting

There are many ways to enjoy the Rogue River: oar rafts (which a guide rows for you), paddle rafts (which you paddle yourself), and one-person inflatable kayaks are all widely used. The 40-mile section downstream from Grave Creek is open only to nonmotorized vessels, and river traffic is strictly regulated. For more information, stop at the **Smullin Visitors Center** (14335 Galice Rd., Merlin, 541/479-3735, 8am-3pm daily early May-mid-Oct.).

During the summer, limited float permits are needed for noncommercial rafters to float the Wild and Scenic portion of the Rogue, which begins 7 miles west of Grants Pass and runs to 11 miles east of Gold Beach. These permits are prized by rafters around the world—this stretch of the Rogue not only has some of the best white water in the United States, but also guarantees a first-rate wilderness adventure. It can be a civilized wilderness: Hot showers, comfortable beds, and sumptuous meals at several of the river lodges tucked away in remote quarters of this famous waterway welcome boaters after a day's voyage. Camping is also available. The Bureau of Land Management (www.blm.gov) holds a lottery to award permits. Apply online between December 1 and January 31 for a spot the following summer. The best way to avoid this process is to sign on with an outfitter.

### OUTFITTERS

Many outfitters can be found off I-5's exit 61, toward Merlin and Galice, just north of Grants Pass. Rafters hit Class III and IV

rapids a little before Galice and, for 35 miles thereafter, the stiffest white water encountered on the Rogue. **Adventure Center** (541/488-2819 or 800/444-2819, www.rafting-tours.com) has half-day ($75), full-day, and multiday trips that range from mild to wild on oar or paddle rafts. **Galice Resort and Store Raft Trips** (11744 Galice Rd., Merlin, 541/476-3818, www.galice.com) offers half-day ($85) and full-day ($125, includes lunch at the resort) raft or inflatable-kayak trips as well as river-craft rentals.

Another river retreat with attractive packages is **Morrison's Rogue River Lodge** (8500 Galice Rd., Merlin, 541/476-3825 or 800/826-1963, www.rogueriverraft.com), about 16 miles from Grants Pass. Everything from half-day ($65-79) and one-day ($95) floats and excursions to two- to four-day trips is available. The longer excursions include either stays at river lodges or camping along the Rogue. Transportation back to Morrison's is included, or your car can be shuttled downriver to meet you at the end of the trip.

**Orange Torpedo Trips** (210 Merlin Rd., Merlin, 541/479-5061 or 800/635-2925, www.orangetorpedo.com) has half-day and one- to three-day adventures on rafts or inflatable kayaks. A four-hour trip ($84)

Laws of nature go a little awry at the Oregon Vortex.

bounces through Class IV Nugget Falls and Powerhouse Rapids.

**Ferron's Fun Trips** (541/474-2201 or 800/404-2201, www.roguefuntrips.com) is a family-run business with guided raft tours and raft and kayak rentals (from $35 a day). Half-day trips are offered both morning and afternoon ($75) and full-day trips ($95) include lunch. Ferron and his guides bring inflatable kayaks along on all the guided trips for anyone who gets the urge to paddle solo. Trips start at the Hog Creek Boat Landing, 8.5 miles west of I-5's exit 61 for "Merlin."

For more information on fishing and white-water rafting trips, contact the **Smullin Visitors Center** (14335 Galice Rd., Merlin, 541/479-3735) or the **Visitor Information Center** (1995 NW Vine St., Grants Pass, 800/547-5927, http://travelgrantspass.com).

## Hiking

The Rogue River Trail was originally built for pack mules delivering supplies to miners. A three- or four-day hike here can include stays in riverside lodges or campgrounds. Summer is far too hot for pleasant hiking; arrange to go in the spring or fall, and even then, try to hike in the morning. Afternoons at swimming and fishing holes can add a special dimension to your hike.

**Rogue Wilderness Adventures** (325 Galice Rd., Merlin, 541/479-9554 or 800/336-1647, www.wildrogue.com, $1,279 for 4 days) is one of several outfitters offering guided hikes. Hikes are lodge- and raft-supported, so hikers need carry only a day pack. Wilderness Adventures also offers raft and fishing trips as well as car shuttles.

## Jet-Boating

**Hellgate Excursions** (966 SW 6th St., 541/479-7204 or 800/648-4874, www.hellgate.com, May-late Sept.) is the premier jet-boat operator on this end of the river. Its trips begin at the dock of the **Riverside Inn** (971 SE 6th St.) and proceed downriver through the forested Siskiyou foothills. En route, black-tailed deer, ospreys, and great

blue herons are commonly seen. If you're lucky, a bald eagle or a black bear might also be sighted. The scenic highlight is the deep-walled Hellgate Canyon, where you'll look upon what are believed to be the oldest rocks in the state. The least expensive way to experience this adventure is with a "scenic" cruise ticket ($43 Mon.-Fri., $47 Sat.-Sun.), but for a bit more money you can step up to a brunch, lunch, or dinner cruise. Another option is the white-water adventure trip that goes beyond Hellgate (adults $69 Mon.-Fri., $74 Sat.-Sun.). These excursions feature commentary by your pilot, who knows every eddy in the river. Call ahead for reservations, as space on all of the runs books up fast.

## Fishing

The upper Rogue River is renowned for one of the world's best late-winter steelhead fisheries. Numerous highways and back roads offer easy access to 155 miles of well-ramped river between Lost Creek Reservoir, east of Medford, and Galice, west of Grants Pass. With fall and spring chinook runs and other forms of river recreation, it's no accident that the Rogue Valley is home to the world's top aluminum and fiberglass drift boat manufacturers. Add rafters, kayakers, and plenty of bank anglers, and you can understand why peak salmon or steelhead season is sometimes described as "combat fishing." Contact visitor information outlets for rules, regulations, and leads on outfitters; many of the rafting outfitters listed above also offer guided fishing trips.

## FOOD

Grants Pass has a number of good dining choices, particularly along downtown's G Street. On a summer evening, take a stroll around the neighborhood on this bustling avenue and check out all the options. The neighborhood is also a good morning destination for fresh-roasted organic coffee and friendly conversation at **Rogue Coffee Roasters** (237 SW G St., 541/476-6134, www.rogueroasters.com, 7am-7pm Mon.-Fri., 8am-5pm Sat., 8am-4pm Sun.) and pastries from

# Rogue River Rooster Crow

The city of Rogue River, southeast of Grants Pass on I-5, has something to crow about. On the last weekend of June, the **Rogue River Rooster Crow** (http://rogueriverchamber.com) is held at the Rogue River Elementary School grounds. On Saturday, a parade and street fair take over downtown, but the big event occurs early in the afternoon: Farmers from all over Oregon and northern California bring their roosters to strut their stuff and crow to the enthusiastic crowds. Following a fowl tradition established in 1953, the rooster to crow the most times in his allotted time period wins the prize for his owner. Then it's the humans' turn, in which well-practiced revelers take their turn trying to mimic a rooster's crow. In the evening, there's live music and entertainment in the park, and Sunday brings the Rooster Crow Car Show's legions of antique cars.

**DASSH Bakery** (102 SW 5th St., 541/474-1380, 7am-3pm Mon.-Sat.).

The **Laughing Clam** (121 SW G St., 541/479-1110, http://laughingclam.com, 11am-9pm Mon.-Thurs. and Sat., 11am-10pm Fri., $9-25) is an old bar and grill that has been transformed into a lively family-friendly tavern with good sandwiches, pasta, and steaks. The name might suggest that this is a seafood house, which it's not, though a number of fish dishes are offered.

Another old-time bar made young again, the ★ **Circle J** (241 SW G St., 541/479-8080, 11am-9pm Mon.-Thurs., 11am-10pm Fri.-Sat., $10-13) is a redbrick cubbyhole with eclectic and funky decor and hip, lively clientele. The specialties are pizza, burgers, and sandwiches (including some vegan ones) with sweet potato fries, all washed down with microbrews.

With marvelous views, **Taprock Northwest Grill** (971 SE 6th St., 541/955-5998, www.taprock.com, 8am-11pm daily, $11-26) occupies a handsome log-built dining room with spacious decks overlooking the river from between the downtown bridges. The menu is geared toward steaks and comfort food; a good selection of sandwiches and salads is also available.

A somewhat swanky G Street dining room is **Blondie's Bistro** (226 SW G St., 541/479-0420, www.blondiesbistro.com, 11am-8pm Mon.-Thurs., 11am-9pm Fri., noon-8:30pm Sat., noon-8pm Sun., $16-22). The international menu includes Italian fare such as chicken marsala and Thai curries.

A wine bar bordering on a full restaurant, ★ **The Twisted Cork** (210 SW 6th St., 541/295-3094, www.thetwistedcork-grantspass.com, over 21 only, 11am-8pm Tues.-Thurs., 11am-9pm Fri.-Sat., small plates $4-16, main courses $15-28) makes the most of local wines and ingredients. In addition to some 30 small plates, salads, and soups, the Twisted Cork also offers house-specialty main courses such as herb-crusted rack of lamb with pomegranate and pistachio couscous.

## ACCOMMODATIONS

You'll find most motel accommodations clustered around the two Grants Pass exits on I-5, although there are a number of good choices right downtown, including the charming courtyard-style **Buona Sera Inn** (1001 NE 6th St., 541/476-4260 or 877/286-7756, www.buonaserainn.com, $67-109), with wall murals that travel from Grants Pass to Italy. The rooms are more "Grandma's house" than Motel 6, with wood floors and nice linens.

Across the river from downtown is a charming option with riverfront access. **Motel Del Rogue** (2600 Rogue River Hwy., 541/479-2111 or 866/479-2111, www.moteldelrogue.com, $110-175) is a classic 1930s motel that has been lovingly updated but not transformed. Most of the units overlook the river. The motel sits on two acres of parklike property and is clean, comfortable, and quiet.

Just off I-5, about 20 miles north of Grants Pass, you'll find the **Wolf Creek Inn** (100 Front St., Wolf Creek, 541/866-2474, www.

thewolfcreekinn.com, $80 queen, $40 twin). Originally a hotel for the California and Oregon Stagecoach Line, this historic property, built in 1883, is now owned by the state parks department and operates as a hotel and restaurant. Legend has it that President Rutherford B. Hayes visited the tavern in the late 1880s; you can also view the small room where author Jack London stayed and wrote part of his novel *The End of the Story*.

The **Riverside Inn** (986 SW 6th St., 541/476-6873 or 800/334-4567, www.riverside-inn.com, $150-170) is right downtown and right on the river. Rooms have decks overlooking the river, and the Hellgate jet-boat excursions depart from just below the hotel. Pets are permitted in some rooms. Nearby, the ★ **Lodge at Riverside** (955 SE 7th St., 541/955-0600 or 877/955-0600, www.thelodgeatriverside.com, $179-235) offers stylish rooms and suites, many with balconies facing the river. The lobby is in a huge log cabin with a stone fireplace, and in the middle of lush gardens beside the river is an outdoor pool. Just like at the chains, continental breakfast is included; there's also an evening wine reception.

Many guests use **Morrison's Rogue River Lodge** (8500 Galice Rd., 541/476-3825 or 800/826-1963, www.morrisonslodge.com, May-Oct., $140-360) as a base for raft trips. Morrison's was built in the 1940s as a fishing lodge and now has a small complex of cottages, suites, and lodge rooms, with an outdoor heated pool, a basketball court, a putting green, and bicycles.

One of the premium lodgings in the area, ★ **Weasku Inn** (5560 Rogue River Hwy., 541/471-8000 or 800/493-2758, www.weasku.com, $234-334) is a venerable river lodge that was the secret retreat of Clark Gable, Carole Lombard, Walt Disney, and other entertainment figures in the 1930s and 1940s. The 17 guest rooms range from lodge rooms and suites to an A-frame cabin. All look out on the Rogue River and have genuine rustic-chic decor. A deluxe continental breakfast is served, as is evening wine and cheese.

The longtime Redwood Motel has undergone a transformation to become **Redwood Hyperion Suites** (815 NE 6th St., 541/476-0878 or 888/535-8824, www.redwoodmotel.com, $140-295). The venerable motel rooms have been updated and upgraded, and a new structure with luxury-level suites has been added. The parklike setting, complete with a grove of redwoods and a 350-year-old Palmer oak, is another plus. Add in a pool, hot tub, fitness center, and complimentary breakfast, and you've got one of the city's most unique lodging options.

## Cabins

About 20 minutes outside Grants Pass and well within the Wild and Scenic section of the Rogue River is the **Doubletree Ranch** (6000 Abegg Rd., Merlin, 541/476-0120, www.doubletree-ranch.com, Apr.-Oct., cabins $135-155). Originally homesteaded in 1891, this 160-acre fourth-generation working ranch offers cozy cabins with full kitchens. There's also a five-bedroom house available for groups.

No roads lead to the main lodge and 16 cabins at **Black Bar Lodge** (541/479-6507, $145-250 pp, includes 2 meals), but it's a good stop for rafters or hikers along the 40-mile Rogue River Trail. The Black Bar is 10 miles downriver from Grave Creek and is pretty much off the grid: Generators power lights and electricity and are turned off at night.

Also off the grid is **Marial Lodge** (541/471-3262 May-mid-Nov., 541/474-2057 winter, May-mid-Nov., $135 pp, includes 3 meals), located about 21 miles downriver from Grave Creek. Hikers should plan to stay a night at Black Bar and a second night at Marial Lodge or **Paradise Lodge** (541/842-2822 or 888/667-6483, www.paradise-lodge.com, $155-165 pp adults, $95 pp children, includes 3 meals), 24 miles from Grave Creek. Book well in advance.

## Camping

Many fine campgrounds are found along the banks of the Rogue River near Grants Pass, including **Valley of the Rogue State Park** (3792 N. River Rd., Gold Hill, 541/582-1118 or 800/452-5687, www.oregonstateparks.org, http://oregonstateparks.reserveamerica.com, $19 tents, $28-31 RVs, $43-53 yurts). About halfway between Medford and Grants Pass off I-5, the park is on the Rogue, which supports year-round salmon and spring steelhead runs. Reservations are advised during the warmer months.

Josephine County has several nice full-service **campgrounds** (800/452-5687, www.co.josephine.or.us, www.reserveamerica.com, $20-25 tents, $30-35 RVs, $40-45 yurts) near Grants Pass. **Indian Mary Park** (7100 Merlin-Galice Rd.), about eight miles west of Merlin, is located on the banks of the Rogue River. A boat ramp, hiking trails, a playground, and one of the best beaches on the Rogue make this one of the most popular campgrounds on the river. **Griffin Park** (500 Griffin Rd.) is a small campground west of Grants Pass. To get here, take the Redwood Highway (U.S. 199) to Riverbanks Road, then turn onto Griffin Road and follow it about five miles to where it meets the Rogue. **Schroeder Park** (605 Schroeder Lane) is near town, off Redwood Avenue. In addition to a picnic area and an excellent swimming hole, there's a dog park. At **Whitehorse Park** (7613 Lower River Rd.), eight miles west of Grants Pass via Upper River Road, the river channel shifted away from the park in the wake of the Christmas flood of 1964, but it's only about a 0.5-mile walk to a fine beach on the Rogue.

## INFORMATION AND TRANSPORTATION

Visit the **Grants Pass-Josephine County Visitor Information Center** (1995 NW Vine St., 541/476-7717, http://travel-grantspass.com, 8am-5pm Mon.-Fri.). More conveniently located is the **Downtown Welcome Center** (198 SW 6th St., 541/476-7574).

**Greyhound** (460 NE Agness Ave., 541/476-4513) offers access to its I-5 routes.

# CAVE JUNCTION

Cave Junction's hippie past is evident in some of the colorful local businesses, which include good farm stands, a couple of quirky galleries, and a groovy sausage shop. Sample some of the local wines at **Foris Vineyards** (654 Kendall Rd., 541/592-3752 or 800/843-6747, www.foriswine.com) and **Bridgeview Vineyards and Winery** (4210 Holland Loop Rd., 541/592-4688 or 877/273-4843, www.bridgeviewwine.com). Both wineries offer tastings (11am-5pm daily year-round), but call for hours in winter.

## ★ OREGON CAVES NATIONAL MONUMENT

About 30 miles southwest of Grants Pass and 20 miles east of Cave Junction is the **Oregon Caves National Monument** (Hwy. 46, 541/592-3400, www.nps.gov/orca, cave tours daily late Mar.-early Nov., 9am-6pm daily summer, shorter hours spring and fall, $10 adults, $7 under age 16). The cave itself—as there is really only one, which opens onto successive caverns—was formed over the eons by the action of water. As rain and snowmelt seeped through cracks and fissures in the rock above the cave and percolated down into the underlying limestone, huge sections of the limestone became saturated and collapsed. When the water table eventually fell, these pockets were drained and the process of cave decoration began.

Dissolved limestone carried by the water evaporated and left behind a microscopic layer of calcite. This process was repeated countless times, gradually creating the formations visible today. When the minerals are deposited on the ceiling, a stalactite begins to form. Limestone-laden water that evaporates on the floor might leave behind a stalagmite. When a stalactite and a stalagmite meet, they become a column. Other cave sculptures you'll see include helicites, formations that twist and turn in crazy directions; draperies, looking just like their household namesakes but cast in stone instead of cloth; and soda straws, stalactites that are hollow in the center like a straw, carrying mineral-rich drops of moisture to their tips.

## Tours

Tours are informative and entertaining, and you will leave the cave with a better understanding of its natural, geological, and human history. A recent discovery in an unexplored part of the caverns was a grizzly bear fossil believed to be over 40,000 years old. Children must be at least 42 inches tall and able to climb a set of test stairs to gain entry. The tour takes 90 minutes and requires uphill walking, lots of stairs, and navigating some low passageways. Wear good walking shoes and warm clothing; the cave maintains a fairly consistent year-round temperature of 44°F. Tour size is limited to 15 people, so reservations (877/444-6777, www.recreation. gov) are strongly advised. Special tours include **candlelight tours** (6:30pm Fri.-Sat. summer, $10 adult, $7 youth) and **off-trail tours** (1pm-4pm Fri.-Sat. June-Aug., reservations required, $45), which give novice spelunkers a chance to learn caving techniques and become intimately familiar with tight passageways through the cave.

## Above Ground

Although the caves are clearly the big attraction, there are some good forest hikes at the monument. The three-mile **Big Tree Trail,** named for a huge Douglas fir estimated to be more than 1,000 years old, wends its way through virgin forest with tan oak, canyon live oak, Pacific madrone, chinquapin, and manzanita. The trail climbs over 1,200 feet, so it's a bit strenuous, but the solitude and views of the surrounding mountains are inspiring. For a one-mile loop, try the **Cliff Nature Trail.** Placards will help you identify the plant life as you traverse the mossy cliffs, and there are also some good vistas of the Siskiyou Mountains. No pets are allowed on the trails in the monument.

## Accommodations

The 23-room **Chateau at Oregon Caves** (541/592-3400, www.oregoncaveschateau. com, May-Oct., $117-212) offers food and lodging. Built in 1934, this rustic structure blends in with the forest and moss-covered marble ledges. Indigenous wood and stone permeate the building so that you never lose a sense of where you are. The guest rooms feature views of Cave Creek canyon, waterfalls,

The area around Cave Junction is colorful, with good wine and produce.

# Bed-and-Breakfast in the Trees

Located in Takilma near Cave Junction, **Out 'n' About Treehouse Institute and Treesort** (300 Page Creek Rd., Cave Junction, 541/598-2208, www.treehouses.com, 2-3-night minimum stay Memorial Day-Labor Day, $150-330 summer, includes continental breakfast) is a unique lodging option that's worth driving a bit out of your way to discover. After all, how many bed-and-breakfasts do you find in tree houses?

This comfortable rural retreat blends the whimsy of the 1960s with 21st-century creature comforts. The well-appointed tree-house guest rooms, some of which sleep four or more, are bolted to 100-year-old white oaks, some 18 feet above the ground. Those desiring a more down-to-earth lodging option can stay in a peeled-fir cabin with a cozy woodstove. For the deluxe treatment, reserve a 300-square-foot structure built of redwood and Douglas fir that features a sink, a tub, a fridge, a queen futon, and a 200-square-foot deck with mountain views. Horseback rides, trips to the best Illinois River swimming holes, zip-line adventures, and white-water rafting trips can be arranged, or swim in the river that runs through the property.

or the Oregon Caves entrance. The old-fashioned bath fixtures, lack of in-room phones, cell service, TVs, and air conditioning (ceiling fans are usually all you need) add to the historical nuance.

The food at the Chateau's main dining room is reasonably good, and having Cave Creek running through the center of the room definitely adds to the unique atmosphere. Downstairs, the old-fashioned 1930s-style soda fountain dishes up classic American burgers, fries, and shakes, but it's not open for dinner.

## Camping

Camping is available at **Grayback** (Wild Rivers Ranger District, 541/592-4000, www.fs.usda.gov, water available, $10), a woodsy U.S. Forest Service campground 12 miles from Cave Junction on Highway 46. There are 39 sites close to Sucker Creek, with one RV hookup and a one-mile hiking trail. Closer to the caves is a smaller U.S. Forest Service campground, **Cave Creek** (water available, $10); take Highway 46 four miles south of the caves to Forest Road 4032.

## Getting There

To get to Oregon Caves National Monument, take U.S. 199 to Cave Junction, then wind 20 miles up Highway 46; a beautiful old-growth Douglas fir forest lining the road might help distract the faint of heart from the nail-biting turns. The last 13 miles of this trip are especially winding, and travel trailers and large RVs are not advised due to the steep and narrow roadbed.

# Roseburg

Many people passing through the Roseburg area (pop. 22,000) might quickly dismiss it as a rural backwater. A closer look, however, reveals many layers beneath the mill-town veneer, as evidenced by an award-winning museum, Oregon's only drive-through zoo, and wineries.

The true allure of Roseburg is not really in town, but in the surrounding countryside. The beautiful North Umpqua River to the east offers rafting, camping, hiking, and fishing. In addition to catching trout, salmon, and bass, anglers come from all over to enjoy one of the world's last rivers with a native run of summer steelhead. Numerous waterfalls along the river and the frothy white water make the Native American word Umpqua ("thundering water") an appropriate name.

## SIGHTS

### Douglas County Museum of History and Natural History

The **Douglas County Museum of History and Natural History** (123 Museum Dr., 541/957-7007, www.umpquavalleymuseums. org, 10am-5pm Tues.-Sat., $8 adults, $5 seniors and veterans, $2 ages 5-17) is located at the Douglas County Fairgrounds (I-5 exit 123). Its four wings feature exhibits that range from a million-year-old saber-toothed tiger to 19th-century steam-logging equipment. The museum houses the state's largest natural history collection and its second-largest collection of historic photos.

### Winchester Fish Ladder

The **Winchester Fish Ladder** is just off I-5 at exit 129, on the north bank of the North Umpqua River. Visitors can watch salmon and steelhead in their native environment as they swim by the viewing window at Winchester Dam. Spring chinook and summer steelhead migrate upriver May-August, and coho, fall chinook, and more summer steelhead swim past September-November. Winter steelhead is the primary species seen going through the fish ladders and on past the window December-May. The Umpqua River offers the largest variety of game fish in Oregon.

### ★ Wildlife Safari

Tucked away in a 600-acre wooded valley is **Wildlife Safari** (1790 Safari Rd., Winston, 541/679-6761, www.wildlifesafari.net, 9am-5pm daily, no pets allowed, $20 adults, $17 seniors, and $14 ages 3-12), a drive-through zoo that's a big hit with both kids and adults.

Once you are inside the park gates, the brightly colored birds and exotic game animals transport you to other lands, with an oddly appropriate Oregon backdrop. Be that as it may, at Wildlife Safari every possible step has been taken to re-create African and North American animal life zones, but with natural prey kept apart from predators. Similar precautions are taken with humans and their animal companions. People must remain inside their vehicles, and windows and sunroofs must be kept closed in the big cat and bear areas. Pets must be left in kennels ($5) at the entrance.

Throughout the day, many talks and opportunities to watch the animals being fed are scheduled ($12-15 extra). If a short, free visit will suffice, the Safari Village has a selection of smaller caged animals located right by the parking area. With 600 animals, including one of the most successful cheetah breeding programs in the country, Wildlife Safari is involved with conservation and endangered species programs. The White Rhino restaurant serves food within view of lions, giraffes, and white rhinos. To reach Wildlife Safari, take exit 119 from I-5 and follow Highway 42 for four miles. Turn right on Lookingglass Road and right again on Safari Road.

## Wine-Tasting

Several wineries in the Roseburg vicinity offer tasting rooms and tours. The dry Mediterranean climate and rich variety of soils in the area are ideal for chardonnay, pinot noir, gewürztraminer, riesling, zinfandel, and cabernet sauvignon. A wine tour pamphlet with a map showing the location of the wineries is available from the **Roseburg Visitors and Convention Bureau** (410 SE Spruce St., 541/672-9731 or 800/444-9584, www.visitroseburg.com) or www.umpqua-valleywineries.org.

**Abacela Vineyards and Winery** (12500 Lookingglass Rd., 541/679-6642, www.abacela.com, 11am-6pm daily May-Oct., 11am-5pm daily Nov.-Apr.) is notable for the large variety of wine grapes it grows, including tempranillo, malbec, and dolcetto. It's just a few miles north of Wildlife Safari.

**Girardet Wine Cellars** (895 Reston Rd., 541/679-7252, http://girardetwine.com, 11am-5pm daily) is one of the oldest in the area. Philippe Girardet, from a town at the headwaters of the Rhine River in Switzerland, brought European wine-blending techniques to Oregon in 1971. Still family owned, Girardet produce unique chardonnay, pinot noir, cabernet sauvignon, and riesling wines.

The **Henry Estate Winery** (687 Hubbard Creek Rd., Umpqua, 541/459-5120, www.henryestate.com, 11am-5pm daily) has produced a string of award-winning bottlings from pinot gris, merlot, and pinot noir grapes. Picnic tables near the vineyard and the Umpqua River are a good place for lunch.

Oregon's oldest vineyard, dating to 1961, is **HillCrest** (240 Vineyard Lane, 541/673-3709, www.hillcrestvineyard.com, 9am-5pm daily). A bewildering range of wine grapes is grown here, but some of the best to sample are the riesling, syrah, and tempranillo.

## SPORTS AND RECREATION
### Fishing

The Umpqua River system comprises the North Umpqua, more or less due east of Roseburg; the South Umpqua, south and east of town; and the main stem Umpqua River, which flows west from Roseburg to the ocean. Spring chinook enter the North Umpqua River March-June, work their way upstream during July and August, and spawn September-October. Fall chinook are mainly found in the warmer South Umpqua River. Their migration starts in midsummer and

The Wildlife Safari is known for its successful cheetah breeding program.

# Cow Creek Band of the Umpqua Tribe

As you pass Canyonville, along the remote stretch of I-5 between Roseburg and Grants Pass, you'll see the Seven Feathers Casino. It's operated by the Cow Creek Band of the Umpqua Tribe of Native Americans who, like many Oregon Native American communities, have rallied to regain land that they lost during the pioneer era.

The Cow Creek signed a treaty with the U.S. government in 1853, selling their land in southwestern Oregon for 2.3 cents an acre so that the government could sell it to pioneer settlers for $1.25 an acre. The treaty, which promised health, housing, and education, was ignored by the United States for almost exactly 100 years. The Cow Creek did not receive a reservation, but they stayed in their homeland.

In 1954, the Western Oregon Indian Termination Act terminated federal relations with the Cow Creek and nearly every other indigenous community in western Oregon. Because the Cow Creek were not notified about their termination until after the act was passed, they sued in the U.S. Court of Claims and eventually won a $1.5 million settlement. The Cow Creek set up an endowment for their settlement money and use it to further economic development, education, and housing.

The band has also been buying back land. In the late 1990s they bought land along Jordan Creek and began clearing out old tires and other garbage that had accumulated. A watershed assessment pointed to some habitat restoration opportunities, and the band set about trying to restore coho salmon and steelhead trout in a stretch of the creek that hadn't seen these fish since I-5 was built in 1958. After the installation of weirs that allowed fish to swim through the culverts under I-5 and work on improving water quality and streambank habitat, coho are now spawning in Jordan Creek.

peaks in September, when the rains increase water flow and lower the river's temperature. The best fishing for summer steelhead on the North Umpqua is June-October; the fish spawn January-March. This fish averages only six to eight pounds, but it will make you think you are trying to reel in a chinook by the way it struggles.

Coho salmon, alias "silvers," are found throughout the Umpqua River system. The coho life cycle lasts about three years. Each spends its first year in freshwater, heads for the ocean to spend one or two years, and then returns to freshwater to spawn. The adults weigh an average of seven pounds each. This fishery has had some lean years recently.

You'll find rainbow trout in nearly all rivers and streams of the Umpqua River system, where the water is relatively cool and gravel bars are clean. This is the river's most common game fish, mainly because the rivers, lakes, and streams of the Umpqua are routinely seeded with over 100,000 legal-size (eight inches or longer) rainbows. The fishing season opens in April, with the best fishing in early summer when the fish are actively feeding. Visit the website of the **Oregon Department of Fish and Wildlife** (www.dfw.state.or.us) for more on the Umpqua.

## ENTERTAINMENT AND EVENTS

Head to **Salud Restaurant and Brewery** (537 SE Jackson St., 541/673-1574, www.saludroseburg.com, 2pm-10pm Mon.-Thurs., 2pm-11pm Fri.-Sat., $13-26) for Latin-inspired food and craft beer, including a Mexican chocolate stout and a tamarind and tangerine Imperial IPA. "Street tacos" are filled with fresh fish or Coca-Cola-marinated pork, chipotle slaw, and pineapple salsa. In addition to the beers brewed here, Salud serves good cocktails and has a bit of a late-night music scene on weekends.

The McMenamins brewery empire has an appealing operation at **Roseburg Station**

(700 SE Sheridan St., 541/672-1934, www.mcmenamins.com, 11am-11pm Mon.-Thurs., 11am-midnight Fri.-Sat., 11am-10pm Sun., $9-21). The 1912 Southern Pacific Station was purchased and restored while preserving original features like the 16-foot-high ceiling, tongue-and-groove Douglas fir wainscoting, and marble molding. Quality food and microbrews in a setting suitable for families enhance the appeal.

Roseburg's big event is the **Douglas County Fair,** held annually at the fairgrounds (I-5 exit 123) the second week of August, with down-home events like 4-H livestock competitions, midway rides, food booths, and horse and stock car races. Contact the **Roseburg Visitors Center** (410 SE Spruce St., 541/672-9731 or 800/444-9584, www.visitroseburg.com) for specifics.

If you happen to be in Roseburg on a summer Tuesday evening, check out **Music on the Halfshell** (www.halfshell.org), a series of outdoor summer concerts held at the band shell in **Stewart Park** (NW Stewart Pkwy. and NW Harvey Ave.). The free concerts have featured big-name national and international stars such as Robert Cray, Taj Mahal, and Pink Martini. The park's bandstand is near the banks of the South Umpqua River.

## FOOD

Roseburg is not exactly the fine-dining capital of Oregon, but you won't go hungry here. The **Umpqua Valley Farmers Market** (1771 W. Harvard, 541/530-6200, 9am-1pm Sat. Apr.-Oct.) takes place in the parking lot of the Methodist church.

Some of Roseburg's best dining is Italian-style. ★ **Dino's Ristorante Italiano** (404 SE Jackson St., 541/673-0848, www.dinosristorante.com, 5pm-9pm Mon.-Thurs., 5pm-9:30pm Fri.-Sat., $15-20) is a cozy family-run spot downtown with decor that's a sprawl of wine cases, travel guides, and cookbooks. The husband-and-wife cooking team spends part of each year in Italy, so the food is about as authentic as you'll find anywhere in southern Oregon.

Famous for its breakfasts, **Brix Grill** (527 SE Jackson St., 541/440-4901, 7am-8pm or later Mon.-Sat., 7am-3pm Sun., breakfast $6-13, dinner $11-23) is also open for lunch and dinner, and serves up cocktails and snacks in between. At breakfast, Brix gets the basics, like delicious omelets and eggs Benedict, exactly right. At lunch expect soup, salad, and more inventive dishes like grilled bacon-wrapped salmon on saffron rice. At dinner, choose from burgers, steaks, or perhaps chipotle prawn tacos. The rooftop patio is a great spot to relax on a warm evening.

**True Kitchen + Bar** (629 SE Main St., 541/900-1000, 4pm-10pm Sun.-Thurs., 4pm-midnight Fri.-Sat., $12-33) is both Roseburg's top fine-dining destination and one of its most popular night spots. You'll find a nice selection of appetizers to start a meal or to accompany a cocktail. In addition to excellent steaks, check out house specialties such as pan-seared duck breast with cherry-onion balsamic sauce and pistachio pesto primavera.

## ACCOMMODATIONS

There are over 1,500 motel rooms in Roseburg, and the competition keeps rates relatively low. A number of chain hotels are found at I-5's exit 125. Budget travelers can bunk down at the **Roseburg Travelodge** (315 W. Harvard Ave., 541/672-4836, www.travelodge.com, $75-119). It's right on the Umpqua, though you'll pay a bit more to have a room and balcony overlooking the river. It's also convenient to downtown. Sharing the same river view and easy access to downtown, the **Holiday Inn Express Roseburg** (375 W. Harvard Ave., 541/673-7517, www.hiexpress.com, $135-163) offers a pool, a whirlpool, a business center, and some of the newest rooms in the area. Both these hotels are located just off I-5's exit 124. Just north of downtown, the flower-bedecked **Rose City Motel** (1142 NE Stephens St., 541/673-8209, www.rosecitymotel.com, $66) is an old-fashioned motor court that is well-maintained, with full kitchens ($50 extra) and a friendly welcome.

## INFORMATION

The **Roseburg Visitors Center** (410 SE Spruce St., 541/672-9731 or 800/444-9584, www.visitroseburg.com) has among its brochures a particularly useful drivers guide to historic places.

## GETTING THERE

Buses at the **Greyhound bus depot** (835 SE Stephens St., 541/673-5326) connect Roseburg with other cities along the I-5 corridor.

# The North Umpqua River

One of the great escapes into the Cascade Mountains is via the Umpqua Highway, Highway 138. This road runs along the part of the North Umpqua River fished by novelist Zane Grey and actor Clark Gable as well as legions of others during steelhead season. The North Umpqua is a premier fishing river full of trout and salmon, as well as a source of excitement for white-water rafters who shoot the rapids. Numerous waterfalls, including 272-foot Watson Falls, are found close to the road. Tall timbers line the road through the Umpqua National Forest, and many fine campgrounds are situated within its confines. Mountain lakes offer boating and other recreational opportunities. The Umpqua National Forest also boasts challenging yet accessible mountain trails up the flanks of Mount Bailey (8,363 feet) and Mount Thielsen (9,182 feet). When snow carpets the landscape in winter, you can cross-country ski, snowmobile, and snowcat ski on Mount Bailey without the crowds at other winter sports areas.

The recreational areas along the North Umpqua fall under the jurisdiction of the **Umpqua National Forest North Umpqua District** (541/496-3532, www.fs.fed.us), based in Glide; the **Diamond Lake district** (541/498-2531, www.fs.fed.us), based near Toketee Falls; and the **Bureau of Land Management** (777 NW Garden Valley Blvd., Roseburg, 541/440-4930, www.blm.gov/or).

## SIGHTS
### Colliding Rivers

Just off Highway 138 on the west side of the town of Glide is the **Colliding Rivers.** The Wild and Umpqua Rivers meet head-on in a

bowl of green serpentine. The best times to view this spectacle are after winter storms and when spring runoff is high. If the water is low, check out the high-water mark from the Christmas flood of 1964. Water levels from that great inundation were lapping at the parking lot, a chilling reminder that *umpqua* means "thundering water" in Chinook.

## ★ North Umpqua Waterfalls
### SUSAN CREEK FALLS

About 11 miles east of Glide is 50-foot-high **Susan Creek Falls,** whose trailhead is off Highway 138 near the Susan Creek picnic area. A well-graded one-mile trail through a rainforest-like setting to the falls is accessible to strong wheelchair users. The cascade is bordered on three sides by mossy rock walls that never see the light of the sun and stay wet year-round. Another 0.25 miles up the trail are the **Indian Mounds.** One of the rites of manhood for Umpqua boys was to fast and pile up stones in hopes of being granted a vision or spiritual powers. Also called the Vision Quest Site, the site still holds stacks of moss-covered stones in an area protected by a fence.

### FALL CREEK FALLS

Four miles east of Susan Creek Falls is **Fall Creek Falls.** Look for the trailhead off Highway 138 at Fall Creek. The one-mile trail goes around and through slabs of bedrock. Halfway up the trail is a lush area called **Job's Garden.** Stay on the Fall Creek Trail and in another 0.5 miles you'll come to the falls. It's a double waterfall, with each tier 35-50 feet in height. Back at Job's Garden, you may want to explore the Job's Garden Trail, which leads to the base of columnar basalt outcroppings.

## LITTLE FALLS AND STEAMBOAT FALLS

During early-summer steelhead season, it's fun to venture off Highway 138 at Steamboat and go up Steamboat Creek Road to see the fish battle two small waterfalls. The first, **Little Falls,** is one mile up the road. It's always exciting to see the fish miraculously wriggle their way up this 10-foot cascade. Travel four miles farther up Steamboat Creek Road and turn right on the road to Steamboat Falls campground to see **Steamboat Falls.** A viewpoint showcases this 30-foot waterfall, where some fish jump the falls and others swim the adjacent fish ladder.

## TOKETEE FALLS

The word *toketee* means "graceful" in the Chinook language. After viewing **Toketee Falls** plunge over a sheer wall of basalt, you'll probably agree it's aptly named. Nineteen miles up Highway 138 near the Toketee Ranger Station, this 0.5-mile trail ends at a double waterfall with a combined height of over 150 feet. To get to Toketee Falls, follow Forest Road 34 at the west entrance of the ranger station, cross the first bridge, and turn left. There you'll find the trailhead and a parking area.

## WATSON FALLS

On Highway 138, take Forest Road 37 near the east entrance of the Toketee Ranger Station to reach the trailhead of **Watson Falls,** a 272-foot-high flume of water. A moderate 0.5-mile trail climbs through tall stands of Douglas fir and western hemlock and is complemented by an understory of green salal, Oregon grape, and ferns. A bridge spans the canyon just below the falls, providing outstanding views of this towering cascade. Clamber up the mossy rocks to near the base of the falls and get a face full of the cool billowing spray.

## LEMOLO FALLS

Another waterfall worth a visit is **Lemolo Falls.** *Lemolo* is a Chinook word meaning "wild and untamed," and you'll see this is also the case with this thunderous 100-foot waterfall. To get here, take Lemolo Lake Road off Highway 138, then follow Forest Roads 2610 and 2610-600, and look for the trailhead sign. The trail is a gentle one-mile path that drops down into the North Umpqua

Toketee Falls

Canyon and passes several small waterfalls on the way to Lemolo Falls.

## Umpqua Hot Springs

**Umpqua Hot Springs** is mostly unknown and far enough from civilized haunts not to be overused, yet it's accessible enough for those who go in search of it. The springs have been developed with wooden pools and a crude lean-to shelter. Weekends tend to attract more visitors, forcing you to wait your turn for a soak. Midweek is generally pretty quiet, though we've encountered some pretty dodgy folks up there at these times.

To get here, go north from the Toketee Ranger Station and turn right onto County Road 34, just past the Pacific Power and Light buildings. Proceed down County Road 34 past Toketee Lake about six miles. When you cross the bridge over Deer Creek, which is clearly signed, you will be a little less than 0.5 miles from the turnoff. The turnoff is Thorn Prairie Road, to the right, which goes 1 mile and ends at a small parking area. In wet weather this road may be impassable, and it is not recommended for low-slung cars in any season. From the parking area, it's 0.5 miles down the blocked road to the hot springs trailhead and another 0.5 miles to the pool.

## SPORTS AND RECREATION
### Hiking

The 79-mile **North Umpqua Trail** is divided into 11 segments that are 3 to 13 miles in length. Beginning near the town of Glide, this thoroughfare parallels the North Umpqua River; the trail leads high into the Cascades and connects with the Pacific Crest Trail as well as many campgrounds. Highway 138 affords many access points to the trail.

One segment of the North Umpqua Trail is the five-mile **Panther Trail,** which begins near Steamboat at the historic Mott Bridge. Many wildflowers are seen late April to early June on the way up to the old fish hatchery. One to look for is the bright-red snow plant, *Sarcodes sanguinea,* which grows beneath Douglas firs and sugar pine trees. Also called the carmine snow flower or snow lily, the snow plant is classified as a saprophyte, which contains no chlorophyll and derives nourishment from decayed materials. Growing 8 to 24 inches in height, the plant's red flowers are crowded at the crown of the stem.

A five-mile hike that ranges from easy to quite steep and rocky is on the south slope of 8,363-foot **Mount Bailey.** Bring plenty of water and sturdy hiking shoes. To get to the trailhead, take Highway 138 to the north entrance of Diamond Lake. Turn onto Forest Road 4795 and follow it five miles to the junction of Forest Road 4795-300. Proceed down 4795-300 for one mile until you see the trail marker.

The easy two-mile **Diamond Lake Loop** takes hikers through a mix of lodgepole pine and true fir to Lake Creek, Diamond Lake's only outlet. There are many views of Mount Bailey along the way, as well as some private coves ideal for a swim on hot days. But while the grade is easy, keep in mind that the elevation is nearly a mile high, and pace yourself accordingly. To get to the loop, take Forest Road 4795 off Highway 138 on the north entrance to Diamond Lake and look for the trailhead sign on the west side of the road.

The **Mount Thielsen Trail** offers experienced hikers and scramblers a million-dollar view from the top of the mountain. This challenging, scree-covered, five-mile trail winds to the top of Mount Thielsen's spire-pointed, 9,182-foot volcanic peak. You'll find the trailhead on the east side of Highway 138 one mile north of the junction of Highway 230. Extra care should be taken on the top 200 feet, which requires hand-over-hand climbing up a steep, crumbly pitch. If you make it to the top, enter your name in the climbing register found there. The view stretches from Mount Shasta to Mount Hood.

### Fishing

The North Umpqua has several distinctions, including as one of the most difficult North American rivers to fish. No boats are permitted for 15 miles in either direction of Steamboat, and no bait or spinners are allowed, putting a premium on skillful fly-fishing. You can wade in and poke around for the best fishing holes on the North Umpqua, one of the few rivers with a summer run of native steelhead—or better yet, hire an experienced fishing guide through **Summer Run Guide Service** (541/496-3037, www.summerrun.net).

## Rafting

The North Umpqua has gained popularity with white-water rafters and kayakers, but fishing and floating are not always compatible, so guidelines have been established by the Bureau of Land Management and the Umpqua National Forest. The area around Steamboat has the most restrictions, mainly because of the heavy fishing in the area that boaters would disturb. Check with the **U.S. Forest Service** (541/496-3532) prior to setting out to make sure you are making a legal trip. A good way to get started rafting and avoid the hassle of rules, regulations, and gear is to go along with an experienced white-water guide. These leaders provide the safety equipment, the boats, and the expertise; all you have to do is paddle.

In addition to rafting, inflatable kayak trips are offered by outfitters. Inflatables are easier for the neophyte to handle than the hard-shell type, though these craft expose you to more chills and spills. Expect more than a dozen Class III or IV rapids and plenty of Class IIs, as well as old-growth trees and osprey nests. Best of all, this world-class river is still relatively undiscovered. Spring and summer are the best times to enjoy the North Umpqua, although it's navigable year-round. Boaters are allowed on the river only 10am-6pm daily, leaving the morning and evening for fishing.

**North Umpqua Outfitters** (541/496-3333 or 888/454-9696, http://umpquarivers.com) offers raft ($105 pp half-day), kayak, and drift-boat trips. Other outfitters with similar trips include the **Ouzel Outfitters**

(800/788-7238, www.oregonrafting.com) and **Orange Torpedo Trips** (541/479-5061 or 800/635-2925, www.orangetorpedo.com).

## Winter Sports
### SKIING

Located 80 miles east of Roseburg off Highway 138 in the central Cascades is Mount Bailey. The experienced skiers at **Cat Ski Mt. Bailey** (800/733-7593, www.catskimtbailey.com, $385 per day) know where the best runs are. Snowcats transport no more than 12 skiers up the mountain from Diamond Lake Resort to the summit of this 8,363-foot peak. Experienced guides then lead small groups down routes that best suit the abilities of each group. The skiing is challenging and should be attempted only by advanced skiers. Open bowls, steep chutes, and tree-lined glaciers are some of the types of terrain encountered during the 3,000-foot drop in elevation back to the resort.

### CROSS-COUNTRY SKIING

Over 56 miles of designated cross-country trails are found in the Diamond and Lemolo Lakes area along the upper reaches of Highway 138. Some of the trails are groomed, and all are clearly marked by blue trail signs. Contact the **Umpqua National Forest** (Diamond Lake Ranger District, 541/498-2531, www.fs.usda.gov/umpqua) for maps and information. The **Diamond Lake Resort** (Diamond Lake, 541/793-3333, www.diamondlake.net, 8am-5pm daily) rents skis and snowshoes.

### TUBING AND SNOWBOARDING

If you ski the bunny hill, you might enjoy inner-tubing or snowboarding near **Diamond Lake Resort** (Diamond Lake, 541/793-3333, www.diamondlake.net, $15 for 2 hours). A conveyor takes "tubers" to the top of the hill for nonstop thrills and spills on the way back down. The hill has a ticket system similar to other ski lifts, with full-day, half-day, and two-hour passes available; check the website for open hours. The tubing and snowboarding hill is located at the Hilltop Shop.

## SNOWMOBILING

Concentrated around the Lemolo and Diamond Lakes area are 133 miles of designated motorized snow trails, usually open from late November, according to snow accumulation. Many are groomed on a regular basis, and all are clearly marked by orange trail signs and diamond-shaped trail blazes on trees above the snowline. Diamond Lake Resort is a hub of snowmobiling activity; they rent snow machines and can advise you on trails.

One of the more exotic runs is into Crater Lake National Park. Snowmobiles and all-terrain vehicles must register at the north entrance of the park and stay on the trail, which climbs about 10 miles from the park gates to the north rim of the lake. Be aware that the mountain weather can change suddenly, creating dangerous subzero temperatures and whiteout conditions. Also, watch for cross-country skiers and other people sometimes using motorized vehicle trails.

## FOOD AND ACCOMMODATIONS

The number of lodgings on the North Umpqua River is limited to a few properties that range from rustic quarters to full-service resorts. The ★ **Steamboat Inn** (42705 N. Umpqua Hwy., Steamboat, 541/498-2230 or 800/840-8825, www.thesteamboatinn.com, Mar.-Dec., $205-340) is the premier dining and lodging venue on the North Umpqua, situated in the middle of a 31-mile stretch of premium fly-fishing turf. It's an ideal getaway from civilization, near hiking trails and waterfalls. Lodging is in handsomely furnished riverside cabins, cottages, and suites; a number of three-bedroom ranch-style houses are also available. Reservations are a must for any of the accommodations. The on-site **restaurant** (8am-9pm daily) serves breakfast, lunch, and dinner. Considered one of the top dining experiences in the state, the Steamboat also has a wide selection of Oregon wines. The prix fixe evening dinner ($50) is served nightly, and Winemakers Dinners (Mar.-mid-June, $90) are scheduled frequently during the summer and on weekends the rest of the season. Reservations are required for dinner, but not for lunch.

Near the summit of the Cascade Mountains about 75 miles east of Roseburg and 13 miles from Diamond Lake is **Lemolo Lake Resort** (2610 Birds Point Rd., Idleyld Park, 541/643-0750, www.lemololakeresort.com, campsites $30-35, cabins $179-259, hotel rooms $135), a more modest operation. Formed by a Pacific Power and Light dam, Lemolo Lake has good fishing for German brown trout as well as kokanee salmon, eastern brook trout, and rainbow trout. The lake is sheltered from wind by gently sloping ridges, and there are many coves and sandy beaches along the 8.3 miles of shoreline. Waterskiing is permitted on the lake. Boats and canoes can be rented, and many miles of snowmobiling and cross-country skiing trails are nearby. The resort has both standard cabins and cabins with kitchens.

**Diamond Lake Resort** (Diamond Lake, 541/793-3333, www.diamondlake.net, cabins $129-239, motel rooms $100) is a rustic mountain resort with basic lodging, restaurants, groceries, equipment rental, a service station, a laundry, and showers. It makes a good base camp for a Crater Lake excursion and rents mountain bikes, paddleboats, kayaks, canoes, and fishing boats, and has an equestrian center to keep you out of the modest accommodations and enjoying the spectacular surroundings.

## CAMPING
### Little River Campgrounds

Camping is popular on the North Umpqua. Several alternatives are nearby, up the Little River south of Glide. **Cavitt Creek Falls** (541/440-4930, www.blm.gov/or, May-Sept., $8) has water and vault toilets at a small waterfall with a swimming hole at its bottom. To get to the campground, head east of Roseburg on Highway 138 to Glide, take Little Creek Road (County Rd. 17) for seven miles, then continue three miles down Cavitt Creek Road.

Other small campgrounds, with water and vault toilets and suitable for tents and small

RVs, are up Little River Road and managed by the U.S. Forest Service (North Umpqua Ranger District, 541/496-3532, www.fs.usda.gov, mid-May-late Oct., $10-15): **Wolf Creek** (5 miles from Glide); **Coolwater** (15 miles from Glide), with good hiking trails nearby, including **Grotto Falls, Wolf Creek Nature Trail,** and **Wolf Creek Falls Trail; White Creek** (17 miles from Glide, then 1 mile down Red Butte Rd.), at the confluence of White Creek and Little River, with a good beach and shallow water; and **Lake in the Woods** (27 miles from Glide, last 7 miles gravel), along the shore of a four-acre artificial lake at 3,200 feet elevation. Motorized craft are not permitted in this eight-foot-deep pond. Two good hikes nearby are to **Hemlock Falls** and **Yakso Falls.**

## North Umpqua River Campgrounds

Set along the bank of the North Umpqua River 15 miles east of Roseburg a little ways north of Highway 138 is **Whistler's Bend** (541/673-4863, www.co.douglas.or.us/parks, $17), with reservable sites. Picnic tables and grills are provided at this county park, as are piped water, flush toilets, and showers.

About 30 miles east of Highway 138 is **Susan Creek** (541/440-4930, www.blm.gov/or, reservations www.recreation.gov, mid-Apr.-late Oct., $14), with water, showers, and flush toilets. This campground has 31 sites for tents and RVs up to 20 feet. In a grove of old-growth Douglas fir and sugar pine next to the North Umpqua River, the campground is enhanced by the presence of a fine beach and swimming hole as well as nearby trails.

Within easy access of great fly fishing, rafting, and hiking, **Bogus Creek** (541/496-3532, www.fs.usda.gov, www.recreation.gov, May-Oct., $15), with flush toilets and water, offers the real thing. As the campground is a major launching point for white-water trips and within a few miles of Fall Creek Falls and Job's Garden Geological Area, it's good to reserve a site or get here early.

About 38 miles east of Roseburg on Highway 138 near Steamboat and good fly-fishing is **Canton Creek** (541/496-3532, www.fs.usda.gov, May-mid-Oct., $10), with water and flush toilets. Take Steamboat Creek Road off Highway 138 and proceed 400 yards to the campground. **Horseshoe Bend** (541/496-3532, www.fs.usda.gov, mid-May-late Sept., $15), with water and flush toilets, is 10 miles east of Steamboat. There are 34 sites for tents and RVs up to 35 feet, with picnic tables and grills. In the middle of a big bend of the North Umpqua covered with old-growth Douglas firs and sugar pines, this campground is a popular base camp for rafting and fishing enthusiasts.

## Diamond Lake Campgrounds

Campgrounds surround beautiful Diamond Lake (elevation 5,200 feet); boating, fishing, swimming, bicycling, and hiking are among the popular recreational options. The trout fishing is particularly good in the early summer, and there are also excellent hikes into the Mount Thielsen Wilderness, Crater Lake National Park, and Mount Bailey areas. Reservations (877/444-6777, www.recreation.gov) aren't required, but these campgrounds fill up fast, so reservations are advised.

With over 200 sites, **Diamond Lake campground** (mid-May 15-Oct., $16), with water and flush toilets, is on the east shore of the lake with easy access to the north entrance of Crater Lake National Park. Numerous hiking trails lead from the campground, including the Pacific Crest National Scenic Trail. Boat docks, launching facilities, and rentals are nearby at **Diamond Lake Resort** (Diamond Lake, 541/793-3333, www.diamondlake.net).

Other large Diamond Lake campgrounds are **Broken Arrow** (mid-May-Labor Day, $15), with water, showers, and flush toilets, on the lake's south shore; and **Thielsen View** (mid-May-mid-Oct., $15), with water and vault toilets, on the west side of the lake, with picturesque views of Mount Thielsen. Contact the **Diamond Lake Ranger District** (541/498-2531, www.fs.usda.gov/umpqua).

# Crater Lake

High in the Cascades lies the crown jewel of Oregon: Crater Lake, the country's deepest at 1,943 feet. It glimmers like a polished sapphire in a setting created by a volcano that blew its top and collapsed thousands of years ago. Crater Lake's extraordinary hues are produced by the depth and clarity of the water and its ability to absorb all the colors of the spectrum except the shortest wavelengths, blue and violet, which are scattered skyward.

In addition to a 33-mile rim loop around the crater, **Crater Lake National Park** (541/594-3000, www.nps.gov/crla, $15 cars, $10 bicycles and motorcycles), established in 1902, features two campgrounds, dozens of hiking trails, and boat tours on the lake itself.

If you're seeing Crater Lake for the first time, drive into the park from the north for the most dramatic perspective. After crossing through a pumice desert, the road climbs to higher elevations overlooking the lake. In contrast to this subdued approach, the blueness and size of the lake can hit you with a suddenness that stops all thought.

## Geology

Geologically speaking, the name *Crater Lake* is a misnomer. Technically, Crater Lake lies in a caldera, which is produced when the center of a volcano caves in on itself; in this case, the cataclysm occurred 6,600 years ago with the destruction of formerly 12,000-foot-high Mount Mazama. Klamath Native American legend, which tells of a fierce battle between the chiefs of the underworld and the world aboveground, resulting in explosions and ash fall, roughly parallels the scientific explanation for Crater Lake's formation.

The aftereffects of this great eruption can still be seen. Huge drifts of ash and pumice hundreds of feet deep were deposited over a wide area up to 80 miles away. The pumice deserts to the north of the lake and the deep

ashen canyons to the south are the most dramatic examples. So thick and widespread is the pumice that water percolates through too rapidly for plants to survive, creating reddish pockets of bleakness in the otherwise green forest. The eerie gray hoodoos in the southern canyons were created by hot gases bubbling up through the ash, hardening it into rocklike towers. These formations have withstood centuries of erosion by water that has long since washed away the loosely packed ash, creating the steep canyons visible today.

Following the volcanic activity, over thousands of years the caldera filled with water. The lake is self-contained, fed only by snow and rain, with no outlets other than evaporation and seepage.

**Wizard Island,** a large cinder cone that rises 760 feet above the surface of the lake, offers evidence of volcanic activity since the caldera's formation. The true crater at the top of the island is the source of the lake's name. The **Phantom Ship,** a smaller island formed from lava, is a much older feature.

Although Crater Lake often records the coldest temperatures in the Cascades, the lake itself has only frozen over once since records have been kept. The surface of the lake can warm up past the 60°F mark during the summer. The deeper water stays around 38°F, although scientists have discovered 66°F hot spots 1,400 feet below the lake's surface.

Rainbow trout, kokanee (a landlocked salmon), and crayfish were introduced to the lake many years ago by humans; crayfish are now threatening the lake's native newts. Some types of mosses and green algae grow more than 400 feet below the lake's surface, a world record for these freshwater species.

## ★ CRATER LAKE NATIONAL PARK
### Visitors Center

The **Steel Visitors Center** (9am-5pm daily

# Crater Lake National Park

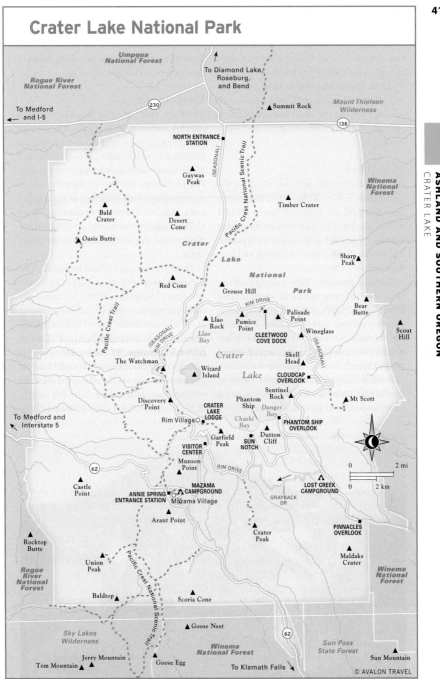

© AVALON TRAVEL

late Apr.-early Nov., 10am-4pm daily early Nov.-late Apr., closed Christmas Day), is located below Rim Village near park headquarters and can provide information and maps as well as backcountry permits and first aid. The **Rim Visitors Center** (9:30am-5pm daily late May-late Sept.) is near the lodge. A rock stairway behind the small building leads to Sinnott Memorial and one of the best views of the lake.

### Rim Drive

Begin a driving tour with a walk along the paved path at Rim Village. Morning views from this path are especially lovely. It's best to drive clockwise around the lake; this makes it easier to pull off at the many viewpoints. The loop is divided into West Rim and East Rim Drives.

Starting from the Rim Village parking area, the first stop comes in about a mile; **Discovery Point** is where a gold prospector stumbled across the lake while riding his mule. Also on the West Rim Drive, **Watchman Overlook** offers good views of Wizard Island.

Head a mile off the East Rim Drive to **Cloudcap Overlook;** Oregon's highest paved road will take you there. At the **Pumice**

**Castle Overlook**, spot the bright orange "castle" on the cliff wall. It's especially vibrant in the early evening, when the sun lights it up. The **Phantom Ship** looks like a tiny island in this big lake; it's really 170 feet tall.

### Boat Tours

There are over 100 miles of hiking trails in the park, yet only one leads down to the lake itself. The 1.1-mile-long Cleetwood Trail is the only part of the caldera's steep avalanche-prone slope that is safe enough for passage. The trail drops 700 feet in elevation and is recommended only for those in good physical condition. There is no other way to get to **Cleetwood Cove dock,** at the end of the trail, where the **Crater Lake boat tours** begin.

There are two types of boat tours. Narrated excursions (6 times 9:30am-3:45pm daily July-mid-Sept., 2 hours, $41 adults, $27 ages 3-12) cruise counterclockwise around the perimeter of the lake and do not stop at Wizard Island. The five-hour cruise (9:45am and 12:45pm daily July-mid-Sept., $57 adults, $36 ages 3-12) makes a three-hour stop at Wizard Island. If you just want to get to the island and dispense with the naturalist's talk, take the shuttle (8:30am and 11:30am daily July-mid-Sept.,

A boat ride on Crater Lake will give you a different perspective.

$32 adults, $30 ages 3-12). Allow one hour from Rim Village to drive the 12 miles to the Cleetwood trailhead and hike down to the boat's departure point. Dress warmly, as it's cooler on the lake.

A limited number of boat tour tickets are available by reservation (888/774-2728, www.craterlakelodges.com). The rest of the tickets are sold up to 24 hours in advance via touch screens in the lodge lobby and at the Steel Visitors Center. Any remaining tickets can be purchased in the final two hours before departure at the Cleetwood Trail ticket kiosk. Ticket sales end 45 minutes before the tour starts, in order to give boaters time to hike down to the dock.

## Hiking

A short hike with lots of visual punch is from **Sun Notch,** on the East Rim Drive, 4.4 miles east of park headquarters. This 0.8-mile loop climbs 150 feet through a meadow to excellent views of the Phantom Ship and other lake features. Park rangers often lead sunset hikes up **Watchman Peak,** 3.8 miles northwest of Rim Village. The 1.6-mile round-trip climbs 420 feet to a fire lookout.

A suitable challenge of brawn and breath is the **Garfield Peak Trail.** The trailhead to this imposing ridge is just east of Crater Lake Lodge. It is a steep climb up the 1.7-mile trail, but the wildflower displays of phlox, Indian paintbrush, and lupine, as well as frequent sightings of eagles and hawks, give ample opportunity for you to stop and catch your breath. The highlight of the hike is atop Garfield Peak, which provides a spectacular view of Crater Lake 1,888 feet below.

Boat tour tickets aren't required for the steep hike down the **Cleetwood Cove Trail** (2.2 miles round trip, 700 feet elevation change) to the boat dock. There's no better way to know the lake than by swimming in it, and this is the place to do it!

A hike to **Wizard Island's summit** involves a boat ride and a one-mile (770-foot elevation gain) climb. Once at the top you can see (or hike into) the crater and circumnavigate the rim on a flat 0.3-mile trail. Drop-offs are steep, but the views are spectacular.

Although it doesn't include views of the lake, the **Plaikni Falls Trail** leads to a pretty cascade that rolls down a glacier-carved cliff. The 1.1-mile trail is along a well-graded dirt path. Reach it from the Pinnacles Road, just off the East Rim Drive southeast of the Phantom Ship overlook.

One of the best places to view the mid-July flora is on the **Castle Crest Wildflower Trail.** The trailhead to this easy 0.5-mile loop trail is 0.5 miles from the park headquarters. The 4.4-mile hike to the top of **Mount Scott** (8,926 feet), the highest peak in the area, gains 1,250 feet. Lake views and perspectives on a dozen Cascade peaks are potential rewards at the end of the trek.

## Winter Sports

When snow buries the area in the wintertime, services and activities are cut to a minimum. However, many cross-country skiers, snowshoers, and winter campers enjoy this solitude. Park rangers lead **snowshoe hikes** (1pm Sat.-Sun., 1pm daily Christmas week, weather permitting). Ski and snowshoe rentals are available at Rim Village.

Winter trekkers should be aware that there are no groomed cross-country trails, so it's imperative to inquire about trail, avalanche, road, and weather conditions at the visitors center. Circumnavigating the lake, which is visited by frequent snowstorms, takes two or three days, even in good weather. Only highly skilled winter hikers should attempt this 33-mile route, which requires a compass and maps to traverse avalanche paths.

## Trolley Tours

Passengers can take two-hour round-trip tours on new but historically designed **trolley cars** (541/882-1896, www.craterlaketrolley.net, on the hour 10am-3pm daily mid-June-mid-Oct., fewer tours June and Sept.-Oct., $27 adults, $24 seniors, $17 ages 6-13) along Rim Drive, with several stops at scenic viewpoints. The natural gas-powered trolleys are ADA-compliant and feature commentary by a guide. Purchase tickets up to 24 hours in advance from a trolley parked by the Community House at Rim Village, near the Crater Lake Lodge.

## Food and Accommodations

One of the nicest things about 183,180-acre Crater Lake National Park is that it's not very developed. Lodging and services are concentrated on the southern edge of the lake at **Rim Village;** the exact opening and closing dates for services change depending on the snow, which can exceed 50 feet. In general, restaurants and information services are open mid-May to mid-October, with the exception of the **Rim Village Cafe** (9am-8pm daily summer, shorter hours fall-spring), which is open year-round. The café has grab-and-go sandwiches, salads, and rice bowls.

The 71-room ★ **Crater Lake Lodge** (541/830-8700, www.craterlakelodges.com, late May-mid-Oct., $189-329) is on the rim south of the Sinnott Overlook and is hewn of local wood and stone. The massive lobby boasts a picture window on the lake and has decor echoing its 1915 origins. The stone fireplace is large enough to walk into and serves as a gathering spot on chilly evenings. Many of the rooms have expansive views of the lake below. Less expensive rooms face out toward upper Klamath Lake and Mount Shasta, 100 miles away in California.

Amid all the amenities of a national park hotel, it's nice to be reminded of the past by such touches as antique wallpaper and old-fashioned bathtubs (rooms 401 and 201 offer views of the lake from claw-foot tubs). This marriage of past and present in such a prime location has proven so popular that it's imperative to reserve many months in advance. The 72-seat **dining room** (541/594-2255, ext. 3217, 7am-10:30am, 11:30am-2:30pm, and 5pm-10pm daily mid-May-mid-Oct., hours vary early and late in the season, dinner reservations advised, $24-43) features Pacific Northwest cuisine in a classic setting. If you want to soak in the ambiance of the lodge but don't want to commit to a full dinner, consider ordering from a bar menu (order in the lobby near the restaurant, $8-12) and relaxing with drinks and appetizers in the lobby or on the porch overlooking the lake.

Seven miles south of the rim is another cluster of services called Mazama Village. At the **Cabins at Mazama Village** (541/830-8700, www.craterlakelodges.com, late May-late Sept., $155), each room has one or two

Crater Lake Lodge has a spectacular setting.

queen beds and a bath with a shower, but no TV, phones, or air-conditioning; two cabins are designed for wheelchair access. Reserve well in advance.

Also in Mazama Village, the **Annie Creek Restaurant** (11am-4pm and 5pm-8pm daily late May-mid-June, 7am-10:30am, 11am-4pm, and 5pm-9pm daily mid-June-Labor Day, 8am-10:30am, 11am-4pm, and 5pm-8pm daily Sept., dinner $9-20) serves American-style comfort foods, including burgers, pot roast, and vegetarian lasagna.

## Camping

**Mazama Village Campground** (reservations www.craterlakelodges.com, early June-late Sept., $22 tents, $31 RVs), seven miles south of the rim, has over 200 sites; in spite of its size, this is a nice campground, with many spacious sites. **Lost Creek Campground** (early July-mid-Oct., $10 tents), about four miles down the Pinnacles Road from the East Rim Drive, has 16 sites with water and vault toilets. Its more remote location is nice for many campers, but damage to the trees has left it feeling hot and scrubby.

Campers should also consider **Diamond Lake** (877/444-6777, www.recreation.gov, mid-May-Oct., $16), just a few miles from the park's north entrance. The large lakeside campground here has many reservable sites.

## Getting There

The only year-round access to Crater Lake is from the south via Highway 62. To reach Crater Lake from Grants Pass, head for Gold Hill and take Highway 234 until it meets Highway 62. As you head up Highway 62, you might spot roadside snow poles in anticipation of the onset of winter. This highway makes a horseshoe bend through the Cascades, starting at Medford and ending 20 miles north of Klamath Falls. The northern route via Highway 138 (Roseburg to U.S. 97, south of Beaver Marsh) is usually closed by snow mid-October-July. The tremendous snowfall also closes 33-mile-long Rim Drive, although portions are opened when conditions permit. Rim

Drive is generally opened to motorists around the same time as the northern entrance to the park.

# CRATER LAKE HIGHWAY (HWY. 62)

Don't think that the vacation's over when you leave Crater Lake, at least for the first 40 miles or so. Highway 62 travels along the Upper Rogue River, where you'll find amazing river dynamics and lots of good camping and hiking. Unfortunately, once you're west of Shady Cove, it's a long, slow suburban slog to Medford. If you intend to head north on I-5, definitely take the Sams Valley cutoff (Hwy. 234) toward Gold Hill.

## Hiking

Many choice hikes are found along the 50-mile stretch of the Rogue River Trail from Lost Creek Lake to the river's source at Boundary Springs, just inside Crater Lake National Park. Those interested in more than just a short walk from the parking lot to the viewpoint can design hikes of 2 to 18 miles, with or without an overnight stay.

A two-mile hike down a cool and shady trail takes you to the source of the mighty Rogue River—**Boundary Springs.** Situated just inside Crater Lake National Park, it's a great place for a picnic. About one mile down the path from the trailhead, hang a left at the fork to get to Boundary Springs. Once at the springs, you'll discover small cataracts rising out of the jumbled volcanic rock, which is densely covered with moss and other vegetation. The vegetation here is extremely fragile, so refrain from walking on the moss. To get here, take Highway 230 north from Highway 62 to the crater rim viewpoint, where parking can be found on the left-hand side of the road.

An easily accessible and particularly scenic stretch of the Rogue is near the hamlet of Union Creek. Several short trails are right near the highway and lead to deep gushing gorges and a natural bridge.

Just north of Union Creek is the spectacular **Rogue River Gorge.** At this narrowest point on the river, the action of the water has carved out a deep chasm in the rock. A short trail with several well-placed overlooks follows the rim of the gorge. Green mossy walls, logjams, and a frothy torrent of water are all clearly visible from the trail.

South of Union Creek, the **Natural Bridge** is about a mile off the highway. Here the Rogue River drops into a lava tube and disappears from sight, only to emerge a little way downstream. A paved path takes you to an artificial bridge that fords this unique section of the river. Keep going; the natural bridge is at the end of the paved path. The 3.5-mile Rogue Gorge Trail connects these two viewpoints. Note the potholes in the dry riverbed above the gorge: They were formed by smaller rocks that were spun and drilled by river currents.

Many more hikes are accessible in this area if you're willing to drive on U.S. Forest Service roads. Find more trails in the **Rogue River-Siskiyou National Forest** (www. fs.usda.gov/main/rogue-siskiyou) or at the **Prospect Ranger Station** (47201 Hwy. 62, 541/560-3400).

## Accommodations

The accommodations you'll find on Highway 62 are rustic and simple. They're good bases for hiking in the area and for visiting Crater Lake. Both of the lodgings we've listed here have restaurants on-site or a few steps away.

The **Union Creek Resort** (56484 Hwy. 62, Prospect, 866/560-3565, www.unioncreekoregon.com, year-round) was built in the early 1930s and little has changed since then (it's listed on the National Register of Historic Places). The lodge rooms ($83-89), paneled in knotty pine, have washbasins; guests share the baths down the hall. The stone fireplace in the lobby was built of opalized wood from Lakeview, Oregon. The simple cabins ($129-134) have private baths. The vacation rental cabins ($249-350) have kitchens and sleep up to 10. If you like rustic cabins and lodges, the Union Creek is the real deal. The **Union Creek Country Store**, located at the resort, carries groceries and essentials as well as fishing licenses and Sno-Park permits.

The **Prospect Hotel and Motel** (391 Mill Creek Rd., Prospect, 541/560-3664 or 800/944-6490, www.prospecthotel.com, hotel rooms $150-295, includes breakfast, motel rooms $100-220) gives you a choice between something old and something new. The hotel, built in 1889 and listed on the National Register of Historic Places, has several small but comfortable guest rooms with private baths. The rooms are named after local residents and famous people who have stayed at the hotel, including President Theodore Roosevelt and authors Zane Grey and Jack London. Because the hotel is small and old, no children, smoking, or pets are permitted, but pets and kids are welcome in the adjacent motel, which features clean, spacious, modern units, some with kitchenettes.

## Camping

Set along the woodsy bank of Union Creek where it merges with the upper Rogue River is **Union Creek Campground** (541/560-3400, www.fs.usda.gov, late May-Oct., $16), with drinking water and vault toilets. Other U.S. Forest Service campgrounds within a couple of miles of Union Creek are **Farewell Bend** ($20), with drinking water and flush toilets; and **Natural Bridge** ($10), which has no drinking water and vault toilets.

Lost Creek Lake is the site of **Joseph Stewart Recreation Area** (35251 Hwy. 62, Trail, 541/560-3334, www.oregonstateparks. org, http://oregonstateparks.reserveamerica. com, Mar.-Oct., $17-22). The large campground here is set on a big grassy field above the reservoir and has all the usual state park amenities. Bike paths, a beach, and barbecue grills make this a family-friendly locale, if not exactly getting away from it all. Boat-launching facilities for Lost Creek Lake are located nearby, and eight miles of hiking trails and bike paths crisscross the park. Lost Creek Lake also has a marina, a beach, and boat rentals.

# Klamath Falls

Klamath Falls, or "K Falls" as locals call it, is the population hub of south-central Oregon, with about 20,000 people within the city limits and an additional 40,000 in the surrounding area. This community is used to hard times after witnessing the decline of its previous economic engines, starting with the railroads and moving on to the timber industry. Farming and ranching are still an important part of the local economy, as are tourism and the influx of new settlers, particularly retirees. The Oregon Institute of Technology is also in Klamath Falls, bringing a frisson of youthful energy to this otherwise rural city. The climate is dry here, with more than 290 days of sunshine; winters are cool but not damp.

Downtown Klamath Falls has a clutch of handsome historic buildings, many revitalized with shops and dining spots, and museums that shed light on different aspects of local history and culture. But the real draw of Klamath Falls is out in the surrounding countryside, where the Klamath Basin national wildlife refuges, a complex of six lake and wetland units stretching into California, draw visitors—and lots of birds—to the area. The refuges host some 50 nesting pairs of bald eagles, as well as more than 400 other bird species.

## SIGHTS
### Museums
A fine collection of Native American artifacts and Western art is found at the **Favell Museum** (125 W. Main St., 541/882-9996, http://favellmuseum.org, 10am-4pm Tues.-Sat., $10 adults, $5 ages 6-16, free under age 6, $25 family). Here you'll find beautiful displays of Native American stonework, bone and shell work, beadwork, quilts, basketry, pottery, and Northwest coast carvings. Another attraction is the collection of miniature working firearms, ranging from Gatling guns to inch-long Colt 45s, displayed in the museum's walk-in vault. The museum also houses one of Oregon's best collections of Western art, and the gift shop and art gallery specialize in limited edition prints and original Western art.

Two other museums are nearby: the **Baldwin Hotel Museum** (31 Main St., 541/883-4207, 10am-4pm Wed.-Sat. Memorial Day-Labor Day, 1-hour tour $5 adult, $4 seniors and students, 2-hour tour $10 adult, $9 seniors and students), adorned with original fixtures and furnishings and the compelling legacy of pioneer photographer Maud Baldwin; and the **Klamath County Museum** (1451 Main St., 541/883-4208, http://museum.klamathcounty.org, 9am-5pm Tues.-Sat., $5 adults, $4 seniors and students, $5 ages 5-12), with a good natural history section.

### Wildlife Refuges
The lakes, marshes, and streams in the Klamath Basin are protected by six different wildlife refuges that stretch between southern Oregon and northern California and share a **visitors center** (4009 Hill Rd., Tulelake, CA, 530/667-2231, www.fws.gov/refuge/Tule_Lake, 8am-4:30pm Mon.-Fri., 9am-4pm Sat.-Sun.) in Tulelake, California. Overnight camping is not permitted in any of the refuges.

December-February the Klamath Basin is home to one of the largest wintering concentrations of bald eagles in the Lower 48. The thousands of winter waterfowl that reside here provide a plentiful food source for these raptors. Ask at the Tulelake Visitors Center about where bald eagles can be seen.

March-May is when waterfowl and shorebirds stop over in the basin on their way north to their breeding grounds in Alaska and Canada. They rest and fatten up during the spring to build the necessary strength and body fat to carry them through their long migration. May-July is the nesting season for thousands of marsh birds and waterfowl. The

# Klamath Falls

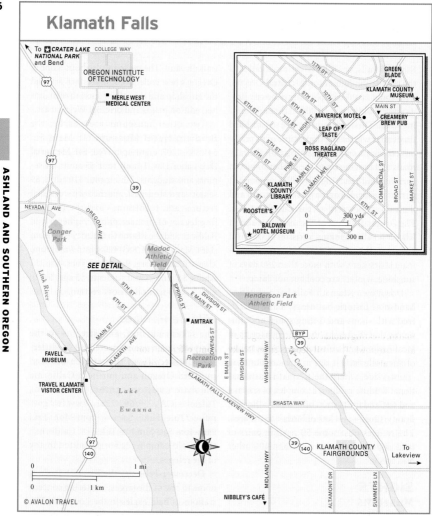

**Klamath Marsh National Wildlife Refuge** (off U.S. 97, north of Klamath Falls, www.fws. gov) is a good place in spring to observe sandhill cranes, shorebirds, waterfowl, and raptors.

The summer months are ideal for taking the self-guided auto tour routes and canoe trails. Descriptive leaflets for both are available from the refuge office. Among the most prolific waterfowl and marsh bird areas in the Pacific Northwest, over 25,000 ducks, 2,600 Canada geese, and thousands of marsh and shorebirds are raised here each year. You may also see American white pelicans, *Pelecanus erythrorhynchos,* at the **Upper Klamath National Wildlife Refuge** (north of Klamath Falls, www.fws.gov) during the summer.

Another high point is the **Upper Klamath Canoe Trail,** which follows a 9.5-mile passage through lakes, marshes, and streams at the northwest corner of Upper Klamath Lake within the boundaries of the refuge. Birding

# Oregon for the Birds

Oregon has great bird-watching destinations. Pack your binoculars and go birding at these scenic sanctuaries.

- **Cape Meares Rocks:** This Pacific coast fastness combines rocky headlands for nesting seabirds such as cormorants, common murres, tufted puffins, and pigeon guillemots as well as coastal old-growth forest, home to northern spotted owls, bald eagles, and marbled murrelets.

- **Sauvie Island:** This large, lake-filled island in the Columbia River is a good spot for fall and winter birding, when you might see snow geese and sandhill cranes, plus massive flocks of migrating waterfowl. Bald eagles and peregrine falcons are the primary raptors.

- **Malheur National Wildlife Refuge:** Over 320 bird species have been observed at Malheur Lake; during spring migration it's a top viewing area for sandhill cranes, tundra swans, northern pintails, many types of geese, white pelicans, double-crested cormorants, western grebes, long-billed curlews, and American avocets. Sage grouse are also prevalent.

- **Upper Klamath National Wildlife Refuge:** Large, marshy Upper Klamath Lake is most noted as the winter home of hundreds of bald eagles. In spring breeding season, you may see white pelicans, great egrets, and black-crowned night-herons, and if you're lucky, western and Clark's grebes doing their mating dance on the water.

is excellent along the canoe trail as mature ponderosa pines come right to the edge of the marsh, creating habitat for raptors, songbirds, and waterfowl. The trail departs from Rocky Point, about 25 miles northwest of Klamath Falls on Highway 140. Canoe rentals ($60 per day) are available from **Rocky Point Resort** (28121 Rocky Point Rd., 541/356-2287, www.rockypointoregon.com). The **Winter Wings Festival** (www.winterwingsfest.org) is held in February, with lots of workshops, field trips with celebrity birders, and photography workshops.

## SPORTS AND RECREATION

With all the lakes, rivers, and mountains in the region, there's no shortage of fishing, rafting, golfing, and other recreational opportunities. Here's a short list of some local attractions.

### Rafting

Just under an hour's drive, 20 miles west of Klamath Falls, is what's known as Hell's Corner of the Upper Klamath River.

**Arrowhead River Adventures** (720 Greenleaf Dr., Eagle Point, 541/830-3388 or 877/217-4387, www.arrowheadadventures.com) offers daylong trips (June-Sept., $149) through this remote canyon. With several Class IV-plus rapids, the Upper Klamath provides some of the best spring and summer rafting in the state.

You can also arrange a rafting trip in the Upper Klamath River canyons through Ashland's **Adventure Center** (40 N. Main St., Ashland, 541/488-2819 or 800/444-2819, www.raftingtours.com). In addition to a day trip ($135, includes transportation from Ashland), they offer a two-day trip ($339) down the river with a night of fully catered riverside camping.

### Fishing

Local guides can get you outfitted and on the water angling for the elusive big one. **Darren Roe Guide Service** (5391 Running Y Rd., 541/884-3825, http://roeoutfitters.com) offers trips on Klamath Lake and the nearby Wood and Williamson Rivers, noted for their runs of wild trout.

## Golf

The most notable area course is at the **Running Y Ranch Resort** (5500 Running Y Rd., 541/850-5500 or 877/866-1266, www.runningy.com, $65-95 for 18 holes), a 7,138-yard 18-hole course designed by Arnold Palmer.

## ENTERTAINMENT AND EVENTS

**Klamath Basin Brewing** (1320 Main St., 541/273-5222, http://kbbrewing.com, 11am-9:30pm daily, $10-24) has good beer and serviceable pub food. One of the great attractions of the brewery (the building dates to 1935) is its outdoor seating on the old loading dock; another is the fact that the brewery uses geothermal renewable energy. The Extra Special Bitter won accolades at the 2017 national Best of Craft Beer Awards; it's always worth stopping by the brewery to taste the seasonal limited-release brews.

The region's cultural hub is the **Ross Ragland Theater** (218 N. 7th St., 541/884-5483, www.rrtheater.org). The Klamath Symphony, community theater groups, country stars, and touring Broadway troupes grace the stage of this 800-seat auditorium.

## FOOD

The popular spot for breakfast and lunch is **Nibbley's Cafe** (2424 Washburn Way, 541/883-2314, www.nibbleys.com, 6am-4pm Mon., 6am-9pm Tues.-Fri., 7am-9pm Sat., 8am-2pm Sun., breakfast $5-11). The oatmeal pancakes are locally renowned, and the omelets are yummy. We're suckers for a good artisanal bakery, and were happy to find the **Green Blade** (1400 Esplanade St., 541/273-8999, http://green-blade.com, 6am-2pm Tues.-Sat.), with excellent morning pastries and sourdough breads.

Right downtown, **A Leap of Taste** (907 Main St., 541/850-9414, www.aleapoftaste.com, 7:30am-6pm Mon.-Fri., 8am-4pm Sat., $4-11) is a great place for a sandwich or coffee, but it also stocks a small selection of organic groceries, including locally raised meat, and serves as a place for young adults to learn job skills in a way that's a bit more intentional than most coffee shops. **Rooster's Steak and Chop House** (205 Main St., 541/850-8414, 4pm-10pm Mon.-Sat., 4pm-9pm Sun., $22-38) is the place for fine dining in K Falls, with excellent steaks and a classy atmosphere.

## ACCOMMODATIONS

Travelers on a budget will appreciate **Maverick Motel** (1220 Main St., 541/882-6688 or 800/404-6690, www.maverickmotel.com, $79-99). It serves continental breakfast and allows pets. Midrange properties are mostly the domain of the chains. The independent **Olympic Inn** (2627 S. 6th St., 541/882-9665, www.olympicinn.com, $114-179) is the nicest standard hotel in the area; soup and freshly baked bread is served every afternoon at 4:30pm, cookies come out at 8pm, and breakfast is included.

The upscale golf resort **Running Y Ranch Resort** (5500 Running Y Rd., 541/850-5500 or 800/851-6013, www.runningy.com, hotel rooms $170-370 d) offers the total Klamath Basin package experience, and travelers can stay at the ranch lodge in the deluxe guest rooms, a mix of comfortable hotel-style rooms and well-appointed one-bedroom suites. Two- and three-bedroom houses are also available. Pets are welcome, and the resort has plenty of trails for ambles with the dog.

### Camping

Most of the campgrounds you'll find in the vicinity of Klamath Falls are privately owned RV campgrounds, often in prime locations. **Rocky Point Resort** (28121 Rocky Point Rd., 541/356-2287, www.rockypointoregon.com, Apr.-mid-Nov., $30 tents, $38-44 RVs, $140 cabins) is close to the Upper Klamath National Wildlife Refuge, about half an hour from Klamath Falls. This resort has a summer-camp vibe, with tent and RV sites with hookups as well as rustic cabins and a restaurant. Ask about canoe rentals for trips on the Upper Klamath Canoe Trail.

Several other campgrounds are also found on Upper Klamath Lake. **Hagelstein Park**

(17301 U.S. 97 N., 541/883-5371, Apr.-late Nov., free), a small park just off the highway with a boat ramp is the only campground on the east shore of the lake; to get here, head north of Klamath Falls for 10 miles and look for signs on the right side of the road.

Approximately seven miles farther north on U.S. 97 is **KOA Klamath Falls** (3435 Shasta Way, 541/884-4644, year-round, $28-38, $76 cabins). Set along the shore of Upper Klamath Lake, the park has showers, flush toilets, a pool, laundry, and a recreation hall.

The pretty campground at **Collier Memorial State Park** (547/783-2471, www.oregonstateparks.org, http://oregonstateparks.reserveamerica.com, $19-26) is set near the convergence of the Williamson River (locally famous for its trout) and Spring Creek. Across the road you'll find a logging museum. It's about 40 miles north of K Falls on U.S. 97.

## INFORMATION

Over 2.2 million acres of Klamath County is publicly owned. The **Klamath Falls Ranger District Office** (2819 Dahlia St., 541/885-3400) can provide outdoor recreational information on the Fremont-Winema National Forest.

You'll find the **Oregon Welcome Center** (11001 U.S. 97 S., 541/882-7330, May-Oct.) at a U.S. 97 rest area about halfway between Klamath Falls and the California-Oregon border. They have a broad collection of brochures and information about locales all over the state. For information on Klamath Falls, contact **Meet Me in Klamath** (205 Riverside Dr., 541/882-1501 or 800/445-6728, www.meetmeinklamath.com).

## GETTING THERE

**Amtrak** (1600 Oak Ave., 541/884-2822) can connect you with northern and southern destinations via the daily *Coast Starlight* train. The **Klamath Shuttle** (445 S. Spring St., 541/883-2609) provides daily bus service between Klamath Falls and Medford, with connections to Amtrak in K Falls and Greyhound in Medford. From the same location, the **Point Bus** (445 S. Spring St., 541/883-2609, www.oregon-point.com) provides connections to Ashland and Brookings.

# Bend and Central Oregon

C entral Oregon is one of the most magnificent natural playgrounds in this part of the world, with a scenic collage of green forest and black basalt outcroppings topped by extinct volcanic cones covered with snow. Lakes, rivers, and

waterfalls provide a sparkling contrast to the earth tones. It's easy to find ways to explore these natural areas: hiking, biking, and cross-country ski trails abound, as do resorts both luxurious and rustic, waterways teeming with fish, and, increasingly, good restaurants and shopping.

The central Oregon Cascades, and especially Mount Bachelor, are a haven for winter sports that range from skiing to snowmobiling, snowboarding, and snowshoeing. Skiing here can be a special treat for west-side Oregonians accustomed to Mount Hood's fierce weather and frequently dense heavy snow. Of course, Bachelor is in Oregon, so don't expect all powder all the time.

Central Oregon has gained recognition for world-class golf. With over a dozen courses, this region offers just about every kind of golf challenge. The warm sunny days, cool evenings, and spectacular mountain scenery make every shot memorable.

With respect to everything except rain, the climate is more extreme here than on the west side of the Cascades. Expect it to be fairly dry, though not constantly sunny—that snow on Mount Bachelor has to come from somewhere. It's cold in the winter and hot in the summer, with cool to cold evenings year-round.

## PLANNING YOUR TIME

Plan to spend a few days exploring this part of the state. A long weekend will do for a taste or if you're very focused on skiing or a particular hiking or fishing destination. **Bend** is a natural base in the area, but it's also worth considering **Sunriver,** especially if you're visiting with family or a group of friends. Both of these places allow easy access to the Deschutes River, the High Desert Museum, and the Lava Lands sights.

If you plan to do a bit of hiking in the national forests, pick up a **Northwest Forest Pass** (www.fs.usda.gov, $5 one-day, $30

**Previous:** the glaciered Three Sisters peaks; Smith Rock State Park. **Above:** Tumalo Falls.

Look for ★ to find recommended
sights, activities, dining, and lodging.

# Highlights

★ **High Desert Museum:** This indoor-outdoor museum has exhibits on contemporary Native American life, the development of the West, photography, and wildlife (page 436).

★ **Mount Bachelor:** When weather permits, you can ride the Summit Lift all the way to the top of the mountain (page 438).

★ **Deschutes River Trail:** This trail ushers runners, walkers, and bicyclists along the Deschutes. Cyclists can ride from downtown Bend all the way to Benham Falls (page 441).

★ **Metolius River:** At the headwaters of the Metolius, the water emerges from hillside springs and immediately becomes a full-sized river (page 465).

★ **Smith Rock State Park:** Famed for its rock climbing, Smith Rock has just as much to offer hikers, who can search for golden eagles on the cliffs (page 469).

★ **Museum at Warm Springs:** Not only does this museum display a wide variety of Native American artifacts, it also features audio and visual exhibits portraying the cultures of the Paiute, Warm Springs, and Wasco peoples (page 477).

★ **Rafting the Deschutes:** Sign on with an outfitter and float from a put-in upstream of the town of Maupin (page 478).

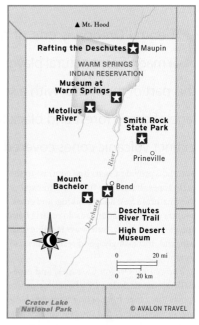

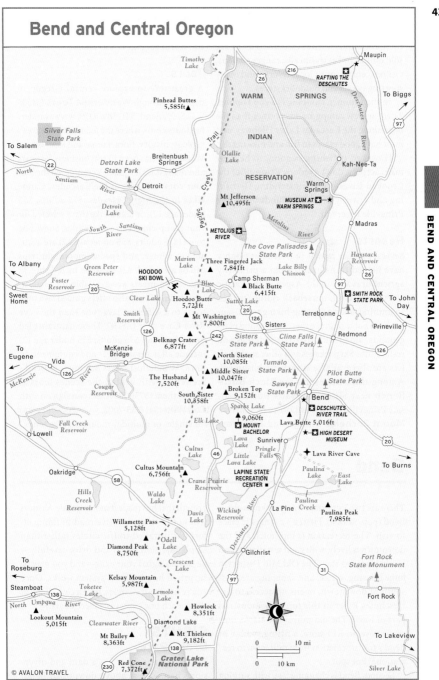

# Bend and Central Oregon

© AVALON TRAVEL

annual), which is required for parking at most trailheads and will get you into sites such as the Lava Lands Visitors Center. Passes are sold online and at trailheads, ranger stations, visitors centers, most local resorts, and many sporting goods and outdoors stores.

In the summer, camping is a good option. There are few campgrounds prettier than the ones along the Cascades Lakes Highway, and most have good places to fish and hike nearby.

However, if fishing is going to be your main activity, don't overlook **Prineville;** the Crooked River offers outstanding fly-fishing and a string of campgrounds below the Prineville Reservoir.

## Resorts

Several premier resorts in Deschutes County have helped transform it from a primarily agricultural area to the Aspen of the Pacific Northwest. Golf, horseback riding, tennis, swimming, biking-jogging-hiking trails, saunas, and hot tubs grace these year-round playgrounds, along with first-rate lodgings and restaurants. Ski packages and other special offers are also available at each establishment. Among the best resorts are **Black Butte Ranch** near Sisters, **Brasada Ranch** outside Prineville, **Sunriver Lodge** in Sunriver, **Mount Bachelor Village** and **Tetherow**

resorts on the outskirts of Bend, **Eagle Crest Resort** near Redmond, and **Kah-Nee-Ta** on the Warm Springs Reservation.

## Tours

A great way to explore central Oregon in depth is through **Wanderlust Tours** (61535 S. U.S. 97, Bend, 541/389-8359, www.wanderlusttours.com), where the focus is on the area's geology, history, flora, fauna, and local issues. Wanderlust has been in this business for years and really does it right; it's considered the best tour company east of the Cascades. Canoe lakes in the high Cascades ($75 adults, $55 under age 12), or take a hike that's selected for your group's interests and abilities. Snowshoe tours ($75 adults, $55 under age 12) are available in winter, and special moonlight trips can be arranged. All-day trips include lunch; vegetarian meals are available on request. Wanderlust Tours also offers guided lava tube tours to a different lava tube than the Lava River Cave near U.S. 97. These naturalist-led tours (half-day, $75 adults, $55 under age 12) include all necessary gear and equipment. In town, Wanderlust offers bus tours of Bend's breweries, with behind-the-scenes tours at four of them ($75). Bicyclists can sign on with **Cog Wild** (541/385-7002, www.cogwild.com) for single- or multiday mountain bike tours.

# Bend

There are two important things to know about Bend (pop. 91,000). First, it's a fantastic place to visit. The recreation is top-notch and the downtown is lively, with good restaurants and lovely places to stay. The Old Mill District, a huge housing, office, and shopping area just south of downtown, opens up access to the Deschutes River in this formerly industrial part of town. The old mill smokestacks now soar above an REI store, a fitting symbol of Bend's transformation from mill town to recreational hot spot.

Second, Bend is changing fast, with surging

growth that has made it more upscale. Visitors will notice that a massive road-building effort has installed traffic circles rather than stoplights. Slow down and drive carefully—be sure to signal your exits—and you may be surprised how well this system works. Once you're used to the circles, take a closer look at them; each one contains a piece of art.

## SIGHTS
### Drake Park

The Deschutes River has a dam and diversion channel just above downtown Bend.

# Bend

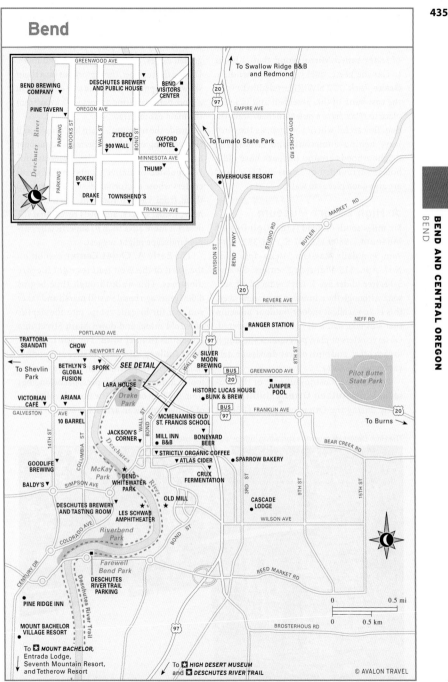

GREENWOOD AVE

BEND BREWING COMPANY ▼

DESCHUTES BREWERY AND PUBLIC HOUSE ▼

BEND VISITORS CENTER ■

PINE TAVERN ▼

OREGON AVE

Deschutes River

PARKING

BROOKS ST

WALL ST

ZYDECO
900 WALL ▼

BOND ST

OXFORD HOTEL ■

PARKING

MINNESOTA AVE

THUMP ▼

BOKEN ▼

DRAKE ▼

TOWNSHEND'S ▼

FRANKLIN AVE

To Swallow Ridge B&B and Redmond

20
97

EMPIRE AVE

BOYD ACRES RD

To Tumalo State Park

RIVERHOUSE RESORT ●

MARKET RD

DIVISION ST

BEND PKWY

STUDIO RD

BUTLER

20

REVERE AVE

NEFF RD

RANGER STATION ■

PORTLAND AVE

8TH ST

Pilot Butte State Park

TRATTORIA SBANDATI ▼

CHOW ▼

NEWPORT AVE

97

WALL ST

SILVER MOON BREWING ▼

BETHLYN'S GLOBAL FUSION ▼

SPORK ▼

SEE DETAIL

BUS
20

GREENWOOD AVE

To Shelvin Park

LARA HOUSE ●

Drake Park

HISTORIC LUCAS HOUSE
BUNK & BREW ●

JUNIPER POOL ■

VICTORIAN CAFÉ ▼

ARIANA ▼

AVE
10 BARREL ▼

14TH ST

COLUMBIA ST

BOND ST

Deschutes River

BUS
97

FRANKLIN AVE

GALVESTON

MCMENAMINS OLD ST. FRANCIS SCHOOL ●

To Burns

JACKSON'S CORNER ▼

MILL INN B&B ●

BONEYARD BEER ■

BEAR CREEK RD

GOODLIFE BREWING ▼

McKay Park

★ BEND WHITEWATER PARK

▼ STRICTLY ORGANIC COFFEE

▼ ATLAS CIDER

SPARROW BAKERY ●

9TH ST

15TH ST

BALDY'S ▼

SIMPSON AVE

CRUX FERMENTATION ▼

3RD ST

DESCHUTES BREWERY AND TASTING ROOM ▼

LES SCHWAB AMPHITHEATER ★

OLD MILL ★

CASCADE LODGE ■

WILSON AVE

COLORADO AVE

Riverbend Park

BOND ST

CENTURY DR

Farewell Bend Park

Deschutes River Trail

■ DESCHUTES RIVER TRAIL PARKING

REED MARKET RD

PINE RIDGE INN ●

N

0        0.5 mi

MOUNT BACHELOR VILLAGE RESORT ●

0        0.5 km

97

BROSTERHOUS RD

To ✚ MOUNT BACHELOR,
Entrada Lodge,
Seventh Mountain Resort,
and Tetherow Resort

To ✚ HIGH DESERT MUSEUM
and ✚ DESCHUTES RIVER TRAIL

© AVALON TRAVEL

It provides valuable irrigation water for the farmers and ranchers of the dry but fertile plateau to the north and creates a placid stretch of water called Mirror Pond that is home to Canada geese, ducks, and other wildlife. **Drake Park** (777 NW Riverside Blvd.) is on the east bank of this greenbelt and is a nice place to relax, have a quiet lunch, or walk the dog. Be careful where you step, as the birds leave behind numerous land mines. The neighborhoods around the park have older homes surrounded by lawns and trees and are also good places to walk.

## ★ High Desert Museum

Six miles south of Bend is the **High Desert Museum** (59800 U.S. 97 S., 541/382-4754, 9am-5pm daily May-Oct., 10am-4pm daily Nov.-Apr., $15 adults, $12 seniors, $9 ages 5-12, free under age 5, rates reduced off-season). Although the admission may seem steep, this is an excellent indoor-outdoor museum that will take half a day to explore in detail. Observe otters at play, porcupines sticking it to each other, and birds of prey dispassionately surveying the scene.

Perhaps the most joyful part of the museum is the **Autzen Otter Exhibit**, especially during the Otter Encounter (1:30pm daily), when the animals are typically at play. Another highlight is the **Donald M. Kerr Bird of Prey Center,** with resident bald and golden eagles, a great horned owl, and more. During the summer, the raptors put on a flight show (12:30pm daily, $5 adults, $3 children) in a more natural setting a short walk away from the main exhibit area.

Inside the museum's main building, you'll find rotating exhibits, galleries, and pioneer history demonstrations. The "desertarium" is populated by native plants and 37 small critters whose nocturnal lifestyles often keep them from view in the wild. Bats, lizards, mice, toads, snakes, and owls reveal that the desert is more alive than its superficially barren landscape might suggest.

The **Earle A. Chiles Center** exhibit on the spirit of the West features eight life-size dioramas. This walk through time begins 8,000 years ago beside a still marsh and takes you to a fur brigade camp, into the depths of a gold mine, and down Main Street in a boisterous frontier town. The **Spirit of the West Gallery** has representative arts and artifacts of the early American West, as well as tools, clothing, and other personal belongings from the 19th century. The Bounds collection of Native American artifacts and the Hall of

The High Desert Museum is a sprawling indoor/outdoor museum.

Plateau Heritage balance out the museum's coverage of the peoples of the high desert, while the Changing Forest exhibit addresses old-growth life cycles and other issues of forest ecology. The scope and interactive nature of this facility make it appealing for people who don't usually like museums. Stop for lunch or a snack at the museum café.

Along the many trails that wind through the 150-acre facility are replicas of a sheepherder's cabin, a settler's cabin, forestry displays, and other historical interpretations.

## Lava Lands Visitors Center and Lava Butte

About 11 miles south of Bend on U.S. 97 are **Lava Butte** and the **Lava Lands Visitors Center** (58201 S. U.S. 97, 541/593-2421, www.fs.usda.gov/centraloregon, 10am-4pm Thurs.-Mon. May, 9am-5pm daily late May-Labor Day, call for hours Sept., $5 per vehicle or NW Forest Pass). The center has some interpretive exhibits that explain the region's volcanic history, as well as a small selection of good local geology books. Summertime ranger talks introduce the Lava Lands and the Newberry National Volcanic Monument, which encompasses Lava Butte, Lava Cast Forest, Lava River Cave, Newberry Caldera, Paulina Peak, and other local sites. Admission to all these sites is covered by the same $5 pass.

After your orientation, take the steep drive to the top of 500-foot-high Lava Butte, just behind the visitors center (in summer, you can take the $2 shuttle to the top). The observation platform on top of this fire lookout (established in 1928) offers the best viewpoint. Nearly one mile above sea level, the butte affords a commanding panorama of the Cascade Range. On a clear day you can see most of the major peaks, with Mounts Jefferson and Hood looming prominently on the northern horizon. These snowcapped turrets form the backdrop to a 10-square-mile lava field.

Two short trails start from the visitors center: the 0.3-mile **Whispering Pines** trail is a short paved path along the edge of the lava flow; the paved but steep **Trail of the Molten Land** traces a one-mile loop across the lava. Don't be surprised to see blue-tailed lizards sunning themselves alongside these trails. You can also see *kipukas*, small islands of green trees surrounded by a sea of black lava, and what geologists call splatter. You'll know it when you see it, as it looks exactly like what it sounds like.

## Benham Falls

**Benham Falls** is four miles down Forest Road 9702 from the Lava Lands Visitors Center. Give other cars a wide berth and plenty of following distance, as the road's pumice and fine dust are hard on paint jobs and engines. The road leads to a small picnic area in a grove of old-growth ponderosa pines on the bank of the Deschutes River. Be sure to bring your own water; there is none here.

The hike to the falls is an easy half-mile jaunt downstream. Take the footbridge across the river and enjoy your stroll past a spectacular section of untamed white water. While the water in the Deschutes is much too cold and dangerous for a swim, it's ideal for soaking your feet a little after you've completed your hike. Benham Falls was created when magma from Lava Butte splashed over the side, flowing five miles to the Deschutes. When the molten rock collided with the icy water, the churning rapids and crashing waterfall were created.

When you reach the falls, you'll see another parking area. If you want to forgo the hike, reach the falls by heading south from Bend on the Cascade Lakes Highway and turning east (left) onto Forest Road 41, shortly after the Seventh Mountain Resort.

## Lava River Cave

About 12 miles south of Bend on U.S. 97 and one mile south of Lava Butte is Oregon's longest known lava tube, the **Lava River Cave** (541/593-2421, 10am-4pm Thurs.-Mon. May, 9am-4pm daily Memorial Day-Labor Day, 10am-4pm daily Sept., $5 per vehicle or NW Forest Pass). The cave is a cool 42°F year-round, so dress warmly and wear sturdy shoes—the walking surface is rocky and uneven in many places. Bring a strong flashlight to guide you through this lava tube or rent a lantern ($5) at the entrance.

To protect the resident bats, the cave is closed during the winter. To prevent the bats from acquiring white-nose syndrome, take care to wear clothing and shoes that you've never worn into another cave. Parking is limited at this popular site; try to get here early or toward the end of the day, but leave about an hour for the two-mile round-trip hike.

## Lava Cast Forest

A couple of miles south of Lava River Cave on U.S. 97 is an easterly turnoff for **Lava Cast Forest.** From here, follow the very rough Forest Road 9720 for nine miles to an unusual volcanic feature, where a one-mile trail traverses an unreal world created when lava enveloped a forest 6,000 years ago. The lava hardened, leaving behind a mold of the once-living trees, much like how the eruption of Mount Vesuvius in Italy left casts of Pompeii's residents.

## Tumalo Falls

About 12 miles west of downtown Bend, the 89-foot **Tumalo Falls** ($5 day-use or NW Forest Pass) plummets down a sheer cliff. Although the falls are visible from the parking area, a short walk leads to better views, and a slightly longer walk takes you to the top of the falls. From here, follow the trail up Tumalo Creek, where there are a couple of smaller waterfalls. Several other hiking and mountain biking trails leave from the area; it's possible to make a loop, but part of the loop falls in an area where the watershed is protected and dogs and bikes are prohibited.

From downtown, head west on Franklin Street, skirt Drake Park, and continue west on Galveston Avenue. At the traffic circle, continue west; the street becomes Skyliners Road. After 10 miles, follow the signs for the falls and turn onto Tumalo Road. The last couple of miles are on a good gravel road.

## Pilot Butte

On the east side of Bend is **Pilot Butte,** a 511-foot-high volcanic remnant. A road and a trail to the top offer a sweeping view of nine snowcapped Cascade peaks and their forests. It is also pretty at night, with the twinkling lights of the city below and the stars above. Full moons are especially awesome, illuminating the ghostly forms of the mountains as icy light-blue silhouettes. The scent of juniper and sage adds to the splendor. Bring water if you're hiking.

# SPORTS AND RECREATION
## Winter Sports
### ★ MOUNT BACHELOR

The Pacific Northwest's largest and most complete ski area is **Mount Bachelor** (541/382-2607, hours and snow report 541/382-7888, www.mtbachelor.com, $96 ages 19-64, $78 ages 13-18 and 65-69, $54 over age 70 and ages 6-12, discounts online). Located 22 miles southwest of Bend on Century Drive at nearly 9,000 feet elevation, this venue has 12 ski lifts, including 7 high-speed quads, and trails that range from beginner to expert. This is the winter training grounds for the U.S. Olympic Ski Team. If you're at the other end of the expertise spectrum, note that the beginners lift, the Carrousel, is free.

The Summit Express lift takes you to the top of the mountain, yielding great sunny-day views of the neighboring Cascade peaks. You may also see puffs of steam coming off the slopes, which serve as reminders that Bachelor is a still-active volcanic peak. Although central Oregon is known for its clear skies, storms pass through regularly, making the snow deep enough on Bachelor for the ski season to extend into late spring, but it can mean skiing or boarding in high wind and flying snow pellets. Conditions are often best in late winter and early spring. Avoid skiing after 1pm in May and June, when conditions become slushy; the west-side snowfields hold up better in the late-afternoon light.

Expert skiers and boarders should ride the high-speed Northwest Express quad lift to the mountain's Northwest Territory, with trees and bowls. The Summit lift is a must, both for the views and the trails, which include some blue runs. Another good area is the part of the mountain served by the Outback Express; runs here are mostly blue. Snowboarders and freestyle skiers head to the mile-long terrain park at Bachelors Park or the 400-foot-long super pipe. When conditions are wicked on the west side of the mountain, ride the **Cloudchaser lift,** which opens up territory on the east side of the mountain, which is often less stormy.

Skip skiing and join **Trail of Dreams Sled Dog Rides** (Sunrise Lodge parking area, 541/382-1709 or 800/829-2442) for a one-hour sled dog ride ($130-150 over 80 pounds, $50-60 under 80 pounds) with Jerry Scdoris and his daughter Rachael, an Iditarod finisher. A day-long tour ($600 for 2 people) goes to Elk Lake.

Even when ski season is over, **chairlift rides** (541/382-1709, 11am-5pm Mon.-Thurs., 11am-8pm Fri.-Sun. July-Labor Day, $19 adults, $16 seniors, $13 ages 6-12, less for evening rides) give visitors a chance to travel 15 minutes from the West Village base area to the Pine Marten Lodge, perched at 7,775 feet, with tremendous views of Cascade lakes and peaks and access to **mountain bike trails** ($19-39, rentals available) and **disc golf.** Sunset dinners (5pm-8pm Fri.-Sun.) are offered at the Pine Marten Lodge restaurant. Unlike most ski resorts of its size, Mount Bachelor has no slope-side lodging. The closest lodging is down the hill at the Seventh Mountain Resort. Sunriver is also about a 20-minute drive.

## CROSS-COUNTRY SKIING

Just west of downtown Bend on the road to Mount Bachelor are two excellent cross-country ski areas. The **Virginia Meissner Sno-Park** is about 13 miles west of town; **Swampy Lakes Sno-Park** is about two miles farther up the road. The two trail systems join together for more than 25 miles of ski trails dotted with strategically placed warming huts. There are also snowshoe trails leading from each Sno-Park. Dogs and motorized vehicles are prohibited at both. Sno-Park permits are required. In the summer, these trails are good for mountain biking.

Up the mountain at **Dutchman Flat Sno-Park,** what you gain in elevation and early-season snowpack you'll lose in peacefulness. Almost directly across from the turnoff to Mount Bachelor's Sunrise Lodge, Dutchman

snow-capped Mount Bachelor

Flat has trails for both skiers and snowmobilers and can be extremely busy on weekends and holidays. Snowmobilers can use this spot to access roughly 150 miles of trails; skiers find about 19 miles of trails, including some fairly challenging ones. In addition to all the downhill skiing and boarding, Mount Bachelor grooms trails at its **Nordic Center** ($19 adults, $12 ages 6-18 or over age 64, $3 less afternoons). These trails are especially good for families with inexperienced skiers.

A trail system at **Edison Butte** is a good alternative for cross-country skiers with dogs. It's south on Forest Road 45 from the Cascades Lakes Highway. Travel four miles to the trailhead; snowmobilers access trails from the same parking area, which can be very busy on snowy weekends.

Self-guided but supported three-day hut-to-hut backcountry ski trips start at Dutchman Flat and trace the eastern edge of the Three Sisters Wilderness Area to the Three Creeks Sno-Park near Sisters. **Three Sisters Backcountry** (http://threesisters-backcountry.com, $225 pp) will set you up with maps, hut lodging, food to make your own meals, and shuttles.

## Hiking and Biking

The area in and around Bend boasts a rich network of hiking and mountain biking trails, ranging from short barrier-free interpretive walks in town to strenuous wilderness treks. The best hiking is on trails accessed by the Cascade Lakes Highway. Snow can lock up many of these high-elevation trails until as late as June or July, so you'll want to inquire locally before heading out fall-spring. The offices of the **Deschutes National Forest** (63095 Deschutes Market Rd., 541/383-5300, www.fs.usda.gov/centraloregon) can provide information. Parking at most trailheads in the national forests requires a **Northwest Forest Pass** (www.fs.fed.us/r6/passespermits, $5 one-day, $30 annual), available at most outdoor stores and resorts as well as at trailheads.

For mountain bikers, the **Central Oregon Trail Alliance** (www.cotamtb.com) is a good resource. This volunteer group works with the U.S. Forest Service, the Bureau of Land Management, and others to enhance mountain biking in and around Bend. Their website briefly describes area trails and shows current conditions.

The Bend area has an excellent cross-country ski trail network.

the turnoff for Dillon Falls. This road will quickly reconnect you with riverside hiking and mountain biking trails that go all the way to Benham Falls. This section of the trail runs 9.1 miles through riverside pine forests and lava flows. It is actually a set of three parallel trails—one each dedicated to hikers, cyclists, and horseback riders—beginning about seven miles southwest of Bend. To get here via the road, follow Century Drive southwest, then turn south onto Forest Road 41 (Conklin Rd.), which has several access points to the trails at **Lava Island, Big Eddy, Aspen, Dillon, Slough, Benham West,** and **Benham Falls** day-use areas. The season is spring-fall, although most of the trails may remain open in winter during years with low snowfall. A Northwest Forest Pass is required for parking along Road 41, and dogs must be leashed. Four trail sections—at Big Eddy Rapids, Dillon Falls, Benham Falls West, and Benham Falls Picnic Area—are wheelchair accessible. They're surfaced with crushed gravel and are of intermediate difficulty.

## SHEVLIN PARK

About three miles west of town, **Shevlin Park** (year-round, free) lures both hikers and mountain bikers with an easy five-mile loop through the pines along the Tumalo Creek gorge and along a ridge burned in the Awbrey Hall fire of 1990. Several picnic areas offer quiet spots for lunch. To get here, follow Greenwood Avenue west from U.S. 97 in Bend; Greenwood becomes Newport Avenue after a few blocks, then changes again to Shevlin Road as it angles northwest.

## PHIL'S TRAIL

A trail close to town that's very popular with mountain bikers is **Phil's Trail,** an eight-mile segment of a larger network of eponymous bike trails (Kent's, Paul's, Jimmy's—named for the riders who established or popularized them) among the canyon and butte country just west of Bend. Difficulty is generally easy to moderate, with some steep climbs to challenge your lower gears the farther west you

Trails run for miles along the Deschutes River; this stretch is below the Seventh Mountain Resort.

## ★ DESCHUTES RIVER TRAIL

The best thing about Bend's early-2000s boom years was the development of the **Deschutes River Trail** (map at www.bendparksandrec.org). The trail, which will ultimately run 19 miles from Tumalo State Park north of town to the Meadow Picnic Area near Widgi Creek Golf Course, offers excellent river access to walkers, runners, and cyclists (mountain bikes or cruisers are best, though bikes aren't permitted on the west side of the river near Mount Bachelor Village). Pick up the trail downtown in Drake Park or in the Old Mill District, from Farewell Bend Park on the east side of the river (lots of parking on Reed Market Rd.), or from the Les Schwab Amphitheater on the west side. The trail is a patchwork of paved and unpaved surfaces. It's also easy to access from Mount Bachelor Village Resort.

If you want to keep going when you reach the trail's southern terminus, hop up onto Century Drive and head past the golf course and the Seventh Mountain Resort to ride. To get to the trailhead, head 2.5 miles west on Skyliners Road, then turn left on the first paved road to the south and travel 0.5 miles. A little farther west, Forest Roads 4610 and 300 also intersect the network. A **Northwest Forest Pass** (www.fs.fed.us, $5 one-day, $30 annual) is required for parking.

### MOUNT BACHELOR SUMMIT TRAIL

Farther afield, Mount Bachelor beckons hikers in the summer and fall to walk the four-mile **Mount Bachelor Summit Trail** (2-3 hours one-way) to the mountain's top. It can take a while for the snow to melt here, but trails are usually clear by midsummer. This is one of the easiest and safest routes to the top of any Cascade peak, requiring no climbing skills or equipment. An even easier way is to take the Pine Marten lift (which runs in the off season) to the mid-mountain level and trek from there.

To get to the trailhead, follow signs for the upper (east) parking lot at the ski area. The trail begins at the western end of the lot and climbs to a forested ridge on the mountain's northeastern side to the upper station of the first section of the ski lift. From there, the trail climbs steeply through the timberline area and continues up to a talus ridge leading to the mountain station of the second lift segment. It's a short hike from this lift station to the summit.

Plaques at viewpoints along the way identify lakes and mountains visible from this 9,000-foot vantage point, including Diamond Peak to the south and the Three Sisters, Broken Top, Mount Jefferson, and sometimes even Mount Hood, 100 miles away, to the north. The hike involves an elevation gain of 2,600 feet. Mountain bikes are not recommended on the trail.

### BIKE RENTALS AND TOURS

Rent a mountain bike at **Pine Mountain Sports** (255 SW Century Dr., 541/385-8080, www.pinemountainsports.com, 4 hours $20-50, 24 hours $30-75). Upstairs from Pine Mountain are the offices for **Cog Wild** (255 SW Century Dr., 541/385-7002, www.cogwild.com), which leads mountain bike tours that include short family cruises ($75 adults, $60 under age 13), vigorous day-long tours (about $110), and multiday trips ($700-1,100).

If your bicycling style is a little more easygoing, rent a cruiser (or a tandem, kids' bike, trailer, or tagalong) or a surrey from **Wheel Fun Rentals** (603 SW Mill View Way, 541/408-4568, 10am-8pm daily mid-June-Labor Day, hours vary off-season, $12-50 per hour) near the Deschutes River Trail in the Old Mill District. Bend's **bike share program** is still small, but growing rapidly. Download the Zagster app to see the most current map of bike locations and unlock a bike, which you can ride for $3 per hour and return to any Zagster station.

## Fishing

With over 100 mountain lakes and the Deschutes River within an hour's drive of Bend, your piscatorial pleasures will be satisfied in central Oregon. The high lakes offer rainbow, brown, and brook trout as well as landlocked Atlantic and coho salmon. The Deschutes River is famed for its red-sided rainbow trout and summer steelhead. Not surprisingly, the best fishing is outside of the Bend metropolitan area, near Sunriver, Cascade Lakes, and Prineville. If you're stuck in town, head over to the Old Mill District, where you'll find the **Confluence Fly Shop** (375 SW Powerhouse Dr., 541/678-5633, www.confluenceflyshop.com) and a clever 18-station fly-fishing course on the edge of the Deschutes (think miniature golf with a fly rod). The fly shop teams up with **Deep Canyon Outfitters** (541/323-3007, www.deepcanyonoutfitters.com), a well-established guide service.

A full-service pro shop with everything for the fly-fisher is **The Patient Angler** (822 SE 3rd St., 541/389-6208, www.patientangler.com), where you can stock up on information as well as gear; a guide service is also part of this business.

**Deschutes River Outfitters** (503/529-9784, www.deschutesoutfitters.com) features float trips, walk-in lake trips, and steelhead fishing trips that can be customized into single-day or multiday excursions. Check their outstanding website for specifics.

## Floating, Paddling and Surfing

Float or paddle through town on a stretch of the Deschutes that's mostly quiet, but with a potential for some thrills. Put in at **Riverbend Park** (799 SW Columbia St., on the river's west bank) and take out at Drake Park, where a **Ride the River shuttle bus** (www.cascadeseasttransit.com, 11:30am-6:30pm daily mid-June-Labor Day, $3 all day) will ferry you back to the starting point. Just past the Colorado Avenue bridge, the **Bend Whitewater Park** has three channels; stay far to the left for a normal level of thrill. The middle channel is for whitewater experts (you'll see surfers falling off their boards as they attempt to ride the standing waves here), and the far right channel is closed to preserve habitat. If you're with kids, get out of the water before the Colorado Bridge and walk around the short stretch of whitewater.

Experienced whitewater kayakers, surfers, and paddleboarders can practice their skills at the Bend Whitewater Park. Access it from the downstream side, at the McKay Park beach (166 SW Shevlin Hixon Dr.) or Miller's Landing Park (80 NW Riverside Blvd.). The center channel of the river here has been engineered to form four waves; the easiest is the farthest downriver and the most difficult is upstream, closest to the bridge.

Rent a kayak ($40 for 2 hours), canoe ($70 for 2 hours), float tube ($15 for 2 hours), or stand-up paddleboard ($40 for 2 hours) at **Tumalo Creek Kayak & Canoe** (805 SW Industrial Way, 541/317-9407, www.tumalocreek.com, 9am-7pm Mon.-Sat., 9am-6pm Sun.), where you can also sign up for paddling lessons.

Float the river on a specially designed river tube available for rent from **Sun Country Tours** (541/382-1709, www.suncountrytours.com, 10am-5pm daily, $15 adults, $10 under age 13). Find the rental location at **Riverbend Park** (799 SW Columbia St.).

## Golf

A couple of products of Bend's upscale turn are the lavish semiprivate golf courses at **Pronghorn** (65600 Pronghorn Club Dr., 866/372-1009, www.pronghornclub.com, $100-215), which has courses by Jack Nicklaus

Rent a paddleboard and take it to the river in Bend's Old Mill District.

and Tom Fazio, where the eighth hole features a lava canyon; and **Tetherow** (61240 Skyline Ranch Rd., 541/388-2582, www.tetherow. com, $120-175), a links-style course designed by Davis McLay Kidd, known for his work at Bandon Dunes. Both Tetherow and the Nicklaus course at Pronghorn are regularly mentioned as being nearly the same caliber as the courses at Bandon Dunes.

**Widgi Creek** (18707 Century Dr., 541/382-4449, www.widgi.com, $29-89, reserve online), just north of the Seventh Mountain Resort, was designed by Robert Muir Graves. The course's strategically placed trees, lakes, and sand traps have given this place the reputation as the "mean green" golf course of central Oregon. Close to town along the Deschutes River, the hillside **River's Edge Golf Course** (400 NW Pro Shop Dr., 541/389-2828, www.riversedgegolfbend.com, $39-59) is a convenient and pretty alternative.

## Gyms

One of the finest aquatic and fitness centers east of the Cascades is **Juniper Aquatic and Fitness Center** (800 NE 6th St., 541/389-7665, www.bendparksandrec.org, $7-8). Part of the Bend Metro Park and Recreation District, the center is located in 20-acre Juniper Park and features two indoor pools and a large 40-yard outdoor pool. An aerobics room, a weight room, group exercise classes, a jogging trail, and a tennis court offer other exercise options. A sauna and a whirlpool tub provide you with yet another way to sweat it out.

## Rafting

The Deschutes River offers some of the finest white water in central Oregon. The numerous lava flows have diverted the river to create tumultuous rapids that attract raft, kayak, and canoe enthusiasts. From short rafting trips to multiday adventures, you'll find many options available to enjoy the exciting Deschutes River. You will need swimwear, footwear, sunblock, and sunglasses for all rafting trips. It's also advisable to have a set of dry clothes handy at the end of the voyage. The prime spot for daylong trips is actually the Lower Deschutes, out of the town of Maupin, but there are a couple of spots close to Bend that'll satisfy that urge to be on the river on a hot summer day.

A few miles upstream from town, the Big Eddy section of the river offers a few white-water thrills. Several outfitters lead trips on this section of the Deschutes: The **Seventh Mountain River Company** (18575 SW Century Dr., 541/693-9124, http://seventhmountainriverco.com, $45) offers a 1.5-hour raft trip down a three-mile section of the Deschutes that takes in some Class I-IV rapids. With names like Pinball Alley and the Souse Hole, you can be assured of a good ride. Transfer between the inn and the river is included. **Sun Country Tours** (531 SW 13th St., 541/382-1709, www.suncountrytours. com, $59 adults, $49 ages 6-12) runs a 1.25-hour three-mile Big Eddy Thriller that takes in Class I-III rapids on the Deschutes River.

# ENTERTAINMENT AND EVENTS

Downtown Bend's striking art moderne **Tower Theatre** (835 NW Wall St., 541/317-0700, www.towertheatre.org) hosts music, films, and other performances. This nonprofit venue is a good place to see some relatively big-name acoustic musicians. Bend's biggest music venue, the **Les Schwab Amphitheater** (Shevlin-Hixon Dr. between Simpson Ave. and Columbia St., 541/322-9383, www.bendconcerts.com), is on the edge of the Old Mill District. This is the place to see performers such as Pink Martini, the Avett Brothers, or Michael Franti. It's also the site of events such as the Bend Brewfest.

## Brewpubs and Distilleries

Bend has seen an explosion of good local brewers in recent years. Many are alumni of central Oregon's first brewery and brewpub, **Deschutes Brewery and Public House** (1044 NW Bond St., 541/382-9242, www. deschutesbrewery.com, 11am-11pm daily,

# Touring Bend's Brewpubs

Twenty years ago, the Deschutes Brewery was the only artisanal brewery in town, but it turns out to have been an incubator for many local brewers. Bend's microbrewery scene is the fastest-growing in the state, and the local visitors center has developed the **Bend Ale Trail** to help you explore it.

Pick up a copy of the "Discovery Map of Central Oregon" (available at hotels and the Bend visitors center) and use its "Bend Ale Trail Map and Passport" to track down seven Bend breweries. The Ale Trail is also available as an app for smartphones. Get your passport stamped at each stop, and for extra credit, head over Sisters to visit an eighth pub. When you get all seven stamps, stop by the visitors center to receive a commemorative silicone beer glass. All of the seven Bend breweries are within walking distance of each other.

Although it's easy to explore Bend's ever-expanding brewpub scene on your own, a couple of local companies are offering tours that give you a little extra insight into the breweries and remove any temptation to drive. The **Bend Brew Bus** (541/389-8359, $65) is operated by Wanderlust Tours, whose guides know both the outdoors and their way around a tasting room. You'll get to go behind the scenes at the breweries and, of course, do some sampling. There's also a Local Pour tour that visits Bend distillers, cideries, wineries, and kombucha makers. The bus can pick you up at your hotel.

If you can get a group of 14 together and want a slightly more active tour, board the **Cycle Pub** (541/678-5051, www.cyclepub.com) and start pedaling—and drinking. The 16-person "bike," which looks more like a trolley, operates out of the Old Mill District and can be booked for pretty much any sort of tour you want to design. Two-hour tours ($350) are BYOB, but can include stops at brewpubs.

$10-28), which still serves fresh handcrafted ales and decent food ranging from burgers and pizza to steak. The pub's 19 taps include always-satisfying stalwarts like Mirror Pond pale ale as well as a number of specialty beers that you won't find in grocery stores. The main **Deschutes Brewery** (901 SW Simpson Ave., 541/385-8606, 8am-5pm Mon.-Fri., noon-5pm Sat.-Sun.) is in the Old Mill District, where tours and tastings are offered.

A visit to the tasting room at **Crux Fermentation Project** (50 SW Division St., 541/385-3333, http://cruxfermentation.com, 11:30am-10pm daily, $6-12) is a real treat, especially for beer nerds, who can appreciate the nontraditional brewing methods such as decoction mashing, open fermentation, and the use of wild yeast strains and hops from all over the world. Here the beer flows directly from the finishing tanks to the taps (24 last time we counted), and hops scent the building, a former auto shop. Pub grub consists of good salads, cheese and meat platters, and snacks, except on Monday evenings, when

the kitchen is closed and food trucks pull up to make sure no one goes hungry.

Perhaps the hottest brewpub in town is **10 Barrel** (1135 NW Galveston Ave., 541/678-5228, www.10barrel.com, 11am-11pm Sun.-Thurs., 11am-midnight Fri.-Sat.). Wash down good pizza with an award-winning S1NIST0R black ale. Another pub is now open at the **10 Barrel Brewery** (62950 NE 18th St., 541/241-7733, 11am-11pm Sun.-Thurs., 11am-midnight Fri.-Sat.).

Although it only has a tasting room, not a full brewpub, **Boneyard Brewing** (37 NW Lake Place, 541/323-2325, www.boneyard-beer.com, 11am-6pm daily), just a short walk from downtown, is worth a visit. Taking its name from scavenging old equipment from larger breweries, it also scavenged some excellent brewers, and their beers are first-rate. Boneyard brews are on tap at local restaurants. There's more good beer and noteworthy fish tacos at **Silver Moon Brewing** (24 NW Greenwood Ave., 541/388-8331, www.silvermoonbrewing.com, 11:30am-10pm

Mon.-Thurs., 11:30am-2am Fri.-Sat., 11:30am-8pm Sun.), a normally low-key sports bar that kicks into gear several nights a week with live music.

The **Bend Brewing Company** (1019 NW Brooks St., 541/383-1559, www.bendbrewingco.com, 11:30am-10:30pm daily, $9-14) a local staple with a popular happy hour (4pm-6pm Mon.-Fri.) and a fantastic setting on Brooks Street, a pedestrian-oriented street just to the river side of downtown. Come for the good beer, the nice waitstaff, the great patio, and good food—grilled tacos, pizza, sandwiches, and excellent fish-and-chips.

**GoodLife Brewing** (70 SW Century Dr., 541/728-0749, www.goodlifebrewing.com, noon-10pm daily, $9-14) opened in 2011 in a warehouse with a 30-barrel brewing system and quickly established itself as a major player in the Bend beer scene, with Descender IPA winning raves. The brewpub (they prefer to call it a *bierhal*) serves decent pub fare (try the chicken wings with a Sweet as Ale habanero sauce); during the summer, you and your dog can enjoy it by the fire pit out back.

Branch out at **Atlas Cider** (550 SW Industrial Way, 541/633-7757, www.atlascider.com, 11am-11pm Wed.-Sat., 11am-7:30pm Sun.-Tues.) for award-winning hard cider (try the apricot) and arcade games. Find handcrafted spirits at **Crater Lake Spirits** (1024 NW Bond St., 541/318-0200, www.craterlakespirits.com, 11am-9pm Mon.-Sat., 11am-7pm Sun.). This downtown tasting room isn't a bar and doesn't serve food, but it's close to many restaurants.

### Cannabis

Recreational cannabis is easy to come by in Bend. For a DIY tour of dispensaries, pick up a copy of the **Inhale Trail** map at the visitors center or at www.inhaletrail.com. To learn more about cannabis in central Oregon, sign on with **Blazing Trails** (30 SW Century Dr., 541/318-6488, www.blazingtrailsbend.com, $59).

### Festivals and Events

Quintessentially Bend, the mid-May **Pole Pedal Paddle** (541/388-0002, www.pppbend.com) is a relay or, for the exceptionally tough, a single-person event that starts at the top of Mount Bachelor and ends at the Les Schwab Amphitheater in Bend's Old Mill District. Between the two points, participants downhill ski, cross-country ski, bike, run, and canoe or kayak to the finish line. Although some participants take the event quite seriously, most enter in a spirit of fun.

The **Bend Summer Festival** brings out food booths, Oregon wine and microbrews, art exhibits, and live music all in one big downtown block party the second weekend in July. Contact the **Bend Visitors Information Bureau** (541/382-8048, www.c3events.com) for more details. In mid-August, the Les Schwab Amphitheater (Shevlin-Hixon Dr.) is home to the **Bend Brewfest** (541/322-9383, www.bendbrewfest.com), with over 80 craft beers available for tasting.

## FOOD

The scenery around Bend feeds the soul, and restaurants here do the rest. While area restaurants run the gamut from fast-food franchises to elegant dinner houses, many travelers also want something between those extremes. Some alternatives for every budget are listed below.

### New American

★ **Chow** (1110 Newport Ave., 541/728-0256, www.chowbend.com, 7am-2pm daily, $6-16), in a charming little house across from the Newport Market, is a deservedly popular breakfast spot. Chow's aim is to keep their business sustainable and true to the food, and this care is evident: One of the top picks on the menu is always the locavore omelet, made with whatever is in season. Farro and eggs is a good breakfast-for-lunch option; there are also inventive sandwiches. In nice weather the deck seating is great.

Just outside downtown, diners linger at the **Victorian Café** (1404 NW Galveston Ave.,

541/382-6411, www.victoriancafebend.com, 7am-2pm daily, $8-16), one of the few breakfast and lunch joints that has a full bar. Bloody Mary or no, breakfasts here are an extravaganza; for a real treat, order any of the eggs Benedict options.

Drop by ★ **Jackson's Corner** (845 NW Delaware Ave., 541/647-2198, www.jacksonscornerbend.com, 7am-9pm daily, $6-17) almost any time of day for a casual meal. The pizzas are excellent, as are the sandwiches and the salads. It's a casual neighborhood place where you order at the counter and may possibly share a big table with others. The side yard has a place for kids to play and adults to lounge at picnic tables.

**Rockin' Dave's Bistro and Backstage Lounge** (661 NE Greenwood Ave., 541/318-8177, http://rockindaves.com, 7am-2pm Mon.-Sat., 8am-2pm Sun., $4-11) is a popular local spot for sandwiches on Bend's best bagels as well as breakfast burritos. Come back in the evening to dine at the **Backstage Lounge** (4pm-close Tues.-Sat., $13-18), where Dave's commitment to fresh, healthy food shows up in the jambalaya bowl and other interpretations of comfort food.

On a corner in the heart of downtown, ★ **900 Wall** (900 NW Wall St., 541/323-6295, www.900wall.com, 3pm-9pm or 10pm Mon.-Fri., 10:30pm Sat.-Sun. summer, earlier close winter, $15-34) fairly pulses with energy, and the food is delicious and reasonably priced. Try a wood-fired pizza (the prosciutto and arugula pizza is drizzled with truffle oil and is absolutely delicious) or some high-class comfort food, such as duck confit or flatiron steak, prepared with just enough inventiveness to keep them interesting. The selection of wines by the glass is huge and well chosen.

**Drake** (801 NW Wall St., 541/306-3366, http://drakebend.com, 11am-9pm Sun.-Thurs., 11am-10pm Fri.-Sat., $12-19) offers upscale comfort food in a bright and airy dining room. While the menu seems to offer many classic American dishes, look again: The fish-and-chips features ale-battered Pacific cod with dried cherry coleslaw, and the cheeseburger can be accessorized with roasted bone marrow or pear kimchi.

## Steak

★ **Jackalope Grill** (750 NW Lava Rd., 541/318-8435, www.jackalopegrill.com, 4:30pm-9:30pm daily, reservations recommended, $17-39), around the corner from the Oxford Hotel, is more upscale than its name. Main courses range from steak or salmon to pork osso buco, but don't skip the starters. The soup du jour is invariably good, whether it's a rich butternut squash topped with chanterelles or a smooth concoction made from beets. During the summer, diners can sit in an intimate outdoor courtyard.

Also downtown, **The Pine Tavern Restaurant** (967 NW Brooks St., 541/382-5581, www.pinetavern.com, 11am-10pm daily, shorter hours in winter, reservations recommended, $15-32) has been in business since 1936, and although it isn't a trendy place, it keeps current enough to continue drawing crowds. It's in a garden setting overlooking Mirror Pond, with an ancient ponderosa pine that's been growing up through the floor since it opened. Prime rib, meat loaf, and hot sourdough scones with honey butter are among the many specialties.

## Barbecue

Find shockingly good barbecue on the road to Mount Bachelor at **Baldy's** (235 SW Century Dr., 541/385-7427, www.baldysbbq.com, 11am-9pm daily, $10-24). Be warned: If you're a rib lover, once you eat here, you'll be spoiled for any other restaurant in town. If ribs aren't your thing, the hickory-smoked chicken and the pulled pork are also delicious. A good selection of local beers is on tap. If you're headed out of town toward Burns, stop at the eastside **Baldy's** (2670 NE U.S. 20, 541/388-4227, 11am-9pm daily, $10-24) near the Safeway.

## Italian

Head west of downtown to find ★ **Trattoria Sbandati** (1444 NW College Way, 541/306-6825, www.trattoriasbandati.com, 5pm-close

Tues.-Sat., reservations recommended, $15-31), a small family-run Italian restaurant that manages to be simultaneously romantic and homey. Go with the intention of making a night of it; this is not a dine-and-dash spot. Start with a salad of gorgonzola and golden beets, move on to homemade pasta or gnocchi, perhaps try some polpette (meatballs), and make sure to take advantage of the excellent wine list. If you are in a hurry, stop by for a good selection of deli cheeses and cured meats.

## Mediterranean

Just out of downtown in a small bungalow, **Ariana** (1304 NW Galveston Ave., 541/330-5539, www.arianarestaurantbend.com, 5pm-9pm Tues.-Sat., reservations recommended, $21-39) is one of the most appealing and intimate dinner restaurants in town. The Mediterranean-influenced cuisine is prepared with care, elevating dishes as simple as beet salad to remarkable heights. To fully experience Ariana, go for the five-course tasting menu ($65). In the summer, seating expands to a deck.

## Southern

**Zydeco** (919 NW Bond St., 541/312-2899, www.zydecokitchen.com, 11:30am-2:30pm Mon.-Fri. and 5pm-close daily, $12-30) is one of the hottest spots in town. In the summer, its fun, bright atmosphere spills out from the open kitchen to tables on the sidewalk and rooftop. Inside, a good selection of wine is stored behind glass-fronted cabinets, and strategically placed mirrors give views of the crowd—a mix of young partiers and older serious diners—and the open kitchen. The food, not surprisingly, has Creole and Cajun influences, but also includes other good options, such as pan-roasted steelhead trout in a lemon-caper sauce.

## International

**Spork** (937 NW Newport Ave., 541/390-0946, 11am-9pm Mon.-Thurs., 11am-10pm Fri.-Sat., $5-12) is a busy restaurant with a hip and casual atmosphere. There are no reservations, and you order at the counter without a table assignment—but it always seems like a table opens up before the food arrives. The food is a small-plates selection of delicious Asian and Latin American dishes, with excellent tacos, Chinese sweet and spicy pork noodles, and amazing spicy fried chicken with sambal sauce. Spork also does a big take-out business, so it's a good place to grab food for a picnic.

Just down the street, **Bethlyn's Global Fusion** (1075 NW Newport Ave., 541/617-0513, http://bethlynsglobalfusion.com, 11am-8pm Sun.-Thurs., 11am-9pm Fri.-Sat., $9-12) is another casual counter-service place with inspired and healthy food, including a bibimbap bowl, Japanese tacos with salmon, and the improbable but delicious fried avocado tacos.

## Bakeries and Cafés

Downtown coffee lovers head to **Thump** (25 NW Minnesota Ave., 541/388-0226, www.thumpcoffee.com, 6am-5:30pm Mon.-Fri., 7am-5:30pm Sat., 7am-4:30pm Sun.) for small-batch-roasted coffee, good pastries, and friendly conversation. If you'd rather sip a cup of tea, try **Townshend's** (835 NW Bond St., 541/312-2001, www.townshendstea.com, 9am-10pm Mon.-Sat., 9am-9pm Sun.), which serves high-quality teas and kombucha in an atmosphere that's more hip than stuffy.

Downtown by the river, stop into bike-centric **Crow's Feet Commons** (875 NW Brooks St., 541/728-0066, http://crowsfeetcommons.com, 8am-8pm Sun.-Thurs., 8am-10pm Fri.-Sat.) for a Stumptown coffee or a beer (there's usually a Boneyard on tap) and a hang on the patio overlooking Mirror Pond. South of downtown, near the Old Mill District, **Strictly Organic Coffee** (6 SW Bond St., 541/330-6061, www.strictlyorganic.com, 6am-8pm Mon.-Fri., 6am-6pm Sat., 7am-6pm Sun.) is a great place for coffee or tea and a snack.

Check a map to find the tiny ★ **Sparrow Bakery** (50 SE Scott St., 541/330-6321, www.thesparrowbakery.net, 7am-2pm Mon.-Sat., 8am-2pm Sun., sandwiches $7.50-8.50).

Although it's just off the Bend Parkway near the Colorado Street exit, it can be tricky to locate this gem. The cardamom-scented "ocean rolls" make the search worthwhile, as do the fantastic sandwiches, which can take surprisingly long to make. If the weather's nice, sit at a table on the patio, which is surrounded by local artisans' studios and shops. Sparrow's pastries are sold downtown at Crow's Feet Commons.

## ACCOMMODATIONS

Bend is the largest full-fledged resort town in the state. On holidays or ski weekends, it's hard to find a room, much less an affordable one, although during the shoulder seasons of spring and fall, deals often abound. For a comprehensive list of motels, see www.visit-bend.org.

A longtime Bend favorite, the **Seventh Mountain Resort** (18575 SW Century Dr., 541/382-8711 or 877/765-1501, www.seventhmountain.com) was sold in 2013 to Wyndam, which has added it to its stable of WorldMark timeshare developments. Many of the condo units at Seventh Mountain are privately owned and available for rent. If you want to stay at the closest location possible to Mount Bachelor and trails to the Deschutes, it's worth checking the website or looking at **VRBO** (http://vrbo.com) to see if any units are available for rent. The entire resort is oftentimes booked months in advance.

### $50-100

Most of the least-expensive motels are along 3rd Street; except during busy weekends in the middle of the summer, you can just drive the street to check out these older, basic, but perfectly adequate lodgings. One reasonable bet is the **Cascade Lodge** (420 SE 3rd St., 541/382-2612, www.bendvalueinn.com, $64), which has microwaves and fridges in the rooms.

Hostel in style at the **Historic Lucas House Bunk and Brew** (42 NW Hawthorne Ave., 458/202-1090, www.bunkandbrew.com, $39-109), a 1910 brick house right downtown. The lowest prices are for a bunk in a dorm;

the top-end room sleeps four. Guests can use the kitchen (stocked with breakfast fixings) or the outdoor grill and fire pit; beer and coffee are also available. The hostel is well run by an enthusiastic and friendly crew.

### $100-150

Just south of downtown, on the edge of the Old Mill District is the **Mill Inn B&B** (642 NW Colorado Ave., 541/389-9198, www.millinn.com, $105-175). Originally an early 1900s hotel and boardinghouse, it has been remodeled into a 10-bedroom inn. Some rooms share a bath down the hall, but many have private baths, and some rooms adjoin to accommodate families. All rates include a full breakfast and access to a washer and dryer, barbecue grill, hot tub, and cocktail deck. On busy 3rd Street, not far from downtown, **Three Sisters Inn** (721 NE 3rd St., 541/382-1515, www.bendthreesistersinn.com, $129-199) is a tidy place with an included breakfast buffet, a pool, and family suites.

Up the road toward Mount Bachelor, the **Entrada Lodge** (19221 Century Dr., 541/382-4080, www.entradalodge.com, $111-154) is a standard, somewhat dated motel—but in an exceptional setting, nestled among the ponderosa pines at a nexus of hiking and mountain bike trails that can take you to the Deschutes River (about a 20-minute walk). A small pool, a large hot tub, a basic breakfast buffet, and in-room microwaves and fridges are the amenities. It's a good place to bring the dog. Even though Wi-Fi is free, it doesn't work very well.

### $150-200

The **Riverhouse on the Deschutes** (3075 Business U.S. 97 N., 541/389-3111 or 866/453-4480, www.riverhouse.com, $149-299) is situated along the Deschutes River at the north end of town. Although this hotel features a conference center and other business amenities, it's also a good place for vacationers. The rooms are well kept and equipped with Wi-Fi, microwaves, and fridges. Pets are permitted, and guests have access to indoor and outdoor pools, an exercise room, and tennis courts. There's also a golf course on-site.

★ **Mount Bachelor Village Resort** (19717 Mount Bachelor Dr., 541/452-9846 or 800/547-5204, www.mtbachelorvillage.com, $179-545) is a couple of miles from downtown, just off Century Drive. Some of the units, which include a wide variety of condos with fully equipped kitchens and hotel rooms with mini fridges, overlook the Deschutes River. It's easy for guests to get onto the Deschutes River Trail, and they can also use the adjacent Athletic Club of Bend, the most upscale gym in town.

**Wall Street Suites** (1430 Wall St., 541/706-9006, http://wallstreetsuitesbend. com, $169-230), a beautifully converted courtyard motel on the edge of downtown, has a couple of standard but quite comfortable guest rooms and fifteen suites with kitchens. A fenced yard makes it a handy place to stay with a dog; there's also a pet-free zone.

## $200-250

★ **McMenamins Old St. Francis School** (700 NW Bond St., 541/382-5174 or 877/661-4228, www.mcmenamins.com, $205-300, pets $15) is right downtown but is in its own little world, surrounded by gardens with quiet sitting areas. Rooms in this historic 1936 Roman Catholic school are nicely appointed with TVs, phones, Wi-Fi, blow-dryers, private baths with showers only, and comfy bathrobes to wear on the way over to the wonderful Turkish-style soaking pool. In addition to the standard rooms, a house ($515) is available that sleeps up to 10. Guests also get admission to movies at the school theater and easy access to the four bars on the premises; we recommend the fire pit outside O'Kane's pub, located behind the main hotel in a former garage.

Close to downtown, Drake Park, and Mirror Pond is **Lara House** (640 NW Congress St., 541/388-4064 or 800/766-4064, www.larahouse.com, $215-280), a large three-story house built in 1910 that features six large bedrooms with private baths. All rooms are furnished with graceful and charming antiques. A delicious homemade breakfast is served in the bright solarium overlooking the colorful gardens and Drake Park.

## Over $250

Downtown, the gorgeous ★ **Oxford Hotel** (10 NW Minnesota Ave., 541/382-8436 or 877/440-8436, www.oxfordhotelbend. com, $299-569) is a stylish and eco-friendly

Stay in downtown Bend at McMenamins Old Saint Francis School.

boutique hotel in a great location. From the subtle tree motif decor to the French-press coffee (locally roasted and grounds composted), everything is designed to make you feel good about relaxing in luxury. The latex Natura beds are comfortable and breathable; even the pull-out sofa beds have Tempur-Pedic mattresses. All rooms have a microwave and fridge and suites have a full kitchen, including a dishwasher. At seven stories, the Oxford is Bend's tallest building, and the top-floor fitness center has some of the best views this side of the Bachelor summit chairlift. It also has a steam room, a sauna, and a saline hot tub. Inquire about gaining access to private golf courses in the area. This block of Minnesota Avenue bustles with coffee shops, restaurants, and galleries, including a good restaurant in the hotel's basement. Your pet is welcome for $55.

A 10-minute drive from downtown and bordering the Deschutes National Forest, the **Tetherow Lodge** ($279-404) is a new and luxurious hotel set above the links-style course at Tetherow Golf Club. The rooms are large and beautifully furnished, most with a fireplace, spa-like bath, balcony or patio, and sumptuous bedding. Though the setting and exteriors feature a Western lodge look, the rooms themselves are coolly modern and sophisticated—anything but woodsy. The lodge also features a restaurant and bar, while hotel guests get special pricing on greens fees.

**Pine Ridge Inn** (1200 SW Century Dr., 800/600-4095, www.pineridgeinn.com, $269-319) is a small romantic inn above the Deschutes River near the foot of Century Drive, not too far from downtown. Guest rooms are spacious suites and mini suites and are well decorated.

## Camping

With the Three Sisters Wilderness and the Deschutes National Forest flanking Bend, there are many wonderful spots to enjoy camping out under the stars. Closer to civilization, **Tumalo State Park** (64120 O. B. Riley Rd., 541/382-3586, 800/551-6949, or

800/452-5687, www.oregonstateparks.org, year-round, $21 tents, $33 hookups, $46-56 yurts), five miles northwest of Bend, off of U.S. 20 along the banks of the Deschutes River, is convenient and not overly urbanized, with 54 tent sites, 23 sites for RVs up to 35 feet long, and showers. A couple of decent RV parks can be found near Bend. **Crown Villa** (60801 Brosterhous Rd., 541/388-1131, http://crownvillarvresort.com, $69-99), southeast of town, is well maintained and has lots of amenities.

## INFORMATION

Around the corner from the Oxford Hotel, **Visit Bend** (750 NW Lava Rd., 541/382-8048 or 877/245-8484, www.visitbend.com, 9am-5pm Mon.-Fri., 10am-4pm Sat.-Sun.) has an exceptionally helpful visitors center. The **Central Oregon Visitors Association** (705 SW Bonnett Way, 541/389-8799 or 800/800-8334, http://visitcentraloregon.com, 8:30am-5:30pm Mon.-Fri., 9am-5pm Sat.-Sun.) is in the Old Mill District.

The Bend and Fort Rock **Ranger Station** (63095 Deschutes Market Rd., 541/383-4000, www.fs.usda.gov/centraloregon) is the place to go for permits and information on the vast array of lands in central Oregon managed by the U.S. Forest Service. Passes are also available online; NW Forest Passes for hiking are sold at trailheads where they are required, and Sno-Park passes can be purchased at many local businesses, including ski shops and some grocery stores. The **public library** (507 NW Wall St., 541/388-6677) is a good place to get Wi-Fi.

## GETTING THERE
### Air

With flights from Portland, Seattle, San Francisco, Denver, Los Angeles, and Salt Lake City, access to central Oregon is quite good from Redmond's **Roberts Field** (RDM, 2522 SE Jesse Butler Cir., Redmond, 541/548-0646), 16 miles north of Bend and east of U.S. 97. Alamo, Avis, Budget, Hertz, National, and Enterprise have car rental offices in the terminal. Taxis, limos, and shuttle buses connect the traveler to Bend at nominal cost. **Redmond Airport Shuttle** (541/382-1687 or 888/664-8449, www.redmondairportshuttle. net) offers door-to-door service to and from the airport.

## Bus

The **Central Oregon Breeze Shuttle** (541/389-7469 or 800/847-0157, www.cobreeze. com, $52 one-way, $95 round-trip) serves Bend to and from Portland International Airport and the Portland train station. **Pacific Crest Bus Lines** (541/923-1732, www.pacificcrest-buslines.com, $35) runs between Eugene and Bend and east as far as Ontario, Oregon.

Get to and from the airport or the Chemult Amtrak station on **High Desert Point** (541/382-4193, www.highdesert-point.com) buses, which also travel between Bend and Eugene.

## Train

The closest you can get to Bend via **Amtrak** (800/872-7245, www.amtrak.com) is Chemult, 60 miles south on U.S. 97. Amtrak can assist you in scheduling your transfer to Bend.

## Car

U.S. 97 and U.S. 20 converge on Bend, much as the Native American trails and pioneer wagon roads did 150 years ago when this outpost on the Deschutes River was called Farewell Bend. Portland is 175 miles away via U.S. 97 and U.S. 26; Salem is 130 miles away via U.S. 20 and Highway 22; and Eugene is 121 miles away via U.S. 20 and Highway 126. Crater Lake National Park is 91 miles (about two hours) south on U.S. 97. There are also many loops worth investigating, including the Cascade Lakes Highway, Newberry Crater, and the Lava Lands.

You can rent a car starting at around $40 per day from **Hertz** (2025 NE U.S. 20, 541/388-1535; Redmond Airport, 541/923-1411) or **Budget** (519 SE 3rd St., 800/527-0700).

## GETTING AROUND

The Bend Parkway (U.S. 97) moves traffic fairly smoothly north and south through town. It parallels 3rd Street. On the road up to Bachelor and in some of the newer developments, including the area around the Old Mill District, traffic circles are used instead of stoplights. Your awareness of other vehicles should naturally heighten as you approach a traffic circle; traffic slows but doesn't stop at these junctions.

**Ride Bend** (2pm-10pm daily mid-June-Labor Day, free) is a shuttle that runs between downtown and the Old Mill District. Catch a bus at Franklin Avenue and Wall Street downtown, on Powerhouse Drive and Bond Street in the Old Mill District, on Century Drive at Simpson Avenue, or at Galveston Avenue and 13th Street. Another bus comes along every 15 minutes.

**Cascades East Transit** (541/385-8680, www.cascadeseasttransit.com) is a city and regional bus system with lines running to Mount Bachelor, Redmond, Prineville, Madras, Sisters, and La Pine. During the winter, Cascades East partners with Mount Bachelor to run a **ski shuttle** (park-and-ride lot at SW Columbia St. and Simpson Ave., $9 round-trip) to West Village on the mountain.

**Bend Cab** (541/389-8090) can always haul you around if you need a ride, as can Uber and Lyft drivers.

# Sunriver and Vicinity

The seeds of growth were planted in central Oregon in the mid-1960s, when a onetime military encampment a dozen miles south of Bend was transformed into the Sunriver Resort community. The resort, with its mix of private houses, rental units, and a lodge, has an increasing number of year-round residents, but it is still largely a hub for families looking to rent a house in central Oregon. And indeed, this is an ideal spot for a family get-together, with miles of bike paths, swimming pools, tennis courts, and the lovely Deschutes River. It's also an easy base for exploring the nearby volcanic landscape and sites along the Cascade Lakes Highway and, in winter, for skiing Mount Bachelor.

## SIGHTS
### Newberry Volcano

**Newberry Volcano,** a vast shield volcano that reached to about 10,000 feet before it blew its top about 1,500 years ago, covers 500 square miles. Its caldera alone is five miles in diameter and contains Paulina and East Lakes. A 1981 U.S. Geological Survey probe

drilled into the caldera floor and found temperatures of 510°F, the highest recorded in an inactive Cascade volcano.

The volcano itself is at the southeastern end of the area designated the **Newberry National Volcanic Monument,** which extends in a swath from Newberry Crater, south and east of Sunriver, all the way north to Lava Butte, on the highway between Bend and Sunriver. It preserves the obsidian fields, deep mountain lakes, and lava formations left in the wake of a massive series of eruptions. While lacking the visual impact and depth of Crater Lake, this preserve is more accessible and less crowded than its southern Cascades counterpart.

The main focus of interest here are the two lakes in the caldera: **Paulina Lake** and **East Lake.** A 9,500-year-old circular structure called a wickiup, excavated at Paulina Lake, dates well before the latest eruptions and indicates that indigenous people used this area through various stages of volcanic activity. Several campgrounds and two resorts are located along the shores of these

the lava flow at Newberry National Volcanic Monument

lakes, which are noted for their excellent trout fishing, best in the fall. In Paulina Lake, fisherfolk can troll for kokanee, a gourmet's delight, as well as brown and rainbow trout. Paulina's twin, East Lake, features a fall run of German brown trout that move out of the depths to spawn in shoreline shallows. Some locals claim that these lakes have the region's best fishing.

The summer-only four-mile Forest Road 500 leads to the top of 7,985-foot-high **Paulina Peak,** the highest point along the jagged edge of Newberry Crater, towering 1,500 feet over the lakes. A clear day on the peak allows a perspective on the forest, obsidian fields, and basalt flows in the surrounding area. To the far west, a palisade of snow-clad Cascade peaks runs the length of the horizon.

The other must-see site on the volcano is the **Big Obsidian Flow,** which was formed 1,300 years ago and served as the source of raw material for Native American spear points, arrowheads, and hide scrapers. Prized by the original inhabitants of the area, the obsidian tools were also highly valued by other Native American nations and were exchanged for blankets, firearms, and other possessions as far away as Taos, New Mexico. These tools and other barter items helped spread Newberry Volcano obsidian across the West. Centuries later, the National Aeronautics and Space Administration (NASA) sent astronauts to walk on the volcano's pumice-dusted surface in preparation for landing on the moon. A 0.9-mile trail now crosses the obsidian flow. Find the trailhead on the road between the two lakes.

Newberry National Volcanic Monument is managed by the Deschutes National Forest; contact the **Lava Lands Visitors Center** (58201 S. U.S. 97, Bend, 541/593-2421, www.fs.usda.gov/centraloregon) for more information. During the summer, a U.S. Forest Service guard station is staffed at Paulina Lake. A Northwest Forest Pass or a three-day monument pass ($10), available at Lava Lands Visitors Center or at the monument entrance, is required for day-use.

To reach Newberry Crater, head south from Sunriver about 12 miles, or 27 miles from Bend, on U.S. 97 to the turnoff to Paulina and East Lakes. The 16-mile paved but ragged County Road 21 twists and turns its way up to the lakes in the caldera of Newberry Crater.

## Sunriver Nature Center

Educational programs and interpretive exhibits, including a nature trail and a botanical garden, help orient visitors to the high desert ecology of the area around Sunriver. Programs at the **Sunriver Nature Center** (River Rd., Sunriver, 541/593-4394, www.sunrivernaturecenter.org, 9am-5pm daily late May-Labor Day) include nature walks, classes, and summertime day camps for kids.

# SPORTS AND RECREATION
## Bicycling

For many visitors, a trip to Sunriver is a chance to ride a bike. The gentle off-street bike paths provide the perfect way to get around the resort area. Sunriver's **Bike Barn** (541/593-3721), near the Great Hall, can set you up with a rented bike. **Village Bike and Ski** (541/593-2453), in the Sunriver Mall, is another good place to rent a bike. Be sure to pick up a map of the local bike trails. A popular ride from Sunriver is the easy eight-mile loop to Benham Falls on the Deschutes River.

If you like to bike but would rather have gravity do all of the work, consider the **Paulina Plunge** (541/389-0562 or 800/296-0562, www.paulinaplunge.com, May-Oct., $65-70), a six-mile downhill mountain bike ride. The outfitter provides high-quality bikes, helmets, guides, and the shuttle transfer from Sunriver and back. The action starts at Paulina Lake, where you begin your coast down forested trails alongside Paulina Creek. You'll pass by 50 waterfalls on your 2,500-foot descent, as well as abundant wildlife and varied vegetation. Three short nature hikes are necessary to experience the waterfalls and natural waterslides that make this trip famous. You will want to plunge into the water!

You may bring your own bike, but this will not get you a discount from the tour price. A sack lunch ($10) and water ($2) are available, or bring your own.

## Bird-Watching

About an hour south of Sunriver near Fort Rock is **Cabin Lake Campground** (Deschutes National Forest, 541/383-5300), an exceptional spot for viewing a wide variety of birds and wildlife. There is no lake at Cabin Lake, and the campground is pretty marginal, but the U.S. Forest Service has built two small ponds that blend in with the natural surroundings. Permanent wildlife-viewing blinds made of logs, built and donated by the Portland Audubon Society, are adjacent to the small 12-site campground and give close visual access to the ponds. In fact, the blinds are so close that binoculars aren't really needed.

Since there is little water in this 3,000-foot-high meeting of desert and mountain biomes, both mountain and desert birds are regularly attracted, usually in large numbers. The red crossbill, an increasingly rare member of the finch family, is a regular visitor to this avian oasis. The pinyon jay is another fairly uncommon bird that can be seen here with frequency. Woodpeckers, including Lewis's woodpecker, the common flicker, the white-headed woodpecker, and the hairy woodpecker, are also often sighted. Best viewing times are in the morning, but birds can usually be seen all day long.

## Fishing

Although some people do fish the Upper Deschutes River from the bank in the area around Sunriver, most anglers use drift boats. If you don't have a boat, consider fishing the Fall River, off Highway 43 (Century Dr.) southwest of Sunriver. You can get equipment, licenses, advice, or a fishing guide at the **Sunriver Fly Shop** (56805 Venture Lane, Sunriver, 541/593-8814, www.sunriverflyshop.com, 9am-5pm Mon.-Sat., 9am-3pm Sun.), near the Chevron station in the business park and shopping area across the road

from the entrance to Sunriver. Families are catered to by **Garrison's Fishing Service** (541/593-8394, www.garrisonguide.com), which features pontoon boats with padded swivel chairs that cruise the lakes and rivers of central Oregon looking for the big ones.

## Golf

Three 18-hole courses and a family-oriented nine-hole course are found at **Sunriver Resort** (541/593-4402 or 800/801-8765, www.sunriver-resort.com). The Meadows Course ($49-119) is many golfers' favorite. The Woodlands Course ($49-119) has water, abundant bunkers, and constricted approaches to the greens, making club selection and shot accuracy very important. The private Crosswater Course ($69-199) is only for resort guests and is touted by the management as the best course north of Pebble Beach. The nine-hole Caldera Links ($49 adults, $19 ages 12-17) is the newest course, designed to introduce new players to the sport; it's also limited to resort guests.

A nearby and economical golf course is **Quail Run** (16725 Northridge Dr., La Pine, 541/536-1303 or 800/895-4653, http://golfquailrun.com, $35-55), an 18-hole championship course in La Pine. Sand traps, ponds, and tree-lined fairways challenge golfers of all levels without seriously threatening their pocketbooks.

## Horseback Riding

During the spring and summer, the **Sunriver Stables** (57215 River Rd., 541/593-6995, www.sunriver-resort.com, $40-90) offers short pony rides ($15) and two-hour trail rides; riding lessons are also available. During the winter, horse-drawn sleigh rides ($100) travel along the Deschutes River and through the forest.

## Paddling

**The Sunriver marina** (541/593-3492, 9am-4pm daily, weather permitting), on the Deschutes River west of Circle 3, rents canoes, kayaks, stand-up paddleboards, and rafts;

offers kayak classes; and leads float trips and shuttles on the Deschutes. Aspiring anglers can also rent a fishing rod here.

### Swimming

**The Cove at Sunriver** (541/593-1000, 10am-10pm daily) is an expansion of the Lodge Village pool complex, with a new restaurant and bar, a vast pool, a hot tub, a waterslide, private cabanas, and nature trails. Sunriver Resort guests have exclusive and complimentary access to The Cove. Also for resort guests is the **Sage Springs Club and Spa** (541/593-7890) indoor lap pool, located just across from the Great Hall.

Sunriver guests can also swim at **SHARC** (57250 Overlook Rd. off Circle 2, 541/585-5000, www.sunriversharc.com, $25 over age 3, less in winter), a huge two-acre aquatic and recreation center with large indoor and outdoor pools, two waterslides, and an outdoor hot tub reserved for adults as well as playgrounds and basketball and boccie courts. Passes are available with many Sunriver rentals; ask about this when you're booking.

### Ice Skating

During the winter, the **ice-skating rink** (541/593-5948, sunrivervillagefun.com, $14 adults, $10 under age 13) at Sunriver Mall is a big draw, and has skate rentals available.

## ENTERTAINMENT AND EVENTS

The mid-August **Sunriver Music Festival** (541/593-1084 or 541/593-9310, www.sunrivermusic.org), held in the magnificent log-and-stone structure called the Great Hall at Sunriver Resort and in Bend's Tower Theatre, has been pleasing capacity crowds since the festival's inception in 1977. The concert series features top performers from around the world. Highlights include the gala pops concert and the gourmet dinner as well as four traditional classical concerts and a family concert.

## FOOD

There are a number of casual eateries in and around Sunriver's main shopping area as well as a well-stocked grocery store. Food isn't really one of the high points of a visit here, but it's fun to stop by the **Twisted River Tavern** (541/593-3730, www.sunriver-resort.com/dining, 11:30am-midnight daily, $11-22), the lounge in Sunriver Resort's main lodge, to enjoy a drink, pub food, and great views. Kids are allowed until about 8pm. Next door in the lodge, **Carson's American Kitchen** (www.sunriver-resort.com/dining, 541/593-3740, 7am-9pm daily, $18-37) offers steak, pasta, fried chicken, and burgers. For Sunriver's fine-dining option, head to **The Grille at Crosswater** (www.sunriver-resort.com/dining, 541/593-3400, 11:30am-9pm, $16-53), in a pretty golf course location, where you can dine simply on tacos or crab macaroni and cheese, or go all out for rack of lamb with Bing cherry chutney or thyme-honey-glazed grilled salmon. You'll need to meet the "country club casual" dress code.

Beyond the resort itself, in the cluster of shops at the Village, you'll find the area's most interesting dining at **South Bend Bistro** (57080 Abbot Dr., Bldg. 26, 541/593-3991, www.southbendbistro.com, 4pm-9pm daily, $19-33). The menu is influenced by the chef's years in Florence and his immersion into Oregon's bounty, with charcuterie, pasta courses, and entrées ranging from tuna niçoise to braised rabbit with prosciutto, roasted fennel, and provolone-stuffed risotto croquettes.

There are great Deschutes River views, a casual atmosphere, and decent Mexican-Peruvian food at **Hola!** (57235 River Rd., 541/593-8880, www.holabend.com, 11am-9pm daily, $12-19), next to the Sunriver marina. The menu includes dishes such as braised pork with yams, onions, and tomatoes, or wild prawns with fried bananas, red onion, and spicy mole sauce.

## ACCOMMODATIONS

The Pacific Northwest's most complete resort, ★ **Sunriver Lodge** (800/801-8765, www.sunriver-resort.com) not only has proximity to Mount Bachelor skiing, Deschutes River canoeing and white-water rafting, and hiking and horse trails in the Deschutes National Forest, but also boasts golf courses, pools, tennis courts, 35 miles of paved bike routes, and a nature center with an astronomical observatory. There's pretty much something for everybody.

Sunriver Lodge has rooms ranging from up-to-date guest rooms ($289) to relatively large suites ($319) featuring a large fireplace, a fully equipped kitchen, a sleeping loft, and tall picture windows that open onto a patio. Nearby "river lodges" ($309-325) are even more elegant. About two miles south of the lodge, in the newer Caldera Springs development, are swank three- to four-bedroom cabins (from $440). Deals are often available on the resort's website.

Note that it can be a much better bargain to rent a condo or a house. Sunriver Resort's website allows you to set your criteria and browse available properties, which start at about $200. Condo rentals are also available through **Mountain Resort Properties** (541/593-8685 or 800/346-6337, www.mtresort.com). All units have a fully equipped kitchen, linens, a washer and dryer, TV, and a barbecue, as well as access to the SHARC pool and fitness center. Since these are privately owned units, other amenities like hot tubs, saunas, and use of bicycles will vary. Most of these condos do not allow pets or smoking, but there are exceptions; inquire when making reservations. Other agencies brokering vacation house rentals include **Village Properties** (541/593-1653, www.village-properties.com) and websites such as **Vacasa** (www.vacasa.com). Many houses have hot tubs, and quite a few allow pets; rates are all over the map but can be as low as $150 for a two-bedroom condo.

Up on Newberry Crater, **Paulina Lake Resort** (541/536-2240, www.paulinalakelodge.com, year-round, $110-290) has 14 rustic log cabins. Although all cabins have kitchenettes or full kitchens, hearty lunches and dinners (11am-7pm Wed.-Sat., 11am-5pm Sun. summer, 11am-8pm Fri.-Sat., 11am-5pm Sun. winter, dinner reservations required in winter, dinner $11-26) can be had in the resort's log-paneled dining room. Boat rentals and a general store are also on-site. Although the road to the resort is snowed in December-March, the resort is open to cross-country skiers and snowmobilers, giving access to over 330,000 acres of designated snowmobile areas.

**East Lake Resort** (541/536-2230, www.eastlakeresort.com, mid-May-mid-Oct., $85-210) offers 16 cabins, most with full kitchens and some with more rudimentary cooking facilities. A snack bar, a general store, and boat rentals are on-site, and the nearby RV park ($32) and tent sites ($25) have a laundry and pay showers. The lake itself is stocked with trout and Atlantic and kokanee salmon. The cold water and abundant freshwater shrimp make for excellent-tasting fish.

## Camping

The nicest campgrounds near Sunriver are in the Newberry Volcano area. The creekside **McKay Crossing** (541/383-5300, www.fs.usda.gov/centraloregon, $10), about three miles east of U.S. 97 on the road up to Newberry Volcano, has no drinking water. **Paulina Lake, Little Crater, Cinder Hill,** and **East Lake** (reservations 877/444-6777, www.recreation.gov, late May-mid-Oct., $18) all have drinking water and are located at the top of the Newberry Volcano.

**La Pine State Park** (541/536-2071 or 800/452-5687, www.oregonstateparks.org, year-round, $24 tents, $28-32 RVs, $44-54 rustic cabins, $97 deluxe cabins) is a large campground south of Sunriver. Look for a sign on the west side of the highway marking the three-mile-long entrance road, eight miles north of La Pine off U.S. 97. This park also claims Oregon's tallest ponderosa pine tree (162 feet) and offers easy access to the Cascade Lakes Highway and an array of volcanic phenomena. The campground has firewood, showers, and flush toilets.

# Cascade Lakes Highway

The Cascade Lakes Highway, a.k.a. Century Drive or Highway 46, is an 89-mile drive leading to more than half a dozen lakes in the shadow of the snowcapped Cascades. These lakes feature boating, fishing, and other water sports, and almost every lake has at least one campground on its shore. Hiking, bird-watching, biking, and skiing also attract visitors. From Bend, drive south on Franklin Avenue, which becomes Galveston Avenue, about a mile to the traffic circle at 14th Street. Take the exit for Century Drive. The route is well marked, and the road climbs in elevation for a significant portion of the drive.

Although there are many places to stop and explore along the highway, the stretch between Mount Bachelor and Crane Prairie Reservoir is the most spectacular. The area around the Cascade Lakes Highway is part of the **Deschutes National Forest** (541/383-5300, www.fs.usda.gov). A **Northwest Forest Pass** ($5 one-day, $30 annual) is required to park at most trailheads; passes are sold at the trailhead for exact change or a check.

## SIGHTS
### Cascade Lakes Welcome Station

Just past the Seventh Mountain Resort at the national forest boundary, the **Cascade Lakes Welcome Station** (18500 Cascade Lakes Hwy., milepost 7, 521/383-5300, www.fs.usda.gov, 8am-4pm daily summer, shorter hours Apr. and Sept.-Nov.) has both a visitor information and a trail hub, providing mountain bikers access to Phil's and Wanoga trail systems. It's across the highway from the turnoff to Forest Road 41, with access to hiking and biking on the Deschutes River Trail. Park here to hike or bike, buy a trail pass, or get a free map. The station closes down in the winter so as not to disturb migrating elk.

## Todd Lake

Shortly after you pass Mount Bachelor, you'll find the turnoff to the exceptionally beautiful but equally rustic U.S. Forest Service campground (June-Oct., depending on snow, NW Forest Pass, no extra camping fee) at **Todd Lake.** It's a short walk up the trail from a parking area to the campsites at this 6,200-foot-high alpine lake. Tables, grills, and a vault toilet are provided, but you will need to pack in your own water and supplies, as no vehicles are allowed, preserving the grandeur of this pristine spot. You'll find good swimming and wading on the sandy shoal on the south end of the lake, and you can't miss the captivating views of Broken Top to the north. Hardy explorers can portage a canoe up the trail for a paddle around Todd Lake. The resident western toad and Cascade frog are threatened by habitat loss. Because of the lake's high elevation, it is often socked in by snow until about the Fourth of July.

## Sparks Lake

Clear and shallow **Sparks Lake,** about 25 miles west of Bend, is a favorite stop for photographers; most visitors can't resist trying to capture views of Mount Bachelor, South Sister, and Broken Top reflected in the lake. Broken volcanic rock forms the lake bed, and water slowly drains out during the course of the summer, leaving not much more than a marsh by late in the season. Rather than a formal trail, this is a good place just to explore the lakeshore on foot or in a canoe. There is a campground, Soda Creek (June-Sept., $10); bring your own drinking water or a filter to use lake water. The lake is open to fly-fishing only for the local brook trout and cutthroat trout, and the use of barbless hooks is encouraged.

## Green Lakes Trailhead

Begin a hike into the Three Sisters Wilderness

# A Three-Hour Tour of the Cascade Lakes Highway

A shortened version of the Cascade Lakes Highway loop takes in some of the highlights in just a few hours, even allowing for several stops. In contrast, driving the entire loop takes a whole day, with only limited time spent out of the car. Begin by taking U.S. 97 south of Bend 13 miles and getting off at the exit for Sunriver. After about 1.5 miles, the turnoff to Sunriver Resort is on the right; stay on the main road as it curves to the left. Pass the turnoff for Mount Bachelor; follow this road (Hwy. 40/Spring River Rd.) to Cascade Lakes Highway (Hwy. 46) and turn right to reach **Little Lava Lake.** The Deschutes River begins its 252-mile course to the Columbia from here. Head just down the road to **Lava Lake,** where there's a small rustic resort, camping, and a store with a grand view of South Sister from the store's porch; in the summer your attention could be diverted by the hummingbirds that flock to a hanging feeder.

Follow the highway north to the shores of **Elk Lake,** a favorite for windsurfing and sailing. The year-round cabins at **Elk Lake Resort** (541/480-7378, www.elklakeresort.net) are popular, as is taking photos from the lake's beach picnic grounds on the southernmost tip of shoreline. Here you have the full length of Elk Lake before you, with South Sister and Mount Bachelor in the background. During the snowbound months of winter, access to Elk Lake is by snowmobile, Sno-Cat van, or dogsled (really!) to a world of groomed cross-country ski and snowshoe trails amid spectacular alpine scenery.

Not far away, the red volcanic cinder highway contrasts with the black lava flows en route to aqua-tinted **Devils Lake.** From the northern end of this lake, on the other side of the highway, you'll find **Devil's Pile,** an agglomeration of lava flows and volcanic glass where *Apollo 11* astronauts reportedly culled a rock to deposit on the lunar surface. The road winds around to the Mount Bachelor Summit ski lifts. From the deck in front of the sport shop-cafeteria complex, you can see the Three Sisters and Broken Top.

You might want to hike the short trail to **Todd Lake,** canoe **Sparks Lake** in the shadow of Broken Top and South Sister, or visit the **Ray Atkeson Memorial,** dedicated to Oregon's "photographer laureate." All are between Devil's Pile and the ski lifts. From Mount Bachelor it's a 20-minute drive back to Sunriver.

Area from the **Green Lakes Trailhead,** 27 miles west of Bend. It's about 4.5 miles from the trailhead along waterfall-studded Fall Creek, past a big lava flow, to Green Lakes. From Green Lakes, the trail continues to the pass between Broken Top and South Sister. This trail is extremely popular, so it's best to hike it on a weekday.

## Devils Lake

The eerily green **Devils Lake,** 29 miles west of Bend, has a very nice walk-in campground (June-Oct., NW Forest Pass required) with no piped water and an easy lakeside trail. Just across the highway from the lake is a popular trailhead used to climb 10,358-foot **South Sister,** Oregon's third-highest peak. Many choose to do this challenging but not technical 11-mile round-trip as an overnight backpacking trip. Many more hike the trail as far as the pretty Moraine Lake area (about 3.5 miles), then return along the same route.

## Elk Lake

A resort and a marina mean that this is not the quietest lake in the Cascades. **Elk Lake** is just about the only place along this road that you'll see sailboats, and it's also a good swimming lake by August. **Elk Lake Resort** (541/480-7378, www.elklakeresort.net) makes a good base for exploring the local trails if you are not camping, and are open during the winter for cross-country skiers and snowmobilers. Accommodations range from small rustic cabins ($58) to larger but still rustic cabins ($139-199) and modern homes ($399-459).

An on-site restaurant is surprisingly good. During the summer, the resort offers a marina and campsites ($15-35); in addition, there's a U.S. Forest Service campground ($14).

## Hosmer Lake

Just off the highway and 39 miles from Bend, **Hosmer Lake** is a favorite fishing and canoeing lake. It's stocked with Atlantic salmon, but don't count on eating them. Fishing is limited to catch-and-release fly-fishing with barbless hooks. It's worth visiting Hosmer Lake for its spectacular views of Mount Bachelor, South Sister, and Broken Top. Of the two campgrounds on the lake, **South** (mid-June-late Sept., $12) has the best views and the best lake access but no drinking water.

## Lava Lake

Lava flows formed a dam that created **Lava Lake,** which is fed largely by underground springs. Rainbow trout, brook trout, whitefish, and illegally introduced tui chub live in the lake, which is 30 feet deep at its deepest point and open to bait fishing as well as fly-fishing. A lakeside **lodge** (541/382-9443) rents boats and operates an RV park; there is also a U.S. Forest Service campground (early June-mid-Oct., $16) with drinking water near the resort.

## Little Lava Lake

Make a pilgrimage to **Little Lava Lake** and stand at the headwaters of the Deschutes River. Groundwater from the snowpack percolates down from the Mount Bachelor and Three Sisters area to fill the lake (it's thought that a large groundwater reservoir exists upstream); the Deschutes exits the lake as a meandering stream, flowing south about 8.4 miles to Crane Prairie Reservoir. Little Lava Lake shares a highway turnoff with Lava Lake. The campground here (June-Sept., $14) has water.

## Cultus Lake

Glacier-formed **Cultus Lake** is popular with campers, swimmers, boaters, water-skiers, Jet Skiers, and windsurfers. Anglers go for the big lake trout, also called mackinaw. An easy hiking trail follows the northern shore of the lake and then heads north along the Winopee Lake Trail to Teddy Lakes. From the trailhead to Teddy Lakes is about four miles.

The **Cultus Lake Resort** (541/408-1560 summer, 541/389-3230 winter, www.cultuslakeresort.com, mid-May-mid-Sept.) rents rustic cabins ($85-175), motorboats, canoes, kayaks, and personal watercraft; it also operates a restaurant. During the peak summer

Hosmer Lake is known for its good fishing.

season, cabins are rented only by the week. The U.S. Forest Service has a campground ($18).

## Crane Prairie Reservoir

**Crane Prairie Reservoir,** an artificial lake, is a breeding ground for ospreys. These large birds, sometimes known as fish hawks, nest in the snags surrounding the lake and fish by plunging headfirst into the water from great heights. Cormorants, terns, bald eagles, and a variety of ducks are also commonly seen. Humans also like to fish—the most-prized fish is a "cranebow," a rainbow trout that grows almost freakishly large in this shallow nutrient-rich reservoir.

A U.S. Forest Service campground (reservations www.reserveamerica.com, May-Oct., $18) here has drinking water; the private **Crane Prairie Resort** (541/383-3939, www.crane-prairie-resort-guides.com) RV park ($38), cabins ($65-90), marina, and fishing guide service are also located here.

## Wickiup Reservoir

The area of the Deschutes River around present-day **Wickiup Reservoir** was a traditional Native American camping area during the fall. When the dam was completed in 1949, these campsites were flooded. Today, the reservoir, about 60 miles from Bend, is known for its relatively warm water and good fishing, especially for brown trout, which can weigh in at over 20 pounds. Kokanee and coho salmon as well as rainbow trout, brook trout, whitefish, and the nasty and invasive tui chub also live here. At Wickiup Reservoir, camp at **Gull**

**Point Campground** (reservations www. recreation.gov, $18), with drinking water; or across an access road at **North Twin Lake** ($14), with no drinking water, and **South Twin Lake** ($18), with drinking water, both small natural lakes that flank the reservoir.

From Wickiup Reservoir, Highway 42 heads east and north along the Fall River toward Sunriver. Highway 46, the Cascade Lakes Highway, continues south past Davis Lake.

## Davis Lake

It takes a little doing to get to large and shallow **Davis Lake,** and many of those who make it come for fly-fishing. It's known for large rainbow trout as well as illegally introduced largemouth bass. Most anglers use boats or float tubes because the vegetation along the shoreline and the muddy lake bottom make it difficult to wade.

Davis Lake was formed about 6,000 years ago when a lava flow cut off Odell Creek. A fire in 2003 wiped out the West Davis campground; the **East Davis Campground** ($12), with drinking water, was reduced in size by the fire but looks less bare every year.

## INFORMATION

For information about sites along the Cascade Lakes Highway, stop at the **Cascade Lakes Welcome Station** (18500 Cascade Lakes Hwy., milepost 7, 521/383-5300, www.fs.usda.gov, 8am-4pm daily summer, shorter hours Apr. and Oct.-Nov.) or contact the **Deschutes National Forest** (63095 Deschutes Market Rd., Bend, 541/383-5300, www.fs.usda.gov).

# Willamette Pass and Vicinity

In the area around Willamette Pass, it's easy to see the shift from the greener, damper, Douglas fir-dominated west side of the Cascades to the dry east side, forested by lodgepole and ponderosa pines. Each of the lakes in the high country has its own partisans—families who have camped in the same spot for decades—and its own personality. Campgrounds are available at Crescent, Odell, and Waldo Lakes. Pick one place to explore in depth, or hop among the lakes.

## SIGHTS

### Crescent Lake

On the sun-drenched east side of Willamette Pass, **Crescent Lake** is home to a tremendously popular campground ($18, $30-40 yurts) and the **Crescent Lake Resort** (541/433-2505, http://crescentlakeresort.com, year-round, 3-night minimum in summer, cabins $95-215), an easy place to spend a few days. Rent a fishing boat, kayak, or bike from the resort. Large lake trout (including one whopping 30-pounder) are regularly pulled from the lake. Crescent Lake is about three miles south of Highway 58 via Deschutes National Forest Road 60 from Crescent Lake junction.

### Odell Lake

Two resorts, several summer homes, and campgrounds surround 3,582-acre **Odell Lake,** 30 miles southeast of Oakridge on Highway 58. Situated in a deep glacial trough, the lake probably filled with water about 11,000 years ago when a terminal moraine blocked the drainage of Odell Creek. Due to the depth of the lake and the nearly perpetual west-to-east winds that blow through Willamette Pass, the water averages a cold 39°F. Those breezes, however, help to keep mosquitoes away and make for some of the best sailing in the Cascades.

**Odell Lake Lodge** (541/433-2540 or 800/434-2540, www.odelllakeresort.com, year-round, rooms $80-160, cabins $110-340, campsites $14-18) is a charming, though rustic, typical old-time Oregon resort. It is popular with cross-country skiers during the winter. Skiers may want to take advantage of the large Northwest Territory cabin ($340), which sleeps as many as 16 people.

Moorages at Odell Lake are available for rent through the lodge, as are canoes, powerboats, and sailboats. The lodge has a complete tackle shop to help outfit you to catch the kokanee and mackinaw that inhabit the icy waters, and rental equipment is available. The restaurant is open for all meals. The lodge also maintains its own system of trails, which provide good biking in the summer and cross-country skiing in the winter. An area map can guide you to various waterfalls. Bikes and ski equipment can be rented, or play basketball, volleyball, badminton, and horseshoes. Tots and toddlers will enjoy the sandbox, the toy library, and the swings.

Across the lake from the lodge is **Shelter Cove Resort** (W. Odell Lake Rd., Cascade Summit, 541/433-2548 or 800/647-2729, www.highwaywestvacations.com, rooms $270-333, cabins $138-283, camping $45-53), which features nine cabins complete with kitchens, over 70 campsites, and a marina with moorages. The resort's general store has everything from groceries, tackle, and boat rentals to Sno-Park permits and fishing or hunting licenses. The September-October spawning displays by Odell Lake's landlocked salmon are unforgettable.

Two U.S. Forest Service campgrounds, **Sunset Cove** (May-Oct., $16) and **Trapper Creek** (reservations www.recreation.gov, June-Oct., $16) are on the lake; both have drinking water.

### Willamette Pass Ski Area

**Willamette Pass** (541/345-7669, www.willamettepass.com, 9am-4pm Wed.-Sun.

Dec.-Mar., $52 adults, $32 seniors and ages 6-10, hourly $14), 69 miles southeast of Eugene on Highway 58, has some of the most challenging runs in the state as well as a multitude of beginner and intermediate trails. You'll find some of the steepest runs, unlike the open chutes or powder bowls at other ski areas. Since Willamette Pass plows its own parking lot, you will not need a Sno-Park permit. Night skiing (Fri.-Sat. Dec.-Mar.) is possible.

The ski area grooms trails for both regular cross-country and skate skiing (10am-4pm Sat.-Sun. and holidays, trail pass $15 adults). In addition, there are several popular Sno-Park areas near Willamette Pass, including one right by the ski area with several fairly challenging trails; a couple follow the Pacific Crest Trail, which crosses Highway 58 at Willamette Pass. For information on cross-country skiing from this and other local Sno-Park areas, contact the Willamette National Forest's **Middle Fork Ranger District** (46375 Hwy. 58, Westfir, 541/782-2283, www.fs.usda.gov/willamette).

## Waldo Lake

The Waldo Lake Wilderness is a 37,000-acre gem 70 miles southeast of Eugene via Highway 58 (take Forest Rd. 5897 before the Willamette Pass turnoff, then 10 miles to the lake). The centerpiece of this alpine paradise is 10-square-mile **Waldo Lake,** the third largest in Oregon, whose waters were once rated the purest in the country in a nationwide study of 30 lakes. Peer down into the 420-foot-deep green translucent depths to see rocky reefs and fish 50-100 feet below.

No motorized craft are allowed on the lake, but canoeing, sailing, trout fishing, and windsurfing complement hiking and cross-country skiing to give you different ways to experience the lake and the surrounding region. Add wildlife-watching, highlighted by the early September rutting season of Roosevelt elk, and you'll quickly understand why Waldo Lake is a favorite. The 22-mile loop trail around the lake is popular with mountain bikers and backpackers, and day hikes on the south end edify less diehard recreationists. Visit in late August-mid-October to avoid a plague of summer mosquitoes and early winter snowfall. Catch views of 8,744-foot Diamond Peak in the distance.

Waldo Lake has three very popular campgrounds: **Shadow Bay, North Waldo,** and **Islet** (541/822-3799, www.fs.usda.gov/willamette, reservations www.recreation.gov, late

Waldo Lake

June-mid-Oct., $22), all with drinking water. Shadow Bay has the most mosquitoes; North Waldo and Islet are windier. To get to the lake, take Highway 58 for 24 miles southeast of Oakridge. Take a left on Forest Road 5897. It is five miles to Forest Road 5896, which takes you to Shadow Bay, and 10 miles down Forest Road 5897 to North Waldo. Boat docks and launching facilities are available, plus good sailing and fishing; gas motors are prohibited on the lake. Many trails lead to small backcountry lakes from here, so this is a good place to establish a base camp.

From the North Waldo boat launch, hike up to **Rigdon Lakes** via Trail 3555. It's about 0.5 miles to the first lake. If you want a longer loop hike, continue north to two more lakes and the intersection with Trail 3583, turn left, then hike generally southward, back to the lake, and take a left onto Trail 3590, which follows the lakeshore east to your starting point.

# Sisters

Sisters (pop. 2,600), named after its backdrop to the south, the Three Sisters peaks, was established in 1888 when nearby Camp Polk, a short-lived military outpost, was dismantled. The town's 19th-century flavor has been preserved with wooden boardwalks, 1880s-style storefronts, and old-fashioned Western hospitality. Some people are quick to lambaste the thematic look of Sisters as a cheap gimmick to lure tourists, while others enjoy the lovingly re-created ambience and the abundance of charming, independently owned shops, including one of the world's best clock shops.

As well as being a food, fuel, and lodging stop, Sisters is also a jumping-off point for a wealth of outdoor activities. Skiing at Hoodoo Ski Area, fly-fishing and rafting on the Metolius River, and backpacking into the great Three Sisters Wilderness are just a few of the popular local pursuits. Nearby luxury resorts such as Black Butte Ranch, an annual rodeo, and a nationally famous quilting event add to the appeal of this vintage village.

## SIGHTS
### Three Creek Lake and Tam McArthur Rim
**Three Creek Lake,** tucked under **Tam McArthur Rim,** is a good place for a summer swim, especially if you have an inflatable raft to prevent full-body immersion in the often quite cold water. A tiny lakeside store rents rowboats; from the center of the lake you'll get a good view of the rim, named for the original author of the classic reference book *Oregon Geographic Names.*

From the lake, trails head into the Three Sisters Wilderness Area. One leads up to the 7,700-foot rim, and from the top the views of the Three Sisters and Broken Top are quite astounding. Snows can be heavy (the lake is at 6,500 feet), so don't count on hiking this trail before July. A small lakeside **campground** ($14) at Three Creek Lake has no drinking water but is a pleasant place to spend a couple of days in midsummer; bring insect repellent.

To get here from Sisters, turn south on Elm Street, which becomes Forest Road 16, and follow it south about 17 miles to the lake. Be prepared for a couple of miles of fairly rough dirt road. During the winter, Road 16 between the lake and Sisters has a couple of Sno-Park areas that mark cross-country ski trails.

### Black Butte
Hike up to the **Black Butte** lookout towers for a bird's-eye view of the Sisters area. It's about two miles of uphill hiking, often in full sun, to the top of the cinder cone; bring plenty of water. To reach the trailhead, take U.S. 20 west from Sisters, turn north (right) onto Forest Road 11 (Green Ridge Rd.), and pass Indian Ford campground; turn left onto Road 1110 and follow it 5.1 miles to the trailhead.

## ★ Metolius River

About 10 miles from Sisters is the second-largest tributary of the Deschutes River, the **Metolius.** To get here, take the Camp Sherman Highway off U.S. 20 five miles west of Sisters. This road will take you around Black Butte. On the north face of this steep, evergreen-covered cinder cone is the source of the Metolius. A 0.25-mile trail takes you to a railing where you can see the water bubbling out of the ground.

Known simply as "The Spring," the water wells up out of the earth at a constant 48°F. Native rainbow trout thrive in the cold spring-fed waters of the upper Metolius, but they are not necessarily easy to catch—the water is so clear that the fish are extremely selective about what they'll take, and flies must be both perfect looking and perfectly presented. A beautiful riverside trail follows the Metolius as it meanders through the ponderosa pines past many excellent fishing holes. Drift boats are used to tackle the harder-to-reach places along this 25-mile waterway. Bring a bike along to the Metolius; bike trails are being developed here all the time, and they are perfect for easy-going family rides.

Five miles downstream from Camp Sherman, seven miles from the head of the Metolius Trail, is the **Wizard Falls Fish Hatchery,** which is open to visitors daily. Over 2.5 million fish, including Atlantic salmon, brook and rainbow trout, and kokanee salmon, are raised here annually. The hatchery is the only place in the state that stocks Atlantic salmon, which are transferred to Hosmer Lake.

## SPORTS AND RECREATION
### Skiing

Twenty miles (30 minutes' drive) west of Sisters on Highway 126 is one of Oregon's most family-oriented skiing areas, **Hoodoo** (541/822-3799, conditions 541/822-3337, http://skihoodoo.com, 9am-4pm Sun.-Tues. and Thurs., 9am-9pm Fri.-Sat., $51-54 adults, $31-34 seniors and children), with five chairlifts and a rope tow. The maximum vertical drop is 1,035 feet, and the runs are evenly split among advanced, intermediate, and beginner. The ski area's cross-country trails ($16-19) are groomed Friday-Sunday; on other days cross-country skiing is free.

Self-guided but supported three-day hut-to-hut backcountry ski trips start near the base of Mount Bachelor and trace the eastern edge of the Three Sisters Wilderness Area

The Metolius is one of Oregon's most enchanting rivers.

to the Three Creeks Sno-Park near Sisters. **Three Sisters Backcountry** (http://three-sistersbackcountry.com, $225 pp) will set you up with maps, hut lodging, food to make your own meals, and shuttles.

### Horseback Riding

**Black Butte Stables** (541/595-2061, www.blackbuttestables.com) at **Black Butte Ranch** (U.S. 20, 8 miles west of Sisters) has several packages that take you down trails in the shadow of the Three Sisters. Rides range from the one-hour Big Loop trail ride for beginning riders ($50) to the all-day Black Butte Posse ride ($175-225). Kids can take pony rides ($20).

### Golf

Two well-groomed courses, the more open and forgiving Big Meadow and Glaze Meadow, which demands precise shots, are found at **Black Butte Ranch** (U.S. 20, 8 miles west of Sisters, 855/210-5305, www.blackbutteranch.com, $79 for 18 holes peak hours). Both have tall trees and lush fairways from tee to green. Three miles outside Sisters, the highly regarded **Aspen Lakes** (541/549-4653, www.aspenlakes.com, $78 for 18 holes peak hours) offers 27 holes in the shadow of the Three Sisters. Bent-grass fairways and distinct volcanic red-cinder bunkers add to the stunning mountain vistas.

## ENTERTAINMENT AND EVENTS

The annual **Sisters Rodeo** (541/549-0121 or 800/827-7522) happens the second weekend of June, with calf-roping, country dances, a buckaroo breakfast, and a parade. A huge outdoor **quilt show** takes place during the second week of July, blanketing the town with color. Also noteworthy is the annual **Sisters Folk Festival,** held the weekend after Labor Day and attracting some of the biggest names in blues and folk. Contact the **Sisters Chamber of Commerce** (291 E. Main St., 541/549-0251, www.sisterscountry.com) for the schedule of events.

## FOOD

A number of pretty average but often busy restaurants line Sisters's main street, Cascade Avenue. The hottest spot among them is **Sisters Saloon** (190 E. Cascade Ave., 541/549-7427, www.sisterssaloon.net, 11am-midnight daily, $8-32), where you can dine on anything from stuffed zucchini to a rib eye steak. Live music on Saturday nights is a highlight, as are the Wednesday-night poker games upstairs in this refurbished 1912 hotel.

A somewhat hip and healthy alternative lies a block off the main drag: **Angeline's Bakery & Cafe** (121 W. Main Ave., 541/549-9122, http://angelinesbakery.com, 6:30am-6pm daily June-Oct., 6:30am-4pm daily Nov.-May) serves homemade baked goods, salads, wraps, and fresh juices, with lots of gluten-free and vegan options. Try the raw zucchini "noodles" with pumpkin-seed pesto; if you really need a nutritional boost, chase it with a green smoothie. During the summer, Angeline's stays open late most Saturday nights and hosts music.

The best breakfast and lunch food in town is at ★ **Cottonwood Cafe** (403 E. Hood Ave., 541/549-2699, www.cottonwoodsisters.com, 8am-3pm Thurs.-Tues., $10-13), an intimate cottage with casual but delicious fare. Breakfast is fantastic, with smoked salmon scramble and *huevos motuleños* (eggs over ham, black beans, and tortillas). Lunch sandwiches include a ratatouille wrap and an open-faced ocean melt.

In nearby Camp Sherman, the ★ **Kokanee Cafe** (25545 SW Forest Rd. 1419, 541/595-6420, www.kokaneecafe.com, 5pm-close Tues.-Sun. summer, reservations recommended, $18-36) is known for its fresh and innovative cuisine served in a small, simply furnished dining room. The menu is fairly limited, and varies from year to year, but food is generally quite good. Dinner reservations are crucial during the summer and fishing season. The Kokanee usually takes a break during the winter and has scaled-back hours in the spring; this also varies year to year, so check ahead.

Down at Suttle Lake, the crisply stylish **Boathouse** (13300 U.S. 20, 541/638-7001, www.thesuttlelodge.com, 7am-11pm daily, $11-20) at the Suttle Lodge is casual, with a short list of sandwiches, chowder, and salads. The setting is great, and it's a fine spot for a burger, a beer, and a few tunes on the vintage jukebox after a swim or paddle in the lake.

## ACCOMMODATIONS

Although Sisters has plenty of in-town accommodations, many visitors to the area would rather stay in the lodges near the lovely Metolius River. Note that cell phone service around the Metolius village of Camp Sherman and at nearby Suttle Lake is spotty to nonexistent. If constant contact is important to you, ask about cell signal when you make reservations.

The ★ **Sisters Motor Lodge** (511 W. Cascade St., 541/549-2551 or 877/549-5446, www.sistersmotorlodge.com, $159-179) was built in 1939, when the North Santiam Highway first opened to auto traffic. It's set back from the highway, within easy walking distance of the shops and boutiques of Sisters. Beds are decorated with quilts, and the kitchenettes have charmingly retro appliances and Formica tables; pets are allowed in some guest rooms.

The **Best Western Ponderosa Lodge** (505 U.S. 20, 541/549-1234 or 888/549-4321, www.bestwesternsisters.com, $155-215) is a large ranch-style resort motel set back from the road in the scattered pines. Rooms feature private balconies with views of the mountains and the adjacent Deschutes National Forest. Other amenities include a spa, a heated pool, and included continental breakfast.

**Sisters Bunkhouse** (114 N. Oak St., 541/588-6122, www.sistersbunkhouse.com, $159) is a four-room downtown hotel within an easy walk to restaurants and shops. This false-fronted little hotel is really more of a B&B without the breakfast but with friendly on-site innkeepers.

Eight miles west of Sisters on U.S. 20, **Black Butte Ranch** (541/595-1252 or 866/901-2961, www.blackbutteranch.com, $150-650) sits in line with other Cascade peaks in a setting of ponderosa pines, lush meadows, and aspen-bordered streams. Over 16 miles of trails thread through the 1,800 acres of forested grounds. Accommodations include deluxe hotel-type bedrooms, one- to three-bedroom condominium suites, and resort homes. The resort includes golf courses, bike trails, tennis courts, several swimming pools, organized kids' activities and day camps, and a fitness center with yoga and other classes.

Right on the edge of town, ★ **FivePine Lodge** (1021 Desperado Tr., 541/549-5900, www.fivepinelodge.com, $209-347) is a lovely newer resort with convention center facilities and an environmentally sensitive approach. Stay in a spacious suite in the large stone-and-timber lodge or in a classy Craftsman-style cabin with Amish-built wood furniture (pets are permitted in a couple of the cabins). All accommodations include breakfast, a wine reception, and access to the on-site Sisters Athletic Club, which has a 25-yard lap pool and a variety of fitness classes. During the summer, an outdoor pool is open, and use of cruiser bikes is included. Also in the FivePine complex is an upscale spa, a brewpub, a movie theater, and a Mexican restaurant.

In a residential area close to downtown, find the **Blue Spruce Bed & Breakfast** (444 S. Spruce St., 541/549-9644 or 888/328-9644, www.bluesprucebnb.com, 2-night minimum, $159-189). Designed and built from the ground up as a B&B, the five guest rooms have outdoorsy Western themes but plenty of comfort (the "bunkhouse" room, while not a bunkhouse at all, has fewer decorative touches). All baths have a shower and a two-person whirlpool tub. Bikes are available for guest use, and rooms have mini fridges and fireplaces.

**Lake Creek Lodge** (13375 SW Forest Rd. 1419, Camp Sherman, 541/516-3030 or 800/797-6331, www.lakecreeklodge.com, minimum stay may be required, $190-385, off-season $140-335) is near Camp Sherman in the Metolius Recreation Area. This full-service resort has a variety of cabins, some dating back to the 1920s and some built within the past few years. Tennis, swimming, and fishing are some of the many activities. Although the cabins have kitchenettes, many summertime guests like to eat at least one dinner at the lodge restaurant (8am-2pm, dinner seating 6pm Wed.-Sun. July-early Sept., dinner $29 adults, $15 ages 5-12). Dinner is served family-style on the deck or in the pine-paneled main lodge and features a different selection of entrées each day, complemented by homemade breads, salads, and desserts. Lake Creek caters especially well to families; pets are allowed in some cabins.

Another Metolius retreat is at **Cold Springs Resort** (25615 Cold Springs Resort Lane, Camp Sherman, 541/595-6271, www.coldspringsresort.com, $178-198). The cabins feature artesian well water. A footbridge across the Metolius River connects the resort to Camp Sherman, where groceries, a church, and a café are within easy walking distance. Pets are allowed ($10) but must be kept on a leash and not left unattended. The resort also operates an RV park with full hookups ($40). The rustic but comfy cabins at the ★ **Metolius River Lodges** (12390 SW Forest Rd. 1419-700, 541/595-6290, www.metoliusriverlodges.com, $139-335) are tucked in by the Metolius River near the Camp Sherman store. The most coveted cabins have decks extending over the river, and the majority have fireplaces and kitchens.

Wedged between giant ponderosa pines and the banks of the Metolius, behind the Kokanee Café, are the 12 elegant cabins of the ★ **Metolius River Resort** (25551 SW Forest Rd. 1419, 541/595-6281 or 800/818-7688, www.metoliusriverresort.com, around $200). These beautiful wooden 900-square-foot cabins are bright and airy with lots of windows. Two stories high, they comfortably sleep four to six and feature full modern kitchens, baths, river-rock fireplaces stocked with firewood, and river-view decks. Reservations well in advance are a must.

A few miles west of the Metolius River turnoff on U.S. 20 is the turnoff to Suttle Lake and the hipster-friendly **Suttle Lodge** (13300 U.S. 20, 541/638-7001, www.thesuttlelodge.com, rustic cabins $125, rooms, suites, and deluxe cabins $275-400), where a Western theme predominates, thanks to the team behind Portland's Ace Hotel. The least expensive accommodations are in newly built and very clean but rustic cabins that share a central bathhouse; lodge rooms and waterfront cabins are simple but much more upscale. Suttle Lodge is pet-friendly, the boathouse restaurant serves three meals daily, and canoe and paddleboard rentals are available.

For a horse-centered stay, consider the **Long Hollow Ranch** (541/923-1901, www.lhranch.com, $895 pp d for 3 days, $1,775 pp d for 6 days), a guest ranch offering trail rides, cattle drives, and horsemanship lessons. Rates include all meals and on-ranch activities.

## Camping

**Bend Sisters Garden RV Resort** (67667 U.S. 20, 541/549-3021, www.bendsistersgardenrv.com, $58-63 RVs, $68-188 cabins) is a sprawling RV park on the road to Bend, with a pool, a fishing pond, and miniature golf. It's four miles from downtown Sisters, with good views of the mountains.

Six miles northwest of Sisters on Highway 126, find **Indian Ford Campground** (541/549-7700, www.fs.usda.gov, mid-May-Oct., $12), with no water, the closest public campground to town. Farther west on Highway 126, you'll hit the turnoff to the **Metolius River campgrounds** (877/444-6777, www.recreation.gov, $12-18), a number of very pleasant U.S. Forest Service campgrounds strung along the river upstream and downstream from the hub of Camp Sherman. Drinking water is available at all except Candle Creek.

Several **campgrounds** (reservations 877/444-6777, www.recreation.gov, May-early Oct., $16) on Suttle Lake have drinking water and boat ramps. It's a popular place to fish, water-ski, windsurf, and swim. **Link Creek** campground has the longest season and also has a few yurts (no pets, $40).

A handful of campgrounds open only in summer can be found near Sisters on Highway 242, the old McKenzie Highway. Near the source of Trout Creek, pretty **Cold Springs Campground** ($16), just five miles west of town on Highway 242 at 3,400 feet in elevation, has drinking water and 23 sites for tents and trailers up to 22 feet. Near the pass at 5,200 feet is the rustic 10-site **Lava Camp Lake Campground** (late June-Oct. depending on snow, free), with no water but the allure of proximity to the Pacific Crest Trail and the Three Sisters Wilderness. Information

about these campgrounds is available from **Sisters Ranger Station** (Pine St. and U.S. 20, 541/549-7700, www.fs.usda.gov/main/deschutes).

## INFORMATION

Detailed information about the geology, natural history, wildlife, wilderness areas, and numerous recreational opportunities in the Metolius Recreation Area can be obtained from the **Sisters Ranger Station** (Pine St. and U.S. 20, 541/549-7700, www.fs.usda.gov/centraloregon) and the **Sisters Chamber of Commerce** (291 E. Main St., 541/549-0251, www.sisterscountry.com).

# Redmond

Sixteen miles north of Bend is rapidly growing Redmond (pop. 26,000), a hub centrally located among Madras, Prineville, Bend, and Sisters. Even with a new highway bypass, traffic can get congested. The city got its start when the Deschutes Irrigation and Power Company established irrigation canals here in the early 1900s. The railroad soon came, and real estate traders soon followed. Like most central Oregon towns, it was once home to several lumber mills, but now, thanks to its regional airport and nearby resorts, tourism plays a major role in the economy.

## SIGHTS
### Peter Skene Ogden Scenic Wayside
Nine miles north of Redmond on U.S. 97, stop to peer into the dramatic Crooked River Gorge, a 300-foot-deep canyon. The old railroad trestle spanning the gorge was built in 1911 and helped to establish Redmond as a transportation hub. The old highway bridge, now open only to foot traffic, was built in 1926; before it was constructed, travelers had to descend the canyon walls to ford the river. The current highway bridge dates to 2003.

## ★ Smith Rock State Park
The majestic spires towering above the Crooked River on U.S. 97 north of Redmond are part of 623-acre **Smith Rock State Park** (9241 NE Crooked River Dr., Terrebonne, 541/548-7501, www.oregonstateparks.org, $5 day-use). Named for a soldier who fell to his death from the highest promontory (3,230 feet) in the configuration, the park is a popular retreat for hikers, rock climbers, and casual visitors. Picnic tables, drinking water, and restrooms can be found near the parking area. The more adventurous can camp out in the park's primitive (except for the showers) walk-in camping area ($5 pp), near the park entrance; campfires are prohibited.

Although Smith Rock is known for its rock climbing, many come to hike or mountain bike. Seven miles of well-marked trails follow the Crooked River and wind up the canyon walls onto the ridgetops. Because the area is delicate and extremely sensitive to erosion, it's important not to blaze any trails, because they may leave visible scars for years.

Some of the sport-climbing routes at Smith Rock are as difficult and challenging as any you'll find in the United States. Most of the mountain's 17-million-year-old volcanic rock is soft and crumbly, making descents extra challenging. Chocks, nuts, friends, and other clean-climbing equipment and techniques are encouraged to reduce damage to the rock. On certain routes where these methods would prove impractical, permanent anchors have been placed. Climbers should use these fixed bolts (after testing them first) to minimize impact on the rock face. Stop in at the park-side store to pick up a climbing guide to the routes at Smith Rock that do not require mounting additional fixed protection.

Climbers should never disturb birds of prey and their young in their lofty aeries. Golden eagles nest on the cliffs past the far end of the parking area; bald eagles have nested in a tree visible from the camping area. Stop in at the park visitors center (housed in a yurt by the parking area) for details on these birds and other park flora and fauna. Finally, pack plenty of water. The Crooked River is contaminated with chemicals from nearby farmlands and isn't suitable for drinking, and even a short hike in this often-hot park will leave you thirsty.

The Crooked River runs through Smith Rock State Park.

## SPORTS AND RECREATION
### Golf
**Eagle Crest Resort** (1522 Cline Falls Rd., 541/923-4653, www.eagle-crest.com) has three 18-hole golf courses: Resort and Ridge ($76 for 18 holes, $57 resort guests) as well as Challenge (a short 18 holes designed for 3-hour playing time, $46). **Crooked River Ranch** (5195 SW Clubhouse Rd., 541/923-6343, www.crookedriverranch.com, $44-51 for 18 holes), an 18-hole par-71 course, is wide open with few trees, but that doesn't detract from the challenge or the scenic vistas.

A true desert course found in Redmond that requires shot accuracy is the **Juniper Golf Club** (1938 SW Elkhorn Ave., 541/548-3121, www.playjuniper.com, 18 holes $79-82). This is an 18-hole par-72 course that snakes through the juniper and lava of the high desert. The prevailing winds and abundance of rocks off the fairway challenge your shot-making abilities.

### Rock Climbing
Whether you need climbing advice, a carabiner and a sling, a beer, or a massage, **Redpoint Climbing Supply** (8222 N. U.S. 97, Terrebonne, 800/923-6207, www.redpointclimbing.com, 7am-8pm Mon.-Thurs., 7am-10pm Fri.-Sat.), at U.S. 97 and Smith Rock Way, is the place to find it. Climbing lessons, both private and group, are offered by **Chockstone Climbing Guides** (541/318-7170, www.chockstoneclimbing.com), known for its women's programs, and **Smith Rock Climbing Guides** (541/788-6225, www.smithrockclimbingguides.com).

## FOOD
Redmond makes its mark on the culinary world more by its locally raised Kobe beef than by its restaurants, but increasingly there are good places to eat here. The **Brickhouse** (412 SW 6th St., 541/526-1782, www.brickhousesteakhouse.com, 4pm-close daily, $19-49) is a popular and very good steak and seafood restaurant, serving high-quality meat

and using many local ingredients. The interior, with its exposed brick walls and local art, is inviting.

★ **Diego's Spirited Kitchen** (447 SW 6th St., 541/316-2002, 11am-10pm daily, $10-32) is an upscale Mexican restaurant, emphasizing Southwestern Mexican cuisine with French and Italian influences. Pork osso buco slow-roasted with mushrooms is served over mashed potatoes with truffle oil; pork carnitas ravioli and seafood pasta are cooked up alongside burritos and enchiladas.

The **Seventh Street Brew House** (855 SW 7th St., 541/923-1795, 11:30am-10pm Sun.-Thurs., 11:30am-11pm Fri.-Sat., $9-12) is just a block off busy 6th Street and serves Cascade Lakes beer as well as pizza and pub food. Redmond has a couple of other noteworthy pubs: English-style **Pig and Pound** (427 SW 8th St., 541/526-1697, 4pm-9pm Mon.-Thurs., 4pm-10pm Fri., noon-10pm Sat., noon-9pm Sun., $8-12) is complete with bangers and mash and local and imported beers on tap; **Smith Rock Brewing Company** (546 NW 7th St., 541/279-7005, http://smithrockbrewing.com, 11:30am-2pm and 5pm-7:45pm Tues.-Thurs., 11:30am-2pm and 5pm-8:45pm Fri., noon-2:30pm and 5pm-8:45pm Sat., $6-12), where Smith Rock brews and a few other local beers share rotating taps, has woodsy decor—in nice weather, this pub has good outside seating. Burgers and sandwiches are the specialty.

On the road to Smith Rock, the **Terrebonne Depot** (400 NW Smith Rock Way, Terrebonne, 541/548-5030, www.terrebonnedepot.com, 11am-9pm Wed.-Sun., 11:30am-8:30pm Mon., $10-26) offers fresh food, including a good selection of vegetarian options and pizza, in the gorgeously renovated historic Terrebonne train depot. Climbers and hikers can also get picnic lunches to go, though be forewarned that service is notoriously slow.

## ACCOMMODATIONS

The **Lodge at Eagle Crest** (1522 Cline Falls Rd., 855/682-4786, www.eagle-crest.com, $169-196), five miles west of Redmond, is operated by Holiday Inn and offers rooms and one-bedroom suites. The terrain and vegetation are representative of the high desert, and the backdrop is views of eight Cascade peaks. Ask about ski and golf packages. This is a low-key family-oriented place with rental bikes, swimming pools, and a sports center. Vacation rental homes are also available through the resort.

In town, the **Best Western Plus Rama Inn** (2630 SW 17th Place, 541/548-8080, www.bestwestern.com, $179-194) is a comfortable place to spend a night or two, with continental breakfast and an indoor pool. Rock climbers tend to camp, but when that gets old, the **Hub Motel** (1128 NW 6th St., 541/548-2101 or 800/784-3482, http://thehubmotel.com, $60-75) is inexpensive, close to Smith Rock, allows dogs, and has kitchenettes.

Tents and RVs are welcome at the **Crooked River Ranch RV Park** (14875 SW Hays Lane, 541/923-1441, www.crookedriverranch.com, $28 tents, $38-40 RVs). Stay at Smith Rock State Park in the walk-in **Bivy Campground** (9241 NE Crooked River Dr., Terrebonne, 541/548-7501, www.oregonstateparks.org, $5 day-use). A primitive option near Smith Rock is the **Skull Hollow Campgrond** (541/416-6640, $10), with no water.

# Prineville

Prineville (pop. 9,900), near the geographic center of Oregon, is the oldest incorporated town in the region. It still feels a bit like the Old West, even as it becomes a bedroom community for Bend and home to tech-industry data centers. Prineville gets a meager 10 inches of rain per year, a positive factor for retirees and recreationalists seeking sun.

Prineville is also known as the Gateway to the Ochocos, a heavily wooded mountain range that runs east-west for 50 miles. One of Oregon's least-known recreational areas, the Ochocos are ruggedly pristine. Beyond these mountains stretches the long valley of the John Day River.

## SIGHTS

### A. R. Bowman Museum

A good place to begin your travels in Ochoco country is at the **A. R. Bowman Museum** (246 N. Main St., 541/447-3715, www.crook-countyhistorycenter.org, 10am-5pm Mon.-Fri., 11am-4pm Sat.-Sun. summer, 10am-5pm Tues.-Fri., 11pm-4pm Sat. winter, free). This museum's two floors of exhibits and displays are a notch above most small-town historical museums. Fans of the Old West will enjoy the tack room with saddles, halters, and woolly chaps. Rock hounds will be delighted with the displays of Blue Mountain picture jasper, thunder eggs, and fossils. Other classic displays include a moonshine still, a country store, an upstairs parlor of the early 1900s, and a campfire setup with a graniteware coffeepot and a pound of Bull Durham tobacco.

## SPORTS AND RECREATION

### Hiking

**Steins Pillar** is a distinctive rock outcropping in the Ochoco National Forest about 15 miles northeast of Prineville. A four-mile round-trip hike passes through meadows and old-growth forest with some lovely panoramic views and a final steep, challenging stretch of trail before reaching the rock. From town, head east on U.S. 26 for nine miles and turn north onto Mill Creek Road. Continue for 6.5 miles to the turnoff for the trailhead.

Farther up Mill Creek Road, find Wildcat Campground and a trailhead for the **Mill Creek-Twin Pillars** trail. From the campground, the trail follows Mill Creek into the Mill Creek Wilderness Area. This wet area supports lots of wildflowers and also a few cattle. If you go the full 8.3 miles to the Twin Pillars, a pair of 200-foot-tall volcanic plugs, it's necessary to ford the creek a number of times, which can be difficult early in the season.

Another worthwhile place to visit is **Lookout Mountain,** the highest point in the Ochocos. It's a unique biosphere with 28 plant communities, one of the finest stands of ponderosa pines in the state, lots of elk and deer, a herd of wild mustang, and creeks full of rainbow and brook trout. A seven-mile trail starts near the **Ochoco Ranger Station** (541/416-6500), east of Prineville 22 miles on Forest Road 22 at the campground picnic area, and ends at the summit of Lookout Mountain, from which 11 major peaks are visible. June is the time to visit to see one of the best wildflower displays in the state. To get here, drive 14 miles east from Prineville on U.S. 26, and bear right at the sign for the ranger station.

About halfway between Prineville and Madras on U.S. 26, **Rimrock Springs Wildlife Management Area** has a 1.35-mile trail through fragrant sagebrush and juniper to a wetland created by a small dam. Spring and early summer bring a good display of wildflowers, including bitterroot; lizards, snakes, and many species of birds are also easy to see on this short hike.

### Fishing

The 310-acre **Prineville Reservoir,** 17 miles

# Willows, Wagon Trains, and Range Wars

The Ochoco country, named after a Paiute word for willows, was heavily populated by Native Americans who lived off a bounty of deer, elk, fish, and camas roots. The first significant passage of Europeans through the area was the Lost Wagon Train of 1845. Led by Stephen Meek, brother of the Oregon Territory spokesperson Joe Meek, the pioneers were seeking a route to the Willamette Valley that would be easier than the arduous trek over the Blue Mountains. Instead, they found hardship, starvation, thirst, and death on a tortuous journey through the deserts of Malheur and Harney Counties and along the rugged ridges of the Ochoco Mountains. Their hardships ended when they found the Crooked River and followed it north to The Dalles. Somewhere during the trek, members of the party scooped up gold nuggets and kept them in a blue bucket. Although the legend of the Blue Bucket Mine has since captivated Oregon history buffs, its actual site has never been found.

In 1860, Major Enoch Steen led an expedition through the region, which resulted in a number of geographic features being named after him, including Steens Mountain and Steins Pillar. Eight years later, Barney Prine built a blacksmith shop, a store, and a saloon near the bank of Ochoco Creek; the outpost grew into the city of Prineville, the only town in 10,000 square miles. It was settled by the sons of the pioneers who had come west on wagon trains.

At the turn of the 20th century, cinnabar, the raw ore in which mercury is found, was discovered in the Ochocos, resulting in an influx of miners. About the same time, a range war broke out between the cattle ranchers and the sheepherders. Groups like the Ezee Sheep Shooters and the Crook County Sheep Shooters Association bragged that they had slaughtered 8,000 to 10,000 sheep in 1905 alone. Incensed by this lawlessness, the citizens of Oregon moved to stop the killing; troubles continued for cattle and sheep ranchers and farmers. Harsh winters took their toll on livestock, and the hope that the plains would be receptive to wheat farming was unrealized.

During World War I, many homesteaders gave up and moved to the cities to work for the war effort. In 1917, Prineville made a decision that wound up boosting the local economy. The town built a railroad to Redmond, linking its line with the Union Pacific. Used primarily to haul ponderosa pine logs, the railroad remains the only city-owned railroad still in operation in the United States. In the 1950s a new industry was added to the mainstays of logging, ranching, and farming: Gemstones of high quality were discovered in the Ochocos, prompting a rockhounding and tourism boom that continues to this day.

**BEND AND CENTRAL OREGON**
PRINEVILLE

south of Prineville on Highway 27, was built for irrigation and flood control. A popular year-round boating and fishing lake, it is famous for its huge bass and is also stocked with rainbow trout.

Just downstream from the reservoir dam is a winding stretch of the **Crooked River** that offers some of the best fly-fishing in the state, in an incredibly scenic atmosphere beneath basalt rimrock cliffs. This section of the river is also dotted with a series of campgrounds, all of which are good places to camp and fish. This is a fine place to learn to fly-fish; it's easy to wade into the water away from streamside brush. Nonanglers can climb the short trail up Chimney Rock (from the Chimney Rock campground) to the top of the rimrock. From

there, it's possible to walk along the ridge all afternoon.

**Ochoco Reservoir,** six miles east of Prineville on U.S. 26, is a favorite recreational spot for locals, with year-round fishing, boating, and camping.

## FOOD

Behind a downright scary exterior lies an extremely popular (and not at all frightening) steak house: **Club Pioneer** (1851 NE 3rd St., 541/447-6177, www.clubpioneer.com, 11am-10pm Mon.-Thurs., 11am-11pm Fri., 2pm-11pm Sat., 9am-9pm Sun., $15-29). The upscale competition, downtown's **Barney Prine's Steakhouse and Saloon** (389 NE Main St., 541/362-1272, http://barneyprines.

com, 4pm-close Mon.-Sun., 9am-1pm and 4pm-close Sun., $12-27), is a bit more stylish, with beech-wood floors salvaged from a Jim Beam distillery, a huge and beautiful bar, and a good wine list. The menu goes well beyond steaks to include pasta, chicken, and seafood.

Even Prineville has a brewpub! **Ochoco Brewing Company** (234 N. Main St., 541/233-0883, 11:30am-9pm Mon.-Thurs., 7am-9pm Fri.-Sun., $7-15) is a family-friendly, very casual pub with decent sandwiches, fish tacos, and over a dozen beers on tap, including Double Dam IPA.

It's about 20 miles (a 20-minute drive) from Prineville to the Brasada Ranch resort, where you'll find sophisticated farm-to-table cuisine in the area at the resort's **Range** (16986 Brasada Ranch Rd., Powell Butte, 866/373-4882, 5pm-9pm Wed.-Sun., $22-39). The restaurant has an upscale Western ambience and offers both indoor and outdoor seating and impressive views of the Cascades. The food, both here and at the resort's more casual restaurant, the **Ranch House** (7am-9pm daily, $14-38), is very good.

## ACCOMMODATIONS

The **Rustlers Inn Motel** (960 NW 3rd St., 541/447-4185, www.rustlersinn.com, $88-105) was designed in the Old West style. Art by local artists and antique furniture grace the large rooms. A budget motel that's popular with anglers is the **Executive Inn** (1050 NE 3rd St., 541/447-4152, $70-80), east of downtown. The large multiroom family unit is recommended as a base for a family weekend visit to the Painted Hills, as motel accommodations in Mitchell are limited. More upscale accommodations are available at the **Best Western Prineville Inn** (1475 NE 3rd St., 541/447-8080, $122-151), near the east end of town.

The **Prineville Reservoir Resort** (19600 SE Juniper Canyon Rd., 541/447-7468, www. prinevillereservoirresort.com) is on the shoreline of Prineville Reservoir, 17 miles southeast of Prineville on the Paulina Highway (Hwy. 27). This resort offers motel accommodations

with kitchenettes ($80), campsites ($29-31), and rustic cabins (bring your own bedding, $40). The resort also rents fishing boats.

One of Central Oregon's newest resorts, ★ **Brasada Ranch** (16986 Brasada Ranch Rd., Powell Butte, 866/373-4882, www. brasada.com) lies in the open hills of the ranch country between Prineville and Bend. *Brasada* is the Spanish cowboy term for "brush country," and that pretty much describes the landscape, with beautiful views of Cascade peaks. This resort is very popular with golfers, and the rooms are luxurious but comfortable. There's a good fitness center and an outdoor pool that resembles those found in upscale Hawaiian resorts, an excellent restaurant, a golf course, and biking, hiking, and horse trails. It's also a convenient location for Crooked and Deschutes Rivers anglers who want to stay in an upscale resort. Lodgings range from suites in the main lodge ($309) to one- to three-bedroom cabins ($545-929), with fully equipped kitchens.

### Camping

For good campsites in the **Ochocos** (www. fs.usda.gov, mid-Apr.-late Oct.), take Ochoco Creek Road approximately 10 miles east of Ochoco Lake. Camp beneath big ponderosa pines at **Wildwood** (free), **Ochoco Divide** ($13), neither of which has drinking water, or at **Walton Lake** ($15), with water, where you can fish, boat, or hike the trail to Round Mountain. While on this loop, stop at the mining ghost town of Mayflower. Founded in 1873, the community was active until 1925; a stamp mill is still visible.

Camp alongside the Crooked River at any of the nine **Bureau of Land Management campgrounds** (541/416-6700, www.blm.gov, $8) on Highway 27; they are 15 to 20 miles south of Prineville. Be sure to bring water or a filter for the river water.

## INFORMATION

The **Prineville-Crook County Chamber of Commerce** (185 NE 10th St., 541/447-6304, www.prinevillechamber.com) has a helpful staff and lots of information. The **Ochoco National Forest** (3160 NE 3rd St., 541/416-6500, www.fs.usda.gov/ochoco) can offer details on hiking in the Ochocos; the website is an excellent resource for trail information. The **Bureau of Land Management** (3050 NE 3rd St., 541/416-6700, www.blm.gov) can guide you to rock-collecting sites.

# Warm Springs and Lower Deschutes River

North of the Bend-Redmond area, the juniper- and sage-lined roadsides and fields of mint and wheat stand in welcome contrast to the busy main drags of the Bend-Redmond-Sisters urban complex to the south.

## MADRAS

Madras (pop. 6,700) is mostly known as a supply town for the surrounding agricultural area, which comes right up to downtown's doorstep. West of town, the Crooked, Metolius, and Deschutes Rivers join up and are impounded by Round Butte Dam to form Lake Billy Chinook. The main access to the lake is via Cove Palisades State Park. Downstream from the lake, the Deschutes River continues to the Columbia. The most popular place for rafting the Deschutes is the area around Maupin, 47 miles north of Madras.

Madras is one of the region's most culturally diverse towns: Over 35 percent of its residents are Latino, and 5 percent are Native American. Many more Native Americans live on the nearby Warm Springs Reservation.

### Lake Billy Chinook

Heading north from Bend, travelers don't need to put away their recreational gear. Just outside Madras, **Cove Palisades State Park** (541/546-3412 or 800/452-5687, www.oregonstateparks.org, $5 day-use, $20 tents, $30-32 RVs, $85 cabins) is 14 miles southwest of Madras off U.S. 97 and offers hiking, boating, fishing, waterskiing, and bird-watching. Towering cliffs, Cascade vistas, gnarled

Three river canyons meet at Lake Billy Chinook.

junipers, and **Lake Billy Chinook**, with its 72-mile shoreline, create a stunning backdrop. The lake was created when Round Butte Dam backed up the waters of the Deschutes, Metolius, and Crooked Rivers. For the best views of how these rivers come together, hike up the Tam-a-lau Trail (a quick 600-foot elevation gain) to the top of the Peninsula, a plateau of land between the backed-up Crooked and Deschutes Rivers. At the top, the trail makes a loop around the Peninsula, with good views onto the Cascades and the river canyons. In total it is six miles round-trip, best done in the springtime when it's not too hot and when the balsamroot and lupine are in bloom.

The lake is popular with boaters (moorage $10); **Cove Palisades Resort & Marina** (5700 S.W. Marina Dr., 541/546-9999 or 877/546-7171, www.covepalisadesresort.com) rents everything from stand-up paddleboards to houseboats.

## Richardson's Recreational Ranch

If you're a rock hound, you'll want to visit **Richardson's Recreational Ranch** (6683 NE Haycreek Rd., 541/475-2680, www.richardsonrockranch.com, 7am-5pm daily Mar.-Oct., from $1.25 per pound). This family-owned and operated enterprise has extensive rock beds loaded with thunder eggs, moss agates, jaspers, jasper-agate, Oregon sunset, and rainbow agates, and it is a huge hit with most kids. If you want to chip agates out of one of the many exposed ledges on the ranch, bring chisels, wedges, and other necessary hard-rock mining tools. Once you've completed your dig, you drop your rocks off at the office and pay for them by the pound. And if you don't care for dirt under your fingernails, you can find rocks for sale from all over the world in the rock shop. To get here, take U.S. 97 north of Madras 11 miles and turn right at the sign near mile marker 81. Follow the road for three miles to the ranch office. Rock diggers must start by 3pm, and the eight-mile road to the digging site is closed when wet.

## Food and Accommodations

Amid all the fast-food joints in Madras, there's a shining beacon of healthy eating: **Great Earth Natural Foods** (46 SW D St., 541/475-1500, www.greatearth.biz, 7am-6pm Mon.-Fri., 10am-3pm Sat., $6-10) is a small food store with an exceptionally good deli. Stop in for a roasted vegetable salad, a sandwich, or a smoothie. A longtime Madras favorite, **Pepe's** (742 SW 4th St., 541/475-1144, 11am-8pm Mon.-Sat., $7-13), is a friendly all-around Mexican restaurant.

**Geno's Italian Grill** (212 SW 4th St., 541/475-6048, www.genositaliangrill.net, 11am-8pm Tues.-Sun., $14-27) is the best bet for a relaxed and tasty Italian meal. Though the menu features pasta and pizza, you'll also find a wide selection of American fare such as burgers, steaks, and entrée salads.

Most of the lodgings in Madras are inexpensive chain motels. The **Inn at Cross Keys Station** (66 NW Cedar St., 541/475-5800 or 877/475-5800, http://innatcrosskeysstation.com, $150) is by far the most luxurious and restful place to stay in town. It has an indoor pool and conference facilities.

### CAMPING

Two overnight campgrounds at **Cove Palisades State Park** (541/546-3412, www.oregonstateparks.org, reservations 800/452-5687, www.reserveamerica.com, $5 day-use, $20 tents, $28-30 RVs, $85 cabins) offer all the amenities: Deschutes campground (May-mid-Sept.) has 82 full-hookup sites and 92 tent sites; the Crooked River campground (year-round), perched right on the canyon rim, has 93 sites with electricity and water. Reserve in advance, as these are extremely popular. Culver, a little town southwest of Madras, is home to the **Redmond/Central Oregon KOA** (2435 SW Jericho Lane, Culver, 541/546-7972 or 800/562-1992, www.madras-koa.com, $30 tents, $36-43 RVs, $67-105 cabins). An outdoor pool plus some sites with shade are the big attractions at this well-run campground.

Rent a houseboat on Lake Billy Chinook from **Cove Palisades Resort & Marina** (5700 S.W. Marina Dr., 541/546-9999 or 877/546-7171, www.covepalisadesresort.com, $1,550-4,300 for 3 days, $2,275-6,725 weekly).

# WARM SPRINGS INDIAN RESERVATION

Within the 600,000-acre **Warm Springs Indian Reservation** (www.warmsprings. com), which straddles U.S. 26 north of Madras, you can see the age-old practice of dip-net fishing on the Deschutes River, as well as the richest collection of Native American artifacts in the country at a 27,000-square-foot museum. The community also operates a dam, a resort hotel, a casino (U.S. 26, across from the museum), and a lumber mill. These entrepreneurs are the descendants of the same Native Americans who greeted Lewis and Clark and Deschutes explorers Peter Skene Ogden (in 1826), John Frémont, and Kit Carson (both in 1843).

## ★ Museum at Warm Springs

You'll find an impressive display of Native American culture at the **Museum at Warm Springs** (541/553-3331, www.museumatwarmsprings.org, 9am-5pm Tues.-Sat., $7 adults, $6 seniors, $4.50 teens, $3.50 children), just east of the town of Warm Springs below the viewpoint at the bottom of the Deschutes River Canyon. Audiovisual displays, old photos, and tapes of traditional chants of the Paiute, Warm Springs, and Wasco peoples (the three groups that live on the Warm Springs Reservation) are artfully presented. Each group's distinct culture, along with the thriving social and economic community they collectively formed, constitutes the major theme of this museum.

Replicas of a Paiute mat lodge, a Warm Springs tepee, and a Wasco plank house, along with recordings of each group's language, underscore the cultural richness and diversity of the area's original inhabitants. The exhibits, curated from a collection of more than 20,000 artifacts, range from primitive prehistoric hand tools to a push-button-activated Wasco wedding scene. Native American foodstuffs and art are on sale in the bookstore.

## Kah-Nee-Ta

**Kah-Nee-Ta Resort** (541/553-1112 or 800/554-4786, www.kahneeta.com), a golf and hot springs resort at the bottom of a canyon about a dozen miles off U.S. 26 from

the Museum at Warm Springs

the town of Warm Springs, is a good place to find the sun when western Oregon seems unrelentingly gloomy. The 1,000-foot elevation and 12-inch annual rainfall enable golfers to play year-round; Kah-Nee-Ta is even snow-free in February. Spa Wanapine offers a variety of massage, aesthetic, and therapeutic treatments. Owned by the Confederated Tribes of Warm Springs, this arrow-shaped hotel is a focal point of the reservation, which includes a working ranch and wild horses.

Although this resort is a little worn, it's a fine place to spend a night. Lodging possibilities include tepees (bring your own sleeping bag, $79) and RV sites ($69) as well as hotel rooms (some updated), suites, and cottages ($119-640). The hot mineral baths and a spring-fed Olympic-size swimming pool located a short drive from the hotel are among the highlights. There are also bike rentals, tennis courts, horseback rides, and hiking trails. Day visitors can take advantage of Kah-Nee-Ta's Big Village hot spring pool ($15 adults, $10 ages 4-12), heated to 92°F in the cool seasons, cooler in summer; hot tubs (included in room rates); and the 184-foot waterslide ($4). A separate, quieter pool in the lodge area is for lodge guests only.

Resort guests who aren't camping have to eat at one of the resort's two restaurants, as it's a long drive anyplace else: the **Chinook Room** (7am-11am and 5pm-9pm Wed.-Sun., $12-27) and the casual arcade-like **Warm Springs Grill** (11am-11pm Sun.-Thurs., 11am-midnight Fri.-Sat., $9-22). The summertime Saturday-night **salmon bake** (reservations recommended, $33, $15 under age 13), featuring traditional dancing and salmon cooked outside on cedar sticks over an alder fire, is quite popular.

## MAUPIN

The riverside town of Maupin is usually a quiet place, catering mostly to anglers who come to fly-fish the native Deschutes River red-side trout. On summer weekends, however, when river rafters descend, it becomes a zoo.

## Sherar's Falls

Downstream from the Sandy Beach raft takeout is **Sherar's Falls**, a cascade that demands a portage if you're rafting to the Columbia. A bridge crosses the Deschutes just downstream. At the bottom of the waterfall is a traditional Native American fishing area, still used by Warm Springs community members. You'll see the rather rickety-looking fishing platforms perched over the river, and you may see people dip-netting from them. If you're in the mood to explore, cross the bridge to the west side of the Deschutes and follow Highway 216 a few miles to **White River Falls State Park** (800/551-6949, www.oregonstateparks.org), a day-use park with another excellent waterfall and a short trail to the remains of an old hydroelectric power plant.

## ★ Rafting the Deschutes

Just about every tour company operating in central Oregon runs raft trips down the 13-mile "splash and giggle" stretch of the Deschutes River, from Harpham Flat Campground to Sandy Beach, just above Sherar's Falls. Wapinita, Box Car, Oak Springs, White River, and Elevator Rapids are the highlights of this trip; look also for the resident ospreys as you pass the Maupin Bridge.

**Sun Country Tours** (531 SW 13th St., Bend, 541/382-1709, www.suncountrytours.com) runs a full-day trip ($108 adults, $98 children) along the Harpham Flat-Sandy Beach stretch of the river. A hearty grilled chicken lunch is included. Transportation from Bend or Sunriver to Maupin is also part of the day-trip packages.

**Rapid River Rafters** (500 SW Bond St., Bend, 541/382-1514 or 800/962-3327, www.rapidriverrafters.com) offers a series of full-day and multiday packages on the Deschutes River. The one-day trip ($90 adults, $75 children, lunch included) takes in 17 miles of the river from Harpham Flat to Lone Pine. The two-day trip ($295 adults, $220 children) floats 44 miles of exciting white water from

Trout Creek to Sandy Beach. The three-day trip ($400) runs 55 miles from Warm Springs to Sandy Beach. On all of the multiday trips, the camping and meal preparations at pleasant riverside locations are taken care of by guides. The season is late April-early October, and camping equipment is available for rent if you don't have your own. Among its many trips in Oregon, **Ouzel Outfitters** (541/385-5947 or 800/788-7238, www.oregonrafting.com) offers a full-day trip ($105) on the Lower Deschutes out of Maupin.

Experienced rafters can rent a boat from **All Star Rafting and Kayaking** (405 Deschutes Ave., 541/395-2201, www.asrk. com, rafts $80-190 per day, inflatable kayaks $35-45 per day) or **River Trails Deschutes** (301 Bakeoven Rd., 541/395-2545 or 888/324-8837, www.rivertrails.com, rafts from $90 per day, single kayaks from $25 per day). Both outfitters also offer guided trips and shuttles. Boater passes are required for all river users, reserved online (http://recreation.gov, $2 pp, summer weekends $8 pp) up to 26 weeks in advance. For use of Harpham Flat put-in and Sandy Beach takeout, a Warm Springs Tribal permit (www.tribalpermit. com, $2 pp) is required. Call **Affordable**

**Deschutes Shuttle** (541/395-2809, www. affordabledeschutesshuttle.com) if you need someone to take your car from put-in to take-out ($40 from Harpham Flat to Sandy Beach).

## Fishing

Downstream from Maupin, anglers fish the Deschutes River year-round for trout; steelhead are in the river August-November. Part of the reason to fish here, especially in the spring and fall, is the beautiful canyon.

**Deschutes Canyon Fly Shop** (599 S. U.S. 197, 541/395-2565, www.flyfishingdeschutes.com, 8am-5pm Mon.-Sat., 8am-1pm Sun.) sells supplies and can advise you on the hatches and other conditions. They can also set you up with a guide ($375-450 per day). John, the shop's owner, is very helpful, and encourages women anglers. Maupin's other fly shop, the **Deschutes Angler** (504 Deschutes Ave., 541/395-0995, www.deschutesangler.com, 9am-5pm daily), is also worth a visit for both gear and information. The owners of this shop are experts on Spey casting, a two-handed technique, and they hold regular casting clinics. The **Oasis Resort** (609 S. U.S. 197, 541/395-2611, www. deschutesriveroasis.com) also runs a guide service.

fly-fishing the Deschutes near Maupin

## Food and Accommodations

Eat a hearty pre-float breakfast at the **Oasis** (609 S. U.S. 197, 541/395-2611, www.deschutesriveroasis.com, 7am-8pm Fri.-Sat., 8am-4pm Sun., $7-10)—it's also a nearly mandatory post-float stop for a hand-dipped milk shake made with hard ice cream. The **Imperial River Company** (301 Bakeoven Rd., 541/395-2404, 11am-10pm daily late Apr.-mid-Sept., 4pm-9pm Mon.-Fri., 11am-9pm Sat.-Sun. mid-Sept.-Oct., 4pm-9pm Fri., 11am-9pm Sat.-Sun. Nov.-late Apr., $11-25) is the most full-service restaurant in town, featuring steaks from the family cattle.

If you don't want to camp, stay in a simple older cabin at the **Oasis Resort** (609 S. U.S. 197, 541/395-2611, www.deschutesriveroasis.com, $50-95); it's a local classic. The Oasis also has a little camping area where you can pitch a tent or park an RV (no hookups, $22). The **Deschutes Motel** (616 Mill St., 541/395-2626, www.deschutesmotel.com, $84-129), above the river near Maupin's main downtown area, also has acceptable but modest accommodations. The six-room **River Run Lodge** (210 Hartman Ave., 541/980-7113, www.riverrunlodge.net, pets allowed, $79-309) steps up the game a bit with decks, a barbecue grill, and a common kitchen area. The fanciest place in Maupin is the **Imperial River Company** (304 Bakeoven Rd., 541/395-2404 or 800/395-3903, www.deschutesriver.com, $104-264), which has a riverside lodge. Some rooms have balconies overlooking the river, and all are nicely decorated and quite comfortable.

Right in town, **Maupin City Park** (206 Bakeoven Rd., 541/395-2252, http://cityofmaupin.org, reservations advised for summer weekends, $34 tents, $42 RVs), just downstream from the bridge, is on a grassy riverbank lot. Unlike almost all of the Bureau of Land Management campgrounds along the Deschutes, Maupin City Park has water and showers.

### CAMPING

Both upstream and downstream from Maupin are several riverside **BLM campgrounds** (541/416-6700, Memorial Day-Labor Day, $8-12). Bring water or a filter for the river water. **Harpham Flat Campground** is the main launching spot for day trips on the Deschutes, and it can be a little more hectic than the neighboring campgrounds. The nicest spots are actually a ways downstream at **Beavertail** and **Macks Canyon,** 21 and 29 miles north of Maupin, respectively. Reservations are not accepted.

# Northeastern Oregon

Look for ★ to find recommended
sights, activities, dining, and lodging.

# Highlights

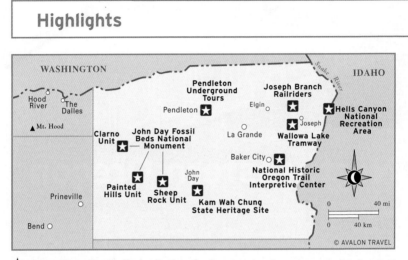

★ **John Day Fossil Beds National Monument:** At these three separate fossil bed units, you'll learn about saber-toothed tigers and wind through remote outposts of Miocene-era life (page 485).

★ **Kam Wah Chung State Heritage Site:** This is a fascinating remnant of the time when Chinese laborers outnumbered European settlers in gold camps of the West (page 490).

★ **Pendleton Underground Tours:** These tours explore everything from a Chinese jail to a brothel, the true underground of 1880s frontier life (page 493).

★ **Joseph Branch Railriders:** Hop aboard a rail-riding car (a cross between a recumbent bike and a rail car) and coast most of the way from Joseph to Enterprise on an abandoned rail line. It's an easy pedal back to Joseph (page 507).

★ **Wallowa Lake Tramway:** Hitch a ride on a gondola and whiz to the top of Mount Howard, with views over the Wallowa Mountains and nearby Hells Canyon (page 510).

★ **Hells Canyon National Recreation Area:** The world's deepest river gorge is trenched by the Snake River. The best way to see this otherwise almost inaccessible canyon is by raft or jet boat (page 513).

★ **National Historic Oregon Trail Interpretive Center:** This excellent museum tells the story of the Oregon Trail pioneers and their treacherous traversal of the West (page 516).

F or jaw-dropping scenic grandeur, outdoor recreation, and escapes from the urban world, Oregon's northeastern corner is hard to top. The magnificent Wallowa Mountains easily invoke comparisons to the Swiss Alps. Hells

Canyon, carved by the Snake River, is one of the deepest river-carved gorges in the world, averaging 6,600 feet in depth. West of the Wallowas rise the Blue Mountains. The high country of the Blue Mountains is often dusted with snow by September, which was when Oregon Trail pioneers crossed these mountain passes. With its headwaters in the Blue Mountains, the John Day River cuts one of Oregon's most dramatic canyons, with fascinating fossil beds and an insightful interpretive center to help make sense of the region's long-buried natural history.

Just as the fossil beds provide a cross section of the earth's history, a trip through northeastern Oregon will give you a feel for the leather-tough people who settled here. In country towns and larger centers like Baker City, La Grande, and Pendleton, history is not very old; what may seem like the Old West is still a way of life. And while it remains primarily rural ranch country, the area is

becoming an increasingly popular haven for painters, sculptors, and writers.

## PLANNING YOUR TIME

For many travelers on a road trip, northeastern Oregon will either be the first or the last part of Oregon they will encounter. If the Willamette Valley or the Oregon coast is the focus of your Oregon vacation, you might find it tempting to hurtle right through this corner of the state on I-84. However, plan to devote at least a day or two to explore the area's rich history and astoundingly dramatic scenery. The world's deepest river gorge is here, as are some of its richest fossil beds.

In order to really explore this wild country, get off the interstate. From Ontario, consider crossing the state on U.S. 26, which travels through pine-clad mountains to the John Day River Valley, one of Oregon's most scenic. The river trenches through a layer cake of dramatic geologic formations to

# Northeastern Oregon

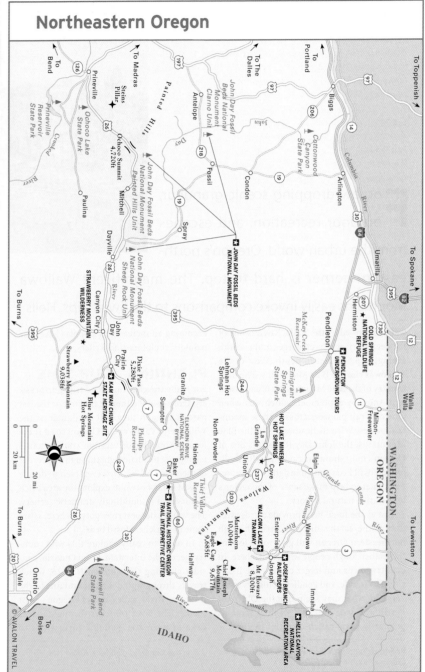

To Bend
126
Prineville
Steins Pillar
To Madras
197
To Portland
To The Dalles
206
Biggs
97
To Toppenish

Ochoco Lake State Park
Prineville Reservoir State Park
Antelope
Clarno Unit
John Day Fossil Beds National Monument
Painted Hills
John Day
218
Fossil
Condon
19
Cottonwood Canyon State Park
97
14
Arlington
84
30
Umatilla
To Spokane

Crooked River
Ochoco Summit 4,720ft
26
Mitchell
John Day Fossil Beds National Monument Painted Hills Unit
JOHN DAY FOSSIL BEDS NATIONAL MONUMENT
McKay Creek Reservoir
82
395
To Walla Walla

Paulina
Dayville
26
Spray
John River
John Day Fossil Beds National Monument Sheep Rock Unit
395
207
COLD SPRINGS NATIONAL WILDLIFE REFUGE
Hermiston
730
Pendleton
PENDLETON UNDERGROUND TOURS
11
Milton-Freewater
12
Walla Walla
WASHINGTON
OREGON

To Burns
395
Canyon City
John Day
STRAWBERRY MOUNTAIN WILDERNESS
Strawberry Mountain 9,038ft
Prairie City
Dixie Pass 5,280ft
KAM WAH CHUNG STATE HERITAGE SITE
Blue Mountain Hot Springs
Granite
Lehman Hot Springs
244
Emigrant Springs State Park
La Grande
HOT LAKE MINERAL HOT SPRINGS
237
Cove
Union
Elgin
Wallowa
3
To Lewiston

Phillips Reservoir
Sumpter
ELKHORN DRIVE NATIONAL SCENIC BYWAY
Haines
7
North Powder
203
Matterhorn 10,004ft
Eagle Cap 9,685ft
WALLOWA LAKE TRAMWAY
JOSEPH BRANCH RAILRIDERS
Enterprise

245
Baker City
7
Thief Valley Reservoir
86
Chief Joseph Mountain 9,617ft
Mt. Howard 8,200ft
Joseph
Imnaha

26
30
NATIONAL HISTORIC OREGON TRAIL INTERPRETIVE CENTER
Halfway
Wallowa Mountains
HELLS CANYON NATIONAL RECREATION AREA

To Burns
20
Vale
Ontario
84
Farewell Bend State Park
Snake River
Imnaha River
To Boise

© AVALON TRAVEL

IDAHO

0    20 km
0    20 mi

expose the **John Day Fossil Beds National Monument.** Even if you stay closer to the interstate, consider branching off and making a loop around the **Wallowa Mountains,** a soaring piece of real estate that contains 17 individual peaks over 9,000 feet high. This side road also takes you to the brink of **Hells Canyon,** where the Snake River carves a gorge beneath 6,500-foot cliffs.

If you stick to I-84 and the fast track, at least realize that this route parallels the original Oregon Trail, the wagon route that brought in upward of 50,000 pioneers to the Pacific Northwest between 1843 and 1860. Stop at the **National Historic Oregon Trail Interpretive Center** near Baker City to learn more about this great human migration. Baker City is also a good place to spend a night, with a lovely old downtown hotel, an excellent brewpub, and plenty of restaurants. Then pull off the interstate at Pendleton to experience the city's colorful past on **Pendleton Underground Tours,** which explores a subterranean business district and a brothel from the turn of the 20th century.

# John Day Fossil Beds and Vicinity

The canyon-cutting John Day River drains the western slopes of the Blue Mountains, trenching through north-central Oregon before spilling into the Columbia River. The John Day River Valley also offers some of Oregon's most tantalizing human history, plus fascinating glimpses into the region's prehistory. In the 1860s, self-taught geologist Thomas Condon discovered what is now known as the John Day Fossil Beds, which provide a paleontological record of 40 million years of ancient life.

## ★ JOHN DAY FOSSIL BEDS NATIONAL MONUMENT

The 14,000-acre **John Day Fossil Beds National Monument** (32651 Hwy. 19, Kimberly, 541/987-2333, www.nps.gov/joda, free) is divided into three areas: the Sheep Rock Unit, about 40 miles west of John Day, with the monument's excellent interpretive center; the Painted Hills Unit, another 45 miles farther west; and the Clarno Unit,

the Painted Hills

# Oregon Paleo Lands Institute

Although scientists have long traveled to eastern Oregon for their research, Pacific Northwest-erners and visitors to the state are often only vaguely aware of the area's rich paleontology and geology. The **Oregon Paleo Lands Institute** (401 4th St., Fossil, 541/763-4480, www. oregonpaleolandscenter.com, 9:30am-4:30pm Fri.-Sun. summer) was established to bring these resources to a wider range of people and also to help boost the struggling rural economy. In downtown Fossil, with exhibits on local geology and paleontology, the institute is a good resource for exploring Oregon's John Day country. It also sponsors occasional trips guided by local geolo-gists, photographers, and other experts.

This is a good place to come for information about floating the John Day River, biking through the John Day Basin, or hiking in the John Day Fossil Beds National Monument. You'll find books and maps (some with an intensely local focus and unavailable elsewhere), and friendly, informa-tive staffers.

northwest of the others, about 20 miles west of the town of Fossil.

The days of 50-ton apatosaurus and 50-foot crocodiles, as well as delicate ferns and flow-ers, are captured in the rock formations of the three beds, easily visited in a day's road trip. This is the richest concentration of prehistoric early mammal and plant fossils in the world. More than 120 species have been identified, documenting a period dating from the extinc-tion of the dinosaurs to the beginning of the last great ice age.

Accommodations are in short supply in this remote part of Oregon. The small towns near the monument's individual units have motels, and the town of John Day has the largest selection. A few campgrounds lie along the main fossil route; more are off the beaten path.

## Painted Hills

The highly photogenic low-slung **Painted Hills** were created 30 million years ago by red, yellow, green, ocher, gray, and black ash deposited into drifts hundreds of feet deep. Erosion has cut through the multicolored lay-ers and sculpted the hills into soft mounds. While many casual visitors are satisfied snap-ping photos from the monument's designated overlook, easy hiking trails lead to more inter-esting vistas; the springtime wildflower dis-play here is exceptional.

The 0.5-mile **Painted Hills Overlook Trail** provides a view of mineral-bearing clays exposed by erosion. Nearby, the 1.5-mile **Carroll Rim Trail** has a spectacular all-encompassing view of the Painted Hills. The most vivid colors of all are found at the **Painted Cove Trail,** a 0.25-mile loop where viewing the red mounds up close is a high-light. Close by, the 0.5-mile **Leaf Hill Trail,** another loop, leads to remnants of a 30-mil-lion-year-old hardwood forest. Take a look at the exhibit describing how our knowledge of Oregon's most ancient forests emanated from studies of this area. To reach the Painted Hills, drive three miles west of Mitchell on U.S. 26, turn left at the sign, and travel six miles along Bridge Creek to the site. Stop at the visitors center to get oriented and fill your water bot-tle. If possible, visit around dusk or after a rain shower, when the colors really pop.

### ACCOMMODATIONS

Mitchell, which has a store, a couple of cafés, and a few places to stay, is the closest town to the Painted Hills. The historic **Oregon Hotel** (104 E. Main St., Mitchell, 541/462-3027, http://theoregonhotel.net, Mar.-Nov., with private bath $60-70) offers pleasantly vintage guest rooms right downtown. The less expensive guest rooms ($50-60) share a bath; kitchenettes ($110) are available. Several hotels have existed on this site since the 1800s,

# Floating the John Day River

Oregon's longest free-running river, the John Day, spends most of its time far from roads, which makes it ideal to see from a boat. From May to early July, it's relatively easy to navigate the river in a canoe, raft, or inflatable kayak. The only rapid of note, a Level III-IV at Clarno, can be tough to run when the water level is low, and since there are no dams on the John Day, flow levels fluctuate widely in response to snowpack and rainfall. When water level is high, canoeists should have white-water experience. The Bureau of Land Management (BLM, www.blm.gov/or) oversees boating on the John Day; the website is a good source of up-to-date information, with links to water-flow forecasts as well as the permit that is required to boat on the John Day.

Most people float the John Day as a multiday trip. Service Creek is a common put-in for river trips; it's 48 miles (usually three days) to the bridge at Clarno. From Clarno to Cottonwood Canyon State Park, it's 70 miles, which usually takes five days to float. One-day floats are also possible from the town of Spray to mile marker 86 on Highway 19 or from mile 86 to Service Creek. During any trip, much of the time the river is bounded by private land; it's important to carry a good map, available from the BLM (541/416-6700) in order to know where to camp.

The **Kellie Frech's Service Creek** (38686 Hwy. 19, south of Fossil, 541/468-3331, www.servicecreek.com) rents rafts ($115-130 per day, with delivery and pickup), as well as kayaks and canoes. This outfit also offers shuttle services to popular takeouts on the John Day River.

with the current incarnation dating back to 1938. More up-to-date accommodations that sleep up to eight are available from **Painted Hills Vacation Rentals** (541/462-3921, www.paintedhillsvacation.com, $125-180), with three cheery rental cottages in the area.

Campers can pitch a tent ($10) or plug in an RV ($20) at the **Mitchell City Park** (541/462-3121), a grassy spot on the edge of the two-block-long downtown.

## Clarno Unit

Right on the John Day River, the Clarno Formations are the monument's oldest and most remote. The 40-million-year-old **Clarno Unit** exposes mudflows that washed over an Eocene-era forest. The petrified mudslide here is one of the few places in the world where the stems of ancient plants, along with their leaves, seeds, and nuts, are preserved in the same location. Fossilized imprints of palm, ginkgo, and magnolia leaves point to a subtropical forest capable of supporting flowering trees. The formations eroded into distinctive chalky-white cliffs topped with spires and turrets of stone. The 0.25-mile **Clarno Arch Trail** leads into the formations, where boulder-size fossils containing logs, seeds, and

other remains of an ancient forest await. It links with two other 0.25-mile trails: **Trail of the Fossils,** where boulders are strewn with plant fossils, and the **Geologic Time Trail,** which lacks fossils but leads to a picnic area. Picnic facilities, drinking water, and restrooms are available at the monument.

The Clarno Formations are 18 miles west of the town of **Fossil** on Highway 218. When you are traveling in the John Day country, Fossil makes an intriguing and perhaps necessary stop—in this remote area, chances are you'll need to gas up or get a bite to eat, and this Old West town has a full range of services for travelers. Fossil also offers fossils: When the townspeople began digging into a hillside to build a football field, they exposed an ancient lake bed rich with fossil leaf prints and petrified wood. The site, just behind the high school, is open to amateur fossil hunters ($5).

### FOOD AND ACCOMMODATIONS

The closest facilities to the Clarno Unit are in Fossil. Escape city life at the **Wilson Ranches Retreat** (16555 Butte Creek Lane, 541/763-2227, www.wilsonranchesretreat.com, $119-149), a welcoming B&B on a 9,000-acre cattle and hay ranch three miles from Fossil. Guests can ride horses (1 hour $55), hike, help fix fences, and even ride along on a cattle drive. **RJ's Steaks, Spirits, and Sports** (415 1st St., 541/763-3335, 11am-9pm Tues.-Sat., $7-20) in Fossil is a good place to dine on anything from steak to ice cream with strawberry sauce, accompanied by a friendly vibe.

Tent campers should head five miles south of town to the forested **Bear Hollow County Park** (45260 Hwy. 19, 541/763-2010, $10), with drinking water and vault toilets. Twenty miles south of Fossil, the **Lodge at Service Creek** (38686 Hwy. 19, 541/468-3331, www.servicecreek.com, $92-128) has lodging in nicely decorated rooms, food, raft rentals, and a shuttle service for paddling the easygoing John Day River.

Twenty miles north of Fossil in the town of **Condon,** the renovated 1920s-era ★ **Hotel Condon** (202 S. Main St., Condon, 541/384-4624 or 800/201-6706, www.hotelcondon.com, $125-249) is the swankiest lodging choice in this part of Oregon, with comfortable and stylish rooms. While in Condon, don't neglect to visit **Country Flowers** (201 S. Main St., 541/384-4120, 9am-6pm Mon.-Sat., noon-5pm Sun.), an eclectic gift store with an outpost of Portland's Powell's Books and a classic old soda fountain. This is a good place for lunch.

North of Condon, where Highway 206 crosses the John Day River, find **Cottonwood Canyon State Park** (541/394-0002, www.oregonstateparks.org, camping $10), one of the state's newest and largest. Many John Day rafters use this as a takeout spot, and the canyons and bottomlands are beautiful places to explore, with 4.5-mile-long trails on either bank of the river. During the summer, this area is quite warm, but it's a great spot to camp in spring and fall.

## Sheep Rock Unit

The **Sheep Rock Unit** is the largest of the monument's three divisions and offers the most visitor facilities. The **Thomas Condon Paleontology Center** (8 miles northwest of Dayville, 541/987-2333, www.nps.gov/joda, 10am-5pm daily, free) serves as the monument's visitors center. It features a fossil museum with exceptional discoveries from local digs, dioramas, and displays on the history of the fossil beds, plus short films. Pick up good printed information here that's not available online, such as a mile-by-mile geology road log detailing the striking stretch of road from the visitors center to the Painted Hills. The handsome 1917 **Cant Ranch House,** across the highway from the

Sheep Rock rises above the Cant Ranch, which houses a museum devoted to the area's human history.

paleontology center, houses a museum on the human history of the ranch. A former bunkhouse and a small log cabin behind it contain additional exhibits on fossil history. The tree-shaded grounds surrounding the ranch house are perfect for picnicking, and short trails lead to the fast-flowing John Day River.

North of the Paleontology Center on Highway 19 are two fossil-viewing areas. Two miles north is the parking area for **Blue Basin,** with several hiking trails leading into fossil-rich formations. The one-mile-long **Island in Time Trail** climbs into a badlands basin of highly eroded, uncannily green sediments. Along the trail are displays that reveal fossils protruding from the soil. The trail dead-ends at a natural box canyon; high around are barren, castellated walls rich in 25-million-year-old life-forms. The **Overlook Trail** offers a longer three-mile loop to the rim of Blue Basin, with views over the fossil beds and the layer-cake topography of the John Day Valley. Two miles farther north at the day-use **Foree Picnic Area** are more hiking trails that explore green mudstone formations capped with basalt from ancient lava flows.

The drive between the junction of Highway 19 and U.S. 26 and the small community of Spray is highly scenic; interesting geology and spectacular scenery don't always occur together, but they do here. Along this route you'll see **Sheep Rock,** a steep-sided mesa rising hundreds of feet to a small rock cap, and **Cathedral Rock,** where erosion has stripped away a hillside to reveal highly colored sediments beneath a thick overlay of basalt. Most astonishing of all is **Picture Gorge,** where the John Day River rips through an immense 1,500-foot-high lava flow and begins trenching its canyon to the Columbia River. Wide enough for only the river and the road, the gorge is named for the pictographs drawn by early Native Americans; look for them near mile marker 125, on the west side of the road.

The Sheep Rock Unit of the John Day Fossil Beds is eight miles northwest of Dayville, and 40 miles from John Day.

## FOOD AND ACCOMMODATIONS

The closest lodgings to the Sheep Rock Unit are in the tiny community of Dayville, where the **Fish House Inn** (110 Franklin St., Dayville, 541/987-2124, www.fishhouseinn.com) offers a cottage ($55-75) and a vintage Craftsman home with three bedrooms ($130). These pleasant digs are decorated with antique farm tools and fishing gear. Tent ($15) and RV ($30) sites are also available. The terrific **Dayville Cafe** (212 Franklin St., 541/967-2122, 7am-8pm Wed.-Sat., 8am-4pm Sun., $8-17) serves burgers from local beef, tasty pie, and real milk shakes. The old-timey **Dayville Mercantile** (207 Franklin St., 541/987-2133, 8am-6pm Mon.-Sat., 9am-5pm Sun.) is a good spot to stock up on picnic items.

# JOHN DAY AND VICINITY

The early history of John Day and nearby Canyon City centers on the discovery of gold in 1862. According to most estimates, $26 million in gold was taken out of the streams and mines in the Strawberry Mountains. At the peak of the gold rush, Whiskey Flat, later called Canyon City, was populated by 5,000 miners, which made it larger than Portland at the time. Thousands of Chinese came to the area to work the tailings, or leftovers, from the mines. Their fascinating history is vividly retold at the Kam Wah Chung and Company Museum in John Day.

One of the more colorful denizens of Canyon City was the celebrated poet Joaquin Miller, who served as the first elected judge in Grant County. Known as the "Byron of Oregon," this dashing figure dressed like Buffalo Bill and recited his florid sonnets to a baffled audience of miners. Today John Day is principally a market town for local farmers and ranchers, with adequate facilities for travelers passing through to visit nearby fossil beds or hike in the lovely Strawberry Mountains.

## ★ Kam Wah Chung State Heritage Site

A must-stop in the town of John Day, the **Kam Wah Chung State Heritage Site** (250 NW Canton St., 541/575-2800, www.oregonstate-parks.org, 9am-noon and 1pm-5pm daily May-Oct., free) has free tours (on the hour, except noon) that begin at the interpretive center, two blocks south on NW Canton Street. The building was the center of Chinese life in the John Day area, serving as a general store and pharmacy with over 500 herbs. People came from hundreds of miles away for the herbal remedies of Doc Hay, who lived here. It also served in more limited capacities as an assay office, fortune-teller's studio, and Taoist shrine.

The building began as a trading post on The Dalles Military Road in 1866. With the influx of Chinese to the area during the gold rush, the outpost was purchased in 1887 by two Chinese apothecaries and evolved into a center for Asian medicine, trade, and spirituality. It remained a gathering place for the Chinese community in eastern Oregon until the early 1940s. While it admirably fulfilled this role, the opium-blackened walls, bootleg whiskey, and gambling paraphernalia are evidence of the less salutary aspects of the Kam Wah Chung lifestyle. At the time of the 1879 census, eastern Oregon had 960 East Coast emigrants and 2,468 Chinese. In 1983, scholars from China came to categorize the herbs and religious objects.

The little touches in the faithfully restored building are moving. Your eye may be drawn to the metal shutters and outside wooden staircase on this rough stone edifice. Inside, there's a locked and barred herb cage where Ing Hay prepared medicine and where gold dust was weighed. A Taoist shrine graces the room where groceries and opium were dispensed. The meat cleaver by Doc Hay's bed bespeaks the fear and despair of Chinese life here near the turn of the 20th century.

## Grant County Historical Museum

Another repository of local history, the **Grant County Historical Museum** (101 S. Canyon City Blvd., Canyon City, 541/575-0509, 9am-4:30pm Mon.-Sat. May 15-Sept., $4 adults, $3 seniors, $2 ages 7-17, free under age 7) is in Canyon City, a couple of miles south of John Day on U.S. 395. Joaquin Miller's cabin and a jail building stand in the courtyard.

Kam Wah Chung State Heritage Site

# Who Was John Day?

John Day is such a common name in this part of Oregon (it is affixed to two rivers, three towns, a dam, a series of fossil beds, a valley, and several parks) that you might assume the original John Day was an early settler. In fact, John Day never visited most of the places that now carry his name. Day was hired to provide meat for a Pacific Fur Company expedition in 1812. Thirty miles east of The Dalles, near what was then known as the Mau Hau River, Day and another mountain man were robbed by Native Americans, who left them naked and injured. The two survived the ordeal and eventually made their way to Fort Astoria. The Mau Hau River soon became known as Day's River; mapmakers later changed it to the John Day River, and the name spread like wildfire. Even at Astoria, John Day's place-naming achievement continued: A second John Day River flows into the Columbia just east of Astoria.

## Accommodations

The **Best Western John Day Inn** (315 W. Main St., John Day, 541/575-1700 or 800/243-2628, $153-200) is a nice conventional motel, with a fitness center, an indoor pool, and free Wi-Fi. A family restaurant is adjacent. The **Dreamers Lodge** (144 N. Canyon St., John Day, 541/575-0526 or 800/654-2849, www.dreamerslodge.com, $89-119), a classic, well-maintained pet-friendly motel, is close to the town center on a quiet side street.

The most amenity-laden campground in the area is **Clyde Holliday State Recreation Site** (7 miles west of John Day, 33 miles east of the Sheep Rock Unit, 541/932-4453, www.oregonstateparks.org, $24 tents or RVs, $5 hiker-biker). In addition to showers and shady sites with electrical and water hookups near the John Day River, the park offers a couple of large tepees ($44). Although campsites are all first-come, first-served, tepees should be reserved (800/452-5687, http://oregonstateparks.reserveamerica.com).

## Food

For a Western meal, dine at the **Snaffle Bit Dinner House** (830 S. Canyon Blvd., John Day, 541/575-2426, 5pm-9pm Tues., 11am-10pm Wed.-Fri., 4pm-10pm Sat., dinner reservations recommended, $8-32), known for its steaks and friendly staff. Locals say it's the best place for miles around. Stop in for a beer and a flatbread or sandwich at the family-friendly **1188 Brewing Company**

(141 E. Main St., John Day, 541/575-1188, www.1188brewing.com, 11am-9pm Mon.-Sat., $8-12). The brewery's Desert Monk IPA is particularly good, and taps flow with beers from around the West.

## Information

For information on John Day and vicinity, contact the **Grant County Chamber of Commerce** (301 W. Main St., John Day, 541/757-0547 or 800/769-5664, www.gcoregonlive.com). The **Malheur National Forest** (www.fs.usda.gov/malheur) and the **Bureau of Land Management** share an office (431 Paterson Bridge Rd., John Day, 541/575-3000).

## STRAWBERRY MOUNTAINS AND VICINITY

Thirteen miles east of John Day, the landscape becomes more mountainous and forests begin to encroach on the ranchland. **Prairie City** is an attractive small town in this lovely locale. The **DeWitt Museum** (Main St. and Bridge St., Prairie City, 541/820-3330, www.prairiecityoregon.com, 10am-5pm Wed.-Sun. May 15-Oct. 15, $3) is housed in the Sumpter Valley Railroad's old depot, which operated between Baker City and Prairie City from 1909 to 1947. The building was restored in 1979 and today has 10 rooms full of artifacts from Grant County's early days.

Just south of Prairie City are the Strawberry Mountains, a small mountain range that offers a good system of trails, seven lakes, volcanic rock formations, and, if you're lucky, glimpses of bighorn sheep. Trails head out from Strawberry Campground, 11 miles south of Prairie City, for the short hike to **Strawberry Lake,** with options to continue to Strawberry Falls or make a loop backpacking trip in the Strawberry Mountain Wilderness Area. Although there are some wild strawberry plants along the trails, late-summer hikers will be more apt to notice the abundant huckleberries. For information on hiking the Strawberry Mountains' 120 miles of trails, contact the Prairie City Ranger District at the **Malheur National Forest Office** (327 SW Front St., 541/820-3800, www.fs.usda.gov/malheur). Ask about the 11-mile loop circumnavigating 9,000-foot Strawberry Mountain.

Prairie City enthusiastically welcomes **bicyclists.** The inaugural 1976 cross-country Bikecentennial route went through town, and it's still a popular stop with long-distance cyclists. In addition, a number of paved road, gravel road, and mountain bike routes have been established. Find details at www.prairiecityoregon.com or www.rideoregonride.com.

## Food and Accommodations

The nine-room ★ **Historic Hotel Prairie** (112 Front St., Prairie City, 541/820-4800, http://hotelprairie.com, $94-156) is a renovated 1910 hotel. Even if you're not staying the night, drop by the lobby to examine the historical photos. The rooms aren't huge—they are authentic in that regard—but the beds and amenities are comfortable. The top choice is a one-room suite; six regular bedrooms have private baths, while the two others share a bath. The hotel is pet friendly, and a wine and beer bar gives guests a chance to mingle.

**Strawberry Campground** (541/820-3800, www.fs.usda.gov/malheur, June-mid-Oct., no reservations, $8) is a great bet for tent campers, but the final stretch of road to this sweet spot, at 5,700 feet elevation, is too steep for trailers and RVs; tiny **Slide Creek** campground (9 miles south of Prairie City on Forest Rd. 6001, free), another U.S. Forest Service campground a couple of miles closer to town but with no water, is a better bet for larger rigs. **Depot Park** (Main St. and Bridge St., Prairie City, 541/820-3605, $20 RVs, $16 tents, $10 bikes, showers $1.75) has an in-town campground surrounding the DeWitt Museum and offers both RV and tent camping; it's also a good place to stop for a shower after a few

Strawberry Lake

nights in the Strawberry Mountains. This campground is a great home base for cyclists exploring the many loop roads in the nearby mountains.

**Chuck's Little Diner** (142 W. Front St., Prairie City, 541/820-4353, 6am-2pm Wed.-Sun., $4-10) is a good place for a big breakfast on the outside patio or an afternoon slice of pie. The **Oxbow Restaurant and Saloon** (128 W. Front St., Prairie City, 541/820-4544, food 4pm-8pm Tues.-Fri., noon-8pm Sat.-Sun., $12-21) offers burgers, steaks, and other comfort foods with a good helping of Western atmosphere, including a lovely antique bar adorned by carved figureheads and taxidermy.

# Pendleton

For a lot of people in the West, Pendleton (pop. 16,900) is synonymous with rodeo and woolens, both pointing to the city's history as a frontier trade settlement. Pendleton still has Western spirit to spare, but proximity to the highly successful wineries in Washington's Walla Walla Valley is bringing change to this bastion of cowboy country.

Pendleton is one of the largest cities in eastern Oregon and an economic force thanks to vast wheat fields (Umatilla County is one of the top wheat-producing counties in the United States), green peas, its famous woolen mills, and the Pendleton Round-Up, the September rodeo and weeklong party that brings in large crowds. The Umatilla Reservation is just outside town, and the Pendleton area has a large Native American population; a Native American encampment is a traditional part of the Round-Up.

## SIGHTS
### ★ Pendleton Underground Tours

One of the area's liveliest attractions is **Pendleton Underground Tours** (31 SW Emigrant Ave., 541/276-0730, http://pendleto-nundergroundtours.org, schedule varies, reservations required, $15). This visit to the wild and woolly days of the Old West takes you through the tunnels underneath the downtown historic district. At one time a series of 90 passageways, originally dug as freight tunnels by Chinese workers who weren't allowed to walk aboveground, crisscrossed the downtown area. During Prohibition, bootleggers, gamblers, opium dealers, and Chinese railroad laborers frequented the businesses that developed here.

The 90-minute tour starts at SW 1st Street and Emigrant Avenue and visits the old Shamrock Cardroom, filled with the bouncy sounds of honky-tonk music, where bartenders were once paid with gold dust; Hop Sing's laundry and bathhouse, a Prohibition speakeasy with secret escapes and a dank opium den; and the well-preserved Cozy Rooms Bordello. After this tour you'll understand how the old town of 3,000 once supported 32 saloons and 18 bordellos.

To get here from I-84, take exit 209 and turn north into Pendleton. Continue up Emigrant Avenue to SW 1st Street.

### Pendleton Woolen Mills

Next to the Round-Up, the town is best known for the **Pendleton Woolen Mills** (1307 SE Court Place, 541/276-6911, www.pendleton-usa.com, 8am-6pm Mon.-Fri., 9am-5pm Sun.), where those colorful wool blankets are made. After shearing, the wool goes to a scouring mill near Portland, where it's graded, sorted, and washed. Then the dried wool returns to the Pendleton mill for dyeing, carding, spinning, rewinding, and weaving.

Production began here in 1909 with Native American-style blankets, which are still produced, along with men's and women's sportswear. Pendleton carved its lucrative niche by copying traditional designs for blankets used by Native Americans in Arizona and New Mexico. It introduced Western-style woolen shirts in the 1920s.

Free 20-minute-long tours (9am, 11am, 1:30pm, and 3pm Mon.-Fri.) are given. Large groups are asked to make an appointment. To get to the mills, take I-84's exit 207 and follow Dorion Street through Pendleton. Do not cross the viaduct, but turn left and proceed four blocks. You can pick up blankets and clothing, often at a good discount, at the company store.

## Heritage Station Museum

In 1881, the Oregon-Washington Railway and Navigation Company, a subsidiary of the Union Pacific Railroad, constructed the northern branch of its transcontinental railroad through northeastern Oregon and Pendleton. By 1910, Pendleton had become the second-largest city in eastern Oregon, meriting a new railroad depot. The attractive **Heritage Station Depot** (108 SW Frazer Ave., 541/276-0012, www.heritagestationmuseum.org, 10am-4pm Tues.-Sat., $5 adults, $4 seniors, $2 students, $10 families), an adaptation of the California mission style, no longer serves railroad passengers but houses the Umatilla County Historical

Society's collection of Oregon Trail pioneer and Native American artifacts. Gold miners, sheep ranchers, and moonshiners are also given attention in well-designed displays.

## Tamastslikt Cultural Institute

The Confederated Tribes of the Umatilla Indian Reservation—which include the Walla Walla, Umatilla, and Cayuse Nations—had little reason to celebrate the 150th anniversary of the Oregon Trail the way it was in other parts of the West. The Oregon Trail led to war and a huge loss of land and human life. To provide their perspective on the Oregon Trail, the **Tamastslikt Cultural Institute** (72789 Hwy. 331, 541/966-9748, www.tamastslikt.org, 10am-5pm Mon.-Sat., $10 adults, $9 seniors, $6 students, $25 family of 4) has exhibits depicting Native American life prior to the pioneers' arrival; the impact of the horse, brought to North America by the Europeans, on indigenous people; and an Oregon Trail retrospective from the point of view of the Cayuse, Umatilla, and Walla Walla Nations.

The interpretive center adds a living encampment, interpretive trails, and an outdoor amphitheater. Sharing this 640-acre site at the base of the Blue Mountains is a casino, a golf course, an RV park, a hotel, and a restaurant.

Pendleton Underground Tours explore a subterranean Old West city.

# Pendleton

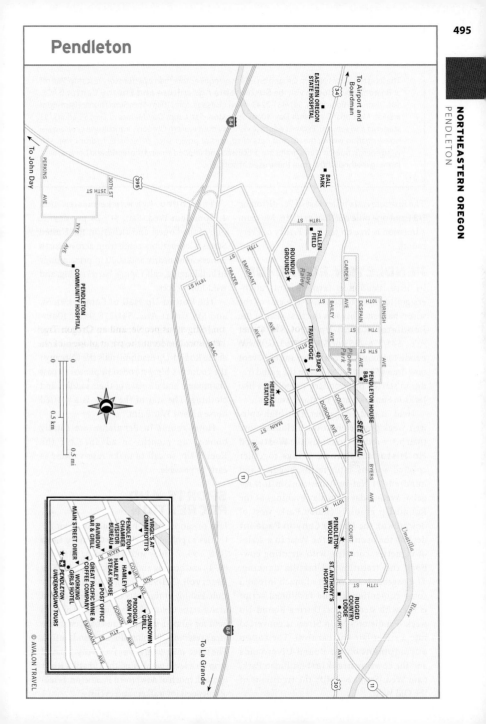

To Airport and Boardman

EASTERN OREGON STATE HOSPITAL

34

84

To John Day

PERKINS AVE

30TH ST

26TH ST

395

NYE AVE

PENDLETON COMMUNITY HOSPITAL

BALL PARK

18TH ST

FALLEN FIELD

ROUNDUP GROUNDS ★

Roy Raley

CARDEN

HILL ST

EMIGRANT

FRAZER

AVE

16TH ST

ISAAC

BAILEY

DESPAIN

FURNISH

ST

AVE

10TH

7TH

6TH

AVE

8TH

ST

AVE

AVE

40 TAPS

Pioneer Park

PENDLETON HOUSE B&B

HERITAGE STATION ★

MAIN ST

COURT AVE

DORION AVE

SEE DETAIL

AVE

BYERS AVE

Umatilla River

11

10TH ST

PENDLETON WOOLEN ★

COURT PL

17TH ST

ST ANTHONY'S HOSPITAL

RUGGED COUNTRY LODGE

COURT AVE

84

To La Grande

11

30

0 | 0.5 km
0 | 0.5 mi

VIRGIL'S AT CIMMIYOTTI'S

PENDLETON CHAMBER VISITOR BUREAU

HAMLEY'S STEAK HOUSE

RAINBOW BAR & GRILL

MAIN STREET DINER

GREAT PACIFIC WINE & COFFEE COMPANY

PENDLETON UNDERGROUND TOURS ★

WORKING GIRLS HOTEL

POST OFFICE

PRODIGAL SON PUB

SUNDOWN GRILL

COURT AVE

MAIN ST

DORION AVE

4TH ST

EMIGRANT AVE

© AVALON TRAVEL

# The Sage Center

The long trip across eastern Oregon on I-84 may require more than a perfunctory rest stop. Pull off at Boardman (exit 164) to visit the **Sustainable Agriculture and Energy Center** (SAGE, 101 Olson Rd., Boardman, 541/481-7243, www.visitsage.com, 10am-5pm Sun.-Thurs., 10am-6pm Fri.-Sat. Memorial Day-Labor Day, 10am-5pm Mon.-Sat. Labor Day-Memorial Day, $5 adults, $3 students and seniors). Exhibits educate visitors about eastern Oregon's agricultural economy—how irrigation works; the ins and outs of sources of power such as biofuels, hydropower, and wind energy; how corn and grains are processed and shipped around the world; and how modern farming methods differ from those used historically.

The institute is six miles east of Pendleton on I-84 and one mile north of exit 216. Museum admission is free on the first Friday of every month.

## PENDLETON ROUND-UP

In 1910, Pendleton farmers and ranchers got together to celebrate the end of the wheat harvest. This was the first year of the **Pendleton Round-Up** (1205 SW Court Ave., 541/276-2553 or 800/457-6336, www. pendletonroundup.com). The annual event now draws 50,000 rodeo fans in the grand tradition started by legendary rodeo stars like Jackson Sundown and Yakima Canutt.

Held in mid-September, this high-spirited weeklong celebration includes more than just a rodeo. On Friday, the **Westward Ho Historical Parade** brings together covered wagons, mule teams, buggies, and hundreds of Native Americans in full regalia. Wednesday-Saturday evenings at the Round-Up grounds (Raley Park, west of downtown), the **Happy Canyon Pageant** depicts the opening of the West in a series of vignettes, complete with strutting cowboys and traditional Umatilla dancing. The pageant is the object of much love and some contention; its old-fashioned script is rife with stereotypes. During Round-Up week, Pendleton's Main Street is converted into a street fair and carnival. The **tepee encampment** on the Round-Up grounds and the **cowboy breakfast** (Stillman Park, 6am Wed.-Sat.) exemplify the traditions of the Old West.

The **rodeo** (www.ticketmaster.com, 1:15pm-5pm Wed.-Sat., $15-28 per day) is one of the largest and richest in the United States. Competitors come from across North America for nearly $500,000 in prize money in bulldogging, calf-roping, barrel racing, and wild-horse races.

The **Round-Up Hall of Fame** (13th St. and SW Court Ave., 541/278-0815, 10am-4pm Sat., $5 adults, $4 seniors, $2 under age 11), located under the south grandstand area at the Round-Up Stadium, tells the history of the country's biggest rodeo in photos of past champions and displays of their saddles and clothing. The star of the show is a stuffed horse named War Paint.

Hotel rooms in Pendleton are totally booked up months in advance for the Round-Up, so call to make reservations as early as possible.

## SPORTS AND RECREATION

Lots of sun is conducive to such outdoor activities as golf at **Pendleton Country Club** (U.S. 395, 7 miles south of town, 541/443-8874), and boating and waterskiing on **McKay Reservoir** (541/922-3232), near the country club. Fishing enthusiasts can head north and arrive at the Columbia River in a little over an hour for salmon, steelhead, and bass, or try the area's reservoirs for bluegills, bass, and catfish. The three-mile-long **River Parkway,** a paved strip on a levee paralleling the Umatilla River through much of downtown Pendleton, is recommended for walkers and cyclists.

Pendleton is a classic Western town.

has an impressive collection of Western art on the mezzanine level of the store. A walk through downtown will reveal several less vaunted and possibly less expensive places to buy Western clothing and boots. It's a fun place to shop, and merchants are quite happy to help city folk with finer points of Western style.

## FOOD

Dine in style at the **Hamley Steakhouse** (8 SE Court Ave., 541/278-1100, http://hamleysteakhouse.com, 5pm-8:30pm Sun.-Thurs., 5pm-9pm Fri.-Sat., bar open later, $10-41), a gorgeous and opulent restaurant with good steaks, house-smoked ribs, and comfort food "ranch cooking" such as biscuits and gravy and pot roast. Spend less and soak up the atmosphere at the bar with a burger ($11). Sharing a grassy plaza with the steak house is the casual but cowboy-chic **Hamley's Café and Coffee Company** (16 SE Court Ave., 541/278-1100, 8am-3pm daily, $5-10), with light breakfasts and lunchtime sandwiches and salads.

Also quite Western but considerably less tony than Hamley's is the **Rainbow Cafe** (209 S. Main St., 541/276-4120, http://rainbowcafependleton.com, 6am-2am Mon.-Sat., 6am-midnight Sun., dinner $8-24, no credit cards), a famous saloon and restaurant for rodeo fans and local buckaroos, in business since 1883. The Rainbow serves decent American diner food, which you shouldn't pass up, if only for the local color. It's a favorite for breakfast or late-night bar food.

**Virgil's at Cimmiyotti's** (137 S. Main St., 541/276-7711, www.virgilsatcimmiyottis.com, 4pm-9pm Tues.-Thurs., 4pm-10pm Fri.-Sat., $14-33), reopened by a new owner in 2009, is the latest incarnation of this dark, cozy, and very red spot that has been around for decades. Cimmiyotti's is an old-style Pendleton institution, with steaks and beef stroganoff and osso buco, but the more up-to-date specials and the excellent service make it a local favorite. In addition, there is a good selection of Walla Walla wines.

During the winter months, ski at **Spout Springs** (79327 Hwy. 204, Athena, 541/566-0320, www.spoutspringsskiarea.com, $35 adults, $30 ages 12-17, $25 ages 5-11), 40 miles northeast of Pendleton in Athena, one of the oldest ski resorts in the Pacific Northwest. It's a small place, with two double chairlifts and relatively easy terrain. **Cross-country ski trails** (trail pass $10) are also maintained. To get here, drive north on Highway 11 to Weston, turn east on Highway 204, and travel a few miles past Tollgate to the ski area. Spout Springs usually holds on to its dry powder longer than other ski areas in the state.

## SHOPPING

If you're starting to like the look of pearl-snap shirts and cowboy boots, make your way to **Hamley's** (30 SE Court Ave., 541/278-1100, www.hamleyco.com, 9am-6pm Mon.-Thurs. 9am-8pm Fri.-Sat., 11am-5pm Sun.), a classic Western clothing and tack store complete with saddle makers in the back. Hamley's also

Barbecue is the focus at the **Sundown Grill** (233 S.E. 4th St., 541/276-8500, 4:30pm-8pm Wed.-Sat., 11am-1:30pm Sun., $9-24), in a nicely decorated historic house with patio seating during the summer. Dinner specials such as smoked trout served with homemade baked beans are offered along with ribs, sausages, and burgers. The **Great Pacific Wine and Coffee Co.** (403 S. Main St., 541/276-1350, http://greatpacific.biz, 10am-9pm Mon.-Sat. $7-14), in the classy former Masonic Lodge downtown, has something to please everyone. This sprawling establishment features imported cheeses, desserts, salads, pizza, sandwiches, microbrews, a good wine selection, an espresso bar, and occasional live music.

Out at the Wildhorse Casino, **Plateau** (46510 Wildhorse Blvd., 541/966-1610, www.wildhorseresort.com, 5pm-9pm daily, $26-60) has French-influenced dishes such as grilled salmon provençal, duck à l'orange, and steak with Pendleton whiskey sauce. Everything is well prepared and presented with elegance. **Sister's Café** (380 S. Main St., 541/276-6278, 10am-8pm Mon.-Sat., 10am-4pm Sun., $8-22) is a cavernous space with a coffee shop, a tap house with a dozen regional beers on draft, and a good restaurant with breakfast sandwiches, wraps, flatbread pizzas, and a children's menu.

Pendleton's first microbrewery is ★ **Prodigal Son Brewery and Pub** (230 SE Court Ave., 541/276-6090, http://prodigalsonbrewery.com, 11am-10pm Tues.-Sat., noon-9pm Sun., $9-12), a lively family-friendly pub on the edge of downtown. Come for the tasty Pacific Northwest-style brews as well as burgers, sandwiches, and an excellent locally made bratwurst with sauerkraut. Take a beer tour of the Pacific Northwest at **40 Taps** (337 S.W. Emigrant Ave., 541/612-8559, www.fortytaps.com, 2pm-10pm Sun.-Thurs., 2pm-1am Fri.-Sat., $4-7), with Pendleton's largest selection of craft beer on tap. Food is almost an afterthought, provided by the taco truck parked outside.

# ACCOMMODATIONS

Pendleton lodging is concentrated in two areas: Chain motels are found along the I-84 exits south of town, and older motor courts are close to downtown, within walking distance of Pendleton's famed nightlife. Rooms at these older downtown motels are usually cheaper than at the chains.

If you show up at Pendleton in mid-September during Round-Up time without a reservation, or unprepared to pay double the usual room rate, you will be out of luck. Anything within easy driving distance will be completely booked. Try booking a room in La Grande or in The Dalles and making a day trip to Pendleton. If you bring a tent, camping may be available in schoolyards and other special sites set up for the Round-Up crowds.

Just west of downtown, the family-run **Rugged Country Lodge** (1807 SE Court Ave., 541/966-6800 or 877/778-4433, www.ruggedcountrylodge.com, $65-80) is a 1950s vintage motel that has been lovingly refurbished—rooms are small but charmingly decorated, and the grounds are nicely landscaped. A bit closer to downtown, within walking distance of downtown shopping, dining, and entertainment, the **Travelodge** (411 SW Dorion Ave., 541/276-7531, www.travelodge.com, $79-92) is another good deal, with continental breakfast and pet-friendly rooms. The rooms are basic but clean and remodeled. Another good value in a central location is the **Marigold Hotel** (105 Court St., 541/276-3231, www.marigoldhotelbooking.com, $58-80). The exterior looks a little faded, but the rooms are nicely updated and comfortable.

For something uniquely Pendleton, consider a night at the **Working Girls Hotel** (17 SW Emigrant Ave., 541/276-0730, www.pendletonundergroundtours.org, $75-95). An offshoot of the popular Pendleton Underground Tours, this five-room downtown hotel once served as a brothel in the Pendleton's rowdy heyday. The rooms have been modernized, but the hardwood floors, 18-foot ceilings, and exposed brick walls point to the hotel's 1890s birthright. Equally historic but from the other end of the economic scale, the ★ **Pendleton House Bed and Breakfast** (311 N. Main St., 541/276-8581, www.pendletonhousebnb.com, $135-349) is a fantastic 1917 mansion with five guest rooms and 6,000 square feet of period luxury. Filled with antiques, oriental rugs, and original silk wall coverings, the Pendleton House even boasts a formal ballroom. A comfy porch, a backyard garden, and a fire blazing in the dining room while you enjoy creative breakfast fare evoke blissful thoughts of the good old days.

Six miles east of Pendleton, the new tower hotel at the **Wildhorse Resort Hotel and Casino** (46510 Wildhorse Blvd., 541/278-2274 or 800/654-9453, www.wildhorseresort.com, $90-230 Mon.-Fri.) is an impressive place, and rooms in the tower have some of the best views in eastern Oregon. The older courtyard rooms aren't remarkable, but some of these rooms are pet-friendly. The hotel lobby is adjacent to the casino, where smoking is permitted, but the hotel itself is nonsmoking, and good ventilation keeps the lobby air clean. The adjacent RV park ($31-40) is also well maintained; tenting sites and tepees ($17-30) are also available.

Facilities include a golf course, an indoor pool, a good restaurant, and, of course, 24-hour gaming.

## INFORMATION

**Travel Pendleton** (501 S. Main St., 541/276-7411 or 800/547-8911, www.travelpendleton.com) can steer you to local sights and special events. A self-guided walking-tour map of the historic downtown district is helpful. The tour starts at the corner of Main Street and Frazer Avenue and takes in many historic buildings.

## GETTING THERE AND AROUND

**Greyhound** (2101 SE Court Ave., 541/276-1551) offers two buses daily in each direction on the I-84 corridor between Portland and Boise. The stop is at the Pendleton Market.

Be aware that the mountainous stretch of I-84 east of Pendleton, known as Cabbage Hill, is treacherous to drive during icy winters. In addition to the slickness of the road surface, sudden blizzards and high winds can result in whiteout conditions. Pack snow chains for your tires, and if you're looking to leave Pendleton during a snowstorm, consider staying another day.

# La Grande and Vicinity

La Grande (pop. 13,000) is in the broad Grande Ronde Valley, which the indigenous people called Copi Copi ("Valley of Peace"). Completely ringed by mountains, it gives the impression of being circular, hence the valley's French name, which translates as "the big circle." The Nez Perce once gathered here for their summer encampments until the Oregon Trail cut through their territory. At La Grande, the Oregon Trail pioneers rested and prepared to traverse the Blue Mountains, a substantial challenge since the passes were often snow-filled by the time the wagon trains reached eastern Oregon.

More than a few of the pioneers were impressed with the agricultural possibilities of the Grande Ronde country, and they stayed to build a town that became the market center for a broad stretch of wheat and grass-seed farms. Lumber from the Blue Mountains and livestock also propelled the community's early growth. Now home to Eastern Oregon University, La Grande has an economy based on beef ranching, wheat farming, and timber. In addition to serving as a gateway to Wallowa Lake and the northern flank of the Wallowa Range, La Grande is a pleasant destination in itself, with a historic downtown and several good restaurants.

The town of Union, 11 miles southeast of La Grande, has a well-preserved town center of late Victorian homes and storefronts. Nearly the entire town is a National Historic District.

## SIGHTS
### Oregon Trail Interpretive Park

The **Oregon Trail Interpretive Park** (9am-7pm Tues.-Sun. Memorial Day-Labor Day, NW Forest Pass required) commemorates the crossing of the Blue Mountains by the Oregon Trail pioneers. Paved, easily accessible trails follow some of the best-preserved and most scenic traces of the Oregon Trail. Signs describe the pioneers' struggle through the thick forests and over the rugged mountain passes, and living history interpretive events are offered on summer weekends. To reach the park, take the I-84 exit for "Spring Creek," 12 miles west of La Grande.

### Mount Emily Recreation Area

When La Grande residents want to go on trail runs, bike rides, or cross-country ski or horseback outings, they don't have to travel far. The 3,669-acre **Mount Emily Recreation Area**

is only two miles from downtown and has 12 miles of trails. Climb the mountain for great views of the Grande Ronde Valley and the distant Eagle Cap Wilderness Area. Owsley Canyon Road (just east of the fairgrounds) leads from downtown north to a Mount Emily trailhead. Stop by the local bike shop, **The Mountain Works** (1307 Adams Ave., 541/963-3220, 10am-6pm Mon.-Sat.), for advice on where to mountain bike.

### Hot Lake Mineral Hot Springs

**Hot Lake Mineral Hot Springs** was considered powerfully healing by the Native Americans who camped nearby. A steady flow of nearly boiling water reaches the surface and pours into a large pond. During the 1800s, a hotel, a bathhouse, and a hospital were built, and the facility became known as the "Mayo Clinic of the West." During that era, the waters were thought to give relief from arthritis and rheumatism, and the medical team was noted for its success treating tuberculosis. The sanatorium was also a fashionable place to have a spa vacation. After the hospital closed in the 1930s, the building was used variously as a resort, a hotel, a restaurant, and a nursing home. Subsequently, for many years, it sat vacant.

Hot Lake Mineral Hot Springs

# The Oregon Trail

The pioneer trek along the Oregon Trail, a tide of migration starting in 1841 and lasting over 20 years, is among the largest voluntary human migrations ever recorded. About 50,000 pioneers followed the trail and settled in Oregon Country—present-day Oregon, Washington, and Idaho.

The wagon trains started in Independence, Missouri, as soon as the spring grass was green, and then the race was on to get across the far mountains before the winter snows. Although the first few hundred miles were easy traveling across the plains, the hardships soon came. Contrary to the stereotype of hostile Native Americans being a major cause of casualties, cholera was by far the leading cause of death on the 2,000-mile journey.

The route—which usually required six months to complete—followed the North Platte River to South Pass in Wyoming, then crossed the Snake River Plain in Idaho, then across the Snake River and up and over the Blue Mountains in eastern Oregon to The Dalles. Here the pioneers faced a decision: Put themselves and all their belongings onto rafts to float the rapids of the otherwise impassable Columbia Gorge, or struggle up the flanks of Mount Hood, descending into the Willamette Valley via the precipitous Barlow Trail.

At Fort Hall in eastern Idaho, there was a fork in the trail and a sign that read "To Oregon." It was here that the pioneers had to make another key decision: Head south to California and the goldfields shining with the promise of instant wealth, or continue west to Oregon, where the fertile Willamette Valley offered its own allure for farmers. Some Oregonians like to tell a more pointed version of the story, which claims that the sign for the California road was marked by a pile of gold-painted rocks, in contrast to the Oregon sign. The implication is that people who could read—or who were more interested in domestic pursuits than quick wealth—would head to Oregon. While this interpretation is not seriously accepted by historians, it remains a source of humor.

In 2004, David Manuel, an artist who owned a bronze foundry and gallery in nearby Joseph, and his wife, Lee, took over the crumbling resort and embarked on an ambitious remodel and revival. The **Hot Lake Springs** (66172 Hwy. 203, 541/963-4685, www.hotlakesprings.com) resort now includes bed-and-breakfast guest rooms ($189), a mineral-water spa with a selection of treatments, a museum and history center, and a restaurant and coffee shop. Tours of the property focus on the museum and history center (9am-4pm Mon.-Sat., $10); call to check on tour times if you want to visit the bronze foundry.

## Ladd Marsh

The 3,200-acre **Ladd Marsh** (I-84 exit 268, 5 miles south of La Grande off Foothill Rd.) is one of northeastern Oregon's largest remaining wetlands. Both upland and wetland habitats are represented, and habitat diversity contributes to the wide array of plant and animal species found on the marsh. It's an excellent place to go bird-watching, especially in the springtime when waterfowl are in the area; attentive birders can see up to 80 species in a morning.

## SPORTS AND RECREATION
### Golf

The **Buffalo Peak Golf Course** (1224 E. Fulton St., Union, 541/562-5527, www.buffalopeakgolf.com, $27 Mon.-Fri., $31 Sat.-Sun.) is an 18-hole par-72 links-style course in the Grande Ronde Valley that offers a variety of landscapes with native vegetation and natural terrain, such as patches of native prairie, streams, and lakes incorporated into the play.

### Swimming

Hot Lake is not the only natural hot spring in the area. In the little community of Cove, 17 miles southeast of La Grande, the **Cove Warm Spring Pool** (907 Water St., Cove, 541/568-4890, http://coveoregon.org, noon-6pm Thurs.-Sun. Memorial Day-Labor Day,

$8) is a great outdoor swimming pool; the water is naturally heated to a constant 86°F.

## FOOD

Stop for morning coffee and pastries at **Joe and Sugar's** (1119 Adams Ave., 541/975-5282, 7am-3pm Tues.-Fri., 9am-2pm Sat.-Sun., $2-10), a tiny bakery right downtown that also turns out excellent breakfast sandwiches and burritos. Some of the state's best fast food is available at the drive-through **Nells In 'n' Out** (1704 Adams Ave., 541/963-5733, 10:30am-10pm daily, $5-8). You'll find creative variations on shakes and floats, hand-curled french fries, and a full array of burgers.

**Ten Depot Street** (10 Depot St., 541/963-8766, http://tendepotstreet.com, 5pm-10pm Mon.-Sat., $10-32), in a classy old brick building, offers an up-to-date menu with grilled local lamb kebabs, grilled halibut, good salads and pasta, and perfectly prepared prime rib, the house specialty. The saloon is as popular as the restaurant and is a great place to indulge in a burger. If you're looking for beer and a burger, head to the firehouse: **Side A Brewing** (1219 Washington Ave., 541/605-0163, 11am-11pm daily, $10-20) is located in the city's 1899 fire station, which doubles as a museum and brewpub. Side A's IPA has won awards. The brown oatmeal ale is delicious, and food is tasty.

## ACCOMMODATIONS

Most of La Grande's hotels are not exactly grand. Out at I-84's exit 261, **Best Western Rama Inn and Suites** (1711 21st St., 541/963-3100 or 800/780-7234, www.bestwestern.com, $143-185) has more amenities than other places in town, including an indoor pool. The adjacent **Best Value Sandman Inn** (2410 E. R Ave., 541/963-3707, www.bestvalueinnlagrande.com, $103-134) has an indoor pool and spa, included Wi-Fi and continental breakfast, and bright clean rooms. Downtown, **The Landing** (1501 Adams Ave., 541/786-1212 or 888/950-5062, www.lagrandelandinghotel.com, $120-145) is a beautifully renovated 1900 boardinghouse that's the finest lodging choice

in historic La Grande. The rooms are simple but beautifully furnished, and the lobby offers a wine bar.

Eleven miles southeast of La Grande on Highway 203, the nine-unit **Union Hotel** (326 N. Main St., Union, 541/562-6135, www.theunionhotel.com, $89-135) will take you back to the 1920s, when this imposing hotel was built to satisfy the needs of sophisticated travelers between Portland and Boise. The hotel has been partially renovated (it's definitely a work in progress) and is one of the most charming and unusual hotels in eastern Oregon, best suited now for those who don't mind simple accommodations.

Hike, fly, or pack a horse into the remote **Minam River Lodge** (541/508-2719, http://minam-lodge.com), in the backcountry 26 miles from La Grande. Although many guests arrive via private plane, it's possible to hike or ride a horse in via a steep 8.5-mile trail from the Moss Springs trailhead, east of the town of Cove. Once there, the lodgings are in a beautiful log cabin ($395-595), a wall tent ($195), a tepee ($95), your own tent ($40), or under your plane wing ($30). Along with the beautiful setting, the simple locally sourced family-style breakfast and lunch ($25) and dinner ($75) are a big attraction. Even if you're camping, reserve your meals in advance.

### Camping

Between La Grande and Pendleton in the midst of the Blue Mountains, **Emigrant Springs State Heritage Area** (541/983-2277 or 800/551-6949, www.oregonstateparks.org, reservations www.reserveamerica.com, $17 tents, $22-24 RVs, $24-50 cabins) has showers and flush toilets in a wooded area immediately off busy I-84.

The **Hilgard Junction State Park** campground (I-84 exit 252, 541/983-2277 or 800/551-6949, www.oregonstateparks.org, no reservations, $10) is eight miles west of La Grande on the Grande Ronde River, at the foot of the Blue Mountains. The campground, on the original route of the Oregon Trail, has no hookups but is convenient to the interstate, which means it's noisy and not particularly private. Consider driving eight miles up Highway 244 (Starkey Rd.) to **Red Bridge State Wayside** for more appealing campsites ($10).

Another option off Highway 244 is **Spool Cart Campground** (541/963-7186, www.fs.usda.gov, May-Nov., $5) a small site with no water on the banks of the Grande Ronde River. From I-84 exit 252, drive 13 miles southwest on Highway 244 along the river, where stands of ponderosa pine and aspen are broken by meadows and farmland; from there, drive six miles south on Forest Road 51.

Southeast of La Grande, near the town of Union, **Catherine Creek State Park** (Hwy. 203, 541/983-2277, www.oregonstateparks. org, $10) is a pretty spot on a trout stream and has water and flush toilets.

## INFORMATION

For information on La Grande and Union County, contact the **Union County Chamber of Commerce** (207 Depot St., 541/963-8588 or 800/848-9969, http://visitunioncounty.org). Information on the Wallowa-Whitman Forest is at the **La Grande Ranger Station** (3502 U.S. 30, 541/963-7186).

## GETTING THERE

Two **Greyhound** buses travel each day between Portland and Boise with stops in La Grande (2204 E. Penn Ave., 541/963-5165).

# The Wallowas

Unlike any other of Oregon's peaks, the snowcapped Teton-like spires of the Wallowa Mountains soar 5,000 feet above Wallowa County farmlands and six-mile-long Wallowa Lake. Rather than the basalt that covers much of the state, these mountains are made of granitic rocks and limestone and are more closely related geologically to the Rockies than the Cascades of western Oregon. Much of the range is in the **Eagle Cap Wilderness Area,** which contains 17 of the state's 29 mountains over 9,000 feet and 50 glacial lakes sprinkled throughout 300,000 acres. Campers and cross-country skiers are regularly treated to glimpses of bighorn sheep, mountain goats, elk, and mule deer, as well as snow-streaked peaks rising above meadows dotted with an artist's palette of wildflowers. Seashells in limestone and greenstone outcroppings attest to the 200-million-year age of the range. The Wallowa Valley is formed by the drainages of the Wallowa, Minam, and Grande Ronde Rivers, and its backdrop is the half-moon-shaped Wallowa Range, 80 miles long and 25 miles across at its widest.

## History

The Wallowa Valley, set apart by deep river canyons and mountain ranges, is the ancestral home of the Nez Perce Nation, known for their horse-training skills and fierce independence. Astride their spotted Appaloosas, the Nez Perce first encountered Europeans when mountain men wandered onto their lands. Lewis and Clark believed that the Native Americans' generosity with food saved their lives. Their willingness to feed and care for the Bonneville Party, which had struggled up out of the Snake River Canyon in 1834, reinforced their reputation for honor and largesse. Later, however, when a dry spell in the Grande Ronde Valley to the south prompted homesteaders to farm the Wallowas, indigenous and settler cultures clashed.

One source of tension was the settlers permitting their hogs to trample the camas fields where the indigenous people came to gather food. The U.S. government attempted to resolve the situation by creating a 7-million-acre reservation in 1855, but reneged on the land treaty five years later when gold was

# Chief Joseph

Chief Joseph is known for his brave resistance to the government's attempts to force his people onto a reservation. A nation that spread from Idaho to northern Washington, the Nez Perce had peacefully coexisted with European Americans after the Lewis and Clark expedition, and had given the newcomers much-needed horses.

But with the incursion of miners and settlers, and because of misunderstandings surrounding the annexation of Native American land through a series of treaties never signed by Chief Joseph, tension increased. White disregard of Native American property spurred some young Nez Perce to retaliate. The ensuing 11-week conflict, during which the Nez Perce engaged 10 separate U.S. military commands in 13 battles (the majority of which the Nez Perce won), guaranteed Chief Joseph's fame as a brilliant military tactician. However, after many hardships, including starvation and many lost lives, Chief Joseph surrendered, only 50 miles from the sanctuary of the Canadian border.

Chief Joseph appealed repeatedly to the federal authorities to return the Nez Perce to the land of their ancestors, but to no avail. In 1885 he and many of his band were sent to a reservation in Washington, where, as the presiding doctor was heard to have said, he died of a broken heart.

discovered in the Wallowas. This breach initiated an era of confusion and distrust.

The settlers later successfully lobbied the government to evict the Native Americans, which led to the Nez Perce War of 1877. Chief Joseph and his people fought a running battle that covered 1,700 miles and ended with their surrender in the Bear's Paw Mountains, 50 miles from the Montana-Canada border. The Nez Perce Reservation is in central Idaho.

## EAGLE CAP EXCURSION TRAIN

Trains didn't reach the remote canyon country of the Wallowas until 1908, and passenger service lasted only into the 1920s. In the 1990s, freight service stopped along this lonely rail line that passes through stunning mountain meadows and deep river gorges. Local citizens banded together to purchase the track, and today the system operates both freight and excursion services between Elgin and Joseph.

The **Eagle Cap Excursion Train** (800/323-7330, http://eaglecaptrainrides.com, most Sat. early May-mid-Oct.) offers occasional trips leaving from the small Wallowa Valley town of Elgin. The train passes through spectacular scenery and culminates by traveling along the designated Wild and Scenic stretch of the

Wallowa River. Different trips focus on faux train robberies or wine and cheese. Most depart at 10am and return around 2pm, with lunch included in the fare ($80 adults, $75 seniors, $40 ages 3-16).

## ENTERPRISE

Enterprise (pop. 1,800) is the larger of the two towns that dominate the Wallowa Valley, and unlike Joseph, it has an authentic Western feel. Much of the original downtown, built in the 1890s, still exists and functions as the mercantile center. The **Bookloft and Skylight Gallery** (107 E. Main St., 541/426-3351, http://bookloftoregon.net, 9:30am-5:30pm Mon.-Fri., 10am-4pm Sat.), just across the street from the county courthouse, is a community gathering spot.

### Zumwalt Prairie

North of Highway 82, about halfway between Enterprise and Joseph, roads head north through rangeland to high plateaus. One good destination 45 minutes from Enterprise is **Zumwalt Prairie,** the largest remaining native Pacific Northwest bunchgrass prairie, managed by the **Nature Conservancy** (541/426-3458, www.nature.org) with several hiking trails (dogs, bikes, and horses not permitted). To reach the prairie from Highway

# Floating the Wallowa and Grande Ronde Rivers

The Wallowa and Grande Ronde Rivers offer an easygoing raft trip.

From the dot on the map that is Minam, rafters can float 46 miles north along the Wallowa and Grande Ronde Rivers through steep basalt canyons to Troy, a tiny town near the Washington border. Depending on flow and the amount of time you spend exploring on foot, the trip takes two or three days; there are options for shorter or longer trips.

Because the rivers are primarily free-flowing, water levels and river character change dramatically with the seasons. Higher, faster river flows typically occur in the spring and early summer. By August, river flows are typically low, with shallow water and exposed rocks. Early in the summer, this is a popular family trip, especially if parents are experienced rafters or the trip is a guided one; in midsummer, and again when the water cools, anglers dominate the scene.

**Minam Raft Rentals** (541/437-1111, www.minamraftrentals.com), operated out of the **Minam Motel** ($69-89), has rentals, shuttles, and guided trips. For full details on do-it-yourself trips, contact the **Bureau of Land Management River Station** (Minam, 541/437-5580, www.blm.gov/or).

82, head north on Cow Creek Road; after five miles, turn right onto Zumwalt Road, which is paved for the first few miles. Travel 14 miles on Zumwalt Road; at the junction, turn right toward Imnaha and follow the Nature Conservancy sign 1.4 miles to the Duckett Barn, which has interpretive signs and a trailhead. Another trailhead, for the Horned Lark Trail, is on the main Zumwalt Road about three miles past the junction with the Imnaha road.

In addition to providing public access via the trails, the Nature Conservancy works to maintain the prairie with controlled burns, hunting, and cattle grazing. If you're up for more back-road exploration, continue north on the Zumwalt Road to the Buckhorn Lookout; it's a slow 35 miles from the highway and has amazing views.

## Entertainment and Events

**Terminal Gravity Brewing** (803 SE School St., 541/426-0158, www.terminalgravity-brewing.com, 11am-10pm daily summer, 11am-10pm Sun.-Mon. and Wed., 11am-9pm Thurs.-Sat., $8-14) is a top-notch brewpub with excellent beer, decent pub food, and a perfectly laid-back atmosphere. Customers congregate on the porch and front lawn in an idyllic creek-side poplar grove.

Northwest of Enterprise in the town of Wallowa, the **Wallowa Band Nez Perce Trail Interpretive Center** (209 E. 2nd St., Wallowa, 541/886-3101, www.wallowanezperce.org) holds the late-July **Tamkaliks Celebration,** which celebrates the continuing Nez Perce presence in the Wallowa Valley. A Native American encampment, dancing, and feasting are highlights of the festival.

**Hells Canyon Mule Days** (www.hellscanyonmuledays.com), held the weekend after Labor Day at the **Wallowa County Fairgrounds** (668 NW 1st St., Enterprise), is where pack-animal fanciers can get their kicks. The action includes mule races, a parade, a speed mule-shoeing contest, and endurance competitions.

## Food

About 10 miles northwest of Enterprise, the 1900 building housing the ★ **Lostine Tavern** (125 Hwy. 2, Lostine, 541/569-2246, http://lostine-tavern.com, 11am-10pm Wed.-Sun., $8-20) has long been a local gathering place; now it houses a wonderful pub-style restaurant where the emphasis on farm-to-table cooking supports local farmers and ranchers. In the evening, the sandwich-leaning menu adds a few homey dinner specials, such as barbecued chicken.

**Red Rooster Cafe** (309 W. Main St., 541/426-2233, www.red-rooster-cafe.com, 7am-2pm Wed.-Sat., 8am-2pm Sun., $6-12) is an especially cheery place for breakfast or lunch in downtown Enterprise. The food here is homemade, using as many fresh, local ingredients as possible; baked oatmeal and a cup of the café's custom-roasted coffee are a great way to get ready for the day.

Drive 30 miles north of Enterprise on Highway 3 to the tiny town of Flora, where the **Rimrock Inn** (83471 Lewiston Hwy., 541/828-7769, www.rimrockinnor.com, 11am-8pm Tues.-Sat., reservations required, $10-28)

awaits. The menu includes a selection of salads, burgers and steaks, accompanied by organically grown vegetables. A staggering view of Joseph Canyon as it trenches its way toward Hells Canyon is as good as the food.

## Accommodations

Lodging in Enterprise can be less expensive than other Wallowa area options—and it's not booked up months in advance like the lodges at Wallowa Lake. The fairly large **Ponderosa Motel** (102 SE Greenwood St., 541/426-3186, $92-105) is just south of downtown and has fridges and microwaves in the guest rooms. **Wilderness Inn** (301 W. North St., 541/426-4535, $86) has everything you need for a comfortable night in Enterprise.

**The 1910 Historic Enterprise House B&B** (508 1st South St., 541/426-4238 or 888/448-8825, www.enterprisehousebnb.com, $149-219) is a large rambling farmhouse from the turn of the 20th century and has a big front porch and great mountain views. Each of the five guest rooms has a private bath, and the massive third-floor suite ($219) can sleep up to six.

A different sort of B&B experience is offered at **Barking Mad Farm B&B** (65156 Powers Rd., 541/886-0171, www.barkingmadfarm.com, $175-225), an elegant and exceedingly pet-friendly inn. The three suites are all beautiful, but it's hard to top the Treetop Suite, which you enter through a hatch and which has a deck snug up against an ancient yew tree.

Travel 30 miles north of town to the ★ **Rimrock Inn** (83471 Lewiston Hwy., 541/828-7769, www.rimrockinnor.com, late May-Sept., breakfast included), where you can choose between staying in a fully furnished futon-equipped but nonelectrified tepee ($150-195) with a separate bath, a suite ($160-175) in the inn, or a vintage trailer ($165-180). It's worth heading off the beaten path to stay at the Rimrock, and not only because of the views of beautiful Joseph Canyon; the inn's restaurant (peak summer season, reservations required) is remarkably good.

## Information

The **Wallowa County Chamber of Commerce** (309 S. River St., 541/426-4622, www.wallowacountychamber.com, 8am-5pm Mon.-Fri.) stocks a full complement of brochures, maps, and other information on the area.

## JOSEPH

At the base of the Wallowa Mountains is Joseph (elevation 4,150 feet), a lively community of about 1,000 people that's named after the famous Nez Perce chief. Joseph is noted across the West as an arts town; however, the colorful main street is increasingly lined with gift shops more than galleries, and on a busy summer weekend, finding the artsy charm of this pretty town takes a little doing.

That said, there are still plenty of galleries and arts-related shops to visit, and **Valley Bronze** (18 Main St., 541/432-7445, www.valleybronze.com), Joseph's original bronze-casting operation—and the second-largest in the nation—displays works and offers tours of its **Foundry** (307 W. Alder St., 541/432-7551, 11am Mon.-Sat. May-Sept., reservations required, $15).

If a foundry tour doesn't fit into your schedule, at least take a walk down Main Street to look at many bronze sculptures; each was done by a different artist.

### ★ Joseph Branch Railriders

Ride the rails between Enterprise and Joseph using your own steam with the **Joseph Branch Railriders** (501 W. Alder St., 541/786-6149, http://jbrailriders.com, 8am-4pm Thurs.-Mon. mid-May-early Oct., reservations recommended). The vehicles are a cross between a recumbent bicycle and a railcar; the routes, no longer used by trains, pass through beautiful country that you won't see from the highway. A popular 12-mile round-trip (9am, noon, 3pm, $22 adults, $10 under age 12) is a gentle downhill from Joseph to Enterprise and back. Another route goes from Minam to Wallowa, a relatively flat 26-mile round-trip (about 6 hours) along the Wallowa River (9am Fri.-Mon., $48).

### Josephy Center for Arts and Culture

The **Josephy Center** (403 N. Main St., 541/432-0505, www.josephy.org, 10am-5pm Mon.-Fri., noon-4pm Sat.) aims to revitalize the area's "creative capital" with its attractive gallery space, library, and workshops. The library honors Alvin Josephy (1915-2008), a

Joseph Branch Railriders pedal from Joseph to Enterprise on an abandoned rail line.

Western historian who focused much of his work on the Nez Perce people and is a treasure trove of books, journals, artifacts, and manuscripts from the Josephy family.

## Wallowology!

Much as the Josephy Center celebrates the area's arts, **Wallowology!** (508 N. Main St., 541/263-1663, www.wallowology.org, 10am-3pm Tues.-Sun. Memorial Day-Sept., free) gives visitors a chance to learn about the Wallowas' natural history. In addition to the exhibits, the center leads free three-hour hikes several times a week; longer outings and talks on geology, wildlife, fire, and other natural history topics are also offered (check the website for schedules).

## Iwetemlaykin State Heritage Site

On the road from Joseph to Wallowa Lake, stop off and hike the trails at the **Iwetemlaykin State Heritage Site** to get a feeling for the Nez Perce homeland. It's easy to see why this grassland laced with streams and surrounded by mountains is sacred to the Nez Perce. Short trails offer a chance to get away from the hubbub of downtown Joseph without launching into a rigorous mountain hike. The site is adjacent to the Old Chief Joseph gravesite.

## Wallowa County Museum

A must-stop for history buffs is the **Wallowa County Museum** (110 Main St., 541/432-6095, http://co.wallowa.or.us, 10am-4pm daily Memorial Day-late Sept., $4 adults, $3 seniors, $2 students). Built in 1888, the museum building has served as a newspaper office, a private hospital, a meeting hall, and a bank (one of the crooks who robbed the bank later became its president). The museum includes displays of pioneer life and the Nez Perce people.

## Fishing

The Wallowa Valley area is home to several fine fishing streams, including the Wallowa, Grande Ronde, Lostine, and Imnaha Rivers.

The **Joseph Fly Shoppe** (203 N. Main St., 541/432-4343, www.josephflyshop.com, 9am-5pm Mon.-Sat., 9am-4pm Sun.) is a good source for information and gear; **Winding Waters** (877/426-7238, www.windingwatersrafting.com) is a local outfitter.

## Entertainment and Events

The **Wallowa Valley Festival of the Arts** (www.wallowavalleyarts.org) is held at the Joseph Civic Center in mid-September. Along with awards for Pacific Northwest artists, there are wine-tasting parties, a silent auction, and a quick-draw competition (using pencils, not sidearms).

Held the last week of July, **Chief Joseph Days** (541/432-1015, www.chiefjosephdays. com) is a weeklong festival in Joseph that features dances along with a carnival, the Grand Parade, a ranch-style breakfast, and a three-day rodeo, one of the largest in the Pacific Northwest. **Bronze, Blues, and Brews** (www.bronzebluesbrews.com) takes place in early August, featuring music, gallery and foundry open houses, and locally brewed beer.

A couple of times a year, Joseph hosts a low-key but talent-laden literary gathering known as **Fishtrap** (541/426-3623, www. fishtrap.org). Authors writing in different genres attend; past participants have included William Kittredge, Ursula K. LeGuin, Ivan Doig, Sandra Scofield, and Terry Tempest Williams. Writers of all levels come to read their works and discuss social issues.

## Food

Don't limit yourself to a latte at **Red Horse Coffee Traders** (306 N. Main St., www.red-horsecoffeetraders.com, 541/432-3784, 7am-3pm Mon.-Sat., 8am-4pm Sun., $7-10); this is a wonderful place for a scone, a breakfast burrito, or a sandwich on homemade bread. If you prefer chocolate with your coffee, check out **Arrowhead Chocolates** (100 N. Main St., 541/432-2871, 7am-5pm daily), where you'll find excellent handmade confections as well as Stumptown coffee.

The log-sided **Old Town Café** (8 S. Main St., 541/432-9898, 7am-2pm daily, $6-12) looks the part of a vintage frontier town eatery—it's a great spot for oniony hash brown potatoes topped with cheese, bacon, and homemade salsa. In nice weather, the outdoor seating is particularly appealing. **Outlaw Restaurant & Saloon** (108 N. Main St., 541/432-4321, www.theoutlawrestaurant.com, 11:15am-8:45pm Tues.-Sat., $10-22) offers standard American fare, but in summer there's ample outdoor seating; this is a good bet for dinner for a family. **Embers Brewhouse** (204 N. Main St., 541/432-2739, www.embersbrewhouse.com, 11am-9pm Mon.-Sat., noon-8pm Sun., $9-13) offers regional microbrews on tap plus pizza and deli sandwiches; try for a spot outside on the deck.

## Accommodations

There are a few lodging options in Joseph itself; many visitors stay a few miles away at Wallowa Lake, where there's a large campground, a couple of RV parks, and several cabin resorts. Right downtown, the distinctive landmark ★ **Jennings Hotel and Sauna** (100 N Main St., no phone, www.jenningshotel.com, $79-160) is part hotel, part artists colony. Built in 1910, it was recently revitalized when a Kickstarter campaign transformed it into a stylish outpost for the arts. Each of the nine guest rooms has been decorated by a different regional designer; the hotel's artist residency program brings artists to town. Book rooms through the website.

In town, for clean, basic motel rooms, try the **Indian Lodge Motel** (201 S. Main St., 541/432-2651, www.indianlodgemotel.com, $112-127), known by old-timers as "Walter Brennan's place," after the motel's original owner, the TV and movie actor. **Mountain View Motel and RV Park** (83450 Joseph Hwy., 541/432-2982, www.mtviewmotel-rvpark.com, $80-115) is about a mile out of town toward Enterprise; in addition to pet-friendly motel rooms, they have a space for RVs ($40) and tents ($30).

**Bronze Antler Bed & Breakfast** (309 S. Main St., 541/432-0230, www.bronzeantler.com, $158-260) is a friendly B&B in a 1925 bungalow originally built by a local sawmill supervisor who filled the Craftsman-style home with custom millwork and beautiful wood floors. The three guest rooms and one suite have private baths and luxurious linens and towels—the room appointments rival those at upscale hotels. **Chandler's Inn** (700 S. Main St., 541/432-9765, $95-180) is a large house, long a B&B, on the edge of town. Options range from smaller rooms with a shared bath to large two-bedroom suites.

## WALLOWA LAKE

The biggest attraction in the Wallowas is the 5,000-foot-elevation Wallowa Lake, which is bordered by the peaks of the Eagle Cap Wilderness. This moraine-held glacial lake begins a mile south of Joseph on Highway 82 at the east end of the Wallowa Valley, though most development is at the south end of the lake, about six miles from Joseph. Although it is beautiful, the area around the lake takes on a carnival atmosphere during the summer, with arcades, bumper boats, miniature golf, go-karts, and—for adults—parasailing. In addition to these amusements, there are lodges, a large state park with a campground, boat launches, a marina, and perhaps the **Wallowa Lake Monster,** a creature with a gentle disposition and a length of 30 to 100 feet, depending on the sighting. Reports of the critter go back centuries to Native American tales.

Exercise caution before you dive in to join the monster. Invitingly clear, the lake waters are extremely cold and should not be experienced until August, and not for long thereafter. The beach in the county park at the northern end of the lake is a good spot to test the waters.

### Wallowa Lake State Park

One of the most popular in the Oregon state park system, **Wallowa Lake State Park** (541/432-4185, www.oregonstateparks.org)

is set lakeside amid big old ponderosa pines. It's a beautiful spot for an outdoorsy family vacation. Even if you're not camping, enjoy the scenery from the large lakeside day-use area. The **Wallowa Lake Marina** (541/432-9115, www.wallowalakemarina.com), in the day-use area, sells fishing gear and rents watercraft ranging from stand-up paddleboards to motorboats. The park is moments from wilderness hiking trails and horseback riding as well as bumper boats and miniature golf. In high season, reserve campsites several months in advance.

## ★ Wallowa Lake Tramway

The gondola up Mount Howard, the **Wallowa Lake Tramway** (544/432-5331, http://wallowalaketramway.com, 9am-5:45pm daily June-late Sept., reduced hours early and late in season, $33 adults, $30 seniors, $27 ages 12-17, $21 ages 4-11, $6 under age 4), lifts passengers 3,700 feet from the edge of Wallowa Lake to the 8,200-foot summit.

The 15-minute ride ends at the Summit Grill, but forget about dining; the best reason for taking the trip is the view. About 2.5 miles of mostly easy trails lead to various overlooks, where you have amazing views of the Wallowa Range, Snake River country, and Idaho's Seven Devils area. The gondola operates fewer days per week mid-May to mid-June and mid to late September; check the website for the schedule then.

## Hiking and Horseback Riding

Although many visitors hike the trail network at the top of the tram, there's a good trailhead at the end of Wallowa Lake Highway, less than one mile from the lake. From here you can hike the steep uphill trail six miles to Aneroid Lake, or turn around at the waterfall that's about four miles in. The last couple of miles, between the waterfall and the lake, are the prettiest. From the same trailhead you can catch the seven-mile trail to Chief Joseph Mountain, with good views along the way of Wallowa Lake. Expect to share the trail with horses.

If you'd rather ride a horse up one of these trails, the **Wallowa Lake Pack Station** (59761 Wallowa Lake Hwy., 541/432-7433, www.wallowalakepackstation.com) is right near the trailhead; one-hour ($35) and two-hour ($65) rides are available as well as half-day ($120) and full-day ($190) rides that take riders up into the high country. A variety of longer rides are also offered.

Find relatively easy trails and spectacular views at the top of the Wallowa Lake Tramway.

Horseback rides head to mountain lakes.

## Food, Accommodations, and Camping

The following lodgings on Wallowa Lake reflect the special woodsy flavor of this outback locality. These accommodations are all at the south end of the lake, near the state park, which offers campsites. Most of the cabins have kitchens, and Joseph's limited selection of restaurants are just a short drive away.

The renovated 1923 **Wallowa Lake Lodge** (60060 Wallowa Lake Hwy., 541/432-9821, www.wallowalakelodge.com, $129-279) on the lakefront drips with vintage atmosphere. Some guest rooms are quite small; others have two bedrooms; all have private baths. Eight 1950s-era cabins feature knotty pine cabinets, stone fireplaces, and fully modern kitchens and baths; most have lake views. It's hard to imagine a more enchanting setting. The **dining room** (7am-11am and 5pm-9pm daily May-Oct., $11-26) is beautifully preserved, though the food—steaks, pasta, fresh seafood—is up-to-date. Early and late in the season, restaurant hours are reduced, so check ahead.

The **Flying Arrow Resort** (59782 Wallowa Lake Hwy., 541/432-2951) and **Wallowa Lake Resort** (84681 Ponderosa Lane, 541/432-2391) now offer an extensive selection of cabins, condos, and houses from a single website, www.wallowalakeresort.com. You'll find a big range, from one-room cabins to four-bedroom houses that can sleep 14. All but the most basic cabins have kitchens, fireplaces, and baths; all are unique.

On the quieter western side of the lake, **Trouthaven** (61841 Lakeshore Dr., 541/432-2221, www.trouthavencabins.com, mid-May-mid-Sept., $110-120) is another venerable cabin resort. The cabins come in two sizes (the larger ones can sleep six) and have knotty pine paneling and a covered porch with an outdoor dining table. The Trouthaven also has a half-mile of Wallowa Lake frontage with a couple of docks; boats and fishing gear are available for rent. The cabins and this location are perfect for a family vacation; during the busy months of July and August, a five-day minimum stay is required.

**Vali's Alpine Delicatessen** (59811 Wallowa Lake Hwy., 541/432-5691, www.valisrestaurant.com, seatings 5pm and 7pm Wed.-Sun. Memorial Day-Labor Day, 5pm and 7pm Sat.-Sun. Apr.-Memorial Day, reservations required, $13-22, no credit cards) features a different fixed dinner menu each day, with German and Hungarian specialties such as cabbage rolls or schnitzel. Freshly made doughnuts are on offer 9am-11am Saturday and Sunday.

## THE WALLOWA MOUNTAINS HIGH COUNTRY

The Wallowa Mountains are some of Oregon's most rugged, beautiful, and least visited: 715 square miles of this craggy backcountry are preserved as the **Eagle Cap Wilderness Area.** Glacier-torn valleys, high mountain lakes, and marble peaks are some of the rewards that await backpackers. There's good fishing in streams and lakes, and in winter the heavy snowfalls attract both downhill and cross-country skiers. U.S. Forest Service campgrounds serve as bases for Wallowa Mountains exploration. For more on recreation and camping, contact the **Wallowa-Whitman National Forest** (201 E. 2nd St., Joseph, 541/426-5546, www.fs.usda.gov/wallowa-whitman).

## Hiking and Camping

Most Eagle Cap Wilderness Area trails are long and steep, and most alpine lakes are at least five miles from a trailhead, so opportunities for easy day hikes into the wilderness are limited. Camping is the best way to enjoy the area. Before heading out, pick up the Eagle Cap map from a U.S. Forest Service office or local sporting goods stores. Higher elevations are usually free of snow by early July, but streams may be running high and fast until late July.

The easily accessible **Minam State Recreation Area** (541/551-6949, www.oregonstateparks.org, no reservations, $10) off Highway 82 about 15 miles east of Elgin puts you within relatively easy striking distance of trailheads. The **Two Pan** trailhead is one of the most popular gateways into the Wallowas; **Williamson** and **Shady** campgrounds ($6) are along the road to the trailhead and have no water. To get here, head south from Lostine on County Highway 551 for seven miles and down Forest Road 5202 for 11 miles. This is a rough and rocky road, so take your time. Trails leave Two Pan for the Lostine River Valley and the glacial lakes at the base of Eagle Cap.

Farther east, **Hurricane Creek** ($6) has no water and is three miles southwest of Joseph on Forest Road 8205. The Hurricane Creek trailhead leads to a hike along the east slope of the Hurricane Divide past Sacajawea Peak and the Matterhorn to the glacial lakes basin. An ambitious trek starts at Two Pan and ends at Hurricane Creek. The lake basin area south of Joseph can get crowded, especially on weekends in July and August.

If your budget allows, hire a guide to ease your way into the wilderness. The **Wallowa Lake Pack Station** (59761 Wallowa Lake Hwy., 541/432-7433, www.wallowalakepackstation.com) runs many day horseback rides to lakes and streams in the Eagle Cap high country and outfitting expeditions into the backcountry ($250 pp per day). The outfitters furnish your complete camp, including riding horses, pack animals, a guide, wranglers, a cook, and food. These outfitters also offer "gear drop" trips, where horses and mules carry supplies to a lake, then leave and return at an appointed time to pack your gear out. This service starts at $400 a day for one packer and mule; if you want to ride a horse to your chosen destination, it's an additional $150 a day for each riding horse.

**Wallowa Llamas** (36678 Allstead Lane, Halfway, 541/742-2961, www.wallowallamas.com) offers a unique way to venture into the wilderness. One surefooted, even-tempered llama will carry 20 pounds of your gear; you carry the rest. The outfit offers three- to seven-day trips to Hells Canyon and the Wallowas. The expeditions (4-6 days, late Apr.-late Aug., from $795) are designed for those with some backpacking experience or anyone in reasonably good shape. The outfitters provide tents, eating utensils, and all meals—and the llamas.

## Skiing

The recreational delights of the Wallowas extend to excellent skiing in this alpine wonderland. **Ferguson Ridge Ski Area** (541/426-3493, www.skifergi.com, 10am-4pm Sat.-Sun. and holidays, $20 adults, $10 children) is a small and laid-back downhill facility with a rope tow and T-bar that climb from a 5,100-foot base to 5,800-foot-high Ferguson Ridge. The light eastern Oregon powder, when there's enough of it, makes for good skiing. Make sure to bring a full water bottle; no water is available at the ski area. To get here, drive east from Joseph about five miles on the Wallowa Loop Highway, then follow signs south on Tucker Down Road.

Cross-country skiers can head to the **Hurricane Creek.** Take Hurricane Creek Road west from Joseph to the trailhead. Another popular spot is **Salt Creek Summit,** about 20 miles southeast of Joseph on Wallowa Loop Highway. The facility has five miles of marked but ungroomed ski and snowmobile trails and a plowed snow park.

Backcountry ski mountaineering is the focus of **Wallowa Alpine Huts** (541/398-1980, www.wallowahuts.com), which offers four- or five-day trips to several backcountry huts, including one at 7,500-foot McCully Basin within the Eagle Cap Wilderness. Ski seven miles in to a yurt base camp and spend the days exploring the high country on backcountry snowboards, telemarking skis, or randonée skis, then return to cooked meals, warm yurts, and even a sauna. Four-day trips (from $1,000) include all backcountry meals, accommodations, bedding, and guides; forgo the guide and cook for yourself for a four-day stay at the yurts ($250 pp).

# Hells Canyon

## ★ HELLS CANYON NATIONAL RECREATION AREA

The **Hells Canyon National Recreation Area** (Oxbow, 541/785-3395, www.fs.usda.gov) straddles a 71-mile portion of the Snake River and encompasses the 215,223-acre Hells Canyon Wilderness Area. Most of the canyon's terrain is precipitous rock walls and steep, slot-like side valleys, which means that just about the only way to experience this epic landscape is on foot, horseback, or—most accessibly—by boat. The remote Hells Canyon is the deepest river gorge in North America. For a distance of 106 miles no bridge crosses the river, and few paved roads even come near the canyon. At its deepest point, the gorge walls rise nearly 8,000 feet.

### Hells Canyon by Vehicle

There are several ways to get to Hells Canyon from Oregon. From Baker City, take Highway 86 for 50 miles east to **Halfway.** Stop here to stock up on groceries and gas, continue

Hells Canyon Lookout

on Highway 86 another 16 miles to Oxbow Dam, and then downstream (north) 20 miles on the Idaho side of the Snake River to **Hells Canyon Dam.** A visitors center is adjacent to where rafts put in on the Snake River at the beginning of the river's designated Wild and Scenic stretch. This site affords a spectacular view of the canyon.

Another approach is via Highway 82 through the Wallowa Valley to Enterprise, Joseph, and Imnaha. From Imnaha, one of the most isolated towns in the country, drive 24 miles to **Hat Point Lookout.** The first five miles of ascent is not for the faint of heart— the guardrail-free dirt road is vertigo-inducing. However, once on the ridgetop, the road edges to Hat Point and a view into Hells Canyon and the Snake River, a dizzying 7,000 feet below.

A simpler but less satisfying way to glimpse the canyon is from the **Wallowa Mountain Loop Road** (a.k.a. Forest Rd. 39), which runs between Joseph and Halfway. The **Hells Canyon Lookout,** the only paved viewpoint into Hells Canyon, is 31 miles north of Halfway. The vista looks into the canyon, but the river isn't visible from here.

## Hiking

More than 900 miles of trails await hikers and backpackers in the Hells Canyon National Recreation Area, and hiking is just about the only way to get to some of the canyon's remoter areas. However, it's not a hiking destination for novices. Before lacing up your hiking boots, consider that summer temperatures soar above 100°F, rattlesnakes abound, and potable water can be hard to find. Ticks and poison oak can be problems here too. Black widow and brown recluse spiders can constitute the biggest danger, however. Major trails are maintained, but others are difficult to follow. It's a good idea to talk to rangers before setting out, as this is an extremely remote and challenging wilderness. You'll also want a detailed map.

Long-distance riverside trails run on both the Oregon and Idaho shores of the Snake River, but reaching them is a challenge. The rugged cliffs along the Hells Canyon Dam are too steep for hiking trails, although a mile-long trail from the jet-boat launch area north of Hells Canyon Dam does pick its way down the Oregon side before ending precipitously.

Reach the **Oregon Snake River Trail,** on the river's western edge, by driving 27 miles north of Imnaha to Dug Bar; this will put you on the river. The road is okay for passenger cars in good weather, but it can be slippery when wet. Another option is the **Western Rim Trail.** There are comparatively few steep ups and downs, and daytime temperatures are much less oppressive than within the canyon. There is also plenty of shade among the rim's evergreen forests. On the other hand, the rim route has fewer water sources, so camping choices are limited. To reach the southern end of this 37-mile trail, from Joseph, follow Forest Road 39 to the Hells Canyon Viewpoint and head about 10 miles northeast on Forest Road 3965 to the PO Saddle Trailhead (www.fs.usda.gov).

## Boating

Outfitters arrange Snake River float trips on rafts, dories, or kayaks, providing high adventure as the river bounces though 34 Class II-IV named rapids in the two- to three-day passage between Hells Canyon Dam and Pittsburgh Landing in Idaho, the most commonly floated part of the canyon; longer trips are available. Turbine-powered flat-bottomed jet-boat tours are a noisy but equally exciting way to see the canyon in as little as a day. The national recreation area (www.fs.usda.gov) provides a list of outfitters licensed to guide trips on the Snake River, which include the following.

From the landing just below Hells Canyon Dam, **Hells Canyon Adventures** (541/785-3352 or 800/422-3568, www.hellscanyonadventures.com) offers a variety of jet-boat tours (daily Apr.-Sept.), as well as one- and two-day rafting and fishing trips. The briefest and least expensive excursion is a two-hour afternoon jet-boat trip into the deepest part of the canyon ($85 adults, $60 children). A six-hour tour (10am, $177 adults, $88 children) runs all the principal rapids and includes lunch and a stop at the frontier Kirkwood Ranch Museum at the base of the canyon. Float trips and fishing charters are also provided, and reservations are required.

**Winding Waters** (877/426-7238, www.windingwatersrafting.com, May-Oct.) is a local outfitter that specializes in three- to six-day white-water raft trips (from $995 adults, $796 children) that include guide services, tent accommodations, transport to and from Joseph, a night's lodging in Joseph, and food. Fishing for trout, catfish, smallmouth bass, and, if you're lucky, 100-year-old sturgeon can add to the pleasure of a raft trip. **Canyon Outfitters** (541/742-4110, www.canyonoutfitters.com) offers summer white-water float trips (4 days, $1,450) with ample time for fishing. If you plan to shoot the Class III and IV rapids of the Snake River on your own, you'll need a permit from the **Hells Canyon National Recreation Area Office** (541/785-3395) in Oxbow.

## Camping

Of the 12 campgrounds on the Oregon side of the national recreation area, we recommend the following three. **Lake Fork Campground** ($6), with no water, is 18 miles northeast of Halfway on Forest Road 39, and the fishing is good at nearby Fish Lake. **Indian Crossing** ($6), 45 miles southeast of Joseph on Forest Road 3960, has a trailhead for backpacking into the Eagle Cap Wilderness; water is available at the trailhead. On the northern end of the recreational area, **Buckhorn** (free) has no water and is 43 miles northeast of Enterprise, with a great view.

## Accommodations

The town of Halfway (pop. 286), 17 miles from the Oxbow Dam on the Snake River, is a popular way station for Hells Canyon-bound travelers. It's prudent to pack a few picnic items here as restaurants are few on the route, and Halfway has a few cafés. There's also a restaurant at Oxbow, near the Snake River on Highway 86.

The ★ **Pine Valley Lodge** (163 N. Main St., Halfway, 541/742-2027, www.pvlodge.com, $80-150) is an unexpected Old West pleasure in rugged Hells Canyon country. A dozen guest rooms have been created in vintage log and wood structures in downtown Halfway, and each is filled with cowboy decor that's part history, part whimsy. Reasonably priced standard guest rooms can be found at the **Halfway Motel** (170 S. Main St., Halfway, 541/742-5722, $70).

Twelve miles north of Halfway, at the southern edge of the Eagle Cap Wilderness Area, the **Cornucopia Lodge** (Queen Mine Rd., 541/742-4500 or 800/742-6115, www.cornucopialodge.com, $130-195, includes breakfast) is a great place to launch or conclude a backpacking trip, or just relax. The cabins and lodge are in a spectacularly scenic setting with horseback rides, hikes, or fishing trips. Cooking is not allowed in the cabins, but dinner ($26) is available.

# Baker City

Friendly Baker City (pop. 9,700), in a valley between the Wallowas and the Blue Mountains, is the quintessential Western ranch town, with a handsome downtown area filled with classic stone and redbrick storefronts. Ranchers still drive their herds down the highways, and folks wave "howdy" to passersby. Baker City has held on to its pioneer spirit, and there's lots of history here, highlighted by the nation's foremost Oregon Trail interpretive center. Baker City is a good jumping-off spot for Hells Canyon, the deepest gorge in North America.

Baker City was the hub of the eastern Oregon gold rush; stop by the U.S. Bank downtown and check out the 80.4-ounce **Armstrong gold nugget,** found in 1913. It's a remnant from the days when this wealthy, raucous frontier boomtown was the biggest and most important in the region. West of town along Highway 7 and its offshoots leading into the Elkhorn and Blue Mountains, ghost towns like Granite, McEwen, and Sumpter are remnants of the gold rush days of the 1860s. The route, which follows the twisty

contours of the Powder River, is particularly pretty when the trees take on fall hues.

## SIGHTS
### ★ National Historic Oregon Trail Interpretive Center

Six miles east of Baker City is the 23,000-square-foot **National Historic Oregon Trail Interpretive Center** (22267 Hwy. 86, 541/523-1843, www.blm.gov/or/oregontrail, 9am-6pm daily mid-Apr.-Nov., 9am-4pm daily Dec.-mid-Apr., $8 adults, $4.50 seniors, free under age 16, discounts in winter). The museum is perched atop Flagstaff Hill overlooking a picturesque section of the famous frontier route. The exhibit halls are arranged to simulate the route and experiences of pioneers on the 547-mile section of the trail within Oregon's borders. Life-size dioramas and taped renditions of immigrant voices and wagon wheels make you feel like part of the great migration.

Outside the museum are living-history exhibits and the chance to stand in the actual ruts left behind by pioneer wagons at

The Oregon Trail Interpretive Center offers a commanding view of the Elkhorn Mountains.

Virtue Flat, a two-mile walk from the center. Surrounded by the 10,000-foot Elkhorn Mountains to the west, the Blues to the south, and the craggy Eagle Cap to the northeast, the "land at Eden's gate" becomes more than just another florid phrase from a pioneer diary.

## Baker Heritage Museum

Housed in a showcase natatorium built in 1920, the **Baker Heritage Museum** (2490 Grove St., 541/523-9308, www.bakerheritage-museum.com, 9am-4pm daily mid-Mar.-Oct., $6 adults, $5 seniors and ages 13-17) shows off an extensive collection from Baker City's frontier days as well as exhibits depicting the Oregon Trail migration. The museum is across from Geiser Pollman Park, which has picnic tables and playgrounds.

## Eastern Oregon Museum

Ten miles northwest of Baker City in the town of Haines is the **Eastern Oregon Museum** (610 3rd St., Haines, 541/856-3233, www.easternoregonmuseum.com, 10am-3:30pm Thurs.-Sat., 12:30pm-3:30pm Sun. June-mid-Sept., donation). One of the largest historical museums in this part of the state, it boasts over 10,000 artifacts. It has an outstanding collection of vintage farming equipment, mining tools and paraphernalia, and pioneer relics.

## SPORTS AND RECREATION
### Skiing

**Anthony Lakes Ski Area** (541/856-3277, www.anthonylakes.com, Thurs.-Sun. and holidays, $35 adults, $29 ages 13-18, $21 ages 7-12, free under age 7) is 18 miles west of Haines on the Elkhorn Scenic Byway. This ski resort offers a triple chairlift, a cross-country trail system, a day lodge, a ski shop, and ski lessons. This is Oregon's first and highest elevation (7,000 feet) ski area, with pristine dry powder and a family-oriented environment. The 1,100 acres of slopes offer plenty of challenge—80 percent of the runs are intermediate or expert.

During the summer, the area around Anthony Lakes is a beautiful place to hike,

and several trailheads are along the road near the ski resort.

## FOOD

The ★ **Lone Pine Café** (1825 Main St., 541/523-1805, 8am-3pm daily, $7-17) is an outpost of good food on historic Main Street. The menu isn't complicated—breakfast standbys, burgers, and excellent sandwiches (try the Reuben!)—but the quality is high. There's always a daily special that features local and seasonal ingredients, such as Blue Mountain-harvested morel mushroom risotto.

**Latitude 45 Grille** (1925 Washington Ave., 541/406-4545, 4pm-9pm Tues.-Sat., $12-19) is a lively downtown spot with good pasta and hearty dishes like New York strip steak with blue cheese sauce. Check out the specials board for delicious Korean-style ribs or burgers topped with local wild mushrooms. Just down the street, **AJ's Corner Brick Bar and Grill** (1840 Main St., 541/523-6099, 11am-9pm Tues.-Thurs., 11am-10pm Fri.-Sat., $10-15) is a friendly little spot with huge portions of burgers, pizza, and salads.

**Barley Brown's Brew Pub** (2190 Main St., 541/523-4266, www.barleybrowns.com, 4pm-10pm Mon.-Sat., $8-19) serves some of Oregon's best brews, which is no small feat. The menu goes far beyond pub grub and includes steak, seafood, barbecued ribs, and pasta. If you're just looking to sample the beer, head to **Barley Brown's Taphouse** (2200 Main St., 541/523-2337, 2pm-10pm daily), just a block down the street, with over 20 ales on tap.

**Earth and Vine Gallery and Wine Bar** (2001 Washington Ave., 541/523-1687, 11am-9pm Tues.-Thurs., 11am-10pm Fri.-Sat., $8-15) is a bright and airy place to enjoy a drink, including beer from Barley Brown's, and an appetizer, sandwich, fondue, or flat-bread pizza. The **Palm Court** (Geiser Grand Hotel, 1996 Main St., 541/523-1899, www.geisergrand.com, 5pm-9pm daily, $9-27) is easily the classiest place to eat in Baker City, if not in all of eastern Oregon. The setting is splendid—a soaring stained-glass ceiling surmounts a

# Northeastern Oregon's Scenic Byways

Northeastern Oregon is road-trip country, and several routes in this region are designated National Scenic Byways. The **Wallowa Mountain Loop Road** (closed in winter) is a 54-mile drive through Hells Canyon Country, beginning with the Joseph-Imnaha Highway winding past farms and canyons. Turn south on Wallowa Mountain Loop Road to the Imnaha River, then ascend into alpine forests along Dry Creek Road to Halfway to come out on the south flank of the Wallowas. Turn east for a shoreline view of the Snake River and Hells Canyon.

Explore the high country behind Sumpter by driving the **Elkhorn Drive National Scenic Byway,** which runs northwest from Sumpter through gold-mining territory to Granite, across the north fork of the John Day, and past Anthony Lake to Baker City. Because much of this road is above 5,000 feet in elevation, the portion south of Anthony Lakes and north of Granite is closed by snow from early November through June or early July. The Elkhorn Byway climbs higher than any other paved road in Oregon (7,392 feet) after passing North Fork John Day Campground and the junction with Blue Mountains Scenic Byway. The craggy granite peaks of the northern Elkhorns—several higher than 8,000 feet—are near this area.

The longest of eastern Oregon's scenic byways is the **Journey Through Time Scenic Byway.** Departing or ending at Biggs, on I-5 and the Columbia Gorge, this highly scenic route takes back roads through the canyon-cut Columbia Plateau to Baker City. The highlight is the John Day River canyon, where millennia of erosion have sculpted a dramatic gorge through layers of volcanic formations, in the process unveiling the fossil remains of ancient life, which can be seen at the John Day Fossil Beds National Monument. This route makes an excellent bike ride, especially during the spring and early fall; it's also popular with motorcyclists.

wood-paneled dining room sparkling with linen, crystal, and candles. Specialties include mesquite-smoked prime rib, fresh salmon, and home-made desserts. A less formal option in the Geiser Grand is the **1889 Café** (7am-10pm daily, $5-15), in the old hotel bar, where you can start out with big eggy breakfasts in the morning, enjoy burgers and salads for lunch, and have light meals with cocktails and microbrews in the evening.

Ten miles north of Baker City is the beloved **Haines Steakhouse** (910 Front St., Haines, 541/856-3639, www.hainessteakhouse.com, 4:30pm-9pm Mon. and Wed.-Fri., 3:30pm-9pm Sat., 12:30pm-9pm Sun., $20-30), known for its tender prime rib and authentic Western atmosphere. Antiques and cowboy Americana decorate the restaurant, enhancing what may be described as first-rate chuck-wagon fare.

## ACCOMMODATIONS

Baker City's preeminent lodging choice is the ★ **Geiser Grand Hotel** (1996 Main St., 541/523-1899 or 888/434-7374, www.

geisergrand.com, $99-209), a showplace of period grandeur. Built in 1889 as the finest hotel between Portland and Salt Lake City, it was updated and refurbished in the 1990s and sparkles with both modern comforts and old-fashioned charm: Viennese chandeliers, mahogany columns, and a stained-glass skylight 40 feet above the dining room. The standard guest rooms are large, and for a real treat you can step up to a suite—particularly one on a corner or including the cupola—and have 10-foot-high windows on two sides to take in the Blue Mountain views.

Within walking distance of downtown is a good value motel, the **Oregon Trail Motel** (211 Bridge St., 541/523-5844 or 888/523-5882, http://oregontrailmotelandrestaurantbakercity.com, $48-60). It's not fancy but is a clean and pleasant place to spend the night. The adjoining restaurant is a good spot for breakfast. Just across the street, rooms at the friendly but basic **Bridge Street Inn** (134 Bridge St., 541/523-6571, www.bridgestreetinn.net, $45-60) are similar.

The **Best Western Sunridge Inn** (1 Sunridge Lane, 541/523-6444, www.bestwesternoregon.com, $97-42) is a large motel complex with the feel of a small resort. Five motel blocks surround a nicely landscaped central garden, pool, and fitness area, which is also linked to the motel's two restaurants. The disadvantage is that it is near the interstate (exit 304), over a mile from downtown. Also out near the interstate is the **Motel 6 Baker City** (175 Campbell St., 541/523-3431, www.alwayswelcomeinn.com, $73-80), a motel that offers clean comfortable rooms, an indoor pool, and—to set it apart from other interstate motels—a fossil bed out back.

### Camping
The area's best camping is up in the Elkhorn Range near Anthony Lakes. **Anthony Lakes Campground** (541/523-6391, www.fs.usda.gov, no reservations, $10) has water and is right at the base of the Anthony Lakes Ski Area, with campsites tucked among huge boulders a short walk from the lake. About a mile farther east along Forest Road 73, find **Grande Ronde Lake Campground** (no reservations, $5), with water, a pretty spot at the headwaters of the Grande Ronde River.

## INFORMATION
Contact the **Baker County Chamber and Visitors Center** (490 Campbell St., 541/523-5855, www.visitbaker.com) for information. The *Baker City Herald* (www.bakercityherald.com) publishes a good annual travel guide, available free at area museums.

## GETTING THERE
**Greyhound** buses serve the Baker City terminal (515 Campbell St., 541/523-5011) on runs between Portland and Boise. There are two buses daily in each direction.

# Sumpter and Vicinity

In the Elkhorn Mountains west of Baker City, Sumpter is a former gold-mining town, one of many small communities in this area that hovers between ghost town and tourist town. Its gold-mining heyday was 1900-1905, when over 3,000 miners worked the hard-rock mines and dredged the Powder River. By 1905 most of the easily accessed gold was gone, but dredging continued until 1954. Today, Sumpter has about 150 year-round residents—a few of whom actually still run small gold mines—and the old storefronts are now antiques shops and art galleries. A few vintage watering holes still provide food and drink. Sumpter is 30 miles west of Baker City and 57 miles east of John Day.

## SIGHTS
### Sumpter Valley Dredge State Heritage Area
A state park-managed site, the **Sumpter Valley Dredge State Heritage Area** (541/894-2486 or 800/551-6949) preserves one of three gold dredges that scooped up and sifted gold-rich Powder River gravels. With a hull 125 feet long and 52 feet wide, this is the longest and most accessible gold dredge in the country. In its day, it was capable of chewing up 225 cubic feet per minute, equal to 100 acres of riverbed per year. Sticking out from the dredge's hull is a massive boom bearing 72 one-ton buckets that move like a chainsaw that would bore into the riverbank and carry the loose rock back into the dredge interior. Once inside, the rock passed through a series of steel cylinders that separated the material by size, sending the smaller components deeper into the dredge. Using water and sluices, the gold was separated from the sediment, which passed through the back of the dredge along with the gravel and larger rocks, deposited as mine tailings. In its lifetime, this dredge made $4.5 million when gold prices were $35 per ounce. The dredge passed

to Oregon state parks in 1995, which has restored it, and in summer offers interpretive displays and tours. Access to the park is free, with trails leading out into wildlife viewing areas—the orderly piles of mine tailings along the Powder River have become an unlikely wetlands habitat.

## Sumpter Valley Railroad

Another piece of local history is the **Sumpter Valley Railroad** (12259 Huckleberry Loop Rd., Baker City, 541/894-2268 or 866/894-2268, http://sumptervalleyrailroad.org, adults $16 one-way, $21 round-trip, seniors and military $13 one-way, $18 round-trip, ages 6-16 $8 one-way, $12 round-trip, family $47 one-way, $57 round-trip), a rebuilt narrow-gauge excursion train pulled by steam engines. The railroad originally ran from 1890 to 1961 between Baker City and Prairie City, transporting logs and ore in addition to passengers. Today, passengers ride the five miles between McEwen Station and Sumpter in two vintage observation cars; a restored 1890 caboose is also part of the train. Runs depart Sumpter station at noon and 3:15pm (Sat.-Sun. Memorial Day-Oct., plus special dates).

## Granite

Connoisseurs of back roads and ghost towns will want to stop and take a gander at the remains of **Granite** (pop. 38). With its false-fronted buildings of unpainted and splintered boards, Granite is a true ghost town. Hard as it is to believe, this place once had four saloons, a 50-room hotel, several smaller hotels, a boardinghouse, a church, and a wooden jail. Founded in 1862, its mining legacy sustained the town through the 1930s. The need for miners in World War II defense industries at that time compelled President Franklin D. Roosevelt to shut down the mines. Today, community ties are maintained by regular visits to the Granite store, where miners, retirees, and other residents meet up to keep the ghost alive.

## ENTERTAINMENT AND EVENTS

Head to the fairgrounds for the **Sumpter Flea Market** (Memorial Day, Fourth of July, and Labor Day weekends). Collectibles, crafts, and food are arrayed in a beautiful mountain setting. This event is legendary among Oregon's bargain hunters.

The Sumpter dredge is a massive piece of equipment.

## ACCOMMODATIONS

The **Sumpter Stockade Motel** (129 E. Austin St., Sumpter, 541/894-2360, www. sumpterstockade.com, May-mid-Oct., $75-85) offers individually decorated rooms, including a suite with a full kitchen, in a newly built structure designed to resemble an Old West military fort complete with a pole stockade. Tent campers can set up on the lawn inside the stockade ($10 pp, $15 for 2), and there's a tiny bunkroom ($20 pp) used mainly by bicycle travelers, a surprising number of whom pass through town on cross-country tours. This is an unusual but comfy place to stay in this little town.

For more traditional guest rooms, the **Depot Inn** (179 S. Mill St., 541/894-2522, www.thedepotinn.com, $85) is a handsome log-built motel; rooms have fridges, microwaves, and wireless Internet. Sumpter's original 1900 hospital is back in business as **Sumpter Bed and Breakfast** (344 NE Columbia St., 541/894-0048, www.sumpterbb.net, $95-110), with six antique-filled guest rooms and a hearty breakfast.

# Ontario

Midway between Portland and Salt Lake City in Oregon's far east, Ontario (pop. 11,000) is where "Oregon's day begins." (Indeed, it begins an hour earlier here—Ontario is in the mountain time zone.) It's the biggest city in Malheur County and ships over 5 percent of the nation's onions as well as a good portion of the sweet russet potatoes used by national fast-food chains. Other local crops include sugar beets and grain, an abundance that derives from the fertile plains at the confluence of the Snake, Owyhee, Payette, and Malheur Rivers.

In 1942, President Franklin D. Roosevelt ordered the removal of 120,000 Japanese Americans from the West Coast to 10 inland concentration camps located in isolated areas of seven states. About 5,000 Japanese Americans were moved to an internment camp near Ontario. Under the leadership of Ontario mayor Elmo Smith, the eastern Oregon farming community invited internees to help fill service and farm jobs. By the end of the war, 1,000 Japanese Americans had settled in the Ontario area, giving Malheur County the largest percentage of Japanese Americans in Oregon. As a result, Japanese surnames grace many ranches and farms in eastern Oregon. Some of the migrant workers from Latin America also stayed, adding another flavor to a cultural stew that already contained Basques and the indigenous Paiute people.

## SIGHTS
### Four Rivers Cultural Center

Ontario's rich mix of cultures is celebrated at the **Four Rivers Cultural Center** (676 SW 5th Ave., 541/889-8191, www.4rcc.com, 9am-5pm Mon.-Fri., 10am-5pm Sat., $4 adults, $3 seniors and children) at Treasure Valley Community College. The four rivers—the Snake, Malheur, Owyhee, and Payette—represent the flow of people of different ethnicities into this part of Oregon: Native Americans, Basques, Hispanics, and Japanese. The complex includes a museum, a theater, and a formal Japanese garden.

### Snake River Crossing

Remnants of the Oregon Trail still cross this remote corner of Oregon. Museums, historic markers, and wagon-rut memorials stud the area. South of Ontario, between Nyssa and Adrian along Highway 201, a roadside monument commemorates the trail's **Snake River Crossing** into Oregon. Directly across the Snake from this point was Fort Boise, a Hudson's Bay Company fur-trading fort that doubled as a landmark and trade center for often desperate pioneers. The fort was swept away by floods long ago, and the site is now part of a wildlife refuge.

Follow the Oregon Trail from Nyssa to Vale to find several other historic sites. Take Enterprise Avenue just west of Nyssa and turn right on Lyttle Boulevard; from here the paved road closely follows the tracks of the Oregon Trail to Vale.

## Keeney Pass Oregon Trail Historic Site

The **Keeney Pass Oregon Trail Historic Site,** four miles south of Vale, has a display of the deep ruts cut into the earth by ironclad wagon wheels. This exhibit marks the most used route of the wagon trains as they passed through the Snake River Valley on their way to Baker Valley to the north. From the top of this pass you can see the route of a whole day's journey on the trail to Oregon over 160 years ago. Ponder the fact that 1 pioneer in 10 died on this arduous transcontinental trek. In June and July, Indian paintbrush and penstemon add a dash of color to the sagebrush and rabbitbrush that surround the ruts in the trail.

## Farewell Bend

Twenty-two miles north of Ontario on I-84 is **Farewell Bend,** where travelers along the old Oregon Trail left the valley of the Snake River, which they had followed from central Idaho, and climbed up into the desert uplands of eastern Oregon. Before undertaking the strenuous journey through desert landscapes to the imposing Blue Mountains, travelers usually rested at Farewell Bend, grazing livestock, gathering wood, and otherwise preparing themselves for the arduous segment ahead. Today, **Farewell Bend State Park** (800/452-5687, www.oregonstateparks.org, $5 day-use, $18-24 camping) commemorates this placid pioneer wayside with a picnic and play area, interpretive displays, a boat launch, and a large campground.

## FESTIVALS AND EVENTS

The **Vale Rodeo** is a four-day fete that takes place July 1-4, highlighted by the Suicide Race, held at nearby Vale Butte, in which cowboys race their horses off a steep slope into an arena. The **Obon Festival,** celebrating Ontario's Japanese heritage, is held in late

Ontario's Four Rivers Cultural Center celebrates the region's multiethnic background.

June at Ontario's **Buddhist temple** (286 SE 4th St., 541/889-8562). Japanese folk dancing is the highlight.

## FOOD

There are plenty of fast-food and chain restaurants at the interstate exits, but for more authentic options, head to Ontario's old downtown area. Mexican restaurants abound, including the very good **Tacos Mi Ranchito** (2520 S. Oregon St., 541/889-6130, 10:30am-8:30pm Mon.-Wed., 10:30am-9pm Thurs.-Sat., 10:30am-6pm Sun., $8), a simple order-at-the-counter taco joint. Another good Mexican restaurant is **Casa Jaramillo** (157 SE 2nd St., 541/889-9258, 11:30am-10pm Tues.-Sat., 11:30am-9pm Sun., $6-15), an Ontario tradition since 1967. The chili verde has a local reputation, and don't forget to end your meal with deep-fried ice cream, topped with dulce de leche.

Ontario's Japanese heritage is represented at **Ogawa's Wicked Sushi, Burgers, and Bowls** (375 E. Idaho Ave., 541/889-2725, http://ogawasrestaurant.com, 11am-8pm Mon., 11am-9pm Tues.-Fri., noon-9pm Sat., $5-27), which is one of the few places in this part of the state where you can get good sushi, in addition to well-prepared burgers and steaks. Downtown, regional chain **Romio's** (375 S. Oregon St., 541/889-4888, 11am-2pm Mon., 11am-8pm Tues.-Wed., 11am-9pm Thurs.-Sat., noon-8pm Sun., $8-18) serves pasta, pizza, calzones, and sandwiches, including gluten-free options. If you're looking for your first steak-house experience in Oregon, head to **Mackey's Steakhouse and Pub** (111 SW 1st St., 541/889-3678, 11am-9pm, Sun.-Thurs., 11am-10pm Fri.-Sat., $8-25), a lively Irish-style establishment with steaks, burgers, and curious "traditional Irish fare" such as salmon alfredo. Oh, and corned beef and cabbage too.

Another downtown enterprise worth noting is **Jolts and Juice** (298 S. Oregon St., 541/889-4166, 6am-9pm Mon.-Sat., 7am-6pm Sun., $4-12), with house-roasted coffee, smoothies, fresh-squeezed juice, breakfast pastries, panini sandwiches, soups, and salads. This lively coffee shop is also the home of **Tandem Brewing Company,** and you can sample the ales or pick up a growler to go. If you're staying out at the chain hotels at I-84's exit 376, you'll find a Jolts and Juice outlet in the Ontario Marketplace Mall (215 East Lane, 541/881-8989, 6am-9:30pm Mon.-Sat., 7am-7pm Sun.), although this location doesn't serve ales.

## ACCOMMODATIONS

There is a cluster of motels at I-84's exit 376. If you're hot and tired of driving, the deluxe sheets, indoor pool, and fitness center at the **Holiday Inn Express** (212 SE 10th St., 541/889-7100, $134-148) might sound pretty good. This is the high end of what you'll find in Ontario. The **Best Western Plus Inn** (251 Goodfellow St., 541/889-2600, $131-142) is also one of the nicer places to stay in town; it has an indoor pool, exercise room, and laundry, plus continental breakfast is included. All rooms have microwaves and fridges. If you want a simple, friendly, 1950s-style courtyard motel well off the interstate, check out the **Ontario Inn** (1144 SW 4th Ave., on the road to Vale, 541/823-2556, www.ontarioinnmotel. com, $86-99). It's pet-friendly, and even has a large fenced backyard where dogs can play.

## INFORMATION

Contact the **Malheur County Chamber of Commerce** (876 SW 4th Ave., 541/889-8012, www.ontariochamber.com) for more information.

## GETTING THERE

**Greyhound** buses stop at the Ontario terminal (842 SE 1st St., 541/823-2567) on twice-daily trips in each direction between Portland and Boise.

# Southeastern Oregon

Southeastern Oregon is a place where travelers shed their notions of what Oregon is supposed to be like. It's largely desertlike but has huge wetland areas. It's back-country but also surprisingly sophisticated. It's the middle of

nowhere but it has a couple of the state's most charming hotels. And it does deliver on what many travelers seek: wildlife galore. Malheur National Wildlife Refuge is one of the Pacific Northwest's top birding areas, especially during the spring and fall migrations, when it's easy to spot well over 50 species in a day. Hart Mountain has a refuge for pronghorn antelope, which can be seen across all of southeastern Oregon, and there are even wild mustangs living on Steens Mountain.

Although it's handy to come to southeastern Oregon prepared to camp, there are enough lodgings, mostly simple, to make your trip a little less rugged. The Christmas Valley area has some of the most intriguing geological formations in the Pacific Northwest. Evidence of the cataclysmic forces that shaped the Columbia Plateau and the Great Basin are on display in this starkly beautiful part of the state. Fissures in the ground and wave patterns left by ancient lakes on the flanks of mountains are some of the fingerprints left by the hand of nature.

The sparsely populated sagebrush, rimrock, and grassy plains around Malheur National Wildlife Refuge and Steens Mountain are home to cattle ranches, a usually dry alkaline lake bed, and some hot springs. The tiny town of Crane has one of the few public boarding schools in the United States. Students reside in dorms on campus, because most come from ranches located many miles from town. In the very southeast corner of the state, the area carved out by the Owyhee River is wild and beautiful, with only a handful of very small settlements. If you're looking to get away from it all, you've found your piece of Oregon.

## PLANNING YOUR TIME

If you're looking to explore the open spaces and wildlife of southeastern Oregon, be prepared to take your time. Once you settle into the rhythm of driving, poking around, and

**Previous:** wild horses after roundup; Wildhorse Lake. **Above:** the Alvord Desert is a hardpan playa.

Look for ★ to find recommended
sights, activities, dining, and lodging.

# Highlights

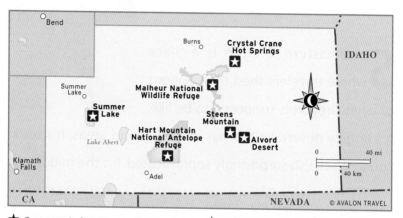
© AVALON TRAVEL

★ **Summer Lake:** Here, you're surrounded by geological curiosities such as Crack-in-the-Ground and Hole-in-the-Ground, birds, and minimally developed hot springs (page 533).

★ **Hart Mountain National Antelope Refuge:** This refuge is home to pronghorn and lots of other wildlife, rock art, and hot springs (page 534).

★ **Crystal Crane Hot Springs:** Here, you can actually swim in the big hot springs-fed pond (page 537).

★ **Malheur National Wildlife Refuge:** This wet spot in the desert supports a huge variety of birdlife. Birders may get to witness the sage grouse courtship ritual (page 538).

★ **Steens Mountain:** This fault-block mountain drops straight off to the Alvord Desert. Take your time, hike the trails, and bring binoculars—you may catch a glimpse of the local wild mustangs (page 541).

★ **Alvord Desert:** It's hard to believe that this dry, blindingly white alkaline playa, or lake bed, is in the same state as the lush forests of western Oregon (page 544).

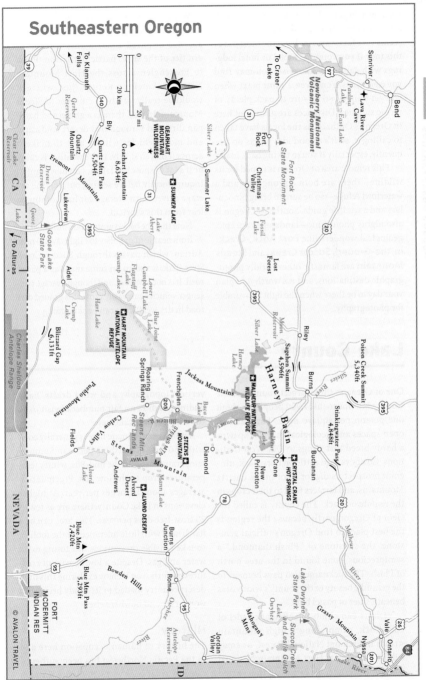

# Southeastern Oregon

0 20 km

0 20 mi

To Klamath Falls

To Crater Lake

Sunriver

Paulina Lake
Lava River Cave
East Lake

Newberry National Volcanic Monument

Bend

Gerber Reservoir

Quartz Mountain

Fremont

Mountains

Quartz Mtn Pass 5,504ft

GEARHART MOUNTAIN WILDERNESS

Gearhart Mountain 8,634ft

Silver Lake

Fort Rock

Fort Rock State Monument

Christmas Valley

Summer Lake

SUMMER LAKE

Dreus Reservoir

Lakeview

Clear Lake Reservoir

Goose Lake State Park

Goose Lake

To Alturas

Adel

Lower Flagstaff Lake
Campbell Lake
Swamp Lake

Lake Abert

Fossil Lake

Lost Forest

Silver Lake

Moon Reservoir

Riley

Burns

Sagehen Summit 4,596ft

Harney Lake

Silvies River

Poison Creek Summit 5,340ft

Stinkingwater Pass 4,848ft

Charles Sheldon Antelope Range

Crump Lake

Hart Lake

Blizzard Gap 6,131ft

HART MOUNTAIN NATIONAL ANTELOPE REFUGE

Blue Joint Lake

Jackass Mountains

Roaring Springs Ranch

Frenchglen

Malheur Lake

MALHEUR NATIONAL WILDLIFE REFUGE

Harney Basin

Buchanan

Burns

Pueblo Mountains

Fields

Catlow Valley

Steens Mtn Rec Lands

Steens Mountain

Donner und Blitzen R.

Diamond

New Princeton

Crane

CRYSTAL CRANE HOT SPRINGS

Alvord Lake

Andrews

Alvord Desert

ALVORD DESERT

Mann Lake

Burns Junction

NEVADA

Blue Mtn 7,420ft

Blue Mtn 5,293ft

Bowden Hills

FORT MCDERMITT INDIAN RES

Rome

Owyhee River

Antelope Reservoir

Jordan Valley

Mahogany Mtns

Grassy Mountain

Lake Owyhee State Park and Leslie Gulch

Lake Owyhee

Succor Creek

Malheur River

Vale

Nyssa

Ontario

Snake River

ID

© AVALON TRAVEL

pausing to look at a kingfisher or some prong-horns, you may find that the rest of the world seems very far away. You'll get the most out of this tour if you combine motel or hotel lodgings with camping. Likewise, you may find yourself miles from even a mini mart when you get hungry, so be sure to pack plenty of picnic supplies. Distances are grand out here in Oregon's Outback, as the locals have taken to calling it, so it's a good idea to gas up frequently, especially if you're taking back roads.

This remote area of Oregon is famed for its wildlife—there are both a pronghorn and a waterfowl refuge—so be sure to bring binoculars and a wildlife guide. Southeast Oregon is also highly photogenic—landscapes are epic, geological wonders like **Fort Rock, Crack-in-the-Ground, Succor Creek,** and **Steens Mountain** are fantastic otherworldly photographic destinations, and it's worth it to plan your day to be there when the light is favorable for photography.

When you get out a map and start planning a trip, you'll notice that there's a distinct absence of paved roads across the southern tier of the state, particularly from Plush to Frenchglen across the Hart Mountain National Antelope Refuge, just where it would be really handy to cut over to Steens Mountain. In fact, there is a gravel and hardpan dirt road through this desert landscape, and most vehicles will be able to make it across if driven slowly. If the weather is rainy or if a lot of snow has fallen, you may want to inquire locally before setting out, but the average driver in an average car has nothing to fear from this shortcut.

Note that the backcountry route linking U.S. 95 from near Jordan Valley to Highway 210 near Adrian, which passes through Succor Creek State Park, is shown on some maps as a paved road. It is not, however, and though average passenger vehicles can easily cross this graded dirt road in dry weather, it can be slow going.

# Lake County

One of Oregon's three largest counties, Lake County is home to just 7,900 people, or about one person per square mile. This land of open spaces and geological marvels spawns a hardy breed that clings to Old West traditions. Cowboys herd cattle on horseback, itinerant prospectors dig for color in the Quartz Mountains, and farmers tend to their crops in the remote outback. The county is called the Gem of Oregon partly because the region is the best place to find Oregon's official gemstone, the sunstone or "Plush diamond," a semiprecious stone found in the area north of Plush. The nickname also pays homage to the gem-like beauty of the county's wide vistas beneath skies of pastel blue.

Visitors can climb the ancient citadel of Fort Rock, camp along a high mountain stream in Fremont National Forest, or enjoy wildlife-viewing at Hart Mountain National Antelope Refuge. Because of the varied

vertical topography and wind drafts, hang gliding has drawn a fair number of visitors to the cliffs around Lakeview.

The semiarid climate here is generally cool, with 250 days of sunshine per year. Summer temperatures stay in the mid-80s; winter temperatures drop to the low 30s. Precipitation averages about 16 inches per year. At higher elevations in Lake County, there are as few as 20 frost-free days per year. This area can be a harsh land with little tolerance for the foolish, so take sensible precautions like toting extra water and gas. Despite a low density of creature comforts, you'll enjoy exploring this high desert country loaded to its sandy brim with wonders found nowhere else.

## History

The history of human occupation here and in the Pacific Northwest has been authenticated to as far back as 13,200 years through carbon-dating of grass sandals found in Fort Rock Cave. Early desert dwellers who roamed the Great Basin in search of game and food witnessed the eruption of Mount Mazama 6,000 to 8,000 years ago. Their descendants, the Northern Paiute people, were also hunter-gatherers. This Lake County indigenous group was known as the Groundhog Eaters, and they left more petroglyphs and pictographs in Lake County than in all the rest of Oregon and Washington.

The first Europeans to venture into the area were French Canadian trappers working for the Hudson's Bay Company in the early 1800s, and they were eventually joined by U.S. mountain men. The journals kept during these expeditions noted broad valleys with grasses "belly-high to a horse." This information attracted a new cast of players: the cattle and sheep barons. The white influx resulted in frequent tensions with the original occupants, often culminating in bloodshed on both sides. After the Bannock-Paiute uprising in 1878, the local Native Americans were herded up and forced onto a reservation.

In the growth spurt that followed, the town of Lakeview was chartered in 1889; it burned to the ground in 1900 and was rebuilt with brick and corrugated-iron roofs. Other hopeful hamlets with names like Arrow, Buffalo, and Loma Vista sprang up around the county, thanks to a reactivated Federal Homestead Act in 1909 that sanctioned 320 free acres per settler. Many of these tiny burgs dried up and blew away after the 1918-1920 drought. However, larger communities like Lakeview, Paisley, and Summer Lake held on, and local farmers figured out how to irrigate and cultivate this ornery land, which is incredibly fertile if you just add water.

## ALONG HIGHWAY 31: LA PINE TO LAKEVIEW

A vehicle with a bit of clearance is indispensable in this region if you value your oil pan (a Subaru wagon made it to all the places described, but did suffer one flat tire along the way). Stock up on provisions in Bend or La Pine.

## La Pine State Park

Located in Deschutes County, huge **La Pine State Park** (541/536-2428, www.oregonstateparks.org) lies just a few miles off U.S. 97. Trails meander along the Deschutes and Fall Rivers; the 15 miles of single-track mountain biking trails are mostly flat and perfect for beginners. Bikes can be rented at Bend and Sunriver cycle shops. During the winter, many trails are open to cross-country skiing. Don't expect a desert here; the park is full of old-growth ponderosa and lodgepole pine trees. The park's **campground** has 137 campsites ($24-26) and 10 cabins ($44-54 rustic, $86-97 deluxe) that can be reserved (800/452-5687).

## Hole-in-the-Ground

An interesting geological feature called **Hole-in-the-Ground** is found about 25 miles southeast of La Pine Junction off Highway 31. Although this 300-foot-deep indentation looks like a meteor crater, scientists believe molten lava came into contact with water here, causing a massive explosion that quarried out a 7.5-mile-diameter crater, or maar. Astronauts came here in 1966 to experience the moonlike terrain.

To find this unusual and awe-inducing sight from U.S. 97, drive 22 miles southeast from La Pine Junction on Highway 31; turn left at the Hole-in-the-Ground sign. Drive 3.1 miles to the next sign. Turn right and go 1.1 miles to the final sign. Turn left and go 0.2 miles to the rim of the hole. From the parking area, you can hike a moderately steep trail to the bottom of the crater.

## Christmas Valley and Vicinity

**Christmas Valley,** considered a remote destination even in Oregon's outback, is a rather nondescript alfalfa-farming community in the midst of some spectacular geologic formations. The town got its picturesque name by accident. Southeast of here, the explorer and adventurer John C. Frémont spent Christmas at a lake during one of his mid-19th-century treks and called it Christmas Lake. A turn-of-the-20th-century mapmaker mistakenly affixed this name to a seasonal lake near the present-day town site, which also took on the moniker. Although the expanse of sagebrush dotted with mobile homes is not immediately appealing (an attempt to turn the town into a retirement mecca in the 1980s largely failed), there are plenty of fascinating areas nearby.

If you'd like to plunge even farther into the Oregon outback, continue driving east on the Christmas Valley-Wagontire Rd. From Christmas Valley, you'll drive along a good paved road for 40 miles through scrub desert to U.S. 395, with scarcely a sign of human habitation in sight. Once you get to the junction, you're still scores of miles from the nearest gas station, so if you decide to make this trek, be sure to refuel before leaving Christmas Valley.

### ACCOMMODATIONS AND FOOD

Although accommodations are generally more appealing at Summer Lake, Christmas Valley is not without lodging options. The **Lakeside Terrace Motel** (1 Spruce Lane, 541/576-2309, www.lakesideterracecv.com, $55-65) offers basic motel rooms and rents full houses to larger groups; RV spaces are also available. The Lakeside Terrace is also the main place to eat (7am-3pm Mon.-Sat., $6-10) in Christmas Valley.

## Fort Rock State Natural Area

Rising like an enormous and eerie stone castle from the desert floor, Fort Rock towers 400 feet above the surrounding sagebrush. A series of underwater volcanic blasts created this very unusual formation when the entire area was a huge ice-age lake stretching for hundreds of miles across central Oregon. Rising molten rock came into contact with mud and lake water, creating a series of massive explosions. As the ash and rock were thrown into the air, they came to rest in a perfect ring whose walls eventually reached hundreds of feet high. Fall and winter here offer wildlife-viewing par excellence; large herds of mule deer can be seen mid-November to mid-April, and pronghorn range over the alfalfa fields year-round. Many birds nest in the rocks, and golden eagles, hawks, kestrels, and peregrine falcons soar overhead.

**Fort Rock State Natural Area** (800/551-6949, www.oregonstateparks.org, free) has picnic facilities and restrooms as well as trails and amenities for rock climbers and sightseers. An easy trail rings the inside base of the crater walls, and the intrepid can follow more

Fort Rock is an enormous splatter cone.

adventurous trails that explore the rims (some bouldering required). This is a great family destination: It's hard not to imagine this as the remains of a mythic fortress, and kids of all ages will love clambering up the rock walls exploring the trails. Fort Rock State Park is seven miles east of Highway 31, or 30 miles northwest of Christmas Valley.

As the ice-age lake waters receded, ancient Native Americans also made their homes in caves and shelters in and around Fort Rock. At **Fort Rock Cave** (a.k.a. Sandal Cave), in a nearby but separate formation, waves carved a 50-foot-deep cave in what was once a basalt island. In 1938, anthropologist Luther Cressman discovered over 70 ancient sandals woven from sagebrush in the cave. Dated at almost 10,000 years old, the sandals are some of the oldest human artifacts found in the Pacific Northwest; they're now on display at the University of Oregon Natural History Museum in Eugene.

Fort Rock Cave is a National Heritage site and is now open to a limited number of tours operated by Oregon State Parks. The tours are offered for only a few days June-August; see the Fort Rock Cave page at www.oregonstateparks.org for exact dates, which change annually. Tours are limited to 10 people, and reservations (http://store.oregonstateparks.org, $8) are required.

The nearby town of Fort Rock has an old-time flavor that has been accentuated by the recent restoration of homestead cabins in a pioneer village at the **Fort Rock Valley Historical Homestead Museum** (541/576-2251, www.fortrockoregon.com, 11am-5pm Thurs.-Sun. late May-mid-Sept., $4 adults, $2 ages 6-17). There's not much to the town of Fort Rock, but there is the **Fort Rock Pub and Restaurant** (64591 Fort Rock Rd., 541/576-3988, 11am-8pm daily, $7-18), with burgers, sandwiches, and a friendly welcome.

## Derrick Cave

Discover an exciting journey down into the bowels of the earth at **Derrick Cave,** 22 bumpy miles northeast of Fort Rock. This large lava tube is 1,200 feet long with rooms up to 80 feet wide and 46 feet high. After the Cuban missile crisis of 1962, the cave was turned into a fallout shelter. Metal doors were installed and provisions for 1,000 people were stockpiled. The supplies were later plundered by vandals, and the cave's civil defense status was eventually dropped.

Today, Derrick Cave is open to visitors year-round. Because the ceiling of the cave has collapsed in a number of places, these natural skylights allow visitors to explore the first section of the cave without flashlights, though a flashlight is an excellent precaution. The lower section of the cave does not have natural skylights and requires artificial light.

Derrick Cave is part of a larger set of volcanic features called the Devils Garden, a 45-square-mile series of lava flows that includes a set of splatter cones called The Blowouts and other volcanic oddities. These lava flows are likely 10,000 to 50,000 years old. To reach Derrick Cave, drive east from Fort Rock village on County Road 5-10 and follow signs north on County Road 5-12. The final six miles are unpaved and quite bumpy.

## Crack-in-the-Ground

Another really magical geologic feature in the Christmas Valley area, **Crack-in-the-Ground** is weirdly compelling and worth the journey to anyone with an interest in natural history. Crack-in-the-Ground is a volcanic fissure about two miles long, 10 to 15 feet wide, and up to 70 feet deep. On hot days, it's nice and cool within this chasm. In fact, the crack is so deep that cold winter air sometimes gets trapped within, preserving ice into summer. According to geologists, this dramatic fissure has been open for at least 1,000 years; the opening was once larger, but lava from nearby volcanoes filled it in to its present dimensions.

There are numerous sections to Crack-in-the-Ground. The first, when walking the 0.25 miles from the parking area, is also the easiest to explore. Walk down into the crack: With a bit of rock clambering, you'll be able to negotiate the entire length of this section. Another couple of fissure sections follow, but these don't have smooth floor passages and require some rock climbing skills. The less intrepid can follow trails along the edge of these chasms, and you can peer down into the rocky void and marvel.

To reach Crack-in-the-Ground, drive one mile east from Christmas Valley's main intersection (with the gas station) and turn north on Road 6109-D (watch for the Bureau of Land Management, or BLM, signs on the south side of the road). Crack-in-the-Ground is seven miles north along a fairly bumpy dirt road.

Five miles northwest of Crack-in-the-Ground (along the same rough BLM road) is **Green Mountain Campground** and fire lookout, which sits high above the Devils Garden site. This primitive campground (free) is large enough for three cars but has no water or toilets. It sits atop a small cinder cone overlooking hundreds of square miles of high desert, lava beds, and forest from 5,190 feet above sea level.

### Fossil Lake

During wetter times, thousands of years ago, **Fossil Lake** was a watering hole for ancient camels, enormous beavers, flamingos, mammoths, and miniature horses. It was once part of a much larger body of water in the Fort Rock basin that was perhaps 40 miles wide and 200 feet deep. Their fossilized remains are still unearthed by paleontologists on sanctioned digs. Be aware that it is illegal to remove any fossils from the beds.

To reach this large dry lake bed, drive two miles east from Christmas Valley and turn north on County Road 5-14C (a.k.a. Fossil Lake Rd.). Follow signs toward "Lost Forest" and "Sand Dunes," and in 16 miles, you'll pass beneath a high-tension power line. Turn south on a dirt road and drive an additional 1.5 miles. You'll see an interpretive sign for Fossil Lake at a parking area. You'll need to hike in 0.5 miles to reach the lake bed itself.

Crack-in-the-Ground is exactly what you would expect.

### Lost Forest

Amid hundreds of miles of scrub desert and sand dunes, **Lost Forest** is a 9,000-acre stand of ancient ponderosa pines intermixed with the largest juniper trees in Oregon—all that's left of a grove that dates back thousands of years. Surprisingly, studies of tree rings show this area has received on average only nine inches of rain per year for the last 600 years, half the amount normally needed to sustain the growth of ponderosa pines. A layer of pumice-like soil beneath the surface traps and retains enough moisture to allow the trees to draw water up through shorter-than-usual root systems.

This island of green is 40 miles from the nearest forest, accentuating the isolation and solitude of these stately sentinels. Many of the junipers here are over 1,000 years old. On hot summer days this place is a welcome source of shade. The forest borders the largest inland sand dunes in the state. To reach the Lost Forest, follow directions for Fossil Lake, but continue an additional eight miles east along the rough and sandy Lost Forest Road.

## ★ Summer Lake

The region surrounding **Summer Lake** sits at the interface of desert and mixed conifer forest. Abundant wildlife, geological wonders, Native American sites, and historic structures beckon further investigation. The 20-mile-long and 10-mile-wide lake is surrounded by the mountains of the Fremont National Forest and Winter Ridge.

The tiny community of Summer Lake is on Highway 31, about halfway between La Pine and Lakeview, and is a good place to stop for a night or two while you explore the area. Just north of Summer Lake on Highway 31, pull into **Picture Rock Turnout.** Take the trail 80 feet to the southeast; behind the tallest rock is a pictograph. In the town of Summer Lake, the old **Harris School** is worth a photo. This classic one-room schoolhouse, complete with bell tower, looks like it's straight out of *Little House on the Prairie.*

The highway also passes through the **Summer Lake Wildlife Refuge** (541/943-3152, www.dfw.state.or.us, parking permit required), home to 170 species of migratory birds. Spring is the best time to see an amazing showing of waterfowl, including snow geese, avocets, black-necked stilts, and snowy plovers. An eight-mile wildlife-viewing trail around the lake is a recommended diversion at mile marker 70.

Anglers should head due west of Summer Lake to the **Thompson Valley Reservoir,** which has been known to yield large rainbow trout. It's most easily reached by driving south from Silver Lake on County Road 4-12.

### FOOD AND ACCOMMODATIONS

Rustic and interesting is the concept here: ★ **Summer Lake Hot Springs** (41777 Hwy. 31, Paisley, 541/943-3931, www.summerlakehotsprings.com), six miles north of Paisley on the southern tip of Summer Lake, is a private operation where you can enjoy a dip in the 30-foot-long **pool** (8am-8pm daily May-Sept., 9am-7pm daily Oct.-Apr., $10 adults, $5 ages 7-15, free under age 7 and overnight guests), housed in a rustic shed originally built

in 1927 as a bathhouse for local cowboys. This hot spring resort has campsites ($20 tents, $45 RVs) on a bluff above the lake, a couple of small cabins ($100-110 d), and two-bedroom cottages ($150-225) for rent. This rustic resort is usually pretty laid-back, with an old-time Oregon hippie vibe; however, it's a popular stopover for people traveling to the Burning Man festival in Nevada, so during the week before Labor Day it can take on a party atmosphere.

The 1940s-era accommodations of the **Lodge at Summer Lake** (53460 Hwy. 31, 541/943-3993, www.lodgeatsummerlake.com) feature seven motel units ($68-80) and cabin and house rentals ($65-140), including one unit that can sleep six. There is an on-site restaurant and a private bass pond. The no-frills **Wildlife Refuge Campground** (53447 Hwy. 31, 541/943-3152, www.dfw.state.or.us, free) is on the Ana River just north of Summer Lake on Highway 31. Bird-watchers like to camp here and walk the dikes of Summer Lake looking for waterfowl.

In a remote rustic shack 4.5 miles south of Silver Lake, ★ **Cowboy Dinner Tree Steakhouse** (50836 E. Bay Rd., 541/576-2426, www.cowboydinnertree.net, 4pm-8:30pm Thurs.-Sun. June-Oct., 4pm-8:30pm Fri.-Sun. Nov.-May, reservations required, $30 adults, $11 ages 7-13, free under age 7, cash only) has gained a statewide reputation. You must specify when you make your reservations whether you'd like the nearly 30-ounce top sirloin steak or the chicken (an order is an entire chicken); no split orders are allowed. Sides include soup, salad, fresh rolls, beans, and baked potato. Dessert is available, and nonalcoholic beverages are served in mason jars. This isn't just pretend rustic; as the sign says, "No Credit Cards—No Electricity—No Kidding." If you're too stuffed to drive after the meal, bunk down in a cabin ($130 for 2, includes dinner).

## Paisley

Thirty miles south of Summer Lake is the town of **Paisley** (pop. 200). The **Paisley Ranger Compound** features several structures built by the Civilian Conservation Corps (CCC) during the 1930s. Check out the pine dugout canoe carved by CCC workers for U.S. Forest Service personnel. Trout fishing on the Chewaucan River west of town and deer hunting also draw visitors. Paisley is home to the 137-mile-long, 64-mile-wide ZX Ranch, and in caves outside Paisley, fossilized human excrement has been found that dates back 14,400 years. These coprolites, as they're called, were found along with bones of horses and camels that went extinct in North America over 13,000 years ago. The town's other main claim to fame is its annual **Mosquito Festival,** a fundraiser for mosquito control in this swampy area, held the last full weekend of July.

### FOOD AND ACCOMMODATIONS

If you need to stay in Paisley, the **Sage Rooms** (441 Main St., 541/943-3145, $80-85) offer basic but comfortable accommodations, and a couple of restaurants, including the historic **Pioneer Saloon** (327 Main St., 541/943-3289, 11am-8pm Tues.-Wed., 11am-9pm Thurs.-Sun., $8-15), provide a taste of the West. Campers should head west out of downtown, up the Chewaucan River; **Marster Spring campground** ($6) is about six miles from town on Forest Road 33 and has drinking water.

Plan ahead to rent the remote, historic, and quite scenic **Bald Butte Lookout Cabin** (541/943-3114, reservations 877/444-6667, www.recreation.gov, mid-June-mid-Oct., $40), which has no drinking water, in the Fremont National Forest near the Gearhart Mountain Wilderness.

## LAKEVIEW AND VICINITY

The "big city" in this part of the world is Lakeview (pop. 2,300), 142 miles south of La Pine on Highway 31, about 96 miles east of Klamath Falls on Highway 140, and 139 miles from Burns on U.S. 395. The county hub, Lakeview bills itself as the highest town in Oregon, at 4,800 feet in elevation.

Most of what's appealing about Lakeview lies outside the downtown area, but if you're spending time in town, the **Schminck Memorial Museum** (128 S. E St., 541/947-3134, noon-4pm Thurs.-Sat. May-Oct., $3 adults, free under age 13) has antiques and Native American artifacts assembled by the Oregon chapter of the Daughters of the American Revolution.

This town's fault blocks and winds have made Lakeview a center for hang gliding enthusiasts—look for hang gliders coming off 2,000-foot Black Cap Hill above the east side of Lakeview from May to October. The local geyser, Old Perpetual, which used to erupt quite reliably in the front yard of **Hunter's Hot Springs Resort** (18088 U.S. 395), north of town, has become finicky, but especially in wet years it's worth checking to see if it's spouting.

### Abert Rim

Fifteen miles north of Lakeview on U.S. 395 is the **Abert Rim,** the highest fault escarpment in the United States. The rim rises 2,000 feet above Lake Abert. This unusual body of water has no outlet and is rich in brine shrimp, which attract countless waterfowl and shorebirds. As at Summer Lake, fall is prime birdwatching season; expect thousands of plovers and other shorebirds. Due to its high alkalinity, it is hazardous to swim in the lake.

Below Abert Rim along the east shore of Lake Abert, the slope is covered with boulders, some of which sport petroglyphs. Several are located right off the highway near the Abert Rim geological marker. Forest roads lead through the North Warner Mountains to Bureau of Land Management (BLM) trails up the back side of Abert Rim; obtain routing information on these obscure byways from the **Lakeview Ranger Station** (18049 U.S. 395 N., 541/947-6300). Although reaching the rim requires an arduous journey down bumpy back roads and a steep hike up the mountain, the view from the top is spectacular. Watch for rattlesnakes in the rocks.

### ★ Hart Mountain National Antelope Refuge

North and east of Lakeview, **Hart Mountain National Antelope Refuge** stretches across a high plateau rising above Warner Lakes. From U.S. 395 just north of Lakeview, head east on Highway 140 for 15 miles to the Plush Cutoff Road, go northeast 19 miles to Plush, and take the road up the steep west face of Hart Mountain to the refuge headquarters. The **U.S. Fish and Wildlife Service Refuge Complex Headquarters** (20995 Rabbit Hill Rd., 541/947-3315) in Lakeview has information on the refuge. There's also information and a small visitors center (541/947-2731, 24 hours daily), about 10 miles east of the refuge's western entrance, along with restrooms. Rangers are usually available. In summer, hundreds of the agile tan-and-white pronghorn gather at sunset along the dirt road south of the refuge. The refuge is also home to bighorn sheep, mule deer, 213 species of birds, and many small mammals.

The **campground** (free), a few miles south of the refuge headquarters, has no drinking water but features a hot spring surrounded by a cinder-block privacy wall; a dunk in the spring is highly recommended to loosen the stiffness from bouncing down the dirt roads to get here. Fill water containers at the refuge headquarters. The refuge is also a popular place for rock hounds searching for agates, fire opals, crystals, and sunstones.

Check with the **chamber of commerce** (126 N. E St., Lakeview, 541/947-6040, www.lakecountychamber.org) or the ranger at Hart Mountain for more information.

Despite the name of the preserve, you won't find any antelope here; there are no antelope in North America, only pronghorn. Because these animals shed the outer sheaths of their horns each year, they differ from their Asian and African counterparts—the true antelope—which have permanent horns. Male pronghorn have prongs, protrusions extending from their sheaths, to further distinguish them from antelope. The lingering misnomer was bestowed on these Oregon animals by Lewis and Clark. At any rate, many scientists believe that pronghorn could be the world's fastest land mammals over a long distance, barely edging out the cheetah on distances exceeding 1,000 yards. It's said they can cruise at more than 35 mph, maintain 60 mph for half a mile, and reach 70 mph in short bursts.

Besides pronghorn, the refuge also protects a number of areas rich in prehistoric rock art. The easiest to visit is **Petroglyph Lake** (follow signs from the refuge road), where early Native Americans etched symbols and animal likenesses on a rocky cliff

pronghorn at Hart Mountain National Antelope Refuge

above a small water hole. Follow the path to the cliff's end for the best display.

Most state maps show an unpaved road between Plush and Highway 205 near Frenchglen, designated a National Scenic Byway. It's about 50 miles across a frequently rough and dusty road that's equal parts gravel and hardpan, but most vehicles will make it without problems as long as you drive slowly. Inquire locally if there has been a lot of snow or rain, as the road is not regularly maintained.

## Rockhounding
Rockhounding is a popular hobby in Lake County. Best known for its abundance of sunstones (also called aventurine or Plush diamonds), the area has jasper, agates, petrified wood, fire opals, wonder stones, thunder eggs, and obsidian as well. To get to the sunstone-hunting grounds, go east on Highway 140 to the Plush junction and turn north. Another spot for rockhounding can be reached by taking Hogback Road just north of the upper section of the Abert Rim; the Hogback junction is about 50 miles north of Lakeview on U.S. 395. For more information, visit the **Hi Desert Craft Rock Shop** (244 N. M St., 541/880-8787, 9:30am-5pm daily).

## Skiing
**Warner Canyon Ski Area** (541/947-5001, http://warnercanyon.org, $32), seven miles east of Lakeview on Highway 140, is a small ski area with 23 runs, one chairlift (but no lines), and over 25 miles of marked but ungroomed cross-country trails. Thanks to a mile-high base elevation and the dry southeastern Oregon climate, excellent dry powder conditions are common. The area has a day lodge near the base of the hill with a snack bar that serves breakfast and lunch. The season may start as early as mid-December and run through the end of March.

## Food and Accommodations
In Lakeview, the **Best Western Skyline Motor Lodge** (414 N. G St., 541/947-2194, www.bestwesternoregon.com, $110-130) is

the most comfortable place to stay; it's pet-friendly and has a pool and a hot tub as well as large guest rooms. Just north of town, **Hunter's Hot Springs Resort** (18088 U.S. 395, 541/947-4242 or 800/858-8266, www.huntersresort.com) has basic motel rooms ($65) as well as an RV park and a restaurant. The rooms aren't exactly luxurious, and the hot springs pool has seen better days, but it's a place to really soak in the local atmosphere.

Lakeview isn't known for its cuisine. However, **Mario's Dinner House** (9 N. F St., 541/947-3102, 5pm-9pm Tues.-Sat., $11-30) serves good steaks, salmon, prime rib, homemade breads, and other standards in a historic downtown building. It's a really popular place on the weekends, when folks drive in from surrounding areas.

## Camping
**Goose Lake State Park** (541/947-3111 or 800/551-6949, www.oregonstateparks.org, mid-Apr.-early Oct., $22) is a big spread 15 miles south of Lakeview on U.S. 395. The campground has tent sites, electrical hookups, and a boat launch on the shore of the huge lake. **Corral Creek Campground** (free) has no water and is a good headquarters for an exploration of the Gearhart Mountain Wilderness, an area of high meadows, cliffs, and worn-down volcanoes. To get to the campground, turn off Highway 140 at Quartz Mountain, 24 miles west of Lakeview, and drive north on Forest Road 3600.

**Junipers Reservoir RV Resort** (541/947-2050, www.junipersrv.com, May-mid-Oct., depending on weather, $32-39) is 10 miles west of Lakeview on Highway 140. This private reservoir with campgrounds ($20), including some tent sites, is on a working cattle ranch. Designated one of six private wildlife-viewing areas in the state, this spread offers an excellent chance to view longhorn cattle, deer, eagles, ospreys, and coyotes.

## Information
Stop by the **Lakeview Welcome Center** (126 N. E St., 541/947-6040) for maps and brochures.

# Steens Mountain Country

If you judge this part of southeastern Oregon by driving through on U.S. 20, you probably won't find it too memorable. But off the main thoroughfares are recreational retreats worthy of closer investigation. The Malheur National Wildlife Refuge is nationally recognized not only as one of the best bird-watching sites in the country but also as the place occupied by armed antigovernment protesters for 41 days in 2016. Nearby Steens Mountain is famous for its stunning scenery.

## BURNS

The town of Burns, named after the Scottish poet Robert Burns, was founded in 1884. By 1889 it had a population of 250, which has since grown about tenfold. A significant boost to the town's economy came in 1924, when a rail line reached Burns. Its sister city, **Hines,** was incorporated in 1930. Named after Chicago lumberman Edward Hines, this town of 1,400 residents is primarily a bedroom community for Burns.

### Sagehen Hill Nature Trail

The **Sagehen Hill Nature Trail** is 16 miles west of Burns at the Sagehen rest stop on U.S. 20. This 0.5-mile nature trail has 11 stations on a route that takes you around Sagehen Hill through sagebrush, bitterbrush, and western juniper. Other plants found along the way include lupine, larkspur, owl clover, and yellowbell. The lucky early morning visitor in March and April might also catch the sage grouse courtship ritual. The male, bobbing his head, displays his puffed-up neck and plumage and makes clucking noises to attract the attention of the females. If these creatures are not visible, the views of Steens Mountain (elevation 9,733 feet) to the southeast will make the hike worthwhile.

### Harney County Historical Museum

The **Harney County Historical Museum** (18 W. D St., 541/573-5618, 8am-4pm Tues.-Sat. Apr.-Sept., $5 adults, $8 couples, $3 seniors and children) started out as a brewery and then became a laundry and a wrecking yard. Descendants of local pioneer families have donated quilts, furniture, a complete kitchen, a wagon shed, and machinery to the museum. Of special interest are artifacts from pioneer Pete French's ranch.

### ★ Crystal Crane Hot Springs

Spend an idyllic couple of hours at **Crystal Crane Hot Springs** (59315 Hwy. 78, 541/493-2312, www.cranehotsprings.com, 9am-9pm daily, $6 day-use), 25 miles southeast of Burns, just west of the town of Crane. The local hot springs feed a large pond that's big enough to swim in if you have the energy. It's more likely that you'll lounge at the pond's edge and watch the coots and shoveler ducks paddling around in the adjacent cool pond. Several bathhouses have cattle troughs filled with hot spring water as private soaking tubs ($10 pp per hour). The range of lodging includes simple cabins ($48-75) with a shared bathhouse a bit of a walk away, a tepee with a soaking tub ($75), three-bedroom houses ($220), and a camping area ($25 tents, $28-32 hookups).

### Rockhounding

Southeastern Oregon is rockhounding country. Each year, thousands of enthusiasts flock to this far-flung corner of the state to collect fossils, agates, jasper, obsidian, and thunder eggs. The **Stinking Water Mountains,** 30 miles east of Burns, are a good source of gemstones and petrified wood.

**Warm Springs Reservoir,** just east of the Stinking Water Mountains, is popular with agate hunters. **Charlie Creek** and **Radar,** west and north of Burns, respectively, produce black, banded, and brown obsidians. Be sure to collect only your limit—be a rock hound, not a rock hog. Also keep in mind that it is illegal to take arrowheads and other artifacts from public lands.

## Entertainment and Events

Held in Burns in early April, the **Harney County Migratory Waterfowl Conference** (541/573-2636, www.migratorybirdfestival.com) celebrates the spring return of waterbirds to the region with lectures, movies, slides, a high-quality art show, and guided bird-watching tours, including early morning visits to the sage grouse leks, or strutting grounds. This is an excellent opportunity to learn more about birds, and it attracts some knowledgeable and interesting people.

## Food

Although Burns isn't known as a culinary mecca, there are a few decent places to eat in town, especially if you're hankering for a steak dinner. The **Pine Room Restaurant and Lounge** (543 W. Monroe St., 541/573-2673, 4pm-2am Tues.-Sat., $12-32) is a steak house with multicourse meals, including bread, shrimp cocktail, salad, soup, and a main course. The barbecued pork ribs are especially good. This is one of the few places to find beers from local Steens Mountain Brewing, the state's smallest craft brewery.

If the timing is right, treat yourself to dinner at ★ **Rhojo's** (83 W. Washington St., 541/573-7656, 11am-2pm Mon.-Fri., 11:30am-2pm Sun., 6pm-9pm Fri.-Sat., $20-25). Lunchtime sandwiches and salads (about $8) are good, but the weekend nights offering two entrées that change weekly, such as seared halibut or marinated rib eye steak, plus full fixings, including delicious vegetables, are special events in downtown Burns.

## Accommodations

The pet-friendly **Silver Spur Motel** (789 N. Broadway, 541/573-2077, www.silverspurmotel.net, $55-62) is well-maintained and family-owned, on the north edge of downtown, with fridges and microwaves in the guest rooms. Another exceptionally sweet small-town motel is the **Horseshoe Inn** (50836 U.S. 20 E., 541/573-2034 or 866/834-2034, www.horseshoeinn.net, $69). It's about a mile from town, with a big yard, a grill, horse boarding, and pet rooms. In the adjacent town of Hines, the **Best Western Rory and Ryan Inn** (534 N. U.S. 20, Hines, 541/573-5050 or 800/780-7234, $130-165) is newer and very comfortable, with an indoor pool, hot tub, hot breakfast, and all the extras you would expect.

## Camping

A couple of campgrounds (541/573-4300, www.fs.usda.gov, $10) north of Burns in the Malheur National Forest are **Idlewild,** right off U.S. 395 about 17 miles north of Burns in a pretty setting, and the more remote **Yellowjacket,** on the shore of Yellowjacket Lake, 37 miles northwest of Burns on Forest Road 3745. From Burns, take County Road 127 out of town, then take Forest Road 47 to Forest Road 37 and follow signs to the campground. Be sure to keep your food under wraps, especially meat, if you want to avoid being visited by the namesake hosts of the lake. The lake is stocked with trout.

## Information

Stop by the **Harney County Chamber of Commerce** (484 N. Broadway, 541/573-2636, www.harneycounty.com, 10am-4pm Tues.-Sat.). For recreation, contact the **BLM office** (12533 U.S. 20 W., Hines, OR 97738, 541/573-5241, 9am-5pm Mon.-Fri.). The **Emigrant Creek Ranger District** (265 U.S. 20, Hines, OR 97738, 541/573-4300, 9am-5pm Mon.-Fri.) is also nearby.

## ★ MALHEUR NATIONAL WILDLIFE REFUGE

Malheur and Harney Lakes, fed by the mountain snow runoff filling the Blitzen and Silvies Rivers, have been major avian nesting and migration stopovers since prehistoric times. The contrast is startling: the stark dry basin land, with its red sandstone monoliths and mesas, and the lush green freshwater marshes (the longest in the western United States) and riparian areas, which attract thousands of birds along with bird-watchers.

Until recently, birders were just about the only visitors here, but when armed militants broke into the refuge headquarters on New Year's weekend 2016 and settled in for a 41-day occupation, the world took note. The protest originally took up the cause of local ranchers who were being sent to prison after being convicted of setting fires on federal land, but the refuge occupiers—almost all from out of town—demanded that the refuge and other public land be given to local landowners. After weeks of fruitless negotiations, a roadblock stopped a group of the leaders heading to a meeting in John Day; one of the militants was killed, and the remaining five were arrested. The remaining occupiers left the refuge. Later in the year, seven of the protest leaders were acquitted of conspiracy charges in federal court; others pleaded guilty to conspiracy or were found guilty of lesser charges.

Today, the **Malheur National Wildlife Refuge** (36391 Sodhouse Lane, Princeton, 541/493-2612, www.fws.gov, visitor center 8am-4pm Mon.-Thurs.) is once again dominated by bird-watchers. Over the past century, 312 species have been sighted. Prime

bird-watching times are the spring and fall migrations. Late spring is a good time to visit, before summer's scorching heat. In March, the first Malheur arrivals include Canada and snow geese, and in the vast Malheur Marsh, swans, mallards, and other ducks. Look for sandhill cranes in the wet meadows. Great horned owls and golden eagles are other early arrivals. Shorebirds are followed by warblers, sparrows, and other songbirds in spring. Red-tailed hawks can be seen swooping over the sage-covered prairies throughout spring, summer, and fall. In late spring, ponds and canals at Malheur occasionally host the trumpeter swan, a majestic bird with a seven-foot wingspan. This is one of the few places where you can observe this endangered species nesting. Flocks of pelicans are a summertime spectacle; see them before they head south to Mexico in the fall.

August to October is another prime time when birders might see 100 species, and lucky visitors might see the magnificent snow goose. Another fall arrival is the wood thrush, graced with one of the most beautiful songs in the bird kingdom. A September-October sees a concentration of greater sandhill cranes, Canada geese, and mallard ducks foraging on Blitzen Valley grain fields. The first two

Buena Vista Ponds, Malheur National Wildlife Refuge

weeks of September are nice because hunting season has yet to begin and the aspens have turned golden.

While the absolute numbers of birds at Malheur are not as great as they are at the Klamath Lakes or along the Oregon coast, the variety here is unsurpassed. Among birders, however, it is the "accidental list" of 55 infrequently sighted species that makes this preserve special. Many of these "exotics" are sighted nowhere else in the region.

Be sure to visit the **refuge headquarters** in a grove of cottonwoods looking out over the huge expanse of Malheur Lake. Here you can pick up maps for the self-guided auto tour of the refuge. A short distance downhill is a small **museum** (8am-4pm Mon.-Thurs.) where more than 250 bird specimens are beautifully arrayed. Also of interest is the charming **park** on the edge of the lake.

Settlers enjoyed unrestricted hunting, and at the turn of the 20th century, hunters killed thousands of swans, egrets, herons, and grebes for feathers for the millinery trade. In 1908, President Theodore Roosevelt put a stop to the slaughter by protecting the area as a bird sanctuary. The Blitzen Valley and P Ranch were added to the refuge in 1935. Today, 185,000 acres are protected.

Krumbo Reservoir is a good bet for trout or largemouth bass **fishing.** Invasive carp are a huge problem in Malheur Lake; control programs were interrupted by the refuge occupation, but the U.S. Fish and Wildlife Service is working with Native American communities and the public to control the carp and maintain habitat for birds.

To get to the refuge, drive 25 miles south from Burns on Highway 205 and then nine miles east on the county road toward Princeton. The Buena Vista Ponds are an excellent place to stop along the way.

## Accommodations

A convenient though bare-bones place to stay on the refuge is the **Malheur Field Station** (34848 Sodhouse Lane, 541/493-2629, www.malheurfieldstation.org, $55-150), where you can bunk in dorm rooms (groups only, $22-30 pp), trailers, or a three-bedroom house. RV sites ($19) are also available. Guests should bring bedding and towels; dorm dwellers should be prepared to share a restroom. Although most accommodations have kitchen facilities, meals are available during the peak season. Note that the trailers are the most coveted accommodations; they're often full during spring and fall birding seasons. Reserve a room in advance to avoid driving 35 miles to Burns for food and lodging.

## FRENCHGLEN

Named for famous rancher Pete French and his wealthy father-in-law, Hugh Glenn, the town of Frenchglen was originally known as P Station and was part of the nearby P Ranch. Today, this historic community with its hotel, store, corral, and post office remains essentially the same as it was 70 years ago. The town is about 60 miles south of Burns on Highway 205.

The ★ **Frenchglen Hotel** (Hwy. 205, 60 miles south of Burns, 541/493-2825, www.frenchglenhotel.com, mid-Mar.-Oct., $75-135) is an excellent place to stay while visiting Steens Mountain or Malheur National Wildlife Refuge. Built in 1914 as a stage stopover, the main hotel has eight smallish rooms with a shared bath down the hall. Just behind the hotel building are several modern rooms with private baths in the Drover's Inn, a separate unit. Ranch cooks prepare delicious family-style dinners (6:30pm sharp, reservations required, $23-26); breakfast and lunch are also available. Watching thunderstorms sweep across Steens Mountain from the hotel's screened-in porch while you chat with birders from all over the West can provide after-dinner entertainment.

## DIAMOND AND VICINITY
### Diamond Craters

**Diamond Craters** have been described by scientists as the most diverse basaltic volcanic features in the United States. To tour these unique formations, drive 55 miles south of

Burns on Highway 205 until you reach the Diamond junction. Turn left and begin a 40-mile route ending at New Princeton on Highway 78. On the way you'll see why this area is called "Oregon's Geologic Gem." There are craters, domes, lava flows, and pits that give an outstanding visual lesson on volcanism. To aid your self-guided tour, pick up the "Diamond Craters" brochure at the **BLM office** (12533 U.S. 20 W., Hines, 541/573-5241) in Hines.

## Round Barn

While in the Diamond Craters area, stop at the **Round Barn,** a historic structure built in the 1870s or 1880s by rancher Peter French as a place to spend the winter breaking his saddle horses. Located 20 miles north of Diamond, the barn is 100 feet in diameter, with a 60-foot circular lava rock corral inside. Twelve tall juniper poles support a roof covered with 50,000 shingles. Hundreds of cowpokes have carved their initials in the posts of this famous corral.

Just up the road from the barn, the privately owned **Round Barn Visitors Center** (541/493-2070, www.roundbarn.info, 9am-5pm daily, free), a combination gift shop, cold drink vendor, and historical museum, is worth a stop. Its architecture mirrors that of the historic barn, and the genial proprietor, a third-generation Diamond Valley rancher, leads daylong tours of the area with stops in some rather remote areas, focusing on the area's colorful history.

## Food and Accommodations

Tall Lombardy poplars mark the tiny hamlet of Diamond, which is a cluster of buildings tucked in at the bottom of a hill. The focal point of the town is the ★ **Hotel Diamond** (541/493-1898, www.historichoteldiamond.com, Apr.-Oct., $89-115), a wonderfully and unpretentiously restored hotel dating from the late 1800s. Don't worry about where to eat when you book a stay: Continental breakfast comes with the rooms, and family-style dinners (about $26) are quite good. Reserve a seat at the table at least a day in advance.

## ★ STEENS MOUNTAIN

**Steens Mountain**—named after Major Enoch Steen, a U.S. Army officer assigned the task of building a military road through Harney County—is one of the great scenic wonders of Oregon. A 30-mile fault block, the eastern flank of the mountain rises straight up from the Alvord Desert to a row of glacial peaks. On the western side, huge gorges

the historic Frenchglen Hotel

carved out by glaciers one million years ago descend to a gentle slope drained by the Donner and Blitzen River, which flows into Malheur Lake.

Steens Mountain has five vegetation zones, ranging from tall sage to alpine tundra. The best way to see the transition is to drive the **Steens Mountain Byway** out of Frenchglen to the top of Steens Mountain. This is the highest road in Oregon, rising to 9,000 feet in elevation. The first 15 miles of the road are gravel, and the last 9 miles are dirt. The latter section is not recommended for low-slung passenger cars. Expect to spend the entire day traveling this 59-mile byway.

Starting and ending at Frenchglen, the route up Steens Mountain, sans significant tree cover save for some beautiful aspens, evokes Alaskan alpine tundra. Multicolored low-to-the-ground wildflowers and vast spaciousness give the feeling of being on top of the world. This impression is accentuated by standing in snow while you look 5,000 feet straight down into the sun-scorched Alvord Desert, which records just seven inches of rain annually.

The first four miles of the trek lead across the Malheur National Wildlife Refuge and up to the foothills of Steens Mountain. **Page Springs,** the first campground on the route, is a popular spot offering campsites along the bank of the Donner and Blitzen River. Approximately 13 miles beyond Page Springs is **Lily Lake,** a good place for a picnic. This shallow lake has an abundance of water lilies, frogs, songbirds, and waterfowl.

After Lily Lake, you really start to climb up the mountain to **Fish Lake, Jackman Park** (both with campsites), and viewpoints of Kiger Gorge and the East Rim. **Kiger Gorge** is a spectacular example of a wide U-shaped path left by a glacier. Blanketed in meadow grasses, quaking aspen, cottonwood, and mountain mahogany at lower elevations, tiny tundra-like flowers proliferate on the 8,000-foot viewpoint.

The **East Rim** is a dramatic example of earth-shifting in prehistoric epochs. The lava layers that cap the mountain are thousands of feet thick and formed 15 million years ago when lava erupted from cracks in the ground. Several million years later, the Steens Mountain fault block began to lift along a fault below the East Rim. The fault block tilted to the west, forming the gentler slope that stretches to the Malheur Lake Basin. At the summit (9,670 feet), on a clear day, you can see the corners of four states—California,

Steens Mountain drops 5,000 feet to a desert playa.

Nevada, Oregon, and Idaho. From the summit, it's about one mile and 1,300 vertical feet down the slopes of Wildhorse Canyon to **Wildhorse Lake**. Expect the hike back up to the parking area to be tough—after all, you're climbing to 9,670 feet!

A good time to visit is August through mid-September. Nights are cold, but daytime temperatures are more pleasant than those of summertime scorchers. Later in the fall, red bushes and yellow aspens attract photographers. Some of the aspens are located at Whorehouse Meadow and are indirectly responsible for its name. Lonely shepherds would scratch love notes and erotica in the tree bark, pining for a visit from the horse-drawn bordellos that serviced these parts. Wildlife-viewing highlights include bighorn sheep, seen around the East Rim viewpoint in summer; hummingbirds, often observed at high elevations; and hawks, which can be spotted anywhere and anytime, especially from the ridge above Fish Lake.

The area has off-highway vehicle restrictions to protect the environment. Five gates controlling access to the Steens Mountain area are located at various elevations and are opened as road and weather conditions permit. Normally, the Steens Byway is not open until early July and is closed by snow in October or November. Gas is available only in Burns, Frenchglen, and Fields. Take reasonable precautions when driving the loop: sudden storms, lightning, flash floods, and extreme road conditions can be hazardous to travelers. The loop returns to Highway 205 about 10 miles south of Frenchglen.

Visit Steens Mountain the first Saturday of August for the **Chris Miller Memorial Steens Mountain Rim Run** (541/573-4412, http://steensrimrun.net), a 10K run or walk along the East Rim of Steens Mountain that starts at an elevation of 7,835 feet and finishes at above 9,700 feet.

## Blitzen

Four miles south of the southern terminus of the Steens Mountain Loop Road, turn west off Highway 205 to take a side trip to the ghost town of **Blitzen.** This eight-mile jaunt will take you to the ruins of the little town of a half-dozen dilapidated buildings, founded in the late 1800s. Blitzen was named after the Donner and Blitzen River, which flows nearby. *Donner und Blitzen* is German for "thunder and lightning," the label given this stream by Captain George Curry, who tried to cross it during a fierce thunderstorm.

## Camping

As for summertime Steens weather, the 100°F temperatures in the high desert give way to 50-80°F daytime temperatures atop the mountain. Nonetheless, be aware that the summit can see severe thunderstorms and lightning, and at night the mercury can drop below freezing, even on days with high noon-time temperatures.

There are three high-elevation **BLM campgrounds** (541/573-4400, no reservations, $8) along the Steens Mountain Loop Road. Close to the Malheur National Wildlife Refuge, **Page Springs** (year-round) is four miles southeast of Frenchglen and a good base for bird-watching, fishing, hiking, and sightseeing. **Fish Lake** (July-Nov. 15) is 17 miles east of Frenchglen. The namesake lake is stocked with eastern brook, cutthroat, and rainbow trout. Aspens surround the campsites, which have well water, fire pits, and toilets; firewood is included in the campsite fee. Climb up on the ridge above the campground to watch hawks. **Jackman Park,** three miles east of Fish Lake, is particularly popular with backpackers, who use it as a takeoff point. It has six sites with potable water and toilets.

Another alternative is the **Steens Mountain Wilderness Resort** (35678 Resort Lane, Frenchglen, 541/493-2415 or 800/542-3765, www.steensmountainresort. com, reservations recommended, $75-125 cabins and trailers, $15 tents, $27-32 RVs), just before you get to the Page Springs campground. Views of the surrounding gorges are spectacular, and there are more amenities than at the BLM facilities, including showers, a small store, laundry, dumping facilities, and a public phone. Some of the cabins and trailers (all heated and air-conditioned) require guests to bring towels and linens.

# ALVORD DESERT AND VICINITY
## Fields

**Fields,** the largest community on the east side of Steens Mountain (area pop. 120) and perhaps the friendliest place in the state, was established as a supply station in 1881, and a supply station it still is. Fields now has a gas station, a store, and a café (9am-4:30 Mon.-Sat.), all part of the same business, **Fields Station** (541/495-2275 8am-6pm Mon.-Sat., 9am-5pm Sun.). The accommodations, though very simple, are perfectly sufficient and very reasonably priced; there are a couple of one-bedroom units and an old hotel ($65-90) that'll sleep up to 10 people.

## ★ Alvord Desert

About 20 miles north of Fields, the vast hard-pan playa of the **Alvord Desert** comes into view. This usually dry and stark white alkali lake bed, called a playa, gets about six inches of rain per year, which quickly evaporates. It's possible to drive down to, and even on, the playa (unless it's wet, in which case it's quite slick). But rather than driving, get out of the car and walk. One popular activity here is land-sailing, which is done in a "boat" that's like a go-kart with a sail.

There is a small informal camping area under the east face of Steens Mountain along Pike Creek. Look for a spur road leading off to the west about two miles north of Alvord Hot Springs. Some folks also camp on the edge of the playa.

## Alvord Hot Springs

North of Fields, look for **Alvord Hot Springs** ($5 for 24 hours), a rustic spa recognizable by its corrugated-steel shack on the east side of the road. Two pools of hot mineral water piped in from spring runoff will warm your muscles. A small store and camping area round out the amenities. The view from the hot springs up onto the east face of Steens Mountain is magnificent.

## Mann Lake

North of the Alvord Desert, just west of the road, **Mann Lake** is a popular fishing destination. Early spring trout fishing is especially good, and the lake is the repository for the breeding stock of Lahontan cutthroat trout,

It's okay to camp at the edge of the Alvord Desert, but not toward the center.

Volcanic rocks form pinnacles in the Succor Creek area.

$1,000-1,800, depending on the length of the trip, to float (with an occasional run through hair-raising rapids) through deep rugged canyons past tall rock pillars, petroglyphs, many species of birds, and a number of hot springs. Offering Owyhee River trips are **Ouzel Outfitters** (541/385-5947 or 800/788-7238, www.oregonrafting.com), **Oregon Whitewater Adventures** (541/746-5422 or 800/820-7238, www.oregonwhitewater.com), and **Momentum River Expeditions** (541/488-2525, www.momentumriverexpeditions.com), which also runs kayak trips down the Owyhee.

### Succor Creek and Leslie Gulch

From Jordan Valley, head north 18 miles on U.S. 95, then turn left onto unpaved Succor Creek Road (just shy of the Oregon-Idaho border) to discover one of Oregon's remotest and most spectacularly scenic areas. Note that some maps show this route as paved. It is not. It's passable for most passenger vehicles, though high clearance is a plus.

Follow Succor Creek Road nine miles north to a signed junction with Leslie Gulch Road, which drops through a wildly eroded landscape on its way to Lake Owyhee. This steep though usually passable gravel road careens down a narrow creek channel incised through vividly colored volcanic rock that's been eroded into amazing pinnacle and turreted formations. The 16-mile route ends at a lakeside campground (no potable water). Watch for bighorn sheep along the cliffs.

Back on Succor Creek Road, continue another 11 miles north to Succor Creek State Park, where small but mighty Succor Creek (and the twisting road) plunge between cliffs of volcanic tuff hundreds of feet high, a landscape reminiscent of Utah's Zion National Park. You'll find a number of streamside campsites and picnic areas (bring water). Wander along the stream to explore the geology and wildflowers, but be sure to watch out for rattlesnakes and for thunder eggs—spherical, baseball-size geodes filled with agate, Oregon's state rock. This is one of the

a subspecies that's adapted to alkaline water. Although the lakeshore is pretty brushy and unshaded, there is a campground.

## OWYHEE RIVER COUNTRY

It's a long way from just about anywhere to the far southeastern corner of Oregon, but the canyons of the Owyhee are enchanting for those who don't mind roughing it. If you aren't prepared to camp, you can stay in one of the two very basic motels in Jordan Valley, or come down from the north, where Ontario has more services.

### Owyhee River Trips

The big treat for visitors to this area is a four-to six-day raft trip down the Owyhee River. The river can be run only for a few weeks in the spring, and during drought years it can't be run at all. Most trips start in the tiny town of Rome, east of Jordan Valley, and end at the southern edge of the Owyhee Reservoir, at the base of Leslie Gulch. Expect to pay

# The Grave of Jean-Baptiste Charbonneau

One of the early West's most colorful characters is buried at the old Inskip Ranch, near the ranching community of Danner, just west of Jordan Valley. Jean-Baptiste Charbonneau was the son of Toussaint Charbonneau and Sacajawea, who accompanied Lewis and Clark's Corps of Discovery on their journey across the western U.S. between 1805 and 1806. In all those images of Sacajawea, young Pomp, as Jean-Baptiste was known to the corps, is the one in the papoose—but having served as the youngest member of the expedition was just the beginning of his incredible life.

Captain Clark was so taken with the infant that he sent the child to private schools in St. Louis at his own expense. Later, at Fort Union in Montana, the adolescent Charbonneau met German nobleman and scientist Prince Paul von Wertemberg, who was impressed by the well-educated boy. He took Charbonneau back to Germany with him, where Charbonneau spent the next six years as a courtier. During this time, he learned five languages fluently and traveled across Europe and to Africa with the prince.

Charbonneau eventually returned to the western United States. He served as a guide through the Montana wilderness, trapped furs, served as alcalde at a California mission, and prospected for gold in the 1850s California Gold Rush. In 1866, he hankered to return to Montana, where gold fever had broken out. He got no farther than Danner, then a stage stop, where he died of pneumonia at age 61. To visit the gravesite, follow signs north off U.S. 95, about 17 miles east of Jordan Valley or 28 miles east of Burns Junction. The grave site is about two miles north on a good gravel road.

top spots in the state for discovering these unusual specimens.

Continue north 15 miles on Succor Creek Road to reach paved Highway 201, which runs between Homedale, Idaho, and Nyssa, Oregon. If you are beginning your Succor Creek journey from the north, you'll find the well-signed Succor Creek Road eight miles south of the small Oregon town of Adrian.

## Food and Accommodations

**Jordan Valley,** located almost on the Idaho border where U.S. 95 takes a sharp bend north, is mostly visited by long-haul truckers. For years, the Old Basque Inn, a former boardinghouse, was the place to eat and sleep in this remote territory. After a long closure, it was reopened as the **Flat Iron Steakhouse** (306 Wroten St., 541/586-2800), a good place for a meal and B&B room, but when we last checked, it was temporarily closed and on the market to be sold. If you're headed to Jordan Valley, call ahead to find out if the restaurant or B&B rooms are open. Otherwise, the **Basque Station Motel** (801 Main St., 541/586-2244, $50-65) has basic rooms that look pretty inviting after a long day's drive.

# Background

# The Landscape

## GEOGRAPHY

If Oregon were part of a jigsaw puzzle of the United States, it would be a squarish piece with a divot carved out of the center top. To the west is the Pacific Ocean, with some 370 miles of beaches, dunes, and headlands; to the east are the Snake River and Idaho. Up north, much of the boundary between Oregon and Washington is defined by the mighty Columbia River, while southern Oregon lies atop the upper borders of California and Nevada.

### Highs and Lows

Moving west to east, the major mountain systems start with the Klamath Mountains and the Coast Range. The Klamaths form the lower quarter of the state's western barrier to the Pacific; the eastern flank of this range is generally referred to as the Siskiyous. To the north, the Oregon Coast Range, a younger volcanic range, runs north-south in parallel to the coastline. The highest peaks in each of these cordilleras barely top 4,000 feet and stand between narrow coastal plateaus on the west side and the rich agricultural lands of the Willamette and Rogue Valleys on the other. Running up the west-central portion of the state is the Cascade Range, which extends from northern California to Canada. Five of the dormant volcanoes in Oregon top 10,000 feet above sea level, with Mount Hood, the state's highest peak, at 11,239 feet.

Beyond the eastern slope of the Cascades, semiarid high-desert conditions begin. In the northeast, the 10,000-foot crests of the snow-capped Wallowas rise less than 50 miles away from the hot, arid floor of Hells Canyon, itself about 1,300 feet above sea level. The Great Basin desert—characterized by rivers that evaporate, peter out, or disappear underground—makes up the bottom corner of eastern Oregon. Here the seven-inch annual rainfall of the Alvord Desert seems as if it would be more at home in Nevada than in a state known for blustery rainstorms and lush greenery. In addition to Hells Canyon, the country's deepest hole in the ground (7,900 feet maximum depth), Oregon also boasts the continent's deepest lake: Crater Lake, with a depth of 1,958 feet.

### Last of the Red-Hot Lavas

Each part of the state contains well-known remnants of Oregon's cataclysmic past. Offshore waters here feature 1,477 islands and islets, the eroded remains of ancient volcanic flows. Lava fields dot the approaches to the High Cascades. East of the range, a volcanic plateau supports cinder cones, lava caves, and lava-cast forests in the most varied array of these phenomena outside Hawaii.

The imposing volcanic cones of the Cascades and the inundated caldera that is Crater Lake, formed by the implosion of Mount Mazama 6,600 years ago, are some of the most dramatic reminders of Oregon's volcanic origins. More fascinating evidence can be seen up close at Newberry National Volcanic Monument, an extensive area south of Bend that encompasses obsidian fields and lava formations left by massive eruptions. (Geologists have cited Newberry on their list of volcanoes in the continental United States most likely to erupt again.) Not far from the Lava Lands Visitors Center in the national monument are the Lava River Cave and Lava Cast Forest—created when lava enveloped living trees 6,000 years ago.

Erosion has exposed many volcanic curiosities in eastern Oregon.

top billing with the last ice age in the grand epic of Oregon's topography. At the height of the most recent major ice age glaciation, the world's oceans were 300 to 500 feet lower, North America and Asia were connected by a land bridge across the Bering Strait, and the Oregon coast was miles west of where it is today. The Columbia Gorge extended out past present-day Astoria. As the glaciers melted, the sea rose.

When that glacial epoch's final meltdown 12,000 years ago unleashed water dammed up by thousands of feet of ice, great rivers were spawned and existing channels enlarged. A particularly large inundation was the Missoula Floods, which began as ice dams broke up in what's now northern Idaho and western Montana, releasing epic floods of glacial meltwater. These floodwaters carved out the contours of what are now the Columbia River Gorge and the Willamette Valley.

## Earthquakes and Tsunamis

Scientists exploring Tillamook County in 1990 unearthed discontinuities in both rock strata and tree rings, indicating that the north Oregon coast has experienced major **earthquakes** every several hundred years. They estimate that the next one could come within the next 50 years and be of significant magnitude. With virtually every part of the state possessing seismic potential that hasn't been released in many years, the pressure along the fault lines is increasing.

In coastal areas, one of the greatest dangers associated with earthquakes is the possibility of **tsunamis.** When the March 2011 Tohoku earthquake hit Japan, Oregon's coastal residents fled to higher ground; although most of the state's coast was spared, eight-foot waves along the southern coast damaged the harbor in Brookings.

## The Great Meltdown

However pervasive the effects of seismic activity and volcanism are, they must still share

## CLIMATE
### The Rain Shadow

Oregon's location equidistant from the equator and the north pole subjects it to weather from both tropical and polar airflows. This makes for a pattern of changeability in which calm often alternates with storm, and extreme heat and extreme cold seldom last long.

Oregon's weather is best understood as a series of valley climates separated from each other by mountain ranges that draw precipitation from the eastbound weather systems. Moving west to east, each of these valley zones receives progressively lower rainfall level, culminating in the desert on the eastern side of the state.

### The Coast

Wet but mild, average rainfall on the coast ranges from a low of 64 inches per year in the Coos Bay area to nearly 100 inches around Lincoln City. The Pacific Ocean moderates coastal weather year-round, softening the extremes. Spring, summer, and fall generally don't get very hot, with highs generally in the 60s and 70s and seldom topping 90°F. Winter temperatures only drop to the 40s and 50s, and freezes and snowfall are quite rare.

## Western Oregon

If there is one constant in western Oregon, it is cloudiness. Portland and the Willamette Valley receive only about 45 percent of maximum potential sunshine; more than 200 days of the year are cloudy, and rain falls an average of 150 days. While this might sound bleak, consider that the cloud cover helps moderate the climate by trapping and reflecting the earth's heat. On average, fewer than 30 days of the year record temperatures below freezing. Except in mountainous areas, snow usually isn't a force to be reckoned with. Another surprise is that Portland's average annual rainfall of 40 inches is usually less than totals recorded in New York City, Miami, or Chicago. In the southern valleys, Ashland and Medford typically record only half the yearly precipitation of their neighbors to the north, as well as higher winter and summer temperatures.

## Central and Eastern Oregon

The landscape of central and eastern Oregon by and large determines the weather, but you can almost always count on weather out here to be more extreme than in western Oregon. In summer, mountainous areas will be cooler, while the extensive desert basins of eastern Oregon can be scorching. Winter can bring snow and cold temperatures across the entire region.

# Plants and Animals

## PLANTS

With 4,400 known species and varieties, Oregon ranks fourth among U.S. states for plant diversity, including dozens of species found nowhere else.

## Trees

The mixed-conifer ecosystem of western Oregon—dense, far-reaching forests of Douglas fir, Sitka spruce, and western hemlock interspersed with bigleaf maple, vine maple, and alder—is among the most productive woodlands in the world. In southern Oregon, you'll find redwood groves and rare myrtle trees, prized by woodworkers for their distinctive coloring and grain, while huge ponderosa pines are a hallmark of central and eastern Oregon. A particularly striking autumnal display along the McKenzie River mixes red vine maple and sumacs with golden oaks and alders against an evergreen backdrop.

Of the 19 million acres of old growth that once proliferated in Oregon and Washington, less than 10 percent survive. Naturalists describe an old-growth forest as a mixture of trees, some of which must be at least 200 years old, and a supply of snags or standing dead trees, nurse logs, and streams with downed logs. Of all the old-growth forests mentioned in this volume, **Opal Creek** in the Willamette Valley most spectacularly embodies all of these characteristics.

## Coastal Plant Life

While giant conifers and a profuse understory of greenery predominate coastal forests, this ecosystem represents only the most visible part of the Oregon coast's bountiful botany. Many coastal travelers will notice **European beachgrass** (*Ammophila arenaria*) covering the sand wherever they go. Originally planted in the 1930s to inhibit dune growth, the thick, rapidly spreading grass worked too well, solidifying into a ridge behind the shoreline, blocking the windblown sand from replenishing the rest of the beach, and suppressing native plants.

**Freshwater wetlands and bogs,** created where water is trapped by the sprawling sand dunes along the central coast, provide habitats for some unusual species. Best known among

trillium in Portland's Forest Park

these is the **cobra lily** (*Darlingtonia californica*), which can be viewed up close just north of Florence. Also called pitcher plant, this carnivorous bog dweller survives on hapless insects lured into a specialized chamber, where they are trapped and digested.

**Coastal salt marshes,** occurring in the upper intertidal zones of coastal bays and estuaries, have been dramatically reduced due to land "reclamation" projects such as drainage, diking, and other human disturbances. The halophytes (salt-loving plants) that thrive in this specialized environment include pickleweed, saltgrass, fleshy jaumea, salt marsh dodder, arrowgrass, sand spurrey, and seaside plantain. Coastal forests include Sitka spruce and alder riparian communities, which provide resting and feeding areas for migratory waterfowl, shore and wading birds, and raptors.

## Flowers and Fruits

While not as visually arresting as the evergreens of western Oregon, the state's several varieties of berries are no less pervasive. Found mostly from the coast to the mid-Cascades, invasive **Himalayan blackberries** favor clearings, burned-over areas, and people's gardens. They also take root in the woods alongside **wild strawberries, salmonberries, thimbleberries, currants,** and **salal.** Within this edible realm, wild-food connoisseurs especially seek out the thin-leafed **huckleberry** found in the Wallowa, Blue, Cascade, and Klamath Ranges. Prime snacking season for all these berries ranges from midsummer to mid-fall.

No less prized are the rare plant communities of the Columbia River Gorge and the Klamath-Siskiyou region. A quarter of Oregon's rare and endangered plants are found in the latter area, a portion of which is in the valley of the Illinois River, a designated Wild and Scenic tributary of the Rogue. *Kalmiopsis leachiana,* a rare member of the heath family endemic to southwestern Oregon, even has a wilderness area named after it.

Motorists will treasure such springtime floral fantasias (both wild and domesticated) such as the **dahlias** and **irises** near Canby off I-5; **tulips** near Woodburn; irises off Highway 213 outside Salem; the **Easter lilies** along U.S. 101 near Brookings; **blue lupines** alongside U.S. 97 in central Oregon; **apple blossoms** in the Hood River Valley near the Columbia Gorge; **pear blossoms** in the Bear Creek Valley near Medford; **bear grass, columbines,** and **Indian paintbrush** on Cascades thoroughfares; and **rhododendrons** and **fireweed** along the coast.

East of the Cascades, the undergrowth is often more varied than the ground cover in the damp forests on the west side of the mountains. This is because sunny openings in the forest permit room for more species and for plants of different heights. And, in contrast to the white flowers that predominate in the shady forests in western Oregon, "dry-side" wildflowers generally have brighter colors. These blossoms attract color-sensitive pollinators such as bees and butterflies. On the opposite flank of the range, the commonly seen white **trillium** relies on beetles and ants for propagation, lessening the need for eye-catching pigments.

## Mushrooms

Autumn is the season for those who covet wild chanterelle and matsutake mushrooms. September through November, the Coast Range is the prime picking area for chanterelles—a fluted orange or yellow mushroom in the tall second-growth Douglas fir forests. In the spring, fungus-lovers' hearts turn to morels. Of course, you should be absolutely certain of what you have before you eat wild mushrooms, or any other wild food. Farmers markets are usually good places to find an assortment of wild mushrooms.

# ANIMALS

Oregon's creatures great and small are an excitingly diverse group. Oregon's relatively low population density, abundance of wildlife refuges and nature preserves, and biomes running the gamut from rainforest to desert explain this variety. Throughout the state, numerous refuges, such as the **South Slough National Estuarine Research Reserve,** the **Malheur National Wildlife Refuge,** the **Jewell Meadows Wildlife Area** preserve for Roosevelt elk, and the **Finley National Wildlife Refuge** provide safe havens for both feathered and furry friends.

## Tide Pools

For many visitors, the most fascinating coastal ecosystems in Oregon are the rocky tide pools. These Technicolor windows offer an up-close look at one of the richest—and harshest—environments, the intertidal zone, where pummeling surf, unflinching sun, predators, and the cycle of tides demand tenacity and special adaptation.

The natural zone where surf meets shore is divided into three main habitat layers, based on their position relative to tide levels. The **high intertidal zone,** inundated only during the highest tides, is home to creatures that can either move, such as **crabs,** or are well adapted to tolerate daily desiccation, such as **acorn barnacles** and **finger limpets, chitons,** and **green algae.** The turbulent **mid-intertidal zone** is covered and uncovered by the tides, usually twice each day. In the upper portion of this zone, **California mussels** and **goose barnacles** may thickly blanket the rocks, while ochre **sea stars** and green **sea anemones** are common lower down, along with **sea lettuce, sea palms, snails, sponges,** and **whelks.** Below that, the **low intertidal zone** is exposed only during the lowest tides. Because it is covered by water most of the time, this zone has the greatest diversity of organisms in the tidal area. Residents include many of the organisms found in the higher zones, as well as **sculpins, abalone,** and purple **sea urchins.**

Standout destinations for exploring tide pools include Cape Arago, Cape Perpetua, the Marine Gardens at Devil's Punchbowl, and beaches south and north of Gold Beach, among many others. Tide pool explorers should be mindful that, despite the fact that the plants and animals in the pools are well adapted to withstand the elements, they and their ecosystem are actually quite fragile, and they're very sensitive to human interference. Avoid stepping on mussels, anemones, and barnacles, and take nothing from the tide pools. In the Oregon Islands National Wildlife Refuge and other specially protected areas, removal or harassment of any living organism may be treated as a misdemeanor punishable by fines.

## Gray Whales

Few sights along the Oregon coast elicit more excitement than that of a surfacing whale. The most common large whale seen from shore along the West Coast of North America is the gray whale (*Eschrichtius robustus*). These behemoths can reach 45 feet in length and 35 tons in weight. The sight of a mammal as big as a Greyhound bus erupting from the sea has a way of emptying the mind of mundane

With warming oceans, sea lions are more numerous than ever in Oregon.

returning northward past the Oregon coast. Mothers and their new calves are the last to leave Mexico and move more slowly, passing Oregon late April-June. During the spring migration, the whales may pass within just a few hundred yards of coastal headlands, making this a particularly exciting time for whale-watching from any number of vantage points along the coast.

## Seals and Sea Lions

Pacific harbor seals, California sea lions, and Steller sea lions are frequently sighted in Oregon waters. California sea lions are characterized by their 1,000-pound size and their small earflaps, which seals lack. Unlike seals, they can point their rear flippers forward to give them better mobility on land. Lacking the dense underfur that covers seals, sea lions tend to prefer warmer waters.

Steller sea lions can be seen at the Sea Lion Caves. They also breed on reefs off Gold Beach and Port Orford. In the largest sea lion species, males can weigh more than a ton. Their coats tend to be gray rather than the nearly black California sea lions. They also differ from their California counterparts in that they are comfortable in colder water.

Look for Pacific harbor seals in bays and estuaries up and down the coast, sometimes miles inland. They're nonmigratory, have no earflaps, and can be distinguished from sea lions because they're much smaller (150-300 pounds) and have mottled fur that ranges in color from pale cream to rusty brown.

## Salmon and Steelhead

In recent decades, dwindling Pacific salmon and steelhead stocks have prompted restrictions on commercial and recreational fishing in order to restore threatened and endangered species throughout the Pacific Northwest. Runs are highly variable from year to year; for more information about fish populations and fishing restrictions, see the Oregon Department of Fish and Wildlife's website (www.dfw.state.or.us).

The salmon's life cycle begins and ends in

concerns. Wreathed in seaweed and sporting barnacles and other parasites on its back, a California gray whale might look more like the hull of an old ship were it not for its expressive eyes.

Some gray whales are found off the Oregon coast all year, including an estimated 200-400 during the summer, though they're most visible and numerous when migrating populations pass through Oregon waters on their way south December-February and northward early March-April. This annual journey from the rich feeding grounds of the Bering and Chukchi Seas of Alaska to the calving grounds of Mexico amounts to some 10,000 miles, the longest migration of any mammal. On the Oregon coast, their numbers peak usually during the first week of January, when as many as 30 per hour may pass a given point. By mid-February, most of the whales will have moved on toward their breeding and calving lagoons on the west coast of Baja California.

Early March-April, the juveniles, adult males, and females without calves begin

# Species of Fish

Touted as the best-tasting salmon, king (also known as chinook) salmon are also the largest species, sometimes weighing in at over 80 pounds. Coho (or silver) salmon are known among anglers as fish that fight fiercely, despite a weight of just 10-20 pounds. Chum salmon (known as "dog salmon" because Canadian and Alaskan native people thought them worthy only of being fed to their dog teams) are found only in the Miami and Kilchis Rivers near Tillamook.

Steelhead are sea-run rainbow trout averaging 5-20 pounds whose life cycle generally resembles that of salmon—save for the fact that steelhead generally survive after spawning and may live to spawn multiple times. Runs of steelhead, often heavily supplemented by hatchery-raised fish, are found in rivers and streams up and down the coast. They provide great—if challenging—sport angling, but are not fished commercially (though you will find farm-raised steelhead in the grocery store).

a freshwater stream. After an upriver journey from the sea of sometimes hundreds of miles, the spawning female deposits 3,000-7,000 eggs in hollows (called redds) she has scooped out of the coarse sand or gravel, where the male fertilizes them. These adult salmon die soon after mating, and their bodies then deteriorate to become part of the food chain for young fish.

Within three or four months, the eggs hatch into alevin, tiny immature fish with their yolk sac still attached. As the alevin exhaust the nutrients in the sac, they enter the fry stage, and begin to resemble very small salmon. The length they remain as fry differs among various species. Chinook fry, for example, immediately start heading for saltwater, whereas coho or silver salmon will remain in their home stream for one to three years before moving downstream. The salmon are in the smolt stage when they start to enter saltwater. The five- to seven-inch smolts will spend some time in the estuary area of the river or stream while they feed and adjust to the saltwater.

When it finally enters the ocean, the salmon is considered an adult. Each species varies in the number of years it remains away from its natal stream, foraging sometimes thousands of miles throughout the Pacific. Chinook can spend as many as seven years away from their nesting (and ultimately their resting) place; most other species remain in

the salt for two to four years. Spring and fall mark the main upstream runs of the Pacific salmon. It is thought that young salmon imprint the odor of their birth stream, enabling them to find their way home years later.

The salmon's traditional predators such as the sea lion, northern pikeminnow, harbor seal, black bear, Caspian tern, and herring gull pale in comparison to the threats posed by modern civilization. Everything from pesticides to sewage to nuclear waste has polluted Oregon waters, and until mitigation efforts were enacted, dams and hydroelectric turbines threatened to block Oregon's all-important Columbia River spawning route.

## Cougars and Wolves

Oregon is home to cougars, also known as mountain lions. As human development encroaches on their territory, sightings of these large cats become more common. Although they tend to shy away from big people, they've been known to attack children and small adults. For this reason, if no other, keep your kids close to the adults when hiking. Oregon also supports several packs of gray wolves.

## Mustangs

Wild Kiger mustangs, descendants of horses that the Spanish conquistadors brought to the Americas centuries ago, live on Steens Mountain and are identified by their hooked ears, thin dorsal stripes, two-toned manes, and faint zebra stripes on their legs. Narrow trunks and short backs are other distinguishing physical characteristics.

## Bears

Black bears (*Ursus americanus*) proliferate in mountain and coastal forests of Oregon. Adults average 200 to 500 pounds and have dark coats. Black bears shy away from people except when provoked by the scent of food, when cornered or surprised, or when humans intrude into territory near their cubs. Female bears tend to have a very strong maternal instinct that may construe any alien presence as an attack on their young. Authorities counsel hikers to act aggressively and defend themselves with whatever means possible if a bear is in attack mode or shows signs that it considers a hiker prey. Jump up and down, shout, and wave your arms. It may help to raise your jacket or pack to make yourself appear larger, but resist the urge to run. Bears can run much faster than humans, and their retractable claws enable black bears to scramble up trees. Furthermore, bears tend to give chase when they see something running.

If you see a bear at a distance, try to stay downwind of it and back away slowly. Bears have a strong sense of smell, and some studies suggest that our body scent is abhorrent to them. Our food, however, can be quite appealing. Campers should place all food in a sack tied to a rope and suspend it 20 feet or more from the ground and away from your tent.

## Deer, Elk, and Pronghorn

Sportspeople and wildlife enthusiasts alike appreciate Oregon's big-game herds. Big-game habitats differ dramatically from one side of the Cascades to the other, with Roosevelt elk and black-tailed deer in the west, and Rocky Mountain elk and mule deer east of the Cascades. The Columbian white-tailed deer is a seldom-seen endangered species found in western Oregon. Pronghorn reside in the high desert country of southeastern Oregon. The continent's fastest mammal, it is able to sprint at over 60 mph in short bursts. The low brush of the open country east of the Cascades suits their excellent vision, which enables them to spot predators.

## Small Mammals

Many of the most frequently sighted animals in Oregon are small scavengers. Even in the most urban parts of the state, it's possible to see raccoons, skunks, chipmunks, squirrels, and opossums. West of the Cascades, the dark-colored Townsend's chipmunks are among the most commonly encountered mammals; east of the Cascades, lighter-colored pine chipmunks and golden-mantled ground squirrels proliferate in drier interior forests. The latter two look almost alike, but the stripes on the side of the chipmunk's head distinguish them. Expect to see the dark-brown cinnamon-bellied Douglas squirrel on both sides of the Cascades.

## Beavers

Beavers (*Castor canadensis*), North America's largest rodents, are widespread throughout the Beaver State, though they're most commonly sighted in second-growth forests near marshes after sunset. Fall is a good time to spot beavers as they gather food for winter. The beaver has long been Oregon's mascot, and for good reason: It was the beaver that drew brigades of fur trappers and spurred the initial exploration and settlement of the state. The beaver also merits a special mention for being important to Oregon's forest ecosystem. Contrary to popular belief, the abilities of Mother Nature's carpenter extend far beyond the mere destruction of trees to dam a waterway. In fact, the activities associated with lodge construction actually serve to maintain the food chain and the health of the forest by slowing waters to create a habitat for a variety of freshwater and woodland creatures.

## Banana Slugs

You won't go far in the Oregon coast woodlands or underbrush before you encounter the state's best-known invertebrates—and lots of them. There are few places on earth where these snails-out-of-shells grow as large (3-10 inches long) or as numerous. The reason is western Oregon's climate: moister than mist but drier than drizzle. This balance, combined with calcium-poor soil, enables the native banana slug and the more common European black slug (the bane of Oregon gardeners) to thrive.

## Desert Critters

Because most desert animals are nocturnal, it's difficult to see many of them. Nonetheless, their variety and exotic presences should be noted. Horned lizards, kangaroo rats, red-and-black ground snakes, kit foxes, and four-inch-long greenish-yellow hairy scorpions are some of the more interesting denizens of the desert east of the Cascade Mountains.

## Birds

The Pacific Flyway is an important migratory route that passes through Oregon, and the state's varied ecosystems provide habitats for a variety of species, ranging from shorebirds to raptors to songbirds. The U.S. Fish and Wildlife Service has established viewpoints for wildlife- and bird-watching at 12 Oregon national wildlife refuges.

In the winter, the outskirts of Klamath Falls become inundated with bald eagles. Along the lower Columbia east of Astoria and on Sauvie Island, just outside Portland, are other bald eagle wintering spots. Visitors to Sauvie Island will be treated to an amazing variety of birds. More than 200 bird species come through here on the Pacific Flyway, feeding in grassy clearings. Look for eagles on the island's northwest side. Herons, ducks of all sorts, and geese also live on the island.

Other birds of prey, or raptors, abound all over the state. Northeast of Enterprise, near Zumwalt, is one of the best places to see hawks. Species commonly sighted include the ferruginous, red-tailed, and Swainson's hawks. Rafters in Hells Canyon might see golden eagles' and peregrine falcons' nests. Portlanders driving the Fremont Bridge over the Willamette River also might get to see peregrine falcons. Along I-5 in the Willamette Valley, look for red-tailed hawks on fence posts, and American kestrels, North America's smallest falcons, sitting on overhead wires.

Turkey vultures circle the dry areas during the warmer months. Vultures are commonly sighted above the Rogue River. In central Oregon, ospreys are frequently spotted off the Cascades Lakes Highway south of Bend,

osprey

nesting atop hollowed-out snags near water (especially Crane Prairie Reservoir).

In terms of sheer numbers and variety, the coast's mudflats at low tide and the tidal estuaries are among the best birding environments. Numerous locations along the coast—including Bandon Marsh, Three Arch Rocks near Cape Meares, and South Slough Estuarine Research Reserve near Coos Bay—offer outstanding opportunities for spotting such pelagic species as pelicans, cormorants, guillemots, and puffins, as well as waders such as curlews, sandpipers, and plovers, plus various ducks and geese. Rare species such as tufted puffins and the snowy plover enjoy special protection here, along with marbled murrelets, which feed from the ocean but nest in mature forests up to 30 miles inland. The **Oregon Islands National Wildlife Refuge,** which comprises all the 1,400-plus offshore islands, reefs, and rocks from Tillamook Head to the California border, is a haven for the largest concentration of nesting seabirds along the West Coast, thanks to the abundance of protected nesting habitat.

Malheur Wildlife Refuge, in the southeast portion of the state, is Oregon's premier bird and birder retreat and stopover point for large groups of sandhill cranes, Canada and snow geese, whistling swans, and pintail ducks.

In the mountains, look for Clark's nutcracker or the large Steller's jay, whose grating voice and dazzling blue plumage often commands the most attention. Mountain hikers are bound to share part of their picnic lunch with these birds. At high elevations, the quieter Clark's nutcracker will more likely be your guest.

Unfortunately, the western meadowlark, the state bird, has nearly vanished from western Oregon due to loss of habitat, but thanks to natural pasture east of the Cascades, you can still hear its distinctive song. The meadowlark is distinguished by a yellow underside with a black crescent pattern across the breast and white outer tail feathers.

# History

## NATIVE PEOPLES
### Early Days
Long before Europeans came to this hemisphere, indigenous people thrived for thousands of years in the region of present-day Oregon. The leading theory concerning their origins maintains that their ancestors came over from Asia on a land or ice bridge spanning what is now the Bering Strait.

Despite common ancestry, the people on the rain-soaked coast and in the Willamette Valley lived quite differently from those on the drier eastern flank of the Cascade Mountains. Those west of the Cascades enjoyed abundant salmon, shellfish, berries, and game. Broad rivers facilitated travel, and thick stands of the finest softwood timber in the world ensured that there was never a dearth of building materials. A mild climate with plentiful food and resources allowed the wet-siders the leisure time to evolve a complex culture rich with artistic endeavors, theatrical pursuits, and such ceremonial gatherings as the traditional potlatch, where the divesting of one's material wealth was seen as a status symbol.

After contact with traders, Chinook, an amalgam of Native American tongues with some French and English thrown in, was the common argot among the diverse nations that gathered in the Columbia Gorge each year. It was at these gatherings that the coast and valley dwellers would come into contact with Native Americans from east of the Cascades. These dry-siders led a seminomadic existence, following game and avoiding the climatic extremes of winter and summer in their region. In the southeast desert of the Great Basin, seeds and roots added protein to their diet.

The introduction of horses in the mid-1700s made hunting much easier. In contrast

# What's in a Name?

One rather peculiar theory of how Oregon got its name derives from a reputed encounter between Native Americans and the Spanish mariners who plied West Coast waters in the 17th and 18th centuries. Upon seeing the abalone shell earrings of the coastal Salish people, the European sailors are said to have exclaimed, *"¡Orejon!"* ("What big ears!")—later anglicized to Oregon. Others point out the similarity between the name of the state and the Spanish locales Aragon and Obregon (in Mexico). Additionally, the word *Oregon* belonged to a Wisconsin group of Native Americans who purportedly traded with Columbia River natives during salmon season.

A less fanciful explanation has it that the state's name was inspired by the English word "origin," conjuring the image of the forest primeval. The French word *ouragan* ("hurricane") has also been suggested as the source of the state's name, courtesy of French Canadian fur trappers who became the first permanent European settlers in the region during the early 19th century. In this vein, the reference to the Columbia River as the "Oregan" by some French Canadian voyageurs who came here with the "beaver brigades" of the Northwest and Hudson's Bay Companies is another possible etymological ancestor.

It was recently noted that *oregonon* and *orenogonia,* two Greek words pertaining to mountainous locales, were seen on old navigators' maps marking the area between northern California and British Columbia. Given that the famous Pacific Northwest explorer Juan de Fuca was actually Greek (born Valerianos) and that many navigators were schooled in Greece, perhaps Oregon's name originated in the Mediterranean.

to their counterparts west of the Cascades, who lived in 100-by-40-foot longhouses, extended families in the eastern groups inhabited pit houses when not hunting. The demands of chasing migratory game necessitated caves or simple rock shelters.

Twelve separate nations populated what is now Oregon. Although these were further divided into 80 tribes, the primary allegiance was to the village, and "nation" referred to language groupings such as Salish and Athabascan.

## Conflicts with European Settlers

The coming of European settlers meant the usurpation of Native American homelands, exposure to European diseases such as smallpox and diphtheria, and the passing of ancient ways of life. Violent conflicts ensued on a large scale with the influx of settlers doing missionary work and seeking government land giveaways in the 1830s and 1840s. In the 1850s, mining activity in southern Oregon and on the coast incited the Rogue River Wars,

adding to the strife brought on by annexation to the United States.

These events compelled the U.S. federal government to send in troops and eventually to set up treaties with Oregon's first inhabitants. The attempts at arbitration in the 1850s added insult to injury. Tribes of different—indeed, often incompatible—backgrounds were rounded up and grouped together haphazardly on reservations, often far from their homelands. In the century that followed, modern civilization destroyed much of the ecosystem on which these cultures were based. An especially regrettable result of colonization was the decline of the Columbia River salmon runs due to overfishing, loss of habitat, and pollution. This not only weakened the food chain but treated this spiritual totem of the many Native American groups along the Columbia as an expendable resource.

For a while, there was an attempt to restore the balance. In 1924 the federal government accorded citizenship to Native Americans. Ten years later, the Indian Reorganization Act provided self-management of reservation lands. Another decade later, a court of treaty claims was established. In the 1960s, however, the government, acting on the premise that Native Americans needed to assimilate into mainstream society, terminated several reservations.

Recent government reparations have accorded many indigenous peoples preferential hunting and fishing rights, monetary and land grants, and the restoration of status to certain disenfranchised bands. In Oregon, there are now nine federally recognized tribes and six reservations: Warm Springs, Umatilla, Burns Paiute, Siletz, Grand Ronde, and Coquille. Against all odds, their culture is still a vital part of Oregon; the 2010 census estimated that over 53,000 Oregonians are Native American. Native American gaming came to Oregon in the mid-1990s, and Native Oregonians now operate a number of lucrative casinos in the state; the Confederated Tribes of Grand Ronde, owners of the phenomenally popular Spirit Mountain Casino, are among the state's biggest philanthropists.

## EXPLORATION, SETTLEMENT, AND GROWTH

In the 17th and 18th centuries, Spanish, British, and Russian vessels came to offshore waters here in search of a sea route connecting the Atlantic with the Pacific. Accounts differ, but the first sightings of the Oregon coast have been credited to either Spanish explorer Juan Rodríguez Cabrillo (in 1543) or English explorer Francis Drake (in 1579). Other voyagers of note included Spain's Vizcaíno and De Aguilar (in 1603) and Bruno de Heceta (in 1775), and Britain's James Cook and John Meares during the late 1770s, as well as George Vancouver (in 1792).

Sea otter and beaver pelts added impetus to the search for a trade route connecting the Atlantic and Pacific Oceans. While the Northwest Passage turned out to be a myth, the fur trade became a basis of commerce and contention between European, Asian, and eventually American governments.

## U.S. Expansion in Oregon

The United States took interest in the area when Robert Gray sailed up the Columbia River in 1792. The first U.S. overland excursion into Oregon was made by the Corps of Discovery in 1804-1806. Dispatched by President Thomas Jefferson to explore the lands of the Louisiana Purchase and beyond, Captains Meriwether Lewis and William Clark and their party of 30 men—and one woman, Sacajawea—trekked across the continent to the mouth of the Columbia, camped south of present-day Astoria during the winter of 1805-1806, and then returned to St. Louis. Lewis and Clark's exploration and mapping of Oregon threw down the gauntlet for future settlement and eventual annexation of the Oregon Territory by the United States. The expedition also initially secured good relations with the Native Americans in the West, thus establishing the preconditions to trade and the missionary influx.

Following Lewis and Clark's journey, there were years of wrangling over the right of the United States to settle in the new territory (when Lewis and Clark made their journey, Oregon and Washington were British territory). Nonetheless, American John Jacob Astor's Pacific Fur Company established a trading fort at Astoria in 1811, though British war ships soon dispersed the settlement. It wasn't until 1818, as part of the settlement of the War of 1812, that the country west of the Rockies, south of Russian America, and north of Spanish America was open for use by U.S. citizens as well as British subjects.

During the 1820s, the British Hudson's Bay Company continued to hold sway over Oregon country by means of Fort Vancouver on the north shore of the Columbia. More than 500 people settled here under the charismatic leadership of John McLoughlin, who oversaw the planting of crops and the raising of livestock. Despite a growing number of farms and settlements along the Willamette River, as the trappers began to put down roots, several factors presaged the demise of British influence in Oregon. Most obvious was the decline of the fur trade as well as Britain's difficulty in maintaining its far-flung empire. Less apparent but equally influential was the lack of European women in a land populated predominantly by male European trappers and explorers. If the Americans could attract settlers of both genders, they'd be in a position to create an expanding population base that could dominate the region.

The first step in this process was the arrival of missionaries. In 1834, Methodist soul-seekers led by Jason Lee settled near Salem. Four years later, another mission was started in the eastern Columbia River Gorge. In 1843, Marcus and Narcissa Whitman's missions started up on the upper Columbia in present-day Walla Walla, Washington. The missionaries brought alien ways and diseases for which the Native Americans had no immunity. As if this weren't enough to provoke a violent reaction, the Native Americans would soon have their homelands inundated by thousands of settlers lured by government land giveaways.

## The Oregon Trail

Despite Easterners' ignorance of western geography and the hardships it held, more than 53,000 people traversed the 2,000-mile Oregon Trail between 1840 and 1850 en route to the Eden of western Oregon. Though many of these settlers were driven by somewhat utopian ideals, there was also the attraction of free land: This march across the frontier was fueled by the offer of 640 free acres that each white adult male could claim in the mid-1840s.

In 1850, the Donation Land Act cut in half the allotted free acreage, reflecting the diminishing availability of real estate. But although a single pioneer man was now entitled to only 320 acres, and single women were excluded from land ownership, as part of a couple they could claim an additional 320 free acres. This promoted marriage and, in turn, families on the western frontier and helped to fulfill Secretary of State John C. Calhoun's prediction that American families could outbreed

the Hudson's Bay Company's bachelor trappers, thus winning the battle of the West.

## The Applegate Trail

Another route west was the Applegate Trail, pioneered by brothers Lindsay and Jesse Applegate in the mid-1840s. Each had lost sons several years before to drowning on the Columbia River. The treacherous rapids here had initially been the last leg of a journey to the Willamette Valley.

On their return journey to the region, the brothers departed from the established trail when they reached Fort Hall, Idaho. Veering south from the Oregon Trail across northern Nevada's Black Rock Desert, they traversed the northeast corner of California to enter Oregon near present-day Klamath Falls. A southern Oregon gold rush in the 1850s drew thousands along this route.

## Early Government and Statehood

There was enough unity among American settlers to organize a provisional government in 1843. Then, in 1848, the federal government decided to accord Oregon territorial status. The new Oregon Territory got off to a rousing start thanks to the California gold rush of 1849. The rush occasioned a housing boom in San Francisco and a need for lumber, and the dramatic population influx created instant markets for the agriculture of the Willamette Valley. The young city of Portland was in a perfect position to channel goods from the interior to coastal ports and prosper economically.

However, strategic importance and population growth alone do not explain Oregon becoming the 33rd state in the Union. In 1857, the Dred Scott decision had become law. This had the effect of opening Oregon to slavery, as a territory didn't have the legal status to forbid the institution as a state had. While slavery didn't lack adherents in Oregon, the prevailing sentiment was that it was neither necessary nor desirable. If Oregon were a state instead of a territory, however, it could determine its own policy regarding slavery. A constitution (forbidding free black residents as well as slavery) was drawn up and ratified in 1857, and sent to Washington DC for approval. However, the capital was engulfed in turmoil about the status of slavery in new American states, and only after a year and a half of petitioning did Oregon finally enter the Union, on Valentine's Day 1859.

## Economic Growing Pains

During the years of the Civil War and its aftermath, internal conflicts were the order of the day within the state. By 1861, good Willamette Valley land was becoming scarce, so many farmers moved east of the Cascades to farm wheat. They ran into violent confrontations with Native Americans over land. Miners encroaching on Native American territory around the southern coast eventually flared into the bloody Rogue River Wars, which would lead to the destruction of most of the indigenous peoples of the coast.

In the 1870s, cattle ranchers came to eastern Oregon, followed by sheep ranchers, and the two groups fought for dominance of the range. However, overproduction of wheat, uncertain markets, and two severe winters spelled the end to the eastern Oregon boom. Many eastern Oregon towns grew up and flourished for a decade, only to fall back into desert, leaving no trace of their existence.

In the 1860s and 1870s, Jacksonville in the south became the commercial counterpart to Portland, owing to its proximity to the Rogue Valley and south coast goldfields as well as the California border. The first stagecoach, steamship, and rail lines moved south from the Columbia River into the Willamette Valley; by the 1880s, Portland was joined to San Francisco and the east by railroad and became the leading city of the Pacific Northwest.

## Progressive Politics

In the modern era, Oregon blazed trails in the thicket of governmental legislation and reform. The so-called Oregon system of initiative, referendum, and recall was first conceived in the 1890s, coming to fruition in the first decade of the 1900s. The system has since become an integral part of the state's democratic process. In like measure, Oregon's extension of suffrage to women in 1912, a 1921 compulsory education law, and the first large-scale union activity in the country during the 1920s were red-letter events in U.S. history. However, blacks were still excluded from residency in the state.

The 1930s were exciting years in the Pacific Northwest. Despite widespread poverty, the foundations of future prosperity were laid during this decade. New Deal programs such as the Works Progress Administration and the Civilian Conservation Corps undertook many projects around the state. Building roads and hydroelectric dams created jobs and improved the quality of life in Oregon, in addition to bolstering the country's defenses during wartime. Hydroelectric power from the Bonneville Dam, completed in 1938, enabled Portland's shipyards and aluminum plants to thrive. Low utility rates encouraged more employment and settlement, while the Columbia's irrigation water enhanced agriculture.

## World War II

Thanks to mass-production techniques, 10,000 workers were employed in the Portland shipyards. But in addition to laying the foundations for future growth, the war years in Oregon and their immediate aftermath were full of trials for state residents. Vanport—at one time a city of 45,000—grew up in the shadow of Kaiser aluminum plants and the shipyards north of Portland, but it was washed off the map in 1948 by a Columbia River flood. Tillamook County forests, which supplied Sitka spruce for airplanes, endured several massive fires that destroyed 500 square miles of trees.

## The Modern Era

With the perfection of the chainsaw in the 1940s, the timber industry could take advantage of the postwar housing boom. During that decade, the state's population increased by nearly 50 percent, growing to over 1.5 million. During the 1950s and 1960s, the U.S. Army Corps of Engineers carried out a massive program of new dam projects, resulting in construction of The Dalles, John Day, and McNary Dams on the main stem of the Columbia River as well as the Oxbow and Brownlee Dams on the Snake River. In addition, flooding on the Willamette River was tamed through a series of dams on its major tributary watersheds, the Santiam, the Middle Fork of the Willamette, and the McKenzie.

Politically, the late 1960s and 1970s brought environmentally groundbreaking measures spearheaded by Governor Tom McCall. The bottle bill, land use statutes, and the cleanup of the Willamette River were part of this legacy. The 1990s saw the Oregon economy flourishing, fueled by the growth of computer hardware and software industries here as well as a real estate market favorable to an Oregon Trail-like stream of new settlers. The demographics of Oregon's new arrivals as well as its changing economic climate helped to sustain the state's image as a politically maverick state, with Oregon leading the way in physician-assisted suicide, extensive vote-by-mail procedures, legalized marijuana, and the Oregon Health Plan, a low-cost health insurance program for low-income residents.

## Today's Economy

Oregon's economy has traditionally followed a boom-bust cycle. Even though it has in recent decades diversified away from its earlier dependence on resource-based industries, the economic bust of 2008 left over 10 percent of Oregonians unemployed, second only to Michigan in unemployment.

The state's major industries today include a booming high-tech sector (Intel is the state's largest employer), primary and fabricated metals production, transportation equipment fabrication, and food processing. Important nonmanufacturing sectors include wholesale and retail trade, education, health care, and tourism. Portland is home to a number of sports and recreational gear companies, including Nike, Adidas America, Columbia, and other sportswear companies with headquarters in the Rose City area.

In agriculture, organic produce, often sold in farmers markets, and other specialty products have helped many small farmers to survive. Other agricultural products include nursery crops (Monrovia is the nation's largest Christmas tree nursery, and Oregon is the number one Christmas tree state); wine grapes; berries, cherries, apples, and pears; and gourmet mushrooms, herbs, and cheese. Wheat, cattle, potatoes, and onions are the stalwarts of the eastern Oregon economy. Oregon wineries, most of them small operations, turn out increasingly excellent wine to meet the demands of a thirsty global market. With the legalization of marijuana in late 2015, the enormous black market in pot production has edged into the mainstream economy, with over $60 million in tax revenues generated in 2016.

# Essentials

# Transportation

## AIR

It is simple to get to and around Oregon by air. The main point of entry is Portland International Airport (PDX), served by over a dozen airlines, but there are also airports in Eugene, Redmond, and Medford. If eastern Oregon is your destination, consider flying to Boise, Idaho.

**Alaska Airlines** (800/252-7522, www.alaskaair.com) connects Portland to Redmond, Eugene-Springfield, and Medford, as well as numerous other cities around the Western states.

## TRAIN

Thanks to **Amtrak** (800/872-7245, www.amtrak.com) and its high-speed Spanish-made Talgo trains, the stretch from Eugene to Vancouver, British Columbia, has an efficient and scenic mass-transit link. **Cascades** trains make daily round-trips between Portland and Seattle; one continues to Vancouver, BC, and one goes from Portland south to Eugene daily. The **Coast Starlight** runs between Los Angeles and Seattle with stops in Oregon at Klamath Falls, Chemult, Eugene, Salem, and Portland. Note that getting a sleeper on the extremely popular Coast Starlight requires reservations 5 to 11 months in advance year-round.

The **Empire Builder,** which connects Portland with Chicago, shows off the Columbia River Gorge. Trains run on the Washington side of the Columbia, giving a distant perspective on the waterfalls and mountains across the river. In summer this train stops at Glacier Park, Montana. Amtrak also runs bus service on routes such as Portland-Eugene, Portland-Astoria, and Chemult-Bend. The latter service makes Bend accessible to Coast Starlight passengers who disembark in Chemult.

## BUS

**Greyhound** (800/229-9424, www.greyhound.com) has cut most of its service to rural Oregon and now travels only along I-5 and I-84, but many smaller companies have picked up the slack. Porter, Valley Retriever, Central Oregon Breeze, SouthWest and NorthWest Point, and other smaller companies operate on former Greyhound routes. Visit www.tripcheck.com to find details on bus service to Oregon's cities and towns.

## CAR

For the vast majority of visitors, the automobile is the vehicle of choice for exploring the state. Speed limits top out at 65 mph on sections of I-5 and I-84; the rest of the roads in the state have a 55 mph limit. Many Oregon roads are strikingly beautiful. The magnificent scenery prompted the building of the first paved public road in the state with the Columbia River Highway, constructed 1913-1915, now known as the Historic Columbia River Highway. (Stretches of this road were closed after the 2017 Eagle Creek Fire; check www.tripcheck.com or mapping apps to ensure that it's passable when you travel.) The Oregon Coast Scenic Highway, U.S. 101 along the entire Oregon coast, is another internationally renowned drive. Entirely different in character, but equally stunning, is the Cascade Lakes Highway out of Bend.

The **Oregon Department of Transportation** (503/588-2941 out of state, 800/977-6368 in Oregon) advises on **road conditions** by phone and via the TripCheck website (www.tripcheck.com). Gas is readily

---

"Go by bike" is a common mantra across Oregon.

parking lots leading to cross-country ski trails. Without the pass on the left side of your windshield, a car left in a Sno-Park area can be ticketed. This permit is essentially a fee levied by the state to pay for the upkeep of parking and rest areas and for snowplowing in the mountains. Pick these up at a Department of Motor Vehicles office, ski shops, sporting goods stores, and other commercial establishments; stores selling the permits often charge an extra service fee.

If you are traveling into the mountains in the winter, make sure your car has tire chains in the trunk. During snowstorms, many mountain passes are closed to vehicles without chains, and the state patrol takes the task of enforcing this requirement seriously.

## BICYCLE

Oregon is user-friendly for bicyclists. In the 1970s the Oregon legislature allocated 1 percent of the state highways budget to develop bike lanes and encourage energy-saving bicycling. In addition to establishing routes throughout the state with these funds, many special paths were developed with bicycle and foot access specifically in mind. For example, Eugene's Willamette River Greenway bike path system winds through a string of parks. In Portland, many streets are marked as bike corridors, and signs direct cyclists to nearby destinations. A decent cyclist can easily beat a car across town during rush hour.

The **Oregon Department of Transportation** (503/986-3555, www.oregon.gov/programs) produces some useful and free resources for cyclists, which can be ordered by phone or downloaded online—you can find maps of bike trails and routing suggestions for the entire state, the Columbia Gorge, the coast, and a number of cities. **Ride Oregon** (800/547-7842, www.rideoregonride.com) is also a good source for maps and trip planning.

available on the main routes, but finding it can be a little trickier in remote eastern Oregon, especially after 5pm. Fill up before you leave the city. Another thing to remember is that Oregon is one of the few states that does not have self-service gasoline outlets; pull up to the pump and wait for an attendant. In some eastern Oregon communities, self-service gas is available outside regular opening hours.

### Winter Driving

The first rule to follow when rain, snow, or hail make pavement slick, or when fog reduces visibility, is to slow down. From late fall to early spring, expect snow on the Cascade passes and I-5 through the Siskiyous; snow tires or chains are often required.

A **Sno-Park permit** (required Nov. 15-Apr. 15, $4 per day, $25 full season) is required to park at most ski areas and plowed

# Sports and Recreation

## PARK FEES AND PASSES

Oregon has more state parks than almost any other state, as well as a natural environment suited to all manner of recreational activities. In recent years, numerous state and federal parks, national recreation areas, trails, picnic areas, and other facilities have begun charging day-use fees, which are separate from overnight camping fees (except camping at rustic sites in national forests, covered by the NW Forest Pass). At sites that charge fees, the day-use fee is currently $5 per vehicle at state parks or federal sites. Visitors can pay for day use at individual sites or purchase one of the annual passes described here.

### Oregon Pacific Coast Passport

The best deal if you plan to visit many parks along the Oregon coast, this pass covers entrance, day-use, and vehicle parking fees at all state and federal fee sites along the entire Oregon portion of U.S. 101. It does not cover the cost of camping at state parks. The two options are an **annual passport** ($35), valid for the calendar year, and a **five-day passport** ($10). Passports may be purchased at welcome centers, ranger stations, national forest headquarters, national memorials, and state park offices. Call 800/551-6949 to purchase an annual pass by credit card or for directions to a purchase location.

### State Park Passes

Another option for day-use fees at Oregon state parks is a one-year ($30) or two-year ($50) **State Park Pass.** It's available from state park offices, at day-use fee booths, and by phone (800/551-6949). See the **Oregon State Parks website** (www.oregonstateparks.org) for more details and a list of vendors.

### Northwest Forest Pass

In response to major reductions in timber harvests and cutbacks in federal money, a revenue shortfall has made it hard to maintain trails and campgrounds at a time when the region's population has put more demand on these facilities. The **Northwest Forest Pass** ($5 per day, $30 annually) is a vehicle-parking pass for the use of many improved trailheads, picnic areas, boat launches, and interpretive sites in the national forests of Oregon and Washington. Funds generated from pass sales go directly to maintaining and improving the trails, land, and facilities. You will see "Northwest Forest Pass Required" signs posted at participating sites. Fees are collected at trailhead kiosks. Passes are also available at many local vendors and online at www.fs.usda.gov. You can also check this website before you head out to find out if a pass is required. These passes are good at most U.S. Forest Service sites all over the Pacific Northwest, but they are not valid for campground fees (with the exception of rustic free campsites), concessionaire-operated sites, or Sno-Parks.

### Golden Passport Program

Most National Park Service sites, such as national parks and monuments, charge a fee for their use. You can pay an entrance fee at each site or park you visit, or you can purchase an annual **America the Beautiful Pass** ($80), which allows the owner to use all U.S. Forest Service, Park Service, Bureau of Land Management, and Fish and Wildlife sites, as well as developed day-use sites and recreation areas. The **America the Beautiful Senior Pass** ($80) is a lifetime pass covering entrance fees for U.S. citizens over age 62; annual senior passes go for $20. Pass holders also get a 50 percent discount at some campgrounds, boat launches, and swimming areas. The free **Access Pass** is available to those who are permanently disabled; check with the National Park Service for eligibility requirements. It offers the same benefits as the Senior Pass. Families with a fourth-grade student are also eligible for a free one-year pass, as are individuals who are serving in the U.S. military.

## BICYCLING

While it's not for everybody, biking all or part of the Oregon coast is the surest way to get on intimate terms with this spectacular region. Before going, get a free copy of the **Oregon Coast Bike Route** map from the **Oregon Department of Transportation** (503/986-3555, www.oregon.gov) or from coastal information centers. This brochure features strip maps of the route, noting services from Astoria to the California border. With information on campsites, hostels, bike repair facilities, elevation change, temperatures, and winds, this pamphlet does everything but map the ruts in the road.

Because the prevailing winds in summer are from the northwest, most people cycle south on U.S. 101 to take advantage of a tailwind. You'll also be riding on the ocean side of the road with better views and easier access to turnouts, and generally wider bike lanes and shoulders. The entire 370-mile trip (380 miles if you include the Three Capes Scenic Loop) involves nearly 16,000 feet of elevation change. Most cyclists cover the distance in six to eight days, pedaling an average of 50 to 65 miles daily.

If you're looking for a medium to long recreational ride, check out www.rideoregonride. com, which has excellent route information for road and mountain bike rides all over the state. A number of companies offer preplanned group bicycle trips, with everything from the bicycle to the meals and lodging included. For example, **Bicycle Adventures** (425/250-5540 or 800/443-6060, www.bicycleadventures.com) offers several tours around the state; expect to pay upward of $3,000 for a weeklong fully supported tour.

**Cycle Oregon** (503/287-0405 or 800/292-5367, www.cycleoregon.org) sponsors an annual weeklong supported tour of rural Oregon (Sept., around $1,000 pp). Considered one of the best bike tours in the country, Cycle Oregon tours cover about 500 miles and attract up to 2,000 riders each year. Fees include all meals, showers, support, and entertainment. A mid-July weekend Cycle Oregon ride ($199 adults, $99 students) is a bit more family-oriented, with a variety of daily routes ranging 25 to 75 miles. The one-day women's Joyride ($85) explores the wine country.

## CAMPING
### State Parks

Oregon's state parks have great amenities (including showers at most campgrounds), and given that, fees are reasonable. Fees for RV sites run about $32, tent sites about $22, yurts and rustic cabins $45-57. The fee for reserving a site is $8. During the winter, camping fees drop slightly. Most state park campgrounds have at least a couple of yurts—canvas-walled, wood-floored shelters equipped with fold-up beds, heaters, and lamps; they sleep five. Although pets have traditionally been banned from state park yurts, most parks now have at least one pet-friendly yurt.

Many state park campgrounds accept campsite reservations, and reservations are accepted for all special facilities such as cabins, yurts, and tepees. The state park system has a central **information hotline** (800/551-6949) and a website (www.oregonstateparks. org) where you can get park maps, campground layouts, rates, and other information. **Reservations** for state parks can be made by phone (503/731-3411 Portland, 800/452-5687 elsewhere, 8am-7pm Mon.-Fri.). Online reservations, with a Visa or Mastercard, are handled by a private vendor, **ReserveAmerica** (www.reserveamerica.com). Reservations may be made from two days up to nine months in advance. In addition to the campsite fee, a processing fee is charged.

If you need to **cancel your reservation** three days or more before your scheduled arrival, call one of the numbers above. Two or fewer days before your trip, call the park directly to cancel your reservation. Phone numbers for each park are found on the individual park's Web page (www.oregon-stateparks.org). Cancellation fees and requirements for special facilities, such as yurts and cabins, vary. The reservation fee is nonrefundable, and a small cancellation fee will be charged if you cancel in the last two days.

### National Forests

The U.S. Forest Service maintains hundreds of campsites, trails, and day-use areas. National forest campsites are usually much less developed than those at state parks; electric hookups are not available, although most campgrounds have water and vault or flush toilets. Most overnight sites charge a user fee. Fees are generally $12-20 for campsites, $7 for an extra vehicle. Campsites can be reserved online with a Visa or Mastercard through www.recreation.gov.

Get out of the car and hike!

## HIKING

While every corner of Oregon features hiking trails, a couple of long-distance trails deserve special notice. For 362 miles, from the Columbia River to the California border, the **Oregon Coast Trail** hugs the beaches and headlands, leading hikers into intimate contact with some of the most beautiful landscapes anywhere. Most of the trail runs through public lands, though some portions traverse easements on private parcels and the trail follows the highway and city streets in a number of places. The only coastal long-distance treks separated from U.S. 101 are the 30 miles between Seaside and Manzanita, and between Bandon and Port Orford. A free trail map and directory are available from the **Oregon State Parks information center** (800/551-6949, www.oregonstateparks.org). This pamphlet makes clear where this trail crosses open beaches, forested headlands, the shoulder of the Coast Highway, and even city streets in some towns. Be sure to bring water, particularly on northerly sections of the

trail, as much of the trek is on beachfront away from a potable supply.

The other long-distance trail through the state is the Oregon portion of the **Pacific Crest Trail,** which runs from Southern California to the Canadian border. The PCT through Oregon is exceptionally scenic and not too hard for experienced backpackers; much of it runs along ridgelines, avoiding constant ups and downs.

## FISHING AND HUNTING

Oregon takes a backseat to few other places when it comes to sportfishing and hunting opportunities. Rules and bag limits for both are subject to frequent change, so get a copy of the **hunting and fishing regulations,** available at the website or the office of the **Oregon Department of Fish and Wildlife** (4034 Fairview Industrial Dr. SE, Salem, 503/947-6000, www.dfw.state.or.us), as well as at sporting goods stores, some grocery stores (such as Fred Meyer), and other outlets.

## Fishing

Fishing for trout, both wild native cutthroat and rainbows as well as planted hatchery fish, is popular all across the state. Standout areas include the Deschutes River, a blue-ribbon stream noted for its large red-band rainbow trout, as well as excellent steelhead fishing. Other notable steelhead streams include the coastal Rogue and Umpqua Rivers, as well as the Sandy and Clackamas Rivers, in Portland's backyard. Smallmouth bass provide excellent sport on the John Day and Umpqua Rivers, and largemouth bass draw anglers to warmwater lakes across the state.

Weighing into the hundreds of pounds, sturgeon is a popular game fish in the larger rivers, particularly the Columbia and the Umpqua. Off the coast, bottom fishing for rockfish and other species is a year-round activity, depending on the weather. Warm ocean currents bring albacore tuna in August-September, and halibut are usually available in summer, though the season is variable and set yearly by the Pacific Fishery Management Council.

About 1,000 fishing guides are licensed in Oregon. Independent fishing opportunities are almost limitless, but hiring a guide can be money well spent if you're exploring unfamiliar waters or lack a boat. Major **charter-fishing** centers on the coast include Astoria, Hammond, Warrenton, Garibaldi, Depoe Bay, Newport, Winchester Bay, Charleston, Gold Beach, Bandon, and Brookings. Charter rates vary, but typical rates are about $100 for a half day (5-6 hours) of bottom fishing; $200 for an 8-hour salmon outing; $300 for 12 hours of tuna fishing; and $175-200 for a 12-hour halibut charter. Inland, expect to pay $175-300 pp per day for guided trips for salmon, steelhead, sturgeon, and other species. Chambers of commerce in each town can also provide listings.

**Fishing licenses** cost $19 (for 1 day), $34.50 (2 days), $50.50 (3 days), $76.50 (7 days), or $97.50 (full year for nonresidents; $38 full year for Oregonians). Nonresident licenses include Combined Angling Tags (allowing the taking of salmon, sturgeon, steelhead, and halibut).

## Hunting

Hunters enjoy a broad range of opportunities throughout Oregon. Shooting for upland game birds—chukars, Hungarian partridge, pheasant, grouse, and quail—can be good to excellent in eastern and central Oregon, the Cascades, and the coastal ranges. The eastern half of the state as well as the Willamette Valley, Columbia River basin, and coastal areas offer waterfowl hunting. Wild turkeys, introduced successfully on the eastern side of Mount Hood, have proliferated and are now hunted in almost every county of the state. Bigger game includes elk, black bears, cougars, black-tailed deer in western Oregon, and mule deer in the east. A limited number of special tags are also issued for pronghorn, bighorn sheep, and mountain goats.

The rules governing hunting in the state are more complex and variable than those for fishing. Check the regulations carefully for seasons, restrictions, and bag limits, and consult the **Department of Fish and Wildlife's website** (www.dfw.state.or.us) for the latest information.

## WHITE-WATER RAFTING

With 90,000 river miles in the state and hundreds of outfitters to choose from, neophyte rafters have an embarrassment of riches. To help navigate the tricky currents of brochure jargon and select the experience that's right for you, here's a list of rivers to run and questions to ask before going.

Raft the famous **Rogue River** June-September to avoid the rainy season and be spared current fluctuations due to dams upstream. This run is characterized by gentle stretches broken up by abrupt and occasionally severe drop-offs as well as swift currents. In fact, Blossom Bar is often cited as one of the state's consummate tests of skill for rafters. The Rogue is ideal for half- and full-day rafting trips, with most outfitters putting in near the town of Merlin and continuing downstream as far as Foster Bar. Water turbulence on the Rogue is often intensified by constricted channels created by huge boulders.

Depending on the season, rafters can expect Class II, III, and IV rapids interspersed by deep pools and cascading waterfalls. At day's end, superlative campsites offer repose and the chance to savor your adventures.

Despite the dryness and isolation of Oregon's southeast corner, the **Owyhee River** has become a prime springtime destination for white-water enthusiasts. The 53 miles from Rome to the Owyhee Reservoir have two sections of exceptionally heavy rapids, but the many pools of short, intense white water alternating with easy drifts make for a well-paced trip. The best times to go are May-early June. Before going, check conditions with the **Vale Bureau of Land Management District office** (541/473-3144, www.or.blm.gov/vale), because the Owyhee can only be run in years with high snowmelt. Access to rafting takeout points in this part of the state is greatly facilitated by a four-wheel-drive vehicle.

The **John Day River** in northeastern Oregon offers an even-flowing current as it winds 175 miles through unpopulated rangeland and scenic rock formations. Below Clarno, the grade gets steep, creating the most treacherous part of the state's longest river (275 miles). The 157-mile section of the John Day that rafters, canoeists, and kayakers come to experience also has falls near the mouth that require a portage. The special charm of this Columbia tributary is the dearth of company you'll have even during the river-running seasons of late March-May and then again in November. Just watch out for rattlesnakes along the bank, and remember that the silt load in this undammed river reduces it to an unboatable trickle in summer months. Contact the **Prineville Bureau of Land Management office** (541/416-6700) for more information.

Unlike the John Day and the Owyhee Rivers, the **Deschutes River** rapids aren't totally dependent on snowmelt, and it is the busiest vacation waterway in the state. The 44 miles between Maupin and the Columbia River contain sage-covered grasslands and wild rocky canyons where you might see

bald eagles, pronghorn, and other wildlife. If there's a good run of salmon or steelhead, you might also encounter plenty of fishing boats. This area averages 310 days of sunshine annually, so weather is seldom a problem except for excessively hot summer days.

Typical rafting outfitter services include meals, wetsuits or rain gear, and inflatable rafts and kayaks. Guided raft trips begin at about $55 for a half-day trip and increase to $250 and up per day for longer trips. To ensure an intimate wilderness experience, ask about the number of people in a raft and how many rafts are on the river at one time. Are there any hidden costs such as camping gear rental or added transfer charges? What is the cancellation policy? Another consideration is the training and experience of the guide. Can he or she be expected to give commentary about history, geology, and local color? You might also want to check on the company's willingness to customize its trips to special interests such as photography, bird-watching, or hiking.

## WINDSURFING AND KITEBOARDING

Windsurfing conditions near the town of Hood River have made the Columbia River Gorge world-famous. In recent years, kiteboarding has become almost as popular. Other than the San Francisco Bay Area, no other place in the continental United States boasts summertime airflows as consistently strong as those in the gorge. Championship events and top competitors have coalesced on the shores of the river here, 60 miles east of Portland. The Columbia River runs in the opposite direction of the westerly airflows, which can cause large waves to stack up and allow windsurfers to maintain their positions relative to the shore. In short, the area offers the perfect marriage of optimal conditions and scenic beauty.

Some coastal waters are also gaining popularity for windsurfers. Floras Lake, near Port Orford, and the area around Pistol River, just south of Gold Beach, are top destinations. The latter hosts the Pistol River Wave Bash National Windsurfing Competition each June.

# WINTER SPORTS

One of the silver linings to Oregon's legendary precipitation is that so much of it falls in the form of snow in the mountains. Mount Hood, for example, has been buried by as much as 100 feet of snow in a single year. That makes a lot of people happy from late fall through spring and even into summer, as Oregon snowpacks support the longest ski season in the country (at Timberline on Mount Hood), as well as snowboarding, snowmobiling, and snowshoeing. For snow reports and other updated information throughout the season, a good source is **OnTheSnow.com** (www.on-thesnow.com).

Downhill ski resorts are concentrated in the northern and central Cascades and in the state's northeast corner. A little over an hour's drive away on **Mount Hood,** Portlanders have their choice of five developed ski resorts—Mount Hood SkiBowl, Cooper Spur, Mount Hood Meadows, Timberline, and tiny Summit, the Pacific Northwest's oldest ski resort, dating to 1927. In the central Cascades, there are family-friendly **Hoodoo Ski Bowl** southeast of Salem, **Willamette Pass** southeast of Eugene, and **Mount Bachelor,** the Pacific Northwest's largest and most developed ski area, southwest of Bend. At **Mount Bailey,** near Diamond Lake in the southern

Cascades, downhillers can experience snow-cat skiing, a more affordable alternative to being dropped off on inaccessible slopes by helicopter. The area also offers extensive cross-country, skating, sledding, and snowmobiling terrain. Near the California border in southern Oregon, **Mount Ashland** offers downhill action in addition to 100 miles of cross-country trails. In the northeast, skiers have their choice of **Anthony Lakes Ski Area,** between Baker City and La Grande, and the tiny **Ferguson Ridge Ski Area,** east of Joseph.

Cross-country skiing can be as simple as heading to the nearest mountain pass and looking for a Sno-Park trailhead (remember to buy the parking permit). You may need to share your trail with snowmobiles, however. Ski rental stores and U.S. Forest Service offices can offer suggestions. In addition, most of the larger downhill ski resorts also offer miles of groomed and backcountry ski trails.

## Sno-Park Permits

Note that for winter sports in many areas, you'll need to purchase a **Sno-Park permit** (Nov. 15-Apr. 30, $4 for 1 day, $25 full season) to park your vehicle in posted winter recreation areas. Sporting goods stores, ski shops, and resorts near the slopes sell them.

# Travel Tips

## LIQUOR AND MICROBREWERIES

Liquor is sold by the bottle only in state-sanctioned liquor stores, open Monday-Saturday. Many stores also open Sunday. Beer and wine are also sold in grocery stores and retail outlets. Liquor is sold by the drink in licensed establishments 7am-2:30am. The minimum drinking age nationwide is 21.

## CANNABIS

Recreational marijuana use (http://whatslegaloregon.com) is legal for adults 21 and older

in Oregon. Buy it in a marijuana dispensary (look for the green cross or check www.leafly.com or www.weedmaps.com). Come prepared with a valid ID and cash. Prices start at $5-8 for a pre-roll (a joint) and range around $12-14 for a gram of flower. Edibles and concentrates are more expensive; check menus on Leafly or Weedmaps to get an idea of offerings. In addition to the price on the menu, expect to pay a sales tax of 17-20 percent, of which 40 percent goes to Oregon's schools.

While at a dispensary, take some time to talk with a budtender; different strains have very different effects. In general, sativa strains are energizing, while indicas are relaxing. You'll also find all sorts or hybrid strains. Be sure to look at the percentages of THC, the main psychoactive component of cannabis, and CBD, a compound that won't get you high but may relieve pain and anxiety.

Since cannabis can't be consumed in public, and most hotel rooms are nonsmoking, it can be a challenge for a visitor to find a place to smoke; edibles can resolve this conundrum but have their own risks. If you consume edible cannabis, be cautious not to overdo it. Effects can take up to an hour or more to set in, then creep up on you and last for several hours. Don't drive under the influence or take your purchases out of the state.

## ENTRY REQUIREMENTS

U.S. entry requirements are subject to change. For current information, see the **U.S. Department of State's Bureau of Consular Affairs website** (www.travel. state.gov). All visitors from abroad must be in possession of a valid passport in order to enter the United States. Also required in most cases is a round-trip or return ticket, or proof of sufficient funds for a visit and a return ticket. Visitors from many countries must also have a valid visa for entry. See the State Department website (www.state.gov) for a current list of countries for which the visa requirement is waived. Applicants for visitor visas should generally apply at the U.S. embassy or consulate with jurisdiction over their place of permanent residence. Although visa applicants may apply at any U.S. consular office abroad, it may be more difficult to qualify for the visa outside your country of permanent residence.

## ACCESS FOR TRAVELERS WITH DISABILITIES

Oregon is generally proactive with regard to providing accessible facilities for people with disabilities, though there's always room for improvement. The great outdoors and some older buildings (lighthouses, for example), of course, can pose insurmountable challenges, but many parks and recreation areas work to accommodate visitors with mobility issues. Many campgrounds have accessible sites.

The **Access Pass,** which allows free entry to designated federal recreation areas such as national parks and monuments, Bureau of Land Management lands, and U.S. Fish and Wildlife sites, is available to those who

first-chance/last-chance cannabis dispensary, south of Brookings

# Oregon Festivals and Events

The majority of large crowd-drawing events take place June-September, but there are plenty of cool weather and ongoing activities to keep you entertained throughout the year. The free local weekly magazines are a great source for listings of events and entertainment and can be found in most of the larger burgs and college towns.

Oregon loves to celebrate its heritage, as well as its artistic and gastronomic bounty. The following seasonal sampler highlights some of the festivals and celebrations throughout the state. In spring, two coastal gourmet affairs of note are the **Newport Seafood and Wine Festival** and the **Astoria Crab, Seafood and Wine Festival.** Also around this time, Florence's **Rhododendron Festival** and Brookings's **Azalea Festival,** both on the coast, attract blossom connoisseurs.

If you have kids in tow, in June take advantage of the parades, carnival rides, air shows, and floral splendor of Portland's **Rose Festival** or the Cannon Beach **Sandcastle Festival.** You could fill up July and August with such varied musical talents as the new vaudeville acts of the **Oregon Country Fair** and the gold-record performers at Jacksonville's **Peter Britt Music Festival,** not to mention the blues icons who appear at the **Waterfront Blues Festival** in Portland, the West Coast's largest.

During the last full weekend of July, festivalgoers can toast their appreciation of Oregon at Portland's **Oregon Brewers Festival,** where more than 60 microbreweries are showcased, or at the **Annual International Pinot Noir Festival** in McMinnville, attracting master vintners from around the world. Summer festival-hoppers might also want to take in **Da Vinci Days** in Corvallis, uniting the community's scientific and artistic elements, and Portland's **Bite,** featuring the best in food.

In the fall and winter, the leading events west of the Cascades include Mount Angel's **Oktoberfest** and Thanksgiving **open houses** in the wine country. At Christmastime the leading events are Albany's **Victorian Parlor tours,** Portland's **Christmas Ships,** and light displays all over the state.

While most of Oregon's celebrations take place west of the Cascades, there are notable exceptions. Bird-watchers relish the Klamath Basin **Bald Eagle Conference** in February and the springtime **Harney County Migratory Waterfowl Conference** in Burns. Highbrows can take in the summertime literary festival at **Fishtrap** in the Wallowas or rock out at the **Bend Summer Festival** in central Oregon. Rock hounds flock to summer mineral shows in the central Oregon hamlets of Madras and Prineville. Rodeo fans can whoop and holler at the venerable **Pendleton Round-Up** in September. Such celebrations of ethnicity as Portland's **Cinco de Mayo** (one of the largest celebrations of its kind in the nation) and **Scandinavian festivals** in Astoria and Junction City express the state's diversity.

are blind or otherwise permanently disabled. The pass is free to qualified applicants ($10 processing fee); get details from the **U.S. Geological Survey** (http://store.usgs.gov).

## TRAVELING WITH CHILDREN

Oregon is a great place to travel with kids, with plenty of attractions and activities to keep them interested. One of the first things car travelers will notice is the ample number of rest stops, every 30-60 miles or so on major routes. In most towns and cities, public parks offer play structures and open spaces where kids can burn off some energy. Many Oregon state parks offer excellent recreational opportunities for families, such as guided hikes, nature programs, and campfire presentations.

Many B&Bs discourage children. Where possible, we've indicated policies, for and against, in the accommodations listings, but it's always a good idea when making a reservation to inquire as to whether the lodging is appropriate for children.

## GAY AND LESBIAN TRAVELERS

In Portland, college towns such as Eugene and Corvallis, and most touristed areas, gay and lesbian visitors can expect to find progressive attitudes. In these places there are venues that specifically cater to same-sex couples; Portland's **Q Center** (4115 N. Mississippi Ave., 503/234-7837, www.pdxqcenter.org) is an LGBTQ community center. Outside these places, one may find attitudes considerably less open and accepting; in more rural parts of the state, the attitude may be hostile. On the other hand, gays and lesbians live all over the state, and the relationships that these folks have built with their neighbors and coworkers often pave the way for acceptance of gay and lesbian travelers.

# Health and Safety

## EMERGENCY SERVICES

Throughout Oregon, dial 911 for medical, police, or fire emergencies. Most hospitals offer a 24-hour emergency room. Remember that medical costs are high here, as in the rest of the United States, and emergency rooms are the most expensive places for medical care; for nonemergency situations, look for urgent-care clinics. In Portland and its suburbs, the ZoomCare clinics charge about $145 for a visit, and take most kinds of insurance.

## HEALTH HAZARDS
### Hypothermia

In this part of the country, anyone who participates in outdoor recreation should be alert for problems with hypothermia—when your body loses more heat than can be recovered and shock ensues. The damp chill of the Pacific Northwest climate poses a greater hypothermia threat than colder climes with low humidity. In other words, it doesn't have to be freezing for death from hypothermia to occur; wind and wetness often turn out to be greater risk factors. Remember that a wet human body loses heat 23 times faster than a dry one.

One of the first signs of hypothermia is a diminished ability to think and act rationally. Speech can become slurred, and uncontrollable shivering usually takes place. Stumbling, memory lapses, and drowsiness also tend to characterize the afflicted. Unless the body temperature can be raised several degrees by a knowledgeable helper, cardiac arrhythmia or arrest may occur. Getting out of the wind and rain into a warm, dry environment is essential for survival. This might mean placing the victim into a sleeping bag with another person. Ideally, a ground cloth should be used to insulate the sleeping bag from cold surface temperatures. Internal heat can be generated by feeding the victim high-carbohydrate snacks and hot liquids. Placing wrapped heated objects against the victim's body is also a good way to restore body heat. Be careful not to raise body heat too quickly, as that could also cause cardiac problems.

Measures you can take to prevent hypothermia include eating a nutritious diet, avoiding overexertion followed by exposure to wet and cold, and dressing warmly in layers of wool and polypropylene. Wool insulates even when wet, and because polypropylene tends to wick moisture away from your skin, it makes a good first layer. Gore-Tex and other waterproof breathable fabrics make for more comfortable rain gear than nylon because they don't become cumbersome and hot in a steady rain. Finally, wear a hat to prevent heat loss through your head.

### Frostbite

Frostbite is not generally a major problem until the wind-chill temperature falls below 20°F. Outer appendages such as fingers and toes are the most susceptible, with the ears and nose a close second. Frostbite occurs when blood is redirected out of the limbs to warm vital organs in cold weather, and the exposed parts of the face and peripherals cool very rapidly. Mild frostbite is characterized by extremely pale skin with random splotchiness; in more severe cases, the skin will take on a gray ashen look and feel numb. At the first signs of suspected frostbite, you should gently warm the afflicted area. In more aggravated cases, immerse hands and feet in warm water. Do not massage the skin, or you risk further skin damage. Warming frostbitten areas against the skin of another person is suitable for less serious frostbite. The warmth of a campfire cannot help once the skin is discolored. As with hypothermia, it's important to avoid exposing the hands and feet to wind and wetness by dressing properly.

## Poison Oak

Neither the best intentions nor knowledge from a lifetime in the woods can spare the western Oregon hiker a brush with poison oak. Major infestations of the plant are seldom encountered in the Coast Range but are prevalent in the Columbia Gorge. In the fall, the leaves are tinged with red. Even when the plant is totally denuded in winter, the toxicity of its irritating sap still remains a threat.

When hiking in hardwood forests, it's a good idea to wear long pants, long-sleeved shirts, and other covering. When you know you've been exposed, try to get your clothes off before the resin permeates your garments. Follow up as soon as possible by washing with Tecnu, a type of soap that seems to help remove the poison oak oil from skin. It's available at REI and at many drugstores. If you get the rash, cortisone cream is effective at temporarily quelling the intense itching.

## Giardia

Known medically as giardiasis but colloquially called "beaver fever," this syndrome afflicts those who drink water contaminated by *Giardia lamblia* parasites. Even water from cold, clear streams can be infested by this microorganism, which is spread throughout the backcountry by beavers, muskrats, livestock,

and other hikers. Boiling water for 20 minutes or applying five drops of chlorine, or preferably iodine, to every quart of water and letting it sit for half an hour are simple ways to kill the giardia spores. Backpackers should use water pumps that filter out giardia and other organisms.

## Mosquitoes

Mosquitoes can be a problem especially in the Cascades, the Willamette Valley, and parts of the Columbia River Gorge. West Nile virus is not common in Oregon, though every year at least a few infected mosquitoes are detected, mostly in the eastern part of the state. When mosquitoes are present, it's a good idea to apply insect repellent and wear long pants and long-sleeved shirts to reduce the chance of getting bitten. Otherwise, you may want to stay indoors during prime mosquito time, around dusk.

## Ticks

Of approximately 20 species of hard ticks found in Oregon, only four species are commonly found on humans. Of these, the western black-legged tick (also known as the Pacific tick and deer tick) is the only known carrier in the western United States of the bacterium that causes the debilitating Lyme disease.

A prescription for prevention is to layer insect repellent on thickly before venturing into potentially infested areas. Also, be sure to check your body and clothing frequently during and after possible exposure. Ticks often may be found attached in the underarms, the groin, behind the knees, and at the nape of the neck.

If you find an attached tick, remove it promptly by grasping it with tweezers, as close to the skin as possible, and pulling it straight out, steadily and firmly. Don't twist it, as this increases the chance of breaking off mouth parts and leaving them embedded in your skin. Afterward, wash up with soap and water and apply an antiseptic to the bite area. The same routine applies for the removal of ticks from pets.

# Information and Services

## COMMUNICATIONS AND MEDIA

The state's two largest-circulation newspapers, the *Oregonian* and the *Eugene Register Guard,* are in the most populous cities, Portland and Eugene. The *Oregonian* is distributed statewide, while the *Register Guard* is carried in newspaper dispensers as far away as the southern coast of Oregon. Alternatives to the big dailies are found in a number of excellent tabloids, including Portland's *Willamette Week,* the *Eugene Weekly,* Astoria's monthly *Hipfish,* and others.

Portland and Eugene also dominate broadcast media, serving far-flung rural communities by means of electronic translators. **Oregon Public Broadcasting** (www.opb.org) is also a statewide presence both in TV and radio. Some standout TV programs of interest to visitors include the long-running *Oregon Field Guide,* which explores natural history, outdoor recreation, travel, and environmental issues; and *Oregon Art Beat,* which profiles local artists, craftspeople, and performers of all stripes. **Warm Springs Indian Reservation's KWSO** (91.9 FM) is a progressive country radio station spiced with elders chanting in the morning and topical discussions on Native American issues by younger community members.

### Telephones

Oregon has three area codes. **503** is the main area code for greater Portland, including Mount Hood and the westerly portion of the Columbia River Gorge, Astoria to Lincoln City on the coast, and Portland to Salem in the Willamette Valley; it's supplemented by **971.** The area code **541** is for the rest of the state. When using a landline in Oregon, you must dial the area code, even for local calls. **Cell phone** service in some parts of

Oregon—including mountainous regions, the southern coast, and the state's eastern areas—can be spotty to nonexistent.

## MAPS AND TOURIST INFORMATION

**Travel Oregon** (775 Summer St. NE, Salem, 800/547-7842, www.traveloregon.com) is an outstanding resource for visitors and residents alike. The state-run organization maintains an informative website and produces a number of useful free maps and publications, with extensive listings of lodgings and activities, suggested itineraries, events, and more. Nine welcome centers, located near the borders along major routes into the state, are a good first stop. They stock literature and maps on the entire state, though their regional offerings tend to be best represented.

Other useful contacts are the **Oregon Parks and Recreation Department** (725 Summer St. NE, Salem, 503/986-0707 or 800/551-6949, www.oregonstateparks.org), the federal **Bureau of Land Management** (333 SW 1st Ave., Portland, 503/808-6002, www.or.blm.gov), and the **U.S. Forest Service** (333 SW 1st Ave., Portland, 503/808-2971, www.fs.fed.us/r6). All offer free information and maps on the specific recreation areas and preserves under their respective auspices.

For auto club members, **AAA Oregon/Idaho** (600 SW Market St., Portland, 503/222-6734 or 800/452-1643, www.aaaorid.com) offers roadside assistance such as towing and retrieving keys locked in cars and provides printed guides and high-quality maps of the state and major towns.

Visitor information offices are all good sources for free maps. Some of the best road and city maps available are those produced by AAA for its members. Particularly useful for outdoor recreation is *Oregon Road & Recreation Atlas,* a large-format book of beautiful shaded-relief maps of the entire state, published by **Benchmark Maps** (www.benchmarkmaps.com). Several regional tourism authorities also offer information and services for their corners of Oregon.

## Trail Maps

Accurate trail and topographical maps are worth their weight in gold for hikers and other outdoors enthusiasts. A wide variety of maps, including those published by the U.S. Geological Survey (USGS), can be purchased at **Pittmon's Map store** (825 SE Hawthorne Blvd., Portland, 503/233-2207, www.pittmonmaps.com, 8am-5pm Mon.-Fri.) in Portland.

Another good series of paper maps is put out by **Green Trails.** Unlike USGS maps, these maps show trail mileage and campsites. Look for them at outdoors stores and ranger stations.

# Resources

## Suggested Reading

In addition to the titles cited in the text, Oregon-bound travelers may want to read some of these books. We advise readers to search for out-of-print books at www.powells.com.

### ATLASES

Benchmark Maps. *Oregon Road and Recreation Atlas*. Medford, OR: Benchmark Maps, 2009. Use this atlas to help plan your trip or as a travel companion. You'll find that it has lots of detail and shaded relief. It works when your mapping apps won't.

Loy, William G. *Atlas of Oregon*. Eugene, OR: University of Oregon Press, 2001. Find graphic details on economics, climate, geology, and historic trails in this gorgeous detailed reference atlas.

MacArthur, Lewis. *Oregon Geographic Names*. Portland, OR: Oregon Historical Society, 2003. This text might be physically weighty, but its alphabetic historical rundown of place-names makes for light and informative reading.

### FICTION

Davis, H. L. *Honey in the Horn*. Corvallis, OR: Oregon State University Press, 2015. This reprint edition of a 1936 Pulitzer Prize-winning novel about rowdy southern Oregon settlers makes the pioneer days seem quite real.

Doyle, Brian. *Mink River*. Corvallis, OR: Oregon State University Press, 2010. Part crime novel, part magical realism fantasy, this book beautifully evokes the personalities and rhythms of the Oregon coast.

Duncan, David James. *The River Why*. San Francisco: Sierra Club Books, 1983. A coming-of-age story and an epic of fly-fishing set along the Deschutes River.

Kesey, Ken. *Sometimes a Great Notion*. New York: Viking, 1964. One of the best novels ever about life in rural Oregon.

Leslie, Craig. *Winterkill*. New York: Picador, 1996. A touching father-son saga set on the reservations of central Oregon.

### GUIDEBOOKS

Fanselow, Julie. *Traveling the Lewis and Clark Trail*. Helena, MT: Falcon, 2007. This guidebook for the modern-day explorer acquaints readers with what to see and do along Lewis and Clark's celebrated route from Illinois to Oregon.

Fanselow, Julie. *Traveling the Oregon Trail*. Guilford, CT: Globe Pequot, 2001. The adventures continue with Fanselow's scenic and informative guide to the present-day Oregon Trail.

Jewell, Judy. *Oregon*. New York: Fodor's Compass American Guides, 2005. Read this guide before traveling to the state to complement *Moon Oregon* as your on-the-road reference. Beautiful color photos and insightful travel tips liven up this literary rendition of Oregon's greatest hits.

Jones, Shawn, and Nell Nix. *Out and About: Portland with Kids*. Portland, OR: Sasquatch Books, 2009. A must-have for those exploring Portland with children.

McRae, W. C., and Judy Jewell. *Moon Coastal Oregon*. Berkeley, CA: Avalon Travel, 2018. Comprising the coastal Oregon chapters in this book, with new and specific Discover, Background, and Essentials chapters for the Oregon coast.

Vaughn, Greg. *Photographing Oregon*. Alta Loma, CA: PhotoTripUSA, 2009. Good tips on selecting subjects and setting up your shots.

## HISTORY

Ambrose, Stephen. *Undaunted Courage*. New York: Touchstone, 1996. A classic book on the country's seminal voyage of discovery, the Lewis and Clark expedition. It gives a historical context to the explorers' journals in an entertaining, enlightening way. Read this before taking on *The Journals of Lewis and Clark* themselves. The latter work is available through many different publishers, but the antiquated grammar and archaic English make it difficult reading.

Federal Writers' Project, editor. *WPA Guide to Oregon*. Portland, OR: Binford and Mort, 1940. The granddaddy of them all, this 1941 guide is the primary inspiration for *Moon Oregon*. The product of dozens of authors working in the Federal Writers' Project, this post-Depression guidebook still sets the standard for thorough coverage and vivid description. Although much of the information is dated, its rundown of pioneer history and glimpses of early 20th-century Oregon make it a valuable tool for any modern traveler. Available in public libraries.

Jackman, E. R., and R. A. Long. *The Oregon Desert*. Caldwell, ID: Caxton, 2003; and Jackman, E. R., John Scharff, and Charles Conkling, photographer. *Steens Mountain in Oregon's High Desert Country*. Caldwell, ID: Caxton, 2003. These two works are the classics for eastern Oregon. Within the volumes, history and local color fill in the east side of the state's wide-open spaces.

O'Donnell, Terrence. *Portland: An Informal History and Guide*. Portland, OR: Oregon Historical Society, 1964. This book is widely available used, and it makes for entertaining reading.

Robbins, William G. *Landscapes of Promise: The Oregon Story 1800-1940*. Seattle: University of Washington Press, 1999. In this fascinating environmental history of Oregon, Robbins examines ways that Oregonians have interacted with the land; he shows that Native Americans altered the landscape in a number of ways, and that the landscape encountered by early European settlers was, in some areas, highly managed.

Stark, Peter. *Astoria: Astor and Jefferson's Lost Pacific Empire*. New York: Ecco Press, 2014. Though solidly founded in history, this is a ripping good yard about the founding of Astoria.

## NATURAL HISTORY

Alt, David, and Donald W. Hyndman. *Roadside Geology of Oregon*. Missoula, MT: Mountain Press, 2003. This book's mile-by-mile approach makes it a good reference to have in the car to answer your questions about Oregon's geology.

Evanich, Joseph E., Jr. *Birders Guide to Oregon*. Portland, OR: Audubon Society of Portland, 2003. A good all-around guide to the state's birdlife, with a useful breakdown of specific coastal locations and details on what species to watch for and when.

Jolley, Russ. *Wildflowers of the Columbia Gorge.* Portland, OR: Oregon Historical Society Press, 1988. An exhaustive study of the gorge's plant species, with excellent color photos identifying 744 of the Columbia Gorge's more than 800 species of flowering shrubs and wildflowers.

Littlefield, Carroll D. *Birds of Malheur Refuge.* Corvallis, OR: Oregon State University Press, 1990. Recommended for serious birders.

Mathews, Daniel. *Natural History of the Pacific Northwest Mountains.* Portland, OR: Timber, 2017. Simply the best field guide to the western part of the state. Use this not just to ID flora and fauna, but to read engaging descriptions of the ways of the natural world and those who have studied it.

Sept, J. Duane. *The Beachcomber's Guide to Seashore Life in the Pacific Northwest.* Vancouver, British Columbia: Harbour Publishing, 1999. This ideal guide for the casual and curious observer aids in understanding the intertidal zone and in identifying more than 270 species encountered there, including crabs, clams, and other mollusks, seaweeds, sea stars, sea anemones, and more.

## OUTDOOR RECREATION

Giordano, Pete. *Soggy Sneakers: Paddlers Guide to Oregon Rivers.* Seattle: Mountaineers Books, 2004. An indispensable guide to Oregon's rivers, replete with maps, class ratings, gradient listings, river lengths, and best seasons to visit.

Hill, Sean Patrick. *Moon Oregon Hiking.* Berkeley, CA: Avalon Travel, 2010. Details more than 490 hikes throughout Oregon, including hiking tips and top 10 lists of Oregon's best trails.

Ostertag, Rhonda, and George Ostertag. *75 Hikes in Oregon's Coast Range.* Seattle: Mountaineers Books, 2001. A well-chosen selection of hikes along the length of the coastal ranges covers a broad variety of terrain and difficulty levels. Detailed trail descriptions and maps make this guide particularly useful.

Stienstra, Tom. *Moon Oregon Camping.* Berkeley, CA: Avalon Travel, 2018. Details campgrounds across the state, with an excellent selection on the coast. Rich with tips on gear, safety, and other topics.

Sullivan, William L. *100 Hikes in Northwest Oregon and Southwest Washington.* Eugene, OR: Navillus Press, 2013. Sullivan's excellent hiking guides also include *100 Hikes* books for the central Oregon Cascades, southern Oregon, eastern Oregon, and the Oregon coast and Coast Range.

Wozniak, Owen. *Biking Portland.* Seattle: Mountaineers, 2013. Guided tours through Portland's neighborhoods, with history and interesting commentary along the way.

# Internet Resources

## ACCOMMODATIONS

**Oregon Bed and Breakfast Guild**
www.obbg.org
800/944-6196
Lists links to Oregon bed-and-breakfasts by region.

## ENTERTAINMENT AND EVENTS

**Oregon Craft Beer**
www.oregoncraftbeer.org
Proffers merchandise and features a calendar of statewide beer-related events, along with an extremely useful map of Oregon's microbreweries.

**Oregon Wine**
www.oregonwine.org
Everything you ever wanted to know about Oregon wines, wineries, and events.

**Wines Northwest**
www.winesnw.com
A guide to the world of wine in the Pacific Northwest, and a useful link to guides and driving services.

## HISTORY

**Haunted Places**
www.ghostsandcritters.com
An eerie look into Oregon's underworld. Offers advice for novice ghost hunters and info about haunted places in the state.

**Oregon Historical Society**
www.ohs.org
A resource for Oregon history.

## OUTDOOR RECREATION AND CAMPING

**The Dyrt**
www.thedyrt.com
Find and review campsites; the Yelp of camping.

**ORbike**
www.orbike.com
Statewide calendar of bike rides and cycling events.

**Oregon Department of Fish and Wildlife**
www.dfw.state.or.us
Information on fishing and wildlife in Oregon.

**Oregon Hiking**
www.oregonhiking.com
Information on outdoor adventures such as hiking, snowshoeing, rafting, and climbing.

**Ride Oregon**
http://rideoregonride.com
Bike ride options throughout the state.

**State Parks**
www.oregonstateparks.org
Find a state park or campsite, make a reservation, or download brochures.

**U.S. Forest Service**
www.fs.usda.gov/r6
Links to national forests, camping information and reservations, ranger station contact info, maps and brochures, fees, passes, and permit info.

## REGIONAL INFORMATION AND SERVICES

**Central Oregon Visitors Association**
http://visitcentraloregon.com

**Columbia River Gorge Visitors Association**
www.crgva.org

**Eastern Oregon Visitors Association**
www.visiteasternoregon.com

**Eugene, Cascades & Coast**
www.eugenecascadescoast.org

**Oregon Coast Visitors Association**
http://visittheoregoncoast.com

**Oregon's Mount Hood Territory**
www.MtHoodTerritory.com

**Southern Oregon Visitors Association**
www.southernoregon.org

**Travel Portland**
www.travelportland.com

**Willamette Valley Visitors Association**
www.oregonwinecountry.org

## STATEWIDE INFORMATION AND SERVICES

**Travel Oregon**
www.traveloregon.com
The official state tourism department offers a fun website with information about lodging, recreation opportunities, and a statewide calendar of events.

## TRANSPORTATION

**Amtrak**
www.amtrak.com
Train schedules, fares, and booking information.

**Greyhound**
www.greyhound.com
Schedules, fares, and booking information.

**Oregon Department of Transportation**
www.tripcheck.com
Great site with webcams, road conditions, public transportation, and a mileage calculator.

**Portland International Airport**
www.flypdx.com
Portland International Airport's website provides a list of carriers, ground transportation, and other useful information on the area.

# Index

## QR

# List of Maps

# Photo Credits

Title page photo: © Marshall Miller; page 4 © Tom Grundy /123rf.com; page 5 © Josemaria Toscano/123rf.com; page 6 (top left) © Judy Jewell, (top right) © Joshua Rainey | Dreamstime, (bottom) © Qwntm | Dreamstime.com; page 7 (top) © Rachell Coe /123rf.com, (bottom left) © Joshuaraineyphotography | Dreamstime.com, (bottom right) © Jpldesigns | Dreamstime; page 8 © Minacarson | Dreamstime; page 9 (top) © Michael Albright | Dreamstime, (bottom left) © Judy Jewell, (bottom right) © Mjsquirephotography | Dreamstime.com; page 10 © Joshua Rainey | Dreamstime; page 13 (top) © Simathers | Dreamstime, (bottom) © Lindsay Snow | Dreamstime; page 14 © Alan Dyck | Dreamstime; page 15 (top) © Ffennema | Dreamstime, (bottom) © Bill McRae; page 16 (top) © Judy Jewell, (middle) © Deebrowning | Dreamstime, (bottom) © Joshua Rainey | Dreamstime; page 17 © Vivian Mcaleavey | Dreamstime; page 18 © Judy Jewell; page 21 © Tondafoto | Dreamstime.com; page 23 © Judy Jewell; page 25 © Jamiehooper | Dreamstime.com; page 28 © Toynutz | Dreamstime.com; page 31 © Ruth Gibian; page 32 © Lisa Heigh; page 33 (top) © Paulbradyphoto | Dreamstime.com, (bottom) © Judy Jewell; page 35 © Judy Jewell; page 44 © Bill McRae; page 47 © Judy Jewell; page 49 © Judy Jewell; page 51 © Judy Jewell; page 56 © Judy Jewell; page 57 © Judy Jewell; page 62 © Judy Jewell; page 66 © Bill McRae; page 68 © Judy Jewell; page 71 © Jit Pin Lim/123rf.com; page 74 © Judy Jewell; page 77 © Bill McRae; page 80 © Judy Jewell; page 85 © Judy Jewell; page 86 © Bill McRae; page 94 © Andreykr | Dreamstime.com; page 97 (top) © Bill McRae, (bottom) © Tusharkoley | Dreamstime.com; page 99 © Judy Jewell; page 106 © Bill McRae; page 111 © Judy Jewell; page 114 © Judy Jewell; page 117 © Bill McRae; page 128 © Paul Levy; page 131 © Bill McRae; page 134 © Bill McRae; page 136 © Judy Jewell; page 138 © Judy Jewell; page 144 (top) © Paul Levy, (bottom) © Judy Jewell; page 145 © Judy Jewell; page 148 © Bill McRae; page 153 © Bill McRae; page 156 © Judy Jewell; page 157 © Judy Jewell; page 159 © Judy Jewell; page 161 © Paul Levy; page 165 © Judy Jewell; page 166 © Judy Jewell; page 170 © Judy Jewell; page 171 © Paul Levy; page 174 © Judy Jewell; page 175 © Judy Jewell; page 177 © Judy Jewell; page 180 © Judy Jewell; page 185 © Bill McRae; page 188 © Judy Jewell; page 192 © Judy Jewell; page 194 © Judy Jewell; page 198 © Judy Jewell; page 204 © Judy Jewell; page 207 (top) © Glebtarro | Dreamstime.com, (bottom) © Bill McRae; page 209 © Bill McRae; page 214 © Bill McRae; page 218 © Bill McRae; page 221 © Bill McRae; page 224 © Bill McRae; page 227 © Bill McRae; page 233 © Bill McRae; page 236 © Bill McRae; page 237 © Bill McRae; page 242 © Bill McRae; page 247 © Bill McRae; page 252 © Bill McRae; page 257 © Bill McRae; page 258 © Bill McRae; page 260 © Bill McRae; page 266 © Bill McRae; page 270 © Bill McRae; page 273 (top) © Judy Jewell, (bottom) © Judy Jewell; page 275 © Judy Jewell; page 285 © Bill McRae; page 294 © Bill McRae; page 296 © Bill McRae; page 304 © Paul Levy; page 307 © Paul Levy; page 310 © Judy Jewell; page 313 © Bill McRae; page 316 © Judy Jewell; page 318 © Judy Jewell; page 323 © Bill McRae; page 327 (top) © Paul Levy, (bottom) © Judy Jewell; page 329 © Paul Levy; page 331 © Bill McRae; page 335 © Judy Jewell; page 338 © Judy Jewell; page 341 © Judy Jewell; page 346 © Paul Levy; page 354 © Rruntsch | Dreamstime.com; page 356 © Paul Levy; page 360 © Paul Levy; page 365 © Bill McRae; page 368 © Paul Levy; page 371 © Judy Jewell; page 374 © Judy Jewell; page 376 (top) © Bill McRae, (bottom) © Bill McRae; page 377 © Bill McRae; page 381 © Judy Jewell; page 384 © Judy Jewell; page 386 © Judy Jewell; page 390 © Bill McRae; page 392 © BLM OR/WA; page 394 © Judy Jewell; page 398 © Judy Jewell; page 401 © Judy Jewell; page 406 © Judy Jewell; page 413 © Ron Murphy/U.S. Forest Service; page 420 © Judy Jewell; page 422 © Judy Jewell; page 430 (top) © Bill McRae, (bottom) © Judy Jewell; page 431 © Judy Jewell; page 436 © Judy Jewell; page 439 © Joshua Rainey/123rf.com; page 440 © Judy Jewell; page 441 © Judy Jewell; page 443 © Judy Jewell; page 450 © Judy Jewell; page 453 © Judy Jewell; page 460 © Judy Jewell; page 463 © Viviansviews | Dreamstime.com; page 465 © Ruth Gibian; page 470 © Judy Jewell; page 475 © Bill McRae; page 477 © Paul Levy; page 479 © Judy Jewell/Paul Levy; page 481 (top) © Bill McRae, (bottom) © Judy Jewell; page 485 © Paul Levy; page 488 © Paul Levy; page 490 © Judy Jewell; page 492 © Ruth Gibian; page 494 © Laura Thorson/Pendleton Chamber of Commerce; page 497 © Judy Jewell; page 500 © Judy Jewell; page 505 © Paul Levy; page 507 © Paul Levy; page 510 © Paul Levy; page 511 © Ruth Gibian; page 513 © U.S. Forest Service; page 516 © BLM OR/WA; page 519 © Paul Levy; page 521 © Bill McRae; page 524 (top) © Lisa Heigh, (bottom) © Bill McRae; page 525 © Judy Jewell; page 530 © Bill McRae; page 532 © Bill McRae; page 535 © Bill McRae; page 539 © Judy Jewell; page 541 © Bill McRae; page 542 © Bill McRae; page 544 © Bill McRae; page 545 © Bill McRae; page 547 (top) © Bill McRae, (bottom) © Paul Levy; page 549 © Bill McRae; page 551 © Judy Jewell; page 553 © Bill McRae; page 556 © Paul Levy; page 563 (top) © Bill McRae, (bottom) © Bill McRae; page 565 © Bill McRae; page 568 © Judy Jewell; page 572 © Judy Jewell

# MOON NATIONAL PARKS

ACADIA
NATIONAL PARK
HILARY NANGLE

ARCHES &
CANYONLANDS
NATIONAL PARKS

BANFF
NATIONAL PARK

DEATH VALLEY
NATIONAL PARK
JENNA BLOUGH

GLACIER
NATIONAL PARK
BECKY LOMAX

GRAND
CANYON
KATHLEEN BRYANT

GREAT SMOKY
MOUNTAINS
NATIONAL PARK
JASON FRYE

MOUNT RUSHMORE
& THE BLACK HILLS
Including the Badlands
LAURAL A. BIDWELL

ROCKY MOUNTAIN
NATIONAL PARK
ERIN ENGLISH

## In these books:

- Full coverage of gateway cities and towns
- Itineraries from one day to multiple weeks
- Advice on where to stay (or camp) in and around the parks

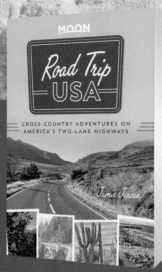

## Road Trip USA

Criss-cross the country on America's classic two-lane highways with the newest edition of *Road Trip USA!*

Packed with over 125 ~~~ed driving maps ~~~ore than ~~~lorful

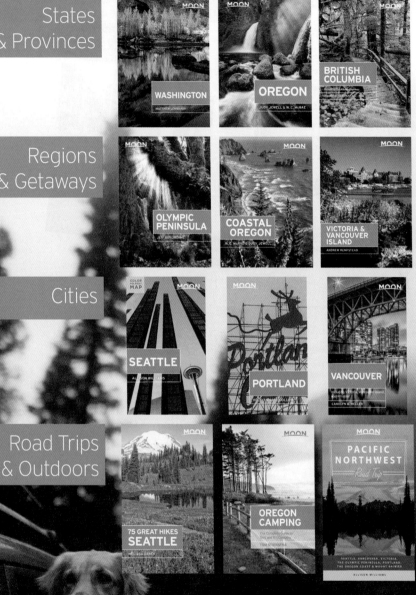

States & Provinces

Regions & Getaways

Cities

Road Trips & Outdoors

MOON WASHINGTON
MATTHEW LOMBARDI

MOON OREGON
JUDY JEWELL & W. C. McRAE

MOON BRITISH COLUMBIA

MOON OLYMPIC PENINSULA
JEFF BURLINGAME

MOON COASTAL OREGON
W. C. McRAE & JUDY JEWELL

MOON VICTORIA & VANCOUVER ISLAND
ANDREW HEMPSTEAD

MOON SEATTLE
ALLISON WILLIAMS

MOON PORTLAND

MOON VANCOUVER
CAROLYN B. HELLER

MOON 75 GREAT HIKES SEATTLE

MOON OREGON CAMPING
TOM STIENSTRA

MOON PACIFIC NORTHWEST Road Trip
SEATTLE, VANCOUVER, VICTORIA, THE OLYMPIC PENINSULA, PORTLAND, THE OREGON COAST & MOUNT RAINIER
ALLISON WILLIAMS

We've got you covered, PNW!

# MAP SYMBOLS

| | | | | | | | |
|---|---|---|---|---|---|---|---|
| ═══ | Expressway | ○ | City/Town | ✈ | Airport | ⚲ | Golf Course |
| ═══ | Primary Road | ◉ | State Capital | ✈ | Airfield | 🅿 | Parking Area |
| ═══ | Secondary Road | ⊛ | National Capital | ▲ | Mountain | ⬟ | Archaeological Site |
| ------ | Unpaved Road | ★ | Point of Interest | ✛ | Unique Natural Feature | ⛪ | Church |
| ──── | Feature Trail | • | Accommodation | | Waterfall | ⛽ | Gas Station |
| - - - - | Other Trail | ▼ | Restaurant/Bar | ▲ | Park | | Glacier |
| ········· | Ferry | ■ | Other Location | 🚩 | Trailhead | | Mangrove |
| ═══ | Pedestrian Walkway | Λ | Campground | ⛷ | Skiing Area | | Reef |
| ▥▥▥ | Stairs | | | | | | Swamp |

# CONVERSION TABLES

°C = (°F - 32) / 1.8
°F = (°C x 1.8) + 32
1 inch = 2.54 centimeters (cm)
1 foot = 0.304 meters (m)
1 yard = 0.914 meters
1 mile = 1.6093 kilometers (km)
1 km = 0.6214 miles
1 fathom = 1.8288 m
1 chain = 20.1168 m
1 furlong = 201.168 m
1 acre = 0.4047 hectares
1 sq km = 100 hectares
1 sq mile = 2.59 square km
1 ounce = 28.35 grams
1 pound = 0.4536 kilograms
1 short ton = 0.90718 metric ton
1 short ton = 2,000 pounds
1 long ton = 1.016 metric tons
1 long ton = 2,240 pounds
1 metric ton = 1,000 kilograms
1 quart = 0.94635 liters
1 US gallon = 3.7854 liters
1 Imperial gallon = 4.5459 liters
1 nautical mile = 1.852 km

## MOON OREGON

Avalon Travel
Hachette Book Group
1700 Fourth Street
Berkeley, CA 94710, USA
www.moon.com

Editors: Kathryn Ettinger, Kevin McLain
Series Manager: Kathryn Ettinger
Copy Editor: Christopher Church
Graphics Coordinator: Rue Flaherty
Production Coordinator: Rue Flaherty
Cover Design: Faceout Studios, Charles Brock
Interior Design: Domini Dragoone
Moon Logo: Tim McGrath
Map Editor: Kat Bennett
Cartographers: Brian Shotwell, Kat Bennett
Indexer: Rachel Kuhn

ISBN-13: 978-1-63121-735-7

Printing History
1st Edition — 1991
12th Edition — April 2018
5 4 3 2 1

Front cover photo: Wahclella Falls, Columbia River Gorge © Michael Breitung / Huber Images / eStock Photo

Back cover photo: Oregon Dunes National Recreation Area © Vivian Mcaleavey | Dreamstime

Printed in China by RR Donnelley

Avalon Travel is a division of Hachette Book Group, Inc. Moon and the Moon logo are trademarks of Hachette Book Group, Inc. All other marks and logos depicted are the property of the original owners.